国家社科基金
GUOJIA SHEKE JIJIN HOUQI ZIZHU XIANGMU
后期资助项目

袁同礼年谱长编

Yuan Tongli: A Chronicle

二

雷　强　撰

中华书局
ZHONGHUA BOOK COMPANY

一九三五年　四十一岁

Edna M. Sanderson 致函先生，告知哥伦比亚大学图书馆新馆已落成，并感谢先生赠送地毯。

January 4, 1935

Dear Mr. Yuan:

　　Ever since the dedication of our new library building, I have been intending to send you the enclosed literature which was distributed at the time of the dedication. I think you will be interested in having a copy of the plans of the various floors, in the program, and in the description of parts of the building that appeared in the Bibliotheca Columbiana. I am sorry the Library School was not given some consideration, but perhaps when Dr. Williamson returns to his desk, he will prepare something that we can distribute to the alumni.

　　The beautiful rug, which you were so instrumental in securing for us, adds a great deal to our social room which is one of our prize rooms, we think. I hope that some other important conference or assembly will bring you to this country again before long and that we shall have the opportunity of showing you about personally.

　　We all hope your tour last year in this country and in Europe was very successful and pleasant, and that you returned to your work in Peiping with renewed interest and very much refreshed.

　　With best wishes for the New Year,

Yours very sincerely,

Associate Dean

〔Columbia University Library, New York State Library School Collection, Series 2 Student Records, Box 65, Folder Yuan, T. L.〕

　　　　按：该件为录副。

一月六日

下午一时，北平市图书馆协会假师范大学图书馆召开年度第一次常会。先生、李文裿、田洪都、洪有丰、何日章、邓衍林、严文郁、吴鸿志、于震寰、黄向文、瞿凤鸾、施廷镛、丁濬、顾宝延等二十余人与会。李文裿为会议主席，洪有丰、先生先后演说。先生的发言涉及三个方面：一为阅览人互助精神，二为书籍陈列以实用为上，三为馆员终身为事业学习。最后，举行改选，先生、田洪都、洪有丰、何日章、邓衍林、严文郁、李文裿当选为执行委员，吴鸿志、于震寰、黄向文、瞿凤鸾、施廷镛、丁濬为监察委员。〔《华北日报》，1935 年 1 月 7 日，第 9 版；《中华图书馆协会会报》第 10 卷第 4 期，1935 年 2 月 28 日，页 22〕

　　　　按：丁濬，字汇川，河北东鹿人，时任平馆参考组组员。

一月十一日

上午十时，旧都文物整理委员会举行成立大会，委员长黄郛，当然委员于学忠、宋子文、袁良、罗耀枢（内政部）、殷同（铁道部）、沈兼士（教育部）、丁春膏（财政部）、马衡（中央古物保委会），委员朱启钤、朱深、程克、翁文灏、先生、陈汉第、周作民等人出席。黄郛为会议主席，秘书夏清贻记录。开会后，各委员就主席提交各案、涉及本会议事规则、执行手续、组织保管款项委员会等案，一一讨论通过，至十二时许始毕，会后午餐。〔《申报》，1935 年 1 月 12 日，第 7 版〕

　　　　按：旧都文物整理委员会负责北平地区文物建筑的修缮。朱深
　　　　（1880—?），字博渊，河北永清人，日本东京帝国大学法学毕业，
　　　　曾任京师高等检察厅检察长；程克（1878—?），字仲渔，河南开封
　　　　人，日本东京帝国大学法学毕业，曾任司法总长。另，委员方觉慧
　　　　因在外，未能出席。

先生受邀赴天津工商学院演讲，题为"现代之图书馆"。〔《大公报》（天津），1935 年 1 月 12 日，第 4 版〕

先生致信 Giuseppe Gabrieli，告收到前函，并寄上中国文献中有关耶稣会士 Johannes Schreck 的书目清单，如有问题可联系华嘉教授。

January 11, 1935

　　Prof. Giuseppe Gabrieli, Librarian

　　R. Accademia Nazionale dei Lincei

Via Lungara 10

Roma, Italia

Dear Prof. Gabrieli,

　　Your letter of November 8, 1934 duly received.

　　We have succeeded in looking up a number of Chinese sources relating to the German botanist, astronomer and physician Johannes Schreck. These are being given in the enclosed list. Perhaps you will consult Prof. Vacca, if you do not happen to know the Chinese text.

　　Hoping you will find the information useful,

Very truly yours,

T. L. Yuan

Acting Director

〔韩琦《袁同礼致伯希和书信》,页 132〕

按:Giuseppe Gabrieli(1872－1942),意大利图书馆学家,时应为 Accademia dei Lincei 图书馆馆长。Johannes Schreck(1576－1630),德籍耶稣会士,中文名邓玉函,1618 年随金尼阁等人自里斯本启程,翌年 7 月抵达澳门,著有《远西奇器图说》。

一月十四日

先生致信陶洙,附影印《宋会要》合同修改稿。

　　心如先生大鉴:

　　晨间承教为快。影印《宋会要》合同事,就尊处原稿经同人详为讨论,移改数点,另纸奉察。惟此种事项须经本馆委员会通过方能生效,倘各委员有修改之点,自当随时奉达。余俟面陈。顺候台祺。

弟袁厶厶拜启

　　附修改合同一份。

　　　　〔国家图书馆档案,档案编号 1935－※040－编印 1－001001 至 1935－※040－编印 1－001003〕

按:陶洙(1878—1961),字心如,江苏武进人,陶湘六弟,画家、藏书家,曾任董康秘书,与大东书局颇有渊源。[1] 此件为文书所拟

---

[1]《红学世界》,北京:北京出版社,1984 年,页 196;邓洪波主编《中国四库学》第五辑,2020 年 11 月,页 86。

之底稿,先生略加修改。

一月十五日

先生致信黄炎培,谈《夷氛闻记》出版事宜。

> 任之先生左右:
>
> 　　三年前为刊印《夷氛闻记》曾奉手教,诸承赞助,无任欣感。此书敝馆原拟校印公诸世人,近以经费所限,一时无法办理。尊处倘愿刊印,订有确实办法,敝馆自当借给,至与赵竹老藏本互校一节,亦关重要。夙谂台端事务甚繁,本不敢以此琐琐奉累,惟能自校必可精绝莫伦。如何之处,乞察复为幸。专此,顺候台祺。
>
> 弟袁同礼顿首
> 一月十五

〔国立北平图书馆用笺。华夏天禧(墨笺楼)拍卖(http://www.
kongfz.cn/24370518/)〕

> 按:此信为文书代笔,惟落款处签名和日期为先生亲笔。是信于当日寄出,寄送地址为"上海辣斐德路亚尔培路西首南钱家塘小学校路一号人文图书馆筹备处,黄任之先生",22 日送达。

一月十九日

下午二时,故宫博物院召开第四次院务会议临时会议,马衡、徐森玉、沈兼士、先生、张庭济、叶澜、赵儒珍、庄尚严、邵锐、何澄一、黄鹏霄、黄念劬(王承吉代)、虞和寅、王孝缉、陆绍宣等人出席。除主席报告事项外,还讨论诸多事项,其中第一项为先生以全部薪水捐充本院奖学金,并拟简章草案。决议:"袁馆长捐薪奖学,同人均极钦佩,所提草案原则通过。详细办法,由院长与袁馆长商定。"〔《马衡年谱长编》,页 565-566〕

> 按:是年 6 月 30 日,马衡院长签发国立北平故宫博物院"布字第40 号"院令,公布《国立北平故宫博物院奖学金简章》。① 该简章规定,奖学金分设甲、乙两种,甲种奖学金每年 2 名,每名金额为1400 元,特别资助在国外大学从事博物院管理法、考古学和美术史研究的自费贫困生;乙种奖学金每年 10 名,每名金额 200 元,奖励在古物、图书或文献方面有研究成果的故宫博物院职员。张

① 故宫博物院档案,"章制纪录类",第 71 卷页 5。

庭济,字柱中,浙江平湖人,北京大学英文门毕业,长期担任故宫博物院总务处处长。叶澜,字清伊,浙江杭州人,时任马衡院长的秘书。赵儒珍,字席慈,江苏镇江人,亦为故宫博物院院长秘书。邵锐,字茗生,浙江杭州人,时任古物馆第二科科长。何澄一,字澄意,广东中山人,时任图书馆第一科代理科长兼第二科代理科长。黄鹏霄,字鹏笑,广东新会人,时任文献馆第一科代理科长。黄念劬,江西都昌人,时任总务处第一科科长、驻南京办事处主任。王承吉,字贞吉,浙江长兴人,时任总务处第一科帮办科务科员。虞和寅,字自畏,浙江镇海人,时任总务处第二科科长。王孝缙,字筱晋,福建闽侯人,时任总务处第三科科长。陆绍宣,字季馨,浙江杭州人,时任总务处第四科科员。①

一月二十二日

黄炎培覆函先生。〔《黄炎培日记》第5卷,页16〕

一月二十九日

午,谢国桢、刘盼遂在同和居设宴,钱玄同、陈寅恪、先生、孙人和、郭绍虞、冯友兰、徐森玉、顾颉刚等人同席。〔《顾颉刚日记》卷3,页302〕

一月三十一日

先生致信凯欧,中华图书馆协会执委会已经通过邀请其和毕寿普来华考察访问的决议,期待其在协会成立十周年年会时抵达南京。

January 31, 1935

Dear Dr. Keogh:

At a recent meeting of the Executive Committee of the Library Association of China, a resolution was unanimously adopted that the Association extends you a cordial invitation to visit China in 1935 to conduct a survey of Chinese libraries and to assist us in devising ways and means for their further development.

In adopting the above resolution, the Executive Committee feels confident that through your rich and long years' experience in library administration, you will be able to give us your expert advice and

---

① 《国立北平故宫博物院职员录》,1935 年。

assistance. Your collaboration will no doubt make a most significant contribution to Sino-American cultural relations.

The Library Association of China was founded in 1925 and was inaugurated in the presence of Dr. Arthur E. Bostwick, the Official Delegate of the American Library Association. In celebrating its ten years' anniversary, the Library Association of China has decided to hold an annual conference at Nanking and has authorized me to arrange with you for your presence at this conference. The conference will therefore be held at the time of your visit; and for this reason, the Committee would like to know as soon as possible the definite date of your arrival as well as the length of your stay, in order to make necessary plans for the Conference.

The Committee will arrange an itinerary for your visit and will provide you with an interpreter. Meanwhile the Committee will collect data and information concerning libraries in China in order to facilitate your investigations.

It is our earnest hope that in spite of your heavy responsibilities at home you will be able to plan a trip to China in 1935, in order that we may have the pleasure of welcoming you in connection with the celebration of the ten years' anniversary of our Association.

With sincere greetings and cordial expressions of regard,

Yours very sincerely,

T. L. Yuan

Chairman, Executive Committee.

〔中华图书馆协会英文信纸。Yale University records, Peiping National Library, 1931–1937, Box: 80, Folder: 831〕

按:此件为打字稿,落款处为先生签名。

一月

《海潮音》刊登《发行宋藏遗珍缘起》,朱庆澜、蒋维乔、欧阳渐、先生、叶恭绰、徐乃昌、徐文霨、周叔迦共同署名。〔《海潮音》第 16 卷第 1 期,1935 年 1 月 15 日〕

按:该文前有"影印宋藏遗珍发行预约广告",后附"宋藏遗珍目录(上集二十六种一百三十六卷)""发行宋藏遗珍预约办法"。
"宋藏遗珍"即山西赵城广胜寺所藏宋金卷轴式藏经,全套预计
一百四十册,用中国手工制上等连史纸照相影印,定价八十圆,预
约一次交付六十圆,至本年三月底截止。《海潮音》由该社编辑
发行,汉口印书馆承印。

二月一日

方树梅抵平,赴平馆访问先生,不值。李文碕负责接待,介绍参观。〔方树梅
著、戴群整理《北游搜访文献日记》,上海:上海人民出版社,2020年,页39、71〕

> 按:方树梅(1881—1967),字臞仙,云南晋宁人,肄业于云南高等
> 学堂、优级师范学堂,曾任昆明师范学校学监、省立师范学校国文
> 教员、云南大学教授等,1934年12月出滇搜访有关云南省文献。
> 自此日至4月初,方树梅常赴平馆看书、抄书,时已留心有关《滇
> 南碑传集》书稿的相关史料搜集。

先生致信凯欧,附上中华图书馆协会正式邀请函,请其于本年秋季访华并
寄下照片两张。

February 1, 1935

Dear Dr. Keogh:

I should have written to you earlier, if not for the fact that I have not
been feeling very well after a strenuous tour.

I take pleasure in enclosing herewith an official invitation from the
Library Association of China, requesting you to arrange for a visit to this
country in 1935. Dr. Bishop wrote me sometime ago that you would
probably find it easier to be away in the coming autumn and so we shall
leave the time of your visit to your own selection.

I shall write you soon about other matters. Meanwhile, I hope very
much that we may hear favorably from you. I should like to request you
to send me, if possible, two copies of your photo.

With warmest regards,

Yours sincerely,
T. L. Yuan
Acting Director

P. S. I am writing a similar letter to Dr. Bishop.

〔Yale University records, Peiping National Library, 1931 –
1937, Box: 80, Folder: 831〕

　　按：该件为抄件。

先生致信毕寿普，邀请其访华。〔Rockefeller Foundation. Series 601: China;
Subseries 601.R: China-Humanities and Arts. Vol. Box 47. Folder 388〕

二月八日

下午二时，平馆委员会召开第十七次会议，陈垣、胡适、傅斯年、孙洪芬、蒋
梦麟、任鸿隽、先生出席，胡适为会议主席。讨论议案如下：

(一)审核本馆与德、俄、法交换科学书籍合同案，议决通过试办一年：(1)以
　　国币一万元为限，其中德国四千元、法国三千元、俄国二千元，准备金
　　一千元；(2)本馆可邀请国内学术机关参加此项交换（与苏俄应以一册
　　抵一册为交换标准）。

(二)影印《宋会要》稿案，首由陈垣说明编印经过，次讨论与上海大东书局
　　订立影印合同，议决通过并由馆函告大东书局影印时应竭力保持原
　　样，不宜修补。

(三)平馆职员服务规程案修正通过，薪俸标准自下年度起实行。

(四)拟建筑新闻阅览室案，议决通过。

(五)何遂送金石物品案，议决除将馆中所拟草约修正外，请林行规律师代
　　表平馆拟订正式契约，再与何遂接洽。

(六)本馆宿舍案，议决停办，将御史衙门退租。

(七)先生提议在大同书店赢余款内提出三百元作为酬谢赠送顾子刚，感谢
　　其在暑期加班，议决通过。

(八)先生提议聘用王政、宋长洞、方梦龙、陈震华，议决通过。

(九)关于馆员加薪案，议决薪金五十元以下者，由馆长酌情办理。

(十)先生提议取消编纂委员会及期刊部，前者改称编目部，后者改称期刊
　　组归并于采访部①，议决通过。〔《北京图书馆馆史资料汇编（1909-1949）》，
　　页349-350〕

　　按：王政，江苏江宁人，入庋藏组；宋长洞，河北衡水人，入西文编

---

① 《北京图书馆馆史资料汇编（1909-1949）》所存抄件，此处描述甚为混乱，应为笔误。但根据
　《国立北平图书馆职员录》（1936年1月）可以推知以上人员、组织结构变化。

目组;方梦龙,安徽桐城人,入中文编目组;陈震华,浙江绍兴人,入西文编目组。

恒慕义覆函先生,告知徐世昌题写"玉海珠渊"匾额悬挂的位置,并请先生预估手抄《钦定八旗通志》四十四卷的费用。

February 8, 1935

Dear Mr. Yuan: –

As the Librarian wrote you some weeks ago the beautiful 扁, described by Ex-president Hsu Shih-ch'ang, arrived in good condition. It received a great deal of publicity, and pleased Dr. Putnam and the staff of the Library of Congress very much. I enclose a brief account which appeared in a local Washington paper. Longer accounts have been sent for publication in the New York papers. It has been hung in the most important and most appropriate place in the Library, namely, in the large general Reading Room where it is visible to all readers. Our ceilings on Deck 38, where the Chinese collection is housed, are entirely too low, and do not admit of the proper display of such an important object of art. I am myself greatly pleased that it is now hung in such an appropriate place where it can be seen and admired by so many people. I think that if you could see it, you would agree that no more suitable place could have been found for it in the entire library. Its striking colors and beautiful calligraphy invariably attract the attention of all who pass by it.

We find that our copy of the *Ch'in-ting pa-ch'i t'ung-chih* 钦定八旗通志 (in the 嘉庆四年 edition of 342 + 12 chuan) is lacking 44 chuan which we need very much in the compilation of our biographies. Could you send me by return mail an estimate of the cost of having the missing chuan copied out by hand in 　　　 which are 32.3 cm long and 19.8 cm wide. I mean to say that our present volumes are 32.3 cm × 19.8 cm. and we would like the copied volumes to be the same size. The following are the numbers of the chuan that are now missing from our set: chuan 166, 186, 187, 190, 228, 229, 230, 231, 241, 242, 243, 244, 245, 246, 247, 248, 249, 250, 251, 252, 253, 254, 255, 256, 257, 280, 282, 311, 315, 316, 317,

318, 319, 320, 321, 322, 323, 324, 325, 326, 327, 328, 329, 330－making a total of 44 chuan.

Please do not begin to make the copies now as I must first obtain approval for the work to be done. And I cannot get approval until I can state what the approximate cost will be. If you keep a record of this letter, perhaps we can cable you, our reply. We might reply, "Copy missing 44 chapters".

I hope that all is going well with your work. With kind regards, I remain,

Sincerely yours,

Arthur W. Hummel,

Chief, Division of Orientalia

〔Library of Congress Archives, Arthur W. Hummel Sr. correspondence series, MSS86324〕

　　　按:该件为录副,空白处付诸阙如。

二月十六日

中华图书馆协会执行委员会、监察委员会改选投票结果产生,先生、杜定友、沈祖荣、李小缘、王云五任执行委员,裘开明、柳诒徵、毛坤任监察委员,以上八人至一九三八年届满。〔《中华图书馆协会会报》第 10 卷第 2 期,1935 年 6 月 30 日,页 3〕

　　　　按:此次改选依照惯例只涉及各委员会三分之一席位,其中执行委员会候选除当选五人外,还有胡庆生、陈东原、查修、谭卓垣、吴光清五人,监察委员会候选者除当选三人外,还有章新民、曾宪三、钱亚新三人。另,执行委员会又推定先生、洪有丰、刘国钧、沈祖荣、严文郁为常务委员,先生为主席。

二月十七日

下午五时,中华图书馆协会在平执委假平馆工程参考室开会,讨论会务进行事宜,先生、洪有丰、何日章、田洪都、严文郁、于震寰、李文裿等人与会。讨论议题包括:一、基金,仍在积极募集中,已有一千二百三十六元六角;二、出版,会报和图书馆学季刊均正常组稿、发行中;三、个人会员总登记,仍有相当会员未填写该信息。另,本届年会拟在南京或杭州举办,由先生负责接洽。〔《中华图书馆协会会报》第 10 卷第 4 期,页 19-20〕

二月十八日

金问泗致函先生。〔《金问泗日记》上册,页157〕

二月十九日

上午十一时,先生受邀前往燕京大学,在第三次师生大会上演讲,题为"晚近的国际情势"。〔《益世报》(北平)1935年2月20日,第9版〕

二月二十日

先生致信米来牟,请美国图书馆协会委任毕寿普和凯欧作为该会正式代表来华考察图书馆事业。

February 20, 1935

Dear Mr. Milam:

　　With a view to bringing about close co-operation between Chinese and American libraries, the Executive Committee of the Library Association of China has extended an invitation to Dr. W. W. Bishop and Dr. Andrew Keogh to visit China in 1935 to make a survey of Chinese libraries and to assist us in working out a plan for their future development. It is hoped that your Executive Board will request Dr. Bishop and Dr. Keogh to serve as the Official Delegates of the American Library Association.

　　The Library Association of China was founded in 1925 when Dr. Arthur E. Bostwick, Librarian of St. Louis Public Library, attended its inaugural meeting as the Official Delegate of the American Library Association. The Association is to celebrate its tenth anniversary during the visit of Dr. Bishop and Dr. Keogh and we hope that they will present the greetings and felicitations of the American Library Association. We are confident that their mission will not only serve to bind more tightly the bonds connecting the two sister associations, but will also bring about closer cultural co-operation between China and the United States.

Yours very faithfully,

T. L. Yuan

Chairman, Executive Committee

〔Yale University records, Peiping National Library, 1931 –
1937, Box: 80, Folder: 831〕

按：此为抄件。

二月二十二日

先生具呈教部，请加委汪长炳代表中华图书馆协会前往西班牙参加国际图书馆第二次大会。

> 谨呈者：本会送准国际图书协会来函内称：第二次国际图书馆大会，已定于本年五月二十日至二十九日在西班牙首都马德里举行，除由西班牙政府正式邀请，遴派代表出席外，特请贵会派员参加，并征求专门论文，以便宣读等因。查国际图书馆协会之主旨，在促进国际间图书馆事业之联络，及东西文化之沟通，关系学术前途至为重要。首次国际图书馆大会，于民国十八年六月十五日至三十日在罗马举行，本会曾派代表沈祖荣为代表，前往参加，并蒙大部加委该员为部派代表，提出行政会议，拨给赴会津贴二千元在案。此次大会，东西各国政府及学术团体，莫不踊跃参加，我国虽值经济紧迫之际，似亦未可后人。本会详加考虑，拟即委派现在欧洲考察图书馆事业之会员汪长炳为出席代表，程途既近，用费自轻，撙节开支，大约最低国币一千二百元，即可敷用。拟恳仍援往例，由大部加委该员汪长炳为部派代表，并提出行政会议，拨给旅费，俾得届期出席。非独本会之幸，亦我中华文化之光也。理合具文呈请，敬候训示施行，谨呈

教育部长王

中华图书协会执行委员会主席袁同礼谨呈

〔《华北日报》，1935 年 2 月 23 日，第 9 版〕

二月二十四日

西北科学考查团在沙滩二十一号召开第四次全体理事大会，梅贻琦、陈受颐、先生、沈兼士、马衡、徐旭生、袁复礼等人出席，袁复礼为临时主席，沈仲章为记录。袁复礼报告考察团甲组汉简及同地发现古物、乙组历史考古及气象监测、丙组地质及史前考古一年来的工作进展。〔邢义田《香港大学冯平山图书馆藏居延汉简整理档调查记》，《古今论衡》第 20 期，2009 年 12 月，页 24-25〕

二月

先生为袁涌进《现代中国作家笔名录》撰写序言。〔《现代中国作家笔名录》，1936 年 3 月初版〕①

---

① 无论是该书各处显示的版权信息，还是《大公报·图书副刊》（第 143 期）等书评文章，均可证实该书于 1936 年初版，但先生、周作人的序和袁涌进本人的前言确都标注写于 1935 年，特此说明。

按：袁涌进，江苏金坛人，南京金陵大学文学学士，在平馆任职，该书为《中华图书馆协会丛书》第十一种，除先生所作序外，周作人、刘国钧亦各撰序言一篇。

三月一日

先生致信耿士楷，提出延长李芳馥在美学习图书馆学时间，并请其考虑资助沈祖荣和曹祖彬前往美国学习考察。

March 1, 1935

Mr. Selskar M. Gunn

Vice President

Rockefeller Foundation

Peiping

Dear Mr. Gunn:

　　With reference to our conversation relating to the question of fellowships for library science, I beg to enumerate below three cases requiring consideration by your Foundation:

（1）Mr. F. F. Li whom the Foundation granted a fellowship last year will be completing the requirements for his M. S. degree in library science at Columbia the coming June. As it is necessary for him to continue his studies at least for one more year, I would request the Foundation to extend his fellowship for the year 1935-36 in order to enable him to study at the Graduate Library School of the University of Chicago.

（2）In order to develop the Boone Library School at Wuchang, I strongly recommend that a fellowship be granted to its Director, Mr. Samuel T. Y. Seng, to enable him to make an extensive visit to the libraries and library schools in the United States and in Europe. It is hoped that through Mr. Seng's visit, the curriculum of the Boone Library School will be improved, exchange of lecturers will be arranged and closer contact will be established between Chinese and American library schools.

（3）With a view of strengthening the Chinese Library Association which has done much towards arousing interest in the promotion of public libraries in China, it is proposed that one of its secretaries be sent to the American Library Association for practice after he has completed his professional education in the American library school of recognized standing. The Association has selected Mr. Tsu-Pin Tsao, Assistant Librarian of the University of Nanking, for this task and will appreciate greatly the assistance of the Rockefeller Foundation if a two years' fellowship be granted to Mr. Tsao in order to enable him to study in the Library School of the University of Michigan and later spend a year for practice and observation at the American Library Association. It is hoped that the Foundation will give special consideration to the application of Mr. Tsao in view of the significant work which he will be called upon to do after his return.

With much appreciation for your interest and assistance, I am

〔Rockefeller Foundation. Series 601: China; Subseries 601.R: China-Humanities and Arts. Vol. Box 47. Folder 388〕

按：此为抄件，无落款。3 月 2 日，耿士楷将此信寄送洛克菲勒基金会纽约总部。

三月二日

先生致信史蒂文斯，申请洛克菲勒基金会资助美国图书馆专家凯欧前往中国考察图书馆事业发展情况。

March 2, 1935

Dear Dr. Stevens:

With a view of bringing about closer co-operation between Chinese and American libraries, the Library Association of China has extended an invitation to Dr. Andrew Keogh to visit China in 1935 to make a survey of Chinese libraries and to assist us in working out a plan for their further development. It is also hoped that the visit of Dr. Keogh will not be too limited, so that he will have an opportunity of visiting other institutions of learning and research in different cities in China.

The Library Association of China was founded in 1925 when Dr. Arthur E. Bostwick, Librarian of St. Louis Public Library, attended its inaugural meeting as the Official Delegate of the American Library

Association. The Association is to hold its tenth anniversary at the time of Dr. Keogh's visit and we trust that his mission will arouse greater interest and will bring about closer cultural co-operation between China and the United States.

As the Association is unable to finance Dr. Keogh's trip because of its budgetary limitations, it is therefore hoped that the Rockefeller Foundation which is always interested in the promotion of better international understanding will give the necessary support to this project, the carrying out of which will undoubtedly mean a great deal in Sino-American cultural relations.

Yours very sincerely,
T. L. Yuan
Chairman, Executive Committee

〔中华图书馆协会英文信纸。Rockefeller Foundation. Series 601: China; Subseries 601.R: China-Humanities and Arts. Vol. Box 47. Folder 388; Yale University records, Peiping National Library, 1931-1937, Box: 80, Folder: 831〕

按：此件为打字稿，落款处为先生签名。

先生致卡耐基国际和平基金会主席巴特勒两信，其一，感谢基金会向平馆捐赠图书，并请考虑资助美国图书馆专家毕寿普访问中国。

March 2, 1935

President Nicholas Murray Butler,

Carnegie Endowment for International Peace,

405 W. 117th St.,

New York, N. Y.

Dear President Butler:

Upon my return to China, I was very much gratified to receive from the Carnegie Endowment a set of Mr. David Hunter Miller's *Diary of the Peace Conference* which you so kindly presented to the National Library of Peiping. It is indeed a most valuable addition to our collections and I hasten to write to extend to you and Mr. Haskell our very hearty thanks for the inclusion of our library among the depositories of this monumental work.

It was a pleasure to receive the other day your Message to the Japanese People given on the New Year's Day. It was a most frank advice which, we are sure, will produce an immense effect on the Japanese mind. In view of the importance of the document, I am arranging to have it translated into Chinese which will be published in all the leading Chinese newspapers.

When I called on you last April, I expressed to you our desire to extend an invitation to Dr. W. W. Bishop to visit China for a few months in 1935 in order to advise us in the development of our libraries. It was gratifying to find that you endorsed the plan. The Chinese Library Association has extended an official invitation to Dr. Bishop and we trust his visit will help in bringing about closer cultural co-operation between China and the United States.

Knowing your great interest in promoting international understanding and knowing your confidence in Dr. Bishop to carry out the task entrusted to him, I take the liberty of soliciting your assistance in the realization of the plan. I enclose therefore a letter of application from the Library Association of China and I hope you will find it possible to give it your favourable consideration.

With sincere greetings, I am,

Yours respectfully,

T. L. Yuan,

Acting Director

其二,先生以中华图书馆协会执行部主席身份恳请卡耐基基金会资助毕寿普访华考察图书馆事业。

March 2, 1935

Dear President Butler:

With a view of bringing about closer co-operation between Chinese and American libraries, the Library Association of China has extended an invitation to Dr. W. W. Bishop to visit China in 1935 to make a survey of Chinese libraries and to assist us in working out a plan for their further development. It is also hoped that the visit of Dr. Bishop will not be too limited, so that he will have an opportunity of visiting other institutions of learning and research in different cities in China.

The Library Association of China was founded in 1925 when Dr. Arthur E. Bostwick, Librarian of St. Louis Public Library, attended its inaugural meeting as the Official Delegate of the American Library Association. The Association is to hold its tenth anniversary at the time of Dr. Bishop's visit and we trust that his mission will arouse greater interest and will bring about closer cultural co-operation between China and United States.

As the association is unable to finance Dr. Bishop's trip because of its budgetary limitations, it is therefore hoped that the Carnegie Endowment which is always interested in the promotion of better international understanding will give the necessary support to the project, the carrying out of which will undoubtedly mean a great deal in Sino-American cultural relations.

Yours very sincerely,

T. L. Yuan

Chairman, Executive Board.

〔中华图书馆协会英文信纸。Columbia University Libraries Archival Collections, Carnegie Endowment for International Peace Record, Box 322, Folder Yuan, T. L.〕

按：此两件均为打字稿，落款处为先生签名，于本月底送达。

三月四日

先生致信毕寿普，附上致科普尔信的副本，希望密歇根大学可以顺利批准其请假访华的申请，并对 Benjamin March 的突然离世表示惋惜。

March 4, 1935

Dr. W. W. Bishop, Librarian,

University of Michigan,

Ann Arbor, Michigan, U. S. A.

Dear Dr. Bishop:

With further reference to my letter of February 28, I enclose a copy of my letter to President Keppel of the Carnegie Corporation. As the Corporation makes grants only to institutions in English-speaking countries, I am writing him a personal letter without asking for financial support. When I interviewed with him last April, he indicated considerable interest in having you and Dr. Keogh make the trip to China and I believe he has already written to urge you to arrange for it. I trust, however, that the Carnegie Corporation can make grants to finance your trip through the Carnegie Endowment or the American Library Association.

Aside from the financial arrangements, I hope you will have no difficulty in asking the University for a leave of absence. We are inclined to think that President Ruthven and the Board of Regents would approve your request for leave in view of the importance of your mission as well as in view of the cordial relations China has had with the University of Michigan.

When I was in Chicago, I suggested to Mr. Milam that the A. L. A. should make a series of moving pictures of American libraries as they would arouse immense interest if you would bring them over. A series of lantern slides showing latest development of library buildings and equipment should also be desirable.

From Dr. John W. Stanton who is now studying in Peiping, I am extremely sorry to learn the sudden death of Mr. Benjamin March. It is a great loss to the University and to China. Personally, I have suffered an irreparable loss of one of my best friends.

With kindest regards,

Yours sincerely,

T. L. Yuan

Acting Director

〔Yale University records, Peiping National Library, 1931–1937, Box: 80, Folder: 831〕

按：President Ruthven 即 Alexander G. Ruthven（1882-1971），1929
年至 1951 年担任密歇根大学校长。John W. Stanton 应为密歇根
大学的博士，著有 *Russian Embassies to Peking During the XVIIIth
Century*（1937）；Benjamin March 即 Benjamin F. March Jr.（1899-
1934），亚洲艺术学家，曾任密歇根大学人类学博物馆馆长，著有
China and Japan in Our Museums（1929）等，《国立北平图书馆馆
刊》曾予以介绍[1]，1934 年因心脏病去世。

先生致信科普尔，附上与米来牟往来有关邀请毕寿普、凯欧访华考察图书
馆事业的信件，请卡耐基基金会考虑资助，并附有关葛斯德图书馆的备
忘录。

March 4, 1935

Dear President Keppel:

When I had the privilege of meeting you in New York last April, I
mentioned to you our desire of asking Dr. W. W. Bishop and Dr. Andrew
Keogh to arrange for a visit to China. I was very much gratified to find
that you took considerable interest in library development in China and
you endorsed the plan of inviting two American library experts to make a
survey of our libraries.

Upon my return to China, the Chinese Library Association has
extended an official invitation to Dr. Bishop and Dr. Keogh. I now enclose
copy of our letter to Mr. C. H. Milam, Secretary of the American Library
Association and we earnestly hope that both of them would be able to
plan for a trip this autumn.

I enclose a memorandum regarding the Gest Library which I
promised you. I should have submitted it to you long ago, but a strenuous
journey in Europe has made the delay unavoidable.

With kindest regards,

Yours sincerely,

T. L. Yuan

---

[1] 《国立北平图书馆馆刊》第 4 卷第 5 期，页 129。

Chairman, Executive Committee

〔Yale University records, Peiping National Library, 1931-1937, Box: 80, Folder: 831〕

按：a memorandum regarding the Gest Library 未存，此为抄件。

三月五日

先生致信凯欧，略述在纽约洛克菲勒基金会商谈资助其与毕寿普作为美国图书馆学专家赴华考察的初步结果，并表示在财务支出外，可先与耶鲁校方沟通请假的可能性。

March 5, 1935

Dear Dr. Keogh:

With reference to my letter of January 31, I enclose a copy of my letter to Dr. Stevens and President Keppel. From my conversations with them while in New York, I am rather confident that the request will be granted. Although the Corporation makes grants only to institutions in English-speaking countries, it can finance your trip through the A. L. A. especially as President Keppel indicated considerable interest in having you and Dr. Bishop make the trip to China.

Aside from the financial arrangements, I hope you will have no difficulty in asking the University for a leave of absence. We are inclined to think that President Angell would approve your request for leave in view of the significance of your mission and in view of the close relations Yale has had with China in the past.

Dr. Bishop asked me to write him somewhat fully about our plans. I enclose herewith copy of a memorandum which represents only my own point of view. There will be many more points to be raised after your inspection tour and after your conference with other librarians in China.

With warmest regards,

Yours sincerely,

T. L. Yuan

Chairman, Executive Committee

〔中华图书馆协会英文信纸。Yale University records, Peiping National Library, 1931-1937, Box: 80, Folder: 831〕

按：President Angell 即 James R. Angell(1869-1949)，美国心理学家，1921 年至 1937 年担任耶鲁大学校长。此件为打字稿，落款处为先生签名，附备忘录一份，于 4 月 1 日送达耶鲁大学。

胡适致函先生，告张云川搜集苏区资料，欲寄存平馆。

> 守和兄：
>
> 　　顷得马幼渔先生来函，说有张云川君，在共产党区域收到文件甚多，他很想将这些文件寄存在北平图书馆一类的机关，所以我请张君来看您。幼渔先生原函附呈。匆匆，敬问大安。
>
> 　　　　　　　　　　　　　　　　　胡适敬上
> 　　　　　　　　　　　　　　　　廿四，三，五夜
>
> 　　　　　〔《北京图书馆馆史资料汇编(1909-1949)》，页 407〕

按：张云川(1903—1965)，江苏萧县(今属安徽)人，肄业于黄埔军校第六期，曾任北伐军团政治指导员。

三月八日

晚，先生由平汉线南下武汉。〔《世界日报》，1935 年 3 月 9 日，第 7 版〕

按：先生在武昌事毕后，将转南京，向教育部报告平馆馆务。

三月十日

先生赴武昌文华图书馆学专科学校讲演，主题为"欧美图书馆之新趋势"。〔《文华图书馆学专科学校季刊》第 7 卷第 1 期，1935 年 3 月 15 日，页 1-4、163-164〕

按：2 月底，武昌文华图书馆学专科学校致函先生，邀请其南下赴校演讲，演讲辞由该校胡延钧、邬学通记录整理，后刊于《文华图书馆学专科学校季刊》。

三月中上旬

先生在武汉私立中华大学演讲，题为"欧游见闻——中国与国际文化之关系"，大意如下：

> 诸位同学：
>
> 　　兄弟很久想到武汉来参观，因为有八九年没有到过武汉了。今天有机会到贵校来，看了学校组织的完备、同学成绩的优良，真使得我第一要感动：敬佩陈校长私人办学的热忱！
>
> 　　今天承陈校长要我兄弟讲演中国与国际文化之关系。在十九世纪，中国与国际完全是商业的交换，现在因为交通的便利，将空间、时

间缩小或缩短,到欧洲仅需半月,所以中国在国际上,有密切的关系了!中国与外国文化发生关系的,要算俄国来得密切,因为她与中国是邻国。俄国研究中国的文化,有两个中心点:一是列宁格勒,一是莫斯科。在列宁格勒地方,有中国语言学校,研究中国的语言文字。博物院收藏中国的艺术字画。至在莫斯科,是研究中国现在的问题,如政治,经济,商业……,规模宏大,这种机关,完全是受共产党文化部的指挥。我们真惭愧,没有像俄国一样的机关,研究过去与现在的文化。向西走去,便有波兰,捷克,亦有研究中国学术的机关,像东方学院,不过规模较小些。再西走,便到德法英意等国了。她们研究中国的学术,亦很厉害。像德国因为与中国有好的感情,对于中国的政治、商业与文化,研究得很好,博物院收藏中国古代的文物,异常的丰富。德人研究中国文化的中心地:有柏林,汉堡,来比锡等地,德国人研究学术态度很彻底。如研究中国的瓷器,送到化验室化验,百分之几是某种原料。这研究的方法是合理的。

再,谈到法国,法国的文化,她的菁华完全集在巴黎。巴黎大学附设的东方学院,崇门研究中国古代的文化,中国人有二三人在那儿担任这种任务。东方语言学校,是训练到中国做领事的人才。还有中国文化讲座,博物院大都收藏丰富,如气美博物馆,设备非常完备,到那里就好似到了中国一样。法人研究中国文化有独到之处,所以有法兰西学派之称。巴黎有五六个小博物院,中国有些赶不上哩!法国对于中国的文学很考究,像蒙古文,西藏文,满洲文……。尤其是对于云南土著的语言,研究得很好。著作的刊物,真不下数百种!外国人有这种研究精神,真使得我们惭愧极了!

再看英国,英国研究中国文化最特殊的,是美术。文字方面的研究,东方语言学院,成绩斐然。博物院,伦敦大学,东方学术研究所,都在研究中国的文化。

现在,再看美国,美国是联邦制,所以研究中国文化,分散在各城。中心点如哥伦比亚,哈佛,西雅图,加里弗尼亚等大学,都是研究中国文化的中心地方。还有耶鲁大学,设有中国文化讲座。哥伦比亚大学,支加哥大学,太平洋月报……,讨论中国现在的问题,有很好的成绩。美国的博物院有很多的收藏,亦特别地丰富,像支加哥,波士顿是好的比例。堪斯细得博物院,曾以千万磅美金收买中国的古物,现在我们反躬自问的慎后惩前,实在有从速设立博物馆的必要。不然,实在无法保存中国的古物了。外国人研究了中国的文化,阅读了我们中亚文字的论文,近来对于中国,有比较密切些的情感。今日我们受高等教育的人,应负有整理或研究中国文化的使命呵!

最后要谈到中国文化与国际政治上和外交上的关系:文化建设的基础,是在经济上面。中国是个大的市场,外人因为工业进步,生产过剩,制造品必须输入外国。但是各国的工业,都达到了高级时期,因此,关税壁垒森严,而中国则为其尾闾。外国人对于中国,主张:"门户开放,机会均等",结果,中国遭受了很大的漏卮!去年中国在英国,购了价值数百万磅的机械,可以说救济了世界不景气的一部分。德法现在很想和我国亲善。希望国家的政治,走上轨道,促进工业的发展,实行关税自主,唤醒民众使用国货,保护国民的经济利益,非不得已时,不用外货。

欧洲的政治,与远东有大的关系。在外交方面,政治方面,现在我们不愿意依赖任何强国,在一九三四年里,各国大战的呼声极高,但是因为西欧、东欧的公约,俄国加入国联,战争才得设法使之没有爆发。在去年国际政治方面,有个特殊的情形,便是国联破裂了,而地方公约很盛行。现在国际间,对德问题与波兰问题解决了,欧美各国将集中视力于远东。中日间的问题,中东铁路非法买卖的问题,各国都极其注重。现在英国竭力地在经营新嘉坡。我国今日的地位,确实很危险,应该在四面楚歌的环境里,全国一致团结,找出"救亡图存"的出路。教育是唯一救亡图存的方针,今天兄弟看见陈校长热心教育的工作,觉得中国前途很有希望。谨祝诸君努力!

〔《中华季刊》第 3 卷第 1 期,1935 年 5 月〕

按:此文刊于《中华季刊》,由萧剑云、曾任侠、张光球三位学生纪录。"陈校长"即陈时,时任私立中华大学校长。该篇失收于《袁同礼文集》。

武昌文华图书馆学专科学校召开特别会议,先生作为校董与会,对学校各项事宜,如筹划经费、添聘教员、向教育部及中华教育文化基金董事会继续请款、招考新生、毕业生出路等均允诺设法援助。〔《文华图书馆学专科学校季

刊》第 7 卷第 1 期,1935 年 3 月 15 日,页 164〕

三月十四日

晚,武昌文华图书馆学专科学校教职员及学生代表为先生设宴饯行。〔《文华图书馆学专科学校季刊》第 7 卷第 1 期,1935 年 3 月 15 日,页 164 〕

三月中下旬

先生由武汉前往南京,向教育部报告馆务。〔《京报》,1935 年 3 月 19 日,第 7 版〕

是年春

先生以中华图书馆协会执行部主席身份覆信菲律宾图书馆协会副会长伯礼兹(C. B. Perez)。

The members of the Library Association of China are very much delighted at the news: that the Second Philippine National Book Week will be instituted in the latter half of June, 1935. The Philippine Library Association is to be congratulated for sponsoring this project which, we are sure, will be of considerable cultural significance.

Ever since its inception, the book has played a very important role in the progress of man. It is regrettable that there are still many people to whom the importance of the book has not manifested itself. They fail to see that by virtue of books the distance of time and place between men will be removed. Any effort in trying to win over this large number of people to the group of booklovers is worthy of every support and encouragement.

When the news of the Second Philippine National Book Week was received, the First Chinese National Book Week was in progress. It is gratifying to note that the two countries are now moving along similar lines towards a common object for the enlightenment of mankind upon which the peace and prosperity of the world depend.

The Philippine Library Association is putting forth a worthy project the value and importance of which we fully appreciate. On behalf of my fellow librarians in China, I beg to convey to your Association our best wishes for your every success.

T. L. Yuan

Chairman, Executive Committee

〔《中华图书馆协会会报》第 10 卷第 5 期,1935 年 4 月 30 日,页 22〕

按:此前,该协会伯礼兹曾来信希望中、菲两国图书馆协会可以互通消息并开展国际借书。

三月二十七日　上海

下午,伦敦中国艺术国际展览会筹备委员会在四马路梅园酒家设宴款待外方委员三人,分别为伯希和、赫伯森、欧默福普洛斯,中方与席者有杨振声、先生、郭葆昌、张煜全、叶恭绰、吴湖帆、唐惜分等共十余人。〔《申报》,1935 年 3 月 28 日,第 9 版〕

按:赫伯森即 Robert L. Hobson(1872-1941),大英博物馆东方古物及人类学部主任,著名的陶瓷专家;欧默福普洛斯即 George A. Eumorfopoulos(1863-1939),英国收藏家,以收集中国、日本及近东地区艺术品著称。该会另一位委员拉斐尔(Oscar C. Raphael,1874-1941)已于此前赴日。

三月底

先生由南京乘车北返抵平。〔《华北日报》,1935 年 3 月 25 日,第 9 版〕

四月一日

卡耐基国际和平基金会覆函先生,告知该基金会国际交流、教育两部门均无相应的资金可以用来资助毕寿普来华考察图书馆事业。

April 1, 1935

My dear Dr. Yuan:

President Butler asks me to acknowledge on his behalf your two letters dated March 2, which he has read with interest. He asks me to express his regret that the Division of Intercourse and Education has no fund available which could be used to cover the expenses of the proposed visit of Dr. William Warner Bishop to libraries in China. The undertaking itself is one which is of great interest to us, and we wish very much that it might be carried out, for we believe that Dr. Bishop's rare knowledge in the field of library organization and service would not only be of great benefit to the libraries in China but that such a visit by him would develop

futher the already strong feeling of friendship between the peoples of
China and of the United States.

Sincerely yours,

Henry S. Haskell

Assistant to the Director

〔Columbia University Libraries Archival Collections, Carnegie
Endowment for International Peace Record, Box 322, Folder Yuan,
T. L.〕

按:该件为录副。

四月二日

史蒂文斯覆函先生,告知洛克菲勒基金会暂时无法赞助美国图书馆专家
访华。

April 2, 1935

Dear Dr. Yuan:

Your letter of March 2 was sent on by Dr. Bishop with word that he
had previously reported to Dr. Keogh of Yale University your invitation
for a visit to China during 1935 for the purpose of surveying Chinese
libraries with a view to their future development. This request touches
upon a type of activity that has not yet been approved under the work of
this division of the Foundation. I therefore must beg that you leave the
question in my hands for the time being. I shall have the matter
considered and will report to you as soon as possible.

Sincerely yours,

David H. Stevens

〔Rockefeller Foundation. Series 601: China; Subseries 601.R: China-
Humanities and Arts. Vol. Box 47. Folder 388〕

毕寿普覆函先生,表示自己和凯欧都愿意承担访华考察图书馆事业的任
务,但为此筹集必要资金的责任则需要中方承担,此外询问中国政府机
构是否会出具官方邀请函,并告可能须待一九三六年才能有时间赴华
访问。

April 2, 1935

My dear Mr. Yuan:

Permit me to acknowledge your very kind letter of March 4 with its enclosures.

As I am sure you know, both Dr. Keogh and I would be very glad indeed to come to China for the purposes which you have outlined in your several letters. We both feel that the benefit to American libraries from the visit would be fully as great as any gain which can be expected from our own assistance to our Chinese colleagues. We are both of us willing to take the time, and we think that our respective universities can probably spare us for the necessary period of absence.

Neither of us feels, however, that we should be charged with the duty of raising funds for a trip of this sort. It is not of our own seeking, and it hardly seems to us proper to ask the various American foundations for assistance in the matter. We have, however, advised the Carnegie Corporation, the Rockefeller Foundation, and the Carnegie Endowment for International Peace of the proposed visit and have received a certain amount of encouragement which leads us to suppose that consideration at least will be given to the plan on the part of all three foundations. Your letters to Dr. Butler and to David Stevens a few days since were duly forwarded to New York from Ann Arbor.

In your conversations with Dr. Keogh, which he reported to me last June in Montreal and again in New York in February, you mentioned a formal invitation from the Chinese government which would give the visit an official character. You may have decided that it is better not to attempt this and, of course, neither Dr. Keogh or I desire to insist upon it. From the fact that you have said nothing about any such governmental invitation in your correspondence with me, I am inclined to suppose that you and your colleagues of the Chinese Library Association have felt that an informal, rather than a formal, visit is preferable. I think, however, that we should have a definite understanding on this point.

Comparing notes, Dr. Keogh and I find that the only time at which we can both be absent from the United States in the next academic year is the late winter and spring of 1936. That is to say, we are both very much occupied during the first semester of the academic year and there are local reasons which make it extremely difficult for me to be away at that time. We can both of us get away in March for the journey, so that we could arrive in April and return probably in June. We might be able to come earlier if that is desirable. I think we should both of us wish not to be too much hurried in a trip of this sort.

I fear that this later date will prove inconvenient for your own plans. It would be somewhat difficult to arrange an absence in the autumn of 1935, but it could perhaps be done.

You will see, then, how the matter now stands. By reason of your activities, the three great American foundations have been notified that the Chinese Library Association wishes to have Dr. Keogh and myself come to China to visit libraries and to meet with Chinese librarians. You have urged appropriations for this purpose on the heads and leading officers of these three foundations, i. e. Dr. Keppel, Dr. Butler, and Dr. David Stevens. You have further suggested that the American Library Association appoint Dr. Keogh and myself as official representatives of that Association to your own Association.

I presume that you realize that as neither of us reads or speaks Chinese it will be necessary to have the services of a capable interpreter for any such trip as the one contemplated. This adds necessarily an additional item of expense which must be met from some source.

Professor Charles F. Remer, of this University, is now on his way to China and promised me to confer with you about the matter as soon as possible after his arrival in Peiping. I talked to him at some length so that he knows thoroughly the difficulties which confront me personally in arriving at a decision.

With all good wishes and warm regards, and with greetings to our colleagues in the Chinese Library Association, I am, my dear Dr. Yuan,

Faithfully yours,

William Warner Bishop

Librarian

〔Yale University records, Peiping National Library, 1931 – 1937, Box: 80, Folder: 831〕

按:Charles F. Remer(1889-1972),美国经济学家,尤其对中国经济、矿产有较深的研究,通译作"雷麦",1933 年在纽约出版其代表作*Foreign Investments in China*,1937 年 6 月由蒋学楷、赵康节中译为《外人在华投资论》,商务印书馆初版。该件为抄件,寄送给凯欧。

四月初

伦敦中国艺术国际展览会筹备委员会王世杰、陈树人、褚民谊、张道藩、徐谟、邹琳、曾仲鸣、段锡朋、陶履谦、马衡、先生联名发出请柬,邀请各界名流四月七日下午二时赴仁记路中国银行旧址参观预展。〔《时事新报》,1935 年 4 月 5 日,第 7 版〕

按:陶履谦(1890—1944),字益生,祖籍浙江绍兴,生于广州,1911 年毕业于北京译学馆,时任国民政府内政部政务次长兼代理内政部部长。

四月四日

上午九时,方树梅赴平馆与先生、李文裿等辞别。〔《北游搜访文献日记》,页 72〕

按:4 月 7 日,方树梅离平前往天津。

下午五时,平馆委员会召开第十八次会议,傅斯年、周诒春、胡适、任鸿隽、孙洪芬、蒋梦麟、陈垣、先生出席,胡适为会议主席,先生记录。讨论议案如下:

(一)审核一九三五年度预算案。议决经常费及事业费以十四万为原则,预算内各项细目由平馆再行提出,中文购书费定为六万元,西文购书费定为美金三万元。

(二)修理本馆建筑案。议决原则上通过,由平馆再委他家商店估价,再请中基会拨款。

(三)平馆善本书籍送伦敦中国艺术展览案,议决照单通过。

六时散会。〔《北京图书馆馆史资料汇编(1909-1949)》,页350〕

　　　　按:平馆选送伦敦中国艺术展览之善本书籍共计五十种,其细目
　　　可参见《参加伦敦中国艺术国际展览会出品图说:第四册其他
　　　类》,但在英实际陈列者应为二十三册件。[1]

张云川致函先生,谈苏区资料整理计划,希望予以补助。

　　　　守和先生大鉴:

　　　　马幼渔、胡适之两先生介函业蒙鉴及。兹再将云川此次南去之经
　　　过及所获文件若干,为先生一陈之。

　　　　窃共产党盘扰江西数年,乃中国社会近年之一大事变。国军与共
　　　产党两方之夸大宣传,非诋之为地狱即自诩为天堂,吾人恐其都有未
　　　当。故云川为探究中国社会,一明事实真相起见,爰于去岁十二月
　　　底——瑞金收复后之半月——有考察收复共区之行,计共经黎川、南
　　　城、广昌、宁都、瑞金、会昌等十数县。徒步千余里(不通汽车处),需
　　　时两月余,用款四百余元,蒐获之共方文件,如命令、章则、条例、刊物、
　　　书籍等近千件。如依一人之能力论,所获亦不可谓不多矣。至于背负
　　　运送舟车起卸,请求军政警宪机关之证明放行,尤属困难重重,非身历
　　　者之所能想象者。及今云川欲将所获材料加以整理应用,公之于世,
　　　徒以困于生活之资,力不从心,继经马、胡两先生之介,拟请贵馆每月
　　　酌予接济,以半年为期,俾云川得竟初志。一俟整理应用过后,即将全
　　　部文件移赠贵馆,为公众常留此一部分探研社会之史料,未悉能荷俞
　　　允否? 如何之处,敬希鸿裁,赐复为感。肃此,并颂公绥。

　　　　　　　　　　　　　　　　　　　　　　　张云川敬上
　　　　　　　　　　　　　　　　　　　　　　　四月四日

　　　　　〔《北京图书馆馆史资料汇编(1909-1949)》,页410-412〕

四月五日

先生赠方树梅故宫博物院图书馆善本、普通书目各一册。〔《北游搜访文献日
记》,页73〕

　　　　按:本日中午十二时,方树梅赴故宫博物院图书馆看馆藏书目,尤

---

[1]《参加伦敦中国艺术国际展览会报告》,1936年,页10。

其检视滇人著述。

先生覆信张云川,谈收购苏区资料事。

云川先生大鉴:

日前接对清晖,欣慰无既。台端此次南行,所获材料颇为丰富,具仰辛劳,并拟从事整理,赠诸敝馆,尤感厚意。惟敝馆经常费薪俸一项业无余款,未能如愿延纳,至为歉歉。购书费尚有盈余,倘以此项材料让诸敝馆,丞愿收购也。或派人前往尊处接洽,或送馆审查,统希尊裁。专此奉复,顺候台祺。

袁厶厶拜启

廿四年四月五日办,五日发

〔《北京图书馆馆史资料汇编(1909-1949)》,页 408-409〕

按:此信为文书代笔。所寄地址为"燕京大学蔚秀园十三号"。

四月六日

上午九时许,中美工程师学会十五届年会假平馆工程阅览室召开,到会者六十余人。会长王宠佑因事未能到场,由第一副会长美人迪安(S. M. Dean)致辞,并宣读会议议程及"中国在世界上矿产所占的地位"。随后选举新职员,迪安当选为会长,郑华为第一副会长、李书田为第二副会长,并摄影留念。中午,先生设宴款待各与会人员。下午一时半,先生引导该会会员参观中国现代工业资料展览会,后继续开会,与会人员宣读各专门论文。〔《华北日报》,1935 年 4 月 7 日,第 9 版〕

先生致信伯希和,告知已经为伦敦展览挑选了古籍善本,尤其选择了早期印本以满足其愿望。

April 6, 1935

Prof. Paul Pelliot,

Cathay Hotel,

Shanghai.

Dear Prof. Pelliot:

I appreciate very much your letter of 29th March.

Since coming back to Peiping, I have made a selection of twenty more items of early printed books for the London Exhibition. These are being sent to Mr. Yang by registered mail.

From the enclosed list, you will see that it is quite representative of early printing, and I have tried to meet your wishes as far as possible.

For the *Kao-li tu-ching*, I am referring your letter to Prof. Ma Heng, as it is not included in our collections.

As to the *Ku-yu tu-pu* in the Ssu-Ku Collection, it is not an important work from the point of view of textual criticism and therefore has not been included in the lot.

I hope you will have a pleasant visit to Shanghai and Nanking and I shall look forward to the pleasure of seeing you in Peiping.

Your sincerely,

T. L. Yuan

Acting Director

〔国立北平图书馆英文信纸。法国吉美博物馆伯希和档案〕

按:Mr. Yang 应指杨振声。*Kao-li tu-ching*、*Ku-yu tu-pu* 分别为《高丽图经》《古玉图谱》。此件为打字稿,落款处为先生签名。

四月八日

王世杰致电先生,请平馆增补善本参加伦敦艺展古籍展览。

文津街国立北平图书馆袁守和先生:

参加伦敦艺展之古书,杰及筹委会同人均盼兄能将北宋版活字版及宋元版本增选送展,至盼电复。

京,士杰,庚。印。

〔国家图书馆档案,档案编号 1934-※043-外事 2-007013〕

四月九日

先生复电王世杰,告已增选善本。

南京教育部王部长鉴:

庚电敬悉。已选北宋元明及活字本古书、六朝写经、西夏文经,径寄沪。

同△复,青。

〔国家图书馆档案,档案编号 1934-※043-外事 2-007012〕

按:此件为底稿。

四月十二日

毕寿普致函先生,告已收到国民政府教育部长王世杰的邀请函。

April 12, 1935

My dear Dr. Yuan:

Since dictating the letter which accompanies this, I have received a very kind letter from the Minister of Education of China, expressing the hope that I may be able to visit China and make a survey of Chinese libraries. I understand from Dr. Keogh, with whom I talked on the telephone recently, that he has also received a letter to the same effect. I am enclosing a copy of my reply to His Excellency.

Dr. Keogh has seen my letter to you of April 12 and completely approves of it. It may, therefore, stand as a joint letter from us both.

Faithfully yours,

W. W. Bishop

〔Yale University records, Peiping National Library, 1931–1937, Box: 80, Folder: 831〕

按:此件为录副。王世杰(Shih-chieh, Wang)写给毕寿普的信应于 3 月发出,4 月 8 日送达耶鲁大学图书馆。

四月十三日

下午三时,先生受邀赴北平大学女子文理学院演讲,题为"美国女子大学(之)概况"。〔《益世报》(北平),1935 年 4 月 14 日,第 9 版〕

按:本次演讲后被《大学新闻周报》刊登①,记录者署名"绛珠",似为朱崇庆。

先生致信王重民,告知汪长炳将往西班牙参加图书馆大会,并附论文一篇,请代为转交汪长炳。

汪长炳已由教部委为在西班牙举行图书馆大会代表,兹有论文一篇,请转交。可先寄一信至伦敦中国使馆转,并告其在巴黎之住址,如汪君不到伦敦,或可先至巴黎。如见不着,即将此稿径寄西班牙中国使馆(Madrid)留交为荷。该会五月二十开会也。此上

———————————

① 《大学新闻周报》(北平)第 3 卷第 8 期,1935 年 4 月 23 日,第 4 版。

有三吾兄

袁同礼顿首

四,十三

〔顾晓光《袁同礼致王重民四通书信浅疏》〕

四月十六日

平馆与何遂补订"闽县何氏赠与古物契约",先生作为受赠人(代表)签字盖章,见证人为万兆之、林行规。〔《国立北平图书馆馆务报告(民国二十三年七月至二十四年六月)》,附录五〕

> 按:1932年春,何遂自陕遣赠平馆瓦当、墓志、陶器等物,后又陆续以玉器、甲骨、铜器、石刻、陶器、木雕、乐浪遗物、拓本、书画等古物寄托平馆。1934年2月,何遂函告平馆,其年5月2日为何太夫人春晖老人古稀之寿,为纪念其母寿诞,除书籍等件外,将寄存平馆各物全部永远捐赠。另,此次订立契约,何遂由其弟何岑代表。

四月二十九日

某记者来访,先生略谈筹备中国博物馆协会进展,表示预计一周后公布章程。〔《世界日报》,1935年4月30日,第7版〕

四月三十日

凯欧致函先生,感谢寄赠《清代图书馆发展史》。

April 30, 1935

Dear Mr. Yuan:

　　I have safely received the personal copy of "*The Development of Chinese Libraries under the Ch'ing Dynasty*" by Cheuk-Woon Taam, that you were kind enough to send me. I have skimmed the book already, but I can see how very valuable it is going to be for me if I should make the trip to China.

Yours very sincerely,

〔Yale University records, Peiping National Library, 1931 - 1937, Box: 80, Folder: 831〕

　　按: *The Development of Chinese Libraries under the Ch'ing Dynasty* 即谭卓垣的英文著作,该书中文题名为《清代图书馆发展史》,

1935 年 1 月商务印书馆初版。此件为录副。

五月一日

先生致信陈垣，请其还书数种以便转交伯希和翻阅。

　　援庵先生尊鉴：

　　　　前尊处借用《元秘史》、《华夷译语》、越缦堂手稿本及《新会县志》等书，如已用毕，拟请费神检出，交去人携下为感。内中有数种拟交伯希和一看，渠日内来平也。专此，顺颂大安。

后学袁同礼顿首
五月一日

　　　　〔陈智超编注《陈垣来往书信集》，北京：生活·读书·新知三联书店，2010 年，页 619〕

五月二日

先生致信王重民，告知将与法方（伯希和）沟通延长其在法国服务时间等事。

　　有三仁弟如晤：

　　　　连接来书，欣悉旅居巴黎，一切顺适，至以为慰。上月离平共三星期，返后又忙，久未作复。伯希和在沪晤面数次，不日来平交换昭陵碑，当与之一谈，交换及延长事当可决定。杜女士极愿延长一年，惟法方愿来华者亦大有人在，法使馆亦为之帮忙，想法庚款方面无问题。本馆有二条件，（一）执事在法亦延长一年；（二）杜女士在华多留一年，本馆不负任何经济上之责任。但如同时要求，执事在法亦受九千元之待遇，或较现在之四千元为多，均不易实现。盖法方国立图书馆或受外交部之补助，增加预算较难，而我庚款法国之部份此外并有中国部份及共同部份由法使馆可完全作主也。现在只可作退一步想，能在巴黎多延长一年，亦比自费为上算也。又法使馆增加之五千元，伯希和认为太多，恐旅费亦在内。《海外希见录》已登《图书副刊》，以后寄散处，亦可径寄王庸或贺昌群亦可，因向君拟秋间赴英。影照燉煌卷子进行顺利极佳，下年度清华仍可出资，总以在执事未离巴黎以前，将其重要者完全照完为要拟由清华及本馆再各认贰千元。太平天国文件不识有若干，或东方语言学校有多种也。关于天主教之书，闻徐家汇有全份，故不必照，但作一有系统之目录，则甚有用。兹寄上在罗马所钞一部分，其余者则因无暇停止，将来可继续完成之。李乐知托照南、艾二先生行述,亦盼早日摄出寄去。专此,顺颂旅安。

> 同礼顿首
>
> 五月二日

汪君长炳已赴西班牙,前寄之论文,可寄使馆转交。外一信转寄王静如。

〔国立北平图书馆用笺。顾晓光《袁同礼致王重民四通书信浅疏》〕

按:《海外希见录》刊《大公报·图书副刊》第 75 期(1935 年 4 月 18 日)。"因向君拟秋间赴英"即指向达前往牛津大学协助整理该校中文典籍,10 月 9 日向达离开北平,约于 20 日在上海乘船去国。[①]"南、艾二先生"应分指来华耶稣会士南怀仁(Ferdinand Verbiest,1623-1688)、艾儒略(Giulio Aleni,1582-1649)。

五月三日

先生致信王献唐,邀其担任中国博物院协会发起人。

> 献唐先生大鉴:
>
> 同人为提倡博物院运动起见,拟组织中国博物院协会,集合同志努力进行。素仰台端斗山重望,举世所钦,敢请加入为发起人,庶几登高一呼,则群谷响应。专此奉达,并希惠允是荷。顺候台祺。
>
> 弟袁同礼顿首
>
> 五月三日

〔安可荇、王书林整理《王献唐师友书札》,青岛:青岛出版社,2009 年,页 1213〕

按:该信于 5 月 7 日送达。

五月四日

下午四时,中华图书馆协会在平执行委员假平馆海约翰纪念室举行会议,讨论会务。先生(主席)、洪有丰、田洪都、严文郁等出席,于震寰记录。先生报告会务,并提交执行委员会 1935 年 1 月至 4 月的油印报告,涉及协会出版事业、全国图书馆一览、美图书馆专家来华、会员汪长炳旅欧等事。此外,讨论协会年会、国际图书馆大会代表旅费、事务所于震寰薪给、协会基

[①]《北平圕与英国交换馆员》,《中华图书馆协会会报》第 11 卷第 2 期,1935 年 10 月,页 38。

金募集、增加会费办法、《图书馆学季刊》稿件等诸事。〔《中华图书馆协会会报》第 10 卷第 6 期,页 14-15〕

五月六日

史蒂文斯致函先生,请先生提供更多的信息以便为美国图书馆专家毕寿普制订明年访华计划。

May 6, 1935

Dear Dr. Yuan:

　　Since writing to you on April 2 regarding the proposal to have a visit to China from Dr. Bishop and Dr. Keogh, I have discussed with Dr. Bishop his own plans for the coming year. He informs me that his work would make it impossible for him to leave the University during the autumn months and too, that in planning such a mission he would need more clearly defined statements of what might be expected during his time in China. I know that he is interested himself in gaining information that could be applied in his own institution and that he would be a useful adviser to other American centers that should do more in purchase of Far Eastern materials. But the present year is clearly not a possible time for such a plan, at least so far as Dr. Bishop is concerned. When I have further information from him or from Dr. Keogh, I shall be glad to report to you.

Sincerely yours,

David H. Stevens

〔Rockefeller Foundation. Series 601: China; Subseries 601.R: China-Humanities and Arts. Vol. Box 47. Folder 388〕

　　按:事实上,史蒂文斯最初对该计划持负面态度,是耿士楷 4 月 5 日的来信使他将这个计划重新列入基金会的考虑中。

五月九日

中午十二点三刻,徐森玉、马衡、沈兼士、先生假欧美同学会设宴款待伯希和。〔法国吉美博物馆伯希和档案〕

下午二时,故宫博物院在礼堂召开第五次院务会议,马衡、徐森玉、先生、沈兼士、张庭济、叶澜、赵儒珍、黄念劬、庄尚严、虞和寅、王孝缉、何澄一、黄鹏霄、励乃骥等人出席,马衡为主席,黄念劬为记录。其中,先生负责报告筹备中国博物馆协会经过情形。另,讨论事项中涉及图书分馆阅览暂行简章草案及应用券式样,请复议案,决议修正通过。〔《马衡年谱长编》,页591-592〕

　　　　按:励乃骥,字德人,浙江象山人,时任总务处第四科科长。

晚六时三刻,美国经济考察团团长福勃斯(W. Cameron Fobes)及随行人员共计十三人,由外交部特派员程锡庚陪同由津抵平。军分会李述庚、政整会张剑初、市政府刘毓珊、吉世安、市商会冷家骥、社会局局长蔡元、先生等百余人到站欢迎。〔《大公报》(天津),1935年5月10日,第4版〕

　　　　按:该考察团访问北平,特注意两方面之考察,一为手工业现状、一为文化机构之发展。

五月十一日

下午五时,平馆举行柔克义纪念馆奠基仪式,美国经济考察团全体成员及福开森、蔡元等百余人到场。首由胡适致辞,继由美国亚洲协会(American Asiatic Association)秘书希瓦礼(John B. Chevalier)①宣读柔克义夫人致先生函,大意如下:

　　　建馆纪念先夫君,于心甚感。此纪念物为一图书馆,闻之尤为欣快。今日不能前往参加奠基礼甚歉,惟望将来该馆完成后,定前往一视。专此,敬布谢悃。

再由美国经济考察团团长福勃斯致辞,最后由先生报告纪念馆之筹备经过。礼毕,先生设茶会招待美国经济考察团,邀请美国使馆人士及学术名流参加,并引导参观美国印刷品展览。〔《申报》,1935年5月11日,第10版;《大公报》(天津),1935年5月12日,第3版〕

　　　　按:柔克义(William W. Rockhill, 1854-1914),美国外交官、汉学家,1905年至1909年任驻华大使,后与德国汉学家夏德合作将宋代赵汝适所著《诸蕃志》译成英文。《胡适日记全集》第7册(页199)本日记有“图书馆茶会,请的是美国的经济团。我有短的演说”。为配合此次接待,平馆特举办美国印刷品展览,于12日正式开幕,展品约四百余种,展期为一个月。

---

① China Society of America, *China*, New York, 1935, p. 12.

五月十四日

晚八时,政务整理委员会在外交大楼设宴款待美国经济考察团,美驻华公使詹森夫妇、代办罗赫德夫妇、福开森夫妇、王树常、袁良、严鹤龄、周诒春、王曾思、程远帆、蔡元、先生、程锡庚、唐宝潮等三十余人到场作陪。首由政整会秘书长俞家骥代黄郛致辞,后由严鹤龄译成英文,再由福勃斯答词。十时许,始散。〔《大公报》(天津),1935 年 5 月 15 日,第 4 版〕

施肇基致函先生,告美人韦罗璧撰写有关九一八事变与国联调查经过的专著,请代为在国内图书馆界介绍,以利订购。

> 同礼仁兄惠鉴:
>
> 　　径启者,九一八事变为我国近代一大事。当提出国联时,弟与顾问韦罗璧教授躬与其役,一切经过知之颇详,诚恐日久遗佚、文献无征,后来之人无从措手。兹幸韦罗璧教授纂成《国际联盟与中日争端》一书,纯以客观态度叙述、论列,以故翔实公允,堪称学术界权威之作。现在已付校印,每部定售美金五元,因念我国图书馆林立,需购部数必多,我兄为图书馆界领袖,如能将此书出版消息通知各馆,并将订购总数示知,以便预算分配,实于公私均有裨益。兹将该书内容节略附呈,即希鼎力协助,并盼早日惠复,无任感祷。专泐,顺颂著祉。
>
> 　　　　　　　　　　　　　　　　　　弟施肇基顿启
>
> 　　　　　　　　　　　　　　　　　　廿四年五月十四日
>
> 　　附英文节略一份。

〔国家图书馆档案,档案编号 1935-※050-协会 4-001001
至 1935-※050-协会 4-001008〕

按:韦罗璧即 Westel W. Willoughby(1867-1945),美国霍普金斯大学政治学教授、东亚问题专家,曾担任北洋政府宪法顾问、外交代表团顾问,《国际联盟与中日争端》实为 *The Sino-Japanese Controversy and the League of Nations*,1935 年霍普金斯大学出版社初版。

五月十八日

上午十点半,中国博物馆协会在景山绮望楼举行成立大会,马衡、先生、李书华、李蒸、严智开、徐森玉、朱启钤、钱桐等三十余人到场。马衡为会议主席,报告协会成立意义,先生则讲述协会发起经过。大意如下:

　　五年以来中国学术界进步甚速,文化上有价值之材料发现者甚多,运往外国者亦甚多。不仅古物民俗,即自然科学材料亦往往出洋。其原固系中国人自己不整理,故外人以科学方法来采集。中央对于迳运古物出国限制甚严,现组织中国博物馆协会,将来研究博物馆学,对于博物馆管理方法,全国通力合作。希望各地博物馆互相联络交换动植物标本,不仅限于国内,各国博物馆亦与之联络、交换标本。国际联盟组织之国际博物馆协会去年开会,各国均有协会,惟中国无此组织,实深惭愧。现中国博物馆协会成立,嗣后与各国博物馆联络,对于中国博物馆亦有帮助。

十一时开会讨论,通过组织大纲,设立执行委员会与专门委员会,选举马衡、翁文灏、李书华、沈兼士、先生、叶恭绰、徐森玉、容庚、钱桐、傅斯年、李济、胡先骕、朱启钤、徐旭生、丁文江、严智开等为执行委员,后合影留念。十二时半,故宫博物院古物陈列所在传心殿招待全体午餐,沈兼士讲述整理史料之经过。下午三时至五时,全体参观实录大库及南三所档案。〔《申报》,1935 年 5 月 19 日,第 8 版;《申报》,1935 年 5 月 30 日,第 13 版〕

　　按:本日,中国博物馆协会在团城承光殿举办欧美博物馆图片展览,展品为四百余种书籍、两千余张相片,均为先生在欧美访问时所获取,分为自然历史博物馆、艺术博物馆两大类,该展定于 24 日结束。严智开(1894—1942),天津人,字季聪,严修第五子,时任天津美术馆馆长。

晚,傅斯年、陈寅恪与北平史学界同仁假欧美同学会设宴款待伯希和,胡适、李麟玉、徐森玉、沈兼士、马衡、李济、陆懋德、萧一山、冯友兰、陈受颐、孟森、先生、钱穆、王庸、刘节、孙楷第、赵万里、向达、贺昌群、徐中舒、郑天挺、罗常培、姚从吾、魏建功、陶希圣、容肇祖、陈垣、顾颉刚、唐兰、余嘉锡、余逊、罗庸等四十人与席。〔《顾颉刚日记》卷 3,页 344〕

五月二十二日

先生致信伯希和,告知平馆已开始筹划与法国国家图书馆交换书刊。

　　　　　　　　　　　　　　　　　　　　May 22, 1935

Prof. P. Pelliot,

Legation de France,

Peiping.

Dear Prof. Pelliot:

　　In compliance with your request, I take pleasure in sending you herewith a list of the books which we are sending in exchange to the Bibliothèque Nationale in Paris. Orders have been placed for all the books listed, although those marked with an asterisk have not yet been received from the publishers.

　　Hoping the list to be of use to you,

Your sincerely,

T. L. Yuan

Acting Director

〔国立北平图书馆英文信纸。法国吉美博物馆伯希和档案〕

按:此件为打字稿,落款处为先生签名,信后附 9 页书单,为平馆用以与法国国家图书馆交换的书刊。

五月二十五日

下午五时,北平图书馆协会假清华同学会开茶话会欢迎美人奥思博恩夫妇(Mr. and Mrs. John William Osborn)。先生作为主席致欢迎词,后由奥思博恩夫人发言。〔《中华图书馆协会会报》第 10 卷第 6 期,页 16-17〕

按:奥思博恩夫妇在菲律宾大学任教二十年,夫人从事图书馆事业,素来热心,时来华游历。

五月三十日

下午二时,故宫博物院在礼堂召开临时院务会议,马衡、先生、沈兼士、张庭济、叶澜、赵儒珍、黄念劬、虞和寅、励乃骥、邵锐、何澄一、黄鹏霄等人出席,马衡为主席,黄念劬为记录。其中涉及图书、外事事宜者,报告事项有:

(一)《老满文档》《德宗实录》运回情形。

(二)运送太庙图书馆分馆图书情形。

讨论事项中则有:

(一)拟撤除太庙门首“故宫博物院分院”木牌,改悬挂“国立北平故宫博物院太庙”牌。大高殿、景山、皇史宬亦拟照式悬挂,是否有当。议决太庙改悬“国立北平故宫博物院太庙图书分馆”,大高殿、景山、皇史宬则照旧、无须更改。

(二)瑞典喜龙仁函请购买该院照片三十五张,用以学术研究,可否照准。

议决照单赠送,但以交换瑞典国立博物院所藏仰韶时期陶器相当数量照片为条件。〔《马衡年谱长编》,页 597-598、604〕

　　　　按:6 月 13 日,喜龙仁致信故宫博物院,表示将以瑞典国立博物院所藏东方美术品照片为交换对象。

五月

中德学会迁至北平北城,举行新址开馆典礼,莅临者有德国公使及其夫人、女公子,该会董事蒋梦麟、梅贻琦、先生、张颐、刘钧、鲍鉴清、董洗凡、贺麟、马德润等及该会秘书张天麟、王宜晖等,此外还有德使馆参赞柏列先、洪涛生、卫德明、艾克、石坦安。〔李孝迁著《域外汉学与中国现代史学》,上海:上海古籍出版社,2014 年,页 279〕

　　　　按:董洗凡(1900—?),直隶人,早年留学德国,后曾任辅仁大学社经系讲师,1946 年出任同济大学校长。马德润(1882—1935),字海饶,湖北枣阳人,德国柏林大学法学博士,曾任京师地方审判厅长。

是年夏

先生协助卢靖筹办私立北平木斋图书馆,颇有成效。〔《中华图书馆协会会报》第 10 卷第 6 期,页 18〕

六月四日

中午,钱玄同、马裕藻、沈兼士、徐森玉、陈垣、先生、徐祖正、周作人在外交部街 42 号王家饭店①设宴,款待唐兰、台静农、沈尹默、黎世蘅。〔《钱玄同日记(整理本)》,页 1107〕

　　　　按:黎世蘅(1897—1977),字子鹤,安徽当涂人,教育家,早年赴日本京都大学经济系学习,时任中法大学经济系主任。

六月五日

顾颉刚来访先生,不值。〔《顾颉刚日记》卷 3,页 351〕

六月六日

顾颉刚致函先生。〔《顾颉刚日记》卷 3,页 352〕

六月上旬

先生致信郭绍虞。〔《顾颉刚日记》卷 3,页 353〕

————————

① 《钱玄同日记(整理本)》,页 1050。

　　　　　按:此信应随它信寄予顾颉刚,后者 9 日转交郭绍虞。

六月八日

先生致信史蒂文斯,欢迎美国图书馆专家毕寿普、凯欧于一九三六年来华访问。

June 8, 1935

Dear Dr. Stevens:

　　Thank you very much for your letters of April 2 and May 6, concerning the proposed visit to China from Dr. Bishop and Dr. Keogh.

　　We are sorry to hear that Dr. Bishop find it difficult to make the trip during 1935, but we hope very much that he and Dr. Keogh can both arrange to be absent from their work early in 1936, so that they can spend a few months in China. From our conversation and correspondence, I find that both Dr. Bishop and Dr. Keogh feel that the benefit to American libraries from the visit would be as great as to Chinese libraries. I am also gratified to learn that their proposed visit receives your approval and encouragement.

　　With kindest regards,

Yours sincerely,
T. L. Yuan
Chairman
Executive Committee

　　　　　〔中华图书馆协会英文信纸。Rockefeller Foundation. Series 601:
China; Subseries 601. R: China-Humanities and Arts. Vol. Box 47.
Folder 388〕

　　　　　按:此件为打字稿,落款处为先生签名,于 7 月 8 日送达。

六月九日

故宫博物院以太庙分院打牲亭为址设立该院图书馆分馆,本日正式开馆。
〔《华北日报》,1935 年 6 月 5 日,第 9 版〕

　　　　　按:先生认为东城缺乏图书馆,故筹设分馆,有阅览室、书库、办公
室三部分,大约可以同时容纳四十人阅览。

六月十四日

先生致信米来牟,希望美国图书馆协会积极推动毕寿普、凯欧作为该会正

式代表赴华考察。

June 14, 1935

Dear Mr. Milam:

You will undoubtedly recall our conversation regarding the proposed visits to China from Drs. Bishop and Keogh. They have expressed their willingness to take the journey, and they both feel that the benefit from the visit to American libraries would be as great as to Chinese libraries. I hope, therefore, that in view of the importance of their mission, you will lend us your assistance.

Dr. David H. Stevens of the Rockefeller Foundation has hinted that the Foundation would be willing to finance a part of the expenses, although he does not commit himself to anything as yet. As soon as definite dates for the journey are decided upon by Dr. Keogh, the matter could be brought once more to his consideration.

President Keppel indicated considerable interest in the proposed visit by Dr. Bishop and hinted to me that through the A. L. A. a grant-in-aid can be made by the Carnegie Corporation. As President Keppel will be returning to New York next month, I am writing to you to suggest that you take the necessary steps towards obtaining the support for Dr. Bishop's trip.

We hope that both Dr. Bishop and Dr. Keogh will come as official delegates of the American Library Association. It is desirable therefore that effort be made to remove practical difficulties, so that an early visit may be arranged.

With warmest regards,

Yours sincerely
T. L. Yuan
Acting Director

〔Yale University records, Peiping National Library, 1931-1937, Box: 80, Folder: 831〕

按:此为抄件。

六月十七日

平馆委员会在胡适家开会,商议图书安全事。〔《胡适日记全集》第7册,页236〕

六月二十四日

先生在馆,顾颉刚偕王庸来访。〔《顾颉刚日记》卷3,页358〕

六月二十六日

先生致信王重民,请其径与法国国家图书馆长商谈在法延长访问事并谈影照法藏敦煌经卷细节。

　　有三仁弟:

　　　　五月三日、二十四、六月七日手书均收到,欣悉一切。所拟影照燉煌书片条例极佳,即照此进行可也。伯希和想已到巴黎,在法延长一年事,观 Cain 致杜女士之信不成问题,便中可一访 Cain,即不请教伯希和亦可办到也。照片已收到二批,跋语并刊于《大公报·图书副刊》矣。温彦博碑如能得最好,否则摄影亦可。摄影费清华及本馆各任二千元,准七月间奉上,想可敷用。匆匆,顺颂旅安。

　　　　　　　　　　　　　　　　　　　　　同礼

　　　　　　　　　　　　　　　　　　　六月廿六

　　外一信请转寄。

　　　　　　　　　〔国立北平图书馆英文信纸。中国书店·海淀,四册〕

　　按:是年6月上旬,伯希和离开中国赴日本,中旬经神户乘船前往马赛。[1] Cain 即 Julien Cain(1887–1974),时任法国国家图书馆馆长。"跋语"应指"巴黎敦煌残卷叙录",自《大公报·图书副刊》第80期(1935年5月23日)起不定期刊登。"温彦博碑"即虞恭公温彦博碑,全称则为"唐故特进尚书右仆射上柱国虞恭公温公碑",唐贞观十一年(637)十月立,位于陕西醴泉县。

六月二十七日

上午十时许,马衡乘平浦路列车抵达北平,赵儒珍、先生等人赴车站迎接。
〔《晨报》,1935年6月28日,第6版〕

是年夏

武昌文华图书馆学专科学校介绍该校费锡恩(Grace D. Phillips)女士赴平

----

[1] From Day to Day, *The North-China Daily News*, June, 14, 1935, p. 6.

馆考察馆务情况,她到馆后即拜访先生,对平馆开办的各项服务和先生均十分赞赏。〔《文华图书馆学专科学校季刊》第 7 卷第 3-4 期合刊,1935 年 12 月 15 日,页 565①、561-571〕

> 按:1934 年初,武昌文华图书馆学专科学校聘请费锡恩来校任教。② 她在平馆工作一月有余,回校后特撰写文章,题为 Behind the Scenes in the Peiping National Library(《国立北平图书馆之内部情形》),文中提及平馆馆员因与先生彼此亲切,习惯称之为"老袁"(Lao Yuan),并称先生"He is one of the guardian angels of library work in China."

蔡元培、李石曾、吴铁城、蒋梦麟、张元济、先生、刘海粟、王云五、沈恩孚、黄伯樵、陈公博、潘公展、蒋复璁等百余人联名向熊式一发去贺电,祝贺其改编的戏剧《王宝川》在英国取得巨大成功。〔《时事新报》,1935 年 8 月 2 日,第 7 版〕

> 按:1932 年,熊式一赴英留学,后将传统京剧《红鬃烈马》翻译并改写成英文舞台剧《王宝川》(*Lady Precious Stream*)在伦敦小剧场上演数月之久。1934 年 7 月,Methuen & Co. Ltd.出版该译本,后又多次再版。

七月九日

米来牟致函先生,表示美国图书馆协会执委会已经同意毕寿普、凯欧作为该会正式代表访华,预计在三周后与美国某些基金会接洽资助事宜,并询问本次邀请是否已经告知中国政府或中基会。

July 9, 1935

Dear Mr. Yuan:

　　The Executive Board of the A. L. A. has already acted favorably on your first suggestion that Dr. Bishop and Dr. Keogh be made official delegates of the A. L. A. if and when they visit China in accordance with your invitation.

　　At the first opportunity, which will probably be about three weeks from now, I shall discuss the matter of funds with representatives of the

---

① 该刊"校闻"标注 565 页似有问题,此处照录。
② 该人履历可参见《文华图书馆学专科学校季刊》第 6 卷第 3 期,1934 年 3 月 15 日,页 542。

foundations and will report on the results. I hope very much that either you or we may find the funds for this proposed visit.

It is quite possible that the American foundations may raise some question as to whether the money should come from America rather than from China. Though I shall not postpone a possible interview while waiting for your answer, I shall be glad to have you tell me whether the matter has been presented to the Chinese Government or the China Foundation for Education and Culture.

Cordially yours,

Carl H. Milam

Secretary

〔Yale University records, Peiping National Library, 1931-1937, Box: 80, Folder: 831〕

按:此为抄件,寄送毕寿普。

七月十六日

晚,先生假欧美同学会设宴,Jan Julius Lodewijk Duyvendak、博晨光、胡适、洪业、冯友兰、裘善元、陈受颐、顾颉刚受邀与席,至九时许散。〔《顾颉刚日记》卷3,页367〕

> 按:Jan Julius Lodewijk Duyvendak(1889-1954),荷兰汉学家,中文名戴闻达,曾翻译《道德经》。

七月十八日

故宫博物院院长马衡召集奖学金审查委员会会议,徐森玉、沈兼士和先生出席会议,共同审核王海镜、王静如、李瑞年的申请材料。〔《定于本月十八日上午十时开审查委员会请准时出席由》,《故宫博物院·人事组织类》第154卷,页22-24〕

> 按:王海镜,河南洛阳人,1935年北京大学法国文学系毕业,旋即赴法留学,抗日战争爆发后投身社会运动。李瑞年(1910—1985),天津人,韩俊华与李莲普之次子,1933年国立北平大学西洋画系专修科毕业,约在1934年①留学法国,在巴黎高等美术专科学校、比利时皇家美术院等处学习,归国后任国立艺术专科学

---

① 该人曾河北省1934年度外国留学生自费奖学金,获得国币一千五百元。

校教授、教育部美术教育委员会专任委员。

七月二十二日

徐乃昌致函先生,赠《金石古物考》。〔《徐乃昌日记》,页 1716〕

七月二十三日

某记者来访,先生告知平馆将在馆区东南角花园内建柔克义纪念楼,一俟经费到位即可动工,另新闻报纸阅览室须俟本年秋或可着手,新书阅览室已于昨日正式开放。〔《益世报》(北平),1935 年 7 月 24 日,第 9 版〕

> 按:"新书"指 1933 年以来所有铅字新刊书籍,共分 9 类。

七月二十五日

上午九时,旧都文物整理委会在政整会召开第三次全体会,委员长王克敏,委员商震、袁良、周作民、朱启钤、朱深、陈汉第、先生、丁春膏、马衡等十余人出席。市长袁良报告修建天坛、明陵、各牌楼进展,随即开始讨论各项议案。十二时散会,各委员赴王克敏宴会,二时许散。〔《大公报》(天津),1935 年 7 月 26 日,第 4 版〕

下午,先生、徐森玉乘平浦路列车南下。〔《世界日报》,1935 年 7 月 26 日,第 7 版;《益世报》(北平),1935 年 7 月 25 日,第 9 版〕

> 按:先生赴京拟向教育部部长王世杰汇报馆务并商影印《四库全书》事宜。之后,将取道粤梧赴南宁参加"六学术团体联合年会",即中国工程师学会第五次年会、中国化学会第三次年会、中国地理学会第二次年会、中国科学社第二十次年会、中国动物学会第二次年会、中国植物学会第三次年会。

七月二十六日

王芸生在列车上遇到先生,谈时局,尤其涉及两粤拥护中央政府的话题。〔王芸生《由统一到抗战》,上海:上海书店,1989 年,页 397〕

> 按:王芸生(1901—1980),原名德鹏,天津静海人,报人,长期担任《大公报》总编、社长。

七月二十八日

先生抵达上海,宿八仙桥青年会。〔谢国桢《两粤纪游》,《禹贡》半月刊,第 4 卷第 9 期,1936 年 1 月,页 48〕

七月三十日　莫干山

晨,先生访黄郛,谈华北局势,相与唏嘘。〔《黄郛日记(1935-1936)》,页 47〕

八月一日

先生为 *Libraries in China: papers prepared on the occasion of the tenth anniversary of the Library Association of China* 撰写序言。〔*Libraries in China*, 1935〕

八月二日

凯欧致函先生,感谢寄赠《现代美国印刷展览目录》,并表示本年秋无暇访华。

2 August, 1935

Dear Dr. Yuan:

Thank you very much for the two copies of your *Catalogue of Modern American Printing*.

I am writing to-day to Mr. Bishop, who is due in New York on Sunday, asking him whether he has any new information or any new light upon our proposed trip to China.

The only thing that I have new is that it will not be possible for me to go this fall because of a lecture course in which I am involved.

Mr. Bishop told me that two Chinese delegates at Madrid were very much set on having us visit China. They have probably written to you on that point.

I hope that the moving of the Japanese southward will not affect your own plans for library development in China. I fear, however, that the floods and other calamities may make it impossible to carry out some of your generous intentions.

Yours very sincerely,

〔Yale University records, Peiping National Library, 1931 – 1937, Box: 80, Folder: 831〕

按:该件为录副。

八月初

先生电话联系耿士楷,询问洛克菲勒基金会就《图书季刊》英文本申请资助案的最终决定。此外,两人讨论了日本在华北地区的军事行动对北平局势的影响,先生表示就这一问题刚刚从南京国民政府得知确切消息,北平地区的高校、科研机构不会南迁,这一原则适用于平馆。〔Rockefeller

Foundation. Series 601: China; Subseries 601.R: China-Humanities and Arts. Vol. Box 47. Folder 394〕

> 按:9 月 20 日洛克菲勒基金会人文部在其会议上讨论了此项申请,27 日电报从纽约发往洛克菲勒基金会驻沪办事处,告知基金会已批注了代号为 RF35150 资助项目,决定给予平馆 5,000 美金,用以支持《图书季刊》英文本发行,期限为 1935 年 10 月 1 日至 1938 年 12 月 31 日,只能用于英文部分,以便外国学者可以获取更多中国学术信息。每年编辑费 800 美金,助理费 350 美金,杂费 350 美金,年度为 1,500 美金。额外的 500 美金用于 1935 年的剩下月份,或者不可预计的花销。

八月五日　广州

上午,先生参观广州市立中山图书馆。下午,国立中山大学校长邹鲁邀请先生参观该校石碑新校区。〔《天光报》(香港),1935 年 8 月 7 日,第 2 版〕

八月六日

香港《天光报》记者来访,先生表示曾于十年前来此,今日广东已有长足进步,本省应多建立通俗性民众图书馆,以推动文化事业发展。〔《天光报》(香港),1935 年 8 月 7 日,第 2 版〕

> 按:先生表示 8 月 7 日将离开广州,前赴苍梧再转南宁。

八月八日　梧州

晚七时,广西大学校长马君武和苍梧县长蔡灏在洞天酒家代表广西省政府,设宴款待参加六学术团体联合会途径梧州的各团体会员。首由马君武致欢迎辞,末由先生代表答谢。九时许散席,各代表径赴桂德轮船处前往南宁。〔《民国日报》(广州),1935 年 9 月 9 日,第 7 版〕

> 按:1928 年,广西大学在梧州成立,首任校长即马君武。途经此地的各团体会员均借宿广西大学学生宿舍,此种欢迎会于 7、8 两日连开两天。

八月十二日　南宁

六学术团体联合年会召开,先生以中国科学社社员身份与会。〔《中国科学社第二十次年会记事》,页 3〕

八月十三日

下午四时,先生公开演讲,题目为"现代图书馆及博物馆之重要与管理"。

〔《六学术团体联合年会特刊》,页34〕

> 按:本次演讲由李青记录,后刊发于《六学术团体联合年会特刊》。

八月十四日

下午二时,中国科学社假文化建设研究院开第二次社务会,先生被选为下届司选委员。随后由竺可桢、先生等人做报告。先生讲述科学团体联合会之必要,并谈一战结束后欧美各国先后组织科学团体联合会的情况,并希望中国亦能如此发展。〔《中国科学社第二十次年会记事》,页23〕

八月中下旬

先生与徐森玉离开南宁,前往上海。〔《北平晚报》,1935年8月23日,第3版〕

八月三十一日

下午二时,故宫博物院在礼堂召开第六次院务会议,马衡、先生、沈兼士、张庭济、叶澜、赵儒珍、章宗傅、王孝绪、黄念劬(王承吉代)、励乃骥、邵锐、何澄一、黄鹏霄等人参加。马衡为主席,王承吉为记录。除报告点收经过情形、伦敦艺展运输展品赴英情况等各案外,讨论各事项中涉及外事者如下:

(一)德国佛朗府中国学院及美国加利福尼亚大学分校图书馆请求本院寄赠出版物,应否照赠。议决,德国佛朗府中国学院准予捐赠出版物全份(拓片、书画单页等除外),美国加利福尼亚大学分校图书馆捐赠约价值数百元之书籍。

(二)喜龙仁请购书画照片,是否照购。议决,保留。〔《马衡年谱长编》,页616-617〕

> 按:章宗傅,字砚遗,浙江吴兴人,时任故宫博物院会计主任。[1]

先生致信米来牟,就毕寿普和凯欧两位图书馆专家来华考察的费用问题提出初步设想。

August 31, 1935

Dear Mr. Milam:

　　Your letter of July 9th concerning the proposed trip of Dr. Bishop and Dr. Keogh to China was duly received. I have been out of town for over four weeks, and hence I have not been able to answer you earlier.

---

[1]《国立北平故宫博物院职员录》,1935年,叶20。

It is a pleasure to know that the Executive Board of the A. L. A. will ask Dr. Bishop and Dr. Keogh as official delegates of the A. L. A. when they visit China next year.

I note that you will discuss the matter of funds with representatives of the foundations and hope very much that you will get tangible results. On our side, we have approached the Government authorities concerning this matter. But it seems that the Government is now concentrating its resources on flood and famine relief and has very naturally put all cultural projects in the rear.

But if the travelling expenses of Dr. Bishop and Dr. Keogh can be defrayed out of a grant from some of the foundations, we shall be able to make arrangements so that they may stay and travel at the expense of the Chinese Government after their arrival in this country.

Being a joint Sino-American project, I earnestly hope that through your effort and assistance their visit to China in the spring of 1936 will be realized.

With cordial regards,

Yours very sincerely,

T. L. Yuan

Chairman,

Executive Committee

〔Yale University records, Peiping National Library, 1931-1937, Box: 80, Folder: 831〕

按:该年,汉江中上游爆发特大洪水,数百万人受灾。此为抄件。

九月二日

国民政府增聘先生为中央古物保管委员会委员。〔《申报》,1935 年 9 月 3 日,第 9 版〕

> 按:9 月 11 日下午二时,中央古物保管委员会假内政部开会,内政部次长许修直为主席,原委员朱希祖、滕固、马衡、徐旭生、李济、蒋复璁、叶公绰、黄文弼、董作宾、卢锡荣皆留任,傅斯年、傅汝霖去职,增聘先生及内政部参事、司长各一人为委员。李济、叶公

绰、先生并未出席该日会议。①

九月七日

某记者来访,请谈馆务。先生略述出版、建筑新闻阅览室计划、选派向达前往牛津大学交换等事。〔《世界日报》,1935年9月8日,第7版〕

九月中旬

万国美术院(北平)在南河沿前新生活俱乐部重新开放。〔《华北日报》,1935年9月10日,第6版〕

> 按:该社团创立十余年,现任院长为周诒春、主任为王锡炽太太。此前该院位于东四报房胡同,于8月间迁往新址,并修缮一新。蔡元、先生、金绍基为会员。

九月十八日

先生致信詹森大使夫人,告知夫人袁慧熙无法前往参加茶会,并就詹森出任美国驻华大使表示祝贺。

September 18, 1935

Dear Mrs. Johnson:

Owing to absence from Peiping, Mrs. Yuan regrets exceedingly that she will not be able to attend your tea party on Friday. She wishes very much to thank you for your courtesy.

We are very much delighted at Mr. Johnson's appointment as the First Ambassador to China and we wish to express to you our very hearty congratulations.

Yours sincerely,

T. L. Yuan

> 〔国立北平图书馆英文信纸。Library of Congress, Nelson T. Johnson Papers〕

> 按:此件为打字稿,落款处为先生签名。

九月二十二日

下午三时,北平图书馆协会假北京大学图书馆举行常会。先生、严文郁、李文裿、于震寰、田洪都、何日章、徐家璧、杨殿珣、王育伊、张允亮、袁涌进、王

---

① 《朱希祖日记》,页543。

访渔等七十余人到场,田洪都为会议主席,特别邀请莫余敏卿、吴光清演讲,前者的题目为"美国之专门圕",后者则例举圕事业计划应注意之要点。后由李文裿报告代订《丛书集成》获利并充作协会经费,继由于震寰报告中日文期刊联合目录进展。另外,讨论三项议案:一为中学图书馆调查,先生提议北平公私立中学甚多,图书馆设施应属上乘,会议主席指定严文郁、李文裿、于震寰组织办理调查事宜;二为推广公共图书馆事业,先生提议北平市内图书馆分布不均,东城、南城尤少,会议主席指定何日章、吴光清、商鸿逵三人组织协商解决办法;三为每次常会会员应携配姓名标识,反对者较多。会后,众人参观北京大学图书馆,至六时许始散。〔《中华图书馆协会会报》第 11 卷第 2 期,页 35-37〕

　　　　按:徐家璧,字完白,湖北江陵人,时任平馆西文编目组组员。王育伊,浙江黄岩人,平馆馆员,抗战前曾任索引组组长。

十月一日

米来牟致函先生,建议由中华图书馆协会或平馆致函美国卡耐基基金会、洛克菲勒基金会申请资助美国图书馆学专家访华。

October 1, 1935

Dear Dr. Yuan:

　　I have not had the opportunity, which I anticipated when I wrote you on July 9, to discuss your proposal with officers of the foundations. On further reflection I doubt the advisability and propriety of our making the request. We are constantly making proposals to the foundations and it is somewhat more than probable that one more project from the A. L. A. would be received less warmly than a proposal from the Library Association of China and the National Library of China.

　　On the basis of activities financed in recent years, you might logically write to Dr. David H. Stevens, Vice President of the General Education Board, 49 West 49th Street, New York, or to Dr. Frederick P. Keppel, President of the Carnegie Corporation, 522 Fifth Avenue, New York, N. Y. The Carnegie Corporation would not be able under its charter to make a grant to a Chinese institution directly but it might handle the matter either through the Carnegie Endowment for International Peace or through the A. L. A.

In your letter you are free to state that the Executive Board of the American Library Association has made Dr. Bishop and Dr. Keogh official delegates of the A. L. A. to be effective if and when they visit China in accordance with your invitation.

With cordial greetings, I am

Very sincerely yours,

Carl H. Milam

Secretary

〔Yale University records, Peiping National Library, 1931–1937, Box: 80, Folder: 831〕

按：此为抄件,寄送毕寿普。

十月二日

下午二时,平馆委员会召开第二十次①会议,周诒春、傅斯年、孙洪芬、胡适、蒋梦麟、先生出席,胡适为会议主席,先生记录。讨论议案如下:

(一)胡适、陈垣、任鸿隽任满,议决连任三年。

(二)改选本届职员案,票选结果为委员长蒋梦麟四票、副委员长傅斯年五票、书记先生五票、会计孙洪芬五票。

(三)核审平馆一九三四年度决算案,议决接受并建议平馆在下年度决算书内应将每项科目盈亏另行标出。

(四)平馆聘请吴光清为编目部主任、莫余敏卿为参考组组长、余霭钰为西文编目组组员,请予核聘案,议决照案通过。

(五)先生提议拟派谢国桢代理金石部主任、孙楷第为写经组组长、谭新嘉为编纂、吴光清兼中文编目组组长,议决照案通过。

(六)商务印书馆函请委托影印善本七种,并入《续四部丛刊》发行案,议决照案通过。

(七)平馆请求拨给卡片费案,议决铅印卡片先试办,由平馆与清华、北大、燕大、师大协商组织委员会主持进行事宜。

(八)先生提议向达赴英留学二年,在留学期内拟请准予拨给半薪案,议决

① 《北京图书馆馆史资料汇编(1909-1949)》原文为第"十九次",但根据前后会议顺序(时间),可知此处抄件有错,应为第二十次。

照案通过。

(九)审查新闻阅览室图样,议决依此图设计,请木厂估价并请梁思成在原图上加地下室或改为楼房,以充分利用可能范围内之面积为原则。

(十)先生报告养蜂夹道空地二亩出让,应否收购,议决如价廉可以购,交平馆办理。〔《北京图书馆馆史资料汇编(1909-1949)》,页350-351〕

　　　　按:余霭钰,湖北蒲圻人。

十月五日

先生致信耿士楷,告平馆中文书目卡片即将对公发行,希望得到洛克菲勒基金会的资助。

　　　　　　　　　　　　　　　　　　October 5, 1935

Dear Mr. Gunn:

For some years past, we have been contemplating the printing and distribution of catalog cards for Chinese books. Partly due to financial difficulties and partly due to the pressure of work resulting from the cataloging of our entire Chinese collection of 500,000 volumes, the project has been put off until today. With our recataloging work near completion, we hope that our plan will materialize in the immediate future. It goes without saying that the printing and distribution of catalog cards will be the most effective way to-ward inter-library cooperation both within and without the country and that many libraries, institutions and individuals will be greatly benefitted from this worthy undertaking. We are submitting herewith a memorandum with the hope that you will kindly forward the same to your New York office for consideration and action. Any help or advice which you may kindly extend toward the early realization of this plan will be gratefully appreciated.

If the Foundation wishes to consult some specialists regarding the project, I may be allowed to suggest the following names:

Dr. Arthur W. Hummel, Library of Congress, Washington, D. C.

Dr. A. Kaiming Chiu, Chinese-Japanese Library, Harvard University, Cambridge, Mass.

Dr. Mortimer Graves, Secretary, Committee on the Promotion of

Chinese Studies, American Council of Learned Societies, Washington, D. C.

I may add that we have already started on a small scale the printing of catalog cards for Chinese books published since January, 1935. Mr. K. T. Wu, a graduate of Columbia and Michigan library schools with considerable experience in cataloging, is now in charge of our Catalog Division and supervises the printing and distribution of the printed cards.

Yours very sincerely,

T. L. Yuan

〔Rockefeller Foundation. Series 601: China; Subseries 601.R: China-Humanities and Arts. Vol. Box 47. Folder 388〕

按:10 月 31 日,耿士楷将此信及备忘录送往纽约,11 月 25 日送交史蒂文斯。前者在信中说自己不是图书馆学专家,不便妄加评论,但可能是个好的计划。此为抄件,另有备忘录 Memorandum re the Project for the Printing and Distribution of Catalog Cards for Chinese Books 五页。

十月十七日

晚,杨光弼、夏怀仁夫妇在东堂子胡同宅邸设宴,李石曾、李书华、李麟玉、朱君夫妇、福开森、崔敬伯、先生、顾颉刚等人受邀与席。〔《顾颉刚日记》卷 3,页 401〕

按:崔敬伯(1897—1988),原名翊昆,以字行,河北宁河人,财政学专家、经济学家,早年赴日本、英国留学,时应任北平研究院秘书、管理中英庚款董事会北平办事处主任。①

十月二十一日

先生致信国会图书馆(馆长),请求与该馆交换各自印刷的书籍卡片目录。

October 21, 1935

Dear Sir:

Enclosed herewith please find a circular letter regarding the distribution of catalogue cards for Chinese books.

---

① 《国立北平研究院院务汇报》第 6 卷第 5 期,1935 年 9 月,"本院职员"页 1;《益世报》(天津),1935 年 3 月 31 日,第 8 版。

Since we have been buying the proof-sheets issued by the Library of Congress, and since you will no doubt need at least one set of our cards for reference purposes, it has occurred to us that we may arrange for an exchange of our respective cards. Please let us know if this is agreeable to your Library.

Yours very sincerely,

T. L. Yuan

Acting Director

〔国立北平图书馆英文信纸。Library of Congress, Putnam Archives, Special Files, China: National Library 1930-1939〕

按:此件为打字稿,落款处为先生签名,于 11 月 16 日送达国会图书馆秘书办公室。

十月下旬

先生南下入京,向教育部报告馆务,并出席中国科学社二十周年纪念大会。〔《世界日报》,1935 年 11 月 1 日,第 7 版〕

按:10 月 27 日上午 9 时,中国科学社二十周年纪念大会在国立中央大学大礼堂举办。在此期间,先生还联系京、沪各大图书馆商洽印刷中文书籍目录卡片事宜。

袁勤礼在南京中央医院病逝,先生特赶赴仁孝殡仪馆吊唁,甚为悲痛。〔《思忆录》,中文部分页 104〕

十月三十一日

上午十时许,先生搭乘平沪线北返。〔《世界日报》,1935 年 11 月 1 日,第 7 版〕

十一月一日

上午十时半,先生抵达北平。〔《绥远西北日报》,1935 年 11 月 3 日,第 2 版〕

十一月四日

晚,谢国桢、徐森玉、王庸在煤市街泰丰楼设宴,先生、吴廷燮、孟森、胡汝麟、赵万里、孙海波、刘盼遂、容庚、顾颉刚受邀与席。〔《顾颉刚日记》卷 3,页 407〕

耿士楷致函先生,告知洛克菲勒基金会批准对《图书季刊》(英文本)的资助,请先生尽快决定支付方式。

November 4, 1935

Dear Mr. Yuan:

　　I am enclosing herewith an official letter from Mrs. Norma S. Thompson, the Secretary of the Rockefeller Foundation, to Mr. S. K. Koo concerning the *Quarterly Bulletin of Chinese Bibliography*. Will you please transmit this to Mr. Koo?

　　You will observe that an appropriation not to exceed US $ 5000 has been made to the National Library of Peiping towards the support of the *Quarterly Bulletin of Chinese Bibliography* during the period October 31, 1935 to December 31, 1938. Will you please send me as soon as possible a statement as to what manner you wish this money paid? The grant, as you will see, runs for three years and three months, which is at the rate of a little more than US $ 1500 a year. I presume that you would like the payments made in Tientsin dollars, and we can readily sell here in Shanghai from time to time US currency for this purpose. I shall await a reply from you before taking any action.

Yours sincerely,

P. S. Please note the under the terms of this grant any balance remaining unexpended as of December 31, 1938 would revert to the Foundation.

〔Rockefeller Foundation. Series 601: China; Subseries 601.R: China-Humanities and Arts. Vol. Box 47. Folder 394〕

　　按：此件为底稿，另附 10 月 8 日基金会秘书 Norma S. Thompson 写给顾子刚的信。

十一月五日

耿士楷致函先生，补充说明资助款的使用范围和注意事项。

November 5, 1935

Dear Mr. Yuan:

　　In connection with my letter attached herewith, I feel it advisable to also send you some supplementary information with regard to the grant for the *Quarterly Bulletin of Chinese Bibliography*.

　　It is understood that the sum of US $ 5000 is to supplement the money given to the Library by the Chinese National Committee on intellectual cooperation. According to our understanding, this Committee provided the money for the Chinese Section of the Bibliography, and the Foundation's contribution is to be allocated to the following uses in preparation of the English section, the annual charges being approximately as follows:

Editor	US $ 800
Assistants	US $ 350
Miscellaneous expense	US $ 350
Total	US $ 1500

For over a period of three years, this would amount to $ 4500 (US), and the additional US $ 500 is to be used during the closing months of 1935, or for unexpected charges during the term of the grant.

The help of the Foundation is to be devoted entirely to the more careful preparation of the English section, and is looked upon as support of a project essential to cooperative plans of Oriental and English scholars.

Your sincerely,

Selskar M. Gunn

Vice-President

〔Rockefeller Foundation. Series 601: China; Subseries 601.R: China-Humanities and Arts. Vol. Box 47. Folder 394〕

十一月九日

先生致信耿士楷,感谢洛克菲勒基金会给予五千美金用以《图书季刊》英文本的编辑,并告知平馆计划支取的方式和每季的额度。

November 9, 1935

Dear Mr. Gunn:

I thank you very much for your letter of November 4 informing me of the appropriation of US $ 5,000 made by the Rockefeller Foundation to the National Library of Peiping for the support of the *Quarterly Bulletin of Chinese Bibliography*, English Section, from October 31, 1935 to December 31, 1938.

The money will be used in the manner as outlined in your letter of

November 5. If, however, the allowance for the printing expenses for the English Section of the *Bulletin* be discontinued by the Chinese National Committee on Intellectual Cooperation at any time before December 31, 1938, may I suggest that the National Library, through economies effected, use a part of the Foundation's appropriation for this purpose?

As to manner of payment, I would suggest that the instalment for the last quarter of 1935 be remitted to the National Library during this month; while for the future, quarterly instalments of US $ 375 at exchange be remitted during the first month of each quarter. A separate account of the money will be kept, and an annual statement of expenditures will be sent to your office. I understand that any balance remaining unexpended as of December 31, 1938, reverts to the Foundation.

I have transmitted Mrs. Thompson's letter to Mr. Koo, who will write to New York direct.

I assure you of my grateful appreciation of your assistance in making possible this appropriation. On our side, we shall do our best to make the *Quarterly Bulletin* a better medium of information about Chinese cultural activities and scholarly accomplishments, so that it shall indeed be an essential link between Chinese and Western scholars as envisaged by the Foundation.

Yours sincerely,

T. L. Yuan

Acting Director

〔Rockefeller Foundation. Series 601: China; Subseries 601.R: China-Humanities and Arts. Vol. Box 47. Folder 394〕

按:此为抄件。

十一月上旬①

蔡元培致函先生,询问有无合适人选可担国内博物馆之职。〔《蔡元培全集》

---

① 11 月 26 日蔡元培覆函叶恭绰,其中提到"直至到京后,询李济之兄,始知有数人可以备选。但济之亦系由袁守和兄间接得来者,已不大记得;函询守和,始得一名单",由《蔡元培日记》可知,10 月 31 日蔡元培抵达南京,故将此函系于此。

〔第 14 卷,页 112〕

　　按:此事由叶恭绰而起,叶氏时任上海市博物院董事会董事长,正在筹建该院。9 月 15 日函蔡元培请求推荐人选,蔡元培遂问李济有无合适人选,后者将袁同礼之推荐转述与蔡元培,但蔡并未记住,故又函先生询问。

十一月十三日

耿士楷覆函先生,即将如先生前请汇付第一笔支票,并表示洛克菲勒基金会对《图书季刊》英文本的资助可用于印刷和其他杂费支出。

November 13, 1935

Dear Mr. Yuan:

　　Your letter of November 9th to hand, and I am arranging with our Comptroller to forward to you promptly a check in Tientsin dollars equivalent to US $ 500.00.

　　It is also understood that beginning with January first, quarterly payments in Tientsin dollars will be made for the equivalent of US $ 375. 00, at the current rate of exchange at the time of payment.

　　While we hope that the Chinese National Committee on Intellectual Cooperation will continue to make appropriations towards the printing and other expenses of the English Section, I believe it would not be impossible, if this money does not come, to use a part at least of the Foundation's appropriation for this purpose. I suggest, however, that I be kept informed with regard to everything dealing with this matter.

Yours sincerely,
Selskar M. Gunn
Vice-President.

〔Rockefeller Foundation. Series 601: China; Subseries 601.R: China-Humanities and Arts. Vol. Box 47. Folder 394〕

十一月中旬

先生覆信蔡元培,推荐博物馆人才四人,其中有冯君、李君等人,并将每人情况一一说明。〔《蔡元培全集》第 14 卷,页 112〕

十一月二十一日

先生致信杨孝述,告平馆已寄出第一批善本书籍,并愿与中国科学社(图书馆)开展学术合作。

> 允中先生大鉴:
>
> 　　前由任叔永先生处交到大函,对于敝馆寄存书箱一节深荷规画,至为感泐。兹于本月十九日交中国旅行社运上善本书籍第一批,共二十箱,每箱高二十四英寸、宽十九英寸。如置尊处书库顶层当能容纳,每箱上面写明"亚尔培路五三三号中国科学社收",由中国旅行社派人径送贵社点收。暂时既无庸开箱,拟即委托贵社代为保管,除由馆另函贵社外,特此奉闻。承提议派一有经验之馆员代为整理贵社书籍,其薪给由敝馆担任一节,事关学术合作,亟愿遵命,拟俟敝馆书箱数量加多时,再行决定,届时当再奉闻。专此,敬候台祺。
>
> 弟袁厶厶再拜
>
> 〔国家图书馆档案,档案编号 1935-※034-采藏 6-002004 至 1935-※034-采藏 6-002005〕

按:杨孝述(1889—1974),字允中,江苏松江人,1914 年赴美留学,入康乃尔大学,与杨铨、竺可桢、胡明复等发起组织中国科学社。该件为文书所拟之底稿,先生改动甚多,无落款时间,但由发文记录可知应为 11 月 21 日。

十一月二十三日

下午四时,平馆委员会召开第二十一次会议,孙洪芬、周诒春、傅斯年、蒋梦麟、陈垣、胡适、先生出席。蒋梦麟为会议主席,先生纪录。讨论议案如下:

(一)本馆因时局关系应即将贵重书籍暂寄存安全地点,西文书及普通书暂缓迁移。

(二)关于平馆请求拨给装箱费、运费一案,议决由委员会函请教育部拨给四千元,在该款未寄到前,暂向中基会借垫三千元周转。

(三)静生生物调查所来函称社会调查所南迁后所址移交该所接收,但水电、热气费用该所无力承担,应如何办理等,议决函复该所请与中基会接洽。

(四)静生生物调查所来函拟请授权该所处理本馆寄存书籍案,议决本馆西文书籍既决定暂缓迁移,寄存该所之书籍可随同迁移以供研究,实施细则届时本委员会再行考虑。在该所全部未迁移之前，所中职员借书应按借书章程办理。

(五)先生报告调查所职员在西海醋局六号职员宿舍内擅自衔接本馆水电，议决立即停止供给水电。

五时半散会。〔《北京图书馆馆史资料汇编(1909-1949)》，页352〕

先生致信庄长恭、丁西林、周仁，请三人照顾平馆南运至沪暂存各研究所的善本书籍。

　　丕可、巽甫、子竞先生大鉴：

　　　　华北时局日趋严重，北平图书馆所藏善本书拟择要运沪暂存贵研究所，本日交中国旅行社运上五十箱，到时并希点收并代为保管。除由该馆函告外，特此奉闻，即希台察为感。

　　　　　　　　　　　　　　　　　　　　　十一月廿三日

　　　　　〔国立北平图书馆用笺。国家图书馆档案，档案编号1935-※034-采藏6-002013〕

　　按：庄长恭(1894—1962)，字丕可，福建泉州人；丁西林(1893—1974)，字巽甫，江苏泰兴人；周仁(1892—1973)，字子竞，江苏江宁人；以上三人分别为中央研究院化学研究所、物理研究所、工程研究所所长，其所址均为上海白利南路①，故有信中"暂存贵研究所"之表述。此件为先生所拟之底稿。

教育部电告平馆重要图书择要移存，运费由北大垫付。

　　蒋校长亲译教密并转傅孟真先生、袁叔和先生鉴：

　　　　国立北平图书馆贵重书籍希以极机密方法择要移存南方，以策安全，所需运费二千元可商北大垫付，当由部汇还。

　　　　　　　　　　　　　　　　　　　　　　　教育部，漾。

　　　　　〔《北京图书馆馆史资料汇编(1909-1949)》，页417〕

　　按：此次装箱、运费大约四千元，除向北京大学领取两千元外，剩余部分应由教育部通过中国银行电汇。

十一月二十六日　南京

晚六时，邵元冲设宴，黄志雄、贡沛诚、先生、陶林英、习文德、徐忍茹等受邀

---

① 《国立中央研究院职员录(民国二十四年度)》，1935年，叶1。

与席,九时散。〔《邵元冲日记》,页1343〕

> 按:黄志雄,字智雄,浙江金华人,早年留学日本;贡沛诚,湖北人,早年留德,归国后曾任南京高等师范讲师、边疆学校副主任;陶林英,字萃民,广东人,曾任国民政府立法院编译处科员,时应在国民党党史编纂委员会任职;习文德,时应在国民党党史编纂委员会任职;徐忍茹(1883—1965),原名沛德,浙江嘉兴人,早年留学日本,时应任国民党党史编纂委员会主任秘书。①

十一月二十七日

梁思成致函先生,协商移运梁启超遗物至天津。

> 径启者:
>
> 先严去世之后,曾经散家族全体同意,将先严饮冰室藏书、字画、碑帖及生平所用文具、桌椅等,永久寄存贵馆,以便学子并资纪念,已六载于兹。顷因时局不靖,拟恳求将饮冰室藏书、字画、碑帖、文具等,择要即运天津意租界西马路敞宅暂存。业经面谈,荷蒙惠允。兹拟装运办法条列于左:
>
> (一)饮冰室藏书按照贵馆所印目录择要点检装箱。
>
> (二)凡先严手批书籍,皆须一律检运,其余则选择比较珍贵者先运,此项选择权由思成授与馆方全权选择。
>
> (三)梁氏家族委托杨鼎甫先生代表点检。
>
> (四)此次检运暂以一百箱为限。
>
> (五)书籍、字画、碑帖之已经南运者,由馆方另开清单,以备将来核对。
>
> (六)文具、用器等之不在目录内者,由馆方另开清单对核。
>
> (七)木箱不宜过大,以便在敞宅内原箱存放。(将来仍拟原箱运回北平。)
>
> (八)装箱时务请用油纸充分包裹,以防途中潮湿。
>
> (九)运输由馆方负责送达天津意租界西马路二十五号梁宅。
>
> (十)木箱费用由馆方完全担负。

---

① 《中国留日同学会会员录》,1942年,第18页;《中国国民党中央政治学校大事记》,1941年,页35;《留德同学通讯录》,1944年,页52;《中央各机关职员录》,1933年,页169;《胡汉民先生哀思录》,1936年,"唁电"页52;《民国廿三年中国国民党年鉴》,1934年,(甲)页257。

（十一）由平至津运费由馆方及思成平均担负；将来由津回平运费，则由馆方完全担负之。

此次由平运津书籍、字画、碑帖及文具用器，只属暂存性质，一俟治安恢复，思成或敝家族认为十分安全时，当即全数运回贵馆，永久寄存也。此致

国立北平图书馆馆长袁同礼先生

梁思成

廿四年十一月廿七日

〔《北京图书馆馆史资料汇编(1909-1949)》，页 421-423〕

按：此函为文书代笔，落款处为梁思成签名。

十一月二十八日　北平

先生为现代英国印刷展览（目录）撰写英文序言（Foreword）〔*Exhibition of Modern British Printing: a catalogue*, December, 1935〕

按：该文后被译成中文，刊于《中华图书馆协会会报》第 11 卷第 3 期（页 1-2）。

十一月下旬

先生致信王世杰、段锡朋，告知平馆已先后六次委托中国旅行社南运珍本。

雪艇部长、书贻次长钧鉴：

廿三日曾奉一函，谅达座右。本馆珍本书籍先后分六批南运，共三百二十六箱，除内中一百三十箱分存中国科学社及中央研究院外，余均暂存上海银行仓库。第一批至第五批委托中国旅行社交铁路负责运输，径寄沪上，第六批委托该社改由平汉路经郑州、徐州南下，除俟各箱安抵上海再将书目寄呈外，先此奉达，诸乞垂察，敬候道祺。

〔国家图书馆档案，档案编号 1935-※034-采藏 6-002050〕

按：由相关档案①可知，信中所指六批时间应分别为 11 月 19 日，第 1 批，20 箱（科学社）；21 日，第 2 批，60 箱（科学社）；23 日，第 3 批，50 箱（中央研究院）；26 日，第 4 批，126 箱（上海商业储蓄银行）；27 日，第 5 批，40 箱（上海商业储蓄银行）；28 日，第 6 批，30

————————

① 国家图书馆档案，档案编号 1935-※034-采藏 6-002016。

箱(上海商业储蓄银行)。此件为先生所拟之底稿,无落款时间,信笺左侧注有"馆长自稿未列号,存专字卅三案甲一卷"。

十一月三十日

刘承幹致函先生,欲借平馆所藏明本《杭州府志》。〔《求恕斋日记》(稿本)〕

　　　　按:收到此函后,先生应将平馆所藏之本借与刘承幹。

十二月二日

北平各大学校长及教育文化界人士联名向中央政府发送电报,对华北自治阴谋予以批驳。电文大意如下:

　　　　近日平津报纸载有文电,公然宣称华北有要求自治或自决之舆情,殊足淆乱观听。吾辈亲见亲闻,除街头偶有少数受人雇用之奸人发传单、捏造民意之外,各界民众毫无脱离中央另图自治之意,望政府及国人勿受其朦蔽,尤盼中央及平津河北当局消除乱源,用全力维持国家领土及行政之完整。

　　　　　　徐诵明、李蒸、蒋梦麟、梅贻琦、陆志韦、胡适、傅斯年、

　　　　　　　袁同礼、陶孟和、刘运筹、刘廷芳、杨立奎、吴文藻、

　　　　　　　　查良钊、张奚若、周炳琳、蒋廷黻

　　　　　　　　　　　　　　〔《申报》,1935 年 12 月 3 日,第 3 版〕

　　　　按:此电文稍后两日似又发送一遍。①

十二月五日

下午五时,平馆举办现代英国印刷展览会开幕。到场嘉宾有英国大使贾德幹、英使馆参赞、文官及北平各大学教授七十余人。首由先生致开幕辞,大意如下:

　　　　本次展览之目的乃因英国近年印刷事业之精进,有资吾国人士省览与观摩者至多,且印刷关系文化之进步至大,是以本馆前曾举办德、美两国印刷展览,此次又举行英国印刷展览,俾各国之精良印刷,得为吾国之借鉴,借此以鼓励出版界印书事之改善,并予读书界优美印刷之欣赏,倘能由此获得良好之影响,实不胜企望。

后由贾德幹发言,随后先生陪同参观,至六时许始散。〔《中华图书馆协会会报》第 11 卷第 3 期,1935 年 12 月 31 日,页 14-15〕

────────────────

① 《申报》,1935 年 12 月 5 日,第 11 版。

按:展览原定于 11 月 28 日开幕,后因故推迟,其初衷为纪念英伦中国艺术展览及促进中英两国印刷技术进步。展品大致有三个来源:一是先生旅欧时收集,一是平馆所藏,一是与相关各方商借。贾德幹(Sir Alexander George Montagu Cadogan, 1884－1968),1934 年 1 月 19 日被委任为英国驻华特命全权公使,3 月 6 日抵华。

十二月六日

史蒂文斯覆函先生,告知关于平馆申请资助刊印卡片目录已获得美高校、图书馆的初步支持,并已与恒慕义交换意见,暂时不需要提供其他辅助申请材料。

December 6, 1935

Dear Mr. Yuan:

　　Your letter of October 5 addressed to Mr. Gunn with materials concerning the printing of catalogue cards on Chinese books reached me only a few days before a conference in New York that dealt with the classification of collections in our country. We had representatives from four universities - California, Columbia, Harvard, and Yale; from the Library of Congress; and a fellow on Foundation support, Mr. Wong. I am sure that progress is possible in the cataloguing and then in the buying of material at major centers here.

　　I followed your suggestion to talk with Dr. Hummel regarding your own project. He will report to you the ideas he has on your project. I think that there is nothing to add in order to have your plan discussed. If the letter sent you by Dr. Hummel raises any questions that require answers before the plan is fully outlined, I shall know of that by direct communication from him.

Sincerely yours,

David H. Stevens

〔Rockefeller Foundation. Series 601: China; Subseries 601.R: China-Humanities and Arts. Vol. Box 47. Folder 388〕

按:该函抄送给耿士楷和恒慕义。

十二月十日

先生致信杨孝述,介绍曾宪文、赵希贤先后前往科学社移交、整理书刊,并转上契约草案请其确认以便报部备案。

允中先生大鉴:

十二月七日由馆奉达一函,谅邀台察。顷接贵社来函,悉第一次所运书籍二十箱业已送到,至慰。兹派曾宪文女士前往整理书籍,特函介绍,即希指导为荷。又前派定之贾宝成君因事未能前往,兹改派赵希贤君接替。赵君迟一、二日后启程,到时请为代备宿处为盼。此次移运图书系奉部令办理,对于寄存贵社之书,拟订一契约以便报部存查,兹拟契约草案一份,交由曾女士转奉,如承同意请将原稿寄还以便缮正。专此奉达,统祈惠照是幸,余容面谢。祇候台祺。

弟袁厶厶再拜

〔国家图书馆档案,档案编号 1935-※034-采藏6-002051 至 1935-※034-采藏6-002054〕

按:曾宪文,女,湖北武昌人,时任西文编目组组员;贾宝成,字子仪,北平大兴人,时任西文编目组组员;赵希贤,字又贤,湖北江陵人,时任西文采访组组员。[1] 此件为文书所拟之底稿,先生略加删改,无落款时间,但据发文时间可知为 12 月 10 日。

李耀南、金守淦致函先生,汇报赴科学社接收平馆运沪善本情况。

馆长钧鉴:

守淦、耀南今日赴科学社粘贴封条计二十箱,申君耀庭亦莅场帮忙,内有第三箱被车站折开,耀南当将该箱所装书籍悉行取出清查,并开单呈览以备查考。复又将该箱照旧装妥,并雇用木匠焊工当众封固,以昭慎重。再正在封箱时适第七次所运之西文书籍四十二箱亦运到社内,并闻。再中国饭店房间每天房费三元二角(按八折)初住房间每天二元四角,因住二人太小故移此,因二人同住加铺一张,每天加五角八分,似觉太贵,本拟迁移他处,又恐该店函件不肯转交,姑且住此,并请裁夺。肃此奉达,余容续报,顺颂道绥。

李耀南、金守淦谨启

---

① 《国立北平图书馆职员录》,1936 年 1 月,页 9、13。

十二月十日

上海中国饭店第三百十四号

附第一次第三箱书单一纸。

　　〔国家图书馆档案,档案编号 1935-※034-采藏 6-002038 至
　　1935-※034-采藏 6-002040〕

按:李耀南,字照亭,河南上蔡人,时任平馆考订组组员,后长期在
沪办公;金守淦,字壬父,浙江富阳人,时任平馆庶务组组长;申耀
庭,北平大兴人,时任国立故宫博物院图书馆第二科书记员,驻
沪①。该信另附"检查第一次第三箱装书单"一纸,包括《南史》
(元明刻配本,十一册二函)、《北史》(元明刻配本,廿八册四函)、
《隋书》(元刻明印本,二十册)、《隋书》(元刻明印本,存十一
册)、《唐书》(宋刻本,存三册木匣)、《唐书》(宋刻明印本,八十
册十函,此箱装八函)、《魏书》(宋刻本,四十册十函,此箱装三
函)。

十二月十二日

恒慕义覆函先生,表示积极支持平馆排印中文书籍卡片目录的计划,并建
议平馆根据国会图书馆主题分类在卡片上端或背面加以标识,方便欧美学
者利用。

December 12, 1935

Dear Mr. Yuan: –

I have your letter of October 16th outlining the project for the
printing and distribution of catalogue cards for Chinese books. No one in
this country appreciates more fully than we here in the Library of
Congress the advantages of this undertaking, and I am doing all I can to
promote a knowledge of its importance.

Your project was fully discussed at a conference of Far Eastern
Librarians which met in New York on November 29th under the auspices
of the Rockefeller Foundation, and every person present felt that if you
can proceed along the lines you propose, you will be helping to solve one

---

①《国立北平故宫博物院职员录》,1935 年,叶 15。

of our major problems. Present at the conference were representatives from the Chinese and Japanese libraries of Harvard, Columbia, Yale, University of California, and the Library of Congress. It was called by Mr. Stevens, and I think it succeeded in showing us, and the officials of the Foundation, what our needs are, and where we stand.

I may add that some members of the conference stressed the importance of arranging Chinese cards, here in the West, by English rather than by Chinese subject heading. In the absence of a fixed Chinese terminology, and for the convenience of western students, it was thought best for us to arrange our cards according to the Library of Congress subject-headings. There the terms are already fixed, and we might as well profit by such uniformity as we can get. If your staff could choose and then print the required L. C. headings, either on the back or the front of the card, all western libraries could attain uniformity in their subject catalogues. I realize that this involves some study of the book, and that you may not care now to assume that responsibility, but I wish to present it as one of the techniques that could be of great benefit to western collections.

With best wishes and kind regards, I remain,

Sincerely yours,

A. W. Hummel,

Chief, Division of Orientalia

〔Rockefeller Foundation. Series 601: China; Subseries 601.R: China-Humanities and Arts. Vol. Box 47. Folder 388〕

按：此件为录副。

十二月十三日

先生覆信金守淦、李耀南，请二人再详查《南史》《隋书》卷册数并再函覆，另请访中国学艺社及叶恭绰。

壬父、照亭两先生鉴：

接十日来函，藉悉一切。附单各书惟《南史》及《隋书》等二部照底册各系十二本，此则为十一本，未识有无遗漏。《南史》系八十卷、《隋书》系四十卷，如卷数不误，则本数不符自无甚关系，希再详查函复为要。旅馆暂可无须迁徙,短期寄寓所费无几也,惟可与之商洽改为七折。又现拟借中华学艺社会所作为藏书之处,便中请访叶玉虎先生。兹附上介绍信一件,希转致为荷。又该社现由何人负责,请前往参观,有无空屋可供庋藏及阅览之用,便中示复为荷。专复,即问旅祺。

袁厶厶启

另邮寄上《善本书目》一部。

〔国家图书馆档案,档案编号 1935－※034－采藏 6－002035 至 1935－※034－采藏 6－002037〕

按:中华学艺社会所位于上海法租界爱麦虞限路(今绍兴路),平馆运沪书籍并未借用该所。此件为底稿。

杨孝述覆函先生,告知中国科学社已收到平馆寄存的第二批书籍。

守和先生大鉴:

来函奉悉。曾女士及赵君业已于今晨来社接洽。第二批书计壹百零捌箱亦已运到,承示契约稿,兹略易数字,可以遵照,原稿奉还。专复,顺颂台祺。

弟杨孝述顿首
十二、十三

附契约原稿乙份

契约

一、国立北平图书馆因时局关系,今将所存一部分图书暂存上海中国科学社。

二、前项寄存图书计中文书八十箱,西文书一百四十六箱(另附中西文目录),全书运到后,由中国科学社点收后掣给收据。

三、前项中文书八十箱存于中国科学社图书馆书库顶层,暂不开箱,由北平图书馆派员粘贴封条后,委托中国科学社代为负责保管。

四、前项西文书籍由北平图书馆派员前往开箱,即存于中国科学社图书馆书库内,公开阅览。

五、北平图书馆派往之馆员于整理前项西文书籍外,并得受中国科学社之委托,代为整理其所藏图书。

六、前项派往整理书籍之馆员,其薪金由北平图书馆给予,作为寄存书籍租费。

七、北平图书馆可随时持原收据将寄存书籍取回。

八、本契约分缮两份，各执其一为据。

〔中国科学社用笺。《北京图书馆馆史资料汇编(1909-1949)》，
页 430-433〕

十二月十五日

中午十二时，北京大学、清华大学、北平师范大学、北平大学、燕京大学、平馆等教育文化机构负责人在欧美同学会聚餐，讨论时局，建议教育部作制止学生集会的预案，必要时可提前放假。〔《北京大学史料》第2卷第3册，页3090〕

按：学生集会指一二·九运动，以反对华北自治为目的。

十二月十八日

蒲特南覆函先生，告知国会图书馆愿意获取平馆印行的中文卡片目录，并已授权卡片部给予平馆相当的信用额度用以购买该馆卡片的校样。

December 18, 1935

My dear Dr. Yüan:

Your note of October 21 reached us over a fortnight ago, and if my acknowledgment has been delayed that is not due to any inattention, - because the project suggested interests us strongly.

I write now to say that we should like to secure three sets of the cards that your Library is proposing to print and that we shall be happy to secure them by giving your Library credit for them in exchange for the proof sheets of our own cards for which you have customarily been subscribing.

Dr. Hummel estimates that the subscription price of the three sets which we hope to receive from you would be G. $ 76.50. It is therefore this amount that I shall authorize our Card Division to credit to your Library on account of the exchange.

Very sincerely yours,

Librarian

〔Library of Congress Archives, Arthur W. Hummel Sr. correspondence series, MSS86324〕

按：该件为录副。

十二月十九日

先生致信翁文灏、蒋廷黻,祝贺履新并愿推荐图书管理人才。

　　咏霓、廷黻先生惠鉴:

　　　　缅闻荣膺右职,深为国庆,拜贺拜贺。行政院为中枢各机关之总
　　汇,对于现代图书馆之设备似为必不可缓之举,诚以处理政务增加效
　　能,胥以图书馆是赖,而尤为促成文治之工具也。高明亮已计及,无待
　　上陈。此时如需专门人员协助整理,愿为介绍,俾以早观厥成。献曝
　　微忱,尚希垂察是幸。专此,敬贺任禧,伏候勋祺不备。

　　　　　　　　　　　　　　　　　　　弟袁厶厶再拜

　　　　　　〔国家图书馆档案,档案编号 1945-※057-综合 5-005020 至
　　　　　　1945-※057-综合 5-005023〕

　　　　按:时翁文灏任行政院秘书长,蒋廷黻任行政院政务处长。此件
　　　　为文书所拟之底稿,于是日发出。

十二月二十四日

某记者来访,先生略谓英国印刷展览会今日闭幕,展品拟运往南京展出,馆
务方面,现已开辟远东问题研究室,内陈列相关书籍和期刊。〔《华北日报》,
1935 年 12 月 25 日,第 9 版〕

十二月二十五日

曾宪文覆函先生,汇报南运科学社西文书刊点收情况。

　　守和馆长先生大鉴:

　　　　敬启者,昨捧示谕,聆悉一是。兹特将赐寄之运书单一纸附呈,凡
　　有红√者为已到之箱数,均已点收无误,至第十一次所运之四十九箱
　　尚未转来,刻已去电问询,据云货已抵申,但因海关手续未清,故未运
　　来,想不日内即可点收也。专此奉达,并颂年禧。

　　　　　　　　　　　　　　　　　　　属职曾宪文谨上

　　　　　　　　　　　　　　　　　　　十二月廿五日

　　　　　　〔国家图书馆档案,档案编号 1935-※034-采藏 6-002048〕

　　　　按:该函另附一页清单,即第七次至第十一次所运西文杂志、善本
　　　　箱数、日期表格。

十二月二十八日

先生致信史蒂文斯,感谢洛克菲勒基金会对《图书季刊》英文本的编辑出

版给予资助,告知平馆现下的排印卡片工作,并希望由耿士楷转交的申请
备忘录能够得到积极地考虑,此外就毕寿普、凯欧访华计划也希望获得
资助。

December 28, 1935

Dear Dr. Stevens:

Sometime ago we learned from Mr. Gunn that the Foundation had made a grant towards the support of the *Quarterly Bulletin of Chinese Bibliography*. We are much obliged to you for your personal interest and assistance in this matter and we wish to convey to you the expression of our hearty thanks.

In spite of the unsettled political situation in North China, we have been carrying on our work as usual. We are now engaged in the printing and distribution of catalogue cards for Chinese books. Owing to our limited budget, only books published after January, 1935 are included. Through Mr. Gunn we submitted a memorandum concerning this project and in view of the valuable services which it will render to all libraries in China and abroad, we hope that it will receive your favourable consideration.

In two weeks' time, I hope to send you a brochure entitled *"Libraries in China"* which will give you some idea about library development in this country. We hope very much that the Foundation may find it possible to lend assistance to Dr. Bishop and Dr. Keogh, in order that their trip to China may be realized. The Chinese Government has extended them a cordial invitation and the Executive Board of the American Library Association has made them official delegates of the A. L. A. to be effective when they visit China. It only remains to find the financial support in order to make the trip possible.

Mr. Milam of the A. L. A. suggested that we should also write to the Carnegie Corporation which might make a grant through the A. L. A. We sincerely hope that the proposal will receive the approval of the two Foundations.

With assurances of my deepest appreciation for your interest, I am

Yours very sincerely,

T. L. Yuan

Acting Director

〔国立北平图书馆英文信纸。Rockefeller Foundation. Series 601: China; Subseries 601.R: China-Humanities and Arts. Vol. Box 47. Folder 388〕

按:此件为打字稿,落款处为先生签名,1936 年 1 月 27 日送达。

十二月三十一日

先生致信严文郁,就马廉旧藏两种戏剧书入藏北京大学图书馆办法予以商讨。

绍诚先生大鉴:

接廿七日手翰,敬谂种切。马氏戏剧书二种,尊处拟藏副本一节,极表赞同。兹将《千金记》一种代为影晒,奉赠其余杂剧三集一种,请由尊处自行出资影照或钞写,均无不可,敝馆届时当予以便利也。专此奉复,顺候台祺。

弟袁同礼顿首

十二月卅一日

〔国立北平图书馆用笺。北京大图书馆图书馆特藏部〕

按:"马氏"应指马廉,1935 年 2 月 19 日因脑溢血猝逝于北京大学。此信为文书代笔,落款处为先生签名。

十二月

先生为《国立北平图书馆善本书目乙编》撰写序言。〔《国立北平图书馆善本书目乙编》,1935 年 12 月初版〕

是年底

方甦生撰《整理档案方法的初步研究》,由沈兼士推荐,经马衡、徐森玉、先生审查通过,获得先生捐薪所设国立北平故宫博物院乙种奖学金。〔《国立北平故宫博物院年刊》,1936 年 7 月,页 75—111〕

按:该文于是年 11 月草成,后收录于《国立北平故宫博物院年刊》。

是年

先生共向故宫博物院捐资 3472.00 元,用以设立、发放奖学金。〔《收到廿四年奖学金 3472 元正补具收据由》,《故宫博物院·财务类》第 55 卷,页 1—2〕

一九三六年　四十二岁

一月一日

先生及国立北平图书馆全体职员合影。〔"国立北平图书馆全体职员合影"(二十五年元旦)相片)〕

一月五日

中午,北平图书馆协会假骑河楼清华同学会举行聚餐会,到会者约五十余人。餐后,开本年第一次常会,李文裿为主席,致辞后,继由谢礼士演讲欧洲各国图书馆近况及国际图书馆大会之情形,次由严文郁翻译。议决事项:一调查本市学校图书馆;二向市政府建议增设图书馆;三与中华图书馆协会合印"中国杂志专号目录""北平各图书馆所藏中文算学联合目录"。最后,选举新职员,结果为执行委员先生、何日章、严文郁、吴鸿志、李文裿、田洪都、朱日珍七人,监察委员吴光清、于震寰、邓衍林、曾宪三、莫余敏卿。〔《华北日报》,1936年1月6日,第9版〕

一月八日　上海

晨,先生访黄郛,报告北平近况,并请其资助李瑞年留学。黄郛当即交给先生千元,并委托汇往法国。〔《黄郛日记(1935—1936)》,页88〕

一月中上旬

先生拜会耿士楷,谈国立中央图书馆筹备的经费问题,询问有无可能向洛克菲勒基金会临时借款,以加速组建。此外,重提邀请美国图书馆学家访华的计划。〔Rockefeller Foundation. Series 601: China; Subseries 601.R: China-Humanities and Arts. Vol. Box 47. Folder 388〕

一月十八日　南京

中午,朱希祖、朱偰在土街口浣花春设宴,胡适、王星拱、沈兼士、先生、张仲翔、陈大齐、刘国钧、罗家伦等与席,王世杰、朱家骅因事未到。其间,先生告平馆《宋会要》将付梓印成,陈垣拟名为"宋会要稿",朱希祖认为不妥,应改为"辑本宋会要稿",以示与原本不同,先生以为是。〔《朱希祖日记》,页611〕

　　按:该书最终刊印名为《宋会要辑稿》,由陈垣题写书名。

晚,蒋慰堂在德奥瑞同学会设宴,刘英士、辛树帜、陈可忠、王廉、童冠贤、郑鹤声、汪敬熙、顾颉刚、先生与席。〔《顾颉刚日记》卷3,页433〕

一月二十日

上午,先生抵达北平。〔《华北日报》北平,1936年1月19日,第9版〕

一月二十一日

先生致信恒慕义,询问国会图书馆可否为平馆影照三册新获得的《永乐大典》。

January 21, 1936

Dear Dr. Hummel:

　　We have been informed that three volumes of the "*Yung lo ta tien*" formerly in the possession of Prof. H. A. Giles were recently sold to the Library of Congress. Will you be so kind as to make for us a photostat copy of these three volumes, which according to our records are numbers 13344/5, 19742/3 and 19792, so that we may add them to our collection?

　　Our work in copying for the Library of Congress our volumes of the "*Yung lo ta tien*" is still progressing and we hope to make a shipment next month.

Yours sincerely,

T. L. Yuan

Acting Director

P. S. According to my census, Prof. Giles has another volume Chuan 13496-97. Is this copy available at Washington?

　　　　〔国立北平图书馆英文信纸。Library of Congress, Putnam Archives, Special Files, China: National Library 1930-1939〕

　　　　按:H. A. Giles 即 Herbert A. Giles(1845-1935),英国汉学家,中文名翟理斯,其旧藏三册《永乐大典》分别为示字和谧字、录字、服字册,影照之事参见3月27日恒慕义覆函。此信为打字稿,落款处为先生签名。

一月二十二日

中午,中国工程师学会北平分会在报子街会址议事厅设宴,欢迎美国工程师专家杰克逊教授夫妇来华考察。陆志韦夫妇、顾毓琇夫妇、庄前鼎夫妇、李书华、刘拓夫妇、先生、饶毓泰等三十余人到场作陪。〔《华北日报》，1936 年 1 月 23 日，第 9 版〕

恒慕义致函先生，感谢寄赠某书并已为国会图书馆订购一份，并谢先生寄赠故宫日历。

January 22, 1936

Dear Mr. Yuan: -

　　Many thanks for sending me the volume of the 　　　　. It is beautifully done, and I appreciate your sending it to me. I am ordering a copy for the Library of Congress.

　　I have also to thank you for the Palace Museum canlendar - it makes a useful and valuable addition to my desk.

　　I sent you a few days ago a statement about the bond of the Departmental Bank, which I hope you received. With kind regards,

Sincerely yours,

Arthur W. Hummel

〔Library of Congress Archives, Arthur W. Hummel Sr. correspondence series, MSS86324〕

　　按：该件为录副，空格处付诸阙如。

一月二十六日

先生致信黄炎培，告知另邮寄上《夷氛闻记》。

　　任之先生大鉴：

　　　　奉到一月二十日大函，聆悉种切。兹将馆藏钞本《夷氛闻记》八册，另邮挂号寄上，以供校勘。即祈察收，并先掣给收据为荷。此书倘能赖鼎力流传，尤所感祷。专此奉复，顺候台祺。

弟袁同礼顿首

一月廿六

　　附《夷氛闻记》八册（另邮）。

〔国立北平图书馆用笺。华夏天禧（墨笺楼）拍卖（http://www. kongfz.cn/24370411/）〕

　　按：此件为文书代笔，落款处为先生签名。此信寄送"上海霞飞路一四一三号善钟路西白赛仲路口鸿英图书馆筹备处黄任之先生"。黄炎培收到书后,于本月 30、31 日持该版与人文图书馆(筹备处)所藏版本对校。①

一月二十七日

恒慕义覆函先生,告知国会图书馆馆长已同意订购三份平馆刊印的中文卡片目录。

Jan. 27, 1936

Dear Mr. Yuan: -

I have your letter of December 31st, 1935, asking whether we can exchange L. C. cards for your newly printed cards.

On December 18th, the Librarian wrote you stating that we should like to secure "three (3) sets of your cards in exchange for the proofsheets of our own cards for which you have customarily been subscribing"-the price of the three sets to be G. $ 76.50, as stated in your announcement.

Doubtless that word reached you after your letter was sent off.

With kind regards, I remain,

Sincerely yours,

Arthur W. Hummel,

Chief, Division of Orientalia

〔Library of Congress Archives, Arthur W. Hummel Sr. correspondence series, MSS86324〕

按:该件为录副。

一月二十八日

先生致信金守淦、赵希贤,请二人将暂存上海商业储蓄银行之书籍提出转移至中央研究院研究所、中国科学社。

壬父、又贤先生大鉴:

查本馆寄存上海商业储蓄银行仓库部书籍贰佰四拾陆箱,现拟于二月六日以前将写经四十九箱改存中央研究院物理、化学、工程研究所,其余壹百九十七箱改存中国科学社,以便开箱整理。兹寄去该行

---

① 《黄炎培日记》第 5 卷,页 113。

仓单四纸,希察收取书,并将经过情形函复备查为要。再中国科学社已另函接洽,如楼上地址不敷,请商杨先生暂借楼下客厅一用,一俟书架做成即可开箱陈列也。宿舍布置已就绪否?兹派李锺履、余炳元、王锡印赴沪办公,约十日后启程,刘君所复之德文书书单查对后,请即寄来以便付款。此上,顺候旅祺。

附仓单四纸、函二件代转。

〔国家图书馆档案,档案编号 1936-※035-采藏 7-001012 至 1936-※035-采藏 7-001014〕

按:李锺履,字仲和,山东阳谷人;余炳元,湖北黄陂人,时均任平馆西文采访组组员。王锡印,字月潭,河北枣强人,时任平馆西文编目组组员。[①]“刘君”似指刘咸,待考。此件为文书所拟之底稿,先生有大量修改,无落款,但据记录可知实发日期。

凯欧致函先生,寄来本年一月十九日《纽约时报》。

January 28, 1936

Dear Mr. Yuan:

There is an article in the *New York Times* for January 19th on Chinese students and their political views. As you may not take the *Times* I send you a copy under separate cover. Even if you do take it you may be able to make some use of the copy is now giving to you.

Yours very sincerely,

〔Yale University records, Peiping National Library, 1931-1937, Box: 80, Folder: 831〕

按:此件为底稿。

一月三十日

刘承幹致函先生,前因身体违和未能晤谈,并告《杭州府志》已由董康带还。

○○仁兄大人阁下:

日前台从南下,辱承枉存,乃弟方以感寒卧疾,有失迎迓。阍者谓台从即须离苏,故未及报谒,稍伸地主之谊,尤深歉悚。授经丈于旧历

---

① 《国立北平图书馆职员录》,1936 年 1 月,页 8、13。

岁暮南还，《杭州府志》十三册业已带还，弟以病未能至沪奉访，闻其不日将有苏行，或可得晤也。专此布臆，祗颂著安。

弟〇〇〇顿首

新正初七日即一月卅号

〔上海图书馆藏求恕斋信稿;《求恕斋日记》(稿本)〕

按:此件为底稿，前冠有"致袁守和"字样。

一月

先生撰《国立北平故宫博物院图书馆概况》。〔《故宫博物院图书馆概况(附太庙图书分馆概况)》,1936〕

按:该篇并未署名，暂依朱赛虹之说，将其归于先生名下。①

二月一日　北平

晚，谢国桢、刘盼遂、孙海波在撷英设宴，先生与容庚、钱玄同、黎锦熙、刘节、侯堮、唐兰等人同席。〔《钱玄同日记(整理本)》,页 1176〕

按:侯堮，字芸圻，安徽无为人，清华大学国学研究院毕业，与谢国桢等人同为梁启超的学生。

The Library Journal 刊登先生短文，题为 *Cards for Chinese Books* 。〔*The Library Journal*, vol. 61 no. 3, p. 84〕

按:该文失收于《袁同礼文集》。后 *Catalogers' and Classifiers' Yearbook* (1937)中 Bibliography of Cataloging and Classification, 1936 一栏提及此篇介绍文字，但未做转述或评价。②

二月四日

先生致信张元济，赠《国立北平图书馆善本书目乙编》，并询《永乐大典》本《水经注》何时刊行。

菊生先生大鉴:

敝馆所藏善本乙库各书，现将目录编印成帙。兹奉上一册，乞察存。如有可印之书，敝馆极愿委托贵公司影印流传也。书均暂存上海。又前承赐观《永乐大典》本《水经注》，业已照毕，预计何日出版? 亦极欲先睹为快，并希示及为幸。专此奉达，静候道祺。附书目一册

① 朱赛虹《故宫博物院出版事业的首度辉煌——民国时期出版综论》,《故宫博物院院刊》,2011 年第 1 期,页 137。

② *Catalogers' and Classifiers' Yearbook*, 1937, pp. 119, 123.

（另寄）。

后学袁同礼顿首

四日

〔《张元济全集》第 3 卷,页 2〕

按:《永乐大典》本《水经注》即《续古逸丛书》之四十三,所用底本为《永乐大典》卷 11127 至 11141,影印八册,约在是年四月底五月初刊行。[①] 此信于 7 日送达。

二月五日

先生致信史蒂文斯,告知平馆编印目录卡片的标题词主要依据国会图书馆的标题词,方便西方学者利用,另自本年 1 月 1 日起,印制的卡片已寄送哈佛、加州(伯克利)、哥伦比亚、芝加哥、密西根各大学、国会图书馆以及欧洲各大图书馆,并请耿士楷携带一套回纽约交洛克菲勒基金会审查。

February 5, 1936

Dear Dr. Stevens:

I thank you for your letter of December 6th, and I am glad to learn that a conference was held in New York that dealt with the classification of the Far Eastern materials.

I have answered Dr. Hummel concerning the subject heading. As our headings are mainly based on Library of Congress subject-heading, there should be no difficulty for western scholars to orientate themselves with our scheme.

Since January 1, we have been printing and distributing Chinese catalogue cards on a small scale. They have been sent to Harvard, California, Columbia, Chicago, Michigan, the Library of Congress as well as to European major centers. I am glad to report that these cards have been very enthusiastically received both in China and abroad.

I am asking Mr. Gunn to bring back a set of these cards for your reference.

Yours sincerely,

---

① 《大公报·图书副刊》第 129 期,1936 年 5 月 7 日,第 11 版。

T. L. Yuan

Acting Director

〔国立北平图书馆英文信纸。Rockefeller Foundation. Series 601:
China; Subseries 601. R: China-Humanities and Arts. Vol. Box 47.
Folder 388〕

按:此件为打字稿,落款处为先生签名,附在2月8日致耿士楷信
内于3月9日送达。

二月六日

先生致信杨孝述,介绍馆员前往上海协助中国科学社图书馆编目、整理书
刊,并商洽联合编目及平馆沪上存书移至该社图书馆事。

允中先生大鉴:

兹派敝馆职员王锡印、张增荣、余炳元三君赴沪办事,特函介绍,
即乞惠予接纳,加以委用为荷。附工作表一份,是否有当,希与刘主任
商酌办理。又敝馆为便利学者参考起见,拟编上海各图书馆西文书联
合目录及西文期刊联合目录,除期刊目录将在北平编辑外,其西文书
籍联合目录拟与贵社合作办理,所需卡片约十万张(约四百元左右),
除编辑及一切杂费由敝馆担任外,其卡片购置费拟请贵社担任,此项
卡片即寄存贵社,以供参考,如荷赞同请即面告曾女士进行可也。
专此奉达,顺候台祺。

弟袁同礼顿首

二月六日

信写就未发,奉到二月三日手札,敬悉尊处讲演室、会客室均不能
存书,承代筹画,至感至感。敝馆之书自当在上海银行多存若干日。
关于玻璃木柜,务请督饬木匠早日做成,以便书籍开箱陈列。再颂
时祉。

弟袁同礼再拜

六日

〔国立北平图书馆用笺。上海市档案馆,档案编号Q546-1-192-55〕

按:"刘主任"即刘咸(1901—1987),字重熙,江西都昌人,时任
《科学》杂志主编,并与杨孝述、秉志等人主持上海明复图书馆。
"上海银行"应指上海商业储蓄银行,1935年12月,该行先后收

到平馆委托中国旅行社运送的书籍 246 箱。该信为文书代笔,但落款两处则为先生亲笔,另附"工作分配表"两页。

二月八日

先生致信耿土楷,告知平馆在南京设立分馆计划将由图书馆委员会交中基会审查,并请将申请资助中国图书馆馆员前往美国留学的函件和中文新书卡片转交史蒂文斯,请洛克菲勒基金会给予妥善考虑。

February 8, 1936

Mr. Selskar M. Gunn

Rockefeller Foundation

Hamilton House

170 Kiangse Road

Shanghai

Dear Mr. Gunn:

I have been hoping to meeting you once more before you sail for America, but owing to heavy office routine, I am obliged to postpone my trip until next month. So, I shall miss seeing you before you leave, but I send you herewith my best wishes for a successful trip and early return.

Our plans of extending our service to Nanking, as I outlined to you at our last interview, has been under serious consideration by our Library Board. It will be one of the main topics for discussion at the China Foundation meeting in April. Owing to the constant threat for autonomy in North China, there will surely be a change in our book purchasing policy. I shall, however, keep you informed concerning our future programme.

I enclose a letter with regard to fellowship in library science and hope very much that you will submit it to Dr. Stevens.

Under separate cover, I am also sending you several packages of our printed cards for Chinese books. They represent the output of January. If you still have space in your trunk, I shall appreciate it if you will bring them to the attention of Dr. Stevens and other officers of the Foundation. We have been distributing these cards to various libraries and scientific institutions in China and abroad.

　　With best wishes for a pleasant voyage,

Yours sincerely,

T. L. Yuan

Acting Director

〔Rockefeller Foundation. Series 601: China; Subseries 601.R: China-Humanities and Arts. Vol. Box 47. Folder 388〕

　　按:此为抄件。

张元济覆函先生,感谢寄赠《国立北平图书馆善本书目乙编》,并回赠《水经注》毛钉本一册。

　　守和仁兄大人阁下:

　　　　昨奉二月四日手书,并见惠贵馆善本乙库各书目录一册。重承雅意,将委敝馆视可印者影印流通,至为感幸。今书目想已付邮在途,俟奉到拜读,先此布谢。永乐本《水经注》业已印就,惟尚未完备出版。兹先取毛钉本一部寄奉,以供浏览,至祈惠察。专此,先布谢忱,敬颂春祺。

廿五年二月八日

〔《张元济全集》第3卷,页2〕

二月十三日

先生致信金守浧,告将寄唐人写经九卷,请其收到后与存上海商业储蓄银行书一起保存。

　　壬父先生大鉴:

　　　　兹有唐人写经九卷,前经人借钞,书箱南运时未及附入,现已陆续收回,特挂号寄上,乞暂存。俟上海银行书箱取出开箱后,再行补入可也。附清单一纸,请察收,照单点验,示复为荷。顺候旅祺。

　　　　附单一纸,唐经九卷(唐经共装一小匣,另寄)。

〔国家图书馆档案,档案编号 1936-※035-采藏 7-001017 至

1936-※035-采藏 7-001020〕

　　　　按:此件为文书所拟之底稿,先生有些许修改,无落款,但据记录可知实发日期。另附写经清单一纸,应为先生亲笔。

二月十四日

刘承幹覆函先生及平馆同仁,感谢寄赠《宋会要辑稿》并请催促大宋书局

将未还之校写清稿寄下。

北平图书馆诸公惠鉴：

展诵十日大札，敬悉壹是。承觅影印《宋会要》业由大东书局寄到，自第二册起至壹百〇六册止，翻劸之余，知贵馆排比整理，煞费苦心，俾兹湮郁数百年之书，一旦复显于世，宁非国故之嘉话、典籍之幸事。校写清稿已由授经丈交还半部，尚余半部，敬希函知大东，校毕检还为幸。专复陈谢，祗颂文安。

第〇〇〇顿首

二月十四号即正月廿二日

〔上海图书馆藏求恕斋信稿〕

按：此件为底稿。

二月十七日

先生致信王重民，告知平馆已向法英学界寄赠最近出版之工具书，并谈说服翟林奈允许王、向二人查看大英博物馆藏敦煌写经的策略，平馆与清华大学筹款拍摄英藏写经和太平天国史料。

有三学弟如晤：

前奉一月三日及十二月廿二日两次来书，均悉一一。清代索引已寄上四部，请分赠伯、戴、罗及国立圕等，Giles 及 Moule 处已由馆直寄矣。Giles 不愿人看写经，亦因其只有一人保管，事必躬亲，看者愈多则不胜其扰，但吾人如不提替他编目而提替他找材料、协助其研究，或较易办理。请在伯希和未赴美以前托伯君写信，自更有力量。既有七千余卷似应与向君分工合作可与向君商定准夏间某日同时进行，日内当函 Giles，托其帮忙俾吾人可以顺利进行。馆中并与清华先筹国币八千元巴黎方面除前后寄去六千元外，尚有一千五百法郎，今英伦所藏既多于巴黎，拟共筹国币八千元，专作为影照英伦所藏写经及天平天国史料之用，约五六月间汇出。巴黎所藏者尚需款若干，方能将其重要者一一影摄，并乞示及以便筹款。尊处既有如此之好机会，极盼在燉煌学上有一大贡献，愿以馆中之财力助君完成斯业，并可使国内学者得一种新资料也。《乙库书目》寄上两部，可以一部赠伯希和君。匆匆，顺颂旅安。

同礼顿首

二月十七

请告王海镜,将巴黎做博物馆陈列柜之商店名称及住址调查示下为盼。

《文学论文索引三编》已出版,如需用再寄上。

〔国立北平图书馆用笺。中国书店·海淀,四册〕

按:"天平天国史料"当作"太平天国史料"。"清代索引"即《清代文集篇目分类索引》,平馆索引组编辑,北京大学出版组印刷,1935 年 11 月初版。Moule 即英国汉学家慕阿德(Arthur C. Moule,1873-1957),生于杭州,后长期在华传教,曾著有《一五五〇年前的中国基督教史》(*Christians in China Before the Year 1550*),时任剑桥大学汉学讲席教授,他是圣公会华中教区第一任主教慕稼谷(George E. Moule,1828-1912)的幼子。《乙库书目》即《国立北平图书馆善本书目乙编》;《文学论文索引三编》由刘修业(平馆索引组)编辑,1936 年 1 月初版。

二月二十日

中国科学社《社友》刊登王家楫、先生与胡博渊共同撰写的《中国科学社第二十一届司选委员会通告》。

社友公鉴:

敬启者,本社理事名额除总干事外为十四人,照章每年应选七人。查本年十月任满之理事为丁绪宝、王琎、任鸿隽、伍连德、李协、周仁、胡先骕诸君。本委员会特依据社章第四十八条提出下届候选理事三十二人(名单列后),社友中如另有候选人提出者,请依据社章第四十九条经二十人以上之连署,于本年四月十日以前函送南京成贤街六十八号国立中央研究院动植物研究所王家楫收,以便汇刊候选名单,分送各社友选举。特此通告。

第二十一届司选委员会

王家楫、袁同礼、胡博渊同启

〔《社友》(中国科学社)第 53 期,页 1〕

按:王家楫(1898—1976),字仲济,江苏奉贤人,动物学家,1920 年毕业于南京高等师范学院,1924 年毕业于国立东南大学农学系,后赴美留学,获宾夕法尼亚大学博士学位,1948 年当选为中央研究院院士。胡博渊(1888—1964),字维颙,江苏武进人,矿

物学家、工程师,1905 年入唐山路矿学堂,后赴美留学,先后在
麻省理工学院、匹兹堡大学学习,1920 年归国,曾任农矿部矿政
司司长、中国矿冶工程学会会长。该通告后附"计开候选人名
单"。

二月二十七日

下午四时,平馆委员会召开第二十二次会议,陈垣、孙洪芬、蒋梦麟、胡适、
先生、傅斯年出席。蒋梦麟为会议主席,先生记录。报告事项如下:

(一)善本书籍南迁,议决准予备案,先生提出与中国科学社订立寄存图书
契约草案,修正通过。

(二)平馆最近三月馆务报告,议决准予备案。

讨论事项如下:

(一)先生提出下年度预算案,计(1)经常费国币十四万四千二百十二元,议
决照案通过;(2)中文购书费国币六万元,议决核减为五万元;(3)西文
购书费美金三万元,议决照案通过;(4)平馆建筑修缮费国币五千九百
元,议决照案通过。

(二)关于南北两馆合作案,由先生及孙洪芬报告经过,议决缓议。

(三)静生生物调查所提议(1)请将平馆一部份馆址拨给该所;(2)请将平馆
生物学书报拨给该所两案,议决缓议。

(四)先生提议上海定制之玻璃书柜五十三件,计洋二千五百元,前经中基
会照数借拨并指定在购书费内扣还,近平馆将西文重复书籍出让于武
汉、成都、岭南各大学,共得洋二千一百八十元六角五分,可否即以此
款作为定制书柜之用,以免动用购书费,不足之数再由西文购书费内
拨付,是否可行,议决照案通过。

(五)先生提议聘梁思庄为编纂,议决照案通过。

(六)傅斯年提议赵万里现编《四部考》为目录学重要贡献,应如何补助以便
早日完成案,议决此书为图书馆工作之一,其编辑费及杂费由平馆担
任,遇必要时可约故宫博物院合作,自下年度起限两年完成。

六时半散会。〔《北京图书馆馆史资料汇编(1909-1949)》,页 352-353〕

> 按:"南北两馆"其中南馆或指国立中央图书馆(筹备处),待考。
> 梁思庄(1908—1986),祖籍广东新会,生于日本神户,梁启超次
> 女,似并未入职平馆,而是赴燕京大学图书馆任事。

晚,先生在同和居设宴,为傅斯年饯行,胡适、陈受颐、孙洪芬、姚从吾、陈垣、王访渔、顾颉刚受邀与席。〔《顾颉刚日记》卷3,页447〕

二月二十九日

蒲特南致函先生,感谢寄赠*Libraries in China* 和《中华图书馆协会会报》等册页。

February 29, 1936

Dear Dr. Yuan:

We have just received, with special appreciation, the copy of the handbook on "*Libraries in China*"; also the copies of the *Bulletin of the Association* (issues of January-February, 1935, March-April, 1935, and May-June, 1935).

They will be notable contributions to our information as to the development of the movement.

With best wishes, believe me,

Very sincerely yours,
Librarian

〔Librarian of Congress, Putnam Archives, Special File, China: National Library 1930−1939〕

按:该件为录副。

二三月间

先生致信庄尚严(伦敦),请其为平馆代购伦敦艺展所有古器物照片,其中铜器务必购得全份,并告费用可由中国驻英使馆垫付。〔庄灵编著《故宫文物南迁时代记往:从〈华严洞图卷〉和〈庄严日记〉谈起》,北京:商务印书馆,2023年,页502〕

按:3月14日庄尚严收到此信,翌日联系向达商讨具体办法,后向达答应垫付40英镑。3月25日,庄尚严为平馆购买此类照片。

先生收王重民二月二日、十七日、十九日各一函,旋即覆信,告其编印《太平天国官书补编》及在法延长交换事。

有三仁弟如晤:

前接二月二日、十七及十九日来书,敬悉一一。太平天国官书十一种,可以设法影印,如已照完可先寄下,以便与商务一商。昨日法使馆韩参赞来谈,谓杜乃扬愿再延长一年,已接伯希和来信为之推荐,当即告以杜君延长既与馆中经费不发生关系,当然欢迎。但巴黎国家图书馆对于吾弟之薪金亦须延长照付壹年,方能公允,渠允函伯希和或法外交部。兹寄伯希和一信,阅后请转交。敝意如能再留法一年,于学问定有大益处,况伦敦密迩,暑假及其他假期中均可前往,但每月薪金应在国家图书馆支领,而不能在伯希和处支领(恐法官方不愿担负,有此拟议,因曾为伯希和帮忙也)。至伯君处则以私人资格帮忙,故可不受其拘束也。伯君虽有学问,但待人不诚,故如 Bibliothèque nationale 能继续聘任,于公于私均有利,否则吾人对于杜女士之延长,亦可予以不同意以为交换条件,请根据此立场随时留意。敝意一切当可以迎刃而解,为吾弟计,亦以多留一年,可从伯希和、戴先生多有研究、讨论机会为得计也。赴俄事(1937年秋),已函阿理克教授,大约无问题,如能多储蓄或可由美返国,亦不失一良策也。总之,中国刻下混乱已极,能在国外安心研究最好,不必亟亟返国也。向觉明处,曾为之谋英庚款未成,后又在伦敦艺展会赢余项下为之设法,王雪艇复函已表示赞同,但逐鹿者多恐无希望。近又在美庚款为之设法,由馆提出补助一百五十磅之计划,以一次……

〔国立北平图书馆英文信纸。中国书店·海淀,四册〕

按:该信残,仅存以上部分。"太平天国官书十一种"为《天理要论全编》(原书)、《天理要论全编》(节录前八章)、《颁行历书》(四年)、《颁行历书》(八年)、《太平礼制》、《会试题干王宝制》、《干王洪宝制》、《资政新编》、《军次实录》、《诛妖檄文》、《太平天日》。

三月三日

柳诒徵致函先生,商借平馆存沪善本《戒庵文集》。

守和馆长大鉴:

久疏笺候,维春祺胜适为颂无量。去岁曾上芜缄,拟假贵藏敝乡靳贵所著《戒庵集》景印流布,旋奉示复,以善本书已运沪。兹悉存放科学社中,可否函达该社,请为一查。敝处当派员前往,俾便假以付照,

不过两三日即可照毕,并按商务印书馆景印散藏之例,将来出书以十分
之一致酬。事关流通古籍,如荷慨允,即希见复为感。专此,即颂公绥。

柳诒徵拜启
三月三日

〔《国学图书馆第九年刊》,1936 年,"案牍"页 43〕

按:靳贵(1464—1520),字充道,号戒庵,江苏镇江人,《戒庵文
集》为其诗文集,后柳诒徵为该书撰写跋文。

三月四日

先生致信凯欧,寄上最新版的 *Libraries in China*,希望卡耐基基金会和洛克
菲勒基金会能够资助其访华。

March 4, 1936

Dear Dr. Keogh:

Thank you so much for sending me the copy of the *New York Times* for January 19th. I have read the article with a great deal of interest and I am having it made available to our reading public.

About three weeks ago I sent you a copy of "*Libraries in China*". Although it is not a satisfactory piece of work, yet I hope it would give you much information you are interested in. All of us here have been expecting that some action will be taken by the Foundations in order to enable you to plan a visit to China this year, if possible. At the end of December, I wrote to President Keppel as well as to Dr. Stevens and I am hoping to hear from them very shortly. It will indeed be a great pleasure to see you in our country.

With kindest regards,

Yours sincerely,
T. L. Yuan
Acting Director

〔国立北平图书馆英文信纸。Yale University records, Peiping
National Library, 1931-1937, Box: 80, Folder: 831〕

按:该件为打字稿,落款处为先生签名,于本月 30 日送达耶鲁大
学图书馆。

三月六日

先生致信柳诒徵,极愿赞助其景印《戒庵文集》,但须等待善本移存中国科学社后方能取出。

> 翼谋先生大鉴:

> 接奉三月三日台笺,敬承种切。贵馆拟景印《戒庵集》一种,事关流通先哲遗箸,极愿赞助。但敝馆运沪图书系分存数处,此书现存上海银行仓库部,约于一个月后可以提出,改存中国科学社,届时开箱整理后,再当奉达商洽一切,尚祈亮察是幸。专此奉复,顺候箸祺。

> 　　　　　　　　　　　　　　　　弟袁同礼顿首

> 　　　　　　　　　　　　　　　　三月六日

〔《国学图书馆第九年刊》,1936年,"案牍"页13〕

按:本年5月1日,平馆去函允借《戒庵文集》景印,国学图书馆派访购部、印行部主干周悫①赴沪主持。6月6日,景印工作完成。

三月十一日

先生致信耿士楷,寄赠五份平馆出版品清单并请其转交洛克菲勒基金会总部,希望洛克菲勒基金会赞助平馆编印中文书籍卡片目录这项工作。

March 11, 1936

Dear Mr. Gunn:

Under separate cover, I am sending you five copies of the "List of Serial Publications" currently received by the National Library and I shall be obliged to you if you will kindly pass them on to the Directors of different divisions of your New York Office.

We are praying that favorable action will be taken towards the support of our project for the printing and distribution of catalogue cards for Chinese books. You will perhaps be good enough to send me a cable, if it will go through.

---

① 周悫,国立南京高等师范文史地部毕业、东南大学文学士,曾任中央大学图书馆编目,1930年8月入江苏省立国学图书馆。参见《江苏省立国学图书馆概况》,1935年,页30。

With kindest regards,

Yours sincerely,

T. L. Yuan

〔国立北平图书馆英文信纸。Rockefeller Foundation. Series 601:
China; Subseries 601. R: China-Humanities and Arts. Vol. Box 47.
Folder 388〕

按：此件为打字稿，落款处为先生签名。

三月十九日

先生致信 Octave Piel，感谢其寄赠期刊，并告知平馆将在下个财年度购买震旦大学博物馆出版的两种书籍。

March 19, 1936

Monsieur O. Piel, Directeur,

Musée Heude,

223 Avenue Dubail,

Shanghai.

Dear Sir:

I beg to acknowledge the receipt of your letter of 8th inst. as well as your sending of your publications as noted below for which I wish to extend to you grateful thanks.

NOTES DE BOTANIQUE CHINOISE, nos. 1-2

NOTES D'ENTOMOLOGIE CHINOISE, vols. 1-2

NOTES DE MALACOLOGIE CHINOISE, vols. 1, nos. 1-2

I should be much obliged to you if you would kindly send us regularly their future issues as soon as they appear.

Regarding the "*Conchyliologie Fluviale*" and "*Memoires Concernant l'historie naturelle de l'Empire Chinois*" quoted at $357.00, we beg to inform you that owing to the limit of our book fund, we shall not be able to purchase them now, but we shall order them from you at the beginning of the next fiscal year. As some of the parts are out of print, will you please reserve a copy each for the National Library.

With best regards,

Yours very truly,

T. L. Yuan

Acting Director

〔国立北平图书馆英文信纸。上海市档案馆，档案编号 Q244-1-499〕

按：Octave Piel（1876-1945），法国耶稣会士、博物学家，中文名郑璧尔，时任震旦大学博物馆馆长。此件为打字稿，落款处为先生签名。

三月二十日

先生致信故宫博物院，平馆欲与故宫博物院交换馆藏复本，以求互补馆藏。

贵院函字第七十八号公函内开，"本院在太庙设立图书分馆，业将旧藏复本及征集新书移馆分陈，籍供众览。兹为充实内容，亟思广为搜集，凤仰贵馆收藏宏富，复本必多，倘荷酌量见贻，固极纫感，否则亦望检借陈列，嘉惠士林，专泐奉商，务祈慨允"等因。查本馆复本书籍，照例未能移赠，惟贵院各项刊物及拓片，本馆尚多未备，拟以此项重复书互相交换，藉期互益。兹先寄上复本书单一份，共计一百八十八种，送请察阅。如贵院图书馆尚未入藏，当再将书奉上。另附本馆拟交换贵院刊物及金石拓片清单一份，随函奉上，倘承惠允，请即检齐送馆，俾供阅览。准函前因，相应函复。即希察照为荷！此致

故宫博物院

副馆长袁同礼

〔《马衡年谱长编》，页 648-649〕

按：马衡收到此信后，批示"所索本院出版物可照单赠送，拟赠本院之《孙中山全集》等书多不需要，另列该馆出版物书目一纸，请照单交换。马衡。"

先生致信金守溢，寄上海商业储蓄银行存书单，请其与即将赴沪的李耀南陆续取出并移至中国科学社妥善存放。

壬父先生大鉴：

接三月十六日函，藉悉一切。书架准于二十二、三日完工，至慰。李照亭君定于二十四日下午三时半由平启程，二十六日（星期四）晨可到沪，届时请到车站一接，在李君未到以前，请暂饬工人将书架玻璃擦净以便应用。兹寄上上海银行仓库部仓单四纸，即请察收，陆续提

取,惟另单所开各书暂时无庸开箱,应存何处请与杨先生一商,此项清单已交李照亭君一份照办。上海银行方面顷已与之接洽,原存每箱每月收费四角,现按八折实收,每箱每月三角二分,共二百四十六箱,四个月合洋三百一十四元八角八分。兹另汇上国币七百七十六元九角,内伍百元作为存费、运取、脚力及三四两月杂项开支之用,余二百七十六元九角系三月份同人薪水,请交中国科学社转发,除另函外,款到后即希函复为要。专此,顺候旅祺。

袁厶厶启

〔国家图书馆档案,档案编号 1936-※035-采藏 7-001021 至 1936-※035-采藏 7-001024〕

按:此件为王祖彝所拟之底稿,先生有大量修改,无落款时间,但据记录可知实发日期。

三月二十四日

凯欧致函先生,感谢寄赠 *Libraries in China*。

March 24, 1936

Dear Mr. Yuan:

　　Thank you very much for *Libraries in China*. I have looked through the papers with much interest, and think them well done. I am delighted to have a personal copy of the book.

Yours very sincerely,

〔Yale University records, Peiping National Library, 1931 - 1937, Box: 80, Folder: 831〕

按:此件为底稿。

三月二十六日

晚,中英同学会假欧美同学会举行宴会欢送英国大使贾德幹,中方人士程锡庚、金绍基、先生、罗昌、林可胜等六十人到场。程锡庚致辞,贾德幹答谢,全体摄影留念。十时半,始散。〔《大公报》(天津),1936 年 3 月 28 日,第 3 版〕

按:贾德幹拟于本月 28 日离平返国。

三月二十七日

恒慕义致函先生,请平馆估算抄写某古籍费用,并告知国会图书馆将尽快为平馆影照新获翟理斯旧藏《永乐大典》三册,另外表示将协助汪长炳获得洛克菲勒基金会资助以延长留美时间。

March 27, 1936

Dear Mr. Yuan: -

I should like to inquire what you would charge to copy for us in manuscript the work on art　　in 80 chuan by　　. It is listed in Vol. II, P. 17b of the National Library's publication entitled

I have urged the Library to furnish you with photostats of the three volumes of the *Yung-lo ta-tien* which were formerly owned by H. A. Giles and which are recorded in your list as: Nos. 13,344 - 5, 19,742, 19,792.

You will doubtless hear from the Library before long about them; but due to the excessive use of our photostat machines, it may take a few months before the photostating actually starts. These three volumes are the only ones we have obtained for several years.

I am urging the Rockefeller Foundation to keep Mr. C. P. Wong here another year, but do not know what they will decide.

With kind regards,

Sincerely yours,

A. W. Hummel,

Chief, Division of Orientalia

〔Library of Congress Archives, Arthur W. Hummel Sr. correspondence series, MSS86324〕

按:"on art　　in 80 chuan by　　"及空行付诸阙如,具体所指待考。此后,先生撰写有关《〈永乐大典〉现存卷目表》等文章,均标注该函所提三册"北平图书馆有影本"。该件为录副。

三月二十八日

下午三时半,中德学会假北平研究院艺术陈列所举办德国绘画展览会开幕典礼,除在平德国人士三十余人外,先生、杨钟健、杨丙辰、李书华等中方人士亦到场。首由德使馆代办致开幕词,继由中德学会干事冯至略谈此次画展的意义,随后自由参观,至五时许散去。〔《大公报》,1936年3月

29 日,第 6 版〕

　　按:展品共 150 余幅,均为德国各公司精印品。

三月三十日

凯欧覆函先生,告知卡耐基基金会不会资助其和毕寿普来华,洛克菲勒基金会方面尚无消息。

March 30, 1936

Dear Mr. Yuan:

　　Thank you for your letter of the 4th.

　　I heard from the Carnegie Corporation a little while ago that they had written to you to say that it would not be possible for them to help in the sending of Dr. Bishop and me to China. I have not heard anything from or about Dr. Stevens.

Yours very sincerely,

〔Yale University records, Peiping National Library, 1931 - 1937, Box: 80, Folder: 831〕

　　按:该件为录副。

三月三十一日

蔡元培致函先生,告知拟将平馆前后寄存中央研究院之一百二十箱古籍暂存会议厅。

　　守和先生大鉴:

　　　　金任父兄来言有善本书七十箱欲寄存研究院,但查院中惟会议厅可暂用,即前存之五十箱亦将移置会议厅中,因厅右一房(即五十箱寄存处)逼近实验机械之屋,殊不稳妥,而两个月后且须将两室打通也。如别有(五十箱加七十箱)可以寄存之处最好,否则暂存会议厅以两月为限。尊意如何? 请酌夺。专此,并颂时绥。

弟元培敬启
三月卅一日

　　会议厅太宽廓,保存珍籍殊嫌不称,而舍此又无他室可用。

　　　　〔国立中央研究院用笺。国家图书馆档案,档案编号 1936-※035-采藏 7-001027〕

四月三日

先生致电蔡元培。

上海国立中央研究院蔡院长鉴：

卅一函奉悉。图书馆寄存书前后百二十箱，请暂存会议厅，余函详。

厶厶，江。

〔国家图书馆档案，档案编号 1936-※035-采藏 7-001026〕

四月六日

蔡元培致函先生，证明收到寄存图书五十箱。

守和先生大鉴：

奉电敬悉。金君任甫已于本月四日送书五十箱至中央研究院会议厅存放，因未取收条，故由弟为之证明。专此，并颂著绥。

弟蔡元培敬启

四月六日

〔国立中央研究院用笺。《北京图书馆馆史资料汇编（1909-1949）》，页 438〕

四月八日

先生与 Elizabeth Wallace、詹森大使夫妇以及美国驻华使团的有关人员聚餐。

按：Elizabeth Wallace，曾任芝加哥大学副教授，后在洛克菲勒基金会的国际卫生委员会、美国红十字会任职。

先生致信史蒂文斯，告知已收到 Elizabeth Wallace 携来的介绍信，并将寄赠有关《天禄琳琅》的英文册页。

April 8, 1936

Dear Dr. Stevens:

I am very glad to meet Miss Elizabeth Wallace who gave me the other day your letter of introduction. She seems very much absorbed by what she sees in this ancient city and regrets very much that she has to leave so soon.

I am asking her to luncheon today to meet the American Ambassador and Mrs. Johnson as well as other members of the Embassy here.

Sometime ago I sent you a copy of the "*Imperial Library of Emperor Chien Lung, its catalogue and its architecture*". Since then an English resumé has been published and I am sending this under separate cover together with a copy of our last annual report.

With kindest regards,

Yours sincerely,

T. L. Yuan

〔国立北平图书馆英文信纸。Rockefeller Foundation. Series 601: China; Subseries 601.R: China-Humanities and Arts. Vol. Box 47. Folder 388〕

按：*Imperial Library of Emperor Chien Lung, its catalogue and its architecture* 应指《天禄琳琅四库荟要排架图》,1933 年 5 月故宫博物院图书馆影印。此件为打字稿,落款处为先生签名,于 5 月 4 日送达。

四月十一日

先生乘平浦线南下赴京。〔《大公报》(天津),1936 年 4 月 12 日,第 4 版〕

按：此次南下,先生预计列席中基会年会并报告馆务,此外视察平馆存沪书籍,拟与中国科学社接洽,请其代为保管。

四月十四日

王欣夫致函先生。〔《王献唐年谱长编》,页 605〕

按：王欣夫(1901—1966),原名大隆,字欣夫,号补安,后以字行,江苏苏州人,古典文献学专家。

四月中上旬　上海

先生参观中国建筑展览会。〔《大公报》(上海),1936 年 4 月 15 日,第 6 版〕

按：该次展览应在 12 日开幕,地点为八仙桥青年会。除先生外,朱启钤、潘公展等人亦前往参观。

四月十五日　南京

晨,故宫博物院在朝天宫举行古物保管库奠基典礼,蔡元培、褚民谊、王世杰、蒋廷黻、马衡、先生等人出席,并摄合影,十一时礼成。〔《申报》,1936 年 4 月 15 日,第 8 版〕

晚九时,王世杰、先生、丁西林、傅斯年、胡适赴蔡元培寓,商谈平馆及北京大学事,至十二时始散。〔《蔡元培日记》,页 443〕

四月十八日　上海

中基会年会举行,先生列席并报告馆务。〔《大公报》(天津),1936 年 4 月 12 日,

第 4 版〕

　　按:本届年会,中基会对平馆预算经费决定为十七万元,较上年减少两万元。①

竺可桢致函先生。〔《竺可桢全集》第 6 卷,2005 年,页 58〕

四月二十四日

上午十时许,先生乘沪平线北返。〔《世界日报》,1936 年 4 月 25 日,第 7 版〕

四月二十七日

先生致信美国国家标准局(Bureau of Standards),请求寄赠照相复制技术的仪器照片、复制品实物及介绍文字,用以在中华图书馆协会第三次年会上展出。

April 27, 1936

U. S. Bureau of Standards

Washington, D. C.

U. S. A.

Dear Sirs:

　　In connection with the third annual conference of the Library Association of China, the National Library of Peiping will organize an Exhibition of Modern Library Appliances in July, 1936. One section of the Exhibition will be devoted to literature and specimens relating to photo-copying or printing and in view of its importance, we are writing to you to solicit your assistance and co-operation.

　　It is our sincere hope that the results of your researches will be represented in this exhibition. If it would be possible for you to send us photographs of appliances, specimens of books or manuscripts reproduced by the photo-filming process, and descriptive literature thereof, they will be most gratefully received. If there is any cost, we hope you will let us know.

　　The object of the exhibition is to show the rapid progress which the science of micro-film copying and photo-printing have made during recent years in the United States. As a very large number of librarians will come

---

① 《大公报》(天津),1936 年 5 月 1 日,第 4 版。

from all parts of China to attend the Conference, the exhibition will be of great significance to the future of library development in this country.

Thanking you in anticipation for your collaboration and hoping to have favorable response from you, I remain.

Yours faithfully,

T. L. Yuan

Acting Director

〔国立北平图书馆英文信纸。Smithsonian Institution Archives, Records, 1902–1965 (Record Unit 7091), Box 431 of 459 Folder 38 Chinese Project〕

按:1901 年 3 月,National Bureau of Standards 由美国国会设立,1988 年改为国家标准技术研究所(National Institute of Standards and Technology)。此件为打字稿,落款处为先生签名,5 月 27 日送达。5 月 28 日,该所致信 Watson Davis,请其给予协助。

四月二十九日

中午,福开森设家宴,马衡、沈兼士、唐兰、顾颉刚、先生等人与席。宴毕,先生与顾颉刚同车至平馆。〔《顾颉刚日记》卷 3,页 469〕

五月五日

下午二时,故宫博物院在礼堂召开第八次院务会议,马衡、先生、徐森玉、张庭济、叶澜、励乃骥、黄鹏霄、章宗傅、王孝缉、何澄一、虞和寅、黄念劬(王承吉代)、邵锐等出席。马衡为主席,王承吉记录。报告商务印书馆承印《郡斋读书志》已改为赠书十分之一已结悬案、商务印书馆拟影印本院所藏唐人写《切韵》及元人书《山海经》并已送合同草稿等九项事宜。讨论七项议案,此外先生临时提议:奖学金至二十五年十二月底止,预计有三千元,因数目减半,拟将奖学金名额减为国外一名(一千四百元),国内五名(一千元),请公决案。议决通过。〔《马衡年谱长编》,页 659-660〕

按:此处之《郡斋读书志》应为 1935 年 9 月之“《四部丛刊》三编”,非 1933 年“《续古逸丛书》之三十五”,特此说明。“唐人写《切韵》”即吴彩鸾抄写王仁昫《刊谬补缺切韵》,“元人书《山海经》”即元至正二十五年(1365)曹善抄写郭璞传《山海经》。

晚八时许,先生乘平浦路列车南下,欲从济南转车赴青岛。〔《世界日报》,

1936年5月6日,第7版〕

按:此次,先生赴青岛指导中华图书馆协会、博物馆协会联合年会筹备事宜。

五月七日

史蒂文斯致先生两函,其一,感谢先生寄赠《故宫日历》及 *Libraries in China*。

May 7, 1936

Dear Dr. Yuan:

This is a late acknowledgment of the many printed articles and books sent me during the past few months and illustrated calendar for the year 1936. The calendar is admired each day by my young daughter in spite of her ignorance of what the characters indicate. Your monograph on *Libraries in China* gave me a great deal of helpful information. It made me wonder whether the best friend of Miss Wood should not give some time to writing her biography.

Sincerely yours,

其二,感谢先生为 Elizabeth Wallace 在北平游览提供必要的帮助,已与耿士楷讨论了平馆的两项申请,并希望平馆能为国会图书馆及美国其他高校和学术机构提供馆藏影本。

May 7, 1936

Dear Dr. Yuan:

You are most kind to report the visit at your library of my old friend, Miss Elizabeth Wallace. I know that she had many pleasant experiences in Peiping, and I deeply appreciate the personal attention you gave to her during her stay.

I have put over until the arrival of Mr. Gunn the discussion of your two requests still before the Rockefeller Foundation. These are the ones for the preparation of cards over a three-year period and for help on a mission of American librarians to China. They will be presented shortly for discussion by our committee. At the same time, I will bring up the desire of the American Council of Learned Societies to aid the Library of

Congress and other institutions and universities in getting photostats of
material in your collection. I hope that we may have favorable news to
give you on all these matters.

Sincerely yours,

David H. Stevens

〔Rockefeller Foundation. Series 601: China; Subseries 601.R: China-
Humanities and Arts. Vol. Box 47. Folder 388〕

五月上旬　济南

先生拜访山东省教育厅长何思源,谈及应开办一民众图书馆讲习会,方便
省内同人可以就近听讲,遂决定于年会闭幕后开始授课,预计三周,自七月
二十七日至八月十五日。授课内容由沈祖荣、刘国钧、严文郁、吴光清、莫
余敏卿五人负责筹划。〔《新北辰》,第2卷第6期,页624〕

五月十一日　济南—北平

上午十时,先生乘平沪线返平。〔《世界日报》,1936年5月12日,第7版〕

五月十四日　北平

上午八时,先生拜访北平市长秦德纯,说明平馆经费来源、组织、结构,后者
认同平馆为社会专门事业,应由专家负责。〔《大公报》(上海),1936年5月15
日,第3版〕

　　　　按:秦德纯拟于翌日下午二时赴平馆参观。

顾颉刚致函先生。〔《顾颉刚日记》卷3,页473〕

五月十九日

Norma S. Thompson致函先生,告知洛克菲勒基金会给予平馆、中华图书馆
协会资助,共计两万五千美金,为期三年,并略述各项用途范围。

May 19, 1936

My dear Dr. Yuan:

　　At the meeting of the Executive Committee of The Rockefeller
Foundation held May 15, 1936, the plans of the National Library at
Peiping, for the development of national and international services were
described. I have the honor to inform you that an appropriation was made
towards the development of library services by the National Library
during the three-year period July 1, 1936, to June 30, 1939, the total to be

available not to exceed $25,000, and the amount to be available in any one year of the period not to exceed $11,000.

It was the understanding of the meeting that of this sum as much as needed up to a total of $18,000 might be called for at the rate of $6,000 yearly for the development of a card catalogue of all Chinese publications from 1931 to 1938, and that up to $7,000 might be called for in connection with the proposed visit of representatives of the American Library Association and to pay for reproduction of Chinese materials for American scholars.

Payments under this grant will made be through the Foundation's office in Shanghai in such manner as may be mutually agreed upon.

Very truly yours,

Norma S. Thompson

[Rockefeller Foundation. Series 601: China; Subseries 601.R: China-Humanities and Arts. Vol. Box 47. Folder 388]

按:该函抄送洛克菲勒基金会驻上海办事处,此件为录副。

五月二十一日

史蒂文斯致函先生,告知洛克菲勒基金会批准有关平馆、中华图书馆协会的三项资助申请。

May 21, 1936

Dear Dr. Yuan:

You will have from the Secretary of the Foundation official notification of a grant for three purposes, two of which have been made the subject of correspondence between us over the past several months. The first item is entirely clear, that is, the one having to do with the support of your plan to produce cards covering titles appearing in China from 1931 to 1938. The second item leaves to your discretion the disposal of $3,000 as a maximum to be used for a mission of American librarians appointed by the American Library Association. This sum also is available during the three-year period.

The third item, a sum of $4,000, is provided for expenditure on your order during the same period to furnish American scholars and institutions with photostats or film copies of materials in Chinese. This sum was included in the grant at the request of American scholars who see the requirements of the Library of Congress and of workers in the colleges and universities. I suggest that the channel of recommendation be Dr. Hummel of the Library of Congress, who will be in touch also with the Committee on Far Eastern Studies of the American Council of Learned Societies representing the major institutions. Please let me know whether or not this suggestion is acceptable. I have reported it to Dr. Hummel and to Mr. Leland of the Council. If you agree to such an arrangement, I am sure that Dr. Hummel and Mr. Leland will be glad to offer suggestions that might be helpful to you in initiating the work.

I am sure that you have had from the office of the Foundation in Shanghai sufficient explanation of the method of securing funds under such an appropriation as this. I am sending a copy of this letter to that office for their reference.

Sincerely yours,

David H. Stevens

〔Rockefeller Foundation. Series 601: China; Subseries 601.R: China-Humanities and Arts. Box 47. Folder 388〕

按：该函抄送洛克菲勒基金会上海办事处及利兰、恒慕义、格雷夫斯诸人。

五月二十五日

下午五时，平馆委员会召开第二十三次会议，胡适、任鸿隽、陈垣、孙洪芬、先生出席。胡适为会议主席，先生记录。会议报告平馆最近三月馆务，议决准予备案。讨论事项如下：

(一)任鸿隽出任国立四川大学校长，本会委员职责无法兼任请辞案，议决接受并深表惋惜，感谢其历年来的服务。

(二)选举秦德纯为委员，补任鸿隽出缺至一九三八年六月任满。

(三)议决委员长(或副委员长)、书记、会计为本会常务委员，在不开会期间，常务委员可处理本会一切事务。

六时散会。〔《北京图书馆馆史资料汇编(1909-1949)》,页353〕

　　　　按:会议记录显示,本次会议胡适代表蒋梦麟。

五月二十七日

Ernest Kletsch 致函先生,告知已将先生来信转交科学服务学社(Science Service),并谈自己所擅长的复制技术。

May 27, 1936

My dear Dr. Yuan:

　　While I am greatly interested in reproduction processes, I feel that I should turn your letter and request of April 27th over to Science Service, an organization which specialized and has at its finger tips all of the latest information on microphotography. My particular field is reproduction by other than printing methods, such as multigraph printing, the use of the set-o-type, and monotype short-type casting.

　　Under separate cover I shall send to you for possible use, specimens of printed work done with short-type (multigraph type) printed entirely on the multigraph.

Very truly yours,
Ernest Kletsch,
Director

　　　　〔Smithsonian Institution Archives, Records, 1902 - 1965 (Record Unit 7091), Box 431 of 459 Folder 38 Chinese Project〕

　　　　按:Ernest Kletsch 时任国会图书馆联合编目部主任(Director, Union Catalog, Library of Congress)。multigraph type 应指旋转式排字印刷机。该函中先生的姓名被错拼为 P. L. Yuan,笔者自行订正,此件为录副。

五月下旬

四川大学校长任鸿隽访先生,商谈该校图书馆建筑计划。〔《大公报》(上海),1936年5月28日,第3版〕

　　　　按:该馆预定建筑费20万元。

六月四日

格雷夫斯致先生两函,其一,略述美国学术界在利用胶片技术复制文献方面的尝试和努力,建议平馆与国会图书馆在两国文献、出版品胶片交换领域结成稳定的合作机制,并介绍缩微胶片拍摄设备的技术负责人 Draeger 博士,以及两馆合作机制运行的基本方式。

4th June, 1936

My dear Dr. Yuan:

We have learned from Dr. Stevens of the grant by the Rockefeller Foundation to you of the sum of $ 4,000 for the purpose of furnishing American scholars and institutions with photostats or film copies of materials in Chinese. We understand, too, that he has told you something of our activities in this direction during the past few months, and has proposed that any information, experience, or suggestion of ours might be placed at your disposal.

It is hardly necessary to say that we are more than delighted to do so, since the grant not only brings closer to realization something which we have long desired, but marks the beginning of a new day in Chinese studies here, and we hope in library service in China. Possibly the best way in which to place the matter before you is briefly to relate what we have been doing.

For two or three years our Joint Committee with the Social Science Research Council on Materials for Research has been very active in studying the possibilities of, and experimenting with, film-strip copying of documents. One of its experiments, for instance, was in photographing on film the entire hearings on the Agricultural Adjustment Act, more than a million pages. A considerable group of Americans have been engaged in this work, from different sides, and all have been in close contact with each other, so that they have a very considerable body of information and technical experience which they have exchanged with the utmost freedom and which they place constantly at the disposal of scholars who wish to use it for scientific purposes. One of the concrete developments is the new Bibliofilm Service under Dr. Watson Davis of Science Service, which is described on the enclosed leaflet.

Among these experimenters has been Dr. R. H. Draeger, of the United States Navy, who first became interested in the matter through an attempt to create a library of medical works on film which could be easily transported to, and used in, out of the way places. In close cooperation with the Department of Agriculture, and of course with Dr. Walter T. Swingle, he has invented and developed his own apparatus both for photographing the works on film and for reading the film, apparatus now being put into production by large American manufacturers of optical materials.

In October of this year, Dr. Draeger expects to be transferred from the United States Naval Hospital here to Peiping, and it had been our intention, in the event that the Rockefeller Foundation could not make a grant for the purpose, to borrow funds for equipment and to utilize Dr. Draeger's technical knowledge and enthusiasm to work out with you some system of establishing an exchange on film of materials which you would like to have from here for materials which we should like to have from China.

In the consideration of our plans during the past few months, we have come to feel that the following desiderata should be the features of any such system:

(1) That the system operate on the basis of mutual exchange; not, however, necessarily on a page-for-page basis. We have taken it for granted that we could count on your full sympathy and cooperation in securing film-copies of any materials which we wanted and which were available to you. But we have not wanted to ask that the cooperation be all on one side, especially when there are so many things, scientific articles and the like, which must be so much in demand on the part of Chinese scholars, and which we should be delighted to make available to them. Moreover, as with every new development, there will be those unsympathetic to it, and it will be easier for both of us if we can always point to an exchange.

(2) We feel that the administration of the exchange should be in the

hands of the two great national libraries, yours, and the Library of Congress. You know enough of inter-university and institutional jealousies in America to make it unnecessary for me to elaborate. We have precedent for this kind of activity on the part of the Library in the Modern Language Association Rotograph Service and its Additional Series. Under this system, four hundred or more medieval manuscripts have been purchased abroad for scholars, and are now preserved and available to other scholars at the Library of Congress. The system has worked much better than having scattered libraries all purchasing rotographs, frequently duplicates of those already in this country. I am just this week, for instance, signing checks for the purchase of 13,000 folios of medieval Latin translations of Aristotle through this service. In other words, the system for handling these matters is already set up; the inclusion of Chinese materials is only an extension of it.

With these ideas in mind, Dr. Swingle, Dr. Draeger, Dr. Davis, Dr. Hummel, and I had lunch together one day last week for a discussion of how we could be most useful to you in setting up this enterprise so that it would yield the best results for American and Chinese scholarship. We communicate the following suggestion, with the full realization that facts known to you but not to us may prevent your putting them into effect, but in the belief that you will receive them just as though you had been sitting at the table with us.

1.That you make full use of Dr. Draeger's technical experience and assistance in setting up the machinery and carrying on the operation of it during the first period, training men to continue it, etc. Dr. Draeger could secure equipment (some of which he would have to build) before he leaves America and transport it with him when he leaves for China. This equipment could be paid for directly by the Rockefeller Foundation here on order from you, of course, with all possible safeguards for you. I think that this would work out much better than ordering the equipment at long range from America, Europe, or anywhere in the Far East. You understand, of course, that there is no question of compensation for Dr. Draeger involved. He will be attached to the United States Naval Hospital in Peiping; he will participate in this enterprise solely because of his own scientific interest and of his realization that it is an important job worth doing. Perhaps in the state of present international tensions his naval connections might be a handicap, but we hope that this will not prevent your taking full advantage of his technical knowledge and experience.

2.That you authorize us to organize the system here through the Library of Congress on a contributory basis. We should ask American scholars and institutions to purchase film-strip copies of Chinese materials through us at a per-page price to be determined by experience. The funds thus secured would not be transferred to you, but be used here for the purchase of such film-strip copies of materials available to us as you should want in China. Our first attempt would be to get the Library of Congress itself to subscribe in this sense. On this question I am in consultation with Dr. Putnam and Dr. Hummel now.

I wish that we had had a little more time in order to be able to make a display at the Tsingtao Conference in July. We have recently had exhibitions of film-strip machinery at New York and at Richmond, and I assure you that there is now nothing experimental about the techniques. I am writing you about this in another letter. Here I need only say that exceedingly satisfactory reading apparatus has been developed, and it will shortly be in quantity production. Unquestionably there will be improvements, but the improvements can only proceed along lines already charted.

There is, however, one difficulty. If you are to make use of Dr. Draeger's services, − and that seems a wise thing to do, since it offers the opportunity for very high technical service and enthusiasm without cost, −

we should set him to work building and assembling the proper equipment here before he leaves. There is, consequently, need for some haste. It may be that we can borrow the money to get him started. We need to buy only the bare materials, since we can use the Government shops for the actual work. There is not time to wait and hear from you, so I shall have to work this out as best I can. Meanwhile, if there is anything to say which you can compress into a cable night-letter, please cable to me, collect, what you think of our plans so far as we have outlined them and how we can best be helpful to you.

We hope that we can make this great effort at cooperative scholarship successful. Such close collaboration between two great national libraries cannot but be an example to the rest of the world and a step in the direction of creating the real world-scholarship which we all so much hope for.

Most sincerely yours,

Mortimer Graves

Secretary, Committees on Far Eastern Studies

〔Library of Congress, American Council of Learned Societies Records Box I:38〕

按：Watson Davis(1896-1967)，本谱中译作"戴维斯"，美国文献协会(American Documentation Institute)创始人之一，美国资讯科学与技术学会(American Society for Information Science and Technology)先驱，时任科学服务学社主任。Dr. Draeger 即 R. H. Draeger，美国海军军医，本谱中译作"德尔格"，20 世纪 30 年代利用工作之余研究缩微拍摄技术，1934 年 11 月，他将自己发明的特制照相机安装在美国农业部图书馆的书目服务(Bibliofilm Service)中心，并开始提供缩微胶片复制服务。① 此件为录副。

其二，寄送介绍缩微胶片技术的册页、《成都府志》(1621 年)缩微胶卷正片，希望能够在青岛举办的中华图书馆协会(与博物馆学会联合)年会上展示。

---

① Mohrhardt, Foster E. "The Library of the United States Department of Agriculture." *The Library Quarterly: information, community, policy*, vol. 27, no. 2, 1957, p. 75.

4th June 1936

My dear Dr. Yuan:

For such purposes as you may wish to use them for at the forthcoming Library Conference in Tsingtao, we are sending you under separate cover certain materials, to-wit:

A number of reprints of a descriptive article which was distributed recently at our own Library Conference in Richmond, Va. To this article was attached a microfilm copy of a page in English from a scientific journal. To each of the copies intended for distribution in China we have attached a microfilm of folio from the third preface of the *Ch'en tu fu chih* in an edition apparently rare in Chinese libraries. Within each reprint we have folded a brief description of this gazetter and a positive enlargement of one page of the folio showing the size in which the film can be read through the reading machine.

In addition, we are sending a positive microfilm of about fifty folios of this same work, being the prefatory materials, table of contents, etc. It is interesting to note that in a pinch the Chinese text could be read with the naked eye directly from the microfilm, something quite impossible with the English text; and with a glass of small magnifying power such as is available almost anywhere (in the five-and-ten-cent stores here), could be used quite readily.

It may be possible later, too, to send descriptive materials and photographs of the various reading apparatus, but we have not those at hand just at the moment and want to get the present material off to you in time to be available at your Tsingtao Conference.

Most sincerely yours,

Mortimer Graves
Secretary, Committees
on Far Eastern Studies

〔Library of Congress, American Council of Learned Societies Records Box I:38〕

　　　　　按:此件为录副。

六月十一日

先生对李瑞年希望延长奖学金补助一年的申请作出书面意见,认为他修习博物馆管理法,"为中国极需要之技术人才",建议继续补助一年。〔《李瑞年函请将贵院补助金再延长一年俾能早日结束所学附呈论文一篇敬悉审阅由》,《故宫博物院·人事组织类》第 167 卷,页 17-20〕

　　　　　按:1936 年 5 月 16 日,为了继续在法国研习艺术,李瑞年再度致
　　　　　函故宫博物院,恳请继续发放奖学金一年。6 月 6 日,马衡对李
　　　　　瑞年的申请作出批示——"送袁馆长审查"。

晚,Derk Bodde 在西裱褙胡同设家宴,福开森、汤用彤、张星烺、先生、顾颉刚及两位美国人与席。〔《顾颉刚日记》卷 3,页 484〕

　　　　　按:Derk Bodde(1909-2003),美国汉学家、历史学家,中文名卜
　　　　　德,后任美国东方学会主席。

六月十二日

北平教育界人士李书华、顾颉刚、先生、徐旭生、卓定谋、崔敬伯、冯友兰、闻一多、容庚、叶公超等人联名致电李宗仁、白崇禧,呼吁息兵。大意如下:

　　　　同人等身处危城,无日不思出水火而登衽席,然对公等此举,乃无
　　不疾首蹙额,诚恐以对外始者,反以对内终也。

此外,另有一电致南京行政院蒋介石,大意如下:

　　　　务望中央宏毅宽忍,力避内争,为民族留昭苏余地。

　　　　　　　　　　　　　〔《大公报》(天津),1936 年 6 月 13 日,第 3 版〕

下午三时二十五分,先生乘平浦线列车南下入京。〔《世界日报》,1936 年 6 月13 日,第 7 版〕

　　　　　按:此次南下与中华图书馆协会年会相关,欲与京沪两地执行委
　　　　　员商讨年会事宜。

六月十四日　南京

上午九时,中央古物保管委员会假内政部大礼堂召开第四次全体会议,张道藩、滕固、李济、蒋复璁、朱希祖、马衡、董作宾、舒楚石、黄文弼、先生、陈念中出席,贺天健、裴善元、周森、袁敷宽列席。因提案众多故分四组审查,分别为法规、奖励、保管登记、行政计划。上午分组审查,下午付大会讨论,通过议案三十余件,重要者有私有重要古物流散外间者亟应收归国有、制

定管理私有古物出口规则、在各地设分会等。〔《中央古物保管委员会议事录》第 2 册，1936 年 6 月，页 26-38〕

　　　按：先生、滕固、陈念中三人为法规组审查委员，滕固担任主笔。又该
　　　会第三次全体会议（1935 年 9 月 11 日）、第十二（1936 年 2 月 29 日）、
　　　十三次（1936 年 4 月 14 日）常务会议，先生均请滕固代表出席。

六月十五日　北平

下午四时，中华图书馆协会在平执委假平馆召开年会筹备会议，先生、田洪都、严文郁、何日章出席，吴光清列席，袁仲灿记录。先生作为会议主席报告赴青岛接洽图书馆、博物馆联合年会情况，议决六项事项，依次为：出席会员注册案、年会职员案、年会经费及联合会所建筑费案、图书馆用品展览会案、游览、民众图书馆暑期讲习会案。〔《中华图书馆协会会报》第 11 卷第 6 期，1936 年 6 月 30 日，页 25-26〕

　　　按：年会职员案中，先生任年会总委员会委员、图书馆行政组副
　　　主任。

戴维斯致函先生，寄送有关缩微胶片的文字介绍。

June 15, 1936

Dear Dr. Yuan:

　　　I am pleased to enclose all the available literature upon the application of microphotography documentation for possible use in connection with the exhibition of modern library appliances.

　　　I have been in communication with Dr. Mortimer Graves of the American Council of Learned Societies as well as the National Bureau of Standards and Mr. Ernest Kletsch, Director of the Union Catalog of the Library of Congress. The material included supplements the more extensive literature sent in cooperation with Dr. Graves.

　　　Please count on us to aid in any way possible your utilization of microphotography.

　　　With appreciation, I am

　　　　　　　　　　　　　　　　　　Sincerely,

　　　　　　　　　　　　　　　　　　Watson Davis,

Director

〔Smithsonian Institution Archives, Records, 1902 – 1965 (Record Unit 7091), Box 431 of 459 Folder 38 Chinese Project〕

按：此件为录副。

六月十六日

戴维斯致函先生，寄送德尔格设计的拍照机、阅读机的照片。

June 16, 1936

Dear Dr. Yuan:

Supplementing my letter of June 15, there is enclosed herewith a photograph showing the Draeger camera and reading machine developed under the auspices of Science Service's Documentation Division.

Sincerely,

Watson Davis,

Director

〔Smithsonian Institution Archives, Records, 1902–1965 (Record Unit 7091), Box 431 of 459 Folder 38 Chinese Project〕

按：此件为录副。

六月二十七日

国会图书馆致函先生，告知国会图书馆（东方部）将寄送三册《永乐大典》影本。

June 27, 1936

Dear Sir:

Dr. Hummel, the Chief of the Division of Orientalia, has referred to this Office your request of January 21, 1936, for a photostat reproduction of the three volumes of the *Yung-lo ta-tien*, which the Library of Congress acquired last summer. We have been glad to have these reproductions made and we understand that Dr. Hummel has forwarded them with our compliments.

Very truly yours,

Secretary of the Library

〔Librarian of Congress, Putnam Archives, Special File, China: National Library 1930–1939〕

　　　　按：此件为录副。

六月二十九日

顾颉刚致函先生。〔《顾颉刚日记》卷3,页490〕

　　　　按：此函内容应与赵丰田有关。

六月三十日

下午四点,古物陈列所福开森古物馆举行成立周年纪念,除钱桐、福开森
外,吴佩孚、王揖唐、傅增湘、李燕、马衡、先生等人先后前往观看。馆中除
文华殿原有古物外,在"集义""本仁"两配殿分别陈列清代历朝御座锦屏
古饰等物。五时许,宾主合影留念,并在传心殿设茶点,六时许始散。〔《华
北日报》,1936年7月1日,第6版〕

　　　　按：福开森本向私立金陵大学捐赠所藏古物,但因该校无处放置,
　　　　故暂将其陈列在古物陈列所文华殿。

七月二日

先生致信史蒂文斯,感谢洛克菲勒基金会给予平馆、中华图书馆协会三项
资助,期待毕寿普、凯欧访华。

July 2, 1936

My dear Dr. Stevens:

　　I beg to acknowledge the receipt of your letter of May 21, 1936,
informing me of an appropriation of $ 25,000 by the Rockefeller
Foundation to the National Library during the three-year period July 1,
1936 to June 30, 1939.

　　On behalf of the National Library, I wish to express to you our keen
appreciation for this grant which not only enables us to realize our desire
we have so long cherished, but it marks the beginning of a new day in
library service in China. We particularly welcome this news, as it was
received on the eve of the Tsingtao Conference of the Chinese Library
Association. We shall not fail to make public announcement of this grant
to our members and shall have occasion to make due acknowledgements
at the sessions of the Conference.

　　With regard to the proposed visit of American librarians to China, I
am writing to Mr. Carl H. Milam, Secretary of the American Library

Association, suggesting the appointment of representatives of the Association. We hope Dr. Bishop and Dr. Keogh may be chosen as official delegates and shall leave the time of their visit to their own discretion.

Concerning the third item, a letter has just been received from Mr. Graves setting forth the new plan for exchanges based on the use of improved cameras and improved projecting machines devised by Dr. Draeger. In view of Dr. Draeger's visit to China, I have cabled Mr. Graves accepting his proposal and asking him to proceed with necessary plans as outlined in his letter. It will indeed be a great privilege for us to make full use of Dr. Draeger's technical experience and assistance in setting up the machinery in China.

I wish to assure you that we shall do everything possible in contributing our share in this cooperative enterprise. I trust that such close collaboration will mean a great deal in fostering closer intellectual relations between our two countries.

With assurances of our sincere appreciation for your interest and assistance,

Yours sincerely,

T. L. Yuan

Acting Director

〔国立北平图书馆英文信纸。Rockefeller Foundation. Series 601: China; Subseries 601.R: China-Humanities and Arts. Box 47. Folder 388〕

按：此件为打字稿，落款处为先生签名。

先生致电格雷夫斯，接受合作拍摄缩微胶片的建议。

THANKS LETTER ACCEPT PROPOSAL PLEASE PROCEED YUAN.

〔Library of Congress, American Council of Learned Societies Records Box I:38〕

七月六日

先生致信米来牟，告知洛克菲勒基金会给予三千美金用以邀请美国图书馆专家访华，建议美国图书馆协会正式通知毕寿普、凯欧作为该会代表。

July 6, 1936

Mr. Carl H. Milam

Secretary

American Library Association

520 North Michigan Avenue

Chicago, Illinois

Dear Mr. Milam:

I have just heard from Dr. Stevens that the Rockefeller Foundation has made an appropriation of $ 3,000 to the National Library to be used for a mission of American librarians appointed by the American Library Association.

Last December, in accordance with your suggestion of October 1, 1935, I wrote to Dr. Stevens stating that the American Library Association had made Dr. Bishop and Dr. Keogh official delegates of the A. L. A. to be effective if and when they visit China.

In view of this grant, I hope it would be possible for you to take early official action and inform Messrs. Bishop and Keogh officially. In view of their academic duties, it would be better if we leave the time of their visit to themselves.

Librarians in China have been expecting their arrival and I am very glad indeed that this grant brings to realization something which you and I have long desired since our last interview at Chicago.

With warmest regards,

Yours sincerely

T. L. Yuan

Acting Director

〔 Yale University records, Peiping National Library, 1931–1937, Box: 80, Folder: 831〕

按:该件为抄件。

先生致信凯欧,邀请其来华考察图书馆事业发展。

July 6, 1936

Dear Dr. Keogh:

I have just heard from Dr. Stevens that the Rockefeller Foundation has made an appropriation of $ 3,000 to the National Library to be used for a mission of American librarians appointed by the American Library Association.

I am writing to Mr. Carl H. Milam today suggesting that you and Dr. Bishop be appointed representatives of the A. L. A. on this mission to China. In view of your academic and professional duties, we shall leave the time of your visit to your own choice.

Librarians all over China have been expecting your arrival and we are very glad indeed that this grant brings to realization something we have long desired since my last interview with you at the Yale Club in New York City.

With kindest regards,

Yours sincerely,

T. L. Yuan

Acting Director

〔国立北平图书馆英文信纸。Yale University records, Peiping National Library, 1931–1937, Box: 80, Folder: 831〕

按:此件为打字稿,落款处为先生签名,于 28 日送达耶鲁大学图书馆。

先生致信 Norma S. Thompson,就洛克菲勒基金会给予的三项资助表示感谢。

July 6, 1936

Dear Mrs. Thompson:

I beg to acknowledge the receipt of your letter of May 19 informing me of an appropriation of $ 25,000 by the Rockefeller Foundation to the National Library of Peiping during the three-year period July 1, 1936 to June 30, 1939.

We feel greatly indebted to you for this grant which not only brings closer to realization something which we have long desired, but marks the beginning of a new day in library service in China. I wish to express to you and through you to the members of your Executive Committee our keen appreciation for the Foundation's assistance in the development of our national and international services.

I am writing to Dr. Stevens in regard to various plans for carrying out the arrangements as embodied in the grant.

With renewed thanks for your interest and support,

Yours sincerely,

T. L. Yuan

Acting Director

〔国立北平图书馆英文信纸。Rockefeller Foundation. Series 601: China; Subseries 601. R: China-Humanities and Arts. Vol. Box 47. Folder 388〕

按：此件为打字稿，落款处为先生签名，于 7 月 28 日送达。

七月七日

上午九时，故宫博物院在礼堂召开第九次院务会议，马衡、先生、沈兼士、徐森玉、张庭济、叶澜、赵儒珍、庄尚严、邵锐、章宗傅、何澄一、虞和寅、王孝缉、励乃骥等出席。马衡为主席，赵儒珍记录。会议报告商务印书馆承印唐人写《切韵》及元人书《山海经》已订立合同案、大东书局承印《实录》已订立合同案等十一项事宜，讨论本院学术材料宜由各馆处搜集整理刊行各种专集、关于保护本院文物亟应拟订严密防范办法等案。〔《马衡年谱长编》，页 682-683〕

先生致信美国科学服务学社，请求获赠该所出版物。

July 7, 1936

Science Service

21st and Broad Streets

Washington, D. C.

U. S. A.

Dear Sirs:

We are interested in knowing the program and activities of the Science Service and shall be very much obliged to you if you will be kind enough to send us catalogues, reports and other publications of your organization. If you do not have these, we shall appreciate it if you will write us about the work of the Service.

Hoping to have favorable response from you, I am

Cordially yours,

T. L. Yuan

Acting Director

〔国立北平图书馆英文信纸。Smithsonian Institution Archives, Records, 1902-1965 (Record Unit 7091), Box 431 of 459 Folder 38 Chinese Project〕

按:此件为打字稿,落款处为先生签名,于7月31日送达。

七月八日

下午三时半,胡适乘平沪线赴沪转美出席太平洋国际学会第六次会议。胡夫人江冬秀、蒋梦麟、梅贻琦夫妇、徐诵明、马衡、先生、查良钊、张奚若、樊际昌、郑天挺、朱光潜等五十余人到站送行。〔《大公报》(天津),1936年7月9日,第4版〕

七月上旬

先生致信竺可桢,表示平馆馆员王庸在浙江大学任事且两面均有薪水,馆中同人颇有微词,请其速回平馆。〔《竺可桢全集》第6卷,页109-110〕

按:王庸似赴浙江大学主持图书事务,而此时尚未到校。该信于11日送达。竺可桢在11日、12日均记收到先生函,实际情况是两封信还是一封信被错记两次,待考。

七月十日

钢和泰致函先生,期待本周日在欧美同学会举行的聚会,并表示海尼士、陈垣等人将会前来。

Austrian Legation, July 10th, 1936

Dear Mr. Yuan,

I look forward very much to seeing you here on Sunday the 12th at one p. m. Messrs. Haenisch, Köster, Chen Yuan, Shen and Yao have promised to come too. Unfortunately I am very busy with the preparation for my journey and □□□□ came to Western Returned Students Club today.

With many thanks for your kind introduction.

I remain yours sincerely,

A Staël Holstein

〔《美国哈佛大学哈佛燕京图书馆藏钢和泰未刊往来书信集》下册,页541〕

按：Haenisch 应指 Erich Haenisch（1880-1966），德国汉学家，中文名海尼士；Köster 应指 Hermann Köster（1904-1978），中文名顾若愚，时在北平私立辅仁大学任教；Shen 应指沈兼士；Yao 所指，待考。此件应为底稿。

七月十一日

德尔格致函先生，告知已与格雷夫斯等人开始筹划组装缩微胶片机，并获得海军部门的初步同意，将以国会图书馆职员身份参加此项目的工作。

July 11, 1936

Dear Dr. Yuan:

After the receipt of your letter of April 27, 1936 work was promptly started toward the getting together of exhibit material which you requested. This was transmitted to you through Mr. Graves and I hope was received in time for your annual Library Association Meeting.

I am now working with Mr. Graves on the plans for the technical apparatus to be built and used in the microphotographic laboratory to be established in your library. As Mr. Graves has no doubt informed you, I have a machine shop and design office with a staff of about ten people, mostly government workers. It is our plan to use these facilities already at hand to complete the design and construction of the needed equipment.

Mr. Graves is now away for a few days and when he returns, I will communicate with you further either directly or through him.

I have recently received tentative permission from the Navy Department to participate in this work and will do so as a member of the Library of Congress Staff.

I am looking forward to meeting you and being associated in this interesting and important work.

Yours sincerely,

R. H. Draeger, M. D.

〔Smithsonian Institution Archives, Records, 1902 - 1965 (Record Unit 7091), Box 431 of 459 Folder 38 Chinese Project〕

七月十三日

晚八时许，先生乘平浦路转往青岛，主持中华图书馆协会、中国博物馆协会联合年会筹备事宜。〔《世界日报》，1936 年 7 月 14 日，第 7 版〕

七月十八日　青岛

晚六时许，先生往火车站迎接参加中华图书馆协会、中国博物馆协会联合年会的嘉宾，如陈训慈、马衡等人。〔陈训慈著《运书日记》，北京：中华书局，2019 年，页 176〕

　　　　按：此次联合年会，先生任图书馆委员会、博物馆委员会委员，并兼任图书馆行政组副主任，正主任为洪有丰。[①]

七月十九日

中午，中华图书馆协会、中国博物馆协会执监委员会在中山公园聚餐，先生、叶恭绰、马衡、沈兼士、严智开、严文郁、田洪都、沈祖荣、柳诒徵、陈训慈同席而坐。餐后开会，推定叶恭绰、先生、马衡、沈兼士、沈祖荣、柳诒徵为提案审查委员会委员。先生嘱托陈训慈润色《两协会之希望》一文，三时方散。〔《运书日记》，页 177；《中华图书馆协会会报》第 12 卷第 1 期，1936 年 8 月，页 1〕

七月二十日

上午九时，中华图书馆协会、中国博物馆协会联合年会假青岛山东大学礼堂开幕，参会会员一百四十余人，来宾三十余人。叶恭绰为主席致开幕词，青岛市长沈鸿烈、山东大学校长林济青、市教育局雷法章、胶济铁路管理委员会葛光庭先后致辞，马衡代表两协会致答谢词。十时半，开幕式结束，并摄合影。

下午二时，沈鸿烈演讲，题目为"青岛乡区建设情形与青岛过去未来之经济教育状况"。四时，全会分别开讨论会，宣读论文。晚六时，沈鸿烈宴请全体人员。〔《运书日记》，页 179、180；《科学》第 20 卷第 8 期，页 693-694；《世界日报》，1936 年 7 月 11 日，第 7 版；《文献论丛》，1936 年，"附录"页 64〕

　　　　按：先生在此次联合年会上的提案有"请在英庚款留学名额及清华公费金名额内设立博物馆学考古学艺术史专科以宏造就案""各博物馆应编印周年报告案""请教育部设立西北及西南博物

---

① 《华北日报》，1936 年 7 月 16 日，第 9 版。

馆搜集边防资料以资宣传文化案""请政府明令奖励收藏家及捐赠艺术品于国家者特殊奖励案",以上四案均在博物馆行政组提案之列。此外,先生拟演讲"英美档案保管之沿革及组织"。

七月二十二日

下午二时,先生报告图书馆协会会务,其中主要内容涉及(一)南京会所建筑费,(二)一年来的工作,(三)协会的国际联络,(四)美国图书馆协会专家来华考察事宜,其中就会费催收一事讨论甚久,导致其他议题匆匆而过,至三时五十分结束。

下午四时,联合年会举行闭幕仪式。叶恭绰为会议主席,致闭幕词,报告两会出席人数;严文郁报告图书馆协会提案数及结果,先生报告图书馆协会会务会议经过,马衡报告博物馆协会讨论提案及会务提案件数及结果,沈祖荣报告教育部交图书馆协会讨论事件经过。

下午五时,浙江文献展览会谈话会假青岛大学科学馆阅览室召开,此会由陈训慈召集,叶恭绰、马衡、先生、沈兼士、庄尚严、傅振伦、单士元、苏生君、金大本(清华大学)、吴其昌(武汉大学)、王幼侨(河南省博物馆)、胡肇椿(上海博物馆)、严智开、柳诒徵等人参加。会上,先生表示平馆善本书存沪上者可以商借。〔《运书日记》,页187-189;《文献论丛》,1936年,"附录"页68〕

七月二十五日

上午,图书馆用品博物馆建筑联合展览会在太平路大饭店开幕,先生任主席,讲述举办此项展览的意义及筹备经历,次由沈鸿烈、陆梦熊发言。〔《运书日记》,页202、203;《申报》,1936年7月25日,第9版〕

> 按:本次展览所陈列博物馆建筑图片多为先生在1934年在欧美考察时所得。陆梦熊(1881—1940),字渭渔,江苏崇明人,时应任交通部北宁路副局长。

七月二十八日

傅斯年、顾颉刚致函先生,请允许谭其骧恢复平馆职务。

> 守和吾兄大鉴:
>
> 谭君其骧前在尊处任编目职务,对于地理一科极有根柢,所作论文亦为读者所赞赏。惟其人少年情性,不克埋头工作,以是自行请辞而去。上年任职广东学海书院,今秋粤局既变,该院恐将停办,弟等为爱护人才起见,甚望吾兄能派其管理舆图,则以彼专长,必可胜任。弟

等与之有旧,自当严予监督,不令眈逸,倘荷引进,请嘱其每一个月将工作成绩送颉刚处审查,想兄拔擢人才,具有同情,得此保证,必不至绝其向上之路也。此上,敬请著安。

弟傅斯年、顾颉刚上

再,谭君现住北平航空署街三十号,并闻。

〔《傅斯年遗札》,页729;《顾颉刚日记》卷3,页508〕

按:此函由顾颉刚撰写。后谭其骧并未赴平馆任职,而是在燕京大学、清华大学兼任讲师。

毕寿普覆函先生,感谢发来赴华考察邀请,并将与米来牟、凯欧等人商讨后再告知最终决定。

July 28, 1936

Dear Dr. Yuan:

I am naturally greatly interested and somewhat surprised to receive your letter of July 6th. Of course, I must await word from Mr. Milam as to the action of the A. L. A. Executive Board, and I must have an opportunity to confer with Dr. Keogh about the whole matter before giving it careful and final consideration.

Will you please accept again my grateful thanks for your thought of me in connection with this visit, which I sincerely hope may be brought about?

With good wishes and regards,

Faithfully yours,

Librarian

〔Yale University records, Peiping National Library, 1931-1937, Box: 80, Folder: 831〕

按:该件为录副。

七八月间

沈祖荣偕家眷由青岛前往平津一带游览,先生得知后曾打电话询问严文郁是否知道其下榻何处。〔《传记文学》,第42卷第5期,页60〕

按:时沈祖荣一家宿珠市口附近的中国大饭店,本不欲打扰文华图专在平之毕业生。

八月三日

米来牟覆函先生,收到来函并已转寄毕寿普和凯欧,两人是否接受邀请以及何时出发是仅有的未定之事,感谢先生的不懈努力。

August 3, 1936

Dear Mr. Yuan

    Your letter of July 6th came during my absence from the city and copies were at once transmitted to Messrs. Bishop and Keogh. They have not yet replied.

    The only details remaining to be settled appear to be the final questions of acceptance of invitation (about which I hope there will be no doubt) and the date.

    I congratulate you most heartily on the success which has rewarded your persistent efforts.

Cordially yours,

Carl H. Milam

Secretary

〔Yale University records, Peiping National Library, 1931 – 1937, Box: 80, Folder: 831〕

按:该件为录副。

八月四日

凯欧覆函先生,收到来信并深感荣幸,其将与毕寿普协商出发时间。

August 4, 1936

Dear Mr. Yuan:

    I have your letter of July 6th in which you tell me of the grant made to the National Library of Peiping by the Rockefeller Foundation to the end that Mr. Bishop and I might visit China and inspect scholarly libraries there.

    I am, of course, greatly honored at the request, and greatly pleased at the successful result of your application to the Rockefeller board.

    There still remains the difficulty of getting away. I am getting in touch with Mr. Bishop as to the time that would be most convenient for him, and we will see whether we can agree upon a date. It is not likely to be within the next six months. I will write to you later, as soon as I have had a chance to think the matter out and to learn what Mr. Bishop's views are.

Yours very sincerely,

〔Yale University records, Peiping National Library, 1931 – 1937, Box: 80, Folder: 831〕

按：该件为录副。

八月十四日

先生致信张道藩，请将中央古物保管委员会"调查与中国古物有关之出版物及其目录"之议交由平馆负责编纂，并附预算书和书目样本。

道藩次长钧鉴：

古物保管委员会第四次全体委员会议曾议决调查流出国外古物办法三项，顷又奉到本会拟定调查流出国外古物办法十条，藉悉种切。查本案交付审查时，曾有"调查与中国古物有关之出版物及其目录"之建议（记录第六页）。弟去岁游欧美时，亦稍有调查，颇愿于此事略贡刍荛，如会中尚未觅得适当机关，未识可否即以调查文献之工作委托敝馆担任。兹奉上样本一纸、预算草案一份，如能补助半数，预计四个月内即可完成，至将来付印一节，似可由本会及敝馆委托商务印书馆印行，当不致有何困难也。如何之处，并盼见复是感。专此，敬候勋祺。

弟袁同礼顿首
八月十四日

附预算草案一纸、书目样本一纸。

〔国立北平图书馆用笺。台北"国史馆"，〈委托北平图书馆调查及编著流出国外古物著述目录〉，典藏号 026-011000-0381〕

按："弟去岁游欧美时"有误，实应为"弟前岁游欧美时"之意，因中央古物保管委员会第四次全体委员会会议于 1936 年 4 月 14 日召开。所附预算草案包括：编辑、助理、书籍、打字、纸张及卡片、邮费等，共计 1200 元，拟请由中央古物保管委员会和平馆各承担一半；书目样本包括两种书籍，均为瑞典所藏中国铜器的西文书籍。该信为文书所拟，落款处为先生签名，21 日送达。张道藩在原信上批注"此件请提出下次常会决定"等语。11 月 4 日，中央古物保管委员会交中央银行汇予平馆 600 元。

八月十七日

上午十时,中国科学社、数学学会、物理学会、化学学会、动物学会、植物学会、地理学会七个科学团体联合年会在清华大学大礼堂开幕。主席团主席蒋梦麟引导王冷斋(秦德纯代表)、梅贻琦、任鸿隽、查良钊、李书华、沈履等登台,先生、刘拓、曾昭抡、彭济群、顾毓琇、潘光旦、叶企孙等八百余人到场。〔《华北日报》,1936 年 8 月 18 日,第 9 版〕

> 按:王冷斋(1892—1960),原名王仁则,字若璧,福建闽侯人,时任北平新闻检查所所长。[1]

八月十八日

先生、徐森玉、赵万里三人在请款单签字,同意王达文将其家藏鸣晦庐藏书暂押与平馆,平馆相应支付贰仟伍佰元,以一年为期。〔国家图书馆档案,档案编号 1936-※035-采藏 7-001038 和 1936-※035-采藏 7-001039〕

> 按:"鸣晦庐"应指王立承(1883—1936),字孝慈,以字行,北平通县人,酷嗜京剧,曾著《闻歌述忆》等,好藏书,尤好收藏戏曲及明清版画。王达文应为其子嗣,该批藏书共 160 种、1130 册。

八月二十二日

金毓黻访先生。〔《静晤室日记》第 5 册,页 3907〕

> 按:此次访问应在平馆中,因其原文为"晤徐森玉、谢刚主、袁守和、顾颉刚诸君"。

八月二十七日

利兰致函先生,告知美国学术团体理事会获得洛克菲勒基金会的赞助,将在北平组装缩微胶片设备用以完成平馆与国会图书馆之间的文献交换。

27th August 1936

My dear Dr. Yuan:

You will have been kept informed by Mr. Graves of our efforts to have constructed for you over here the best possible apparatus for the film-copying that you are planning to do in Peiping as a part of the film-copy exchange between the National Library and the Library of Congress.

---

[1] 《益世报》(天津),1936 年 2 月 7 日,第 3 版。

I am glad to tell you that we have received a grant from the Rockefeller Foundation which assures our ability to supply this apparatus. It is now being constructed, and I hope that Dr. Draeger will arrive with it, and with adequate supplies, early next year. It is a great satisfaction to us to be able to have some modest part in inaugurating so interesting and important an exchange service between our two countries.

I have always had the pleasantest recollection of your visit here, and only hope that you will repeat it many times, and as soon as possible. You doubtless know that Mr. Graves will be in Peiping in November. I assume that you must have one of his itineraries, but in case you should not have one, it is enclosed.

With an expression of my high regard, please believe me,

Sincerely and cordially yours,

Waldo G. Leland,

Permanent Secretary

〔Library of Congress, American Council of Learned Societies Records Box I:38〕

按:此件为录副。

八月二十八日

晚七时,徐森玉、先生在煤市桥泰丰楼设宴,沈兼士、朱希祖、金毓黻、赵万里、谢国桢、傅振伦等与席。席间,朱希祖谈杨守敬《水经注疏》清稿下落,金毓黻认为该书亟需影印。〔《朱希祖日记》,页692;《静晤室日记》第5册,页3909〕

按:该宴本为徐森玉设,先生临时为主人。

是年夏

江西省教育厅函聘程时煃、陈任中、先生、沈祖荣、陈三立、陈布雷、欧阳祖经等人担任庐山图书馆征集图书委员。〔《民国日报》(江西),1936年9月3日,第5版〕

按:该馆于1935年8月筹设,分为管理、图书两部。程时煃(1889—?),字伯庐,江西新建人,早年赴日本留学,后又转美入哥伦比亚大学,归国后曾任北京师范大学教务长,1933年任江西省教育厅厅长。

九月一日

先生访顾颉刚。〔《顾颉刚日记》卷 3,页 525〕

九月二日

上午,朱希祖来平馆访赵万里,后晤先生,谈约片刻。〔《朱希祖日记》,页 695〕

九月十一日

下午,先生离平赴京,指导岳良木筹备工程参考图书馆。〔《华北日报》,1936 年 9 月 23 日,第 9 版〕

　　按:1934 年,平馆设立工程参考专门阅览室,后因资料扩充并方便工程界人士起见,于本年 9 月迁至南京,馆舍暂借实业部地质调查所珠江路 942 号之房产,由岳良木担任主任,下辖馆员四五名。①

傅斯年致函先生,谈《国藏善本丛刊》刊印事。

　　守和吾兄:

　　　顷谈极快,下午打电话,则兄已行矣。所谈《国藏善本丛刊》一事,弟草拟办法十二条,乞兄修改。又致王云五兄一信,如以为可行,乞兄改定后交之。此事来源,正由前年谈《四库珍本》事而起,当时弟对兄云:"蒋慰堂既定合同,教部势必支持之,故可听其自然。北平图书馆再编印一部更伟大的,将《四库》打倒。"北平图书馆善本迁移,若干工作不易进行,办理此事,正其时也。请兄勉力。弟必从旁赞助之,"竭力抬轿"。此事兄当当仁不让,无庸客气。叔平先生处,弟必去说得通也。专此,敬颂日安!

　　　　　　　　　　　　　　　　　　弟斯年谨上

　　　　　　　　　　　　　　　　　　九月十一日

　　　　　　　　　　　　　　〔《傅斯年遗札》,页 731-732〕

　　按:该函后附 9 月 11 日傅斯年致王云五信。

九月十五日　上海

先生参观震旦大学法文书版展览会,并接洽借部分展品运往北平展出。〔《大公报》(上海),1936 年 9 月 17 日,第 4 版;《震旦大学新筑落成法文书展纪念册》

──────────

① 《益世报》(北平),1936 年 10 月 10 日,第 8 版;《科学》第 21 卷第 6 期,1937 年 6 月,页 498。

（Université L'Aurore 1936, constructions Nouvelles exposition du livre Français），1936 年 9 月〕

　　按：震旦大学法文书版展览预计 9 月 27 日结束，先生曾向法国书
业公会借美术书籍二百余种，先在震旦大学法文书版展览会陈
列，结束后运往北平展出。

柳诒徵致函先生，商互钞善本书事。

　　守和馆长道鉴：

　　　　日前都门畅聆教益，至深快慰。借钞《永乐大典》事，即请由贵馆
备具借函，一俟函到，当即照办。兹拟借钞贵藏《宸翰录》等书，业荷
面允，即请转知照亭先生检取，挂号付邮，无任感祷。专肃，敬颂旅绥。

　　　　　　　　　　　　　　　　　　　　　　　　柳诒徵拜启

　　　　　　　　　　　　　　　　　　　　　　　　九月十五日

　　　　　　　　　　〔《国学图书馆第十年刊》，1937 年，"案牍"页 31〕

　　按：1936 年 10 月 20 日，国学图书馆周会议决，准予平馆借钞《永
乐大典》；10 月 31 日，国学图书馆收到李耀南自上海寄出平馆馆
藏杨文襄书三种四册，其中应含有杨一清辑《宸翰录》，并开始钞
写；1937 年 5 月 25 日，平馆寄还五册《永乐大典》与国学图
书馆。[1]

九月十六日

晚，先生乘快车返抵南京。〔《立报》，1936 年 9 月 17 日，第 2 张〕

九月十七日

米来牟致函先生，告知毕寿普、凯欧因在各校开设课程无法于一九三七年
以前访华，建议更换他人或由中华图书馆协会尝试与二人所在学校沟通，
并请先生就访问目的、行程、交通方式等细节给予初步说明。

September 17, 1936

Dear Mr. Yuan

　　Dr. Bishop and Dr. Keogh recently conferred on the proposed visit to
China. They also talked with Dr. Stevens of the Rockefeller Foundation.
This letter is one of the results of their conversations.

　　Both Dr. Bishop and Dr. Keogh have been announced in the catalogs

---

[1]《国学图书馆第十年刊》，"纪事"页 5、7、8、24。

of their institutions as giving courses of lectures during the coming academic year. While it might not be impossible for them to get leave of absence, it would certainly be much easier if the proposed visit to China were postponed until the fall of 1937. This would also permit Dr. Bishop to be present at the discussions of his budget next spring after the adjournment of the legislature. They both recognize that a further postponement of the visit may not meet with the approval of the Chinese Library Association, in which case they suggest that it might be better for other persons to be selected who could go at an earlier date. We shall be glad, therefore, to learn from you whether the visit could be postponed without serious inconvenience until the fall of 1937.

It is not so easy to get leave of absence with pay as it was a few years ago because the university library staffs have been reduced and financial conditions in the universities are much worse than they were when the proposal was first made. It is just possible that neither institution would grant a leave of absence unless substitutes were provided. In view of these facts, Dr. Bishop, Dr. Keogh and Dr. Stevens think that an official request should be made upon the presidents of Yale and Michigan by the Chinese Library Association or the American Library Association or both so that the question of leave of absence would not be initiated by the men directly involved. I am of the opinion that the request should go to the presidents (Alexander G. Ruthven of the University of Michigan, James Rowland Angell of Yale University) from the Chinese Library Association and that the A. L. A. should supplement the request.

It seems necessary to know exactly what you would like to have the American representatives do, what libraries they should visit and what meetings they should attend. If these facts could be set forth in the form of an itinerary giving dates, distances in miles and time and □□□whether communication is by rail or water, it would be very helpful. They would also like to have your advice as to the best date for arriving so far as climate is concerned.

Dr. Bishop and Dr. Keogh understand that all of their expenses from the time they set foot on Chinese soil until they leave will be paid by the Chinese Government. I assume there is no question about this. It is not clear, however, whether the Government's invitation would include the cost of a translator and of a stenographer who could take down in Chinese statements made by the government officials and others, which should be available for the final report.

If you will be good enough to give me the information requested in this letter, I will see that it is transmitted without delay to Dr. Bishop and Dr. Keogh.

With cordial greetings on behalf of your many friends in America, I am

Very sincerely yours

Carl H. Milam

Secretary

〔Yale University records, Peiping National Library, 1931-1937, Box: 80, Folder: 831〕

按:该件中有一处为手写,但因太过模糊无法识别,只得以□□□标识。收到该函后,先生应与图书馆协会在平人员商讨信中各项事宜。

九月二十日　开封

先生致信王重民,告知已与简又文商议印行《太平天国官书补编》办法及在法拍照稀见稿本等事。

有三吾弟:

前接八月二日及七月二十二日来书,欣悉在东方语言学校发现天地会文件等,至为可喜。关于印行《太平天国官书补编》事,因不日南下,故拟与简先生面谭,迟迟未作书。前日在申已与简先生说妥,渠亦同意,至赠书各二十五部一节,已改为五十部,将来图书馆收到后再赠足下二十五部可也。影印燉煌卷子计划书另寄,英庚款可补助数千元,请就已照之卷子开一选印书目,将来仍交商务发行,惟由 Photostat 制版石印,恐不可能,势须再用有光纸重照一次,仍待与商务一商。

张澍稿本及《四译馆考》似亦须照印,此款可另寄,由中文书账支出,清华亦可合作,故可印二份。北平研究院出版书之销路似不及逸经社,故交逸经社印行亦是一法,惟款式应大方,跋语先作就寄来,看书者方感兴趣。函逸经社时应说明似以影印为佳(排印不足取信)。刘女士想已到法,既患神经衰弱,应多走路,勿用脑过甚是要。蒋廷黻任驻苏大使,将来赴俄看书更容易,请告于道泉君。昨由南京来此,将往安阳、洛阳一带视察,再返平。此颂旅安。

同礼顿首
九月二十日,开封

印行《太平天国官书补编》办法

一、原稿为国立北平图书馆所有,由馆委托逸经社印行,出书后仍将原稿寄馆,以便保存。

二、此书为逸经社丛书之一,但应注明为国立北平图书馆委托印行。

三、原稿如有影印之必要,可由两机关委托商务印书馆影印发行。

四、逸经社应以印成之书五十部赠送国立北平图书馆。

五、售书所得红利,酌酬王重民君。

〔开封中国旅行社招待所信纸。袁同礼家人提供〕

按:《太平天国官书补编》最后收录入《广东丛书》第三集,1949年夏[1]印行,其历经种种磨难及删减其中一种,可参见1948年8月简又文所撰"弁言"。张澍(1776—1847),字百瀹,凉州武威人,清代敦煌学研究者。法国国家图书馆所藏其稿本皆由伯希和带回,具体情况可参见王重民所撰《阅张介侯先生遗藁记》。[2]《四译馆考》应作《四夷馆考》,明代学者王宗载所撰,该抄本藏于巴黎东方语言学校。1937年冬,王重民介绍向达前往该所查阅此书,后者撰《瀛涯琐志——记巴黎本王宗载〈四夷馆考〉》。[3]

九月下旬

平馆委员会改选结果公布,委员长蒋梦麟、会计孙洪芬、书记先生,委员周

---

① 《华侨日报》(香港),1949年6月3日,第4张。

② 《金陵学报》第10卷第1-2期,1940年5月,页171-188。

③ 《图书季刊》新2卷第2期,1940年6月,页181-186。

诒春因在实业部任常务次长,故请辞。〔《京报》,1936 年 9 月 23 日,第 7 版〕

> 按:中基会因美金贬值,收入锐减,平馆经常费被缩减为十万元,
> 购书费亦减少三分之一。

九月二十二日

先生赴河南省博物馆参观,并作演讲。〔《河南博物馆馆刊》第 10 集,1937 年 6 月,"大事记"页 6〕

九月二十三日

晚,先生与王幼侨赴辉县考察古物保存状况,行前将永城一地调查事务委托史语所李景聃等人。〔台北"中央研究院"历史语言研究所傅斯年图书馆,"史语所档案",考 6-3-18〕

> 按:永城余瑞璋向政府某机构报告保安山古迹,中央古物保管委员会遂决定派人前往考察。[①] 王幼侨(1888—1951),河南安阳人,时任河南博物馆馆长兼河南大学教授。10 月 11 日,李景聃、韩维周及工友孟常禄由开封出发前往永城,次日抵达即前往余瑞璋处查看铜镜、铜炉、石钟等古物,并至山城集看梁孝王洞石像。

九月下旬

先生以古物保管会监察员身份赴中研院史语所殷墟第十四次发掘现场,其间曾与李永淦、魏鸿纯、尹焕章、高去寻、王思睿、梁思永、石璋如合影。〔石璋如著《安阳发掘简史》,台北:"中央研究院"历史语言研究所,2019 年,页 204;李永迪、冯忠美编《殷墟发掘照片选辑(1928-1937)》,台北:"中央研究院"历史语言研究所,2013 年,页 221〕

九月二十六日　安阳

晨,先生至史语所发掘团,下午四时五十分登车前往洛阳。〔台北"中央研究院"历史语言研究所傅斯年图书馆,"史语所档案",考 4-9-13〕

十月九日

下午二时,先生乘平浦路列车抵达北平,总务主任王访渔等前往接站,旋到馆巡视工作。〔《益世报》(北平),1936 年 10 月 10 日,第 8 版〕

十月十四日

先生撰写《调查洛阳辉县盗墓情形报告》。

[①]《中国考古学报(即田野考古报告)》第 2 册,1947 年 3 月,页 84-85。

（一）洛阳盗墓情形

洛阳为吾国旧都，古迹甚富，城北城东古墓尤多。近十余年来，出土古物以铜器、陶器为大宗。土人以大利所在，私行盗掘者几成一种职业，并发明一种铁锥，专作为探试地层之用。沿城北邙山一带，盗掘痕迹不计其数，地层因之凌乱，古物因之损伤，实为学术上之重大损失。查洛阳盗墓无月无之，而以秋冬为尤甚。盖本地农人多有盗墓者，秋收后禾苗尽去，不致妨碍农作物也。传闻盗墓者多在夜间为之，且全副武装，组织完备，其规模之宏大，迥非地方官吏之实力所能制止。此次前往查看，经古玩商人之导引，在邙山井沟村之北、郑家凹村之南，竟发现土人在白昼间亦作大规模之盗掘。其参加工作者共二十余人，各执铁锥，分区探试，偶有所获则欢呼如狂。此种情形，除面告第十区行政专员王君泽民从速取缔外，本会亟应速筹制止之方，不容再缓者也。

（二）龙门石像被盗情形

龙门一名伊阙，在洛阳城南二十五里，营窟造象肇始后魏，为我国至可宝贵之雕刻。比年以来，外人游洛，诧为鸿宝，其显露而易凿者，辄向村民购之。村民因有利可图，乃将石佛头颅一一击落，且间有毁灭其全身者。毁损情形年有增加，亦近年来我国古迹之一大劫也。此次前往勘看，以宾阳洞、八仙洞、千佛洞、万五佛洞、郭爱洞、莲花洞被毁情形为最惨。兹列表如左：

宾阳洞：中洞四佛像头颅被击落，洞内外龛像有被砍头者，有全身被盗者。

八仙洞：八仙面部已毁其七内中一仙系最近所毁，佛头被砍者一，全身被盗者一。

千佛洞：全数佛头无一幸免，两壁之小佛像极少完整者，面北之佛像全身被盗。

万五佛洞：四角佛像佛头全数被毁，南北龛内佛头亦被砍去，入门右边佛头同。

郭爱洞：十余佛头全数被毁。

莲花洞：大佛三件全毁，其余亦全被毁。

各洞外龛像残缺及被盗者，又不计其数焉。民国二十二年，钱王倬著《洛阳名胜记》，各洞佛像尚多完整，今则满目疮痍，盖被毁程度以近三年为最烈也。传闻盗窃佛头者多为回人，龙门之南有外凹村（亦名魏家凹村），内多石匠，咸以盗窃龙门石像为其职业。此辈勾结土匪，往往于夜间携带高梯，手执电筒，从事毁坏。而土匪多自南来，毁后每向南逃去。八月间，土人马云亭老五（住东关马坡）、马禄超（住东关新街）、马子明、石文化等曾将砍下石佛运平求售。九月二十二日夜十二时，复有二三十名土匪，全副武装，拟从事大规模之盗窃。旋为驻军保安第六团所击退，但魏灵藏（龙门二十品之一）已被毁坏。据该团副队长面称，该团有百十余人，驻守龙门寨，其地距龙门口尚有一里余，故对古迹不易保护。又，河南建设厅正辟洛临公路，在龙门口修筑伊河桥，雇用工人一百七十余人，皆宿于宾阳洞三洞内，并在该处内作炊，于古迹亦不无损坏。但土匪竟置一百七十余工人于不顾，屡来盗窃，其声势之浩大，可见一班。他日工人解雇，则毁坏程度尤有不堪设想者。此种情形至为严重，此本会亟应速筹妥善办法者又一也。

（三）辉县盗墓情形及河南省政府组织发掘团之经过

辉县为古共城，城外固围村素为盗墓渊薮，传闻共伯墓及共姜墓前数年曾为石友三军队所盗掘。本年八月，城外琉璃阁（在辉县与汲县大道上）复有土匪盗墓之举。据豫北绥靖司令四十军军长庞炳勋（现驻节新乡）面告，该土人曾疏通驻军，要求于盗掘时不加干涉。旋以分赃不均，由地主报告县长，县长吕达当即追回铜器（鼎）一件，由县政府送交民众教育馆保存（今改存河南博物馆）。省政府闻讯，当派河南博物馆职员许敬参勘看古物出土情形。根据其所拟发掘预算书，于八月二十五日由李民政厅长及鲁教育厅长提议，组织河南省政府共城发掘团，并由博物馆拨洋一千六百元专作发掘之用。该团于九月四日开始工作，现已掘探八米，曾发现汉墓及瓦器等。查古物发掘之处理在《采掘古物规则》均有详细规定，已告该团应遵照中央颁行之法令，呈请本会转请内、教两部发给执照。惟该处古墓尚多，而土人盗墓之风甚炽，沿汲县大道上盗掘痕迹之多，至为可惊。传闻主使者多在新乡（距辉县一小时汽车）守候，彼处为平汉路及道清路衔接处，交通便利，私运甚易，故此后制止之方，新乡较辉县尤为重要也。

（四）建议制止盗墓具体办法

1.由本会呈行政院转函军事委员会,训令各军队及各地方保安团队,对于盗墓者应援用《惩治盗匪条例》严励办理,认真执行。

2.由行政院训令各省行政专员、各市长、县长,指定特务队或警察专员巡查盗墓之责,遇有盗墓者,随时会同驻军,立予拿办。并责成地主、保长、甲长随时检举或报告。

3.由行政院训令铁道部及交通部,凡无证明文件私运古物者,准各站一律扣留,禁止出境,并报告本会。

4.在洛阳设立办事处,在新乡设通讯员。

5.在龙门设立龙门古迹保管委员会。除河南民政厅长、建设厅长、保安司令、第十区行政专员为当然委员外,本会并推委员二三人共同组织之。并以洛阳办事处主任为委员会秘书。

又,龙门之匪多自南来,下列各办法简易可行,似可采择施行:

（一）在龙门南部（俗名外凹）（即石头马路终止处）设立活动铁门或铁栅栏,每晚六时封锁,翌晨六时启门。由洛阳办事处派人启闭。

（二）由军事委员会训令河南保安处,将保安第六团一部分兵士调至龙门常川驻守,专负守卫之责（现该团驻在龙门寨,距龙门尚有一里余）。

（三）洛阳办事处应在龙门设一办公分处,并安设长途电话。其职务在编辑游览指南、限制传拓、出售游览券、打扫清洁等。

（四）龙门潜溪寺之北有煤窑,土人任意取煤,影响该地地基,亟应禁止。

以上所陈是否有当,敬候公决。

袁同礼

十月十四日

又,洛阳新出土墓志已访得者有:

一、后魏张灵墓志正光三年三月

二、后魏夫人张元华墓志正光四年正月

三、后魏元兴略墓志正光六年三月

四、后魏章武王元融墓志孝昌三年二月

五、后魏长孙士亮妻宋氏墓志永兴二年正月

六、隋廉平县君礼氏墓志大业七年十一月

七、隋陈叔明墓志大业十一年正月

〔李贞德主编《庆祝九十五周年史语所档案选辑》,台北:"中央研究院"历史语言研究所,2023 年,页 41-44〕

按:1937 年 1 月 16 日下午,中央古物保管委员会在内政部召开常会会议审议该报告并商保护办法。[①] 钱王倬,字卓英,浙江崇德人,北京大学文科毕业,后在外交部、教育部任职。庞炳勋(1879—1963),字更陈,河北新河人,民国时期将领。该文失收于《袁同礼文集》。

李耀南致函先生,告知已将存于中央研究院之书悉数搬运至平馆驻沪宿舍,并请先生寄下写经、舆图、金石南运装箱号码,以便核对。

馆长先生道鉴:

前奉电示,研究院书箱,改存宿舍,遵即于昨日雇中国旅行社汽车,前往该院点收搬运汽车以钟点计算,共用四小时,计一百箱,悉置于底楼一层,置放毕,四周门窗,亦加意封闭。

再本馆去年运沪书箱,计中文方面,共计三百七十六箱,除善本甲库,此间存有底册外,其余写经、舆图、金石各部分,箱数号码,不甚明了,祈饬下详开一纸寄来,以便通同查考,是所切盼。肃此,恭颂道祺。

后学李耀南拜启

十月十四日

再本月房捐房租,已催索一次,祈速汇下。耀南又肃。

〔国家图书馆档案,档案编号 1936-※035-采藏 7-001033 和1936-※035-采藏 7-001034〕

十月中下旬

先生致信傅斯年,告知马衡不同意《国藏善本丛刊》影印之议,言之此事不足以表现故宫之工作。〔《傅斯年遗札》,页 745-746〕

按:傅斯年收到此信后,请蔡元培居中说服马衡。本月底,故宫博物院院务会议对此事态度转变,决议加入。

[①]《申报》,1937 年 1 月 17 日,第 4 版。

十月十七日

先生覆信李耀南,寄去南运写经、舆图、金石箱号以便核对。

> 照亭先生大鉴:
>
> 　　接十四日来函,悉壹是。研究院书箱已运完竣,甚慰。兹将写经、舆图、金石等箱号数饬查清楚,另单寄去,请收阅核对为荷。专复,顺候旅祺。
>
> 　　　　　　　　　　　　　　　　袁厶厶启
>
> 附单。
>
> 　　又弟携去之江南地图及王以中携去之各县地图,应具收条寄馆存查。

〔国家图书馆档案,档案编号 1936-※035-采藏 7-001028 至 1936-※035-采藏 7-001032、1936-※035-采藏 7-001035〕

按:此件为底稿,附写经、舆图、金石箱号各一纸,分别为 49、15、8 箱。

十月十八日

下午二时,私立木斋图书馆开幕,该馆邀请平馆各界人士莅临参观。先生、陶希圣、贾恩绂、冯陈祖怡、福开森、刘哲夫妇、陈继淹、虞建中、萧述宗等人到场祝贺。首由馆长胡钧报告筹备经过,继由贾恩绂、福开森、先生、陶希圣致辞。礼毕,合影留念。先生的致辞,大意如下:

> 　　鄙人日前去津,曾瞻仰南开木斋图书馆。此次返平,又参加此馆之开幕礼,木斋先生以毕生精力努力于图书馆事业,凡我教育文化界人士,莫不钦佩。按我国历史言,藏书家之多,及藏书之丰富,可谓世无伦比,但多为私人收藏,罕有公诸社会者,致遭天灾人祸之渐灭毁坏者甚多,良为可惜,平市乃读书风气最盛之区,但图书馆除各大学专有者外,公开者不过数处。欧西各国,虽四五万人口之区域,即有一个图书馆,平市人口一百五十多万,比例言之,应有三百多个,望社会人士,以木斋为榜样,努力图书馆事业之发展。

〔《华北日报》,1936 年 10 月 19 日,第 9 版〕

按:私立木斋图书馆馆址在旧刑部街 20 号,该址今已不存,大约在西单路口西北侧。贾恩绂(1865—1948),字佩卿,河北盐山人,教育家、方志学家。该馆董事为胡钧、甘鹏云、俞人凤、王承传、傅汝勤(天津木斋学校教务长)、袁涌进、严文郁、娄裕焘(开滦矿务局文牍部主任)。该馆开办不久,即与平馆合作,先生力主将平馆所藏复本借与木斋图书馆、北平市立第一普通图书馆巡回阅览。①柳诒徵致函先生,谈借平馆在沪之书《金山集》景印事。

　　守和馆长道鉴:

　　　　久违教益,惟履候胜常为颂。兹有恳者,镇江金山寺假敝藏《金山集》景印,惟敝藏仅有二卷,尚缺一卷。闻贵馆藏有明刊本三卷,系全书,拟请将敝藏所缺之卷借付摄影。乞迅赐函知照亭先生,检出此书。诒约于廿三四日赴沪晤渠,会同鉴摄,至多二日即可竣事。将来出书时,仍照前例赠送十分之一。事关流通古籍,至祈惠允,快函示复为感。专肃,敬颂公绥。

柳诒徵谨启
十月十八日

〔《国学图书馆第十年刊》,"案牍"页34〕

十月十九日

平馆向中央古物保管委员会发出公函,递交拟采掘洛阳汉石经残石填具事项表请核准备案并请转内、教两部发给执照以利进行。先生具名并钤馆章。〔台北"国史馆",〈国立北平图书馆采掘洛阳汉石经残石请领执照〉,典藏号026-011000-0053〕

　　　　按:"采取古物声请事项表"中,徐森玉为"率领采掘人"、谢国桢为"团员",另有中研院助理一人,拟定采掘日期为 1936 年 11(12)月至 1937 年 3(5)月。11 月 16 日,内政部训令,计检发采取古物执照一份。

十月二十三日

下午四时,西北科学考查团在陕山门大街三号召开第六次全体理事会议,周肇祥、先生、马衡、徐旭生、袁复礼、徐森玉、任鸿隽等人出席,沈仲章记录。讨论黄文弼来函请再延长整理期限并继续拨款、居延汉简出版事宜。〔"西北科学考查团理事会第六次会议记录",胡适北京档,HS-JDSHSC-2278-001〕

---

① 《中华图书馆协会会报》第 12 卷第 3 期,页 19。

十月二十四日

下午四时,北平图书馆协会假木斋图书馆举行第三次常会,先生、严文郁、钱稻孙、何日章、李文裿等五十余人出席。严文郁为会议主席,李文裿记录。其中,袁敦礼被邀请演讲,主题为"欧洲之文化及体育方面的情形"。六时许,会议始毕。〔《中华图书馆协会会报》第12卷第3期,1936年12月31日,页18-19〕

十月二十九日

傅斯年、李济致函先生,谈合作发掘洛阳石经办法。

　　守和吾兄左右:

　　　　前承我兄面示贵馆有发掘洛阳汉魏石经之计画,嘱本所加以协助,并云,发掘以石经为限,故无碍本所将来工作,各节。高情弘论,无任佩荷! 弟等以为考古工作,非藉众多有学术能力之机关共同从事,不足以发展中国之考古学,故甚愿大家向此共同目标进行。贵馆发掘石经,诚为盛事,所命协助一端,敢不同声相应? 兹与同人等拟成办法四项,另纸寄呈,如荷同意,即乞示知,俾派有经验之人员前往,以后如有其他应行协助,或在此接洽之事,乞随时见告,当无不竭力奉赞一切也。专此,敬颂道安!

　　　　　　　　　　　　　　　　　　　　　弟傅斯年、李济

　　附:合作发掘洛阳石经办法

　　拟国立北平图书馆与国立中央研究院历史语言研究所合作发掘洛阳石经办法

　　1.石经发掘,由北平图书馆主持之,中央研究院历史语言研究所派员为技术上之协助。除上列两机关外,不得更有其他机关加入。

　　2.出土物:一、石经归北平图书馆研究保存。

　　　　　　　二、石经以外之古物,归研究所研究。

　　3.如图书馆发掘费不足时,可由研究所协助。

　　4.此种合作发掘办法,暂以一年为限。

　　　　　　　　　　　　　　　　　　　　〔《傅斯年遗札》,页743-744〕

十月三十日

上午九时,故宫博物院在礼堂召开第十次院务会议,马衡、徐森玉、沈兼士、先生、张庭济、赵儒珍、王孝缉、章宗傅、励乃骥、黄鹏霄、何澄一、董寅复、邵锐、庄尚严、黄念劬(王承吉代)等人出席,马衡主席,王承吉记录。会议报告十一项,涉及故宫印刷所案、旧都文物整理委员会第二期工程计划中关于本院应修文物及经费案。讨论事项中涉及图书、外事者如下:

(一)拟与外国博物馆交换古物、图书、文献之影片、模型及出版物,以备设立国际文化品陈列室案。决议先以本院出版物交换。

(二)中央研究院历史语言研究所提议国立学术机关联合委托商务印书馆影印《国藏善本丛刊》,邀请本院加入,共同进行案。决议加入,由图书馆拟定目录,接洽进行。

(三)本院拟委托商务印书馆影印《秘殿珠林》及《石渠宝笈》,以广流传案。决议通过,由先生先行接洽。

(四)本院各馆处购买书籍,应集中图书馆办理,藉以增进效能案。决议通过。

(五)本院二十五年度图书馆印刷装潢各费,拟请增加案。决议重新分配,由张庭济与各科长接洽。〔《马衡年谱长编》,页709-710〕

十一月六日

先生致信傅斯年、李济,谈平馆与中研院史语所发掘洛阳汉魏石经办法。

　　孟真、济之先生大鉴:

　　　　接奉手翰暨合作发掘洛阳石经办法四条,敬谂种切。诸承赞助,感谢无既。附开各项办法均表同意,惟第二条补充数字,谅荷赞同。如何之处,并盼示复为荷。顺候台祺。

　　　　　　　　　　　　　　　　　　弟袁同礼顿首
　　　　　　　　　　　　　　　　　　十一月六日

　　二、出土物:

　　1.石经墓志归北平图书馆研究保存。

　　2.石经墓志以外之古物,由图书馆寄存研究所,归研究所研究。
　　　　〔国立北平图书馆用笺。台北"中央研究院"历史语言研究所傅
　　　　斯年图书馆,"史语所档案",元459-2〕

　　按:该信由文书代笔,落款处为先生签名。

先生致信傅斯年,告知故宫博物院对影印《国藏善本丛刊》之态度已转变。

　　印书事,故宫方面完全同意,现正与商务函商办法。同人中对于

缩印仍持异议,将来或分二种印刷,容再函告。此上

孟真兄

弟同礼顿首

十一月六日

编辑 1935 年历史考古论文及书籍条例,请即寄下以供参考。

〔台北"中央研究院"历史语言研究所傅斯年图书馆,"史语所档案",元 393-5〕

十一月七日

先生致信利兰,期待在北平与美国学术团体理事会秘书格雷夫斯面商合作事宜。

November 7, 1936

Dr. Waldo G. Leland

American Council of Learned Societies

907 Fifteenth Street

Washington, D. C.

U. S. A.

My dear Dr. Leland:

I am much obliged to you for your letter of 27 August. Owing to my absence from the city, I wish to apologize for the delay in answering.

We are very grateful to you indeed for assisting us in constructing the best possible apparatus for the film copying under the expert direction of Dr. Draeger. The arrival of Dr. Draeger in China is awaited with much interest and enthusiasm.

I have word from Dr. Graves that he expects to be in Peiping early in November and all of us here have been looking forward to his arrival. I am confident that more fruitful cooperation will result from his forthcoming visit.

I have often had occasion to recall our pleasant meeting in Washington and the charming luncheon which you so kindly arranged for me. It was a great honour which I shall always remember.

With warmest regards,

Yours sincerely,

T. L. Yuan

Acting Director

〔国立北平图书馆英文信纸。Library of Congress, American
Council of Learned Societies Records Box I:38〕

按:此件为打字稿,落款处为先生签名。

十一月十六日

晚八时,平馆、北京大学和清华大学历史学系假欧美同学会设宴款待英国
历史学家田波烈(Harold W. V. Temperley),除先生、姚从吾、刘崇鋐分别代
表以上三个学术机构,另有梅贻琦、罗家伦、沈兼士、潘光旦等四十余人到
场。田氏致辞,介绍世界历史学会(International Congress of Historians)的
成立初衷和现状,并表示极欢迎中国机构和个人参加该学会。〔《新北辰》第
2 卷第 12 期,1936 年 12 月 15 日,页 1298〕

　　　按:Harold W. V. Temperley(1879—1939),英国历史学家,1931 年
　　　起担任剑桥大学现代史教授,曾任世界历史学会主席。

先生致信史蒂文斯,感谢洛克菲勒基金会给予曾宪三的资助,告知平馆将
会扩大目录卡片编印的范围,请李小缘、裘开明、恒慕义等人作为顾问委员
以便满足国内外的需求,期待格雷夫斯访问北平。

November 16, 1936

Dear Dr. Stevens:

　　I was very glad to get your letter of September 30, and deeply
grateful to you for the assistance you have so kindly extended to Mr.
Tseng. I have no doubt that he will make the best use of the opportunity
offered to him.

　　We are most obliged to you for your assistance in connection with
the printing and distribution of Chinese catalogue cards. With your grant,
we are now able to widen the scope of our cards and to print the cards for
old Chinese books as well. I enclosed herewith two copies of our booklet
for your information.

　　In this connection, I would like to inform you that we have asked
Mr. Li Siao-yuan and Dr. A. Kaiming Chiu and Dr. A. W. Hummel to
serve as members of an Advisory Committee. With their knowledge of

Chinese libraries in China and abroad, we shall be able to improve our service to meet the needs of the scholarly world.

We have recently heard from Mr. Milam that Dr. Bishop and Dr. Keogh have decided to visit China in the fall of 1937. All of us here have been expecting their arrival with much enthusiasm, and we certainly wish that they could plan their trip a few months earlier.

I am expecting the arrival of Mr. Graves in a day or two. I am sure we shall have many pleasant talks together.

With kindest regards,

Yours sincerely,

T. L. Yuan

Acting Director

〔国立北平图书馆英文信纸。Rockefeller Foundation. Series 601: China; Subseries 601.R: China-Humanities and Arts. Vol. Box 47. Folder 388〕

按：1936 年 9 月 16 日，曾宪三抵达美国，后前往哥伦比亚大学学习图书馆学，洛克菲勒基金会为其提供每月 170 美金的津贴，原计划为两年。[1] 此件为打字稿，落款处为先生签名，于 12 月 14 日送达。

十一月十八日

先生致信斯文·赫定，感谢其请出版社寄赠《马仲英逃亡记》，并请协助补充平馆馆藏赫定著作。

November 18, 1936

Dr. Sven Hedin,

Blasieholmshamm 5b.

Stockholm,

Sweden.

Dear Dr. Hedin,

I have the pleasure to acknowledge the receipt of your latest book

[1] Rockefeller Foundation Records, New China Program-Humanities-Social Sciences (H-SS), Series 18; Columbia University. *Catalogue 1936-1937*. New York, p. 239.

"The Flight of Big Horse" which you so kindly sent to us through Dutton Co. of New York. It is indeed a great privilege to have you remember us in this way.

The book was so illuminatingly written that every one of your Peiping friends who has read it has been thrilled with joy and pleasure. We are so glad to have it for our Library.

When you were in Peiping last time, you so kindly promised to send us any of your works not yet obtained by the National Library. I am enclosing herewith a list of your works already on file at the National Library and shall greatly appreciate your assistance if you could arrange to send us the others. We shall be doubly thankful to you if you could autograph the volumes that you are ready to send to us. In view of your great interest in China, we would like to have all your writings as complete as possible.

We have had many occasions to recall with vivid memories of your visit to Peiping. All of us here hope that you will repeat it often and many times. It will indeed be a great privilege to be able to see you in China soon.

With greetings and kindest regards to you and your sister.

Yours sincerely,

T. L. Yuan

〔国立北平图书馆英文信纸。韩琦教授提供〕

按：*The Flight of Big Horse* 即《马仲英逃亡记》，1936 年纽约 E. P. Dutton 初版。此件为打字稿，落款处为先生签名，附两页书单——Works of Dr. Sven Hedin in the National Library。

十一月中下旬

先生收李景聃寄来考察永城地区古物报告。〔台北"中央研究院"历史语言研究所傅斯年图书馆，"史语所档案"，考 6-3-28〕

按：李景聃（1900—1946），字纯一，安徽舒城人，史语所安阳殷墟发掘"考古十兄弟"中最长者。

十一月十九日

傅斯年、李济覆函先生，商谈史语所与平馆发掘洛阳汉魏石经办法的细节问题。

守和先生：

十一月六日书奉悉。此事弟等以为不在本所职权之内，故最好不提，仍如原议，何如？盖即本所发掘品，后来如何处置，亦须待政府决定也。专此奉复，敬叩日安。

弟傅——、李—

二十五年十一月十九日

〔《傅斯年遗札》，页752〕

按："此事"应指10月29日、11月6日信函中讨论出土墓志及其他古物之归属。

十一月二十日

傅斯年致函先生，草拟史语所委托平馆编撰民国以来历史学论文索引办法。

守和吾兄：

本所委托贵馆代编历年史学论文索引一事，兹草拟办法如下：

一、范围以（a）国内各重要文史学期刊之论文，（b）国内一般期刊及日报副刊之较重要论文，（c）国内专书，（d）国内单行小册，（e）国人在国外发表之重要论文或著作，为限，其类似笔记性质者不录。

二、兹定于二十六年二月中旬，先完成二十四年七月至廿五年六月一年中出版者，以后每年二月中旬完成其前一年度者，（例如二十七年二月中旬完成二十五年七月至二十六年六月者）并于两年内补成民国元年至民国二十四年七月以前者。（因本有国学索引，补成不难也。）

三、每月由史言所津贴工作费拾圆。

四、此项初稿成后，再由史言所自行删定。（初稿求其备，定稿当有所取舍也。）

如荷同意，即希自本月份办理。

看来本所津贴此事者有限，但此不过贵馆编索引之副产品，而本所又无此项经费也。专此，敬颂日安！

弟傅斯年敬启

廿五年十一月二十日

〔《傅斯年遗札》，页752-753〕

按：此信后寄送胡适一份副本。

十一月二十六日

平馆向中央古物保管委员会发出公函，请派傅雷前往洛阳石经发掘现场监察并供给旅费，另待采掘日期确定后再行函达。先生具名并钤馆章。〔台北"国史馆"，〈国立北平图书馆采掘洛阳汉石经残石请领执照〉，典藏号 026-011000-0053〕

十一月下旬

先生为傅振伦申请奖学金事撰一信，请徐森玉面交马衡。

　　按：傅振伦所撰论文题目似为《博物馆文物陈列方法之原理》，后获故宫博物院乙种奖学金 200 元。12 月 3 日，马衡致信傅振伦，告之其申请奖学金应按手续本人具名办理。原文如下，

　　维本兄：

　　　　日前见徐森玉先生面交袁守和先生一稿，系兄请求奖学金者。此事宜按照手续由本人具名，送奖学会审查委员会声请，希注意。

　　　　　　　　　　　　　　　　　　　　　　　衡

　　　　　　　　　　　　　　　　　　　十二月三日

　　　　　　　　　　　　　　　　〔《马衡年谱长编》①，页 281〕

十二月一日

利兰覆函先生，告知缩微胶片机组装进展，并告德尔格或将于一九三七年春来华。

　　　　　　　　　　　　　　　　　　　1st December 1936

My dear Dr. Yuan:

　　Thank you for your kind note of November 7.

　　I receive regular reports from Dr. Draeger, who tells me that the work on the apparatus is proceeding very satisfactorily. He has his orders to proceed to China in February, but I do not think that he will be able to go until spring. I fear, therefore, that we cannot expect the apparatus to be set up in the National Library until early summer. I am sure that it will be satisfactory, and that it will make possible a most interesting and important exchange of documentary material between China and the United States.

---

① 《马衡年谱长编》将此信错系于 1927 年，特此说明。

I suppose that Mr. Graves is now with you. I am writing to him, at Shanghai, by the same mail, and hope that he will receive my letter before he leaves China on his way back to the United States.

We remember with much pleasure your visit here, and hope that we may have you with us again in the near future.

With kindest regards, in which Mrs. Leland would join if she knew I were writing, please believe me, as ever,

Very sincerely yours,

Waldo G. Leland,

Permanent Secretary

〔Library of Congress, American Council of Learned Societies Records Box I:38〕

按:该件为录副。

十二月五日

下午三时,北平近代科学图书馆举行开幕典礼。除日本大使馆加藤清水、东方文化总会代表森安三郎、桥川时雄等人外,中方人士徐诵明、先生、钮先铮(晋察政委会宋哲元代表)、张我军(秦德纯代表)到场。〔《大公报》(天津),1936年12月6日,第4版〕

按:北平近代科学图书馆由日本外务省文化事业部在平设立。张我军(1902—1955),原名张清荣,台北人,作家,时应任北平社会局秘书。

十二月十日

晚,黎锦熙、顾颉刚设晚宴,先生、汪怡、张维华、韩儒林、李一非、王真、黎光霁等受邀与席。〔《顾颉刚日记》卷3,页570〕

按:汪怡(1877—1960),字一庵,浙江杭州人,早年毕业于两湖书院,后历任北京师范大学讲师、中国大辞典编纂处国音普通词典组主任、国语统一会常委,积极从事国语统一读音工作。张维华(1902—1987),字西山,山东寿光人,历史学家,时任《禹贡》编辑。李一非,曾任通县民众教育馆长,时应任通俗读物编刊社总务主任。王真(1905—1989),河北魏县人,历史学家,时任通俗读物编刊社总编辑。黎光霁(1904—1972),字琴南,陕西宁羌人。

十二月十二日

先生致电王献唐,祝贺山东省立图书馆新楼"奎虚书藏"开馆。〔《王献唐年谱长编》,页 659-660〕

按:1934 年,山东省政府拨专款筹建新楼,其址位于大明湖南岸,遐园近旁,12 月 13 日正式开馆。

先生致信米来牟,告知经过中华图书馆协会执委会就美国图书馆专家访华计划做出的讨论和安排,对推迟到一九三七年秋的建议表示理解,中华图书馆协会已向密歇根大学、耶鲁大学致函请求批准毕寿普和凯欧的请假申请,并告知准备印制英文手册、配置翻译和速记员等细节。

December 12, 1936

Dear Dr. Milam:

Your letter of September 17 has been received for some time. Owing to my absence from Peiping, I wish to apologize for unavoidable delay in answering.

A meeting of the Executive Committee of the Library Association was recently called to consider various plans in connection with the visit of the representatives of the American Library Association. The following is a brief resume of our discussions:

(1) Realizing Dr. Bishop's and Dr. Keogh's difficulty in getting away from their work during the present academic year, we endorse your proposal of postponing their visit until the fall of 1937. If they could arrive at the end of September, it would not only be convenient to colleges and universities, but it would also be the best climate in China.

(2) in accordance with your thoughtful suggestion, the Chinese Library Association has addressed an official request to President Ruthven and President Angell, copies of which are herewith enclosed. It is hoped that the A. L. A. would find it possible to supplement the request.

(3) in order to facilitate their investigations, we are preparing a handbook (in English) of the more important libraries in China which will serve as a useful guide during their visit. I also enclose a tentative itinerary.

(4) The visit of Dr. Bishop and Dr. Keogh will be arranged under the auspices of the Chinese Library Association, but not of the Chinese Government. The Association has requested the Government for a subvention, but so far nothing definite has been decided upon. However, with the grant from the Rockefeller Foundation, we are able to provide a translator and a stenographer as required by Dr. Bishop and Dr. Keogh.

(5) we have arranged with the Dollar Steamship Lines and the American Mail Line to look after their trip. As soon as we hear definitely their probable date of departure, we shall arrange to have the tickets sent to them directly from New York.

With the increasing facilities of rail and air travel in China, it will be possible to shorten the duration of their visit, although we wish they could stay as long as they can possibly arrange it.

I need not emphasize the fact that all librarians in China have been looking forward to their visit and it is a real pleasure to learn that they are able to take the trip in the not distant future.

With many thanks for your cooperation,

Yours sincerely,

T. L. Yuan

Acting Director

〔Yale University records, Peiping National Library, 1931–1937, Box: 80, Folder: 831〕

按:该件为副本。随信附一页行程计划,包括上海、苏州、南京、济南、青岛、天津、北平、汉口、武昌、长沙、广东、香港等地,共计 67 天。先生以中华图书馆协会执行部主席身份致信密歇根大学校长 Alexander G. Ruthven、耶鲁大学校长 James R. Angell,其中写给后者的信为请其考虑给予该校图书馆凯欧馆长三个半月假期用以赴华考察图书馆事业。

December 12, 1936

President James R. Angell

Yale University

New Haven, Conn.

U. S. A.

Dear President Angell

During the past two years the Library Association of China has been endeavoring to arrange a visit to China from Dr. Andrew Keogh, the Librarian of your University. The purpose of the proposed visit is to enable Dr. Keogh to conduct a survey of Chinese libraries with a view to their further development. In taking this action, the members of the Library Association feel confident that they will have at their disposal Dr. Keogh's scholarship and experience which will be of immense value to them in their efforts to improve the library situation in China.

We fully realize the difficulty in granting a leave of absence to a University Librarian during the academic year. But in view of the significance of Dr. Keogh's mission and in view of the close cultural relations between the Yale University and higher institutions of learning in China, we sincerely hope that a leave of absence for three months and half (from September to December, 1937) will be granted to Dr. Keogh by your University.

I may add that a grant has been made to our Association by the Rockefeller Foundation to cover the expenses of Dr. Keogh to be effective when the necessary leave of absence has been granted.

The scheme has also had the cordial support of the American Library Association and if the proposed visit is to be materialized, Dr. Keogh will come as the official delegate of that Association.

Trusting you will give favourable consideration to our request,

Yours very sincerely,

T. L. Yuan

Chairman,

Executive Committee

〔Yale University records, Peiping National Library, 1931–1937, Box: 80, Folder: 831〕

按：此件为抄件。

十二月十五日

史蒂文斯覆函先生,转达恒慕义对平馆卡片目录编印的反馈——希望目录卡片发行数量稳步提升,并就该项资助款的支付周期及年度上限略作解释,此外毕寿普和凯欧均愿意于一九三七年秋访华。

December 15, 1936

Dear Mr. Yuan:

　　In talk on December 11 with Dr. Hummel I learned that the grant of the Foundation for production of library cards at the National Library is giving useful aid to your program. He is much pleased with the current product, and of course hopes that the number issued will steadily increase. The fund for the production of cards is available for any part of the process that you do not have present means of operating under library funds. This of course is within the total of $ 6,000 for each of the three years from July, 1936. The other parts of the total grant are available at any time during the three-year period. I am happy to learn that both Mr. Bishop and Mr. Keogh expect to make their visit to China in the fall of 1937. No doubt by letter and by talk with Mr. Graves you have developed the details of their plans.

Sincerely yours,

David H. Stevens

〔Rockefeller Foundation. Series 601: China; Subseries 601.R: China-Humanities and Arts. Vol. Box 47. Folder 388〕

　　按:该函抄送给恒慕义,此件为录副。

十二月十六日

先生致信葛斯德中文图书馆,询问该馆是否有意购买《宋会要辑稿》。

December 16, 1936

Custodian,

Gest Chinese Library,

Institute for Advanced Study,

Princeton, N. J.,

U. S. A.

Dear Sir:

　　The National Library has recently published the *SUNG HUEI YAO* (宋会要), a compendium on the institutions of the Sung dynasty, compiled by Hsu Sung from the great Ming encyclopedia *Yung Lo Ta Tien*. It is a lost work of great importance and we are anxious to learn whether your Library desires to acquire a copy, as a very limited edition has been printed.

　　The *SUNG HUEI YAO* is reprinted from the original manuscript by photo-lithographic process and each copy consists of two hundred volumes. It is sold at ＄140.00, Chinese currency. But if you send your order immediately upon receipt of this letter, we shall be glad to allow you a 20% discount. Foreign postage is to be paid extra.

　　Should your Library desire to avail itself of this opportunity to purchase a copy, we hope you will place the order with your remittance.

Yours faithfully,

T. L. Yuan

Acting Director

　　　　〔国立北平图书馆英文信纸。Princeton University, Mudd Manuscript Library, AC123, Box 418, Folder National Library-Peiping, 1931 – 1936〕

　　按:此件为打字稿,落款处为先生签名,翌年1月16日送达葛斯德中文图书馆。该件右下角有收信者核算的购书经费和邮费,最终得出全部费用不会超过50美金的结论。

十二月十八日

平馆向中央古物保管委员会发出公函,因西安事变突发,发掘洛阳汉石经计划被迫推迟至明春另择期开工,届时函达。先生具名并钤馆章。〔台北"国史馆",〈国立北平图书馆采掘洛阳汉石经残石请领执照〉,典藏号026-011000-0053〕

十二月二十四日

南京教育部拟筹备全国第二届美术展览会,函聘王一亭、何香凝、吴湖帆、李济、马衡、徐悲鸿、梁思成、先生、高剑父、陈树人、张道藩、傅铜、叶恭绰、傅斯年、杨振声、褚民谊、刘海粟、滕固、蒋复璁、齐白石、严智开、顾颉刚、顾树森等四十余人为筹备委员。〔《申报》,1936 年 12 月 25 日,第 13 版〕

　　　　按:除出任筹备委员外,先生还被推为编辑委员会委员,该展览会于 1937 年 4 月 1 日开幕。

十二月二十九日

晚,李书华、李麟玉在丰泽园设宴,胡适、蒋梦麟、傅斯年、郭有守、孟治、梅贻琦、李蒸、徐旭生、郑天挺、孙洪芬、先生、徐诵明、陆志韦、周炳琳、陶希圣、张奚若、崔敬伯、顾颉刚等人受邀与席,同席者甚多,约九时许散。〔《顾颉刚日记》卷 3,页 577〕

十二月三十一日

下午二时,平馆委员会召开第二十四次会议,胡适、孙洪芬、傅斯年、先生、秦德纯、蒋梦麟出席,林伯遵列席。蒋梦麟为会议主席,先生记录。会议报告平馆最近三月馆务,议决准予备案。讨论事项如下:

(一)蒋梦麟、孙洪芬任满改选案,议决连任三年。

(二)选举本届职员案,议决连任一年。

(三)平馆提议建筑修缮费上不敷三千元应否追加,预算请公决案,议决准予追加,由本委员会商请中基会设法拨付。

(四)联合故宫博物院、中央研究院及北京大学影印《国藏善本丛刊》案,首由傅斯年、先生报告经过,议决照案通过,由馆员负责与商务印书馆接洽,惟(1)经部之书可缓印(2)注多字小者应照原式影印,不得缩小(3)草目再予审查以便分集出版。

(五)拟委托大东书局影印《清世祖实录》案,议决照案通过。

三时半散会。〔《北京图书馆馆史资料汇编(1909-1949)》,页 353-354〕

是年

先生共向故宫博物院捐资 2344.53 元,用以奖学金的发放。〔《收到廿五年度奖学金国币 2340.53 元补具收据并送二十五年奖学金收支清单由》,《故宫博物院·财务类》第 85 卷,页 13-15〕

一九三七年　四十三岁

一月一日

晚,先生与徐森玉在承华园设宴,胡适、傅斯年、沈兼士、罗常培、李书华、赵万里、谢国桢、孙楷第、顾颉刚受邀与席。〔《顾颉刚日记》卷3,页581〕

一月五日

王云五致函先生、傅斯年,呈送商务印书馆就《国藏善本丛刊》草拟影印办法。

> 守和、孟真先生大鉴:
>
> 　　去冬承商以国藏善本委敝馆印行,原则上彼此均已同意,尚未解决者,仅为纸张问题。当时弟以国产手工纸价昂,恐碍流通,嗣守公提出折衷办法,拟以《四部丛刊》第四集专收国藏善本,并顾念敝馆成本,允就报酬方面酌为减让。敝处则以《四部丛刊》第四集拟收之书多已制版付印,如因此搁置一年,敝馆损失颇巨,且国藏善本甚富,《四部丛刊》第四集即使全收国藏亦仅五百册,恐未能尽量容纳。思维再四,难得两全之法,近因外国纸价骤涨,与国产手工纸之距离稍近,又因两公以流布国藏善本之责相委,如敝馆不能充分效力,有辜厚意,亦觉不安。年假稍暇,再就此问题详加考虑,觉两公原意尚可勉遵办理,虽营业上不易有把握,然为文化计,只得冒险为之,并草拟办法大纲如左,
>
> (一)国藏善本由委员会选定千册交敝馆景印。选书时充分容纳敝馆之意见,敝馆已藏有或已摄照者概删除,底本模糊不易制版者亦删除。
>
> (二)国藏善本按《四部丛刊》之式缩摄,每面仍作一面,用国产手工连史纸印刷。
>
> (三)选书限于本年二月底办妥。
>
> (四)选定各书以送交上海敝厂摄影为原则,万不得已少数得在南京摄影。
>
> (五)国藏善本于本年四月一日开始发售预约,全书千册于预约开始后

两年内出齐,每半年出书一次,每次二百五十册。

(六)敝馆对收藏者之报酬按照印书之数,第一千册酬印本百分之五,第二千册酬印本百分之七分半,第三千册酬印本百分之十,以后加印概酬印本百分之十。

上开一、二两条全按两公原意,第四条为谋工作进行迅速且节省工料,第六条系参照守公去年十一月来示,酌拟以期敝馆稍减负担,第三、五两条则因《四部丛刊》四集原拟本年六月开始发售,因性质与国藏善本相近,如同时或在相距不远之时期内发售,势必互有妨碍,故将《四部丛刊》四集延至本年九月开始发售,而将国藏善本提前于四月一日发售,预约四个月即于七月底截止,再越两月始售《四部丛刊》之预约,如此或可避免彼此冲突。因是上述办法有亟待解决之必要,尊意如何,极盼早日示覆,以便进行为幸。专此,敬颂著祺。

弟王云五

二十六年一月五日

〔商务印书馆编审部启事用笺。台北"中央研究院"历史语言研究所傅斯年图书馆,"史语所档案",元 393-6〕

> 按:此件为打印稿,落款处为王云五签名,并在左侧批注"本函另寄守和先生"。

一月六日

午,李书华、徐旭生、顾颉刚在北平研究院设宴,司徒雷登、胡适、孙洪芬、沈兼士、陈垣、容庚、先生等受邀与席。〔《顾颉刚日记》卷 3,页 583〕

一月八日

某记者来访,先生表示平馆并无在西城设立分馆计划。〔《华北日报》,1937 年 1 月 9 日,第 9 版〕

> 按:因新印《职员录》中有在地质调查所设立工程参考处的介绍,故有人误传。另,此前平馆本拟在东城盐务学校旧址设立分馆,但此地已被育英学校租用,遂作罢。

米来牟致函先生,再寄其前函之副本。

January 8, 1937

Dear Dr. Yuan,

Not having heard from you in response to my letter of September 17,

1936, regarding the proposed visit of Dr. Bishop and Dr. Keogh, I fear my letter may have gone astray. I am therefore enclosing a copy of the letter and shall be glad to hear from you.

With best wishes for 1937, I am

Cordially yours,

Carl H. Milam

Secretary

〔Yale University records, Peiping National Library, 1931 - 1937, Box: 80, Folder: 831〕

按:此为抄件。

一月九日

傅斯年致函先生,谈《国藏善本丛刊》影印事。

守和吾兄:

王云五来一信,想兄亦收到。能不缩印,大妙大妙,喜外望外矣。至于选择一事,弟亦觉商务意见可以采纳,彼已有者,自不必列入,若彼以部头太大,不愿印者可待至下次耳。此外条款更无问题矣。还书一事,彼谓送收藏机关,弟意第一批(即第一千部中之五十部)不妨送此会(编辑会)会中每人得一部。其余由四机关依出书多寡之比例全部分之。然此仅吾辈自己之事,与商务无关也。

又,故宫之《宣和博古图》,弟主张宜列入。

本所目录,兹重拟一清目,乞兄审定。凡事兄定则定矣,不必多所商量转耗时日也。贵馆之《四镇三关志》,弟觉亦可列入,因《关中丛书》不知何日出版也。匆匆,敬颂著安!

弟斯年上

廿六年一月九日

〔《傅斯年遗札》,页 769-770〕

按:"缩印"之说,参见 1936 年 11 月 5 日傅斯年致蔡元培信,时王云五主张"如《四部丛刊》缩本之大小。[①]""四机关"即平馆、故宫博物院、历史语言研究所、北京大学。

[①]《傅斯年遗札》,页 745。

一月上旬

华美协进社社长孟治拍摄故宫博物院、古物陈列所、历史博物馆建筑影片,先生作为其好友,出面协调,助力颇多。〔Chi Meng,*Chinese American Understanding: a sixty-year search*, New York: China Institute in America, 1981, p. 177〕

> 按:孟治(Meng Chih,? —1990),河北永清人,字君平,1915 年 6 月由南开学校毕业,后入清华学校,1919 年赴美留学,先后获戴维森学院(Davidson College)学士学位、哥伦比亚大学宗教学硕士,长期担任华美协进社社长。本次实际拍摄时间应为 1 月 22 日、23 日上午,涉及故宫博物院、古物陈列所、历史博物院、景山等处。①

一月十六日

孙念礼覆函先生,告知葛斯德中文图书馆愿意购买《宋会要辑稿》但需等待最终确认,并将寄送其在《哈佛亚洲学报》发表的文章。

January 16, 1937

Dear Dr. Yuan:

　　Your communication under date of December 16 arrived this morning. I certainly hope that we may be able to acquire a copy of the *SUNG HUI YAO* which the National Library has recently published. The policy for and the methods of purchasing acquisitions for The Gest Oriental Library have not as yet been determined. Dr. Flexner, Director of the Institute, being out of town for a brief period just now, I write to acknowledge the receipt of your information. When I can put the matter before him, we will let you hear.

　　Under separate cover I am forwarding to you a reprint of an article (from *Harvard Journal of Asiatic Studies*, I, 3/4, Dec., 1936) I wrote about "Seven intimate library owners" of metropolitan Hang-chou in the 18th century. While its material is probably very familiar to you, you may be interested in the compilation for its contribution to the western world.

Very sincerely,

---

① 故宫博物院档案,"为纽约华美协进社主孟治前往摄取天安门午门等处外景"。

Nancy Lee Swann, Ph. D., Curator

〔Princeton University, Mudd Manuscript Library, AC123, Box 418,
Folder National Library-Peiping, 1931–1936〕

按：Dr. Flexner 即 Abraham Flexner,美国教育学家,普林斯顿高等
研究院的创立者。Seven Intimate Library Owners 介绍清代杭州
藏书楼,分别为汪氏振绮堂、赵氏小山堂、汪氏飞鸿堂、鲍氏知不
足斋、吴氏瓶花斋、孙氏寿松堂、汪氏欣托山房。

一月

先生常与妹夫彭昭贤聚谈,内容涉及西安事变及全国时局。〔《思忆录》,中
文部分页 104–105〕

按：西安事变中,彭昭贤曾被东北军和西北军扣留。1937 年 1
月,彭赴北平过春节,住在新平路(北新平胡同)袁敦礼处,先生
常赴此处与之谈天。

先生为杨殿珣《石刻题跋索引》撰写序言。〔《石刻题跋索引》,1940 年 9 月初版〕

按：据《国立北平图书馆馆刊》①可知,此书本拟于 1937 年交商务
印书馆出版,但极有可能受抗日战争全面爆发影响,被迫中断。

二月三日

下午二时,故宫博物院在礼堂召开第十一次院务会议,马衡、徐森玉、沈兼
士、先生、张庭济、叶澜、赵儒珍、章宗傅、黄念劬(王承吉代)、王孝绪、邵
锐、何澄一、黄鹏霄、欧阳道达(黄鹏霄代)等人出席,马衡为主席,王承吉
为记录。会议报告九项事项,讨论十二条议案。〔《马衡年谱长编》,页 730〕

二月四日

下午五时,先生邀请福开森在平馆会议室举行演讲。〔国家图书馆档案,档案
编号 1937-※044-外事 3-004001 至 1937-※044-外事 3-004003〕

按：2 月 1 日,在纪念周上,先生向馆员通知,今后每周择定一日,
于下午五时至七时请名人演讲,以提高馆员业务水平。② 福开森
为第一位受邀演讲人,先生特发馆内通知,请同人一律参加。

二月六日

下午五时,北平图书馆协会假平馆欢迎武昌文华图书馆学专科学校教授奚

---

① 《印行石刻题跋索引》,《国立北平图书馆馆刊》第 11 卷第 1 号,1937 年 2 月,页 143。
② 《华北日报》,1937 年 2 月 3 日,第 9 版。

路女士(Miss Hill),先生、李文裿、赵廷范等三十余人出席。首由先生报告此次欢迎会之意义,继由奚路女士演讲,题目为"美国儿童图书馆之发展",由吴光清翻译。六时许,散会。〔《中华图书馆协会会报》第 12 卷第 4 期,1937 年 2 月,页 16-17〕

> 按:赵廷范,字锡九,湖北人,曾赴美入纽约医学院图书馆(New York Academy of Medicine Library)学习,时应在北平协和医学院图书馆服务,后任该馆副主任。①

先生致信耿士楷,告知美图书馆专家即将访华,请预支在华旅费。

February 6, 1937

Dear Mr. Gunn:

You will recall that at the meeting of the Executive Committee of the Foundation held May 15, 1936, a grant of $ 3,000 was made to the National Library in connection with the proposed visit of representatives of the American Library Association.

We have had word from the American Library Association that Dr. Andrew Keogh and Dr. W. W. Bishop, librarians of Yale and the University of Michigan respectively, are leaving for China early in September. As we wish to send them the railway and steamer tickets in advance, we shall appreciate your assistance if you will arrange to have payments made to us on July 1, 1937.

With renewed thanks,

Yours very sincerely,
T. L. Yuan
Acting Director

〔Rockefeller Foundation. Series 601: China; Subseries 601.R: China-Humanities and Arts. Box 47. Folder 389〕

> 按:此为抄件,2 月 9 日耿士楷致信史蒂文斯,附上此信。

二月九日

先生致信王重民,影照敦煌写经须替换两种,并谈其他诸事。

---

① 《中华图书馆协会会员录》,1935 年,页 76;李文裿、武田熙编《北京文化学术机关综览》,北京:新民印书馆,1940 年,页 19。

有三吾弟如晤：

　　连奉数函,藉悉种种。在法所编之书目,如能设法早日付印,俾国人略知该馆内容且可表现在法之成绩,最所盼望,但不识印刷方面有无困难。似以玻璃版为最妥,每块价若干可先一询。前函言小者三十方,大者六十方,实不算便宜,不识能办再减少些否? 关于影照敦煌事,曾向英庚款中请求补助,大家均认为重要,惟各董事因彼此略有意见,故尚无正式决定,闻本月间可以开会或可决定。前开之书目极好第二集目录亦请早日选定,惟《还冤记》及《楚辞音》二书已由董授经照有玻璃版,现存本馆中,无庸再照矣应再补充二种以便凑成十五种,已照好之复本,请随时寄平,因清华曾来催问数次矣。此外尚有数事:

　　(一)如能在法继续编制《燉煌写经目录》最佳,亦学术界最需要者,请与伯希和商酌进行。

　　(二)德礼贤所编之《利玛窦地图考证》,馆中决购壹部,或交换以善本丛书相交换,请便中函告德先生。

　　(三)本馆《善本丛书》第一集已赠法国两部,由交换局转寄一赠东方语言,一赠中国学院,可告伯希和先生。附说明二纸另印《善本丛刊》须今秋方能出版。

　　(四)世界图书馆协会在荷兰开会事,闻尚未决定,已函询该会,容再函达。

　　余容再函,顺颂旅安。

　　　　　　　　　　　　　　　　　　　　同礼顿首

　　　　　　　　　　　　　　　　　　　　二月九日

　　河南大学拟添一考古讲座,不识王海镜已作返国之计否,闻渠对于政治太活动,似非学者所宜,务劝其用法文多发表专门论文。李济之到英讲学,将来法,可告其与之通讯也。

　　林藜光前丁忧,不识曾返国否? 晤时希代问候。

　　　　　　　　　　　　　　　　　　〔中国书店·海淀,四册〕

按:德礼贤(Pasquale M. D' Elia,1890-1963),意大利汉学家,耶稣会士,1913年至1917年在徐家汇从事研究,1923年再次来到中国,任震旦大学教授,1933年起在罗马宗座额我略大学(Pontifical Gregorian University)执教。《利玛窦地图考证》应指//

mappamondo cinese del P. Matteo Ricci S.I. (terza edizione, Pechino, 1602) conservato presso la Biblioteca Vaticana, 1938 年梵蒂冈初版。《国立北平图书馆善本丛书》第一集,皆选明代边防史料,《皇明九边考》《边政考》《三云筹俎考》《西域行程记》《西域番国志》《筹辽硕画》《皇明象胥录》《行边纪闻》《朝鲜史略》《安南图志》《日本考》《使琉球录》共计十二种、七十册,交商务印书馆影印刊行。"丁忧"即指林黎光母亲病逝,彼确曾回国奔丧,此时似仍在厦门一带。

先生致信耿士楷,寄上《图书季刊》英文本编辑收支报表,并告知编辑部人员的变动,以及当下组稿之不易。

February 9, 1937

Dear Mr. Gunn,

　　I have pleasure in sending you herewith an audited statement of receipts and expenditures in connection with the grant of the Rockefeller Foundation for the *Quarterly Bulletin of Chinese Bibliography*, English edition.

　　The statement covers the period from November, 1935 to December, 1936. During the period, receipts included five instalments of payments on the grant amounting to Ch $ 6,640.88 (US $ 2,000.00) and Ch $ 59.57 bank interest, while expenditures totaled Ch $ 4,775.48.

　　We have been spending the money in accordance with the suggestions embodied in your letter of November 5, 1935, i. e., US $ 800 for the editor, US $ 350 for assistants, US $ 350 for miscellaneous. A surplus has been accumulated because the first instalment for the last quarter of 1935 was larger than usual, and being received in November we had only two months in which to spend it, while some of the miscellaneous expenses estimated did not have to be met.

　　Since receiving the grant from the Rockefeller Foundation, the publication of the *Bulletin* has been made more regular and the quality of each issue has greatly improved. However, unforeseen circumstances have interfered with some of our plans. Dr. E. Schierlitz, who had been editing the Periodical Index, resigned from the editorial board early in 1936, on account of increased duties at the Catholic University of Peiping. The whole of the editorial responsibility for the English edition thus devolved on the managing editor Mr. T. K. Koo, who has been entirely relieved from library work. Though efforts have been made to find someone to take the place of Dr. Schierlitz, no suitable person has yet been found.

Arrangement was made last spring for Prof. Ch'en Shouyi, Head of the Department of History of the National University of Peking, to be Contributing Editor; but since last July Prof. Ch'en was granted a year's leave by his University, so that the arrangement will not materialize until after his return next summer. It is expected that by that time an editor for the Periodical Index will also be secured.

In spite of our offer of suitable remuneration, there has been difficulty in securing articles, as the bibliographical surveys desired proved to be uncongenial to most scholars approached. During the past year, we secured only two articles, one on recent Chinese historical studies by Prof. Ch'en printed in Vol. II, No. 4, and another one on modern Chinese literature by Mr. Pih Shu-t'ang, printed in Vol. III, No.1. Continued efforts are being made to secure suitable contributions.

Yours sincerely,

T. L. Yuan

Director

[Rockefeller Foundation. Series 601: China; Subseries 601.R: China-Humanities and Arts. Vol. Box 47. Folder 394]

按:此为抄件。

先生致信芒太尔,告知已收到赠书。

February 9, 1937

Dr. Gösta Montell

Statens Etnografiska Museum

Stockholm, Sweden

Dear Dr. Montell:

We have much pleasure in acknowledging the receipt of the

publications listed in your letter of January 7 which you kindly sent to us in the name of Dr. Sven Hedin. We wish to thank you for your courtesy and assistance and shall be most obliged to you if you will convey our hearty thanks to Dr. Hedin.

We value greatly Dr. Hedin's writings and shall be only too glad to receive anything which you may send to us in the future.

With kindest regards,

Yours very sincerely,

T. L. Yuan

Acting Director

〔国立北平图书馆英文信纸。韩琦教授提供〕

按:此件为打字稿,落款处为先生签名。

二月中旬

吴宓致函先生,为高棣华、张宗瑶求职,先生收到后即覆,表示平馆不能增聘职员。〔《吴宓日记》第6册,北京:生活·读书·新知三联书店,1998年,页74〕

按:先生覆信于17日送达。

二月十六日

晚,先生与马衡、沈兼士、徐森玉、张庭济设宴,北平学术界人士如陈垣、章鸿钊、姚从吾、孟森、福开森、赵万里、齐如山、唐兰、傅增湘、容庚、吴廷燮、柯昌泗等人受邀与席,总人数约在三桌以上。〔《顾颉刚日记》卷3,页602〕

按:柯昌泗(1899—1952),字燕舲,山东胶县人,历史学家,柯劭忞长子。

二月十七日

James R. Angell 覆函先生,耶鲁大学支持凯欧赴华考察,但其夫人身体状态堪忧,恐怕不能承担此任。

February 17, 1937

Dear Mr. Yuan:

Your letter of December 12th has been much delayed in arrival but I hasten to reply now that it is at hand. The University would be entirely willing to release Mr. Keogh for the service which you would like him to render, but the condition of Mrs. Keogh's health makes him feel that he cannot with propriety undertake the trip. I am extremely sorry that it seems impossible for him to serve you in this interesting and valuable undertaking.

Faithfully yours,

J. R. A.

〔Yale University records, Peiping National Library, 1931 - 1937, Box: 80, Folder: 831〕

按:该件为录副。

二月十八日

凯欧致函先生,告知其夫人身体状态堪忧,无法如约赴华考察图书馆事业。

February 18, 1937

Dear Mr. Yuan:

It is with great regret that I write to tell you that it will not be possible for me to visit China for the purpose of making the survey of libraries, about which we have had conferences and correspondence.

The Yale Corporation was willing to let me off in spite of the fact that the visit would be in my last year of service to the institution. That last year will, however, be a very busy one for me, and it will be much better for this library if I am here for most of the year at least, instead of being abroad. The main reason, however, is that my wife is not strong, and I am quite unwilling to leave her alone for four or more months that would be necessary to go to China and make the survey. I had originally hoped that she would be able to go to China with me, but I know now that it is not possible.

I have come to this conclusion slowly and painfully, because the trip interests me both as giving a new travel experience, and still more in the possibility of rendering some service to the libraries and the library profession in China, and incidentally to libraries in this country.

I deeply appreciate the honor you have conferred upon me by choosing me as one of the delegates to make the survey, and I thank you for the opportunity to confer with you and for your courteous letters.

Yours very sincerely,

〔Yale University records, Peiping National Library, 1931 -

1937, Box: 80, Folder: 831〕

按:该件为底稿。

二月十九日

晚,朱启钤、梁思成、刘敦桢在朱家设宴,李书华、沈兼士、先生、徐森玉、裘善元、钱桐、叶公超、张叔诚、陶湘、顾颉刚等人受邀与席。〔《顾颉刚日记》卷3,页603〕

　　　按:张叔诚(1898—1995),原名文孚,号忍斋,北平通县人,实业家、收藏家。

二月二十一日

向达覆函先生,告在英查阅、拍照敦煌经卷和太平天国文献的经过,并就平馆人事情况直抒己见。

　　守和先生座右:

　　先后赐示,一一拜悉。一月十四日所汇摄影费壹百贰拾镑陆先令玖辦士,亦已收到,另具收条,随函附陈。兹将数月来工作经遇情形,分别报告如次,敬祈察鉴。

　　(一)看敦煌卷子

　　去岁八月底来英京,九月中旬晤小翟理斯博士,接洽阅看卷子。达当时曾提议,照所编号码,依次阅览。翟氏谓所有卷子,俱已分类,不如依类阅览,先从 Secular text 看起云云。以后即照此进行。唯以翟氏太忙,又常休假,往往一批看完,须待三四日始能另换新者。至一月间才毕三百余号。一月底翟氏见告,谓 Secular text 已将次告竣,此后更看何类? 达谓如果已毕,则佛经等类,亦为所欲阅看者。于是复以印本十余种,及《净名经集解》、《关中疏》等十余种见示。最近翟氏又谓 Secular text 重要者俱已相示,所余不过断篇零片而已。达谓"余初意为对于贵藏作一整个观察,无论整卷断篇,皆愿一一拜读。"故最近又得阅看《左传杜注》、《论语集解》等残篇十余种。唯本周内复放空数日。截至现在,连中亚古文字诸卷在内,曾经过目者将近五百号左右,仏经不到廿卷,其余皆所谓 Secular text 也。翟氏以前虽面允尽量看尽量照,而数月来经过并不甚慷慨;是否故意如此,不得而知。以前翟氏曾要达将其中文书目校阅一过,最近又向达索阅关于敦煌卷子所作之 notes。达当许以于二月底将中文书目校竣,然后再将敦煌卷子之笔记送阅。达阅卷子,每卷俱用卡片记其长短、高度、行数、首尾起讫、讳字、书名、其他载籍中有可参证者,亦偶注片上。将来拟将卡片稍稍整理,即全部送交翟氏,并致请教之意。希望因此能使翟氏态度好转,则前途或可有拨云雾而见青天之一日也。济之先生来英,曾晋谒数次,谈及看敦煌卷子事。达请其晤小翟理斯博士及英伦其他各汉学家时,代致中国学术界对于此事表示好感之意。济之先生允为从旁赞助。是否有效,无从预卜。总之,只有尽其在我者而已。

(二)摄照敦煌卷子

不列颠博物院照相部职员只有两人,工作甚忙。故最初向馆中接洽摄照时,馆中即为介绍 R. B. Fleming 照相馆,担任此事。现照相费已支六十三镑零,照片正负两份共计在一千二百张左右。Positive 以前不用 glossy paper(发光厚纸正张与普通照片不相上下),每张不到一先令,用发光纸折合一先令。现在正负两份俱齐,存在达处者凡七十卷。其所以迟迟未寄者,拟待《切韵》诸重要卷子摄齐,即一并寄回,以快国内学术界心目。今清华方面既迫不及待,当从下周起即将已齐者先行陆续寄回。其余已经请求摄照尚未照齐者,尚有五十卷左右。照相付费收据,下周即行寄陈。

(三)牛津图书馆交换太平天国印本书

此事去岁春夏之间,即同修中诚先生谈过。修氏当时谓牛津中文书复本书目未编成前,尚不能谈论到此。迨秋间全部中文书藏目录编竣,中文复本书目亦为草成。今年二月三日,达曾去牛津一次,晋谒修氏:一为吊其太夫人丧于圣诞节前逝世,年八十六,一即再度接洽交换太平天国印本书。达将平馆送《宋会要》事,向修氏提起,谓此乃平馆诚意交换之表示。又谓牛津图书馆关于中文书方面如有困难,平馆力所能及者,无不竭诚帮忙云云。因牛津图书馆交换复本,俱须经 Curator 会议决定,故复告修氏,请其将平馆愿交换牛津所藏太平天国印本书之意,转陈图书馆长 Dr. Craster,商量定妥后,由修氏将结果径函先生。修氏当时首肯。将来结果为何,尚乞先生随时函告为幸。

（四）Sir Malcolm 铜器照片

此事三月间当可有结果。详情如何，容后续闻。

（五）中国美术流传海外目录

此事当遵命留心。唯购书费是否可以在摄影费中开支，便恳示知为盼。

（六）向 U. C. C. 请求津贴

去岁达为此事曾向王景春先生及郭复初大使谈过。王君谓 U. C. C. 无钱，郭大使谓无能为力，（因大使只有列席权无发言权。）故以后亦不再题。稍迟拟往看使馆刘楷先生，再为打听详情，（刘君牛津出身，因许地山先生之介绍相识。使馆中之翘楚也）。唯 U. C. C. 操纵于 Silcock 一辈人之手。Silcock 为道地的帝国主义鹰犬，对中国留学生善良者欺之，刚正者媚之。达虽一介书生，身无傲骨，然与其向此辈人足恭唯诺，以讨生活，则毋宁反国饿死之为愈耳。至于留此久暂，在达个人本无成见。唯念祖国风尘澒洞，断不敢效叔宝之流，以海外桃园，为避秦之乐土也。平馆下余津贴，亟盼于夏季前拨到，无任感祷之至！所有近来经过，约陈如上。如荷赐予指点，俾得有所遵循，尤为感幸！

此外有一事并愿上闻。南京同学吕叔湘先生，由江苏省政府派至英国，从 Mr. Cowley 治图学。伦敦大学图学院蒐藏各国目录学典籍，约略俱备，而中国方面独付阙如，Mr. Cowley 颇以为憾。吕君意欲代向国内各图学先进，征求著作，转赠该院。而以素无渊源，贸然往请，未免冒昧。因属达向先生转达此意，可否由先生或中华图协会代为征求。此不仅吕君个人之荣，中国图界能因此与英国图机关发生联系，亦未始非计也。吕君聪颖好学，图协会如有事与英国图协会接洽，或调查其他事项，似可即托吕君就近为之。如何之处，统候裁夺。

又最近得家书，知舍妹因工作不力，由先生下手谕开除。海外审此，惭惶万分。比函舍妹，予以申饬，令其"别觅职业。以后处世，更当谨慎忠实，宁死沟壑，断不可阿媚取容，致玷先世清白家风。"至于先生数年来之爱护，以及此次警戒之微意，达及舍妹俱当刻铭书绅，永矢勿谖也。唯达尚有不能已于言者，愿冒万死为先生一陈之。舍妹咎由自取，可不具论。唯平馆同事百余人中，其才果尽足以胜所任乎？其酬果足以尽符其才乎？是不能无疑也。又有受大学专科之训练，入馆数载，而犹朝夕易主，浮沉下僚。徒以未能"留学"于昙华林中，遂致区区四五十元，养一家瞻五口之不足。岂天地之大，遂无容身之所？顾犹恋恋不忍去者，将非为环境静穆，有书可读，故于举世荒荒之中留连此一片净土，虽饭蔬食饮水，亦安之若素也欤？然而安贫乐道是个人之操守；选贤与能，乃当宁之务务。所愿先生于此辈同事，多加爱惜，用如其分。须知此辈中尽有不少洁身自好，力求上进之士；苟假以岁月，俱可成为他日馆中干部人员。夫人才百年养之而不足，一朝毁之而有余！先生素来提携后进，不遗余力，当不以达此言为河汉也。尤有进者。近来英国图书馆之趋势，其注重于人的训练，远过于机械的技能。故极力鼓励馆员读书，养成各部门之专门知识。即以不列颠博物院而言，其各部门之主管人员，莫非斯学知名之士。然其历事，多者至数十年，少亦十数年不等；以渐而升，致有今日。此固由于任事者之能力求上进，为学孜孜，而馆方之能任其从容优游于所学，亦有以致之。今日不列颠博物院干部人员之坚实，固有所自来也。平馆为国家图书馆，其职能在典藏研究，与普通之公共图书馆殊科。徒以国内图事业尚在萌芽，遂致以国家图书馆而兼公共图书馆之任务。此固一时权宜，非久长之计。而年来论者，于所谓编纂员类多侧目而视，不诋为特殊阶级，即视为奢侈品。夫就今日国家危难而言，谓吾辈所学为奢侈品则可。谓为图之特殊阶级，谓为图之奢侈品，则昧于先进国家之近例，不明平馆之使命，固不足与辨也。然而比年来重要干部人员离馆者先后相继。其去也固有其个人不得不去之因，而平馆氛围亦有使其不得不去之势。长此以往，不谋所以改善之方，与平馆将来，可谓有百害而无一利。心所谓危，不敢不为左右一陈之。或谓达盖由于舍妹被裁，以及顾虑将来一己地位，用发此类牢骚之辞。此皮相之谈耳。舍妹既毕业大学，有其专门，何处不可以求生。若达则回国后，即或因批逆鳞，致见摒于门墙之外，自问尚不致饿死。即饿死亦分所当然，乌所用其为未雨之绸缪乎？唯思居平六载，不仅对于平馆，自然生爱护之忱，即与先生朝夕相处，虽格于尊卑，未获少罄胸臆，然何尝无人的感情。是以敢忘忌讳，冒渎尊严。知我辜我，惟在明公。临风神驰，难尽万一。敬颂道安！

　　　　　　　　　　　　　　　　　　向达谨上

　　　　　　　　　　　　　　　　　　二月廿一夜

附汇款收据一纸。

　　　　　〔国家图书馆档案，档案编号 1937-※044-外事 3-002001 至

　　　　　1937-※044-外事 3-002007〕

按：Secular text 即世俗文本。Dr. Craster 即 Sir Herbert H. Edmund
Craster（1879-1959），时任该校博德利图书馆（Bodleian Library）
馆长；Sir Malcolm 即 Sir Neill Malcolm（1869-1953），英国军人，
曾来华；王景春（1882—1956），字兆熙，河北滦县人，北京汇文学
校毕业，1904 年自费赴美留学，归国后历任南京临时政府外交部
参事、京奉铁路管理局及京汉铁路管理局局长等职，1931 年 5 月
任管理中英庚款董事会伦敦购料委员会委员；"刘楷"当作"刘
锴"（1906—1991），字亦锴，广东中山人，牛津大学毕业，后又赴
美国哥伦比亚大学学习，归国后曾任国民政府外交部秘书，时应
任驻英公使；Silcock 即 H. T. Silcock，时应任英国大学中国委员会
名誉主席[①]；Mr. Cowley 即 John D. Cowley（1897-1944），英国图
书馆学家，时任伦敦大学图书馆学主任。向达之妹为向仲，在平
馆中文编目组任职，后改任中文采访组组员。

二月下旬

谢国桢代王献唐与先生商洽山东省立图书馆购《宋会要辑稿》办法。〔《王
献唐年谱长编》，页 685〕

　　　　　按：具体办法为书由上海大东书局直接寄送山东省立图书馆，购
　　　　　书费则直寄平馆，该书款极有可能给以最低折扣。

二月二十四日

毕寿普致信先生，告知密歇根大学校长已经原则性批准其赴中国考察图书
馆事业的请假申请，希望能够在本年秋偕其夫人一同前往中国，另向先生
索要行程计划中涉及各中国图书馆的英文册页，并强调安排合适翻译员的
必要性。

　　　　　　　　　　　　　　　　　　February 24, 1937

----

① 朱乔森编《朱自清全集》第 9 卷，页 110-111。

My dear Dr. Yuan:

A copy of your letter of December 12th to Mr. Milam was sent to me by him and received here a few days since.

I am greatly honored by the invitation from the Library Association of China and hope sincerely that the way may be cleared for its acceptance. I am informed by President Ruthven that there will be no difficulty in securing the necessary leave of absence from the University of Michigan. He hesitates to place the application before the Regents immediately because he wishes to have the actual dates of the leave arranged before he asks the Regents to act on the application. It is understood, however, that there will be no difficulty in securing the necessary leave of absence from this University.

As Dr. Keogh has informed you, he feels it impossible to make the trip. I know he has reached this decision with great reluctance and after very much thought, and that it is based upon purely personal, and not professional, considerations.

I shall have to wait until I hear from Mr. Milam, the Secretary of the American Library Association, what is to be done as a result of Dr. Keogh's decision. Personally, I hope very sincerely that the way may be opened for me to come to China in the autumn. I should like to bring Mrs. Bishop with me, if that also can be arranged, but, of course, I do not suggest that it is impossible for me to come without her.

I have looked over the itinerary, which interests me very greatly. You will do me a favor if you will send me any material in English on the libraries to be seen in the different cities. Of course I have access to a good deal of material in this Library.

Dr. Keogh's observation about the necessity of an interpreter and a secretary were the result of conversations which we held last autumn in New Haven. I feel that he is absolutely correct about the necessity for some such arrangement. If the visit is to have any real value for American and Chinese libraries, it is inevitable that assistance in overcoming the difficulties of language and of assembling materials must be provided. In fact, my chief hesitation about making the trip was a doubt as to whether, in my entire ignorance of the Chinese language, I could be of any real service to my Chinese colleagues. I have been persuaded by members of our faculty here, who have been much in China and Japan, that, with the right kind of interpreter, this difficulty can be overcome.

With good wishes and warm regards,

Faithfully yours,

W. W. B.

Librarian

〔Yale University records, Peiping National Library, 1931－1937, Box: 80, Folder: 831〕

按:此件为副本,抄送给凯欧,并于 2 月 25 日送达耶鲁大学图书馆。

二月二十五日

先生南下赴京。〔《世界日报》,1937 年 3 月 14 日,第 7 版〕

按:先生将出席中央图书馆建筑设计委员会会议,并向教部报告馆务。

二月二十七日　苏州

晚,王世杰、罗家伦、马衡、先生等乘京沪快车抵达苏州,宿花园饭店。〔《苏州明报》,1937 年 2 月 28 日,第 6 版〕

二月二十八日

晨,王世杰、罗家伦、马衡、先生等赴沧浪亭,参观吴中文献展览会。〔《苏州明报》,1937 年 2 月 28 日,第 6 版〕

中午,先生乘车转沪。〔《大公报》(上海),1937 年 3 月 1 日,第 4 版〕

三月一日

顾颉刚致函先生,为程枕霞事。〔《顾颉刚日记》卷 3,页 613〕

按:程枕霞,雕塑家,3 月 5 日,假中南海怀仁堂举办蜡像展①,顾颉刚可能请先生协助办展或查阅平馆文献资料。

――――――――――――

① 《华北日报》,1937 年 3 月 6 日,第 6 版。

三月二日

叶渭清覆函先生,就《国藏善本丛刊》拟目提出自己不同的意见。

守和馆长先生阁下:

二月十九日奉读十六日还教及所附《国藏善本丛书》拟目,敬悉。清惟前人刻丛书多系小品零种,或就全书中抽印(案此已是类书节钞原著之演变),故卷帙繁重之书,例所不收,然后来如《守山阁丛书》、《粤雅堂丛书》、《海山仙馆丛书》等已不用此例。最近,如《畿辅丛书》、《适园丛书》所刻书多可单行,而前年商务印书馆代印之《四库珍本》书尽有钜帙(其实《四库全书》即是大丛书,何尝拘之卷帙之多少)。即今刻所选择,当以希见、重要、完备三者为标准。小品、零种、希见有之,若重要、完备不如钜帙多矣。清谓如《通典》、《通志》、《通考》、《山堂考索》、《朱子文集》、《文苑英华》诸书,馆藏宋元明刻诸古本不妨列入,一则此类书极关重要,沾溉艺林。二则小品书好事者力所能逮,大部书非有国家政府力量即不能刻。往往以一部书占全书卷数十分之七八少刻,便与丛书名实不称,故常置而不刻,实则书之流传,大部则钞刻并难,容易湮没。其著者如《旧五代史》,宋刻山阴祁氏有之,兵乱遂落水(见《南雷集》)。商务印书馆印旧本《廿四史》,广征是书逾二年而无应者(闻扬州有半部,又沪报某君云广西有金刻本,然商务印书馆卒不得之)。此其原因,不外于国家未刊板、私家无力,仅赖当时千百部印本,辗转藏贮,经过水火刀兵风雨诸劫,归于沦失而后已,此真可为痛心之事。吾曹既知其所以然,若又蹈常袭故,先小品零种而后鸿篇钜制,则中国古书之如《旧五代史》者多矣。吾乡唐与政著书数百卷,今惟经世图谱尚有残宋刻,其文集则张作楠辑存数卷耳,失今不刻,悔将无时。清往在馆时私与徐森玉先生言而痛之,尚幸先生主持本馆,又森玉先生长故宫,傅藏园、李木斋、卢慎之诸先生多有藏书,何不向之假出,或即与合刊,为较大规模之印书,悉取希见、重要、完备各古本,陆续景行,一为前人弥此缺憾,则先生嘉惠后学之心,宁有涯涘。清无任踊跃,赞叹之至。春寒,惟为道珍厚。

渭清鞠躬

三月二日

〔国家图书馆档案,档案编号 1943-※041-编印 2-001058 至 1943-※041-编印 2-001061〕

按:"唐与政"即唐仲友(1135—1188),字与政,南宋文学家、政治家。

三月五日　南京

中午,傅斯年在中央研究院设宴,叶恭绰、李四光、金毓黻、先生、董作宾、徐中舒、梁思永与席。〔《顾颉刚日记》卷3,页615〕

三月六日

晚,陈诚设宴,梅贻琦、王世杰、翁文灏、先生、何廉、傅斯年等人受邀与席,其间学界同仁均对张学良、杨虎城发动的西安事变持负面态度,支持南京国民政府彻底解决遗留问题。〔《陈诚先生日记》(一),台北:"国史馆"、"中央研究院"近代史研究所,2015年,页123〕

按:3月3日,蒋介石委派陈诚改编东北军。

三月七日

下午二时,北平图书馆协会假师大第一附小美术馆举行春季大会,何日章、严文郁、田洪都、冯陈祖怡、李文裿、莫余敏卿、裘开明等人参加,严文郁任会议主席,改选本年度职员,先生、何日章、李文裿、严文郁、冯陈祖怡、田洪都、莫余敏卿当选执行委员。〔《华北日报》,1937年3月8日,第9版〕

按:先生时在南京,并未出席。

三月八日

国会图书馆致函先生,客岁平馆寄出的六种出版物仍有两种尚未收到,并告寄送费用将和大同书店账单一并处理。

March 8, 1937

Dear Sir:

For the Librarian, I beg to acknowledge your letter of October 20, 1936, - a photostat negative of which is enclosed, - regarding six items listed therein which you stated would be bound by the Peking Union Bookstore and forwarded to the Library of Congress as a gift from you.

The Librarian appreciates very much the courtesy and friendly interest shown by you in presenting these volumes.

The delay in our response, however, has been due to the fact that, to date, the Division of Accessions has record of the receipt of but four of the six items listed. As you will perceive, the Chief of our Division of

Accessions, Mr. Blanchard, has for convenience, designated the items on your letter of October 20 by the letters a to f, inclusive. Bound copies of items b, c, e, and f have been received, and on February 6, 1937, an engraved acknowledgment was forwarded to you for these four items. Items a and d have not as yet been received apparently. Is it possible that they are still in the bindery and have not been forwarded to us?

In connection with this matter, Mr. Blanchard notes that the Library has several unpaid bills from the Peking Union Bookstore and as far as he can discover, after consultation with Dr. Hummel, the charges for the carriage and binding of the six items listed by you have not been billed to us by the Bookstore.

> Very truly yours,
> Acting Secretary of the Library

〔Librarian of Congress, Putnam Archives, Special File, China: National Library 1930—1939〕

按:其中未收到的 a 和 d 应为《国立北平图书馆善本书目乙编》和《国立北平图书馆方志目录二编》,参见本年 7 月 1 日国会图书馆函。此件为录副。

三月十二日

先生北返抵平。〔《中华图书馆协会会报》第 12 卷第 5 期,1937 年 4 月,页 22〕

三月十六日

先生致信王重民,告知管理中英庚款董事会补助影摄敦煌卷子等事。

有三吾弟:

前接二月廿一日及廿八日手书,拜悉种种。燉煌卷子久未寄平,清华曾催问数次,请从速办理。清华共担任三千元,现已照出若干叶,希至相当时期开一详单寄来,以便转交清华。英庚款董事会近议决补助本馆八千元,专作影摄敦煌卷子之用,前选之十五种拟交商务影印者,除《还冤记》《楚辞音》已有董授经之玻璃版现存馆中无庸再照外,其余者可陆续制玻璃版以便将来付印,每书题跋拟印于卷首作为叙录此事务须在离巴黎以前办妥为要即足下之一大成绩也。又,向达近向中基会申请奖学金,胡适之甚帮忙,大概可有希望,如渠得此奖金按章须专作研究不兼他事即不能为馆中主持摄影事,届时拟请吾弟赴英继任其事,并可在英庚款中拨付壹佰六十磅作生活费,极盼能将英国所藏之经卷作一澈底之研究。因往往一书分散两地,如留英一年或有重要之发现也,但必须在法工作完毕方能赴英。向君之事亦须于七月间结束也。余俟再函,顺颂大安。

同礼顿首
三月十六日

天主教史料照费,可在清华费内开支,英庚款则以燉煌为限。

为东方文化作提要事,傅孟真极表不满,屡屡言之,务设法结束,恐于将来作事有碍也。此次英庚款补助八千元,傅君甚帮忙也。

〔袁同礼家人提供〕

按:"东方文化"应指日本东方文化事业总委员会,平馆数位馆员或直接参与或协助该所编纂《续修四库提要》。王重民与之确有往来,可参见《目加田诚"北平日记"》①,先生数次写信规劝其立刻结束该项工作。

三月十七日

史蒂文斯致函先生,告知凯欧决定取消中国之行,毕寿普拟偕夫人访华。

March 17, 1937

Dear Mr. Yuan:

On arrival in New York Mr. Gunn took up with me the question stated in your letter of February 6 concerning method of payment to the one or two American librarians who are to visit China during the coming year under the grant of the Foundation to the National Library of Peiping. Our Comptroller reports that the money can be paid either through this office or the one in Shanghai in such amounts as are needed in either currency. It will be sufficient if you will send a letter to the Comptroller here, Mr. George J. Beal, requesting advance to Dr. Bishop and to any other man selected as his companion on the mission.

My last news is that Mr. Keogh will not make the journey. I know

---

① 九州大学中国文学会编《目加田诚"北平日记":一九三〇年代の北京学术交流》,福冈市:中国书店,2019年,页124。

from Dr. Bishop that you have been asked to approve the visit by himself alone and that the total appropriation be made available to cover also the travel of Mrs. Bishop. This matter is under approval of the American Library Association and yourself. You will have word on the question from Mr. Milam, Secretary of the Association.

I am reporting to both Mr. Milam and Dr. Bishop by giving copies of this letter to you so that they are now informed of the means of secure funds for expense incurred before departure from this country.

Sincerely yours,

David H. Stevens

〔Rockefeller Foundation. Series 601: China; Subseries 601.R: China-Humanities and Arts. Box 47. Folder 389〕

三月二十九日

上午十时,平馆委员会召开第二十五次会议,陈垣、孙洪芬、胡适、傅斯年、先生出席,傅斯年为主席,先生记录。会议报告事项如下:

(一)平馆送最近三月馆务报告,议决准予备案。

(二)管理中英庚款董事会补助八千元,专作影照及选印英法所藏敦煌写本案,议决应尽量影照,关于选印之古佚书由平馆先拟一书目,再请专家审核。

(三)委托商务印书馆影印《国藏善本丛刊》案,议决商务送来所拟之合同草案,除第二条之款"如底本模糊不易摄照者亦删除之"应改为"凡底本模糊不易摄照者可改精校排印"外,照草案通过,交平馆征询其他参加机关之意见后再函覆商务印书馆。

(四)洛克菲勒基金会捐赠新式照书机案,议决准予备案并由馆方函谢。

讨论事项如下:

(一)平馆提议在下年度试办职员福利储金案,议决修正通过,准予试办。

(二)平馆提议下年度预算案议决通过经常费十四万五千元,中文购书费六万元,西文购书费美金三万元,由委员会函请中基会列入下年度预算。

(三)议决由委员会函请教育部自下年度起在国家文化事业费预算项下每年拨付购书费两万元。

(四)平馆提议美国 Departmental Bank 倒闭后,该行除陆续偿还平馆欠款百分之八十外,尚欠美金三百元一角七分,应如何办理案,议决在本馆账目上仍保留该账户名目,其资产改列一元,将来该行如能继续偿还,仍作为购置西文书之用。

十二时散会。〔《北京图书馆馆史资料汇编(1909-1949)》,页 354-355〕

三月三十日

先生致信王重民,与其商洽影印法藏敦煌经卷办法并谈管理中英庚款董事会、中基会补助申请细节等事。

友三吾弟左右:

顷接三月十四日来书,详悉种种。兹分别答覆如左,

(一)丛书交商务照相石印,可不用玻璃版,即用普通照相片即可翻印,请再与法国方面一商,此项成本不宜过钜。全书叶数若干、约费若干,请详悉估计示知。

(二)英庚款补助之款应尽量影照,盖下年能否得款殊有问题。如能在最近三个月内照二千五百张或三千张,最所盼望因照的多,下年度请款较易。凡关于韵书或字书者一律摄照,每张需费若干,并希示知。总之法国所藏重要之卷子连伯希和自藏者在内一律照一复本,以供本国人士之研究,其不重要者只好暂时割爱,以余款继续在英摄照。

(三)向君得中基会历史补助费,本年八月以后需专事研究,即请足下往英伦继续主持其事,前已函达。到英后可有每月十六磅之补助,此款能否全数在英庚款内拨付尚有问题,该会颇愿全数用于影照而不补助生活费,兄自当尽量设法。足下本年度事务既繁,请暂停著作,以便多经理照相之事。又在外身体最要紧,勿过累,应多休息为要。

(四)下年度 1938-1939 如愿留英或留法,可设法谋一中基会之历史补助费本年第一次发给,须 1938 年二月间请求。盖向君所得者仅限一年,不能继续。明年足下亦甚有希望也研究范围以史学为主。此事取决于傅梦真,大著可先寄一份于彼,并随时与之通讯是荷。渠对代东方作提要甚不满,屡屡言之。

(五)清华应得之照片,屡来询问,请从速多寄。如该校之款三千元用尽时,可早日函示,当再接给或能再拨少许,已竟全功。

(六)巴黎卷子总目,应设法完成之,将来携回北平印刷亦可。此目出版稍缓一二年,想法国方面亦同意也。此次哈佛藏书目录即由裴

君携来北平排印。

(七)刘女士来信亦收到,渠之生活费如何,甚以为念。将来结婚后在返国以前,万不可有小孩,否则不但经费愈加拮据,而无女仆大人亦受罪不浅,望注意是荷。顺颂旅安。

袁同礼顿首
三月三十日

适之言有一部《朱英集》(一部诗选)可加入丛书,不知在巴黎抑在英伦,请一查。又《历代三宝记》是否为《历代法宝记》之误?《善本丛书》已赠伯希和壹部,由交换局寄,请转告。

陆翔来函谓前译之巴黎敦煌写本书目至 3511 号而止,以后之续目如已编就能否传钞一份,俾继续翻译云云。按陆君前译之目错误甚多,不如由尊处编一中文总目录,在馆刊发表,较为便利。如何之处,希函告。

〔中国书店·海淀,四册〕

按:"刘女士"即刘修业,1937 年 4 月 10 日,王、刘二人在巴黎结婚。《朱英集》即《珠英集》,唐代崔融辑,选编珠英学士的诗作,该书确为敦煌经卷残卷,分藏于法国国家图书馆和大英博物馆,前者编号为"伯 3771",后者编号为"斯 2717",王重民在《敦煌古籍叙录》第 5 卷有较为详尽的记述。

是年春

国立中央图书馆筹备处成立建筑委员会,由朱家骅、何廉、段锡朋、罗家伦、雷震、钱端升、先生、蒋复璁等任委员,梁思成为专门委员。〔《世界日报》,1937 年 5 月 23 日,第 6 版〕

按:其馆址定于国府路,工程预算为一百五十万元,其中一百万为建筑,其余则为庭园、暖气、锅炉、电灯、通风、防火、卫生等设备费用。该委员会首先征集建筑图案,应征者共十七人。戴季陶、何廉、先生为初审委员。

国际古物会议定于七月二十日在瑞士举行,先生本被派为代表参见,但因为事务太忙,国民政府改派在英国讲学的李济前往参加。〔《大公报》(天津),1937 年 4 月 21 日,第 4 版〕

四月一日

先生致信陈垣,附上王重民在法影照敦煌写经照片清单,请其审定选择影印之文献。

援庵先生惠鉴：

兹送上燉煌照片十四种_{见附单}，何者可印，何者可删，请审定示复，俾有遵循，无任感荷。顺候著祺。

同礼顿首

四月一日

王重民《巴黎燉煌残卷叙录》可供参考。

〔《陈垣来往书信集》，页619〕

按：《巴黎燉煌残卷叙录》即《巴黎敦煌残卷叙录》，1935 年 5 月 23 日起在《大公报·图书副刊》不定期连载，随后又发表在《图书季刊》（中文本）。

四月二日

先生致信张元济，因平馆编《〈永乐大典〉引用书目录》拟借其收藏《大典》一册。

菊生先生尊鉴：

兹有恳者，敝馆现正编辑《永乐大典引用书目录》，兹有卷九八一（支韵《小儿证治》十四）不识仍在高斋否？敝馆现拟奉借录副，藉供研考。万一原书出让，未审现归何人？如能忆及，并祈示知，以便设法借钞。费神之处，无任感谢。专此奉达，静候台祺。

晚袁同礼拜启

四月二日

〔《张元济全集》第 3 卷，2 页〕

先生致信傅斯年，告知平馆委员会各委员联署向教育部申请购书费，请其签字并转交。

孟真吾兄：

关于委员会请求教部拨给购书费之公函，在平委员业已签署。兹寄上，请签字盖章后送交梦麟先生，或寄梅先生签署后径交王部长，并盼切实说项为感。留交两件一并奉还。顺颂大安。

弟袁同礼顿首

四月二日

托张公权之事已办否？

〔国立北平图书馆用笺。台北"中央研究院"历史语言研究所傅
斯年图书馆，"史语所档案"，元459-4-3〕

四月三日

晚，王静如在承华园设宴，李书华、李麟玉、徐旭生、先生、吴世昌、曾觉之、王
兰亭、何君、范廉清、孙楷第、顾颉刚等人受邀与席。〔《顾颉刚日记》卷3，页626〕

四月五日

先生致信凯欧，就其无法来华考察表示遗憾。

April 5, 1937

My dear Dr. Keogh:

It is with great disappointment that we learn you are unable to accept the invitation of the Library Association of China to come over to this country for a survey trip. All of my colleagues in the Chinese library field learned of your decision with much regret and wish to join me in sending their best wishes both to you and Mrs. Keogh.

With warmest regards,

Yours very sincerely,

T. L. Yuan

Acting Director

〔国立北平图书馆英文信纸。Yale University records, Peiping National Library, 1931–1937, Box: 80, Folder: 831〕

按：此件为打字稿，落款处为先生签名，该于5月5日送达耶鲁大
学图书馆。

先生致信米来牟，就毕寿普及其夫人来华费用的来源略作介绍，并邀请其
代替凯欧赴华考察。

April 5, 1937

My dear Dr. Milam:

I gratefully acknowledge the receipt of your letter of Feb. 25. We are pleased to learn that Dr. Bishop has had assurances from President Ruthven that a leave will be granted in the autumn and that he hopes to be able to accept our invitation. I have also had word from Dr. Bishop to this effect.

As soon as we learned from Dr. Keogh that he was unable to accept the invitation, I wrote you on March 20 to ascertain whether it would be possible for you to take this trip in the place of Dr. Keogh. This letter is on the way to you and we are looking forward to your favorable reply.

Thank you for your suggestion as to include Mrs. Bishop in the party. I am writing to Dr. Bishop to-day extending our invitation also to his wife. Copy of my letter is enclosed herewith for your information.

In response to your inquiry regarding some details of the proposed trip, I wish to reiterate some of the points raised in my previous letter. As the appropriation of $2,000 was granted by the Rockefeller Foundation to the Chinese Library Association, the Association will submit to the Foundation an itemized statement of all the expenses incurred in connection with Dr. Bishop's visit. In addition to transportation and incidentals to and from China, all other expenses, travel, hotel, meals, secretarial and stenographic services will be provided by the Association. Although the grant of the Rockefeller Foundation is not sufficient to cover all these expenses, we have raised $3,000 locally which, we trust, will make the entire trip comfortable and interesting. As far as Dr. Bishop and his party are concerned, they need not have to spend anything from the time they set foot on Chinese soil until they leave.

We have asked the American Express Co. to make reservations of first-class accommodation to Dr. and Mrs. Bishop on S. S. President Jefferson of the American Mail Line leaving Seattle September 11th and arriving Shanghai September 28th. The American Express Co. has also been instructed to pay Dr. and Mrs. Bishop's railroad fares from Ann Arbor (or any other city Dr. Bishop may designate) to Seattle including sleepers, meals and tips.

I trust this letter answers the questions raised in your letter. If there is any further information you wish to know, please do not hesitate to let me hear further from you.

With warmest regards, I remain,

Yours sincerely,

T. L. Yuan

Chairman,

Executive Board

〔Rockefeller Foundation. Series 601: China; Subseries 601.R: China-Humanities and Arts. Box 47. Folder 389〕

按：该件为副本，抄送给史蒂文斯，落款处为先生签名。

四月六日

先生致信傅斯年，请史语所捐助博物馆协会加入中国学术团体联合会所须建筑费。

梦真吾兄：

梦麟先生昨已返平，致教部之函，请仍寄下以便请其签署也，费神至感。又博物馆协会加入中国学术团体联合会所须缴八百元之建筑费，而为日甚迫，除由此间已凑若干外，拟请慨然捐助贰百元幸勿再减，即存尊处。弟大约十日后因中央图书馆建筑事仍需晋京也。顺颂大安。

弟袁同礼顿首

四月六日

〔国立北平图书馆用笺。台北"中央研究院"历史语言研究所傅斯年图书馆，"史语所档案"，元459-4-1〕

先生致信毕寿普，告知已为其和其夫人预订来华船票。

April 6, 1937

My dear Dr. Bishop:

We have arranged with the American Express Co. to make reservations of a first-class cabin for you and Mrs. Bishop on S. S. President Jefferson leaving Seattle September 11th and arriving Shanghai September 28. The American Express Co. has also been instructed to pay your and Mrs. Bishop's railroad fares from Ann Arbor (or any other city you may designate) to Seattle including sleepers, meals and tips.

You will arrive in China at the best time of the year and we shall arrange to enable you to be in the Capital on October 10th which as you know is our National Holiday.

　　I shall inform you later on what steamers are to be available in December for your return trip. Perhaps you may like to arrange to be back at Ann Arbor for Christmas.

Yours sincerely,

T. L. Yuan

Chairman,

Executive Board

　　〔Rockefeller Foundation. Series 601: China; Subseries 601.R: China-Humanities and Arts. Box 47. Folder 389〕

　　按：该件为副本，抄送给史蒂文斯，落款处为先生签名。

张元济覆函先生，告前信所询商务印书馆藏一册《永乐大典》去向及现有卷册。

　　奉四月二日手教，谨诵悉。承询散藏《永乐大典》四册，前岁以资用告竭，货于周君叔弢。其卷数及隶属何韵，均不复记忆，可就近一询便知。商馆藏二十一册无"支韵"也。故宫所藏《唐音统签》为仅存孤本，颇思列入《国藏善本丛书》。闻中分刻本、写本两部分，拟乞饬检其中版印及抄笔最不佳者寄示数册，以便审定可否，企盼无似。弟因患感冒，白下之行迟迟未果。斐云、刚主两君均问候。

廿六年四月六日

〔《张元济全集》第3卷，页2-3〕

四月七日

先生偕馆员胡英赴济宁调查当地图书馆事业。〔《中华图书馆协会会报》第12卷第5期，页22；《益世报》（北平），1937年4月11日，第8版〕

　　按：华北农村建设协进会拟以济宁为中心推进该会工作，欲在此地设立相当规模的图书馆，请先生莅临指导。先生建议将济宁县政府之大礼堂改建为图书馆舍，该馆预计7月1日开馆，平馆拟支援相当数量的书籍。

四月十日①

先生乘车返平，某记者来访，先生略谓前往济宁协助华北农村建设委员会

---

① 此次先生返平日期，另有14日之说，参见《益世报》，1937年4月15日，第8版；《大公报》，1937年4月27日，第10版；《中华图书馆协会会报》第12卷第5期，页22。笔者倾向于4月10日回平，特此说明。

筹设图书馆之起因、经费及人员等细节。〔《益世报》(北平),1937 年 4 月 11 日,第 8 版〕

四月十三日

中午十二时,北平地区十二家文化教育机关团体假清华同学会设宴款待傅作义,蒋梦麟、胡适、梅贻琦、李蒸、陆志韦、沈兼士、李麟玉、查良钊、先生、李书华、孙洪芬等十余人到场,席间傅作义介绍绥蒙近况并谈蒙人生活习俗等,全体人员摄影留念。约三时许,尽欢而散。〔《华北日报》,1937 年 4 月 14 日,第 9 版〕

先生致信史蒂文斯,建议米来牟替代凯欧来华访问,并告知洛克菲勒基金会可通过其上海办公室拨付资助款。

April 13, 1937

Dear Dr. Stevens:

I beg to acknowledge the receipt of your letter of March 17th and to thank you for your kindness in arranging the payment of the ＄3,000 appropriation granted last May.

We are extremely sorry that Dr. Keogh was unable to make his visit to China this fall. However, I have written to Dr. Milam suggesting that he take this trip in the place of Dr. Keogh. For your information, I am enclosing copies of my letters to Dr. Milam and to Dr. Bishop.

It would be more convenient to us if your Comptroller could pay the amount through your office in Shanghai. Should it meet your approval, will you hand the enclosed letter to your Comptroller?

I wish to take this opportunity to thank you once more for your assistance in financing the visit of American librarians to China which will no doubt prove beneficial to both parties.

With assurances of my high appreciation of your interest,

Your sincerely,

T. L. Yuan

Acting Director

〔国立北平图书馆英文信纸。Rockefeller Foundation. Series 601: China; Subseries 601.R: China-Humanities and Arts. Box 47. Folder 389〕

按:此件为打字稿,落款处为先生签名,于 5 月 10 日送达。

先生致信 George J. Beal,希望由洛克菲勒基金会驻沪办事处拨付该会赞助美国图书馆专家访华费用。

April 13, 1937

Mr. George J. Beal

Comptroller

Rockefeller Foundation

49 W. 49th street

New York City

Dear Sir:

We have learned from Dr. Stevens that the $3,000 appropriation granted to the National Library of Peiping last May can be paid either through your head office in New York or the one in Shanghai. In reply, I am writing to Dr. Stevens suggesting that the money be paid through your Shanghai office.

If my suggestion meets the approval of Dr. Stevens, will you kindly arrange the payment through your Shanghai office and inform Dr. Grant in Shanghai that we should like to receive the amount in U. S. currency.

Thanking you for your attention,

Yours very truly,

T. L. Yuan

Acting Director

〔国立北平图书馆英文信纸。Rockefeller Foundation. Series 601: China; Subseries 601.R: China-Humanities and Arts. Box 47. Folder 389〕

按:Dr. Grant 即 John B. Grant(1890-1962),生于宁波,中文名兰安生,1917 年获密歇根大学医学学位,1918 年起在洛克菲勒基金会国际医学部任职,后赴华出任北平协和医学院卫生学教授[1],1934 年回到该基金会协助发展各类与中国相关项目,时任驻沪办事处主任。此件为打字稿,落款处为先生签名。

———————————

[1]《私立北平医学院简章》,1930 年,页 23。

四月十四日

平馆向中央古物保管委员会发出公函,现因国立中央博物院拟在洛阳主持采掘工作,平馆拟即停止进行采掘,并将所藏此项材料供给该院参考,执照奉还内政部,请予缴销。先生具名并钤馆章。〔台北"国史馆",〈国立北平图书馆采掘洛阳汉石经残石请领执照〉,典藏号 026-011000-0053〕

按:4 月 30 日,内政部指令,平馆呈件均悉,准予核销。

四月十七日

先生致信陈垣,请其归还李盛铎书目并催圈选王重民寄来法藏敦煌写经照片。

援庵先生:

李木斋书目兹有所需,请掷交去人带下。又前寄上之燉煌照片,何者可印,何者不印,并请赐示,俾有遵循为感。暑假中令媛实习事,拟请在图书馆协会实习两月或壹月,由渠自定。中南海增福堂。请转告是荷。顺颂大安。

同礼顿首

十七

〔《陈垣来往书信集》,页 619-620〕

按:"令媛"应指陈慈,1918 年出生。此信暂系于此。

先生致信国会图书馆(馆长),订购该馆图书分类法的相关书籍和册页四套。

April 17, 1937

Dear Sir:

As this Library has adopted the Library of Congress scheme of classification, we wish to place with you a standing order for four copies of each of the following published since January 1937.

L. C. Classification Scheme. (Including revised as well as new editions)

Other publications concerning L. C. Classification.

L. C. Subjects Headings as well as supplements.

Other publications concerning cataloguing of various subjects, such as maps, music, manuscripts, etc.

We shall appreciate highly if you will send them to us as soon as they appear.

Please supply us the following together with bill in duplicate copies:

4　*Guide to the cataloguing of the serial publications of societies and institutions*, by H. W. Pierson. (pub. by your Catalog Division)

4　*Guide to the Cataloguing of Periodicals*, prepared by M. W. MacNair. Latest edition. (pub. by your Catalog Division)

4　*Notes on the Cataloguing, care and classification of maps and atlas*, by your Map Division.

1　*Popular names of Federal statutes*, by Division of Documents.

1　*List of series of publications for which cards are in stock*, by Card Division. Latest edition.

1　*List of atlases and maps applicable to the World War*, comp. by P. L. Phillips. (Division of Maps)

Thank you very much for your kind attention,

Yours very truly,

T. L. Yuan

Acting Director

〔国立北平图书馆英文信纸。Library of Congress, Putnam Archives, Special Files, China: National Library 1930-1939〕

按:此件为打字稿,落款处为先生签名,于5月9日送达国会图书馆秘书办公室。

四月二十日

先生致信伯希和,告知已按其前请与故宫博物院商洽影照《钦定石渠宝笈续编》中对存于淳化轩画作的记述,而该书的《续编》和《三编》因为索引未能完成导致尚未付印,另寄上《平馆法文馆藏目录》以便获赠更多但不重复的法文出版品,此外告知通过南京国际交换局寄上四种书籍。

April 20, 1937

Prof. Paul Pelliot

Musée d'Enneri

59 Avenue Foch

Paris, France

Dear Prof. Pelliot:

I am very much delighted to have your letter of March 31.

I am arranging with the Palace Museum to have a copy made for you of that portion of the 石渠宝笈（二编）which describes paintings preserved under Ch'ien-lung in the 淳化轩. As the Palace Museum does not have a photostat outfit, it will be reproduced by the blue-print process.

The Palace Museum has made plans to publish a complete edition of the second and third parts of the *Shih ch'u pao chi*. The reason why the MS. has not yet been sent to the printer is because of the fact that the index has not yet been completed.

We feel much obliged to you for your courtesy in keeping us in mind in connexion with the French books which your Government intends to distribute abroad. This action will strengthen the French section of our collections. Please accept our warmest thanks for remembering us in this way. In order to facilitate your work, we are sending you a copy of our *"Catalogue du fonds Française"*.

We have recently sent to you through the Bureau of International Exchange at Nanking the following works for your personal use:

Tsungshu of the National Library of Peiping（国立北平图书馆善本丛书）70 vols.

Diaries of Li Ts'u Ming（越缦堂日记补）13 vols.

*Hsiou-fu-ch*ü *chi*（休复居集）4 vols.

Compendium of Prayers of Repentance（慈悲道场忏法）1 vol.

A copy each of these works has also been sent to the Institut des Hautes Etudes Chinoises and the Ecole des Langues Orientales Vivantes, through the Bibliothèque Nationale at Paris.

With cordial regards,

Your very sincerely,

T. L. Yuan

Acting Director

〔国立北平图书馆英文信纸。法兰西学院图书馆藏档案〕

按：1918年，《石渠宝笈》由商务印书馆石印出版；因受抗日战争全面爆发影响，《钦定石渠宝笈续编》等并未如期刊印。《越缦堂日记补》原稿藏于平馆，1936年10月商务印书馆初版；《休复居集》，版本待考，因1936年出版者既有4册本又有2册本；《慈悲道场忏法》应指范成西安开元寺所得北宋刻本，后由傅增湘、徐森玉、张允亮、周叔弢、赵万里等人集资，1936年秋珂罗版影印之本。Hautes Etudes Chinoises 即 Institut des hautes études chinoises（巴黎中国学院），Ecole des Langues Orientales Vivantes 即 École nationale des langues orientales vivantes（国立东方语言学院）。此件为打字稿，落款处为先生签名。

四月二十二日

先生乘沪平线南下赴京。〔《中华图书馆协会会报》第12卷第5期，页22〕

按：先生先在南京商讨中央图书馆建筑事宜，后赴沪列席中基会年会报告馆务。

四月二十七日

王云五致函先生，告知张元济检视各机构存沪书籍后所提《国藏善本丛刊》拣选条件并谈合同修改细节。

守和先生大鉴：

敬启者，国藏善本经张菊翁先后就京沪两地所藏及北京大学寄沪各种详加检阅，现已结束。因书名国藏善本视私家刊印丛书可以随意掇拾者有所不同，内容外观均不能不格外郑重，故先假定左列之消极条件，凡具此项条件之一者，均拟撤出，计开：

（一）冷僻纤小或范围甚隘、卷帙过少之书；

（二）抄本非宋元人手笔，或明清抄而非依宋元写工甚精之本；

（三）残本非孤本，或多配通常本，或抄配粗率者。

基于上开办法拟选定景印之书四十四种，除已点或可约估叶数者三十九种共五万七千四百三十七叶外，其余五种假定为五六千叶，约得六万三千叶，适符千册之数。兹将此间选定书目附呈二分，敬祈核夺示覆，并为节省时日起见，另以副本各一分就近寄交马叔平、傅孟真两先生鉴核。又昨奉大示，知合同草案已荷赞同，惟于第二条末句"如有底本模糊不易摄照者亦删除之"一段将"亦删除之"四字改为"精校排印"。查敝处此次拟选之书对于有价值而难得者，虽间有模糊之处亦经勉用，且所选五十种已足千册之数，故拟维持原案或径将该末段完全删去。查本丛书全部景印，如换入一二排印之本，似有损及全书之声价，故菊翁与弟之意均以不加入排印者为宜。至将来如有重要之书，因底本模糊不便景印者，或可精校排印另案办理，尊意以为如何，即祈核示，以便正式订约。又敝处所选书目是否可用，亦乞早日核示，其中未点叶数各书，除故宫及中央研究院二处由敝馆径函点明见示外，所有属于贵馆及北京大学者，并乞将叶数开示，以便估计成本，早日筹备预约也。匆匆，即颂公绥。

王云五

二十六年四月二十七日

〔商务印书馆编审部启事用笺。国家图书馆档案，档案编号1933-※040-编印1-002023至1933-※040-编印1-002026〕

按：此件为打印稿，落款处为其签名。

四月二十九日

教育部秘书处致函先生，令查北方支社情况。

径密启者：

兹据密报共产党在平成立红中北方支社，社址设于中国大学，其内部分为政训、情报、联络、指导四组，其干部人员黄振河（北平图书馆职员）已分头向各校联络左倾青年参加，并以民先队及旧学联作其外围组织等语。据报前情，事属反动，亟应严加防范。奉谕密达，查照注意为荷。此致
袁副馆长守和

教育部秘书处启

廿六年四月廿九日

〔《北京图书馆馆史资料汇编(1909-1949)》，页442〕

按：查《国立北平图书馆职员录》(1936年、1937年)无此人，应属误传，极有可能为北平某图书馆职员。

四月

《教育部第二次全国美术展览会专刊》刊登先生两篇文章,分别题为《全国美术展览会陈列之版画书》、《我国艺术品流落欧美之情况》。〔《教育部第二次全国美术展览会专刊》,1937年4月,页89—91,131—137〕

　　　　按:4月1日,第二次全国美术展览会正式开展,先生曾被函聘为编辑委员。① 另,《全国美术展览会陈列之版画书》失收于《袁同礼文集》。

五月二日　上海

南京工程参考图书馆与上海市博物馆合办铁路工程展览会,先生以工程参考图书馆馆长身份与上海博物馆馆长胡肇椿招待各界人士,到场者有铁道部谢奋程司长、林子峰(俞鸿钧市长代表)等数百人。会上,先生致辞,大意如下:

　　　　一般图书馆往往只注意书不注意图,现代教育之趋势,已由学校教育而至自动式的教育,故于图颇重要。此在工程图书馆更见需要,然看图尚不如看实物,看实物则需博物馆,学校与图书馆与博物馆实三位一体。南京工程参考图书馆所办特览,前有航空展览会、无线电展览会、科学仪器展览会,此亦第四次,今得各界人士热心赞助,并听得中央铁路五年计划,深为庆幸。中央既有计划,学术机关可尽量供给材料,中央计划与学术机关实可打成一片。

　　　　　　　　　　　　　　　　　　　　〔《申报》,1937年5月3日,第13版〕

　　　　按:谢奋程(1898—1941),字英士,广东梅县人,清华学校毕业后赴美留学,先在科罗拉多大学获经济学学士,后又入哈佛大学并获硕士学位,1926年归国,时任铁道部总务司司长。林子峰,广东中山人,时任上海市政府参事。② 本日,该展正式开幕。

五月上旬

中基会年会召开,先生列席。〔《北平晚报》,1937年5月7日,第2版〕

　　　　按:除先生外,北平学界参加者还有李石曾等人。

五月六日　南京

先生赴国学图书馆,与柳诒徵馆长商酌该馆新库房的图样,并到现场勘察。

---

① 《申报》,1937年4月1日,第18版。
② 《民报》(上海),1936年3月27日,第3版。

〔《国学图书馆第十年刊》,"纪事"页22〕

五月八日

下午一时五十五分,先生乘坐沪平线北返。〔《世界日报》,1937 年 5 月 9 日,第 6 版〕

五月十日　北平

先生、徐森玉、张允亮、赵万里等人赴傅增湘藏园,与之商定《国藏善本丛刊》目录,决定删去数种大部头,另补入十数种。〔《张元济傅增湘论书尺牍》,页 353〕

上海市博物馆、上海市通志馆联合本埠各收藏家,筹划组织上海文献展览会,召开发起人大会,先生和容庚被推为北平地区理事,代为征集相关文献。〔《申报》,1937 年 5 月 11 日,第 11 版〕

五月十七日

下午二时,中基会副会长、世界教育联合会会长孟禄博士抵达北平,北平教育界人士蒋梦麟、任鸿隽、孙洪芬、胡适、先生、李蒸、梅贻琦、陆志韦、裴德士二十余人到站迎接。〔《华北日报》,1937 年 5 月 18 日,第 9 版〕

> 按:15 日下午,孟禄及其家人离开南京北上,翌日抵达济南,赴齐鲁大学参观。预计在北平停留两周,随后拟偕任鸿隽飞赴成都,再转往日本。

五月十八日

先生发表书面声明,否认平馆馆员私将善本书籍偷抄、摄影盗售传闻。大意如下:

> 查东方文化会编纂《续修四库提要》一节,馆中前虽有二三职员参与其事,但已脱离关系。至馆员私将珍本书为外人偷抄摄影及盗售一节,尤属绝无其事。图书馆为文化机关,纯属公开性质,历年本馆在东西各国抄摄敦煌写本,为数极多,而国内学术机关及学者委托本馆传抄罕见书籍,亦日不暇给,因之本馆有写生多名专司传抄,馆中并备有摄影室专供照书之用。最近美国赠送最新式照书机一架,即专为传播文化之用。但传抄任何书籍,皆须先经馆长之同意。

> 　　　　　　　　　　　　〔《世界日报》,1937 年 5 月 19 日,第 6 版〕

> 按:传闻所指馆员应为赵万里、孙楷第,后赵万里辞去中文采访组组长,派杨殿珣暂代。胡适亦对此事公开表态,认为纯属学术事

业,不应妄加干涉。

五月二十二日

容庚来访,与先生晤谈。〔《容庚北平日记》,页501〕

晚七时,中基会假欧美同学会大厅设宴款待孟禄,北平文化教育界人士蒋梦麟、梅贻琦、胡适、任鸿隽、陈衡哲、孙洪芬、李燕、李麟玉、徐诵明、陈垣、李书华、陆志韦、司徒雷登、梅贻宝、先生、胡先骕、杨钟健、杨光弼、李健勋、美国大使馆参赞罗赫德、协和医院院长王锡炽、协和医学院代理院长Henry S. Houghton、福开森等五十余人到场,九时许散。〔《华北日报》,1937年5月23日,第9版〕

> 按:Henry S. Houghton(1880-1975),中文名胡恒德,生于美国俄亥俄州,1905年获霍普金斯医学院博士学位,1907年来华,任芜湖教会医院医生,并兼任芜湖海关外科医生,1918年受聘担任北京协和医学院代理院长,主持建校工作,1928年归国,1935年9月再次出任协和医学院代理院长。

先生致信王重民,谈在法、英影照敦煌经卷及为其向各庚款索取津贴进展。

> 有三吾弟:
>
> 接四月十五日及二十七来书,详悉一一。兹分别答覆如下,
>
> (一)照相事。法方免税及于道泉介绍之私人照相已办妥否?英庚款补助之八千元拟以二千元专照巴黎所藏者,如用不了,则留作照英伦所藏卷子之用。玻璃片寄平时务请包好,以便破裂。在法照相之款,于离法以前应有一详细报告(一)本馆(二)清华(三)本馆照书系购书费(四)英庚款,分别开列。
>
> (二)足下在英生活费。英庚款内勉强凑成壹千元,何时需用请函告,当即寄去。此外并拟在中基会设法再谋壹千元,已与胡适之先生谈过,渠允帮忙,俟得到后再奉告,不足之数容再设法。又图书馆每月补助之费照例无超过三年者汪长炳在美四年仅付三年之费,拟向委员会提议自七月起再延长一年,即以此款补助在英之生活费之一部分。至府上用款,只得另想法子矣。又如在英照相成绩优良,英庚款仍可补助,可在下届补助费内再提用一部分,惟该会董事对此办法不赞同(主张专作照像之用),此次经叶玉虎特别帮忙,方筹到此壹千元也。丛书书名经英庚款定为"敦煌古籍丛编"。

（三）在外饮食不可过苦，而休息尤为重要，万不可生病，望注意是荷。

（四）本日寄上汇票一千元，合法郎 6,660，系英庚款照巴黎所藏卷子之款，应另立账目，并赐收据。

（五）公款不应动用或借与他人。闻刁汝钧之款尚未付清，此举殊欠斟酌也。

（六）东方文化会之事务从速结束（近有学生北大史学系声言要到该会查账亦恐吓之一法），以免将来作事困难。日来利用此机会与子书、斐云倒乱者颇不乏人，亦不幸之事也。（见《北平新报》）

同礼顿首

五月廿二日

〔国立北平图书馆英文信纸。中国书店·海淀，四册〕

按："以便破裂"当作"以免破裂"。刁汝钧（1907—?），字士衡，河北邯郸人，1930 年毕业于上海国立暨南大学中国语言文学系，1932 年获燕京大学文学硕士学位。同年赴法国留学，曾在巴黎国家图书馆收集"变文"及"敦煌学"有关资料。"近有学生（北大史学系）声言要到该会查账"，可参见本年 5 月 19 日《大公报》（天津）第 4 版之相关报道。《北平新报》，约在 1931 年 4 月创刊，该社位于绒线胡同路南。①

五月二十四日

先生致信叶恭绰，寄呈平馆拟借予上海文献展览会展出之书籍清单。

玉虎先生尊鉴：

两奉手教，拜悉一一。兹将尊单所列之书为敝馆拟送往陈列者，一一标出，其他各书较为普通，征集较易，故无须送上也。关于川沙、青浦、奉贤地方文献，容开单后再行寄奉。先此，顺颂道祺。

后学袁同礼顿首

五月廿四日

李木斋书已减至五十万，进行较前稍顺利。又及。

〔国立北平图书馆用笺。《历史文献》第 5 辑，页 227〕

---

① *China Publishers' Directory*, Shanghai: China Commercial Advertising Agency, 1934, p. 19. 田蕴瑾编《最新北平指南》，北平：自强书局，1935 年。

五月二十六日

先生招宴商洽购入李盛铎旧藏古籍,胡适与李盛铎之子李家浦、李家淮、李
澪及董康等人与席。〔《胡适日记全集》第7册,页416〕

　　　　按:1937年2月4日晨,李盛铎病逝于天津秋山街私邸,家人有出售
　　　　旧藏之意,教育部遂委托先生接洽。是日,李家原索价八十万元,政
　　　　府许三十万元,李家减至五十万,胡适提议四十万,未能达成协议。

五月二十九日

马衡致函先生,商洽故宫博物院与平馆联合发起四家文化机关影印所藏善
本图书之议。

　　守和仁兄执事:

　　　　四机关影印《国藏善本丛刊》合同二份,兹已签名,应即送请察
　　收。将来四机关应得之酬赠印本,拟比照各机关付印册数之多寡订定
　　一分配比例。如荷赞成,请即由兄与弟发起,约同其他两机关订一合
　　同,藉资依据。特布,即颂日祺。

　　　　　　　　　　　　　　　　　　　　弟马○上言
　　　　　　　　　　　　　　　　　　　　二六,五,廿九
　　　　　　　　　　　　　　　　　　〔故宫博物院档案〕

　　　　按:《马衡年谱长编》(页742)将该函错系为5月28日。

是年夏

《黄膺白先生故旧感忆录》刊登先生文章,题为《对于膺白先生参加华盛顿
会议之回忆》。〔《黄膺白先生故旧感忆录》①,叶114—117〕

　　　　按:1936年12月6日,黄郛在上海病逝。《黄膺白先生故旧感忆
　　　　录》由黄膺白先生纪念刊编辑委员会刊行,线装,非卖品。

六月一日

午,先生、谢国桢、容庚在东兴楼设宴,何遂、郭葆昌、马衡、徐森玉、顾颉刚
等与席。〔《顾颉刚日记》卷3,页649〕

柳诒徵致函先生,谈假借平馆存沪明本《宋史记》钞补事。

　　守和馆长道鉴:

　　　　久疏笺候,维公私均胜为颂为慰。兹有恳者,散藏明王惟俭《宋史

---

① 该册问世,不晚于1937年7月中旬,参见《申报》1937年7月14日第16版。

记》钞本,仅存残零十册。贵藏系全书,拟借钞补。如蒙惠允,即请函达照亭先生,先将首五册或十册寄下。所有递寄手续,当交邮保险,力求妥慎。特此奉恳,至希亮察,顺颂公绥。

柳诒徵拜启

六月一日

〔《国学图书馆第十年刊》,"案牍"页56〕

按:6月19日,国学图书馆收平馆寄来宋宾王钞校《宋史记》一函凡九册,得见"浦星躔者批改,王损仲书"字样。柳诒徵对照其馆藏残本——"星躔批改",始知浦星躔之姓,快慰无似。

六月五日

先生致信刘咸,为在中国科学社图书馆存放更多平馆南迁书籍拟数条建议。

重熙先生大鉴:

敝馆寄存贵社书籍陆续增加,书库已满,无地再容。擅拟办法数项,请采择施行为荷。

(一)第一层书库西边堆有报纸数架,可否设法腾出。

(二)第二层书库(现藏贵社中文书),目下尚不拥挤,可否腾出一部分之地位。

(三)将一部分书籍提出装箱改存他处,如震旦大学图书馆等处。

以上各节,如何之处,即希卓裁,径告曾女士照办为荷。专此,敬候台祺。

弟袁同礼顿首

六月五日

〔国立北平图书馆用笺。上海市档案馆,档案编号 Q546-1-192-60〕

按:该信为文书代笔,落款处为先生签名。

六月七日

先生离平赴济宁,前往指导济宁图书馆筹备开幕事宜。〔《华北日报》,1937年6月8日,第9版〕

按:该馆拟于7月1日举行落成开幕仪式,后派平馆馆员前往协助办公。①

---

① 应为胡英、宋方英、吴藻洲、王耆康四人,参见《华北日报》1937年7月6日第9版。

六月十日

先生返回北平。

六月十一日

先生致信叶恭绰,告其已嘱平馆上海办事处人员将其所需文献提出并送交
上海文献展览会,另告可影照故宫博物院所藏吴历画作。

> 玉虎先生钧鉴:
>
> 　　日昨由济宁返平,连奉赐书,拜悉种切。所需陈列各书,除少数普
> 通书七种由平寄沪外,其余六十七种均在上海,已告保管人于二十日以前
> 连同登记表径交博物馆。惟各书在沪,此间不能详考,因之说明书上
> 仅注明版本而已。太仓郑和等史料,此间无专书述及,想南洋中学及
> 徐家汇或有收藏,又下列各书敝馆未入藏,而张乾若在病中未能见面,恐
> 渠亦未入藏,未能出展,不无可憾。故宫博物院有吴渔山之画,可照相奉
> 赠,请转告胡先生来一公函可也。匆匆奉复,顺颂道安。
>
> 　　　　　　　　　　　　　　　　　　后学袁同礼顿首
> 　　　　　　　　　　　　　　　　　　　　六月十一日
>
> 　　又陈援庵、任振采处已有信征求否? 普通志书恐有重复。另寄
> 《方志目二编》,如有所需,并希示知。
>
> 　　　　　　〔国立北平图书馆用笺。《历史文献》第 5 辑,页 227-228〕

　　按:"胡先生"应指胡肇椿。《方志目二编》即《国立北平图书馆方
　　志目录二编》,1936 年 6 月平馆印行。

六月十二日

晚。司徒雷登、博晨光、陆志韦设宴,Serge Elisséeff、胡适、蒋梦麟、李蒸、钱
桐、陈寅恪、孙洪芬、福开森、张星烺、马衡、沈兼士、田洪都、梅贻琦、梅贻
宝、冯友兰、陆侃如、容庚、黎锦熙、洪业、先生、顾颉刚等人受邀与席。〔《顾
颉刚日记》卷 3,页 653〕

　　按:Serge Elisséeff(1889-1975),俄裔汉学家,中文名"叶理绥",
　　时任哈佛燕京学社社长。

平馆致函中央古物保管委员会,请其在下年度经费中继续拨付六百元用以
编纂日藏中国古物著述目录,具先生名并钤印。

> 　　案查上年十月承贵会委托调查及编著流出国外古物著述目录,并
> 荷补助国币六百元在案。现在此书业已编辑告竣,拟即委托上海商务

书馆代为出版,附奉报告一份,希察阅。惟此书范围仅限于<u>欧美</u>部份,其<u>日本</u>所藏者以种数甚繁,且多散在私家,非前往实地调查无由着手。拟于下年度继续开始搜集资料,积极进行,遇有必要,并当派员赴<u>日</u>调查,以期完备。拟请仍庚续旧案,在下年度经费内准予补助国币陆百元,俾得早日竣事,藉成全帙,无任感幸。相应函达,即希察照见复为荷! 此致

中央古物保管委员会

　　附报告一份。

　　　　　　　　　　　　　　　　　　　　副馆长袁同礼

　　　　　　　　　　　　　　　　　　　　廿六,六,十二

〔台北"国史馆",〈委托北平图书馆调查及编著流出国外古物著述目录〉,典藏号 026-011000-0381〕

　　按:所附报告共计三页,其中提及《流出国外古物著述目录》分上下两部,前者为"普通记载",后者为"专门记载",共涉及书籍五百余种、论文二千余篇,并曾发出英法文信件六百余件,收到四百余件覆函。笔者认为此份书稿与后来陈梦家对海外所藏中国铜器的调查研究有相当关联。此信为文书代笔,落款处并钤"国立北平图书馆馆长"印。

先生签第肆拾号借书单,命上海办事处将《弘治汀州府志》《虚舟集》《康熙鄮都县志》《康熙广通县志》检出,交邮挂号寄送平馆善本书库查收。〔国家图书馆档案,档案编号 1942-※035-采藏 7-001288〕

　　按:以上各书因平馆采访组借抄使用。

六月十三日

先生致信吴宓,请高棣华于十六或十七日到平馆面谈。〔《吴宓日记》第 6 册,页 146〕

六月十四日

先生撰一短片致叶恭绰。残存如下:

　　……关于浏河资料,所藏甚少。兹奉上海运史料选目,如有所需,请示知,当再奉上。此上

玉虎总长

　　　　　　　　　　　　　　　　　　　　同礼拜上

十四日

〔国立北平图书馆用笺。《历史文献》第 5 辑,页 228〕

先生、赵万里、傅增湘、徐森玉等人赴津,与李盛铎家属李滂等人,接洽购入木斋藏书事。〔《大公报》(天津),1937 年 6 月 30 日,第 6 版〕

六月十五日　天津

先生在火车站迎候胡适,晚饭后同到李盛铎宅观其藏书,李家兄弟、子侄搬其善本书,赵万里记录,先生与胡适、徐森玉同看,半夜始散。〔《胡适日记全集》第 7 册,页 418〕

六月十六日　天津—北平

上午,先生、胡适、徐森玉、赵万里等人继续翻看李盛铎藏书。〔《大公报》(天津),1937 年 6 月 30 日,第 6 版〕

　　　　按:李氏将存于新华银行的藏书运回秋山街寓所,供诸人翻检,胡
　　　　适认为可在四十万的基础上再酌情增加两万,但李氏子嗣则希望
　　　　政府拨足五十万元,胡适表示将借参加"庐山茗叙"之便向蒋介
　　　　石陈请。

下午五时许,孟禄至平馆参观,先生负责引导。〔《华北日报》,1937 年 6 月 17 日,第 9 版〕

六月十七日

上午,高棣华来平馆面试。十一时,吴宓在东兴楼设宴,客为先生、顾毓琇、萧公权、萧遽、潘光旦、叶企孙、金岳霖、张奚若。先生先到并告吴宓高棣华事可就,因有事先离席。〔《吴宓日记》第 6 册,页 149〕

　　　　按:先生意聘高棣华为英文秘书,嘱吴宓先教其英文公事函件写
　　　　作格式,并将其学习成绩记录和论文送阅,吴宓甚喜。

十二时,秦德纯夫妇在市府西花厅设宴款待孟禄,蒋梦麟夫妇、梅贻琦夫妇、李蒸夫妇、陆志韦夫妇、先生、司徒雷登、孙洪芬夫妇及北平社会局长雷嗣尚受邀作陪。〔《华北日报》,1937 年 6 月 17 日,第 9 版〕

先生签第肆壹号借书单,命上海办事处将《南览录》《安宁温泉诗》《藤花亭镜谱》检出,交邮挂号寄送平馆善本书库查收。〔国家图书馆档案,档案编号1942-※035-采藏 7-001289〕

　　　　按:以上各书因福开森借用。

六月十八日

王重民致函先生,告其在法拍摄敦煌卷子进展。

守和吾师道鉴:

为英庚款项下照敦煌卷子事,自接到汇款后,略事准备,即订好合同,开始拍照。因鉴于上次相片,略有差误,此次多加注意,刻下照相人已有习惯,从此可顺利进行。然因卷轴不齐,每卷不一定全照,故生每日约有半小时时间,亲加指挥与监视,以冀更能减少错误也。

现在此人专作此项工作,上午来馆摄影,下午在家洗晒,从此每周可作出一百余张,则二千之数,不久可告成功。生选择范围,以有影印价值者为限,如吾师所指示之字书,则拟扫数摄影。其中有数叶裱上薄纸,用 Photostat 不能照者,经此次试验,用 Leica 尚能得其仿佛。又如一切石本及一切刻本,不论片纸支字,则拟均摄一份。因石本均系唐拓,刻本则最迟亦在北宋初年,均系希世之珍故也。

敦煌书目,七月一日定能着手编辑,今年拟不休暑假,再加些努力,九月底必能完成,则可即赴英伦,继续向达工作。伯希和此次既允编此目,且允携回我国付印,看此情势,其家中所珍藏之一箱,或有可以拿出之希望。又去年允协助伯先生所撰之 *Les grottes de Touen-Houang* 手稿,生因精力不及,未有一点成绩,伊似不大痛快。然已谓开始编目时,当可为其搜得些许材料。刻伊之手稿,存生处似恐有危险,欲生交还,生欲用英庚款摄下影片,因看此情形,伊恐不能自己成书,在伊下世以后,恐更无人为力也。伊刻赴英,允于七月十五日交回,此事已不及与吾师往返函商,所幸用款不大多,故拟即依生意进行。得有影片,更欲携往英国,见有新材料时,便可补苴也。二三十年后,此影片或亦成为希世之珍矣。

这一礼拜已洗好相片九十余张,昨日打好六十六张,先寄上。此次所照,比上次进步多多,且宽出一行,尤为雅观。在此六十六张内,亦无一点差错,因之颇悔上次相片之未加审慎,以之付印,实有不宜。现在只请命人详细检查一过,再与商务函商,请不要惜工钱,最好是重加剪贴与排比,把行款与篇幅弄得整整齐齐。且从此以后,相片大小,均能一律,则前次之窄一行者,务要加出,冀将来此敦煌古籍丛编第一编与第二、第……等编均一律。其底片不久可寄上,即把那些剪碎,到中国还可另洗一份,由吾馆保存,洗费必不太昂也。如实在不得已,择其最坏者,另照一次亦可。此次从速寄上此六十六张,目的即在请作一比较也。

生身体已好,只是每日工作,不能超出限度,若超过,便仍感疲乏。与清华合作相片,已有四周未寄,下周可寄上三四包也。

余再及,即请钩安!

受业王重民敬上。
六月十八日

〔刘波、林世田《国立北平图书馆拍摄及影印出版敦煌遗书史事钩沉》,《敦煌研究》2010 年第 2 期〕

按:*Les grottes de Touen-Houang*,现通译为《敦煌石窟》,1920 年至 1924 年陆续出版,共计 6 卷,收录伯希和赴敦煌考察所拍摄外景、洞窟彩塑、壁画等照片。

六月十九日

先生致信叶恭绰,告知上海文献展览会所需文献平馆驻沪办事处必及时送交,并请其协助申请中英庚款以发掘洛阳古物,另谈收购李盛铎藏书进展。

玉虎先生尊鉴:

日前奉十三日赐书,拜悉一一。敝馆出陈之书准于二十日以前送到,已告驻沪李君照办,惟开幕之期不克赶到为怅然耳。中英庚款支配极为公允,我公苦心孤诣,当为学术界同声感谢也。敝馆所请求者,以唐墓志一项为最重要,此又系与中央研究院分工合作之件,孟真兄对此亦愿赞助,将来仍盼列入保存古物史迹委员会请款案内为感。发掘汉石经事,因中央博物院将在洛阳从事发掘,似不愿他人参加,加以经费关系,因之停止,但甚盼有志之人能完成此举也。李氏书事已减至四十五万元,政府方面允增至四十万元,不足之数,势须由敝馆垫付。自十五日起开始看书,参加者适之、沅叔、森玉、庾楼诸先生,发见惊人秘笈,为数甚多。但李氏昆仲同床异梦,故此事之磋商至感困难,将来析产分配大感困难也,余容再陈。顺候著祺。

后学袁同礼顿首
六月十九日

〔天津六国大饭店公用笺。《历史文献》第 5 辑,页 228〕

翟肖兰致函先生,请为其主持公道,分得应有的李盛铎遗产。

同礼先生赐鉴:

敬陈者,肖兰生不逢辰,为李木老侍妾垂二十余年,木老悯其愚诚,备加翼覆。不幸去腊木老逝世,肖兰自惟乖舛,几以身殉然,默祝诸公子努力向上,克承先志。六月三日读天津《大公报》载李氏木犀轩全部藏书五千余种,业由李少斋、李少微在平出让于国立图书馆,并闻馆长袁同礼先生到津视察,已派徐玉森先生驻津审查,从此收归国有,不致流落异邦。木老竭毕生之精力,保存国粹文化,当可瞑目,告慰于泉下矣。惟肖兰为木老生前扶养家属之一人,月给用度二百二十元。自木老逝世,诸公子一再缩减,每月仅给月壹百元,所有房租零用以及衣食之费一包在内,尚有木老族侄家漳、养女家城均归肖兰教养。而木老日常向肖兰通融,以及诸公子借贷计欠肖兰壹万零九百余元,立有借契,仅允月给息金六十元,并经木老友好李鹤轩、郑兰溪、吴洗戈诸先生从中劝说,肖兰重以家庭骨肉忍痛承诺,原冀诸公子谅我苦衷,仰体父志。肖兰亦得苟延喘息,以尽余年,岂意数月以来敷衍推诿_{允给息金分文未付},容心遗弃。公子少微,平日于木老之前曾指天誓日,愿尽孝养。肖兰亦以少微为人忠实,深信不疑,今乃态度陡变。回忆昔日情景,益形恐惧,不知此身将何依托。按木老亲笔遗嘱,令家淮等诸公子应以庶母待遇肖兰,如有不善,即罚六万元与肖兰作为养赡。今木老遗产即此所有珍本书籍一经变卖,得价为诸公子瓜分,各度置肖兰于不顾,而肖兰手中余蓄业为木老生前借用净尽,且现负债累累,举目无亲,生无所依,岂非使肖兰坐以待毙。查我国现行民法律,家长生前扶养之人应酌给遗产,况木老尚有亲笔遗嘱在肖兰之手。肖兰于珍本书籍正在审查尚未交价之时,不难据理告争,并将身历苦境登报表白,终以木老声名为重,诸公子前程可惜,故欲行辄止者。再因念我公为木老旧交,对于肖兰孀寡无告之人必能惟情援助,不揣冒昧,敢分向傅沅叔、曾云霈、李赞侯、胡适之诸先生呼吁肖兰法律上应得之数,于图书馆交付书价项下,召集少微诸公子共同商议酌予分配,俾肖兰、少权子母生活有靠,以成我柏舟之节,并教养家漳、家城两幼儿得以成人,以慰木老遗爱。

我公德望素重,当不忍袖手旁观,而视肖兰生命为不足恤,务恳规劝少微诸公子以确定肖兰生活保障。临书涕泣,伏候德音。敬颂道安。

附遗嘱照片、借约照片各一张。

李翟肖兰敛衽

六月十九日

〔台北胡适纪念馆,档案编号 HS-JDSHSC-1178-010〕

按:"徐玉森"当作"徐森玉"。"去腊木老逝世",李盛铎于 1937
年 2 月 4 日晨逝世,时为农历腊月二十三日。遗嘱照片、借约照
片均存。

六月二十一日

先生致信吴宓,告拟聘高棣华在平馆文书组任职,月薪 70 元,并附平馆英
文函件若干封,以备高棣华学习观摩。〔《吴宓日记》第 6 册,页 152〕

按:吴宓接此函件后,似覆函先生,索要平馆英文出版品。

先生致信伯希和,告知即将寄出《钦定石渠宝笈续编》部分卷册的晒蓝件,
其中有对淳化轩藏画的记述,并告知费用及支付方式,另谈尚未收到法国
政府意欲分发的出版物目录。

June 21, 1937

Prof. Paul Pelliot

Musée d'Ennery

59 Avenue Foch

Paris (XVIe), France

Dear Prof. Pelliot:

Under separate registered cover, we are sending you a blue-print
copy of that portion of the 石渠宝笈(二编) which describes paintings
preserved in the 淳化轩, in accordance with your letter of March 31.

The cost of reproduction is Peking ＄15.32. You may either pay us
in cash or send us French publications of equivalent value in exchange.

The list of books which the French Government wishes to
distribute has not yet been received. I wonder whether it has already
been printed.

With cordial regards,

Your sincerely,

T. L. Yuan

Acting Director

〔韩琦《袁同礼致伯希和书信》，页 129-130〕

六月二十二日

先生寄送平馆英文概况、报告等出版品与吴宓。〔《吴宓日记》第 6 册，页 152〕国会图书馆致函先生，就前信订购国会图书馆整套分类法、主题词大纲及补充数量略表质疑，请其再次确认，并告知已寄出数种出版品。

June 22, 1937

Dear Sir:

Your letter of April 17, regarding your standing order for four copies of each of our Classification schemes, a set of the L. C. Subject Heading, and other publications, was duly received and has had our careful attention.

The National Library of Peiping is on our mailing list to receive one free copy of each of our Classification schedules as issued, and this free set has already been supplied to you. As to your standing order for three additional copies of all Classification schemes as issued, we are in some doubt. Mr. Hastings, Chief of the Card Division, thinks it probable that you wish to obtain three full sets of the schedules, in addition to the free set already sent (or being sent currently), and that you wish to place a standing order for three copies of each new and revised schedule as issued. Upon receipt of further word from you clearing the above points, we shall be glad to comply with your request.

There is also some uncertainty as to your order for the subject headings. Do you wish three additional copies of the main List of Subject Headings and of all the publications supplementary to the main List? Will you let us have confirmation as to this?

Under separate cover and free of charge, we have forwarded to you the following items:

List of Publications

Popular Names of Federal Statutes

List of Atlases and Maps Applicable to the World War

Notes on the Care, Cataloguing, Calendaring and Arranging of Manuscripts, 3d ed.

We have also sent under separate cover four copies of the "*Guide to the Cataloguing of the Serial Publications of Societies and Institutions*", four copies of the "*Guide to the Cataloguing of Periodicals*" and one copy of the "*List of Series of Publications for Which Cards Are in Stock*". The charges for these, including postage, have been entered on the card account of your library (F161) (see enclosed account slip and bill in duplicate).

We regret to report that the "*Notes on the Cataloguing, Care and Classification of Maps and Atlases, 1921*" is no longer in print.

Very truly yours,

Acting Secretary of the Library

〔Librarian of Congress, Putnam Archives, Special File, China: National Library 1930-1939〕

　　　按:此件为录副。

六月二十四日

下午五时,先生至清华园访吴宓。其间,先生阅高棣华学业成绩单,决定聘用,约八月十五日到馆就职。另外,谈女子学院荐周自德到平馆任职,但英文不能胜任,又谈李书华荐绛珠到平馆任职。吴宓认为后者才可堪用,唯其适于管理人事、交际、中文函牍写作等。因值大雨,至六时许方离去。〔《吴宓日记》第 6 册,页 154〕

　　　按:先生言高棣华入职后午饭可在馆中就餐,住宿当在女青年会,
　　　但恐人多易沾染陋习。"绛珠"应指朱崇庆。

顾颉刚致函先生,为杨效曾事。〔《顾颉刚日记》卷 3,页 659〕

　　　按:杨效曾,字中一,山东招远人,北京大学历史系毕业,曾主持
　　　《华北日报·史学周刊》,后在北平研究院史学研究会历史组任
　　　职,与顾颉刚交往颇多。

六月二十六日

先生签第肆贰号借书单,命上海办事处将《弘治徽州府志》《弘治休宁志》《万历休宁县志》《康熙徽州府通志附续编》检出,交邮挂号寄送平馆善本

书库查收。〔国家图书馆档案,档案编号1942-※035-采藏7-001290〕

　　按:以上各书因施廷镛借用。

李耀南覆函先生,谈送赠《越缦堂日记补》事。

　　馆长先生钧鉴:

　　　　奉本月十九日函嘱,将《越缦堂日记补》检取二十部,送请蔡馆长转交李氏一节。遵即于今日上午,亲赴中央研究院,将该书二十部,连同本馆致李氏函及手复蔡馆长函各一件,一并呈交蔡馆长查收。及查收之后,蔡馆长嘱再将该书检送二部,一留自己阅看,一赠马孝焱先生。遵又复行照送,当经分别出给收据。肃此奉复,恭颂道绥。

　　　　　　　　　　　　　　　　　　　　　　后学李耀南拜启

　　　　　　　　　　　　　　　　　　　　　　廿六年六月廿六日

　　　　附《越缦堂日记补》收据三纸。

　　　　　　〔国家图书馆档案,档案编号1945-※057-综合5-020005、1945-
　　　　　　※057-综合5-020006〕

　　按:该函附三份收据,分别为李家后人收二十部(蔡元培代)、蔡元培一部、马孝焱一部。

蔡元培覆函先生,告知收到《越缦堂日记补》二十二部,并表示今年不拟赴平。

　　守和先生大鉴:

　　　　接本月廿一日惠函并合同抄本,致李先生一函及《越缦日记补》二十部,均敬悉。询李耀南君,知馆中尚存有多部。弟自索一部并为马孝焱秘书索一部,共收到二十二部矣,敬闻。今年本有来平之意,曾与石曾、仲揆诸先生谈及,但现因他种关系取销此议矣,承注,谢谢。此复,并颂著绥。

　　　　　　　　　　　　　　　　　　　　　　弟元培敬启

　　　　　　　　　　　　　　　　　　　　　　六月廿六日

　　　　　　〔国立中央研究院用笺。国家图书馆档案,档案编号1945-※
　　　　　　057-综合5-020001〕

　　按:1920年,商务印书馆影印出版了晚清文史学家李慈铭存世64册日记稿中的后51册,为李慈铭自同治二年四月初一日至光绪十五年七月初十间的日记。1935年10月,在钱玄同倡议、蔡元培

主持下,其余 13 册日记仍交商务印书馆石印。翌年出版,名为
《越缦堂日记补》,为咸丰四年三月十四日至同治二年三月三十
日间的日记。

六月二十八日

郑振铎致函先生,商借《汉唐地理书钞》。

> 守和先生:

> 久未通音问,甚念! 兹有恳者:前敝馆向贵馆借阅之拾册《汉唐地
> 理书钞》一书,得中央研究院来函,谓已送还贵馆。便中请即交邮寄
> 下。(借阅期至多不逾二月)因敝处亟待参考也。费神,至为感谢!
> 匆此,专候暑祺。

> 郑振铎拜启

> 26/6/28

〔国立暨南大学西式信纸。国家图书馆档案,档案编号 1945-※
057-综合 5-021001〕

六月三十日

法国大使那其亚(Paul-Émile Naggiar)在使馆设午宴招待叶理绥,傅增湘、
李麟玉、胡适、博晨光、先生、徐旭生、钱桐、协和医学院解剖教授
Weidenreich、徐家汇中国学术研究所裴化行(Henri Bernard)、陆志韦、顾颉
刚、洪业、容庚、陆侃如、冯友兰、张星烺、田清波(Antoine Mostaert)及中法
大学教授数人受邀与席,至二时始散。〔《华北日报》,1937 年 7 月 3 日,第 9 版;
《容庚北平日记》,页 506〕

> 按:1936 年 7 月 9 日,那其亚被任命为驻华大使。

顾颉刚来访,与先生谈孙海波事。〔《顾颉刚日记》卷 3,页 661〕
先生致信高棣华,约七月二日晚宴事,并寄送正式聘书。〔《吴宓日记》第 6
册,页 158〕

六月

先生代表平馆与汉堡大学教授 Fritz Jäger 达成交换协议,平馆获得福兰阁
在清末民初购买的两册《永乐大典》,作为交换平馆赠予翻印的大部头古
籍。〔《为中国着迷:一位汉学家的自传》,页 203〕

> 按:因卢沟桥事变爆发,先生强烈要求将这两册《永乐大典》暂存
> 汉堡大学。1951 年夏,Wolfgang Franke 继续履行此项约定,将两

册《永乐大典》送往美国国会图书馆,由先生归入平馆存美善本书中保管。此项交换协议中,赠予德方的大部头古籍似为《宋会要辑稿》、《国立北平图书馆善本丛书》等。Fritz Jäger(1886-1957),德国汉学家,中文名颜复礼,师从福兰阁,后长期在汉堡大学执教。

Wolfgang Franke 拜访先生。〔《为中国着迷:一位汉学家的自传》,页74〕

　　按:Wolfgang Franke(1912-2007),德国汉学家,中文名傅吾康,福兰阁之子。本年5月31日,傅吾康抵达北平。

六七月间

先生将平馆存沪善本书九十箱提运回平,其中有《永乐大典》《文苑英华》(宋写本)等。〔《蔡元培日记》,页531;朱元曙整理《朱希祖书信集·郦亭诗稿》,北京:中华书局,2012年,页151〕

　　按:此次大规模提运,其初衷似为平馆欲以洛克菲勒基金会赞助缩微胶片照相机拍摄馆藏善本。

七月一日

先生致信王重民,告与商务印书馆商洽影印法藏敦煌写本进展,并告知杜乃扬返国时间。

　　有三吾弟如晤:

　　　　日昨接六月八日来书及相片七包,均如数收到。相片已送商务,极盼题跋及总序等早日寄下,以便付印。《还冤记》、《楚辞音》之玻璃片想能与此次所印之相片一致,容与商务商妥再行奉闻。兹先汇上国币壹仟元合六千七百法郎,系英庚款内拨出补助生活费者,请先收用。馆中补助之款须俟委员会通过后再分两次寄上。又代请求美款补助之壹仟元,委员会已通过,下周中基会开常会时方能正式取决也,容再函告。上次寄来之第二辑目录似嫌太单调,恐于销路亦有影响,不如俟到伦敦后多觅资料,俾第二辑专收英国所藏者。杜乃扬本定今冬返国,但法使馆留其在华驻至明年二月底,渠并拟赴日数月,恐须到五、六月间方能返法,现闻已函 M. Cain 征求同意。如法方需人相助,亦可请刘女士留法帮忙也。顺询旅安。

　　　　　　　　　　　　　　　　袁同礼顿首
　　　　　　　　　　　　　　　　　七月一日

外介绍信两件。

〔国立北平图书馆用笺。中国书店·海淀,四册〕

按:"日昨接六月八日",结合信文内容,应该是本谱 6 月 18 日来函。该信首叶右上角标有"38",应为王重民或其妻刘修业所作记号,但此信实写于 1937 年。

国会图书馆致函先生,此前表示尚未收到的两种平馆出版物已经东方部馆员协助确认收到。

July 1, 1937

Dear Sir:

With further reference to your letters of October 20, 1936 and April 12, 1937 and ours of March 8, 1937, the Chief of the Division of Accessions, Mr. Blanchard, now reports that he has identified the two Chinese works whose transliterated titles are as follows:

"*Kuo-li Peiping' t'u shu-kuan shan-pen shu-mu i-pien*"

"*Fang-chih mu-lu i-pien*".

He has forwarded an engraved acknowledgment of these works.

In your letter of October 20, you described these items as a and d. Items b, c, e, and f were received and acknowledged of February 7, 1937. The reason for the delay in acknowledging them is that they are entirely in the Chinese language, and it was necessary for us to await identification by members of the Division of Orientalia. A further complication was that the other four volumes were all bound in the western manner, whereas the two items that we have just found were bound in Chinese taos.

Regretting that we were unable to make this report earlier,

Very truly yours,

Acting Secretary of the Library

〔Librarian of Congress, Putnam Archives, Special File, China: National Library 1930–1939〕

按:*Kuo-li Peiping' t'u shu-kuan shan-pen shu-mu i-pien*、*Fang-chih mu-lu i-pien* 即《国立北平图书馆善本书目乙编》和《国立北平图书馆方志目录二编》。

是年夏

平馆设立福利储金,用以保证馆员福利,选举先生、王访渔、宋琳、陆元烈及馆员五人出任经理委员会。〔《京报》,1937 年 7 月 6 日,第 9 版〕

七月初

美国教育考察团赴平考察。拟于七月十六日在故宫博物院御花园设茶点招待,相关事宜由先生、查良钊、李湘宸、张庭济商妥。〔《华北日报》,1937 年 7 月 6 日,第 9 版〕

　　　　　按:实际接待日期为 7 月 23 日。

七月二日

晚七时半,先生在北海漪澜堂设宴,客有法国大使、高棣华、周自德、王敏娴、法国留学生等。〔《吴宓日记》第 6 册,页 161〕

七月三日

下午四时,平馆在会议室召开购书委员会,顾毓琇、胡先骕、叶企孙、张准、姚从吾、梁思永、张印堂①等出席。晚七时,先生设宴,为顾毓琇、叶企孙、张准等人出洋饯行,并邀全体委员及馆中重要职员作陪。〔《华北日报》,1937 年 7 月 3 日,第 9 版〕

　　　　　按:张印堂(1903-1991),字荫棠,山东泰安人,地理学家、人口学家,时任平馆购书委员会西文组委员。

七月七日②

上午九时,中国教育学会在北平师范大学文学院大礼堂开会,杨亮功、李蒸、朱有光、沈履、先生等五十余人参加。杨亮功为会议主席,首由赵青誉宣读论文,后讨论议案五项,十二时散会。下午二时,会议继续举行,查良钊为会议主席,首由朱有光报告定县组织教育制小学学业成绩测验研究,后讨论议案四项,五时四十分始散。〔《大公报》(上海),1937 年 7 月 15 日,第 10 版〕

　　　　　按:中国教育学会第四届年会、中华儿童教育社第七届年会在清华大学大礼堂举行联合开幕典礼。其中,教育学会会场在北平师范大学文学院大礼堂,而中华儿童教育社则仍在清华大学内。

---

① 《华北日报》将其错排为"张荫樵"。
② 会议举行时间,《大公报》(上海)并未明示。现根据《吴宓日记》第 6 册,页 163;《华北日报》,1937 年 7 月 6 日,第 9 版;《大公报》(天津)1937 年 7 月 7 日,第 4 版。

晚八时,何日章、先生、吴光清、袁涌进等人在撷英番菜馆设宴款待刘国钧。
〔《华北日报》,1937年7月7日,第9版〕

　　按:7月6日晚,私立金陵大学文学院院长刘国钧抵达北平,此次
　　北来,或与中国教育学会年会相关,抑或与先生推荐其前往国会
　　图书馆东方部编目有关。①

七月十日

先生致信王重民,委托其参加国际图书馆协会执行委员会第十次年会。

　　有三吾弟:

　　国际图书馆协会执行委员会第十次年会定于八月廿四日及廿五
日在巴黎举行,中国方面决定由吾弟代表出席,业已函告该会。请于
开会前数日至 Hotel Corneille 注册,所有注册等费请暂垫,将来由协会
归还。按照往例各国协会每年应有报告送至大会,兹将本届报告随函
奉上此系复本,正本已送该会矣。如台端不善用英、法文报告,可托使馆馆员
代为报告,即约彼一同出席,注册时即用二人姓名亦可。至分委员会之
工作,本会无暇办,亦无此项之人,故不必参加,仅旁听即可。关于国际
借书,中国当然加入,致 Sevensma 之函已略陈一二矣。顺颂旅安。

袁同礼顿首
七月十日

　　协会信件用毕,均请寄还。第八包照片已收到,照的甚好,是否为
第二集者,请函示。卢沟桥事不致扩大,祈释念。

　　七月一号汇去壹千元,数日后法郎大跌,拟与第一次所汇之壹千
元,均作为英庚款照相费,不必作生活费,一俟行市较好,再汇寄生活
费。中基会三号开会,已通过补助尊处壹千元,将来拟与英庚款之壹
千元一并寄英磅至伦敦。

〔国立北平图书馆用笺。中国书店·海淀,四册〕

　　按:先生本拟7月8日南下赴庐山受训②,但因7日夜卢沟桥事变
　　爆发而阻。信中所附报告未存。

---

① 参见本年11月1日,恒慕义致先生函。
② 《华北日报》,1937年7月7日,第9版。是年6月初,蒋介石计划于7月中旬召集各地学者赴
　庐山进行暑期谈话会,参见《陈布雷日记》(1937),2019年,页108。先生本为第三次谈话会参
　加者之一。

七月十三日

中午十二时,北平文化教育界人士在清华同学会举行第一次谈话会,李蒸、袁
敦礼、郑天挺、樊际昌、饶毓泰、潘光旦、沈履、张贻惠、陆志韦、梅贻宝、李书
华、先生、李麟玉、查良钊等二十余人出席。首先彼此交换意见,继而午餐。
餐后,由沈履、李书华、查良钊三人分别报告晋谒北平当局的经过,与会人员
作出下列决定:一战事已难避免,到会人员联署致电蒋介石、宋哲元请积极备
战;二推选代表面谒地方当局致慰劳之意。三时始散,李蒸、李书华、沈履、查
良钊、张贻惠五人前往市府拜谒秦德纯,但后者无暇接待。郑天挺将会议修
正通过致蒋介石、宋哲元电文拍发。〔《华北日报》,1937 年 7 月 14 日,第 9 版〕

　　　　按:成舍我、杨立奎受邀列席本次会议。

七月十四日

中午十二时,北平文化教育界人士在松公府北京大学教员俱乐部举行第二
次谈话会,李蒸、袁敦礼、樊际昌、潘光旦、沈履、张贻惠、李书华、先生、李麟
玉、查良钊等二十余人出席。首由社会局长雷嗣尚说明日前时局,继由与
会人员交换意见,约三时许散会。〔《华北日报》,1937 年 7 月 14 日,第 6 版〕

七月十六日

上午九时,故宫博物院在礼堂召开第十三次院务会议,商定本院文物保护
存储办法,沈兼士、先生、张庭济、章宗傅、赵儒珍、庄尚严(邵锐代)、邵锐、
黄鹏霄、欧阳道达(黄鹏霄代)、何澄一、黄念劬(王承吉代)、杨铎、王孝缜
等出席。张庭济为主席,王承吉记录。报告马衡院长寒电。讨论重要文物
如何装箱妥存案。决议如下:

(1)先就三馆提集文物择最精者装箱。

(2)未提文物由总务处二科会同馆方选其最精者完成提取手续、装箱。

(3)前两次箱件暂定为二十至四十箱(古物十至二十箱,图书五至十箱,文献五至
十箱)。

(4)先就延禧宫水亭旧址改成防空库,存放前项箱件。

(5)装箱工作及水亭工程克日开始,本星期日停止休息。〔《马衡年谱长编》,
页 751〕

　　　　按:寒电即本月 14 日电文。

北平二十一位教授密电庐山谈话会,支持政府坚决抗战,先生为联署者
之一。

张岳军秘书长转谈话会诸公公鉴：

学密。芦沟桥抗战以来，全国振奋，士气激昂，几日来忽有天津谈判之举，敌人重兵深入腹地，城下之盟——求不丧权辱国，岂能幸免。务请一致主张贯彻守土抗敌之决心，在日军未退出以前绝对停止折冲，以维国权。不胜祷切。

李书华、李蒸、李麟玉、陆志韦、徐炳昶、袁同礼、查良钊、赵畸、

罗隆基、孙洪芬、方石珊、关颂韬、潘光旦、袁敦礼、梅贻宝、

郑桐孙、张贻惠、饶毓泰、沈履、樊际昌、郑天挺同叩，铣。

〔《清华大学史料选编》第 3 卷（上），北京：清华大学出版社，1993年，页 2-3〕

七月十九日

先生致信王重民，告知商务印书馆拟以石印方式刊行《燉煌古籍丛编》，并收到其寄送照片一批。

有三吾弟：

关于委托商务印书馆影印《燉煌古籍丛编》，顷接商务来函，谓印珂璎版全书定价须三十元，改用石印则须五元，值此不景气之时，书价不宜太昂，主张石印，看其寄来样本亦还不错，未识尊意以为如何？请速决定示复，以便赶印。昨日接到第九包至十三包均系一份，极为满意，此项照片是否印入第二集，抑仅留复本，请便中示及顷得七月一日信，知有底片后可以任意洗晒。用英庚款影印者亦可为清华留一复本也。连日日本大军云集，将有重要要求，幸地方及中央应付尚得体且能一致，不致为日人暗算。前途暗淡，只能沉着应付。余俟再函，顺颂旅安。

袁同礼顿首

七月十九日

六月廿六日及七月一日信均收到。

基金会之壹千元已通过，日内寄法，因法郎甚跌也。

致 Giles 信明日即发，赠伊之刊物交大使馆赵秘书转交足下面交，并赠《国藏善本丛书》一部（价值六百元），样本五册另寄。

〔国立北平图书馆用笺。中国书店·海淀，四册〕

七月中下旬

上海文献会发起刊印《苏松太丛书》，成立出版委员会，先生与赵万里被推

为委员之一。〔《申报》,1937 年 7 月 20 日,第 14 版〕

按:7 月 18 日,上海文献展览会闭幕。翌日上午九时,该会邀请
上海地区各县负责人在八仙桥青年会开会,会长叶恭绰,常务理
事陈端志、吴湖帆、沈维钧、陆丹林、吴静山等,以及各县征集主任
出席。

七月二十一日

上午十时,李书华、李蒸、先生、樊际昌、沈履、查良钊、潘光旦、张贻惠前往
航空署拜会市长秦德纯,交换对时局的意见,后者表示和平谈判仍在继续,
但军事方面亦有相当准备。中午,教育界人士决议致电蒋介石。

南京行政院蒋院长钧鉴:

连日日军破坏我国主权之行动,如北宁路军运、实际占领天津车
站、飞机扫射平汉列车、强占民地建筑飞机场,不一而足,应请于坚持
日方撤兵为谈判先决条件外,立即作有力之制止,以维主权。

李书华、李蒸、陆志韦、袁同礼、潘光旦、沈履、郑天挺、

樊际昌、袁敦礼、陈中平、张贻惠、梅贻宝、孙洪芬、

赵畸、方石珊、关颂韬、林伯遵等二十余人仝叩

〔《大公报》(天津),1937 年 7 月 22 日,第 4 版〕

先生次子袁清出生。

吴宓致函先生,托其为高棣华母女在城中觅合适的住所,以备迁入避难。
〔《吴宓日记》第 6 册,页 175〕

七月二十二日

晨八时半,先生给吴宓打电话,告知三事:一是命高棣华八月一日到馆办
公;二是紧急情况时,高棣华可住先生家;三是北河沿五十三号陈太太宅有
房分租。〔《吴宓日记》第 6 册,页 175〕

七月二十三日

下午三时,世界教育会议美国来华代表参观故宫博物院,晚五时在御花园
举行茶话会,秦德纯偕市府教育股主任罗静夫前往接待。晚八时,北平十
四家文化教育机关在欧美同学会设宴款待美国来华代表,李书华、先生、胡
先骕、孙洪芬、郑天挺、樊际昌、沈履、潘光旦、李蒸、袁敦礼、陆志韦、梅贻
宝、英千里、李麟玉、查良钊等二十余人出席。首由李蒸代表全体致词,并
解释中国不派代表参与东京世界教育会议的理由,继由米兰博士答词,并

表示对中国退会的举措表示理解。〔《华北日报》,1937 年 7 月 24 日,第 6 版〕

　　　　按:该行人员约 23 名,由米兰博士(Milan)率领,7 月 21 日晚由沪抵达北平。

先生致信吴宓,详述北河沿陈宅情况。〔《吴宓日记》第 6 册,页 176-177〕

　　　　按:7 月 24 日,高棣华进城至陈宅看房,不宜租住,遂决定住女青年会。

七月二十四日

先生致信王重民,寄上商务印书馆石印样本,请其补拍《还冤记》《楚辞音》并寄下,另告知已汇寄中基会补助款。

友三吾弟:

　　日前寄一信,内有商务寄来石印样本二张,请予审阅。如全部改用石印,则《还冤记》、《楚辞音》自不必用玻璃版,拟请提出用 Leica 再各照一份,从速寄下是荷。又国际图书馆协会开会,李石曾极愿参加,可一访之,请其出席亦可。兹寄中基会补助费一千元,合七千八百七十法郎,请查收,并将收据寄下是荷。此颂旅安。

　　　　　　　　　　　　　　　　　袁同礼顿首

　　　　　　　　　　　　　　　　　　七,廿四

〔国立北平图书馆用笺。中国书店·海淀,四册〕

七月二十五日

中午十二时,北平教育界人士在欧美同学会聚餐,李书华、李蒸、先生、胡先骕、潘光旦、查良钊、陆志韦、沈履、樊际昌、张贻惠、郑天挺等二十人到场。席间交换时局消息,决定派李书华、李蒸、樊际昌、查良钊、沈履五人往访市长秦德纯,二时许始散。〔《华北日报》,1937 年 7 月 26 日,第 6 版〕

吴宓致函先生,告知高棣华将于八月二日就职并以女青年会为寓所。〔《吴宓日记》第 6 册,页 178〕

七月二十七日

中午,北平教育界人士聚会,李书华、李蒸、陆志韦、潘光旦、张贻惠、樊际昌、郑天挺、先生、胡先骕、查良钊、沈履等二十余人到场,席间交换时局消息,决定派李书华、李蒸、樊际昌、查良钊、张贻惠五人再往访市长秦德纯。〔《华北日报》,1937 年 7 月 28 日,第 6 版〕

北平学术界人士联名向南京国民政府蒋介石发电报,呼吁全国抗战。

急,南京蒋委员长钧鉴:

学密。敌既轰炸廊坊,又炮毁广安门城楼,并公然向我提出最后通牒。危机一发,万难坐以待毙,务恳发动全国力量,即日明令应战,以保卫国家民族生存。

李书华、李蒸、梅贻宝、

袁同礼、孙洪芬、张贻惠、

潘光旦、饶毓泰、赵畸等叩,感。

〔台北"国史馆",〈卢沟御侮(三)〉,数位典藏号 002-090105-00003-394〕

八月二日

先生致信王重民,谈北平局势已无法挽回,并告将来联系方式及寄送照片地址,另述近汇各款情况。

友三吾弟:

此间大势已去,自本月起兄暂不到馆办事,将来通讯处为"南京珠江路九四二号工程参考图书馆转交",各种燉煌照片亦一并寄至此地为要,并请转告向觉明先生,一律照办是盼。现在北平尚称平静,邮件不致遗失,已由英法寄出之照片当能如数寄到馆中也。兹汇上

(一)国币二千元。系英庚款补助,专作影照伦敦所藏燉煌卷子之用。

(二)国币壹千元。系英庚款补助足下生活费之用。

连前两次所汇各壹千元,共五千元,皆系英庚款补助费。又日前汇壹千元系基金会补助足下之生活费,前后共寄六千元。共23580法郎。至本馆补助之半薪,俟筹得再汇。国家值此非常之变,尚希格外镇静,一切仍按预定计划进行,俾能完成吾人之使命,是所企盼。馆中同人均安,惟不能十分自由耳。一切珍重是荷。顺颂大安。

同礼顿首

八月二日,北平

〔中国书店·海淀,四册〕

先生致信高棣华。〔《吴宓日记》第 6 册,页 190〕

王重民覆函先生,告其拟在法国多摄写经照片,因其中甚多重要文献尚不为中外学术界所知。

守和吾师道鉴：

连奉七月一日、十日两手谕，既为生筹画一切，又复训诲谆谆，感激之余，能不努力！一切请勿怀念，生当能遵嘱一一处理。刻北平大势虽已转移，只有望于国人之努力，而图书事业一项在吾师指示范围之内，仍当不稍稍缩小园地，愿依旧有计画继续向前。谨陈如次：

国际图书馆协会执行委员会命生代表出席事，按人地两方说均较熟习，惟语言一项非生所长，当如嘱与使馆接洽，请其派一职员随生列席，代为报告。闭会后一切详情再作专函奉闻。

为英庚款照书事项进行颇利，此二千元除前者寄上之七包，共四百余叶外，尚够照二千张之数，刻所拍照已超过此数，连伯希和千佛洞手稿计算将近二千五百张矣（前七包除外）。实因英庚款补助数目较大，将来到伦敦后，摄影事项因小 Giles 之气量小，恐不能进行顺利，则与其有款而无所用，不如在巴黎多照一些也。且利用此犹太人之失业，可称物美价廉，又际此法郎贬价，各方面都称便宜。又此次二千余叶内之选择范围，四部书居半（略有影印价值者），佛经居半。缘巴黎所藏佛经卷子均甚长，伯希和编目时概因忙未及打开，便说不知名，殊不知卷尾实有书名也。故日本印《大正藏经》时，在巴黎校写之人只依伯氏目而失收重要之卷子颇多。生更参考《敦煌劫余录》，又知吾馆亦未藏，兹将其最重要者摄影，次要者容后再说。生除随手作一札记，并将《大正藏经》所缺零星短件抄补外，所摄影片意在国内学术机关有款时可趸录付印以补日本之缺。又英庚款既为叶玉虎特别帮忙，伊于此道又属专家，必能了解此事之重要，将来伊必继续愿为协助，或更能肯在英款设法也。此事须抵伦敦后，生将论文写出，或先呈胡适之、叶玉虎二先生一阅也。

第八包照片即在此 2000 张数内者，非为即预备影印，乃在预备为将来选择也。因此二千余张大致都如此好。以后又寄五包，想刻已收到，在此在北平恶耗传来以后，便未再付邮，以后寄何何处，请示知。

第二辑因偏于佚书之选择，故较贫乏，若为投国人嗜好，或再加入一些经书诸子之类，容稍后再选一目邮呈。

第一辑序跋因终日编目，太有兴趣，直到今日尚未肯牺牲一日来写好。然材料大致已预备齐全，不久即可动笔，草讫寄上也。

为英庚款照相事，刻既已超过二千张，则二千元之数已不够，且生尚拟选择一些，或尚有千叶可照，故再请从英庚款项内寄下伍百元，以了此账。

又前者五月二十日曾将旧账单（1936—1937）分清华合项、吾馆专项，并各造清单、报告书寄交王念伦先生请转会计课，并先呈吾师一阅。又附一信致吾师，谓吾馆专项约有三千余元刻由清华合项代垫，如馆中有款，请即寄来。最近来信未言到，不知曾接到该项报告否？又生刻在巴黎，既不能长久代垫之款，如不寄，亦可可由馆方与清华将来算帐。

伦敦照书费及生生活费如欲先寄去，请寄大使馆或领事馆先代保存，亦可随函附上。第二次所寄之一千元收条，再寄伍百元，与馆方补助生六个月之用费，再从速一算，寄下为祷。

巴黎在暑假期内，伯、戴诸先生均出外避暑，杜博思刻在此欲将携来四十余件之明画作一展览会，约于十月一日在 Bibliothèque Nationale 举行。李石曾亦在此间，尚属开放，略接见各方学员，生因无事，故不前往。余再奉陈，即请钧安。

受业王重民敬上

八月二日

〔刘波、林世田《国立北平图书馆拍摄及影印出版敦煌遗书史事钩沉》〕

按："可可"二字，疑衍其一。"杜博思"即杜伯秋（Jean-Pierre Dubosc），其早年中文名确为"杜博思"。"王念伦"即王祖彝，字念伦，河北文安人，抗战前任平馆文书组组长。该函首页右侧有"照录王重民来函八月廿一日到"之语，可知信函21日送到北平，此为抄件。

八月三日

晚，吴宓给先生打电话，告知已命高棣华明晨赴平馆办公。先生表示其职务已交代王访渔。〔《吴宓日记》第6册，页185〕

八月八日

先生即将离平，行前告知高棣华如遇紧急情况，可与王敏娴女士及其家人

联系。〔《吴宓日记》第 6 册,页 190、194〕

王重民覆函先生,请转告商务印书馆石印《燉煌古籍丛编》切勿用墨笔描绘以图清晰,并谈其未来赴英安排,另告《历代三宝记》与《历代法宝记》不同。

守和吾师钧鉴:

　　奉七月十九、廿四两手谕,敬悉一是。其第二函中所附汇票一纸 7870.00Fs,礼拜一即能支出,容再寄呈收条。委托商务影印《燉煌古籍丛编》,石印既能便宜数倍,为流通学术及畅销起见,自应以用石印法印行为宜。唯原来照片如有模糊不清之处,请商务主事人千万不要用墨笔描绘,因图清晰反而致误。这一点是商务的通病,印别的可以不管他,印此书请他千万不要犯此毛病。况说我们既有胶片,即有不清之处,若有别种问题可向吾馆要求洗照。即以罗振玉而论,因为描改,亦误人不浅。罗氏于一九一七年用珂罗版印《古籍丛残》,当然印得很好,到一九二八年又印《鸣沙石室佚书》,改用石印,任意描改。生今得持与原卷相对,弄错的实在狠多。所以这次为便宜而采用石印,千万请商务不要犯了这种毛病。再说就是纸幅大小、宽狭方面可任意割配,俾较美观。高低方面不要减缩,序跋等项两周内定能寄上。《还冤记》、《楚辞音》两种即遵嘱,速速另用 Leica 制片,八月十五日以前定能洗出寄上。巴黎方面工作还有两月,正想只编燉煌目已够忙,而伯希和家所藏还不在少数,恐时间不大从容。适礼拜五秘书长请生谈话,交来法外交部转法大使一函,谓吾师曾谓杜女士可留至明年二月。为筹备法国印刷展览会,想此事法使馆欲留她而庚款又由其支配,有此一言,自可支取生活费。当时,生念伦敦工作久可留巴黎至十二月,继思既属交换条件,不留此为自牺牲。又改说愿和杜女士一样亦留至明年二月。刻已覆函外交部照此决定矣。现在生之计画拟在十月一日以前因为杜博思帮忙在 Bibliothèque Nationale 开我国图书展画会,十月一日至十一月一日休假一月,偕刘女士赴英,她即入学,生即着手照像事,十一月一日回巴黎。如伯希和藏书能看定而燉煌目亦编好,则明年一月内赴英,即不再来巴黎,便常在彼弄英伦所藏卷子。此种计画不知吾师以为然否?今既有如此变动,于生生活费上可得帮助不少,即便明年一月内不再支薪而国内所补助之二千余元在明年六个月内支配便富足多多了。故此次所寄之一千元暂拟补入英庚款照相项下,其用不完者,生拟收下作为生活费(由法郎换英镑比由国币换英镑当然吃亏)。图书馆协会代表出席一节,当遵嘱谒李石曾一商,容再详陈。前者胡适之先生谓《历代三宝记》为《历代法宝记》之误,盖因把书名混而为一,缘《三宝记》为费长房撰,《法宝记》世人久已知之,有《三宝记》以前不知也。又《南宗定是非论》一书,胡先生曾得一节印行,生现在几得全卷,谈话时可将此《南宗定是非论》(独孤沛撰)加入也。Leica胶卷每卷长可二米,达能照像三十六张。英庚款项下刻已有一百卷已按号码装入定做之匣子,候稍平定即可寄上。想国内加洗定比巴黎还便宜,清华如要,俟在国内加洗如何? 又第8-13照片均平安收到,闻之甚慰。此次英庚款所照二千余张都是一样好,将来第二辑自当从中选择付印。余再禀,即请道安。

受业重民敬上

八月八日

〔刘波、林世田《国立北平图书馆拍摄及影印出版敦煌遗书史事钩沉》〕

按:该函首页右侧有"录王有三来函八月廿五日到"字样,可知信函25日送到南京,此为抄件。

八月九日

先生离平赴天津。〔中国书店·海淀,四册〕

按:先生在此留住2日。

八月十七日

柳诒徵致函先生,告国学图书馆已将借钞平馆之明本《宋史记》存放在故宫博物院南京分院地库中。

守和先生大鉴:

秋风凄厉,遥祝平安,南北同情,鄙况尚适。前借尊处之《宋史记》九册,缮录未完,迭闻警报,邮递恐有舛误,已偕敝馆善本书装箱,寄存故宫分院地库,恐劳锦注,谨以奉闻。专此,即颂台绥。并盼惠福。

前向曹君处携取袁许手札,未审已否付印? 近存何许? 盼示。

〔《盎山牍存》,1948年1月,页1〕

按:8月14日,江苏省立国学图书馆分两批寄存善本书5箱至故宫博物院南京分院地库,中有明本《宋史记》九册,除告知先生外,柳诒徵亦于 8 月 17 日致信平馆在沪人员李耀南。但此书应随国学图书馆寄存图书陷于南京,并未随故宫文物西迁。①

八月中旬

先生赴秦皇岛并由此乘船南下前往上海,但被阻于吴淞口,无法登岸,只得乘原船南下香港。〔台北"中央研究院"历史语言研究所傅斯年图书馆,"史语所档案",杂 5-8-2〕

八月二十二日　香港

先生致信王重民,告知离平后的行踪,并谈补助向达、汪德昭等人的方法。

友三吾弟:

离平前曾寄一书,内附中法工商银行汇票(合国币叁仟元),想能如数收到。北平已为日人占据,高等教育无法进行,本馆自受相当影响,但一时尚不致为他人所接收也。前函请将以后所照之照片径寄"南京珠江路 942 号"有二种之玻璃版留平,请各补照一份寄京,以便交商务印,请照办并转告向觉民兄是荷。觉民兄之补助费每月由馆送至其家中,但将来为他人接收时则有问题,并请转告早日准备是盼。兄于九日离平,在津住二日,由秦皇岛搭轮南下,航抵吴淞,以上海战事未得进口,遂搭原轮来港,拟由此赴汉,再换江轮至京,预计九月一号以前必能到京也。汪德昭君现在巴黎,通讯处大约为 Laboratoire de Prof. Langevin,10 Rue Vauquelin Paris 5e,因街名不记忆,请转告如彼需款救济,可暂在尊处借用,外一纸并请转交。应寄尊处之补助费,俟到京后再设法。顺颂旅安。

兄袁同礼顿首

八月廿二,香港

〔中国书店·海淀,四册〕

按:汪德昭(1905—1998),江苏灌云人,物理学家,时在法国留学,入巴黎大学朗之万研究室攻读研究生,后担任法国国家科学研究中心研究人员,1956 年 12 月归国,其妻子李惠年即李瑞年之妹,北平师范大学生物系毕业,以歌唱、音乐教育而知名,归国后曾任中国音乐学院教授。该信以航空信方式寄送。

① 《盍山庼存》,页 27。

九月六日　长沙

先生与朱经农等人在湖南省教育厅商讨平馆与临时大学合作办法。随后，先生致信王世杰，报告此事并恳请将此动议转告在南京的胡适、傅斯年、周诒春等人。

　　雪艇部长尊鉴：

　　　　前由秦皇岛抵粤，曾上一电，抵湘后又寄一电，未识均能寄到否。本拟即日晋京面陈一切，嗣经农及京中来湘同人以临时大学亟须从速设立，而图书设备方面需人主持，坚嘱留此暂予协助。本日同人在教厅集议，拟由临时大学及北平图书馆各任万元作为开办费，同时并将平馆所订购之西文专门杂志二千余种改寄长沙，即在圣经学校内设立办事处。此仅为一时权宜之计，想大部及委员会同人当表赞同也，孟麟、洪芬、援庵先生处，顷已函告。在京委员有适之、孟真、季梅三先生，拟请分别转达，并盼随时指示，俾有遵循。无任企祷，一俟此间布置就绪，当即来京晋谒。先此，敬候道祺。

袁同礼拜启

九月六日

　　叔贻、梅孙先生同此致候。

　　　　〔中国第二历史档案馆，教育部档案·全卷宗5，教育部关于筹设
　　　　长沙临时大学并与国立北平图书馆合组图书馆的文件，案卷号
　　　　2212〕

　　　　按："经农"即朱经农，时任湖南省教育厅厅长。由此信内容可
　　　　知，先生似应分别致信平馆委员蒋梦麟、孙洪芬（沪）、陈垣（平），
　　　　将平馆与临时大学合作之议告知。"叔贻"即段锡朋，字书诒，时
　　　　应任教育部政务次长；"梅孙"即周炳琳。

九月十四日

先生致信傅斯年，告知离平经历并呈上临时大学合组草案。

　　孟真吾兄：

　　　　旧京沦陷，音讯鲜通。弟在平布置妥贴，始于上月十三日由秦王岛来沪，在吴淞口外等候三日，未能进口。原轮驶港，上月杪由粤来湘，本拟晋京，适缉斋、思永均来，劝多留数日。嗣后森玉及馆中同人陆续抵湘，遂与临时大学商定合组办法。兹奉上草案，请交孟麟先生一阅，如有

需修正之处,并祈赐示是荷。此间传闻孟麟先生不日来湘,故不另函。近来心绪繁乱、懒于执笔,每日到旧书铺看书,因书价甚廉,故已开始搜集湘中著述,希望在最近之将来能利用此种环境,将西南文献搜集一处,以供学子之参考,亦未免太痴矣。斐云、刚主、子书诸同人,如有到京者,请告其来湘参加工作。惟孙洪芬先生久无消息,此间同人嗷嗷待哺,而经费来源断绝,殊为惶恐。曾函季梅先生暂向南京中孚暂借两千元馆中一部分余款均汇沪中孚,不识结果如何也。吾兄主持院务,贤劳可想。闻嫂夫人在庐山,当甚安全。舍下仍留北平,弟仅携一皮箱脱身耳。顺颂大安。

弟同礼顿首

〔国立北平图书馆长沙办事处用笺。台北"中央研究院"历史语言研究所傅斯年图书馆,"史语所档案",杂 5-8-2〕

按:"缉斋"即汪敬熙(1893-1968),山东历城人,心理学家。落款时间似因该份档案扫描件未尽全幅,现依照史语所档案所记,归于 9 月 14 日。附临时大学、平馆合组图书馆办法草案三纸,共七条。

先生致信王世杰,谈平馆与临时大学合组图书馆事并附草案。

雪艇部长尊鉴:

本月六日曾上一书,计达钧览,昨奉佳电,敬悉一一。此间充实图书设备办法,业经拟定,兹奉上该办法草案七条,敬希鉴核。刻正锐意搜罗,积极布置,馆中职员亦陆续抵湘,预计国庆日可以开幕。专此,敬候道祺。

袁同礼谨启
九月十四日

〔中国第二历史档案馆,教育部档案·全卷宗 5,教育部关于筹设长沙临时大学并与国立北平图书馆合组图书馆的文件,案卷号2212〕

按:"佳电"即 9 日电。该信后附办法草案,主要涉及临时大学(甲方)、平馆(乙方)的责任,如开办费分担、办公费、职员薪水,另规定双方购书的侧重。

九月二十日

先生致信王重民,告其已决定在长沙办公不再赴南京,并谈人、事近况。

有三吾兄：

在香港寄一航信，想已收到。抵湘后见中央研究院全部移湘，知京中无法工作，遂决定留此，在湘设立办事处继续进行。顷由平转到八月二日来书，由京转到八月八日来书，均悉一一。杜乃扬展至明年二月，系韩参赞主张，杜女士并不愿意，因亟欲赴日本参观正仓院古物。今彼方既决定留至明年二月，则足下自可同样办理，于公于私均值得多留也。伦敦照书费二千元及美庚款补助之一千元，于离平前汇法，想已收到，收条请寄此处是荷。闻平馆已被徐佛苏接收，恐王念伦诸人均须离职，而信件又加检查，故须小心也。如接到刘树楷之信，则较此间接北平之信消息尤快。照片可暂存尊处，第一辑序跋可寄湘，此间与沪尚通邮，惟商务工厂停顿，一时亦不能付印也。适之先生日昨飞美，将来或到欧洲蒋慰堂随乃叔赴德(蒋百里)，中央馆由岳良木代理。本馆移湘办公，将来购书费及一部分经常费均可陆续汇来，但此时孙洪芬先生在津，一切须稍缓方能进行。森玉先生亦在此，平馆诸人陆续南下。刻清华、北大、南开在此设临时大学，本馆与之合作，办事处即设在该大学内。专此，顺颂大安。

袁同礼顿首

九月二十日，长沙

通讯处"长沙韭菜园一号"，外一信转寄汪德昭君。

〔中国书店·海淀，四册〕

按：徐佛苏(1879—1943)，湖南长沙人，日本东京高等师范学校毕业，历任大总统府顾问、币制局总裁、北平民国大学代理校长。北平沦陷后出任地方维持会顾问、东亚文化协议会评议员。[1] 他并未参与接收平馆事宜，信中之言应属谣传。先生兼任临时大学图书馆馆长，平馆之部侧重西南文献、西文专门期刊。时，先生居长沙青年会。[2]

先生致信汪德昭，告知东陆大学仍无覆信，如其归国可至临时大学谋事。

德昭如晤：

前寄一信，由王重民先生转交，谅已收到。刻下东陆大学等处仍

---

① 《北平市地方维持会各项章则文告》，1937 年，页 29；李文褀、武田熙编《北京文化学术机关综览》，新民印书馆，1940 年，页 326。
② 《吴宓日记》第 6 册，页 219。

无覆函,想均感困难,无法位置也。如在法无法维持,则可携眷返国,由香港一日两夜来湘。刻下临时大学已组织成立,谋一小事当不难也。月涵亦在此,瑞年在汉口与张溥泉家同住法界亚尔萨罗兰尼省街 107 号,常有信来。惟北平之信往往须二十余日,且不可靠,但甚安谧,治安无虞也。舍下仍留北平。顺颂旅安。

> 同礼顿首
> 九,二十,长沙
> 〔中国书店·海淀,四册〕

九月二十六日

先生致信蔡元培(香港),告知平馆拟与长沙第一临时大学合组成立图书馆并附合同稿。〔《蔡元培日记》,页 510;《北京图书馆馆史资料汇编(1909 - 1949)》,页 614〕

> 按:此信 10 月 3 日送达,翌日蔡元培即覆先生,述孙洪芬意见,建议将合组之事提交平馆委员会讨论。

九月二十八日

先生致信史蒂文斯,告知自己已南下长沙,行前曾与美国驻平使馆人员商谈,请其代为保管平馆在美的缩微胶卷设配,另外洛克菲勒基金会资助各项目均告暂停。

Sept. 28, 1937

Dear Dr. Stevens:

　　Before leaving Peiping, I received a cable from your office endorsing the postponement of Dr. W. W. Bishop's visit to China. We have been most disappointed that we shall not be able to see him in our country this fall, but we are entertaining the hope that he may come out again after the undeclared war is over. I have, therefore, asked the Peiping office of the American Express Company to hold the money for the time being.

　　Dr. Graves wrote me some time ago that Dr. Draeger had left for China by way of Europe. I have had so far, no word from him nor from the American Embassy in Peiping. I have, however, asked the Embassy to hold the microfilm equipment for us until we are able to set it up in Nanking and to inform Dr. Draeger to this effect as soon as he arrives.

With the shortage of paper and the interruption of postal services, we are obliged to stop temporarily the printing of catalogue cards.

I have asked Mr. Gunn to withhold the grant beginning from October until he hears from me again. The balance of the grant is being deposited in a special a/c at the National City Bank. The work will be resumed as soon as conditions become normal.

With Japan's military occupation of Peiping, all the national institutions have been greatly affected, as it is impossible for us to operate under another flag. With the aerial bombing not limited to military establishments, we are obliged to set up an office in the interior. A library of fairly good size has been organized in Changsha and a number of our technical staff has been transferred from Peiping.

We are having most trying experiences with Japan's aerial bombing of residential quarters and cultural institutions. But every one of us is still very hopeful. I understand that Dr. Hu Shih has already arrived at New York and I hope you will have an opportunity to meet him and to discuss with him the developments here.

With kindest regards,

Yours sincerely,

T. L. Yuan

Acting Director

〔平馆(长沙办事处)英文信纸。Rockefeller Foundation. Series 601: China; Subseries 601.R: China-Humanities and Arts. Box 47. Folder 389〕

按：此件为打字稿，落款处为先生签名，于 10 月中下旬送达。先生致信史密斯森协会，建议该会暂停寄送平馆、南京工程参考图书馆的国际交换品。

Sept. 28, 1937

Dear Sirs:

In view of Japan's armed invasion and aerial bombing of cultural institutions, we have established an office in the interior at the above address.

As the work of Chinese international exchange service has been interrupted, we suggest that you hold temporarily the shipment of consignments intended for the National Library of Peiping as well as for our Engineering Reference Library at Nanking. First class mails, however, should be sent to this office.

　　Thanking you in anticipation for your attention,

Yours truly,

T. L. Yuan

Acting Director

　　　　〔平馆(长沙办事处)英文信纸。Smithsonian Institution Archives, Records, 1868－1988 (Record Unit 509), Box 1, National Library, Peiping〕

　　按:此件为打字稿,落款处为先生签名,于 11 月 16 日送达。

十月初

先生致信高棣华(北平),命其与翟孟生等人同赴长沙。〔《吴宓日记》第 6 册, 页 228、248〕

　　　　按:吴宓、高棣华等于 11 月 7 日离平南行。先生夫人袁慧熙并未随行,只是托其带去面盆一套、衣服一包。

十月三日

先生致信岳良木,告知垫款已汇、新聘馆员事及请代订中央日报诸事。

　　荫嘉先生:

　　　　前奉手教,曾复一函,由于镜宇转交承寄电话簿,迄未收到,惟高门楼误写高楼门,未识能寄到否? 前承中央图书馆代垫之叁百陆拾元,已于前日交上海银行汇上,请查收示复为祷。胡君业于日前安抵浙江, 吴、莫两君亦到馆办事矣。兹请自十月一号起代订《中央日报》一份, 告其径寄长沙临大图书馆韭菜园一号,款请暂垫,示知后当照汇。专此, 顺颂大安。

弟袁同礼顿首

十月三日

　　　　〔长沙临时大学图书馆用笺。台北"中央图书馆"档案,档案编号 180-0002〕

　　按:"于镜宇"即于震寰,时应在国立中央图书馆任职。"高门楼"

应指南京中央路高门楼。1937 年 9 月 9 日,国立中央图书馆暂迁高门楼 32 号办公。胡、吴、莫三人待考。

十月四日

傅斯年覆函蒋梦麟、先生,提出对平馆善后办法的意见。

孟邻、守和两先生:

惠书拜悉。秦绍文先生缺由任叔永先生补选一节,弟谨表赞成。斯年之缺,如到期,乞一并改选。平馆善后办法各项中,斯年有下列意见:

1)"在湘五折,在平全发",斯年觉得似不甚妥,且有奖励人不出来之意思。平馆情形,固应维持,然两处待遇如太不均,似非无宜也。可否即用政府之办法,即五十元以下者不折,五十元以上者,先以五十元为生活费,不折,其余则折扣之,六至八折。两处情形一律,以不得自由离平为限制,殊胜于薪水待遇之差也。

2)西文期刊或可大体续定,但中西文书以少购为宜,今非搜集之时也。当俟时局稍可之□。

本院古籍迁湘者,本应开箱,但事实上一时甚难办,且迁湘之书每多非急用之书也。

两先生以为何如?专此,敬拜道安。

斯年谨上

十月四日

〔《北京图书馆馆史资料汇编(1909-1949)》,页 445-446〕

蔡元培覆函先生,表示平馆与临时大学合组图书馆事须征求平馆委员会之同意,方可继续执行。

守和先生大鉴:

奉九月廿六日惠函,敬悉平馆布置已妥,先生在长沙设一平馆办事处,甚慰。函示与临时大学第一区合组图书馆办法,此事于孙洪芬兄在沪时已谈过一次,均以为本馆有一图书委员会,此种特殊组织非征求委员会之同意不可。请先生提出该会,以多数决之。洪芬兄当已有详函奉告矣。弟在沪尚好,承注甚感。此复,并颂著绥。

弟蔡元培敬启

十月四日

〔国立中央研究院用笺。国家图书馆档案,档案编号 1937-※
007-年录 3-002005、1937-※007-年录 3-002006〕

按:此信被《北京图书馆馆史资料汇编(1909-1949)》错记为 1938
年,实不可能。

十月五日

周诒春覆函先生,告知已收到与临大合组图书馆办法草案并谈汇款事。

守和我兄惠鉴:

顷奉上月二十四日复翰,敬悉一是。临时大学第一区与国立北平
图书馆合组图书馆办法草案七条,业经诵悉,颇为妥洽。前请汇款至
湘,据京中孚称,奉总行函平款尚未汇到,以致不克照汇。洪芬兄在沪
时曾与通过电话,据云已汇款与兄,想已接洽矣。京中日来甚平静,人
心亦极安定,承念并闻。专复,顺颂公祺。

弟周诒春敬启

十月五日

〔《北京图书馆馆史资料汇编(1909-1949)》,页 448〕

按:此件应为代笔,落款处为其签名。

十月九日

任鸿隽覆函先生,告其维持平馆的想法。

守和吾兄左右:

十月五日手示并伯遵英文信均奉到,诵悉一一。平中馆事,据伯
遵所言,甚属可虑。弟于洪芬北上时曾缄渠,如能利用经济条件力图
保全,宜若可为,不知能办到几分否。鄙意目下最要者在得一二略知
守正之人,参与其间暗中维护,方期略有把握。不知馆中尚有此项人
才否?森玉如何,王绂渔恐不足当此重任。在此间植物园造房,不必先交款领
地亦可兴工。房价小者,用木造一千数百元即得,兴工时期以秋季为
佳,冬间冻雪、春间多雨,又农事较忙,恐不宜也。兄如有意来此兴筑,
最好便中来此一视,并畅谈一切。弟等在此已作过冬准备,虽颇不愿,
亦无如何也。临时联合图书馆想已开幕,长沙此时学术机关林立,贵
馆成立功用极大,敬佩敬佩。营造学社是否已全部南迁,朱桂老尚在
平否?甚以为念。余不一一,此请著安。

伯遵信附还。

弟鸿隽顿首

十月九日

〔国家图书馆档案,档案编号 1938-※007-年录 3-002001 和

1938-※007-年录 3-002002〕

十月上旬

长沙临时大学图书馆与湖南省建设厅议定合作办法,后者将附设之国货陈列馆图书室全部借给临大作为第二阅览室。〔中国第二历史档案馆,教育部档案·全宗号 5,长沙临时大学图书馆馆务报告及国立西南联合大学师范学院各项中心活动计划说明,案卷号 5541〕

> 按:10 月 6 日,临时大学常务委员会第六次会议举行,其中讨论议案之一,即借用湖南国货陈列馆图书室办法。①

十月十日

柳诒徵覆函先生,寄赠图书以利平馆复兴之举,并告国学图书馆近况。

> 守和先生道座:

>> 倭奴肆虐,南北同仇,遥望燕云,每为贵馆及执事兴慨。昨得湘函,敬悉大旆南下,计划复兴,侨寄麓台,广征缃帙,应变持颠,规麾弘远,曷胜倾企。兹谨检敝馆印售书全份及鄙人赠品付邮寄呈,另附详目,聊助涓埃。邮件到日,乞赐复书,兼希略示湘垣各方状况为盼。京市空警已历六旬,敝馆幸尚安全,亦拟徙寄要籍,迟回审慎,尚未进行,并祈锡以南针、预筹善策,临楮毋任瞻系。此颂公绥,不备。

〔《盇山胘存》,页 11〕

> 按:先生收到此函后立即覆信,告知长沙、衡山近况,表示两处适宜房屋并不甚多,如国学图书馆将善本迁湘则须派人典守并开箱提供阅览。②

十月十二日

教育部高等教育司发司函,"函知长沙临时大学国立北平图书馆合组图书馆办法已予核定由"。

---

① 北京大学、清华大学、南开大学、云南师范大学编《国立西南联合大学史料》第 2 卷,昆明:云南教育出版社,1998 年,页 10-11。

② 《盇山胘存》,页 12-13。

径启者：

　　奉部长发下九月十四日大函,检送长沙临时大学国立北平图书馆合组图书馆办法草案,希鉴核等语。查是项办法,尚无不合,部中已予核定,相应函达。查照为荷！此致
袁同礼先生

　　　　　　　　　　　　　　　　教育部高等教育司启

　　〔中国第二历史档案馆,教育部档案·全卷宗5,教育部关于筹设长沙临时大学并与国立北平图书馆合组图书馆的文件,案卷号2212〕

　　按:9月29日长沙临时大学筹备委员会曾复函教部高教司,表示与平馆合办图书馆事业系双方同意拟定,无异议。在教育部相关档案中,王世杰曾有批示,原文为"原办法即予核定,关于经费由~~两方实行此办法时自行落实~~,在文件中不必提及。~~可另以私函告袁馆长~~",其中删节处似由王世杰自行涂改。

十月十三日

先生以未买到《四部丛刊》,主张退掉《四库珍本》。〔《朱自清全集》第9卷,页490〕

　　按:朱自清时应为清华大学在长沙负责图书仪器者,对先生的态度较之首次见面时已有极大改观,认为先生"甚和蔼"。《朱自清全集》此处或有误,语义似应为买到《四部丛刊》,退掉《四库珍本》。

十月二十五日

北京大学、清华大学、私立南开大学三校组建的长沙临时大学正式开学。①该校与平馆(南馆)、中央研究院历史语言研究所合作,成立临时大学图书馆,先生兼任该馆馆长。

任鸿隽覆函先生,告知北平文化机关近况并表示愿意就平馆委员会委员一职,另邀先生往庐山一行。

　　守和吾兄大鉴：

　　　　十五日来书奉到,敬悉一一。北平各文化机关既有保管委员会负

———————————

① 《国立西南联合大学史料》第1卷,页3。

责保管,似尚无接收情事,稍可放心。图书馆委员仍令弟滥竽,弟自当勉从诸公之后,略尽棉薄,但恐此时亦无事可作耳。洪芬尚在天津,候船南下。中基会已定计南迁,但尚留一二人在平,料理未了事宜。闻敌机近亦到长沙肆扰,想于新成立各机关尚无防害。山中近来天气颇佳,兄如来山,自以早来为妙,再晚则天寒不宜游览矣。何时驾临请先示知,谨当下榻以待,但须自带铺陈,恐敝处所有不足供用。荒寒至此,想不美也。见梦麐、月涵、经农、伯苓诸先生时,均乞代为致意。不一一,此请著安。

弟鸿隽顿首
十月廿五日

〔《北京图书馆馆史资料汇编(1909-1949)》,页 451-452〕

十月二十六日

柳诒徵覆函先生,告知拟将国学图书馆迁移,并应平馆征书启事寄赠出版物。

　　守和先生大鉴:

　　　　荷教极感,垂注所示,两地似以南岳为尤僻远,未识该馆隶省抑隶衡阳县? 在山之某部分? 顷已报告教厅,俟得决移确讯,当以快电或航函先闻也。前得尊处征书公启,当将敝馆印售书全份及私人所印数种挂号邮赠,未审已否到湘? 细审地址,知尊馆与临时大学即在一处。诸知好均希代为问候。经农兄处,公务谅甚忙,亦祈代候,不另函矣。专此布复,即颂公绥。

　　　　尊处存沪之书现在能否运湘? 科学社似尚安全也。

〔《盋山牍存》,页 11〕

史蒂文斯覆函先生,告知收到九月二十八日报告,此前对平馆的资助仍然有效,但如有特殊情况请先生向基金会或驻沪办事处汇报,并告为平馆购置的缩微摄影器材仍在美国。

October 26, 1937

Dear Dr. Yuan:

I have your letter of September 28 reporting the funds are held for the projected visit of Dr. Bishop. This is quite satisfactory to us. I might recall the terms of the grant whereby during three years ending June 30,

1939, a total of ＄25,000 was made available by our trustees, and in each of these years a maximum of ＄11,000 could be requisitioned for the purposes of the grant. If these terms are not to be possible from your point of view, word should be sent at a later time to the New York and Shanghai offices.

I have had word from Dr. Graves that the equipment of Dr. Draeger is still held in Washington. Under present circumstances this is gratifying. I may have a later report for you, as Dr. Graves is inquiring what the American Council of Learned Societies should do in the matter. You will recall that the Draeger equipment for your library was purchased through a grant to the Council, and fortunately we now have their interest in caring for it.

With kindest regards, I am

Sincerely yours,

David H. Stevens

〔Rockefeller Foundation. Series 601: China; Subseries 601.R: China-Humanities and Arts. Box 47. Folder 389〕

按:该函寄送上海,并抄送基金会驻沪办事处。

十月二十七日

先生致信王献唐,商洽与山东省立图书馆交换、购买方志。

献唐先生大鉴:

事变以来,时以尊处文物之安危为念。迩来敌军北退,济南当可暂安,想早已未雨绸缪矣。弟自八月杪来此,奉令组织办事处继续进行。闻尊处复本方志尚多,应否交换抑价购,均盼示及是荷。专此,敬颂时祉。

弟袁同礼顿首

十月廿七

〔《王献唐师友书札》,页 1212〕

十一月一日

恒慕义致函先生,告知国会图书馆聘请重编馆藏中文文献负责人的要求和待遇。

Nov. 1, 1937

Dear Mr. Yuan: −

I have your letter of May 8, 1937, in which you recommend Dr. Kuo-chin Liu, Librarian of Nanking University, as a suitable man to take charge of the re-cataloguing of our Chinese Collection.

We have made application to a foundation to assist us over a period of three years in re-writing our catalogue and in making the cards ready to print in book form, such as Mr. Chiu is now doing for Harvard. The man in charge of this work would have a salary of about $3,000 annually, in addition to a travel allowance. He would be expected to stay with the project for the full three-year period and then see it through the press. He would have two assistants, with nominal salaries, who could be changed whenever needed. Naturally the head man should know rare books and be able to detect and describe them. Having lived in north China myself, I prefer, other things being equal, a head-cataloguer from that part of the country.

Do you still think that Mr. Liu would be the best man for the post?

I hope that all is going reasonably well with you, considering the trying times you are facing. Miss Sophia Han often comes to Washington, and she then gives us news of your whereabouts.

With kind regards, I remain,

Sincerely yours,

A. W. Hummel

Chief, Division of Orientalia

〔Library of Congress Archives, Arthur W. Hummel Sr. correspondence series, MSS86324〕

按：由该函可知，恒慕义更倾向于曾在平馆服务过的或者是来自北平地区的候选人，而非此前推荐的刘国钧（Dr. Kuo-chin Liu），此点应基于他对北平文化中心的认识。先生收到此函后应改荐吴光清前往，并拟派王重民前往主持，参见 1938 年 1 月 17 日先生致王重民信。该函寄送长沙，此件为录副。

十一月四日

先生致信耿士楷,询问洛克菲勒基金会有无可能援助平馆订购科学技术类期刊。

November 4, 1937

Mr. Selskar M. Gunn

Rockefeller Foundation

c/o American Express Co.

Hongkong

Dear Mr. Gunn:

I wish to thank you for your letter of October 21. At your suggestion I have written to Mr. Chang Hung-chun and asked him to get in touch with the Treasurer concerning the fellowship money at Tsi-ning.

With regard to our reestablishment at Changsha, I wish to report that everything is getting on very satisfactorily. The books are pouring in at a speed much faster than we ever expected. In addition to books, all scientific journals which were transferred from Peiping are arriving via Hongkong almost every day. When you visit our centre, you will find a fairly good library already set up in Changsha within six weeks' time.

What has worried us most recently is our inability to renew our periodical subscriptions for 1938. The Trustees of the China Foundation from whom we have been receiving our support have decided to withhold the payment of our book fund already budgeted for 1937-38. They have to take this action in accordance with the instructions from the Government. But all professors here insist that we must keep on subscribing these scientific journals, as they cannot carry on their work without them.

Out of our annual book fund of G $ 30,000, G $ 6,500 is spent for current scientific periodicals. Together with other serials and continuation orders such as annuals, year-books, directories, reference books, etc., they amount to G $ 10,000. As this is quite a sum, I doubt whether the Rockefeller Foundation would be interested to help us out at this time. However, as these journals are indispensable tools to Chinese intellectual workers, you might like to bring our case to the attention of the officers of the Foundation as opportunity arises. It would indeed be a blessing to our scientific world if some support can be given.

I enclose also a copy of my recent letter to Dr. W. W. Bishop for your information. With kindest regards,

Yours sincerely,

T. L. Yuan

Acting Director

P. S.-All classes were resumed November 1 with 106 professors and 1,100 students.

〔平馆（长沙办事处）英文信纸。Rockefeller Foundation. Series 601: China; Subseries 601.R: China-Humanities and Arts. Box 47. Folder 389〕

按：此件为打字稿，落款处为先生签名。12 月 1 日，耿士楷将此信抄送给史蒂文斯，但不建议给予平馆任何形式的资助。

十一月十日

先生致信耿士楷，简述日军侵占文化教育机关暴行，并寄上温德报告副本。

Nov. 10, 1937

Dear Mr. Gunn:

I trust you have received my recent letter sent to you on November 4th.

Prof. Jameson has recently sent me a copy of the enclosed report submitted by Prof. Winter of Tsing Hua. I hope you will forward it to your New York Office, as most people in the States do not realize what an effect the Japanese invasion has produced on Chinese cultural and educational institutions.

We have just had report from our men in Peiping that all buildings in the National University of Peking and the National Normal University have been occupied by Japanese soldiers. The keys to the National University Library and the Geological building were taken away by force and no employee of the University was allowed to visit the campus after their occupation.

Yours sincerely

T. L. Yuan

Acting Director

P. S.-As Prof. Winter is still in Peiping, it is better not to mention his name.

〔平馆(长沙办事处)英文信纸。Rockefeller Foundation. Series 601: China; Subseries 601.R: China-Humanities and Arts. Box 47. Folder 389〕

按:温德报告写于 10 月 11 日,由翟孟生寄送先生。此件为打印稿,落款处为先生签名,以航空信方式寄送。

十一月十一日

孙念礼致函先生,代其助手郑基元询问玄奘生平、《训民正音》版本问题。

November 11, 1937

Dear Dr. Yüan:

In his preparation for material for his dissertation here at Princeton University, there has arisen especially four questions for Mr. Chung Kei-won to answer. We had hoped that our books would be on the shelves by this time, and that he could find answers to his questions therein. Unfortunately we are still virtually in storage, so I venture to turn to you for information for Mr. Chung.

As I understand his questions (four in number) the first is the most important to him; but we hope that you can have answers sent to him for information on the four. Since he is preparing a dissertation, it is necessary for any information sent to be based upon references with accurate citations of title, authorship if known, edition, publication date as accurate as may be known, chuan, pagination, etc., according, as you know, is required for graduate students to give in their dissertations.

Questions: 1. Was Huang Tsan a specialist in Sanskrit? Please give citation for reply, quoting passages with full accurate references. (N. B. As I understand, Mr. Chung is very anxious for full, definite information on the point whether or not Huang Tsan was such.)

2. May we have a biographical sketch of Huang Tsan? Please give citations for reply, quoting passages in so far as required.

3. Was Huang Tsan a great Chinese scholar as well as a Buddhist one? Please give citations for reply, quoting passages in so far as required for accurate information.

4. The few copies of the Korean book, *Hun Min Chung Eum* with which Mr. Chung is familiar, and of which he has a photo reproduction, lacks the first double page of the original copy. The reproduction contains a substitute double page, but Mr. Chung would like to know whether or not there is a known extant double page of the original copy. If so, where does this page exist? Is it possible for him to obtain a photostat copy of the original page if one does exist?

In order to give you the full information concerning these questions, I asked Mr. Chung to compose a statement in Chinese for me to send to you. This I enclose, hoping that it will facilitate the research of your reference librarian in his endeavor to answer these questions. We will certainly appreciate your co-operation in getting us a reply at your earliest opportunity. I did not realize until this morning that Mr. Chung really needs this information in order to complete his dissertation. In spite of the war conditions under which your Library now functions, and the risk that very like we run both in getting this letter out to you, and in receiving a reply from you, we hope that we may hear from you in the course of the next two months or a bit more time.

In our work in the Library we are looking forward to the time when the catalogue cards that now come to us include Chinese standard texts of pre-Republican date of publication. We look forward to receiving information concerning the set for the coming year. Just now, we have a Chinese student filing the cards for the past two years received up-to-date. We are having him follow the I. V. Gillis Index System that we had begun to use up at McGill, typing the index number on the upper right hand corner.

I hope that we are not over-stepping the privileges of one library making a request of another in asking for the above information.

Very sincerely,

Nancy Lee Swann, M. A. Ph. D., Curator

〔Princeton University, Mudd Manuscript Library, AC123, Box 415,

Folder Peiping, National Library of, 1937–1944〕

按:Mr. Chung Kei-won 即郑基元,韩国人,时任孙念礼的助手,是年毕业于普林斯顿大学东方语言系。[1] Huang Tsan 即玄奘; *Hun Min Chung Eum* 即《训民正音》,是朝鲜王朝第四代国王世宗大王李祹与其子第五代国王文宗大王李珦主导创制的朝鲜语文字,该书于朝鲜世宗二十五年至二十六年间(1443–1444)完成,二十八年(1446)正式刊行。该函寄送北平,此件为录副。

Charles C. Williamson 致函先生,感谢先生及其他中国校友赠送木质匾额作为哥伦比亚大学图书服务学院成立五十周年的贺礼。

November 11, 1937

Dear Mr. Yuan:

Months and months have elapsed, I find, since you wrote us of the exceedingly generous thought of the Chinese alumni in sending us the wooden plaque to mark the fiftieth anniversary of the School of Library Service. What form of official acknowledgment has reached you in one way or another I do not know, but I am sensible of the fact that I have failed so far to express to you my personal pleasure in this interesting and significant gift and to thank you also on behalf of the School of Library Service and its alumni.

We had long delays and considerable difficulty of one sort or another in getting the shipment out of customs. Then, when we finally got it delivered at the University, we discovered that through some mischance it had suffered considerable damage in shipment. I think the damage can be repaired, but to date I have not found anyone who knows just how it should be done, and no

---

[1] Peter X. Zhou ed., *Collecting Asia: east Asian libraries in north America, 1868–2008*, 2008, p. 127.

one to whom I am willing to entrust so delicate a piece of work.

Recently I conferred with Professor Goodrich on this point and he has made suggestions which I think will solve the problem. After considerable discussion we have decided to hang it in a conspicuous place where students congregate between classes in a kind of corridor-lobby outside the main office of the School. There it will be seen and admired by all. We will attach to it a label which will carry the translation which you give and the statement that it is given to the School by the Chinese alumni on the occasion of the fiftieth anniversary.

I am taking great pleasure in making mention of this gift in my annual report to President Butler which will be placed in his hands shortly.

Sincerely yours,

Dean

〔Columbia University Library, New York State Library School Collection, Series 2 Student Records, Box 65, Folder Yuan, T. L.〕

按:1887 年 Melvil Dewey(1851-1931)创立的美国第一家图书馆学校,最初名为 School of Library Economy of Columbia College,即 School of Library Service of Columbia University 之前身。该函寄送北平,此为录副。

十一月十二日

王云五来湘,在长沙曲园招饮,梅贻琦、赵元任、杨树达、先生、徐森玉等人与席。〔《积微翁回忆录》,页 97〕

十一月十五日

先生送别马衡。〔国家图书馆档案,档案编号 1946-※039-采藏 11-005017 至 1946-※039-采藏 11-005019〕

按:马衡离长沙前往武汉并转南京,筹划故宫博物院存京文物大规模移运。

十一月十六日

吴宓(郑州)致电梅贻琦、先生。

长沙临时大学梅月涵、袁守和先生:

吴宓率高棣华及学生陈慈、张婉英即到湘。

宓。

〔《吴宓日记》第 6 册，页 254〕

十一月十八日

孙洪芬覆两函与先生，其一，告北平近况并谈中基会在沪董事执委会决议案等事。

守和先生道席：

敬启者，先后奉九月四日、十月二日、十月十三日、十月廿七日大函及附件，均经拜悉。因交通梗阻，弟之行踪又时南时北，每每信到而人已行，重复转寄，稽延时日，致未能早复，至为罪歉。兹将关于平馆各事，分陈如左：

一、平馆照常开门阅览，未被接收，（最近平函系十一月六日寄出），报载分级订发经费并将平馆列入二级一说，据十一月八日到此之同事（林伯遵兄）言及，该说并未实行，且经平市现当局表示平馆经费等等系"超然"性质，不作官厅看待。

二、删二一电，计先送达，兹将执行委员会议决案原文附上，至祈台洽。近来之执委会开会，凡在上海之董事，俱请出席，计有贝诺德、贝克、金叔初、徐新六、施肇基及蔡子民诸位先生。蔡先生因健康关系，只审核议程及决议，不能到会久坐。执行委员会之意，在此抗战进行期内，长沙颇有遭敌机轰炸之可能，自不应积极买书存在该处；但为使馆中之西文科学杂志免于中断起见，西文购书费仍拟发放一部分，以便续订。开会时曾经主席询弟续订杂志，约需美金多少？弟答以此间无上年馆中购书预算，不能确答。但颇记得杂志、年鉴等似为六七千元美金，如各项专门书费内亦有杂志在内，则总数或不只此。惟如以科学专门杂志为续订范围，六七千美元或亦够用。如何之处，祈查示以便转达执委会。

三、馆中购书汇款等事，似以在上海办理为便。应否由尊处派人驻申洽办一切，拟请特予考虑。科学社只有李先生一人，且不能办西文文件。弟临时办事处只有同事四人，对于图书无专门学识，亦不能多为效劳也。

四、图书馆经常费，敝处在八九十月份内曾陆续汇奉湘平两处，兹将经付各帐开具清单，寄奉尊处及子访兄处各一份，请赐核。十一月份汇奉长沙国币贰千元,北平捌千零叁拾伍元正,十二月份应如何分汇或仍照此比例,候示照办。王重民、向达、李永安君等扣薪事,已将尊函之意转致平馆入册。

五、九月初电奉之国币贰千元,系在经常费内拨汇。

六、前函所陈结束平馆拟发给职工薪水三个月办法,来示中未蒙提及,当荷赞同。

七、执行委员会对于自平调馆员入湘襄助临大图书馆办事一事,已有决议;但希望在平馆未结束以前,调动馆员不致影响平馆工作;又调湘人员在湘似应照发全薪。此二事系未裁议决案而嘱弟函达者,并闻。执委会认此二事为馆中行政细目,故未正式决议。

八、李照亭君来访,谈及彼经手代本馆垫付西北科学考查团傅明德君八九十月津贴共六十元,昨日汇发考查团第二期款内曾扣除壹百元,以六十元还尊处归垫,四十元存李君处备付傅君十一及十二两个月津贴?之用。自本月十一月起,李君处遵嘱月付壹百五十元现尚未付,其账由彼向尊处呈报。又上海生活近来奇昂,李君虽未明白有所请求,似有生活困苦之感。兄如通信有便,可否提询,亦语所谓"勤恤民隐"之意也。

九、前来西文购书费支票及请款单一束,俱经提前赶办。荷兰之Florins 98.70已在上海花旗代买一并寄去。请款单等托申花旗寄平花旗经理转平馆,回执已来,兹连同邮局各据一并寄奉,请存查。此项购书费之荷兰金币共去国币 C＄185.54,应由馆中西文购书费算还经常费。

十、前承寄下寄梅、孟真二位先生各一函,兹附璧。

十一、推举任叔永先生继秦绍文先生任为图书馆委员一案,弟谨赞同,恕未另函,请嘱记室登记。

十二、胡步曾兄托转问馆存调查所书报,可否补办移赠所中手续。查此事,前曾商过多次,未经决定。在现状之下,步曾颇虑平馆如不幸发生变动,则彼所用之书报有被提走之可能,于是研究工作非断不可,此事拟请重予考虑。又下年度关于生物科学之书报,如何借与调查所应用,是否于续订时即关照寄与该所,统请核决。专复,即颂公祺。附件如函述。

弟孙洪芬敬上。

廿六,十一,十八,晨五时

按:李永安,字文钦,昌平人,抗战前任平馆西文编目组组员。傅明德,曾与傅振伦一起整理居延汉简、登记入簿。

其二,谈私人事及平馆存沪书籍近况,并请在沪主持馆务。

守和我兄先生有道:

在津前奉大函,嘱转致平馆将九月薪送嫂夫人收用一节,比经转函子舫兄照办。据内子九月中在平报告,闻已经馆中送去,惟语焉不详,子舫处亦无复信,想或有信径陈左右矣。内子等于前周来申,适之夫人今日可到,远承垂注,敬以附闻。

日来抗战成绩较前略逊,中央政府自京分移重庆、汉口、长沙三处。敌方扬言最后攻汉,狂呓之说或不足信,但如友邦调解无成,长期抗战,则馆中新到书报,应否酌留若干在申,请予考虑。此间苏州河以南地段,未遭战事损失,馆中存申之书,闻李照亭言完全无恙,祈释念。上海为此后交通孔道,订书购汇等等及规画将来平馆前途,如左右能驻科学社亲自主持,似尤便利。如何之处,敬请卓裁。专此,即颂大安。

弟洪芬拜上。

廿六,十一,十八,上午八时

〔《北京图书馆馆史资料汇编(1909-1949)》,页453-462〕

按:以上两函似均未及时送到,反而迁延甚久。

十一月十九日

下午,吴宓偕高棣华至临时大学见先生。〔《吴宓日记》第6册,页257〕

按:时临时大学所在为湖南圣经学院,韭菜园路一号。

先生致信蒲特南,请国会图书馆作为美国各界援华捐书的暂存中心之一。

November 19th, 1937

Dear Dr. Putnam:

The West is undoubtedly alarmed at the war clouds hovering at the Far Eastern horizon. The news of Japan's ruthless bombing, deliberate destruction and systematic pillaging of cultural institutions of China, including many important and great libraries, must have been received with great shock and indignation.

According to a recent survey, over two-thirds of Chinese universities and scientific institutions have been either totally destroyed or paralyzed. The valuable libraries of these institutions have been pillaged and laid waste. The Chinese intellectuals have thus been deprived of the great storehouses of learning and cut off entirely from the intellectual world.

In the immense task of restoration, we are looking forward to American assistance. An appeal has been addressed to the President of the American Library Association, hoping that a nation-wide campaign can be launched in the United States under the auspices of the Association.

As Chinese libraries are now compelled to start collecting books entirely out of nothing, we are in urgent need of books and periodicals of all kinds especially standard works in Western languages in various fields.

Knowing your deep intellectual sympathy for Chinese libraries, we hope it would be possible for you to designate the Library of Congress as one of the centres for receiving American donation of books prior to their shipment to China. As soon as the undeclared war is over, we shall arrange to have them forwarded to China through the assistance of the International Exchange Service of the Smithsonian Institution. Should this suggestion meet your approval, we hope you would get in touch with the officers of the A. L. A.

Thanking you in anticipation for your cooperation and assistance,

Yours sincerely,

T. L. Yuan

Chairman

Executive Board

〔中华图书馆协会（长沙韭菜园）英文信纸。Library of Congress, Putnam Archives, Special File, China: Library Association〕

按：此件为打字稿，落款处为先生签名，1938 年 1 月 11 日送达国会图书馆秘书处。

先生致信米来牟，略述日军暴行尤其是对中国各文化机关的肆意破坏，并恳请美国图书馆协会给予支援。

November 19th, 1937

Dear Dr. Milam:

You must have read about the merciless and deliberate destruction of Chinese cultural institutions by Japanese militarists. Never before has aerial bombardment been carried out indiscriminately on such a large scale; and one can well imagine the dreadful extent to which these militarists have been driven in their efforts to force a victory for self-aggrandizement.

In addition to the military occupation of North China, the Japanese have been invading the provinces of Chekiang, Kiangsu, Fukien and Kwangtung. As the first two provinces, in particular, are known as cultural centres of China, the losses of rare books and historical records both from public institutions and private libraries are most serious and irreparable.

In the immense task of restoration, we are looking forward to American assistance. I enclose, therefore, an appeal addressed to the President of the A. L. A. with the earnest hope that under the traditional leadership of your Association, valuable assistance will be given by every librarian in the United States.

Assuring you of our sincere appreciation for your immediate attention, I remain,

Yours sincerely,
T. L. Yuan
Chairman
Executive Board

按:此时,美国图书馆协会主席为 Harrison W. Craver（1875－1951）。

先生致信美国图书馆协会主席,恳请该会成立专门委员会负责组织美国各界援华捐助图书。

November 19th, 1937

Dear Sir:

The scholarly world in the West must have learnt with great horror and indignation of the ruthless bombing and deliberate destruction of a great number of cultural institutions and libraries in those parts of China which have been devastated by the aggression of Japanese militarists. Institutions thus affected cover a large area extending from Suiyuan in the north to Canton in the south. The total loss thus sustained through Japanese aggression is a hundred times greater than that inflicted by nature on Tokyo in 1923.

According to a survey up to the time of writing, 25 national and private universities and a large number of cultural institutions and libraries were either totally destroyed or disorganized. The valuable libraries and laboratories of many institutions have been laid waste. Finding themselves unable to function properly under most trying circumstances, many institutions have been forced to move away from Japanese domination, leaving behind all their books and apparatus. They are therefore obliged to start their work entirely afresh.

All right-minded people will greatly deplore such a gross anomaly in the family of nations and will be ready, we are sure, to lend a helping hand to China in her immense task of maintaining her cultural institutions in such difficult times. It is in the interest of these libraries that we appeal to you, as our sister institution, for help and cooperation.

There are undoubtedly many libraries in the United States with duplicate copies which they are willing to dispose of, as well as individuals who would like to offer their private collections for this cause. Cognizant of the invaluable service rendered by American librarians towards the restoration of the University of Louvain Library and the Imperial University Library of Tokyo, we are confident that similar help will be forthcoming if the American Library Association would take the initiative in organizing a special committee for this purpose. It is the earnest hope of Chinese librarians that a campaign be launched in every city in the United States under the auspices of the public library. The work of each library will be coordinated by a special committee appointed by your Association.

American donations of books and periodicals sent to China will be administered by a special committee to be constituted by the Library Association of China under the honorary presidency of H. E. the Minister of Education of the National Government.

May we hope that your generous spirit will enable librarians in China to carry on with renewed vigour and increased impetus in this time of national crisis?

Yours faithfully,

T. L. Yuan

Chairman, Executive Board

〔The American Library Association Archives, Books for China and Latin America, 1935-1938〕

按:鲁汶大学(Katholieke Universiteit Leuven)图书馆始建于 1636 年,第一次世界大战期间德国军队放火焚烧了图书馆建筑。1921 年至 1928 年之间重建,由美国建筑师 Whitney Warren(1864-1943)设计,曾接受大量捐赠图书。1877 年,东京大学设立图书馆,1897 年更名为东京帝国大学附属图书馆,1923 年关东大地震,该馆建筑及多部藏书均焚毁,1928 年洛克菲勒基金赞助其重建,并于是年 12 月竣工。

十一月二十三日

先生致信阿博特,告知中国图书馆界、文化机构损失惨重被迫转移,为继续开展工作请史密斯森协会将美国捐赠书刊寄送中国。

November 23, 1937

Dear Dr. Abbot:

The scholarly world in the West must have learnt with great horror and indignation of the ruthless bombing and deliberate destruction of a great number of cultural institutions and libraries in those parts of China which have been devastated by the aggression of Japanese militarists. Institutions thus affected cover a large area extending from Suiyuan in the north to

Canton in the south. The total loss thus sustained through Japanese aggression is a hundred times greater than that inflicted by nature on Tokyo in 1923.

According to a survey up to the time of writing, 30 national and private universities and a large number of cultural institutions and libraries were either totally destroyed or disorganized. The valuable libraries and laboratories of many institutions have been laid waste. Finding themselves unable to function properly under most trying circumstances, many institutions have been forced to move away from Japanese domination, leaving behind all their books and apparatus. They are therefore obliged to start their work entirely afresh.

In the immense task of replenishing Chinese libraries, we are looking forward to American assistance. An appeal has been addressed to the American Library Association, hoping that under the leadership of that Association a campaign can be launched in the United States. The books and periodicals thus collected will be kept temporarily at several centres pending the conclusion of this undeclared war.

Cognizant of the invaluable service rendered by the Smithsonian Institution towards the restoration of Louvain as well as the Imperial University Library at Tokyo, we are confident that similar help may be extended to China particularly in view of such difficult times as we are going through. If it would be possible for the Smithsonian Institution to undertake to forward American donation of books to China, it would be of great assistance to our work.

Assuring you of our sincere appreciation for your valuable assistance,
Yours Faithfully,

T. L. Yuan

Chairman

Executive Board

〔中华图书馆协会(长沙韭菜园)英文信纸。Smithsonian Institution Archives, Records, 1868-1988 (Record Unit 509), Box 1, National Library, Peiping〕

按:此件为打字稿,落款处为先生签名,1938 年 1 月 11 日送达。

十一月二十七日

上午十一时许,忽有空袭警报,先生曾至圣经学院办公楼地下室寻高棣华。

〔《吴宓日记》第 6 册,页 263〕

十一月二十九日

先生致信斯文·赫定,告知日军侵华的惨状、教育界被毁的近况,请求瑞典学术界给予援助。

November 29th, 1937

Dear Dr. Hedin:

You must have been quite anxious over your friends in China. I should have written to you long ago, but the transfer of our office from Peiping to the interior and the process of settling down have delayed my keeping up correspondence with my friends. My brother has arrived at Changsha. All members of the Expedition as well as the collections are safe.

You have no doubt heard a great deal about Japanese armed invasion of China. I trust your correspondents in the Far East have kept the Swedish public fairly well posted with developments over here. But as they are stationed in large cities, they have very little to report concerning conditions in the interior. It is in the out of the way places that Chinese civilians are suffering the most from the invaders. Never before has aerial bombardment been carried out indiscriminately on such a large scale; and one can well imagine the dreadful extent to which Japanese militarists have been driven in their efforts to force a victory for self-aggrandizement.

While the horrors being perpetrated in China are the inevitable accompaniments of modern warfare, the indiscriminate massacre of innocent non-combatants has certainly no parallel in history. But such calculated savagery has so far failed to mobilize world opinion in protest, still less positive action.

According to a recent report, over 30 national and private universities, in addition to many leading libraries of China, have been either totally destroyed or paralyzed. The valuable contents of many libraries and laboratories have been taken away. Many institutions, finding themselves unable to function properly under most trying circumstances, have been forced to move away from Japanese domination. They have been compelled to leave their work behind and to start it all over again from the very beginning.

In our work of restoration, we are looking forward to the assistance of foreign powers. I enclose herewith an appeal addressed to the President of the Swedish Library Association and shall be obliged to you if you will make the necessary contact for us. If you could write a statement in various Swedish papers, it would help greatly our cause.

With kindest regards,

Yours sincerely,

T. L. Yuan

Acting Director

〔平馆(长沙办事处)英文信纸。韩琦教授提供〕

按:此件为打字稿,落款处为先生签名。

十一月

长沙临时大学在南岳设立图书分馆。〔中国第二历史档案馆,教育部档案·全宗号5,长沙临时大学图书馆馆务报告及国立西南联合大学师范学院各项中心活动计划说明,案卷号5541〕

按:11月3日,临时大学文学院教职员搬往南岳,12日学生迁往。①

十二月五日

晚,先生与高棣华送卫士生至临时大学校门。〔《吴宓日记》第6册,页265〕

按:卫士生(1899—1990),浙江衢州人,1937年7月北平沦陷时被日军逮捕,后经营救出狱,转入内地参加爱国民主运动。是日,其与二十九军要人眷属赴汉口。

十二月六日

米来牟覆函先生,收到此前来函并将转交协会主席及国际关系委员会,如

---

① 《国立西南联合大学史料》第2卷,页17。

有反馈必及时通知先生。

December 6, 1937

Dear Dr. Yuan:

I am very happy to learn from your letter of November 19 that you and the Library Association of China are still alive.

Your communications will be brought to the attention of the President and of the Committee on International Relations and you will be informed later concerning the action which we are able to take.

In the meantime, let me assure you of our sympathetic interest and our continuing hope that the destruction may soon cease.

Very sincerely yours,

Carl H. Milam

Secretary

〔The American Library Association Archives, International Relations

Office, Books for China and Latin America, 1935–1938〕

按：该函寄送长沙，此件为录副。

十二月十二日

先生致信王重民，谈英庚款使用事宜及平馆补助费须改由南馆汇出等事。

> 有三吾弟如晤：
>
> 前接十一月三日来函，详悉一切。英庚款现余三千元，原作印刷之用。近王云五来湘，知影印完全绝望，自可移用于英伦照像，俟有机会再陆续汇上汇英镑，径汇英伦。惟英庚款会须要一较详之报告，请将自用该款所照之写本作一有系统之报告，便中寄下为荷。王子访来信，谓尊处补助费北平方面自九月份停发，容由此间汇上。刻下交通不便，将来或须由香港设法。汪德昭君返国旅费如能在他处设法，即不必动用尊处之款也。向觉明仍无信来，渠转瞬即返国，尚须请王景春为之设法免费也。专此，顺颂大安。

袁同礼顿首

十二月十二日

〔中国书店·海淀〕

按："影印"即此前"影印《燉煌古籍丛编》"之议。"有系统之报告"应指《影摄巴黎燉煌写本工作报告》,作为"附录三"载于《国立北平图书馆馆务报告(民国二十六年七月至二十七年六月)》。向达亦撰写了一份报告,题为《影摄伦敦燉煌写本工作报告》,载于同一期馆务报告。

十二月十八日

先生致信法国驻华大使,请其协助保全存放在上海法租界中国科学社的平馆善本古籍。

December 18, 1937

Son Exc. M. l'Ambassadeur de France,

Dear Ambassador:

Learning that Your Excellency has arrived at Hankow, I take the liberty of writing to you concerning a matter of great importance to the Chinese scholarly world.

Your Excellency will recall that when visiting the National Library in July, you were informed that owing to the critical political situation, all of our rare books and manuscripts were, by order of the National Government, removed from Peiping and kept in the Library of the Science Society of China at 533 Avenue du Roi Albert, Shanghai.

The so-called Peking Peace Maintenance Committee has illegally taken over the administration of the National Library and has appointed a Japanese adviser. Word has been received that this Japanese adviser has been making definite plans to take into possession those rare books and manuscripts for sending them to Peiping. In order to carry out this plan, it is possible that Japanese authorities may try to bring pressure to bear upon the French Consul General at Shanghai.

As this action on the part of the Japanese authorities may serve as a very dangerous precedent, I may be permitted to draw the attention of Your Excellency to this matter. We shall greatly appreciate your assistance if Your Excellency would be good enough to request your Counsel General to take precautionary measures in order to safeguard these national treasures of China as long as they are kept in the French

Concession at Shanghai.

With assurances of our sincere appreciation of your interest and assistance,

Yours sincerely,

T. L. Yuan

Acting Director

〔Rockefeller Foundation. Series 601: China; Subseries 601.R: China-Humanities and Arts. Box 47. Folder 389〕

按：该件为副本。

马衡覆函先生，告知故宫博物院南京保存库文物运出经过，并表示不知悉平馆寄存内阁大库舆图现状。

守和先生大鉴：

顷得十六日惠书，敬悉一切。上月十五日别后，次日抵达汉，即闻迁都消息。十八日到京，见江岸秩序紊乱情形，始大惊。其时本院文物正在装江安船运汉计四千余箱，十九晚开行。弟连日接洽续运船只，毫无办法，因思首都有重兵守卫，未必沦陷，与其因搬运而损失，不如封锁库中，且书画、铜器及善本《四库》等皆已迁出，余留部分已不足称为国宝。遂与念劬商由彼留守，印刷所仍照旧工作，弟即于廿一日旁晚附津浦车转陇海平汉来汉。不料在弟启行以后，存京文物又复奉令迁移，由军委会拨车三列运往西安行营，计运出七千余箱。又与太古公司接洽，由黄浦等轮装运，嗣黄浦于三日运出五千余箱，之后即无法再运。存京库者尚有二千余箱，多为木器等大箱。西安行营非保存之所，蒋主任鼎文介绍存于宝鸡，现正开凿土窑，日内可以完工。存汉者计九千余箱，日内将转宜昌运渝水浅非寻常船所能运，长沙之八十箱拟由公路运往贵阳。内阁大库舆图，汉库未见，不知宝鸡有否？如皆无有，则尚在京库也。念劬已于八日离京，十三日到汉矣。梁廷炜已赴宝鸡，故久未通信。专复，即颂台祺。

弟马衡上言

十二月十八日

〔国家图书馆档案，档案编号 1946-※039-采藏 11-005017 至 1946-※039-采藏 11-005019〕

按:梁廷炜,字伯华,河北大城人,抗战爆发前,任故宫博物院图书馆第二科科员。平馆内阁大库舆图并未运出,后失陷于南京。

十二月中下旬

沈履带吴宓函与先生,谈高棣华事。〔《吴宓日记》第6册,页275〕

按:时吴宓身在衡阳,颇担心长沙之高棣华,遂托沈履带信与先生。

先生致信吴宓,表示会尽心保护高棣华,请其不要担心。〔《吴宓日记》第6册,页275〕

按:在此之前先生亦接到高棣华母亲自北平来函,托其照顾。

十二月二十一日

温德覆函先生,报告司徒雷登擅自委任张允亮担任平馆代理馆长,幸得顾子刚等人反对得以终止,并坦言北平馆务因无最高负责人难以维持。

December 21, 1937

Dear Mr. Yuan:

Your letter of November 26th reached me on December 13th. I called at once on Mr. Ku and received the information contained in the enclosed memo dated 16/12/37. At this time things seemed to be going smoothly in the Library. On the 18th, however, Mr. Ku called me on the phone and asked me to meet him to discuss some new developments of a less pleasant nature. It appears that Hashigawa, advisor to the Wei Chih Huei and recently appointed advisor to the Library, has been cultivating Dr. Stuart and that finally, with the additional persuasion of Ferguson, brought Dr. Stuart to the point of writing you and the Foundation announcing that he (Stuart) had appointed Mr. Chang Yun Liang as acting Director of the National Library. Fortunately, Ku learned of this in time to intercept the messenger carrying the letters to the post and to hold him until Stuart was informed of the indignation which all members of the staff felt in regard to such action. Stuart promptly destroyed the letters and, in their place, wired you advising you to appoint Mr. Chang to act for you until further notice. In the meantime, Ku prepared the enclosed confidential memorandum which he asked me to present to Dr. Stuart.

We all feel that we are fighting a losing battle due in part to the fact that no responsible person will come up from the South to negotiate directly with the people in authority here and that it is difficult even to get an answer to telegrams sent. As you will see from the enclosed papers giving some of the events since October 8th, I have been taking much more responsibility than I am entitled to, because of my naturally belligerent character.

Will you kindly pass these things on to Dean P'an or President Mei and tell them that I will try to keep them informed of what is going on although I don't know how I am going to get this letter through.

Please thank Dean P'an for the information he gave me in his letter and tell him that I have done the things he asked me to do for him.

Sincerely yours,

R. Winter

按:Hashigawa 应指桥川时雄,Dean P'an or President Mei 应分别指教务长潘光旦、校长梅贻琦。信中所言备忘录如下:

Memo on Japanese attempt to take articles from the Palace Museum, Peiping.

From: R. Winter, Peiping

To: T. L. Yuan, etc.

Date: 16/12/37

A Japanese advisor to the Wei Chih Huei (Takeda) went to the Palace Museum and demanded to be given an ancient map of Mongolia which the Japanese Military wished to present to Prince Teh. The museum authorities offered to make a copy of the original and allow that to be taken, but Takeda came to the museum with soldiers and took possession of the original map. The museum people protested against this confiscation to the Chief of Police, the Wei Chih Hui and everyone else who might be interested, on the grounds that they could not allow anyone to take curios from the museum. After a few days the map was returned.

The new government just formed in Peiping, it is reported, is making elaborate plans for taking over the administration of the Palace Museum.

....

Japanese interference at the National Library, Peiping

The Japanese Military first suggested that Japanese gendarmes should be stationed in the National Library on supervisory duty. They then asked the Library Board to retire two of its seven Chinese members and replace them with two Japanese members. All the members of the Library Board in Peiping strongly advised the Japanese Military against this policy, as they said that if it were carried out the China Foundation might withdraw support from the Library. The project was dropped.

The Japanese advisor of the Library Hashigawa called privately to see the Library administration, congratulated them on the strong attitude they had taken, and expressed the hope that such cultural institutions could be kept from falling into the hands of corrupt Chinese or Japanese politicians or militarists.

〔台北胡适纪念馆，档案编号 HS－JDSHSE－0433－007 和 HS－JDSHSE－0433－008〕

按：Wei Chih Huei（维持会）两处拼写不同，特此说明。

十二月二十二日

先生致信米来牟，略述中国已有三十五所国立、私立大学图书馆惨遭毁坏，并盼望美国图书馆协会能够成立一个中心负责征集向中国捐赠的图书。

December 22, 1937

Dear Mr. Milam:

We hope you have received our letter dated November 19th enclosing an appeal addressed to the President of the American Library Association.

Since that date, the number of national and private universities destroyed or disorganized has been increased to 35. Many valuable libraries, both public and private, were razed to the ground. This association has been conducting a survey, but it cannot be kept up-to-date, as the Japanese are invading the interior provinces resulting in complete disorganization of our postal service.

As Chinese libraries are now compelled to start collecting books entirely out of nothing, we are in urgent need of books and periodicals of all kinds, old or new, especially standard works in Western languages in various fields. We have recently written to various local library associations in the United States requesting them to cooperate with your Association in every way possible.

Cognizant of your deep intellectual sympathy for China, we hope your Association will designate a member of large libraries in different parts of the United States as centres for receiving American donation of books prior to their shipment to China. As soon as the undeclared war is over, we shall arrange to have them forwarded to China through the assistance of the International Exchange Service of the Smithsonian Institution. Should this suggestion meet your approval, we shall appreciate very much if you would send us a list of libraries thus designated.

Assuring you of our sincerest appreciation for your valuable assistance,

Yours sincerely

T. L. Yuan

Chairman, Executive Board

〔The American Library Association Archives, International Relations

Office, Books for China and Latin America, 1935-1938〕

按:此为抄件。

十二月二十五日

先生致信毕寿普,请其协助中国图书馆界向美国图书馆界、卡耐基国际和平基金会请求援助。

December 25, 1937

Dear Dr. Bishop:

I trust you have received my air-mail letter of October 29th. Being

Christmas to-day, may I write to extend to you and Mrs. Bishop my best wishes for a Merry Christmas and Happy New Year?

Since writing to you last, the Japanese have been invading the provinces of Kiangsu, Chekiang, Anhuei, Fukien and Kwang-tung. As the first three provinces, in particular, are known as cultural centres of China, the losses resulting from destruction of public libraries and private collections are most serious and irreparable. Word has just been received that the famous Sinological Library at Nanking has been very badly looted by Japanese soldiers. Our Engineering Reference Library together with many libraries in the Capital suffered the same fate. The destruction of the Liu family library at Nan Hsun in Chekiang Province, in particular, is a great loss to the scholarly world.

The effects of this undeclared war of aggression upon Chinese intellectual life must be a matter of great concern to all of our friends in America. Without American help, China cannot of her own resources repair the misfortune which has come upon her libraries and cultural institutions.

Cognizant of American sympathy for China, we have sent appeals to the A. L. A. as well as various local associations. I enclose herewith a letter addressed to the Michigan Library Association and shall be indebted to you if you will kindly forward it for us.

We hope the A. L. A. has taken action with regard to the organization of a special committee suggested in our last letter. You will no doubt be asked to serve on this Committee and we are counting upon you for your interest and assistance.

The generous help given by the Carnegie Endowment in the restoration of Louvain is still fresh in our memory. It is our earnest hope that an appropriation may be granted by the Endowment towards the restoration of our libraries. For your information I enclose a copy of my letter sent to President Butler a month ago. I shall greatly appreciate your assistance if you would find it possible to call his attention as opportunity arises. As various grants are usually made in spring, there is ample time for the Trustees to consider our application.

With China's power of resistance greatly reduced as a result of Japan's blockade over our coasts, Japanese columns are penetrating ever deeper into the interior. Intoxicated by military conquest, the invader is bent upon ruthless slaughter and wanton destruction. The recent bombing and sinking of U. S. S. Panay indicate Japan's utter disregard for foreign rights and interests in China. Unless collective acting of all democratic countries is taken to halt Japanese aggression, Europeans and Americans will eventually be forced out of China. The outcome of this conflict is a matter of deep concern to the whole world.

With Season's greetings,

Yours sincerely,

T. L. Yuan

Acting Director

〔Rockefeller Foundation. Series 601: China; Subseries 601.R: China-Humanities and Arts. Box 47. Folder 389〕

按:此为抄件,毕寿普将其寄送给史蒂文斯,后者认为现在时机不成熟,不考虑任何形式的资助。

十二月二十七日　长沙

下午,黄炎培来访,先生与之晤谈。〔《黄炎培日记》第 5 卷,页 239〕

先生致信孙洪芬,讨论平馆在平馆务、存沪善本书状况等事。

> 洪芬先生尊鉴:
>
> 　　日前连奉两电,曾复一急电,谅今晨必能送到。顾问八日就职,福老先生于十七日来电,司徒建议大约亦在此时,恐均系馆中同人所鼓动,而二老均系被动也。当即持尊电商诸蒋、傅两先生,认为如接受该建议,则须由委员会函请教部加委,不啻承认该会为法定团体此系该会之员,将来难免凭地位提取沪货周抵湘后,因连日阴雨,尚未走谒也,王在汉、段、周赴重庆,故主张该顾问接事后即停发经费,并可停办,留保管员数人保管财产。至前电暂停本月经费者,系因孙述万等来湘,知王先生存公款在花旗者,将有两万元且有向该会领四千元之意。如向双方领款,未免太难,故请暂停。无论本月领四千元,渠自□能否在存款内拨付,毫

无困难。兹为下月办事便利起见,拟请速电,可托吴君代查王君在花旗存款共有若干(已集中一处),凭确信到沪再决定下月应否发放经费。因弟屡次函询财政状况,毫无复音,甚不放心,伪政府成立,必有变化。弟意王君手下之款足敷遣散之费,前台端拨付购书费应速提沪为盼。至行政方面,弟本派王、张、徐三人共同负责,闻徐已到平,最好请尊处致电吴君转告三人共同维持至最后为止。此间与平津函电业已不通。又,沪上存货,弟□曾函那其亚注意,尚无覆音,仍盼随时维护,或改存他处,或改用名义,均盼决定实行,以策万全是盼。临大遇必要时或须解散,本馆届时是否发遣散费抑移他处杂志改寄香港,可派四五人至港办事,未识尊意如何,极盼有所指示俾有遵循。刻下工作集中于征取及复兴事业,另拟报告书,油印后再送上备查。又,王重民在英影照燉煌照片,须再汇壹千元英庚款补助项下,请由沪代汇并在一月份经费内将该款扣还是荷。同人薪水应否打折扣,前屡函询,并盼示复。顺颂大安。

弟同礼顿首

十二月廿七

〔长沙临时大学图书馆用笺。《北京图书馆馆史资料汇编(1909-1949)》,页 463-466〕

按:"顾问"即指日人桥川时雄,12 月 4 日伪北京地方"维持会"训令(地字第 229 号)任命其为平馆顾问,后虽数次到馆视察,但并未干涉馆务。[1] 周、王二人似指周诒春、王世杰,段应指段锡朋。"王先生"似指王访渔;王、张、徐三人应指王访渔、张允亮、徐森玉。"吴君"似指吴砚农,湖北监利人,私立华中大学毕业,时应在中基会任职。翌年春,那其亚曾回覆先生。此件修改、涂抹甚多。

---

① 《中国国家图书馆馆史资料长编》,页 299。

一九三八年　四十四岁

先生致信喜龙仁,告其若在新书中使用《故宫书画集》的古画照片作为插图,请务必提及原始出处,并请其在抗战中尽可能给予中国学术界援助。

January 4, 1938

Dr. Osvald Siren

National Museum

Stockholm

Sweden

Dear Dr. Siren:

I thank you for your letter of November 20th. I should have written to you long ago, but the transfer of our office from Peiping to the interior and the process of settling down have delayed my keeping up correspondence with my friends.

I am very glad to learn that you are preparing to publish a book on the History of Later Chinese Painting which I am sure will be of great use and interest to the scholarly world. I am looking forward with much pleasure to its early publication. As to the permission of reproducing 18 plates from the *Ku Kung Shu Hua Chi*, I wish to say that if you would mention the courtesy accorded to you by the Palace Museum, I am sure the museum authorities will not raise any objections.

You have undoubtedly heard a great deal about Japan's armed invasion of China. Never before has aerial bombardment been carried out so indiscriminately and on such a large scale. The suffering of our people is most appalling. The admirable work you have done for the sufferers in this country has our heartfelt gratitude. As war area enlarges, we have no doubt that you will continue to lend us your assistance in this hour of distress.

　　With warmest regards and Season's greetings,

Yours Sincerely,

T. L. Yuan

Acting Director

〔国立北平图书馆英文信纸。叶公平提供〕

按:a book on the History of Later Chinese Painting 即*A History of Later Chinese Painting*,1938 年伦敦 Medici Society 初版,两卷本。此件为打字稿,落款处为先生签名。

一月五日

孙洪芬致函先生,谈平馆在沪所存善本、人员经费等事。

守和先生大鉴:

　　上年十一月廿日大函于十二月十七日始到上海,续又奉十二月四日及十七日之函,俱拜悉——。查弟于上年十一月十八日曾奉复六十行之长函,兹据顷到之十二月廿日来示,该函迄未收到。战事影响交通一至于此,深可痛也。弟因与尊处欲谈之事甚多,每思作长函畅述一切,乃每日见客写信,种种琐事,不一而足,致长函难于写寄。兹拟变更计画,每次作函,以二三事为限,或者可以多点通讯。

　　一、存沪堆栈之货,已由 Mr. Bennett 具名转存英栈,非经彼签名不能提出,存逸园之件,正点交 père Octave Piel。详情托森玉兄函报。

　　二、十二月下旬得尊电,商论停付平馆十二月经费,因该月平湘两处经费系于十一日同时汇发,尊电到此已无法执行。本月半司徒先生来申,对于平中状况必有详报,平馆之事,拟届时提出讨论。子访迄无信来,顾问一事,前日据森玉先生言确有其事,但地方组织发给经费则未之闻。又据林伯遵兄言,花旗款壹万零元非经左右签发支票,不能提用。馆中经常费报告,结至九月底止,存银行及现金四千四百元左右。购书费之陷在北平银行者,拟设法提动。此外如馆中有向他处筹募之补助费,因会中无账可稽,不能估算。

　　三、馆中平湘两处经费,前曾开列清单寄奉。兹将廿六年十一月底总结复印送上一份,请查核。十月汇奉之二九九三.四〇元之来由亦见单内。

四、减折付薪一事,中基会执委无人表示赞同。

五、孙述万兄四人每人就平支安家费半年计三百六十元于本月(廿七年一月)一次支付,此间可以代办。但每人数目太小,花旗开存户恐不甚便,拟托北平中孚代付。敝会平事务所于廿六年十二月底完全结束,吴砚农君等日内俱来申。会所房屋由司徒先生租作城中办事处。

六、罗氏基金之耿先生在申见著,彼对于在华事业极悲观,尊处请求补助似希望不大。

上海与各处勉强通邮通电,来往信件,似不检查,惟北平来信多盖有"检阅"字样。匆复,即颂岁祺。

弟孙洪芬拜上

廿七,一,五

〔《北京图书馆馆史资料汇编(1909-1949)》,页473-476〕

邓衍林致函先生,报告平馆香港办事处工作情况,并告暂存数箱文件于美国大使馆友人处。

守和先生道鉴:

敬肃者,昨上一函,略表不愿回平,并贡献最低限度之维持办法,谅登记室为念。此间商借香港大学图书馆书报事,曾数度由孙君会同陈主任(冯平山主任)请谒该校副校长、教务长并图书馆主任,几经接洽,幸结果圆满。以后我等需用书报,可由冯平山中文图书馆代借或入馆阅均可,自明日起即可赴该馆调查一切也。该校对于我馆工作甚为重视,闻该校副校长已出布告,通知教授(学生不在内)前往冯平山图书馆参阅我馆所藏书报云云。此种合作精神难能可贵。此间暂时根据地得来不易,似不宜轻易放弃也。

寄存美国大使馆友人 Henry C. T. Gow Esq.高冲天之件共计三大皮箱,内中所存之件:

(一)吴主任嘱寄之中文印刷卡片全份(八百余张);

(二)中国问题之西文书目稿片(徐家璧编);

(三)参考组历年所编之重要书目底稿;

(四)国防资源参考资料稿片(万余种);

（五）王主任嘱存之馆藏古器物学书目一册（梁启雄编）。

当时寄存系以本人友谊关系代为保存，并未有收条。如确定寄至何处，由林去函，高君代为设法运寄即可。其运费当由本馆支付。如欲提取，幸勿通知北馆同人办理，恐诸多不便也。如馆长认为可运至香港，请函托美国或英国大使馆西友代为带来更佳，盖可免去检查麻烦也。如去函，务请写明"有本馆文件三皮箱，如沿途能免检查为佳，此件请通知美大使馆友人高冲天君，由彼代为取交尊处带下之。"因临行时高君因检阅多关国防资料，运之不便，留置故都又恐资敌，故乐为以彼私人文件设法储存大使馆中，盖彼不愿当局知彼代人保存文件，诸多不便也。高君现寓美大使馆官舍中，寄存安全当无问题，且彼对于我馆事亦深表同情之友好也。

蒋校长已于日前飞港。木简已安全运到，现储中文学院，港当局甚珍视之，徐主任忙甚。兹将林所担任之征集调查工作制为统计报告，附呈鉴核。其他工作报告孙君现正整理汇报也。向国外公私工程研究机关，即根据最近调查者发出征求函多件，一俟书报到港，林即计划做杂志登记及整理工作也。

近读 *The Year's Work in Librarianship, 1936*, edited for Library Association, London, by A. Esdaile (Secretary of the British Museum) and J. H. Pafford, published by the Library Association, Chaucer Houses, Malet Place, London, 1937 对于我馆工作概况及印刷卡片工作略有记载，是我馆以后之工作报告及宣传文字可寄一份予该会或编者，俾便每年有所记载也。专肃，敬请道安。不一。

生衍林再拜
一月五日

1. 委员会对于本馆决议至关重要，此间仝人念念。
2. 附高小姐一函，乞便中代达。
又及。

〔《北京图书馆馆史资料汇编（1909-1949）》，页 470-472〕

按："孙君会同陈主任"即孙述万、陈君葆二人；"该校副校长"即 Duncan John Sloss（1881-1964），英国学者，早年在印度服务，1937 年至 1949 年担任香港大学副校长。高冲天，河北固安人，燕

京大学毕业,时应任美国大使馆秘书。① "吴主任"应指吴光清,
"王主任"似指王访渔,"高小姐"即高棣华。

一月上旬

先生赴汉口。〔中国书店·海淀,四册〕

一月十一日

徐森玉覆函先生,告知其与香港大学商洽平馆存沪善本书移运办法及南下
赴港馆员近况。

守和先生尊鉴:

前日接奉航示三封,昨由许地山兄转到航示四封,敬悉壹是。宝
拟明日乘 Tjinegara 船赴沪,至沪后当遵照尊嘱并商承洪芬先生相机
审慎办理,务望放心。香港大学校长即港督 Sir Geoffry Northcote,副
校长为 Mr. D. G. Sloss,对于存书事极端慎重。宝意拟请校长直接命
令沪英领设法运港,但渠等决不愿涉及政治关系,仅肯以私人资格设
法移运,几经商酌,副校长口述办法七条,兹另纸写呈,即请核察。第
五条所谓托人者即托太古公司总理 Masson J. R. 从中协助,此事至必
要时 Mr. Sloss 可亲赴沪一行也。西北科查团款项,此次由宝领得者
一千二百余元扣去垫傅明德在沪用款,仅存一千零数十元。希渊先生之物品存
在外人处,尚称安妥。御史衙门乙组之物品数十箱较为危险,宝南来
时曾嘱沈仲章兄将御史衙门物品设法运津。自伪临时政府成立后,稽
查日严,外人代运物品之价日贵每箱已涨至十余元。团中款项实不敷分
配,未识能办到否,乞转告希渊先生为祷。自上海陷后,香港忽增加
人口一百五十余万,故住房拥挤异常,物价昂贵异常,孙、徐、邓、颜
四君昨日来此竟无地可容。幸前日宝托许地山夫人在坚尼地城租
房一大间,月港币廿一元,已请四君移居于此。卧用番布床,桌椅买
旧者,安电灯、接水管约需百元,此宗开办费拟恳准由公款开支。香
港大学有学生寄宿舍,两人住一房,每人月需港币四十余元,则非四
君之力所能办矣。宝留湘之物一网篮、一箧篓内有他人之书籍多种,请交
旅行社运港大地山兄处附上国币十五元,如不敷乞代垫,其余之物弃之可
也。薪金收据六纸遵命签呈十、十一、十二、一月之薪金暂存尊处,宝之名章在

① 《燕京大学教职员学生名录(1932-1933)》,页 42;《华北日报》,1937 年 3 月 1 日,第 9 版。

庄慕陵兄处,如慕陵已他往,请代刻木印一方用之为叩。故宫存单已由柱中兄电汉挂失,尚不致为他人取去也。头痛尚未愈。匆匆陈此,草率万分,乞见谅。此请钧安。

徐鸿宝谨上

一月十一日

　　分两函寄

　　1.正确书目。

　　2.存书地点。

　　3.书之负责人。

　　4.由负责人具函将目列各书借与香港大学中文学院,理由:许地山教授以目列各书学院师生有参考之必要,特向中国国立北平图书馆商借。

　　5.中文学院即托人由存书地点将目列各书移运至港并具覆函。

　　6.负责人方面应派馆员一人或二人常川驻港照料此项书籍。

　　7.如负责人方面须自用此项书籍时,可具函知照中文学院自行运回国内。

　　　　〔国家图书馆档案,档案编号 1937-※035-采藏 7-002006 至 1937-※035-采藏 7-002008〕

按:Tjinegara 荷兰商船,1931 年建造,太平洋战争爆发后作为美国运输船,1942 年 7 月 25 日被日军舰艇击沉。Sir Geoffry Northcote(1881-1948),中文名罗富国,英国官员,多次出任其海外殖民地总督,1937 年 10 月调任香港总督,1941 年 9 月因病辞职返英。"孙、徐、邓、颜四君"即孙述万、邓衍林、徐家璧、颜泽霡,均为平馆馆员。

一月十五日

孙洪芬覆函先生,谈平馆与临时大学合办及停办之议有待中基会执委会商讨,另告其与秉志商洽,拟支付震旦大学一千元用以表示对该校存放平馆善本书之谢意。

　　守和吾兄:

　　　　昨奉惠电示知,蒋、周、傅诸公对于平馆仍主停办,敬悉一一。查司徒先生定十七日到申,届期执委会当与之商量馆事,弟当将尊电提供参考。上海震旦方面有箱三百件，承 père Piel 将半楼洋房一小座腾出专堆。日昨彼托秉农山先生约弟相谈，谓战事后震旦房产收入锐减，经济困难，意求捐助。当经秉兄与弟商洽，拟请图书馆捐助该校国币壹千元，以表馆方对震旦帮忙之忱。查在他处堆箱三百只，每年非千余元不办，故弟昨日电商尊处拟予照准，虽多用点钱，亦无可如何之事也。顾子刚兄一月三日来函，附呈一份，请勿发表。专此，即颂炉安。

弟洪芬匆上

廿七，一，十五

附件。

〔《北京图书馆馆史资料汇编(1909—1949)》，页 477—478〕

按：1938 年 1 月 18 日，中基会执委会召开第 122 次会议；1 月 21 日，又召开特别委员会。两次会议作出继续维持平馆决议，并要求南下馆员除在沪、在港办事一二人外应尽快返回北平服务，先生可赴昆明协助临时大学，但亦须尽快返平。

一月十七日　长沙

先生致信王重民，告知汇寄之款，并嘱其在英法拍照敦煌卷子及推荐其至国会图书馆编写善本书目等事。

有三仁弟如晤：

十一月廿四日及十二月六日两函均先后收到，致 Cain 索旅费信俟日内稍暇再写甫由汉口返湘，积压之事甚多，如能要二人路费亦甚佳，但恐不易。近以中基会下年补助费无何把握，而夏间返国亦无事可做赋闲之人及失业之人甚多，爰拟推荐至美国国会图书馆办事。该馆刻正需人，已荐吴光清前往。惟关于善本书之整理，拟请足下担任可担任生活费及由英至美旅费，二人分工合作必有极好之结果，并告 Hummel 径函接洽。兹由汉口花旗银行汇上二千元附支票，只一张，不可遗失，合计一百十四磅一仙令三辨士(£ 114.1.3)。另托孙洪芬由申汇上壹千元，共三千元，系英庚款余款。除照英伦所藏者外伯希和所藏卷子可以补充者一律影照，并望将牛津、剑桥及 Manchester(一)大学图书馆(二)John Rylands Library(此馆藏西文善甲于天下)所藏者一律影照，并望将以前寄平之报账单及收据等，另以复本寄"香港大学冯平山图书馆寄信均寄此处转交"兄手收是荷。

一俟时局再坏,兄即到港办事,刻下孙述万、邓衍林等均在香港也。

兄同礼

一月十七,长沙

〔中国书店·海淀,四册〕

　　按:John Rylands Library 修建于维多利亚时期,哥特式建筑风格,1900 年对公众开放。

阿博特覆函先生,表示史密斯森协会愿意帮助中华图书馆协会,暂时收存美国各机构捐赠书刊。

January 17, 1938

Dear Mr. Yuan:

　　I beg to assure you, in reply to your letter of November 23, that the Smithsonian Institution will be very glad to help in the rehabilitation of the libraries of China by forwarding to the Chinese Bureau of International Exchanges any books that may be received here for the various establishments which have suffered the loss of their collections during the present conditions in that country.

Very truly yours,

C. G. Abbot

〔Smithsonian Institution Archives, Records, 1868–1988 (Record Unit

509), Box 1, National Library, Peiping〕

　　按:该函寄送长沙韭菜园,此件为录副。

蒲特南覆函先生,已将来信转交美国图书馆协会秘书处,并表示愿意捐赠该馆复本,但希望中方可以任命专职人员负责拣选其中适合捐赠者;另询寄送地址,并表示此时恢复馆藏或操之过急。

January 17, 1938

Dear Dr. Yuan:

　　Your note of November 19 did not reach me until a few days ago. I read it with interest and, as you must be aware, with sympathy that must be shared by many librarians. I shall communicate it to the secretariat of the American Library Association, especially its suggestion that there might be some organized effort by American libraries to replenish some of the

collections in China by contributions from their own duplicates. That is
what I suppose you have in mind. Should a movement be organized, it may
indeed be possible for some agency at Washington, —if not the Library of
Congress, then perhaps the Smithsonian Institution through its international
exchanges, —to assemble and forward the material. Our own collection of
duplicates is, of course, a considerable one, but I am very doubtful whether it
includes many items that would be directly serviceable in China. If there were
anyone who, in your behalf, could examine it, and make a selection, we
should give him every facility, and not hesitate to dispatch the items selected.

To what address should they be sent? Is your present address likely
to be relatively permanent?

Another question, that is certain to be asked, is whether the time is as
yet ripe for the rehabilitation of your collections. The impression here
would be that it is not, and that there will be some waste of effort which
could be avoided by a reasonable delay.

Pray keep us advised, and believe me.

Cordially yours,

Librarian

〔Librarian of Congress, Putnam Archives, Special File, China: Library
Association〕

按：该函实际寄送到昆明，并非件中所注明的长沙韭菜园，特此说
明。此件为录副。

一月二十一日

先生致信王重民，告知已函法国国家图书馆馆长为其索取返国旅费并告临
时大学迁滇。

有三吾弟：

日前寄一函，内附英镑£ 114.1.3 之汇票一张，想先此寄到。致
Cain 之函本日已发出，兹将副本寄上备查。返国旅费如能付给，最好
与之定一活动办法。如今夏由法至美，或明年由美至沪。只要法政府
有一办法证明，以后即以此证明信换取船票由美至中国无法国船。或候美
国方面之消息，再与 Cain 交涉亦可如能成，则要一由法至美之船票，诸希酌

之。致王景春之函亦发出，并请转告觉明是荷。临时大学已决定迁往昆明，以后通信均寄"香港冯平山中文图书馆转"是盼。顺颂旅安。

同礼顿首

一月廿一日

〔中国书店·海淀，四册〕

先生致信史蒂文斯，请求洛克菲勒基金会考虑延长此前的资助期限，并呈上复兴备忘录，告平馆昆明办事处亟需防火建筑和续订外文科学技术期刊。

January 21, 1938

Dear Dr. Stevens:

I beg to acknowledge the receipt of your letter of October 26th, much delayed owing to the interruption of postal services in China.

I thank you very heartily for having expressed willingness to give special consideration to the use of the grant as affected by the war situation in China. Since Japan's war of aggression will be prolonged, we shall ask your Foundation to hold the grant until we are able to continue the printing and distribution of our catalogue cards. We hope, therefore, that in view of the present crisis in China, the Foundation will allow us to continue to use the grant after June 30, 1939, if we shall not be able to spend by that time the total amount under this grant.

In order to safeguard our rare books and manuscripts and in order to continue our work of cultural exchange, we are moving our headquarters to Kun-Ming, Yunnan. We are in urgent need of (1) a modern fire-proof building to house this collection and (2) funds with which to round out our collection of foreign scientific journals. Cognizant of the Foundation's interest in cultural diffusion, I beg to submit herewith a memorandum which I hope will receive your favorable consideration.

In view of Japan's ambitions in China, we are now obliged to develop a program whereby our National Library will henceforth be organized with branches in the southwestern provinces sufficiently large for housing national treasures in time of peace as well as in time of war.

Instead of concentrating all valuable books in the Capital, we shall have to scatter them in these provinces where they will be free from air bombardment. With the aid of microphotography, copies of our valuable books and manuscripts could easily be made available for use in China as well as sinological centers abroad. The proposed building at Kun-Ming will be the first library under this scheme.

While we fully realize that the present situation in China must have given you and your Trustees great disappointment, yet we trust the Foundation will not give up hope and faith in China entirely. It is quite obvious that on the military side a decision cannot be reached for the time being, but on the civil side there is not the slightest doubt that China will succeed if only she will hold loyally her positions. In the history of China, it has always been the civilians who won the victory in the long run.

Thanking you for your assistance and with kindest regards,

> Yours sincerely,
>
> T. L. Yuan
>
> Acting Director

〔平馆（长沙办事处）英文信纸。Rockefeller Foundation. Series 601: China; Subseries 601.R: China-Humanities and Arts. Box 47. Folder 389〕

按：此件为打字稿，落款处为先生签名，于 2 月 18 日送达，随信附上 Memorandum Re the Restoration of the National Library of Peiping，共计 4 页。

一月二十四日

下午，先生访吴宓，因拟编《抗战中之国际舆论》（*Japanese Invasion & World Opinion*）①一书，圈选英文论文数十篇，请其校阅。晚，吴宓在远东西餐馆招宴，先生、毛准、高棣华、陈慈、张婉英为客。〔《吴宓日记》第 6 册，页 287〕

按：吴宓接此重托后十分负责，仔细校对，并按照内容分类，编写

---

① 此书之最终题名为《暴日侵华与国际舆论》（*Japan's Aggression and Public Opinion*）。

目录,至移居云南蒙自时方初步完成。

先生致信孙洪芬,告其平馆长沙办事处拟与临时大学一同迁往昆明,望给予支持。

洪芬先生大鉴:

临大当局既决定迁往昆明,关于图书之充实,要求本馆继续予以协助,曾有专函奉达,谅荷垂察。本日临大正式议决,由校中津贴平馆在湘同人赴滇之旅费壹千元,此外并担任书籍、杂志之运费。顷与蒋、傅两先生商议,特致电尊处。电文为:"同人旅费由校津贴千元,另付书籍运费,请核准"此电想能寄到。执委会对于同人在临大服务既核准于前,此次临大移滇,自与解散不同,同人随同前往,谅邀同意。务请鼎力赞助,俾进行中之各项事业(见前寄上之油印报告)不致中断,无任感幸。临大现定于下月初旬开始迁移,如本馆一同迁滇,则(一)书籍运费、办事地点以及同人住宿均由临大担任,本馆不费一文,而各项事业均可照旧进行。(二)本馆所订之专门期刊均可寄滇香港—部分职员亦一同赴滇,此项刊物现为临大及中央研究院同人所需要,□本馆在战时对于学术界之贡献上亦甚大。又,同人在此对于复兴事业积极进行,国际间之联络始终未断,倘停止进行或职员遣散,则真无以自解。以上种种,深盼予以极大之同情,渡此难关,公私均感。专此,顺颂大安。

一月廿四晚

〔长沙临时大学用笺。《北京图书馆馆史资料汇编(1909-1949)》,页484〕

按:此件为先生所拟之底稿。

中基会致函先生,告中基会执委会关于继续维持平馆的决议。

守和先生道鉴:

敬启者,关于本会继续维持国立北平图书馆一案,前经本会执行委员会议决,由本会将经过情形函知教育部查照,并请该部转呈政府备案。兹将该函副本一份随函邮奉,藉供参阅。敬祈察存为幸。祗颂道绥。

中华教育文化基金董事会启

二十七年一月二十四日

附钞函乙件。

〔《北京图书馆馆史资料汇编(1909-1949)》,页485〕

　　按：此函2月中旬仍未送达。

一月二十六日

孙洪芬覆函先生，告知中基会执委会就平馆随临大迁滇之决定及其他馆务问题。

守和先生有道：

　　敬启者，徐森玉先生带来一月七日大函及账件，又续奉一月十一日及十七日惠函，并一月十七日及廿四日惠电，均拜悉。关于临大迁滇图书馆同人是否偕往之等一事，一月十八日中基会执委会开会，弟曾提请讨论，未能通过。因须评商善后办法，廿一日再开小组委员会，廿二日弟赶将该委员会报告连同执委会决议航快寄湘，廿四日并发致尊处电报一通，以期早洽。此函到湘，上述函电，计已全部达览。一月份经费三千元，系于廿五日交中国银行电汇奉上，度能准时汇到。此次尊嘱之事，弟虽勉其棉力，大费周章，终愧未能完全报命，敬祈鉴谅。综合执委会结论，约如左列：

　　一、推司徒先生暂主平馆大计，内部行政，托王子舫、张庚楼、顾子刚三君会办。照常开门阅览，每月经费暂发八千元，中西文书不添购，续订新杂志之算学、生物科学及物理科学部分，俱请嘱出版家仍寄北平。

　　二、请兄或回平主持馆务，或请假留滇黔协助临时大学并指导改进西南各省图书馆。以后办法，至下届年会再定。

　　三、请就平馆在湘同人指派二至三人驻沪，一人驻港，二人驻湘办理结束，如通知外国书店改寄杂志等事。驻港员除月薪外，外支生活津贴五十元每月。其未经执事指派留南工作之同人，以及指派工作办完之同人，俱请回平馆办事。由长沙回北平之旅费，每人送国币二百元。不愿回平者，每人致送等于三个月薪金之解聘金。

　　四、前自北平运出之书，照存原地，不运回北平。

　　此外尚有左列各事，祈分别察洽或示遵：

　　甲、新杂志除指定请嘱改寄平馆者外，可否请用工程图书馆名义改寄上海中科社代收？

　　乙、Swets & Zeilinger之旧杂志，拟于寄去支票时，请其将该杂志若干箱寄上海中基会代收，附上散处拟函一件共三份，如蒙同意，请将正副本一并签署寄还弟已署名之副本,请留存入尊档,以便邮发。西文购书费在伦敦尚存有三百磅零,足敷支票之用。

丙、尊处欠临大垫款国币五六九.九九圆,即托中国银行航汇该校清账。

丁、平馆花旗存款,已托该行经理密查函报。

戊、中文书存申美艺四十九箱,科社百四十九箱,震旦百八十箱,科社者尚拟一并运去震旦。

己、捐助震旦之国币壹千元,经与森玉兄商洽后,决定送去。该校当事人于理实不当如此,但我辈只好看开些,将此项捐款作为寄存栈租之用。

溯自卢沟桥事变以还,吾兄为平馆及临大事,筹画一切,既劳神思,又吃辛苦,中基会董事及同人,无不十分敬佩。虽图书馆工作不能积极进行,然既已耕耘,必有收获,此弟敢引为左右宽慰者也。中基会同人已全部来沪,但编译委员会为收稿、校稿便利起见,仍留北平,其办公处即在南长街廿二号。如兄在平有事托办,请随时示知,以便转函办理。沪津、平电报每字现收＄1.25。此颂台祺。

弟孙洪芬拜上。

廿七,一,廿六

附西文函正副本共三页。

〔中华教育文化基金董事会笺。《北京图书馆馆史资料汇编
（1909－1949）》,页490－495〕

按:Swets & Zeilinger 实应为 Swets & Zeitlinger,现全称为 Royal Swets & Zeitlinger Holding NV,1901 年由 Adriaan Swets 和 Heinrich Zeitlinger 创立,位于荷兰,是全世界范围内为出版社与图书馆间提供信息获取、订购业务的重要公司。孙洪芬两次提及 Zeitlinger,其拼写皆有错误。

一月二十七日

徐森玉致函先生,告其未能将平馆存沪善本书移运至港及中基会执委会就平馆馆务之决议。

守和先生赐鉴:

移善本书来港事,宝赍尊函多件于十六日抵沪,其时箱已制齐,书由科学社运至震旦大学者已百八十箱。是孙洪芬先生已改变前所主

张,不拟将书运港矣。此事责任太重,宝不便力争,只得作罢。次日司徒雷登到沪,将开执委会,孙先生忙于招待,无暇与宝等多谈,宝乘间必言南来同人从公之辛劳,办事处之有成绩,应加维持。继闻顾子刚兄有英文函致孙先生,力言平馆经费不宜停止,此函已寄至尊处,未识确否? 廿二日赴花旗银行探得开会结果:一、将长沙办事处结束。二、请公回平主持馆务,倘有不便时,暂由司徒代理,专事对外。三、平馆经费仍照常付给。四、长沙同人一律回平复职。此种议事录,想已寄至尊处,究竟与宝所闻有无出入,不可知也。宝向孙先生表示不愿回平,渠谓可留沪办事。将来如何分配,无从悬揣。遂于廿四日乘轮南行,廿七日抵港,暂寓新华饭店,仍拟他移。年近六旬,已无力深入内地。香港用费过大,不能久居,真所谓人间无个安排处矣,言之可叹!闻公不久来港,宝在此恭候,可一罄衷曲。宝薪水请便中赐下,盖手头款项业已用尽也。匆此,即请钧安。

徐鸿宝敬上
一月廿七日

同仁均此致候。

〔《北京图书馆馆史资料汇编(1909-1949)》,页 496-497〕

一月二十八日

晚六时,先生在韭园寓所招宴,袁复礼、吴宓、陈慈、张婉英、高棣华为客,九时方散。〔《吴宓日记》第 6 册,页 290〕

一月二十九日

晚六时许,先生访吴宓,约定明晚宴会。〔《吴宓日记》第 6 册,页 290〕

一月三十日(除夕)

平馆委员会在长沙委员召开特别会议,蒋梦麟、傅斯年、先生与会,通过六项决议。其中第六项决议最为紧要,具体内容为:南下馆员继续为临时大学服务,但每月薪金总额不得超过 3000 国币;除生物学期刊外,其他各订购中的外文期刊均寄送长沙供临时大学使用。〔台北"中央研究院"近代史研究所档案馆,〈中华教育文化基金董事会〉,馆藏号 502-01-08-067,页 54〕

按:另外,根据平馆委员会规定,委员会召开法定人数须在五人以上,虽然此次会议人数不够,但此时在任何一地都难以凑齐任意五位委员。

晚六时,先生在韭园宅招宴,客为袁复礼、吴宓、陈慈、张婉英、高棣华、孟广喆,九时方散。〔《吴宓日记》第6册,页291〕

　　按:孟广喆(1907—1989),生于北京,清华大学毕业后自费赴美留
　　学,获机械工程硕士学位,1933年回国并在南开大学电机系任
　　教,时应在临时大学任教。

先生致信蔡元培,附中基会执委会关于北平图书馆之决议案六条、特别委员会关于北平图书馆决议案、图书馆委员会议决案(草案)。

　　孑民先生钧鉴:

　　　　前闻大驾抵港,深以为慰。中基会于上年十月间议决,平馆在湘同人共廿四人得在临时大学办事,所订之期刊均改寄长沙。近以司徒雷登由平抵申,对平馆事另有主张,爰有各项之议决案见附件。惟平馆既为国立机关,自与燕大、协合情形不同均已悬挂五色旗,国家之立场不能不顾。而既有临时政府,复有日本顾问,同人虽愿返平,但事实方面,在此环境中实无法做事。自接到此项议决案后,即送交委员会予以考虑。前由委员会拟定决议案六条随函附上,即希鉴核示知,俾有遵循为感。临大迁滇并补助同人薪水千元,所有书籍由湘运滇之运费,亦由临大担任。如能来港,当趋谒面陈。先此。

　　　　〔长沙临时大学图书馆用笺。《北京图书馆馆史资料汇编(1909-
　　　　1949)》,页467〕

　　按:此件为先生所拟之底稿,修改、删减甚多。右下处用铅笔标识
　　为"一月三十日",暂依该时间。蔡元培于2月3日①得此信,并
　　得中基会函、抄示致教育部函稿、中基会1月24日电。

邓衍林致函先生,陈述平馆在南方工作的意义和对中基会执委会决议的异议。

　　守和先生道鉴:

　　　　日前徐森玉先生由沪抵港,闻悉中基会执委会开会,对于本馆今后进行有所商策,其决议如何容待揭晓。兹就徐公所闻悉者,大体如下:

　　　　(一)认为北馆行政组织尚未变更,经费仍继续维持。

────────────

① 《蔡元培日记》,页536。

（二）长沙办事处撤销，工作人员回平或遣散之。

（三）馆长未能回平以前，由司徒雷登对外暂摄馆务。

（四）香港方面暂留一人或二人照料。

此为会议方面之公式意见，大体如系。其他私人方面意见如司徒雷登之表示：

1.赴南下工作人员，认为系私人行动，其批评认为"盲动"。

2.北方现安定，能继续工作，南方工作恐不必要，甚或以"无事可做"。

3.南方工作人员太多，认为乘此有大皆裁汰之必要。

4.……

因此根据是项意见之结果，力主继续维持北馆，而南方工作俱应撤销云云。兹就此项政策之大体而加检讨，并披沥私人之管见以供我公之参资。

（一）刻下日人桥川已去馆，馆长仍属袁公，认为行政组织尚未变更，而仍照中基会一贯政策继续维持。兹立于全馆立场上认为可行。

（二）平津刻下治安或称安靖，然人心是否安定，当待研究。北馆事实上能否安心工作？有何表现？容待考虑？

（三）此次抗战爆发后，南北各地藏书多遭摧毁。一旦抗战结束，国家必骤复兴建设。而准备将来复兴建设所应备之参考资料，是否为当前重要之问题，而刻下南方我公所计划之工作，是否为虚设浪费，抑为深谋远虑，当从客观加以批评，是不应该断为"不必要"或"无事可做"，而抹杀事实也。

（四）更就南方所主办工作加以分释检讨，是否合乎"国立北平图书馆"历年之政策而加讨论。我馆自合并成立以后，即确立其两大政策：(1)保存固有文化；(2)发扬近代科学，故购书方面即以此为方针。今南方的工作者：（一）征集调查西南文献，因地制宜就近搜集当与"保存文化"脗合；（二）致力于"工程参考书报"之征集，此不但与馆策及中基科学教育政策相合，且对于供给国家建设及学者专门研究参考有裨，盖且极为重要之工作也。并与北馆现藏之西文书遥为补充，实为一举数便，且极有价值之工作，今被谈为"不必要"或别具高见欤！（三）调查"中日抗战史料与国际舆论资料"，此北方同志见之，或认为头痛，仁者见仁，智者见智，固无论矣！

是我等所做之工作既与馆策相符,而且极为重要明矣。

(五)司徒先生认为我等南下为"盲动"。只能认为洋人意见而已,果真认属"盲动",直不过奖励做馆"汉奸"而已,而对民族意识毫无认识者,可不辨! 其属于私人行动,或亦有未当,因我等多为奉馆命而始南行者,且林等数人确为坚持至日人劫持馆务之最后一秒钟,始行脱险间道离平。且行前亦曾以私人资格征询中基会负责当局之意见,认为无可苟留之必要,当与私人亡命有别也。抗战正酣之时依然据管佣书,既不能效命于疆场,而至少限度之与敌不合作精神,尚遭"盲动"之批评,诚令人欲哭无泪也。今彼等所云"行政组织"尚未变更,严格言之,其所谓之"国立北京"研究,何"国"所"立",谁人之"京",当更不值识者一笑也!

(六)今中基会所决定之政策究属根据何种见地,愚者莫测高深,以臆度之:

a. 北馆藏书甚富,且为硕果仅存之□公藏,历年投资亦钜。虽陷敌手,而仍以国际复杂关系以谋维系,故力主照常维持,理固然也。但愿日军将来撤退之时,对我文物而不加摧残,衷心愿矣。

b. 但何以对于南方现在进行之工作而加阻挠,说者谓日人初据平津之时,确曾向中美庚款建议拨划"本馆购书费"以作维持北平社会文化教育之用,而另以补助义务教育之款,移作补助北平小学经费。日人素奸猾,威胁利诱为惯策,抑日方对中基会或有所要挟欤? 抑中基会确别具原因?

统观上述,目下我馆事业前途确遭遇严重关头,于全馆事业发展前途我公似应据理力争。如公有暇赴沪一行,面向中基会商洽一切,不难迎刃解决也。所幸中基会意见对于"香港办事处"尚留有余地,即如果如决议,亦可从此点以谋缓冲也。林虽不敏,愿矢忠诚、竭尽智能追随我公之后,任何艰辛在所不辞。夙仰我公擘划周详,百折不挠,□虽公之胜利,亦即全国图书馆事业之福也。草率不恭,言不尽意。肃此,敬请道安,不一。

生邓衍林再拜

一月卅日旧历元旦

〔《北京图书馆馆史资料汇编(1909-1949)》,页 498-503〕

二月二日

任鸿隽覆函先生，谈其对平馆馆务维持、存沪善本书保管的想法。

守和吾兄大鉴：

昨奉一月十八日来示，并附图书馆报告等件，敬悉一一。弟等上年十二月末本有下山赴沪准备，嗣因车票无着，遂复中止。目下山中居住虽颇安适，然长此以往亦非了局，现正积极筹备，月内或可下山他往。过长时如兄尚在彼间，当可一晤为快。关于馆务，鄙意以为临大图书馆既已办有条理，此后只有与临大继续合作，庶收彼此互助之效。至北平馆务，弟向来主张尽力维持，但以他方不加干涉为条件。据温德先生报告，月前由司徒先生派人来馆，显系受人朦混与利用。闻司徒先生于前月半到申，对于馆事有详细报告。中基会随即开一执委会，想对此已有办法决定。弟远处深山，未明真象，自不能贡献具体意见。但读温、顾两君报告，觉温君所谓馆中应有一比较能负责之人主持其间，及顾君所述中基会之政策为"Take it or leave it"，皆值得我们严重考虑而已。又，顾君报告所云寄存上海之书，不知是否指寄存科学社者，震旦博物馆如能保险，自以暂存彼处为佳。因在此时局下，各处迁徙徒耗运费，且多危险，固不如就地保存之为得也。尊处所闻粤汉路行车情形如何？元任、孟真等是否在长，抑已他往，便中望示及为感。匆复，即请公安，敬颂潭福。

弟鸿隽顿首

廿七，二，二

〔《北京图书馆馆史资料汇编 (1909-1949)》，页 508-510〕

二月三日

孙述万、邓衍林、徐家璧、颜泽霭、余霭钰覆函先生，恳请保留平馆香港办事处。

守和馆长先生钧鉴：

顷奉一月廿七日及二月一日手谕，敬聆一一。中基会继续维持平馆，闻之至为欣慰。盖我公手创之事业得不至因沦亡而遭顿挫矣。至于其对在湘、港同仁一节，实未能体谅我公南来奋斗之苦心，至堪愤惜。幸该会决议对沪、港尚留余地。我公既已再电恳□，当不难挽回于万一也。职等对于此事聊具管见，谨呈于次，幸垂察焉。

（一）奉命南来，效力于国家，虽经艰苦，义容焉辞。惟于此现局下，决不愿回平忍辱苟安也。

（二）中基会如核允迁滇，港办事处似宜保留。理由：

①国内外交通邮寄两均便利；

②此间工作略就端绪；

③复兴之大业奠基于斯。

（三）中基会如不核允迁滇，则对于湘、港同仁亦应照常维持至本年六月底（会计年度），然后遣散。

（四）万不获已时，最低限度之维持办法：

①征求同仁意见，凡自愿遣散者给资遣散；

②自愿继续者可留港或随临大入滇工作；

③将留任工作人员全部遣散费总数作一临时预算，度此艰局；

④入滇或留港人员均支领最低限度之生活维持费及家庭救济费，务使继续吾人复兴之大业，藉示患难与共之意。

用敢揭櫫信念，藉矢忠诚。肃此，敬请道祺，不一。

职颜泽霭、孙述万、余霭钰、徐家璧、邓衍林谨上

二十七年二月三日

〔《北京图书馆馆史资料汇编（1909-1949）》，页 506-507 〕

按：颜泽霭，广东连平人，抗战前任平馆西文采访组组员。

二月四日

先生致信蔡元培。

按：此信内容应为先生请蔡元培向林风眠介绍李瑞年，于 2 月 5 日送达。[①]

二月八日

先生致信徐新六、施肇基、金绍基三位中基会董事，陈述平馆委员会对中基会执委会决议的意见。

新六、植之、叔初董事前辈钧鉴：

奉到洪芬先生一月廿六日手书，详悉执委会议决各项办法，足征维护文化事业之苦心，本馆同人至深感谢。同礼曾将议决各案转送委员会，业

[①]《蔡元培日记》，页 537。

由蒋、傅两先生函复洪芬先生,谅荷鉴及。综合各委意见,不外三点:

(一)北平沦陷后,国立机关无法发展。维持馆产固极重要,不妨以一部份之经费,利用已有之人员,在西南积极从事复兴事业。

(二)留平职员现共有九十四人,以之维持现状、保管馆产已足敷用。在湘服务之人如继续留在南方办事,决不致影响平馆馆务。

(三)平馆所订之西文专门期刊,以自然科学为最多,刻下从事科学研究之人既已全数离平,似无再将此项刊物寄平之必要。而清华、北大、南开三校所订之期刊,自本年起均已停止续订。倘本馆能将所订者暂存临大,实可救济学术界之恐慌。

此外,留湘同人困难情形亦愿略为陈述:

(一)来湘服务之同事皆富于国家思想且勇于任事之人,到湘以来,成绩卓著。同礼既招之南来,此时如一律解聘家属多在北平,但无人愿北返,使之失业,于人情事理难得其平。

(二)执委会嘱同礼返平服务一节,为个人计极愿遵办,但恐于事业前途无何裨益。同礼为教育部任命之人,对于国家立场不能不坚守。倘届时临时政府加以委任或迫令悬五色旗应付环境,实感不易。至改进西南图书馆事业固所深愿,但须有专门人员相助为理,方易实现。倘在湘同人一律返平或解聘,则孤掌难鸣,亦无法进行也。

以上皆系事实上之困难,用敢披沥直陈,尚希赐以考虑,无任感荷。专此奉达,敬候道祺。

二月八日

〔《北京图书馆馆史资料汇编(1909-1949)》,页525-526〕

按:此为抄件。

先生致信王访渔、张允亮、顾子刚等,请三人竭力维持北平馆务。

庚楼、子访、子刚先生大鉴:

前上数函,谅达座右。中基会议决各案,想已由孙先生奉达。在弟未返平以前,仍请鼎力维持,俾保持独立性而免意外中基会维持到底,但以不受外间之干涉为条件。每月经费由沪汇平,稍迟数日,可在存款内借用,于尊处似无困难。上月较迟者因:(一)提取申货事始终无一字报告,蒋、傅甚不满,曾主停发,经弟缓冲,决定俟司徒到沪再商决。

（二）在平各项存款既敷发放一月之薪水而有余，稍缓似亦无妨，不意竟有误会，亦非始料所及患难之时，似应彼此或相谅解，况邮电迟滞乎。奉上中基会寄来八月至十二月平、湘分配单，请察阅。此六月之会计报告每月一份，并请从速寄下。

兹尚有数事请分别办理：

一、本馆同人均须留平维持到底。如有不得弟之允许而南来者，则此间亦无法可想。

二、工作应积极进行，集中力量完成书本目录，已请庾楼兄总其成，谅荷鉴及。印刷费亦有着，需用时再汇寄。

三、大阅览室每日仅十余人，似不成话，应竭力设法增加，引人来馆看书；如实无人来看，恐影响经费也。

四、福利储金前曾函请停止，何以十二月份之账仍然列入？请自一月份起一律停止。如已发放，应从二、三月内薪水中扣除之。

特此奉托，言不尽意。顺颂道祺。

弟同顿首

二月八日

〔长沙临时大学用笺。《北京图书馆馆史资料汇编（1909－1949）》，页528－529〕

按：3月1日，张允亮开始主持编纂书目。[1] 该信后附 8 月至 11 月平湘分配单 1 纸、12 月平湘分配单 1 纸。

蔡元培覆函先生，赞成平馆南下部分与临时大学合组、互助，并嘱先生就此作一提案，可在中基会年会中予以讨论。

守和先生大鉴：

叠接一月三十日及二月四日惠函，并承徐森玉兄面告一切。敬悉图书馆委员会决议之六条委曲求全，弟所赞成；蒋、傅两委员函稿读过，甚善，弟亦当致一函于洪芬兄也。执委会一月十八日之决议案六条中之第四条，对于先生四月以前往滇，并无冲突。惟为四月以后计，似可由先生具一详明之提案，要求在中基会年会中讨论之（该会定于四月二十九日、三十日开会，已发通告）。目前先生尽可往滇，为临时

---

① 国家图书馆档案，档案编号 1947－※011－年录 7－001020。

大学设计也。承代拟致林、赵二君函,为李君瑞年介绍,弟已签名奉上。颇闻梦麟兄到港,但未晤。此复,并颂著安。

弟元培敬启
二月八日

弟在此用"周子余"姓名,故信封未写本名。

〔国家图书馆档案,档案编号 1937-※007-年录 3-002001 和1937-※007-年录 3-002002〕

按:本日,蔡元培确致信与孙洪芬,表示支持袁同礼及南下馆员自愿前往云南为临时大学服务。[①]"周子余"之称,似与其妻周峻有关。

徐森玉覆函先生,告其与蔡元培初步商讨平馆居湘同人去留问题的结果。

守和先生赐鉴:

昨奉手教,敬悉壹是。蔡先生已移居九龙柯斯甸道一五六号楼下二号。今晨往访,宝力陈中基会议决各案纯系偏见,专与在湘职员为难,不顾事实等语。蔡公颇为首肯,云即致函孙先生转圜,惟要求其发电一节未蒙允许,盖一、无密码,二、此中曲直非数语所能罄也。日来广州、虎门二处均有事,公乘车莅港恐有障碍,不如飞机之稳便,尚祈注意及之。叔平先生来书嘱宝赴黔,拟俟虎门通航后当即前往。宝存湘行李二件,仍求饬旅行社运港为祷。树平、刚主两兄函已遵发,贱疾已愈八九,承念,感极。专此,敬请钧安。

徐鸿宝再拜
二月八日

〔国家图书馆档案,档案编号 1937-※035-采藏 7-002001 和1937-※035-采藏 7-002002〕

按:"树平"即齐念衡,时应任故宫博物院古物科长。先生在此函尾部标注"般含道圣药翰寄宿舍 22 号"。

任鸿隽致函先生,讨论中基会对平馆议决案并仍劝先生返平主持馆务。

守和吾兄大鉴:

昨奉尊寄梦麟先生来示并附件,晚间又接尊处来电,敬悉一一。

[①] 台北"中央研究院"近代史研究所档案馆,〈中华教育文化基金董事会〉,馆藏号 502-01-08-067,页 58。

关于圕事,弟于日昨亦接洪芬来信,并附寄致教育部缄稿及中基会通知圕委员会公缄,想梦麟先生及尊处亦已接到此项通知矣。此事在中基会方面既经执委会正式决议,圕委员会即有他项建议,亦只能将原议略事修改,不能望其根本取消。故鄙意兄此时只能依照中基会议决,返平供职或暂在西南各省服务。至本馆与临大是否继续合作乃为另一问题,当视蒋、傅两公致中基会之缄能否发生效力为断。弟个人意见仍大略如前缄所说,一面维持平馆,一面顾全临大。最好兄本人返平维持彼方局面因彼方须有能负责之人方妥,而临大方面则由兄派少数职员继续工作此处自然亦须中基会承认合作办法并指定预算方可。至中基会年会开后,圕大局决定,再说以后办法。不知兄及梦麟先生之……日致洪芬缄亦将此意约略提及……情形较为繁复,电文不易明了,故本……电只言信详,尚乞谅之。梦麟先生不知尚在长沙否,不另具覆,即请以此缄眎之为幸。弟因山中不可久居,现已积极筹备下山,廿间或可到长,不知彼时台驾尚在彼间否也?匆匆不尽,即请公安。

弟鸿隽顿首
廿七,二,八

弟致洪芬信大略要点:

(一)兄应返平服务。

(二)与临大合作暂延长至暑假为止。

(三)由兄指派少数职员在临大工作并由会指定预算。

(四)西文杂志除生物外,应否全数寄平应考虑。

附录于此以备参考。

〔《北京图书馆馆史资料汇编(1909-1949)》,页 519—521〕

按:该函末页右下部分残缺,只得以……标识。

二月十日

先生致信王重民,告知其补助费之汇寄及自己即将南下赴滇诸细节,并谈向达须向清华大学提交一账目清单。

有三吾弟:

上月由汉口汇寄国币二千元英庚款照相用,由香港挂号寄英,想已收到。尊处之补助费自十月份起勉强可在湘馆支付,俟月底到港后再汇。寄王景春为向君觅免船费事之信已发出,如渠今夏不返国,则作罢也可。大使馆寄来刊物已收到，现在本馆所编之书如印好，较大使馆者有价值多多矣。杜乃扬不日赴日本住三个月，由彼赴美转法，大约到暑假时方能到巴黎。向君之款务使之交出，并索一清账，因清华曾催问也。奖学金事虽可进行，但无大希望。美国方面迄今尚无覆音。兄月抵离此随临大赴滇，以后通讯处为"香港冯平山中文图书馆转"。

兄同礼顿首

二月十日

〔中国书店·海淀，四册〕

> 按："兄月抵离此"当作"兄月底离此"。该信有一便笺，为先生书写的邮寄信息："如王君已赴英，寄此处 Wang Chung-min, Esq., c/o Dr. Lionel Giles, British Museum, London."

教育部以公函形式回覆中基会，认为其执委会第122次会议及一月二十一日特别会议就平馆馆务的决定极为不妥且无法实行，平馆作为国立教育机构，南下馆员应在临时大学服务而不便北返，且改寄所有西文期刊到平亦不能接受。今后中基会召开此类会议，应尽量选择在香港或者内陆城市，以便教育部代表出席。〔台北"中央研究院"近代史研究所档案馆，〈中华教育文化基金董事会〉，馆藏号 502-01-08-067，页73〕

二月十二日

上午十时半，吴宓离长沙，先生送其出临时大学校门口。〔《吴宓日记》第6册，页296〕

二月十三日

先生致信蔡元培，告知已将平馆委员会委员意见汇寄孙洪芬，并奉教部电文。

> 子民先生钧鉴：
>
> 　　奉二月八日赐书，诸承指示，心感莫名。顷已将各委意见汇寄洪芬先生，想司徒既不在沪，或可挽回也。顷教部寄来电稿，录副呈阅，似亦值得考虑也。专此，敬候道祺。

同礼叩上

二月十三日

〔长沙临时大学用笺。国家图书馆档案，档案编号 1937-※007-年录3-002003〕

任鸿隽覆函先生,再劝先生返平主持馆务。

　　守和吾兄大鉴:

　　　前于本月八日奉上缄、电各一,计已达览,昨又奉本月二日快示及附件,敬悉一一。弟前信所言乃系为图书馆、为吾兄、为中基会着想,比较的三方面均可过得去之一种办法,唯尚不知北平情形如何。如来书所言,平中如燕大、协和均已悬五色旗,平馆既为国立机关,诚难同流合污。吾兄返平服务处境之难自可想见事实上兄既系奉命返平,许多问题尽可不负责任,唯平馆为中基会重要事业之一,历年用款巨万,此时如有法维持,自应委曲求全,为当地人民留一点文化基础。依此立场而言,兄返平后即多受一点身体上或精神上之苦痛,乃为民族前途而牺牲,亦事之值得者也。不知尊意以为何如? 至于临大合作事业乃另一问题,既有孟邻、孟真两先生信去,弟亦两缄洪芬,嘱其善为考虑,或不至全无下文也。弟等现定于本月廿间下山,如粤汉路无恙,拟乘车直赴香港,如彼时兄尚在长,当可图一快晤。俟由汉动身时,再当以到长时间电告(兄如彼时已离长沙则请缄示,交汉口中国旅行社留转)。孟真尚在长沙否? 有一笺致彼,请转交为感。此请大安。

　　　　　　　　　　　　　　　　　　　　弟鸿隽顿首

　　　　　　　　　　　　　　　　　　　　廿七,二,十三

　　　　　　　〔《北京图书馆馆史资料汇编(1909—1949)》,页 531—533〕

二月十四日

先生致电孙洪芬,大意如下:

　　　请妥善考虑本月八日信中所列各细节。蒋梦麟、傅斯年、蔡元培等人均促我能够赴云南,任鸿隽则希望我返平。甚盼及时电覆,以决定今后去向。

　　　　　　〔台北“中央研究院”近代史研究所档案馆,〈中华教育文化基金董事会〉,馆藏号 502-01-08-067,页 55〕

　　　　　　按:此电后被译为英文,抄送给中基会各董事。

二月十五日

孙洪芬覆电先生,大意如下:

　　　十四日电收悉,八日信仍未收到。中基会望兄即刻来沪,面商一切。盼覆。

〔台北"中央研究院"近代史研究所档案馆,〈中华教育文化基金
董事会〉,馆藏号 502-01-08-067,页 55〕

按:此电后被译为英文,抄送给中基会各董事。

二月十六日

先生致信史蒂文斯,告知平馆已奉教育部令前往昆明,并请洛克菲勒基金
会考虑不久前平馆寄上的资助申请。

February 16, 1938

Dear Dr. Stevens:

With reference to my letter of January 21 sent to you through Mr. Gunn, I wish to inform you that the Chinese Government has officially approved our plan of developing library resources in the southwestern provinces. We are now moving our headquarters to Kun Ming and expect to arrive there at the end of this month.

During my five months' work in the interior, I have had an unusual opportunity of meeting a great number of wandering scholars passing through Changsha. It is most gratifying to note that under such difficult times as we are now going through, Chinese scholars and scientists have not allowed national tribulation to dampen their ardour for learning and research. While many cultural and scientific institutions have been destroyed, yet the setback has not prevented the revival of learning. In spite of the present crisis, much work of permanent value has already been done. We are continuing to renovate and rebuild the intellectual life of our people in the face of almost overwhelming difficulties. In this connection the National Library is contributing its share towards the achievement of these objectives.

With regard to our application for a grant of $ 80,000, we earnestly hope it will receive the favorable consideration of your Trustees. Should you find it difficult to make the grant while the undeclared war is still in progress, may I suggest that you have the sum appropriated for a period of two years?

I have had telegrams from Dr. Draeger who recently arrived at

Peiping. The microfilm machinery, as soon as received from Washington, will be set up at Kun Ming where our rare books will eventually be transferred. But we shall not be able to move our rare books until we have a fire-proof building. In solving this urgent problem, may we count upon you for your assistance?

For further correspondence, please use the following address:

National Library of Peiping

c/o Fung Ping Shan Chinese Library,

Hongkong.

With warmest regards,

Yours sincerely,

T. L. Yuan

Acting Director

〔平馆(长沙办事处)英文信纸。Rockefeller Foundation. Series 601: China; Subseries 601.R: China-Humanities and Arts. Box 47. Folder 389〕

按:此件为打字稿,落款处为先生签名。

二月中下旬

先生致电孙洪芬,大意如下:

一俟病体复原,愿前往上海。但仍望尊处尽快决定并电覆。

〔台北"中央研究院"近代史研究所档案馆,〈中华教育文化基金董事会〉,馆藏号 502-01-08-067,页 55〕

按:17 日晨,此电送到孙洪芬处。后被译为英文,抄送给中基会各董事。

二月十七日

任鸿隽覆函先生,三劝先生返平维持馆务。

守和吾兄左右:

十三日奉上一缄,计已达览。顷奉本月八、十一、十二、十三等日来示,敬悉一一。弟八日上缄曾有兄或返平、或照执委会议决案仍随临大往西南工作之言。十三日上书,复将兄返平困难情形详加考虑。诚如枚荪所言,弟所提办法近于"折衷",然在执委会未复决前项议决办法以前,此实为一唯一可能之办法。顷见兄抄示蔡先生缄,意似与鄙见大略相同。兄何妨即照蔡先生所指示者进行,以待中基会之最后决定如何?弟前缄劝兄返平,实有见于平馆重要。即便照目下组织,由王、张、顾三君负责维持,能否维持下去仍属疑问。一有蹉跎,则兄多年努力之结果,均归乌有,甚属可惜。故为馆计、为兄计,均以返平为善。至平方情形如何,弟因了无闻知,无从悬断,唯审度而慎择之。幸甚,承示致植之、新六诸公函稿,弟甚表同意。其中如(一)(三)两项,弟致洪芬信时已竭力言之矣。嘱要中基会致各委员缄,兹以呈阅。弟与眷属定于十九日乘轮赴汉,在彼或须耽阁二、三日方能来长,想彼时大驾尚在长沙也。时艰事繁,一切唯希宽怀自卫为祷。匆覆,即请时安。

弟任鸿隽

二月十七日

〔《北京图书馆馆史资料汇编(1909-1949)》,页534-535〕

按:此件应为先生收到后的抄件。

二月十八日

孙洪芬覆函先生,请赴沪或港指挥平馆馆务。

守和先生大鉴:

敬复者,二月十四日尊电及十六日复电,均拜悉。清恙近痊愈否,至念。关于足下行止,弟意去平不妥,往滇太远,最好请在沪或港指挥馆务,藉收兼筹并顾之效,不知尊意以为何如?齐函截至此刻止,尚未到申,但图书馆委员会蒋、傅二君函及临大蒋、张、梅三校长电,俱经执委会同情考虑,二、三日内可有决议。此函到湘,或电已先到也。此间有董事五位,各有本身职务,开会比较不易。近日贝诺德君出门,本拟俟其回申再开会,因图书馆事亟待决定,拟提前集议,以免久悬。孙书城君等三人寄家用各六十元往平,已汇交子刚兄转。在港五人孙君等在内应得之薪亦已径汇。此颂时祺。

弟洪芬上

廿七,二,十八

钱君存训已到申,薪已发。

〔七科学团体联合年会筹备委员会信纸。《北京图书馆馆史资料汇编(1909-1949)》,页536-537〕

按:"在港五人"应指颜泽霭、孙述万、余霭玉、徐家璧、邓衍林。

二月十九日

先生致信国会图书馆(馆长秘书),感谢寄赠出版物并告知平馆通讯地址变更。

Feb. 19, 1938

Dear Madam:

　　We wish to acknowledge with thanks the receipt of your letter dated January 3rd as well as the following publications which the Library of Congress so kindly presented to the National Library of Peiping:

　　Third cumulative supplement to the main list of subject headings,

　　Lists of additions and changes (nos. 30-37).

We are most grateful to the Chief of your Division of Accessions for promising to send to us two free copies of your classification schedules, "Class PT, part 1" which will be ready for distribution sometime in March or April. As soon as these copies reach us, we shall acknowledge their receipt.

　　In order to assure their safe delivery, you are requested to send to us all communications as well as printed matter at the following address until further notice:

　　National Library of Peiping,

　　c/o Fung Ping Shan Chinese Library,

　　Bonham Road,

　　Hong Kong.

　　Will you kindly forward for us the enclosed letter to the Card Division of your Library?

　　Thanking you for your kind cooperation,

Yours very truly,

T. L. Yuan

Acting Director

〔平馆(长沙办事处)英文信纸。Librarian of Congress, Putnam Archives, Special File, China: National Library 1930-1939〕

按:此件为打字稿,落款处为先生签名,于 3 月 26 日送达国会图书馆秘书办公室。

二月中旬

先生覆信任鸿隽,表示不愿回平主持馆务,并告其未收到中基会公函。

> 叔永先生尊鉴:
>
> 顷奉二月八日手书,诸承指示,心感何似。关于执委会议决各案,当时讨论经过及背景,弟亦不甚了了。承嘱各节已转梦麟先生矣。比以尊札与月涵、今甫、梅荪商量,认为兄所拟办法近于 compromise,似不如留有用之身在西南为国家作一最后之奋斗也。无所适从,惟近来似此各有理由。弟顷已函询洪芬先生请其详为指示。此间困难情形已详致施、金、徐三董事之函,六号以副本寄上,谅荷鉴及。弟近来患失眠症甚剧,亟愿早卸仔肩,俾能扫除一切苦恼。日前一切困难皆系自作自受,真所谓天下本无事,庸人自扰之,不识高明何以教之。梦麟先生已赴港转滇,现月涵、今甫仍留湘,过十日后赴港,弟则候洪芬来电再定行止。中基会通知委员会公缄,此间未收到。请录副寄下是荷。

〔长沙临时大学用笺。《北京图书馆馆史资料汇编(1909-1949)》,页 522〕

按:由"关于执委会议决各案,当时讨论经过及背景,弟亦不甚了了"和"中基会通知委员会公缄,此间未收到。请录副寄下是荷"可以推知至 2 月中旬,先生仍未收到 1 月 24 日中基会致先生公函。"今甫、梅荪"即杨振声、周炳琳。此件应为底稿。

二月二十二日

孙洪芬覆函先生,告平馆南下同人本学期赴滇之举应无大碍,并谈人员和经费杂事。

> 守和吾兄有道:
>
> 一月八日大函顷始到申,内附致施、金、徐三董事函,复 Swets and Zeilinger 函,王子访、任叔永二先生致尊处函各一件,均经诵悉。致三董事函及 SLW 函即分别送寄,王、任二先生函兹随函附还,祈查收。二月十四日之函及附件,昨竟先到,因蔡先生函应有效力,弟已送请各董事传观,俟还来再连附来三电一并寄港。在过去三日中,弟曾寄函

电各一与尊处,略称赴滇案可望成立,约于三月五日前正式电告,请展行期,计已先达。

兄返平之说,弟设身处境,不敢主张,赴湘之人一律解约,鄙意亦不赞可。弟为中基会执行事务长,又为图书馆委员,有此种"双层"关系,有时说话固为有力,有时反不能过分坚执。但对于馆事,总以心安理得为目的,必为在湘、在平友人所鉴谅。就弟此刻所能臆度,留湘同人赴滇至本学期止,应可办到,以后之事,则难预测。大抵于北平图书馆之外,添办新馆或分馆,不易通过。若临大请求补助,或比较容易。又平馆技术专员多已南下,上年未完之编目等工作,不易赓续,司徒先生曾引以告弟,不识尊处能设法补救否?

兄为湘馆事,吃苦懊气,弟极了解并表同情。惟因公受气或受怨,只要与事有济,与国有益,其他俱可不计。孙、邓、徐三君之家用 180 元,已代汇平并函三君本人知照。所余薪水及颜君与余女士之二月薪已汇港。湘费余额由中国汇湘。钱存训君已到社,二月薪已送。书已全交 Aurora,科学社无剩册。清恙瘥后,弟切盼大驾来申一行,凡事面谈可谋彻底的了解与各方顾到的办法,请优予考虑为幸。余不一一,即颂大安。

弟洪芬拜上
廿七,二,廿二

赶船班,匆匆不尽。明后日再函。

〔七科学团体联合年会筹备委员会信纸。《北京图书馆馆史资料汇编(1909-1949)》,页 538-541〕

按:Zeilinger 实应为 Zeitlinger,原信拼写有误。Aurora 即震旦大学。

二月二十三日

周诒春覆函先生,告知其对平馆委员会议决案的意见,并托美使馆转达与孙洪芬。

守和先生惠鉴:

十七日航复一缄,谅以入察。今日下午接二月十三日手书并蔡、陶诸委员意见,奉悉一一。图书馆委员会议决案六条,除第三条弟认为不宜积极进行外,余均同意,业经函复并托美使馆转电洪芬兄矣。

专此,复颂台祺。

弟周诒春敬启

二月二十三日

〔《北京图书馆馆史资料汇编(1909-1949)》,页542〕

按:"陶委员"似有误,待考。"第三条"内容应为:北平圕在北平部分之经常费应减至最低限度,由本会授权孙洪芬、袁同礼两先生负责核减。[①] 此函为文书代笔,落款为其签名。

二月二十六日

徐森玉(六寨)致函先生,告其已应马衡之请离港,经广西前往贵州。

守和先生左右:

在港连接叔平先生催促往筑之函,于廿一晨启行,不及待台从莅临,至为歉仄。公率领同人入滇之举,想无障碍,但私衷耿耿,驰系万分。宝廿三日抵苍梧,廿四晨乘小轮至戎墟,换长途车至郁林宿。廿五日至庆远宿,今日下午抵六寨。庆远以上,山坡益峻,水流益急,路甚难行。怀远之龙江两岸及底均黑石,森如剑戟,亦不易渡也。六寨为粤西入黔之边境,车辆甚少,顷至车站询问,日内恐无车赴筑,奈何奈何。尘装甫卸,特寄此以报踪迹。即请钧安。

弟徐鸿宝再拜

二月廿六日

旅店无桌椅,据箱书此,草率不恭。

〔国家图书馆档案,档案编号 1945-※057-综合 5-015001〕

按:苍梧、戎墟(今名"龙圩")、郁林(今名"玉林")、庆远、六寨今皆属广西壮族自治区。

三月一日

史蒂文斯覆先生两函,其一,告知先生前信申请将资助日期延长的要求暂时不会被考虑。

March 1, 1938

Dear Mr. Yuan:

I have your letter of January 21st suggesting that the aid of the

---

① 《北京图书馆馆史资料汇编(1909-1949)》,页515。

Foundation in respect to printing and distribution of catalogue cards be suspended until further notice from you. Our practice ordinarily is to bring up questions of extension of time on our grants at sometime within three months of the final date. No special notice need be sent us to give later report. The request will be reviewed automatically by us next spring and at that time we shall have from our office in China a record of the expenditures from the appropriation.

Very truly yours,

David H. Stevens

其二,告知先生前信所附备忘录已经收到,待耿士楷回到纽约后再与之商议。

March 1, 1938

Dear Mr. Yuan:

　　It is probably clear in your mind that the proposal set forth in your letter of January 21st regarding further library development will need deferment. I thank you, however, for sending us the data on the project in the special memorandum accompanying your letter. I shall be interested to talk through the entire matter with Mr. Gunn when he returns to New York next month.

Very truly yours,

David H. Stevens

〔Rockefeller Foundation. Series 601: China; Subseries 601.R: China-Humanities and Arts. Box 47. Folder 389〕

　　按:该两函寄送长沙,均为副本。

三月三日

张允亮、王访渔、顾子刚覆函先生,报告北平馆务近况。

　　守和先生赐鉴:

　　　　接奉二月八日手书,备谂种切。中基会继续拨款,维持以访渔等组织行政委员会一节,业已来函通知。此项会议即于二月三日成立,兹附上历次会议录,请察阅。承示及患难之时应彼此谅解一节,药石之言,当敬铭肺腑。此间同人自问,始终以尊主权、重典守、忠于其职、无有贰心为职志,馆务亦安然照常进行。嗣后此间事务当每隔半月造具报告一份,由司徒先生转中基会一份寄呈左右,敬备察核。倘有道路言传及报载新闻,请一概屏而弗听,庶误会无由而生,不审高明以为如何?

至提取申货事,此间并未得有比较确实消息,亦无若何方面前来接洽,是以无从报告。倘以影响之辞,遽烦尊听,其取罪当尤甚,故不敢为也。又承示以允亮总成书本目录事,敬当遵照,自愧菲材,弥惧弗克负荷耳。半年以来,中文编目组同人均孳孳从事,不敢稍懈,集中众力,当可计日观成,堪慰廑系。阅览人数每日虽不如从前之多,但亦不致仅十余人,此传者之过也。附呈阅览统计一份,当可释然。

停发福利储金事,始终未奉到明教,仅于二月中收到致紫佩函,内询及已否照办一语,不悉详情,且惟时已遵办,不及当以事关预算,只得向司徒先生请示。据司徒表示,须与上海商定,在未得确实办法以前,二月分储金仍属照发,现尚未得沪复也。专此奉复,敬候台祺。

张允亮、王访渔、顾子刚谨启

三月三日

〔《北京图书馆馆史资料汇编(1909-1949)》,页543-546〕

按:2月3日至3月3日,平馆王访渔、张允亮、顾子刚三人组成的行政委员会共召开数次会议,讨论平馆馆务问题。

三月五日[①]

先生与平馆数位馆员乘船抵达香港,暂在香港大学冯平山图书馆办公。

〔中国书店·海淀,四册〕

三月六日

孙洪芬致函先生,告知中基会执委会对平馆馆务最新议决。

守和先生大鉴:

敬启者,执委会因临时有特,故改至昨夕举行,关于图书馆事,重加考虑,议决要意(1)现在南未返之馆员,得延长服务于临大期间至本年六月底止,月薪约二千五百元,在北平图书馆经费项下支付;(2)上述馆员由昆明或长沙返平得支旅费贰百元;(3)续订购西文杂志费

---

① 《吴宓日记》将抵达香港的时间记作3月8日,笔者认为并不准确。

定为美金五千元,包括各种杂志在内。除生物及有关静生之研究之杂志应直接寄往静生应用外,其余杂志应兼顾平馆阅览及借给临大之两种需要。至详细办法交弟函商左右及平馆妥为办理。弟今晨曾将第一项电告孙书城兄,以备转告,因不知左右是否已到港或在途中也。上海邮件检查五日起施行,我辈通信固毫无政治意味,但为免除误会起见,拟以后信交书城转,并专用香港大学工程图书馆名义,即祈察洽并通知书城为幸。此颂台祺。

弟洪芬拜上。
廿七,三,六

〔国家图书馆档案,档案编号 1937-※007-年录 3-001024〕

按:3 月 4 日,中基会执委会召开第 123 次会议,其议决第一项中前半部分关于南下服务时间的限制被随后在港举行的平馆委员会取消。

三月七日

先生致信耿士楷,告知平馆已暂借香港大学冯平山图书馆继续开展馆务,并请洛克菲勒基金会考虑资助平馆购买科学期刊。

Hongkong
March 7, 1938

Mr. Selskar M. Gunn

Passenger, S. S. Empress of Canada

c/o Canadian Pacific Steamship Co.

Shanghai

Dear Mr. Gunn:

A few days before leaving Changsha, I was glad to receive your letter of February 21. I regret, however, that I was not able to meet you in Hongkong before you departed. I wish to extend to you my very best wishes for bon voyage and early return.

I had intended to discuss with you how we could secure some financial assistance either from your Foundation or from other source so that we can carry on our work uninterrupted. It seems that we are the only institution still able to go ahead with our plans even under such difficult times as we have been going through.

The University of Hongkong has placed its Fung Ping Shan Chinese Library at our disposal. For the time being, we shall have our temporary office in Hongkong. We could easily move our rare books to Hongkong and proceed with the micro-film machinery. If your Foundation feels that it is too early to make grants towards the erection of a fire-proof building while the undeclared war is still in progress, we earnestly hope that some grant can be made to enable us to keep up with current scientific journals and to proceed with the work of cultural exchange. I shall be most obliged to you if you could discuss these details with the officers of the Foundation as soon as you reach New York.

Kindly note that all correspondence with the National Library should be addressed to our Hongkong office.

With warmest regards and all good wishes,

Yours sincerely,

T. L. Yuan,

Acting Director

c/o Fung Ping Shang Library

Hongkong

〔平馆(长沙办事处)英文信纸。Rockefeller Foundation. Series 601: China; Subseries 601.R: China-Humanities and Arts. Box 47. Folder 389〕

按:此件为打字稿,落款处为先生签名。

三月九日

徐森玉致函先生,谈故宫博物院南迁文物在贵阳情形。

守和先生赐鉴:

在六寨候车时曾寄一函,谅先此入照。六寨以上山路崎岖,千回百折,直至三日晨始抵贵阳。此间房屋简陋,人口大增,古物来此月余,尚存行营,未觅得保藏之处行营有他用,即须迁出。现拟租民房暂存,修理运徙仍需时晷也。楚黔相距稍远,情形隔阂。如存放地点,省府始终主张在观音洞,而叔平先生主张在城内,然绝无相当房屋,奈何奈何。计日公已莅港,闻临大在昆明有问题,有迁往蒙自之说,果尔则同人赴滇亦有问题矣。至为驰念,寄上《贵州名胜古迹概说》一册另封寄,乞察存。文献征辑馆业已停办,旧书铺只两家容再至外县细访,无一可购之书也。匆此,即请钧安。

弟徐鸿宝再拜
三月九日

同人均此致意。

〔国家图书馆档案,档案编号 1945-※057-综合 5-015002〕

按:由欧阳道达《故宫文物避寇记》可知,1937 年 8 月 14 日故宫文物八十箱由水路运离南京,16 日抵汉口,经火车转运粤汉铁路至长沙,21 日存入湖南大学图书馆。1938 年 1 月 12 日至 2 月 10 日,该处文物分两批运至贵阳,后暂存城北。观音洞为政府所属意存放处之一,但该洞狭小且常年滴水,极不适宜保存文物。"迁往蒙自之说",盖因临时大学初到昆明时校舍不敷,只得暂将部分师生迁至蒙自分校,后于同年 9 月搬回昆明。《贵州名胜古迹概说》由京滇公路游览会贵州分会宣传部编纂,1937 年贵阳文通书局印制。

三月十日

傅斯年、先生、任鸿隽访蔡元培,商定平馆维持办法。〔《蔡元培日记》,页 543〕

三月十一日

上午十一时,平馆委员会假九龙柯思甸道蔡元培寓所召开关于商讨北平馆务与在滇临大合办的会议,出席者为蔡元培、任鸿隽、傅斯年、先生,另傅斯年又代表蒋梦麟。议决如下:

(一)北平图书馆之保守及维持日常阅览事项案:本委员会认为北平馆址中之保守及维持日常阅览事项暂有维持之必要,应由教育部及中基会妥商办法,但因事务缩小,经常费应减至最小限度。

(二)北平图书馆与临时大学合作办法案:本委员会认为,北平图书馆与临时大学合作办法乃继续北平图书馆原有工作之一部,此事又与西南各省图书馆事业发展大有关系,不应于此时国家困难期中半途改换,应照原定办法,自下学年起再延长一年。

(三)存置北平以外书籍之典守案:1. 存置北平以外之书籍应以存置原处为原则,但本委员会如认为必要,得移至更安全地点;2. 续订之西文科学期刊(除生物部分外)照原定办法继续存置临时大学;3.下年度购置期刊费不加减少,均寄至临时大学,由本馆在彼职员整理典守;

4. 所有北大、清华订购之期刊,均同样交由本馆在临时大学之职员整理典守。

(四)为办事便利起见,在香港设立临时通讯处。

此外,通过《国立北平图书馆昆明办事处工作大纲》(廿七年度至廿八年度),其中先生主要负责编辑云南研究参考资料(与万斯年)、影印《孤本元曲》事,另"协助西南联合大学完成图书设备"、"协助中华图书馆协会向国外征书及其他复兴工作"亦多由先生主持。〔《北京图书馆馆史资料汇编(1909-1949)》,页550-553〕

先生致信张允亮、王访渔、顾子刚,指示停发留平馆员福利储金等事。

　　庾楼、子访、子刚先生大鉴:

　　　　关于福利储金一案,上年十月间曾请停止发给在案。近阅十二月份会计报告,仍行列入,款数虽不甚多,但南北应一律办理。南方始终未发分文,则平中职员应自廿七年一月一日起一律停止。如已发给,应在三、四两月薪水内扣除之。除面告孙先生及司徒先生外,用特再行函达,即希查照。又,谢国桢君未得弟之同意,擅自返平。应请自三月一日起停薪。又,编目部主任曾请庾楼兄担任,请速开始办公。西文编目组组长请李锺履担任。统乞台察为荷,此颂大安。

　　　　　　　　　　　　　　　　　　　弟同顿首

　　　　　　　　　　　　　　　　　　　三月十一日

　　　　　　　〔《北京图书馆馆史资料汇编(1909-1949)》,页554-555〕

　　按:该信为文书代笔,落款处为先生签名,于3月31日送达。

三月十二日

先生致信史蒂文斯,建议在香港组装缩微胶片机用以拍摄平馆善本,并希望基金会考虑给予平馆资助用以购买西方科学期刊。

　　　　　　　　　　　　　　　　　　March 12, 1938

Dear Dr. Stevens:

　　With further reference to my letters of January 21 and February 16, I wish to inform you that the University of Hongkong has placed its Fung Ping Shan Chinese Library at our disposal. For the time being, I shall have my temporary office in Hongkong, while we have moved our headquarters and technical staff to Kun Ming.

I am writing to Mr. Graves and Dr. Draeger suggesting that the microfilm machinery be set up temporarily in Hongkong. We could easily move a number of our rare books from Shanghai to Hongkong and to start the work of reproduction immediately.

With regard to our application for a grant of $ 80,000, I wish to state that if your Foundation feels that it is not timely for a grant for a fire-proof building in view of the war situation, we earnestly hope that you would give due consideration towards our urgent need for western scientific journals, without which our scholars can never expect to keep up with the progress in the modern world.

In this connection I wish to report that at a meeting of the Board of Trustees of the Indemnity Funds returned by the British Government, a grant of $ 138,000, Chinese currency, was made for the placement of wandering scholars and scientists in order to enable them to carry on their work and to publish their scientific results. These scholars have come to us for scientific literature which we expect to supply out of a possible grant from your Foundation. The situation, therefore, needs immediate solution; and if it would be possible for your Trustees to give favorable consideration to this request, I shall appreciate a cable from you. With assurances of our appreciation of your interest and assistance,

Yours faithfully,

T. L. Yuan

Acting Director

〔平馆（长沙办事处）英文信纸。Rockefeller Foundation. Series 601: China; Subseries 601.R: China-Humanities and Arts. Box 47. Folder 389〕

按：该信涉及的申请与 3 月 6 日孙洪芬来函内容有些许冲突，此时或未收到孙函，或先生对战事发展及中基会未来拨款之困难尤

其是外汇统制有所预判。此件为打字稿,落款处为先生签名,于
3 月 28 日送达。

三月十五日

先生致信张允亮、王访渔、顾子刚,请将洛克菲勒基金会余款退回,并谈征
求外文杂志及下半年预算等事。

庾楼、子访、子刚先生大鉴:

日前为福利储金及刚主兄停薪事,曾上一函,谅达座右。罗氏基
金会来函,请将结余之款如数退还该会,弟已复函照办。查尊处呈报
中基会一月止库存清单,该补助费尚存

银行　　　　五,四九四.六三

现金　　　　　　五九.九〇　　　共五,五五四.五三元

除二、三两月份,袁、张、徐诸人薪水各付四八九元外,尚存四,五七六.
五三元,请交花旗平行,径汇花旗港行交弟手收,以便与八月初提取之
款一并退还该会,以资结束。所有该款账目亦请托妥便携港,以便正
式报销。至袁、张、徐、贾、赵、吴、王七人之薪水,自四月份起改由本馆
担任。此外,尚有二事并请分别办理:

(一)向国外征求所缺杂志,凡无须付款者仍可继续办理。但近接
Harrassowitz 来函,谓平馆征求之杂志均须付款。弟已覆函请其停寄,
请转告王锡印君为荷。

(二)中基会开会在即,下年度经费势须紧缩,请将最低预算及三
月份薪水单寄下,俾资核定。司徒先生亦在港,商讨较便也。

专此,敬请台安。

弟同顿首

三月十五日

〔《北京图书馆馆史资料汇编(1909-1949)》,页 556-558〕

按:袁、张、徐、贾、赵、吴、王七人应指袁涌进、张秀民、徐崇冈、贾
芳、赵兴国、吴光清等人,时均在平馆中文编目组任职,此前薪水
或由洛克菲勒基金会赞助款项下拨付。Harrassowitz 全称应为
Otto Wilhelm Harrassowitz,德国学术出版社,1872 年在莱比锡成
立。该信为文书代笔,落款处为先生签名,于 4 月 1 日前送达。

三月十七日

先生致信王重民,告知将为其设法谋取英庚款、中基会两处补助费。

> 有三吾弟:
>
> 　　前接二月十七日来函,欣悉一一。致英庚款报告书顷已发出请觉明亦作一报告书,余款已交到否,并要求在救济科学工作人员中见附件为足下谋一个二千元之补助费。如能办到,再请中基会出一千元或不难办到。美洲编目工作原限三年编成,明夏再前往亦无不可。到英后工作如何,盼详告。同人于五号到港携家眷者五人,已赴昆明,均在此办公,一时不致赴滇也。顺颂大安。
>
> 袁同礼顿首
> 三月十七日,香港
>
> 　　通讯处"香港大学冯平山图书馆"。

〔国立北平图书馆长沙办事处用笺。中国书店·海淀,四册〕

先生致信耿士楷,告知管理中英庚款委员会特别补款支持平馆学术工作,中基会虽然也拨款购买科学期刊,但仍请洛克菲勒基金会考虑给予援助。

March 17, 1938

Dear Mr. Gunn:

　　I wonder whether you have ever received my letter of March 7 sent to the S. S. Empress of Canada.

　　In my last letter I forgot to inform you that at a meeting of the Board of Trustees of the Boxer Indemnity Fund remitted to China by the British Government a sum of $138,000 was appropriated for the purpose of enabling displaced scholars to continue their scientific work. The Board further agreed to bring the figure to $200,000 at its June meeting. Similar amount will be appropriated by the China Foundation at its annual meeting to be held next month here at Hongkong.

　　With these grants we hope to be able to renovate and rebuild our intellectual life. Being unable to move out anything from occupied areas, the need for scientific literature felt by Chinese scholars is most urgent. We have secured a small grant from the China Foundation to enable us to continue subscribing a limited number of scientific journals, but we need a much larger grant, say G $ 20,000, to round out our collection of scientific literature.

　　We feel that the Rockefeller Foundation will render a great service to the Chinese scientific world if a grant can be made to the National Library towards the acquisition of current scientific journals. May we, therefore, count upon you for your assistance in this matter?

　　With cordial regards,

Yours faithfully,
T. L. Yuan
Acting Director

〔平馆（冯平山图书馆转）英文信纸。Rockefeller Foundation. Series 601: China; Subseries 601.R: China-Humanities and Arts. Box 47. Folder 389〕

　　按：此件为打字稿，落款处为先生签名，该信以航空信方式寄送。

三月十九日

先生致信管理中英庚款委员会，继续向该会申请在英影照敦煌写本补助费及王重民个人生活补助。

　　敬启者：

　　　　上年六月承贵会补助国币八千元，作为影照英法所藏燉煌写本之用。曾由敝馆拟定，暂以内中四千元为影照复本费，以三千元为出版费，以一千元为补助经管人维持费，当承贵会核准施行在案。自上年六月开始工作以来，迄本年二月法国部分大致告竣。惟陆续发现重要资料，故影照费因之增加，预计四千元方能敷用。英国部分自本月起开始影照，预计一年以后始能竣事。参照在法经验，复经详细估计，此项影照费至少需三千元。用特函达，拟请准予将原拟定之出版费三千元移作此项之用。事关变更用途，即希核定示复，俾有遵循，无任感荷。

　　　　又经管人王重民君之国外生活费，每年需国币三千元，上年除由贵会在补助费内拨付一千元外，余数则由敝馆担任。自北平沦陷以来，敝馆经费锐减，下年度王君生活费已无力担任。拟请贵会在救济科学研究机关及工作人员专款内予以补助，俾能继续维持其工作，而

收驾轻就熟之效。专此布达,即乞查照惠允,见复为荷。此致
管理中英庚款董事会　福煦路五号

馆启
三月十九日

〔《北京图书馆馆史资料汇编(1909-1949)》,页568-569〕

按:此为抄件。

三月二十三日

晚,香港中文学会请先生演讲。〔陈君葆著、谢荣滚主编《陈君葆日记全集》第1
卷,香港:商务印书馆(香港)有限公司,2004年,页396〕

按:陈君葆因故未能前往。

三月二十四日

先生致信张允亮、王访渔、顾子刚,指示北平馆务。

庚楼、子访、子刚先生大鉴:

前于三月十一、十五各寄一函,谅均寄到。本馆经费下年度势须
紧缩,惟薪水弟当竭力设法,决不致核减,请转告同人是荷。福利储金
为数有限,惟沪、湘、港三处职员均自八月起停付,则留平职员似不便
继续发给,以昭公允。将来时局大定,弟自当设法恢复也。同人之中,
何人无工作,请调查示知,以便为之设法。总之,筹划经费既如是之困
难,如同人每月领薪,无所事事,既对不起维持之苦心,亦于各人良心
亦不安也(闻吴文海每在办公室中午睡,请劝告是荷)。此外,另有三
事请分别办理:

(一)馆藏生物书只能由静生生物调查所借阅,不得依赖司徒之
力全数提取。盖该所为私立机关,本馆以历史关系,自当协助其研究,
但无权私相授受也。

(二)听差及装订人数均可减少。关于装订工作,请寄下一报告。

(三)发电厂用费仍可大减。煤价虽较昂,但晚间可停止阅览也。
专此,顺颂台祺。不一一。

弟同顿首
三月廿四日

〔国家图书馆档案,档案编号1945-※057-综合5-023018至
1945-※057-综合5-023020〕

按:此件为文书代笔,落款处为先生亲笔。

先生致信蒋复璁,询中央图书馆是否已与香港海关接洽各国寄送交换品处理办法,并请代订重庆地区出版的报纸。

> 慰堂吾兄大鉴:
>
> 　　近闻兄等留渝办事,深以为慰。关于国外各交换局转寄国内各机关之刊物改寄香港海关转交一节,未识尊处近已接洽就绪否?敝馆近有刊物多种均存各交换局,此事亟盼尊处早日办妥并候赐覆为荷。重庆重要日报请代订二种,寄港"香港般含道冯平山图书馆",政府机关在重庆出版之刊物名称亦盼示知。顺颂大安。
>
> 三月廿四日

〔《北京图书馆馆史资料汇编(1909-1949)》,页570〕

按:此件为抄件,无落款。

三月二十六日

先生致信史蒂文斯,表示希望尽快在香港组装缩微胶片拍摄设备并开始工作,因为中基会对平馆订购科学期刊的拨款与实际需求间存在巨大缺口,请洛克菲勒基金会考虑给予资助。

March 26, 1938

Dear Dr. Stevens:

　　I have recently had several talks with R. D. Jameson with regard to our plans for the immediate future. We have come to the conclusion that with such a large-scale destruction of sinological libraries as a result of the undeclared war, it is most desirable to have our rare books and manuscripts reproduced as soon as possible. We would suggest, therefore, that the microfilm apparatus be set up at Hongkong, so that we can proceed with the work immediately.

　　In view of the disorganization of scientific institutions, the need for Western scientific literature is most urgent. While the National Library has been securing gifts of books from abroad, it has no money with which to subscribe scientific journals and to keep up with serials and continuations because the payment of its book-fund has been withheld by the China Foundation since last August. It was only until recently that a grant of

$ 5,000 was made by the China Foundation which, compared with last year's appropriation of G $ 45,000, is far from being sufficient in meeting our immediate needs.

As Hongkong will be free from Japanese attack, all journals will be sent here to be forwarded to the interior whenever it is safe to do so. The Library keeps in close touch with the work of various institutions and is serving as a centre of information to all scientific workers.

In spite of financial difficulties, we have been able to carry on our work with renewed zeal and enthusiasm. We feel that if a grant can be made by the Rockefeller Foundation at this time, it will indeed win the everlasting gratitude of a large number of scientific men in this country.

With kindest regards,

Yours sincerely,

T. L. Yuan

Acting Director

〔平馆（冯平山图书馆转）英文信纸。Rockefeller Foundation. Series 601: China; Subseries 601.R: China-Humanities and Arts. Box 47. Folder 389〕

按：此件为打字稿，落款处为先生签名，该信以航空信方式寄送。

三月二十九日

徐森玉覆函先生，告其不再领平馆薪水，并谈故宫博物院南迁文物诸事。

守和先生左右：

昨奉手教，敬悉一切。同人赴滇留港，居处均不宜觅，且物价腾贵，经济自感困难，至为驰念。本馆委员会谈话记录已交寄梅先生阅过，渠所言甚圆融，两面均顾到也。宝二三月份薪水万不敢领，盖现已在故宫支薪，不敢重出，务祈俯允。如赴沪旅费寄到，请交仲章兄为祷。故宫文物由理事会决议，凡不畏潮湿之物，在重庆开掘山洞保存，其畏潮湿之物，在昆明建库保存。宝今日赴渝料理一切，叔平先生已先期赴成都宝鸡文物即须南迁，能否晤面，尚不可知。宝行年将六十，墓木已拱，决不争权利、保地位，惟求国家宝物丝毫不由我等手中失去而已。刚主兄北返，渠曾告宝，当时既未赞同，亦未阻止。故函平停薪一节,此时毫无意见,仍候尊裁。希渊先生前日由湘来此,住远东饭店,赴滇尚无定期。倚装肃此,即请钧安。

弟徐鸿宝再拜
三月廿九晨五时

〔国家图书馆档案,档案编号 1945-※057-综合 5-015004 和 1945-※057-综合 5-015005〕

按:"本馆委员会谈话记录"似指 3 月 11 日在香港九龙柯思甸道蔡元培宅召开的平馆委员会,"两面"应指馆务兼顾留守北平与临大合作两端。"故宫支薪",徐森玉时任故宫古物馆馆长,肩负文物西迁的具体事务,虽未完全脱离平馆但亦无暇他顾,因此不愿两面领薪。"赴沪旅费"似指前北返抢救居延汉简的费用,故可转交沈仲章。"刚主兄"即谢国桢,南下后又临时返回北京,先生对此极为愤慨,据《北京图书馆馆史资料汇编》可知,本年 3 月先生致信留守北京的平馆行政委员会王访渔、张允亮、顾子刚三人,对谢国桢处以停薪,可参见本谱是年 3 月 11 日先生函;曾任平馆金石部主任的刘节在其 1939 年 3 月 8 日日记中谈及"与袁公已三年未见,观其情形甚佳,惟于刚主颇有烦言,谈及北平诸旧友,并无其他批评",亦可见此事之严重性。

三月三十一日

先生致信王重民,告知向管理中英庚款董事会申请补助之进展,并谈其赴美国会图书馆之议不必急切。

有三吾弟如晤:

接三月十日航信,知已抵英伦开始工作,甚慰。二月十八日由港寄上国币三百元,合 £ 17.9.0,由 Giles 转,渠既休假,接到或较迟也。致英庚款之函于十九日发出,迄今尚无复音,大约非俟全体委员会开过会后不能决定也。美国方面须九月一号开始工作,已派吴光清君前往,足下不必忙于前往,盖该馆之事须三年后方能完成。罗氏补助该馆之经费亦系三年,至 1939 年夏间再往,亦无不可。因此后无机会能再游英伦也应在伦敦多参观,并到牛津及其他各地一游。如 Hummel 再来信,可复以正与国内函商,以邮政迟滞,故一时不能得覆音等语。英庚款方面大约在五月中总可发表。日前孙洪芬先生来港,曾与之详商,谓如英庚款能补助二千元,则中基会可援上年之例再补助一千元。至请求研究金则绝对无把握,因在此非常时期势须格外紧缩也。关于同人返平一案,因教部反对已缓和许多,大约一部分同人至昆明,其余留港办事。杜女士已到日本,由彼至美参观,大约九月间方能返法。余再函。顺颂旅安。

袁同礼顿首
三月三十一日

英国各博物院及各学术机关出版目录,请随时索取,即寄下为荷。并告各书店将目录寄港。

〔中国书店·海淀,四册〕

先生致信王访渔、宋琳,谈平馆帐务细目。

子舫、紫佩先生大鉴:

前承托王女士寄下各件,迄今尚未收到,惟托孙君转交之二月份收支报告及中英文馆务报告,业已照收无误。查一月份库存清单列有三笔。兹奉陈如左,请予登记是荷。

(一)罗氏补助费　　一〇,一五〇.〇〇　　此款存香港金城,俟平方所存
　　　　　　　　　　　　　　　　　　　　余款汇到,一并退还该会

(二)《宋会要》售款　五,〇三七.五〇　　此款存长沙金城

(三)中英补助　　　三,〇五五.六一　　此款已全数汇寄王重民

(四)临时修缮费　　二,〇〇九.七四　　已退还中基会

又驻沪收支报告,自八月份起改寄此间(七月份存一三三.七三)。另纸奉上简表,即希台阅。一月份库存清单列有八月以前该处未曾报账之款共七八三.七三,内容为何,请查明示知。又工程图书馆七月份之账,前由岳君寄平,共存三三.八九,此款以收入该馆八月份之账,连同弟携京之款一五〇元,共一八三.八九,已由此间陈报中基会。库存清单列有一九九.一八,内容为何,亦希示复。两笔均应早日结算清楚也。顺颂大安。

三月卅一日

又汽车二辆,应请壬父先生竭力设法转让他人。贺女士六月份半薪已照收。

〔《北京图书馆馆史资料汇编(1909-1949)》,页573-574〕

　　　　按:"贺女士"应指贺恩慈,广东番禺人,抗战前任平馆西文采访
　　　　组组员。此为抄件,无落款。

先生致信张允亮、王访渔、顾子刚,要求在平撙节开支。

　　庾楼、子舫、子刚先生大鉴:

　　　　连日与孙先生商下年度预算事,据云董事中主张紧缩者颇不乏
　　人,将来如何决定尚难预料。查馆中经费以薪金一项为大宗,自四月
　　份起,原在罗氏基金领薪者改在馆支薪,每月又增四八九元。若采纳
　　委员会一部分委员之主张(每月四千元),则施行上更感困难。故数
　　度商洽,拟自七月份起改为每月七千元,务望设法使收支适合。内中
　　可以撙节者如(一)发电厂、(二)馆役工资、(三)技手工资、(四)杂
　　费,均可酌减。至于同人生活,弟固主张维持到底,但无事可作之人或
　　成绩毫无、无志进取者,亦不妨予以甄别,或自四月份起发薪三月,解
　　除职务或在他处为之设法,一切责任由弟担负。盖弟为继续拨发经费
　　事,已大费周章,想同人亦无不相谅也。又《宋会要》售款,尊处尚存
　　三六一二.一二,已指定为书本目录印刷费,请另折存储是荷。专此,
　　顺颂大安。

　　　　　　　　　　　　　　　　　　　　　　　　　　三月卅一日

　　　　　　〔《北京图书馆馆史资料汇编(1909-1949)》,页575-576〕

　　　　按:此为抄件,无落款。

四月二日

教育部电令长沙临时大学更名为国立西南联合大学,图书馆也随之变更,
先生兼任图书馆馆长。

　　　　按:本年 7 月 29 日,该校聘严文郁为校图书馆主任,先生未到馆
　　　　前,馆务由其代理。[1]

先生致信蒲特南,希望国会图书馆能够作为美国各机构捐赠书刊的暂存中
心之一。

　　　　　　　　　　　　　　　　　　　　　　　　　　April 2, 1938

Dear Dr. Putnam,

　　　　With reference to our letter dated November 19, 1937, regarding the

----

[1]《国立西南联合大学史料》第 2 卷,页 63。

work of replenishing Chinese libraries, we hope it would be possible for you to designate the Library of Congress as one of the centres for receiving American donations of books for Chinese libraries.

Since writing to you last, many more libraries, both public and private, were razed to the ground. In view of their wanton destruction, it is evident that the revival of learning and revivification of education and culture will greatly depend upon the success in their restoration. It is indeed an immense task which can never be accomplished without American assistance.

The generous assistance which the Library of Congress extended to Louvain and Tokyo is still fresh in our memory. In this hour of distress, we earnestly hope that you will similarly lend a helping hand to China especially when the loss sustained by our libraries is more serious and the number of libraries destroyed many times more numerous.

I shall be glad to hear from you as to the steps which you may take towards the realization of our plans. Any assistance which you may extend to us in facilitating this work will always have our sincere appreciation and gratitude.

Yours faithfully,

T. L. Yuan

Chairman

Executive Board

〔中华图书馆协会(长沙韭菜园)英文信纸。Librarian of Congress, Putnam Archives, Special File, China: Library Association〕

按:此件为打字稿,落款处为先生签名,于 5 月 23 日送抵国会图书馆秘书办公室。

四月四日

先生致信阿博特,就美国图书馆界向中国捐赠图书,请史密斯森协会协助暂存或寄送香港。

April 4, 1938

Dear Dr. Abbot:

With reference to our letter dated November 23, 1937, regarding the work of replenishing Chinese libraries, we hope it would be possible for the Smithsonian Institution to extend to us the assistance in forwarding American donations of books to China.

In view of the wanton destruction of Chinese libraries as a result of Japan's aggression, it is evident that the revival of learning and revivification of education and culture will greatly depend upon the success in their restoration. It is indeed an immense task which can never be accomplished without American assistance.

As the Library Association of China has established an office in Hongkong, American donations can either be sent to its Hongkong address, or be held by your Institution until permanent peace is restored.

Thanking you in anticipation for your valuable assistance,

Yours faithfully,

T. L. Yuan

Chairman

Executive Board

〔中华图书馆协会(长沙韭菜园)英文信纸。Smithsonian Institution Archives, Records, 1868－1988 (Record Unit 509), Box 1, Library Association of China, Hong Kong〕

按:此件为打字稿,落款处为先生签名,于 5 月 2 日送达。

史蒂文斯致函先生,告知洛克菲勒基金会和美国学术团体理事会均不急于将缩微设备运往中国并开始拍摄,先生前信所提购买外文科学期刊和建造防火书库的资助申请不予支持。

April 4, 1938

Dear Mr. Yuan:

I appreciate fully the difficulties in which you operate, and I am particularly appreciative of your recent letter on various matters. I have not sent acknowledgement of your recent letters because I had no fixed address that seemed certain until I received your letter of March 7th regarding the use of microfilm equipment.

The equipment is still being held by the American Council of Learned Societies. We agree with the officers of the Council that they are wise in keeping the equipment in this country until such time as operators can be trained by experts on a permanent location for the equipment. This seems clear to us and furthermore the copying of material can be postponed without undue hardship. I hope that you approve of this decision.

In earlier letters you have raised question regarding aid on purchase of current scientific journals and on the possible aid of the Foundation toward the erection of a fire-proof building. I regret to report that the indicated decision concerning these requests is an indefinite deferment. Conditions are not favorable for a recommendation for either purpose, either here or in your country; consequently I am noting that these requests have been declined and that at some future time you may bring to us a renewal of the two proposals.

Cordially yours,

David H. Stevens

〔Rockefeller Foundation. Series 601: China; Subseries 601.R: China-Humanities and Arts. Box 9. Folder 85〕

按:该函寄送香港冯平山图书馆,此件为录副。

四月五日

先生致信孙洪芬,请其汇寄支票至法国大使馆。

洪芬先生大鉴:

顷接法大使馆那其亚先生来函,谓杜乃扬女士代本馆选购之法文书共三一,五一六.二五法郎,合国币三,五四一.一五元。拟请在中法工商银行本馆存款内如数拨付,支票请写 M. Gillon, Paris 抬头,并由尊处径寄北平法国大使馆转交可也。至退回书箱之运费及保险费,俟清单到后再为奉寄。先此,顺颂大安。

四月五日

〔《北京图书馆馆史资料汇编(1909-1949)》,页 577〕

按:“退回书箱之运费及保险费”似指本年初拟将平馆存沪善本

书运港未果之事。此为抄件,无落款。

先生覆信中基会,谈平馆代购书籍款项收讫问题。

　　敬复者,接奉三月三日大函,以敝处订购《东北亚细亚书目》
(*Bibliography of Northeastern Asia*)二部,又代中央、湖南及南开三大
学图书馆各认购一部,价款共美金一百一十四元,折合国币为三百八
十五元三角二分。除敝处之款业承贵会在本年度购书费项下拨扣外,
其余三部书款嘱代收汇等因,当经分函通知并请将该项书款径汇贵会
查收,以资便捷。除南开迄今尚未得复函外,兹接中央、湖南二校函复
前来,用特录副寄上,即希查照办理是荷。此致
中华教育文化基金董事会

　　　　　　　　　　　　　　　　　　　　袁○○启

　　　　　　　　　　　　　　　　　　　　四月五日

　　中央原函注:正副发票已寄该馆并请将书款径汇贵会。

　　　　　　〔《北京图书馆馆史资料汇编(1909-1949)》,页578〕

　　按:*Bibliography of Northeastern Asia* 即 *Northeastern Asia: a
selected bibliography* ,编者为 Robert J. Kerner,1939 年加州大学伯
克利分校出版社初版。此为抄件。

四月十一日

先生致信阿博特,请将 Newark College of Engineering 寄送南京工程参考图
书馆的图书及其他一切与平馆相关的交换品寄送香港,并建议以美国驻香
港总领事馆为收件方,以确保顺利通过海关。

　　　　　　　　　　　　　　　　　　　　April 11, 1938

Dear Dr. Abbot:

　　I hope you have received my letter of April 4th which I wrote you
on behalf of the Library Association of China.

　　We learned from the Newark College of Engineering, Newark, N. J.
that twelve cases of books have been sent to your Institution on
December 17, 1937, to be forwarded to our Engineering Reference
Library at Nanking which is one of the administrative divisions of this
Library.

　　We understand that shipment to China was suspended since last

August and your Institution may not wish to resume shipment until China is freed from invaders. But since we have established an office in Hongkong which is entirely free from Japanese aggression, we wonder whether it would be possible for your Institution to forward to our Hongkong address these cases of books as well as all the packages addressed to the National Library of Peiping and its Engineering Reference Library which have been held up since last August. In order to secure free examination by the customs, we suggest that you send the cases to us care of the American Consulate General, Hongkong.

At the suggestion of the American Consul General, we are submitting a memorandum, a copy of which I now enclose. The Consul General is writing to the Department of State recommending the approval of these measures suggested in the memorandum. As they are temporary measures for the purpose of tiding over the present emergency, we trust that they will also be acceptable to your Institution.

We fully realize the amount of work involved in sorting out the packages, but whatever assistance your Institution may be able to extend to the National Library will always have our everlasting gratitude.

Yours faithfully,

T. L. Yuan

Acting Director

〔平馆（冯平山图书馆转）英文信纸。Smithsonian Institution Archives, Records, 1868－1988 (Record Unit 509), Box 1, Library Association of China, Hong Kong〕

按：Newark College of Engineering 与南京工程参考图书馆有交换协议。本年 3 月中旬，阿博特代表史密斯森协会与美国图书馆协会秘书米来牟沟通，后者表示寄送南京工程参考图书馆、平馆、中华图书馆协会的交换品都应寄送香港冯平山图书馆，而寄送国际交换局（Bureau of International Exchange）的交换品则应寄送重庆。4 月 12 日，美驻香港领事 Addison E. Southard 致信史密斯森协会，表示愿意协助平馆在港接收交换品。5 月 11 日，阿博特覆信先生表示同意将交换品寄送美国驻港领事馆。该件为打字稿，落款处为先生签名，于5月7日送达。

四月十二日

吴宓将《抗战中之国际舆论》校稿挂号寄予先生。〔《吴宓日记》第6册，页287〕

四月十三日

张允亮、王访渔、顾子刚覆函先生，报告北平馆务。

　　守和先生大鉴：

　　叠次接奉三月十一、十五、二十四等日大函，祇承种切。刚主停薪及卡片余款（另钞一帐单交司徒先生带港）二事已由子刚另函详述，兹不赘陈。允亮已于三月一日起到编目部办公。李锺履君自奉示后即就西文编目组组长事。停寄国外杂志已告王锡印君知照。装订室报告及三月份薪水表并托司徒先生带上。自上年八月至本年二月收支决算前已寄奉。至于下年度概算前已编制比照表，交由司徒先生转呈中基会，似可备供参考。此外尚有四事，附陈如左：

　　一、福利储金事。因奉示少迟，故当时未及照办。嗣由司徒先生负责先行继续发给，听候中基会解决。兹拟俟中基会在港开会时，请钧座及孙先生、司徒先生商定办法即当遵办。

　　二、生物调查所所借之书，现均为日常必须之本，并未大量提取，仍系按照向例办理。

　　三、发电厂前为节省经费起见，拟改用商电灯公司接洽。彼意送电、吸水应分装，否则无法办理。但分装须请专家代为设计。改作用款既多，而改作后有无其他弊害（如自有机械朽坏等），亦不可臆料，故未敢冒然从事。现在晚间不发电，略可节省。

　　四、本馆用款自当极力紧缩，但物价日来逐渐高涨，对于具体办法，势难预计。

　　专此奉复，敬候台祺。

　　　　　　　　　　　　　　顾子刚、张允亮、王访渔敬启

　　　　　　　　　　　　　　　　　　　四月十三日

　　〔国立北平图书馆用笺。《北京图书馆馆史资料汇编（1909-
　　1949）》，页579-583〕

四月十八日

徐森玉覆函先生,告故宫博物院文物迁移各路之情况,并表示平馆内阁大库地图确实失陷于南京。

> 守和先生赐鉴:
>
> 　　宝离筑时,曾寄一函,谅邀霁照。顷由刘衡如先生转到惠示,敬悉一一。宝于二日到渝,八日抵蓉晤叔平先生。宝鸡文物七千余箱,现已运至南郑、襄城两处分存,拟悉数再移成都。叔平来此,系接洽公路汽车及储藏处所,惟车辆缺乏,房屋无一处空闲者,奔走多日尚无头绪。宝来蓉忙碌异常,又助渠设法,川人轻诺寡信,口惠而实不至,故至今不能完全决定也。汽车费约十万左右,储藏处在大慈寺,但其中驻有军队。叔平不日飞渝,留宝在此接头,俟文物第一批运到,仍回贵阳。宜昌文物万余箱,大半已移至重庆,但该处储藏之所,至今亦未觅妥。大库地图已陷在南京,查鄂陕两处箱中确无此物。盖运物时纷乱紧张,彼时办理此事人员未接尊处电嘱,不敢轻易运出,惜哉惜哉。宝之薪水此后不敢再领,前函业已陈明。二三两月二百元已函嘱沈仲章兄如数缴还,万望俯允。蜀中文化发达甚早,故金石甚富,非贵州等处可比黔省无一古刻。惟散在各地,自刘燕庭蒐罗后,无人继之者,稍暇当加访求寄上。新都出汉画像多种,精美异常。匆此,敬请钧安。
>
> 弟徐鸿宝再拜
> 四月十八日
>
> 　　叔平先生住成都东胜街沙利文饭店十号,宝住四川旅行社提督东街廿七号,重庆办事处在大溪沟高家庄胡家花园。
>
> 　　诸同人均此致候。

〔国家图书馆档案,档案编号 1945-※057-综合 5-015009〕

按:"刘衡如"即刘国钧,时随私立金陵大学迁往成都。"宝鸡文物"指故宫文物西迁之北路,前后三批由津浦路至徐州转陇海路运陕,1938 年春又运至南郑、襄城二地。"宜昌文物"指故宫文物西迁之中路,前后两批由水路运至汉口,并于 1938 年 1 月 6 日前陆续运至宜昌。"大库地图"指平馆所藏内阁大库旧藏明末清初地图,1936 年冬自北京运往南京,暂存故宫南京分院。抗战全面爆发后未能及时运出,1937 年底被日军劫持,置于伪图书专门委

员会图书馆的地图库中,胜利后绝大部分得以收回,现藏于台北
故宫博物院。"刘燕庭"即刘喜海,清代金石学家、古泉学家,曾
任四川按察使,极为关注蜀地石刻碑文,撰《三巴金石苑》等书,
对后世影响颇大。

四月十九日

西南联合大学常务委员会举行第五十八次会议。讨论议案之一为建议设
立"建筑设计委员会",负责筹划昆明校舍建设事宜,该委员会以黄钰生为
委员长,推举胡适(冯友兰代)、周炳琳、潘光旦、饶毓泰、施嘉炀、庄前鼎、
吴有训、杨振声、先生、杨绍曾、孙云铸、李继侗、赵友民、陈序经等人为委
员。〔《国立西南联合大学史料》第2卷,页47〕

　　按:施嘉炀(1902—2001)福建闽侯人,水力发电学家,清华学校毕
　　业,1923年赴美留学,时任西南联合大学工学院院长。昆明建筑
　　校舍其预算为二十万元。

四月二十日

国会图书馆覆函先生,告收到前信,并已将平馆新的通讯地址告知国会图
书馆出版部及卡片部。

April 20, 1938

Dear Sir:

　　Your letter of February 19, acknowledging our letter of January 3
and the publications recently sent to you, was duly received.

　　Our Publications Section has noted the new address for the National
Library of Peiping and when "Class PT, part 1" is ready for distribution
two copies will be forwarded.

　　The communication addressed to the Card Division, regarding the
change of address, has been sent to Mr. Hastings, the chief of that
Division, for his records.

Very truly yours,
Secretary of the Library

　　〔Librarian of Congress, Putnam Archives, Special File, China:
National Library 1930-1939〕

　　按:此件为录副。

四月二十三日

先生致信蒲特南,告知美国捐赠书刊将由史密斯森协会寄送香港,中国科学界正在响应"抗战建国"口号积极恢复研究工作,此时亟需美方给予支持和援助,建议由恒慕义指派东方部馆员代为挑选捐赠复本。

April 23, 1938

Dear Dr. Putnam:

I wish to thank you for your letter of January 17th and for your interest in the work of replenishing Chinese libraries destroyed by the undeclared war. As your letter had been forwarded to Kun-ming and readdressed to me here, I greatly regret the unavoidable delay in answering.

We are most grateful to you for promising to assist Chinese librarians in their work of restoration. If it would be possible for American libraries to contribute their duplicates to this cause, they would undoubtedly prove to be a great help towards the rehabilitation of our collections. On behalf of the Library Association of China, I beg to convey to you our sincerest thanks for your interest and assistance.

Regarding the forwarding of American donations of books, the Smithsonian Institution has promised to undertake in dispatching them to China through its International Exchange Service. All materials thus assembled can now be sent to Hong Kong which is entirely free from Japanese aggression.

American donations of books will be kept temporarily in Hong Kong and will be forwarded to the educational centres whenever we feel safe to do so and warranted by circumstances. They will be properly catalogued here and made available for use. As a great deal of scientific work has been carried on in China in spite of the war, scientific publications from the United States will be of great service to the present and future generations of intellectual workers in this country.

While it may have been the feeling of some of our friends abroad that the time is not yet ripe for the rehabilitation of our collections, yet I wish to assure you that the work of reconstruction in every field is being pushed forward steadily in China while the war is going on. The slogan "reconstruction while resisting" is most popular and can be heard in every province. Taking advantage of the presence of trained personnel from war zones, constructive work has been carried on in those parts of China which are away from the maelstrom of war.

As your colleagues in the library profession may not have been kept informed about the true situation here, we shall appreciate it greatly if you could write a note to this effect and have it printed in the *Library Journal*. We recall vividly the response to your appeal for books for Tokyo printed in that journal and we hope you will extend similar assistance to China.

We appreciate greatly your suggestion that some one should be designated to examine your duplicates and make a selection. May I suggest that you consult with Dr. Hummel to see if he could delegate members of his staff in the Division of Orientalia to select the items on our behalf?

With many thanks for your valuable cooperation and assistance,

Yours faithfully,

T. L. Yuan

Acting Director

〔平馆（冯平山图书馆转）英文信纸。Librarian of Congress, Putnam Archives, Special File, China: Library Association〕

按：此件为打字稿，落款处为先生签名，于 5 月 9 日送达国会图书馆秘书办公室。

先生致信美国图书馆协会，请求该协会援助中国图书馆界。抄件如下：

Constructive work in every field of endeavor is going forward steadily in China despite the war.

While it may have been the feeling of some of our friends abroad that any campaign to collect books for Chinese libraries should be postponed until the armed conflict is cover, yet the urgent demand for western literature is impelling that we are inclined to think otherwise.

Present hostilities are destined to be long drawn out. In the meantime, Chinese scholars have to be provided with an adequate supply of material so that there should be no intellectual stagnation and inactivity. The library association has established an office in Hong Kong to which all materials thus assembled can now be forwarded safely.

The destruction of Chinese libraries has taken place through no fault of their own. What has taken decades to build up is now wiped out in a single raid by the invaders. The havoc wrought in the wake of Japanese aggression is indescribably appalling. To repair the loss is indeed a herculean task; it cannot be successfully consummated without the help of our sister institutions abroad.

〔"Ask Books for Chinese Libraries." *Bulletin of the American Library Association*, vol. 32, no. 10, 1938, p. 710〕

按:《中华图书馆协会会报》第 13 卷第 2 期"本会消息"称该信"原文载《美国图书馆协会会报》三十二卷第六号,一九三八年六月出版,又载《美国图书馆杂志》六月号",此说有误,实际登载在 10 月份《美国图书馆协会会报》第 32 卷第 10 期,且为节录。

先生致信阿博特,表示虽然国立中央图书馆主持的中国国际出版品交换局以重庆为接收交换品地址,但平馆、南京工程参考图书馆、中华图书馆协会的交换品还请其寄送香港。

April 23, 1938

Dear Dr. Abbot:

I have just received your communication of January 17. As the letter had been forwarded to Kunming and readdressed to me here, I greatly regret the unavoidable delay in answering.

It is most kind of you to state that the Smithsonian Institution will be glad to help in the rehabilitation of Chinese libraries. On behalf of the Library Association of China, I wish to express to you our sincere appreciation of your assistance.

As the National Library and the Library Association have a joint office in Hongkong, consignments can now be dispatched to our Hongkong address.

American donations of books will be kept temporarily in Hongkong until permanent peace is restored. They will be properly catalogued here and made available for use. As a great deal of scientific work has been carried on in China in spite of the war, scientific publications from the United States will be of great service to the present and future generations of intellectual workers in this country.

We understand that the Chinese Bureau of International Exchange of Publications has requested you to dispatch your consignments to Chungking. In view of the frequent interruption of railway services between Hongkong and Hankow, we do not wish to have our parcels forwarded to Chungking and back again to Hongkong. Will you, therefore, take steps to sort out all the packages addressed to (1) The National Library of Peiping, (2) The Engineering Reference Library and (3) The Library Association of China and have them packed in separate boxes. They should be dispatched to Hongkong care of the American Consulate General as suggested in our letter of April 11.

We wish to express to you once more our sincere appreciation for the valuable assistance which your great Institution has so generously extended to Chinese scientific and cultural institutions.

Yours very sincerely,

T. L. Yuan

Acting Director

P. S. Your letter of March 17 announcing the shipment of 12 cases of books just received. Will you kindly send us a list of international exchange services with their respective addresses?

〔平馆（冯平山图书馆转）英文信纸。Smithsonian Institution Archives, Records, 1868 - 1988 (Record Unit 509), Box 1, Library Association of China, Hong Kong〕

按：补语中的"March 17"似为笔误，应为 January 17。此件为打字稿,落款处为先生签名,于 5 月 9 日送达。

四月二十八日

先生致信平馆留守员工,劝勉努力维持在平馆务。

> 同人公鉴:
>
> 　　司徒先生来港,欣悉馆务照常进行,同人均安,远道闻之,深以为慰。当此非常时期,本馆对于国家应有相当贡献。北平虽处特殊环境之中,应付诸感困难。但同人不应以维持现状为满足,而宜放大眼光,忠诚服务,盖文化事业自有其永久性也。港、滇同人从事复兴工作,赖国际同情之助,已获有极大效果。故本馆一方面为国家保存重要文献,一方面协助全国图书馆积极复兴,职责重要自不待言。允宜分工合作,共同努力,俾能完成使命,为新中国文化事业树一永久基础。惟念敷衍了事为国人之通病,因循苟且为事业之障碍,此次经非常之变,亟应彻底觉悟,痛改前非。此则区区微意,愿与同人共勉者也。中基会昨日在港开会,对于平馆事业继续维持,除请司徒先生报告一切外,特此函达。即希台察为荷,顺颂公安。
>
> 袁同礼顿首
> 四月廿八日

〔国立北平图书馆长沙办事处用笺。《北京图书馆馆史资料汇编
(1909-1949)》,页 584-586〕

　　按:此信应交司徒雷登携至北平。

四月二十九日

先生致信张允亮、王访渔、顾子刚,就平馆经费和各要务予以指示。

> 庚楼、子舫、子刚先生大鉴:
>
> 　　先后接奉三月三日及四月十三日惠书,拜悉一一。此次中基会在港开会,对于自办事业之预算均希望竭力紧缩。故本馆经费希望能减至十万元之数。弟与洪芬先生商酌,拟请核定为十二万三千六百元,分配如左:
>
> 　　北平每月七千元,香港及昆明三千元,上海三百元,共一万零三百元,全年计十二万三千六百元。请于五、六两月先行着手试办为荷。此外,与洪芬先生商妥各件,分述如左:
>
> 　　(一)福利储金既未能照原定办法施行,似与创立之旨不无违背。拟请自五月一号起暂行停付。在南方服务职员应请一律补发^{见附单,}

以示公允。此款应在经常费赢余款内拨付。但如能自上年七月起恢复原定办法，或自本年七月一号起按原定办法施行，则仍可来函商酌，弟无不赞助也。

（二）卡片目录既于七月杪停止印行，袁涌进等七人之薪水（每月四百九十元，外加福利储金）应由本馆担任。请即在经常费内扣还，即日汇港，以便与其他之款退还该会。

（三）职员请假者仍嫌过多，拟请严格取缔，俾重馆务。

（四）茅乃文君现任编审，应即停薪。一俟解除编审职务，再行恢复原薪。

（五）赵录绰行为不检，拟请准其自动辞职。

（六）本馆欠大东之款，曾与子彬兄说妥，由弟在携湘之《宋会要》存款内偿还。惟该款现存长沙金城银行，暂时不能提取。拟请在北平所存《宋会要》专款内托花旗径汇大东，以资清结^{附大东来信}。（此款及长沙所存之款，已指定为书本目录印刷费）。

（七）《墓志目录》现已编竣，似可以《宋会要》余款付印，或送燕京学报社，托其代印。本馆可要求赠送若干份。

（八）北平需要之中西文书籍统由此间购买，请查照目前需要，由阅览组随时函告。

以上各节请查照办理，并希早日见复是荷。顺颂时祺。

弟袁同礼顿首

四月廿九日

〔国立北平图书馆长沙办事处用笺。《北京图书馆馆史资料汇编（1909-1949）》，页587-591〕

按：茅乃文，浙江杭州人，抗战前任平馆舆图部组员；赵录绰，字孝孟，山东安丘人，长期在平馆善本部考订组工作，专攻目录学、版本学、金石学，其父赵葵畦，清末金石学者。该信为文书代笔，落款处为先生签名，5月17日前送达。

五月一日

郑振铎致函先生，请平馆购买也是园旧藏元明剧。

守和先生：

久未见，至以为念。顷闻先生在香港，<u>港</u>、沪交通甚便，盼有机会可以畅谈也。兹有一重要的消息报告给先生,想闻之亦必当为之欢跃不已也。前者,北平圕馆报报上,曾附刊丁初我氏的元曲"跋一则",并录有黄荛圃的"跋一则"。弟数年来梦寐中无时不念及此种元剧的存亡。打听了许多,竟一无消息。不意这次战事发生后,此书竟从苏州散出。凡有六十四巨册,每册载元曲或明剧三种左右,共约二百种,皆为元曲选所未刊者。诚数十年来古籍发见中的一个最重要的收获也。其中以明抄者为多,亦间有元、明刊本,黄跋亦赫然存焉,并有陈眉公"跋一则"。现此书为二古董商所得,居奇未售。现正在商价中,约三千元左右即可成交。此价亦可谓为至廉! 盖每剧不过十五元左右也。机会稍纵即逝,现正严守秘密。弟企设法尽力张罗此款以购置之,不知北平圕亦有意于此否? 弟一贫如洗,实有心无力也。惟购得后,必须立即影印出书,故须预备五千元左右。将来每部售价五十元,售出一百部即可收回书价矣。如有意收下此书,乞速即电知,弟无办法时,贵馆即可得之入藏矣。丁此国难,我辈于古文化之保存,实感到一种艰巨的负担。然实责无旁贷也! 弟得此实耗为之兴奋,至不眠者数夕,似攻克数十名城也! 想先生亦当同感! 此书当即《也是园书目》中所载者,明日即可见到此书之一部分矣! 专此,顺颂著安。

弟郑振铎启

27/5/1 夜

盼即覆。
来示乞寄上海法界陶尔斐斯路四合里 38 号郑西谛收。

〔台北胡适纪念馆,档案编号 HS-JDSHSC-1635-004〕

按:5 月 2 日,陈乃乾应苏州书贾唐耕余之约,看其所收《古今杂剧》,遂将细节告知郑振铎。落款处有标注"此书后由教部以九千元买去,运昆明存放。洪注,廿七,七,八",此信以抄件存,特此说明。

五月二日

杭立武致函先生,商洽管理中英庚款董事会补助王重民在英影照敦煌写本办法。

守和吾兄大鉴:

前接贵馆来函,关于影照英法所藏燉煌写本事略,以国外研究员王重民君之生活费每年三千元,原定由补助费内拨付一千元,其余二千元系由馆方担任。近以馆中经费锐减、无此余力,嘱由敝会在协助科学工作人员专款项下予以补助等语,此事自当尽力。惟协助科学工作人员现暂拟以在国内者为限,且即按照协助办法每人每年至多亦仅以二千四百元为限。王君在外费用倘敝会每年津贴两千元,其余之数贵馆是否可以担负,又总共全年所需若干? 特此专函奉询,统祈赐覆为荷。专此,祗颂时绥。

杭立武
廿七,五,二

〔中国书店·海淀,四册〕

按:该件为抄件,左下角有先生批注"五月六日函复,每年至少需三千元,请补助二千四百元或二千元,不足之数由馆担任"。

五月四日

先生致信张允亮、王访渔、顾子刚,对馆员赵录绰、茅乃文加以处分,并请留平人员爱惜羽毛,切不可兼领日伪职务。

庚楼、子舫、子刚先生大鉴:

上月廿八日托司徒先生携奉一函,谅达记室。关于赵君免职事,兹附一函,希查照办理。嗣后渠如能改过,则恢复职务当非难事。茅君新职,见诸报章,各方对之极表不满,故留职停薪实为最妥之办法,务祈照办是荷。中基会对于本馆既决定维持,此后对于馆员之工作及私人道德拟请特别注意。盖图小利者往往进退失据,偶一失足,则不易得各方之谅解。弟虽知处境不无可原,但亦爱莫能助,此中困难想同人可以明了也。又,寄来各组报告,内中颇多空洞之辞,嗣后拟请各组组长对于各该组报告之准确积极负责。又,廿六年七月至廿七年六月之报告拟于八月间付印(内分南北二部份),请先为准备,于七月中旬与会计报告一并寄下是荷。顺颂大安。

弟同礼顿首
五月四日

〔中华图书馆协会用笺。《北京图书馆馆史资料汇编(1909-1949)》,页592-593〕

按:此信为文书代笔,落款处为先生签名。

先生覆信赵录绰，请其自动请辞。

　　孝孟先生大鉴：

　　　　握别以来，迄未接奉手书，时以为念。顷得上月廿日来函，藉悉近况安好，至以为慰。在文化机关工作之人，均应忠实服务、洁身自爱，每以此相劝勉，实有爱惜之意，区区微衷，谅早在洞鉴之中。惟台端既不改过自新，复未能诚以待人，弟对之不无失望。兹为维持全馆纪律及希望彻底觉悟起见，拟请自动辞职，暂予解除职务，于公私两方面似不无裨益也。总之，弟虽爱惜人才，但容忍过甚，反于事无补，此不仅对台端一人也。平方机关林立，而主持者又多系旧友，如需作书推荐，并乞示复。尊处生活苦难，素所洞悉，五六两月薪俸自当提前发放。嗣后倘能改过自新，则恢复职务当非难事也。专此布达，诸希鉴察是荷。顺颂大安。

五月四日

〔《北京图书馆馆史资料汇编（1909-1949）》，页 594-595〕

　　按：此时，赵录绰仍在北平东方文化事业总委员会协助编纂《续修四库提要》。此为抄件，无落款。

五月六日

先生致信王重民，告知管理中英庚款董事会及中基会当会补助其在英影照敦煌写经费用，其赴美之议暂缓一年无妨。

　　有三仁弟如晤：

　　　　接四月八日及二十日来书，详悉一切。中英庚款会杭立武君来信对补助费事已允帮忙，当无问题。不足之数由中基会担任，孙洪芬先生亦首肯。故请决定留英一年，俾英法影照之事作一总结束，明夏再赴美。俟两笔款均能正式通过后，再由此间寄 Hummel 一函，说明不能离欧理由，请延一年，渠自当照办也。前荐前往华京之吴光清君已定七月间放洋赴美竹简由沈仲章携港暂存港大，已付商务影印，英庚款补助万元，既有一人先去，吾弟明年再往不迟也。影照复本，清华加入当无问题，容再函询奉告。《东方杂志》在湘复刊，刻正征文，如有小品文字亦可投稿。中基会在港开会，议决本馆在港、滇各设办事处，北平方面照旧维持。兄下月或须赴滇，通讯均寄港为荷。

同礼

五,六

〔中国书店・海淀,四册〕

按:"吴光清君已定七月间放洋赴美",此说不准。8月5日,吴光清偕夫人乘亚西亚皇后号赴美。①

五月七日

先生致信孙洪芬,谈购买也是园元曲古籍事,并转上郑振铎来函。

洪芬先生大鉴:

顷得郑君来函,特为转上(用毕即请赐还)。此书既为孤本,自应为国家留下,书价能稍廉最好,否则照价收下。该款请会中暂垫,将来可由《宋会要》余款下拨还也。致郑君函,亦望代为付邮是荷。顺颂大安。

弟同礼顿首

五月七日

该书可约李照亭前往鉴定,但郑君最内行,惟有书贾习气,如渠认为有价值,自可购也。

〔台北胡适纪念馆,档案编号 HS-JDSHSC-1635-004〕

按:郑振铎从陈乃乾处得知,有书贾出售丁祖荫家藏元曲。孙洪芬后于 24 日赴港,将郑振铎回信带给先生,后郑振铎又发电报给先生,该部存书最终由教部以九千元购入。此信以抄件存,特此说明。

五月八日

下午四时,王兼士、顾毓桐在半岛酒店(Peninsula Hotel)举行婚宴,蔡元培、刘仲杰夫妇、陈寅恪夫人、先生、任鸿隽夫妇、樊仲云、宋子良等人受邀与席。〔《蔡元培日记》,页 557〕

按:顾毓桐为顾毓琇之妹,婚礼由王受庆、顾毓琇主婚,蔡元培为证婚人。《蔡元培日记》(排印本,2010 年)此处记为"王廉"、"顾毓珂",有误。

五月九日

顾毓琇访先生,告教育部望平馆与西南联合大学密切合作。〔《北京图书馆馆

---

① 《中华图书馆协会会报》第 13 卷第 2 期,页 18。

史资料汇编(1909-1949)》,页 597-598〕

先生致信平馆上海办事处李耀南、钱存训,安排二人协助中国科学社编撰
馆藏中西文书目工作任务。

　　照亭、存训先生大鉴:

　　　　顷接科学社杨、刘两先生来函,谓社中中西文书目亟待早日编成,
以资阅览,请予协助等因。兹将执事工作重新分配如左,请查照办理
是荷。

　　　　一、照亭兄除照料善本书外,所余时间请代科学社编中文书目。
该社中文书增加有限,可商刘主任采用书本式之目录,以收驾轻就熟
之效。分类法可采用刘国钧者或其他分类法,编号则每类之下用一数
目字代之。如"社会学一"、"社会学二",以简捷明显为主,无须采用
本馆之手续也。

　　　　二、存训兄索引工作可暂停,以全部时间协助科学社将西文书目
早日完成为盼。

　　　　又,本馆《丛书》及《宋会要》现存科学社者共若干部,请查复是
荷。顺颂大安。

　　　　　　　　　　　　　　　　　　　　　　　　　　　五月九日

　　　　　　　　　　　〔《北京图书馆馆史资料汇编(1909-1949)》,页 596 〕

　　　　按:"杨、刘两先生"应指杨孝述和刘咸。此为抄件,无落款。

五月十日

先生致信孙洪芬,请中基会支持教育部关于平馆协助发展西南图书馆事业
的建议。

　　洪芬先生大鉴:

　　　　日昨顾一樵先生来谈,谓教部之意,本馆应在内地工作,既可协助
发展西南图书馆事业,复能与联大及其他机关予以鼓励。本馆与北方
学术界既有悠久之历史,自当继续合作,俾收互助之效。弟以教部此
种意见,对于本馆立场虽不无可采之处,但中基会举行年会时,渠并未
提出具体办法。兹年会已过,似又需若干时日之接洽方能作最后之决
定。已托叔永兄赴沪时就近面商,尚希指示,不胜盼祷。现在港币飞
涨,每法币一元仅合港币七角九分,将来似仍有增高之势。本馆同人
深感生活惟艰,极盼尊处设法调剂,不仅弟个人感谢已也。专此奉恳,

敬请公安。

五月十日

〔《北京图书馆馆史资料汇编(1909-1949)》,页 597-598〕

按:此为抄件,无落款。

五月十一日

阿博特覆函先生,告知将照前请将寄送平馆、南京工程参考图书馆、中华图书馆协会的交换品尽可能发送美国驻香港使领馆代转。

May 11, 1938

Dear Sir:

I have your letters of April 4, 11 and 23 concerning the forwarding in care of the American Consul General in Hongkong of American publications for the National Library of Peiping, the Engineering Reference Library and the Library Association of China. A communication regarding the same matter has this day been received from the American Consul General at Hongkong and I am enclosing herewith a copy of the Institution's reply to the latter.

When the forwarding of shipments to you is commenced, there will be eliminated from the material now on hand for China and forwarded to you such packages as may be for the three organizations referred to.

Very respectfully yours,

C. G. Abbot

Secretary

〔Smithsonian Institution Archives, Records, 1868 – 1988 (Record Unit 509), Box 1, Library Association of China, Hong Kong〕

按:此件为录副。

五月十二日

先生致信顾子刚,请其向代理商订购期刊并寄送北平,另告圣路易斯公共图书馆未收到《图书季刊》英文本赠刊。

May 12, 1938

Dear Mr. Koo:

I enclose a list of journals suggested for Peiping. Please order them from January 1938 and inform the publishers that these journals are extra copies for Peiping, so that there will be no confusion. Bills, however, should be sent to Hong Kong for payment.

In order to avoid confusion, you may like to give the order to other agents rather than to Faxon and Stevens & Brown.

Yours sincerely,

T. L. Yuan

P. S.-St. Louis Public Library writes that they have not yet received March 1937 issue of the *Q. B.*

〔工程参考图书馆（长沙韭菜园）英文信纸。国家图书馆档案，档案编号 1938-&249-027-1-5-006003〕

按：此件为打字稿，落款处为先生签名，于 5 月 30 日送达。史蒂文斯覆函先生，婉拒资助平馆购买书刊的申请，至于缩微胶片机配件则有待主机组装完毕且专家对操作者进行培训后才能投入使用。

May 12, 1938

Dear Mr. Yuan:

Your letter of March 26 has questions on microfilm work and also on purchase of books and journals. On the second point I was obliged to send you in an earlier letter a negative reply that still obtains. The use of the filming apparatus would not be possible until expert training had been given to operators. Consequently the American Council of Learned Societies undoubtedly will not be ready to act in that matter at present. As you doubtless know, the builder of the machine is in Peiping and probably will remain there for some time.

It is gratifying to hear that in spite of financial difficulties your work is going forward. With kindest regards, I am

Sincerely yours,

Davide H. Stevens

〔Rockefeller Foundation. Series 601: China; Subseries 601.R: China-Humanities and Arts. Box 9. Folder 85〕

按：该函寄送香港冯平山图书馆，并抄送格雷夫斯。

五月十三日

先生致信王访渔、宋琳，谈平馆账目细节，并请其寄来平馆一九三五年度支出计算书。

　　子舫、紫佩先生大鉴：

　　　　日昨接到紫佩兄四月十八日手书及托杜女士转寄之收支对照表、支出计算书（廿五年度）等件，均悉一一。廿四年度者亦请便中寄下，因需用颇急也。暂记账内工程图书馆部分，除弟携京之壹百伍拾元，业于去秋奉上收据，并与七月份余款三三.八九一并登入此间，呈报中基会之账外，其李永安旅费及印花费二角九分均请一并注明核销为盼。九月份沪上转拨之六百元是否由中基会扣还，已函孙先生，容再函告。又，暂记账内尚有张桂森欠款壹百伍拾元，拟请每月由渠归还拾元，分十五个月付清。吴藻洲欠款，因已离馆，曾去函催促。王政、吴藻洲欠款为数无多，即作为本馆补助，以示体恤。原单及收据三纸一并附上，即希台察是荷。顺颂大安。

　　　　　　　　　　　　　　　　　　　　　　　　五月十三日

　　　　〔《北京图书馆馆史资料汇编（1909-1949）》，页599-600〕

　　　　按：王政、吴藻洲均为平馆馆员，于1937年7月离馆。此为抄件，未落款。

五月十四日

教育部第3403号令，指令平馆应在昆明继续开展馆务工作。

　　令国立北平图书馆：

　　　　廿七年四月廿一日呈一件——为呈复关于保障国立北平图书馆馆产议决各办法，祈鉴核备案由。

　　　　呈件均悉。该馆应迁昆明继续工作，并应与西南各教育机关取得密切联络，以推进西南文化。至在香港设立临时通讯处一节，姑准暂时设立。仰即知照，存件。此令。

　　　　　　　　　　　　　　　　　　　　　　二十七年五月十四日

　　　　　　　　　　　　　　　　　　　　　　　　部长陈立夫

　　　　〔《北京图书馆馆史资料汇编（1909-1949）》，页601-602〕

五月十六日

先生致信孙洪芬，请其考虑今后将汇港经费以美金寄来。

洪芬先生大鉴：

　　十日奉上一书，谅达记室。日来港币狂涨，法币一元仅换港纸七角。如法币与美金汇率不若是之悬殊，能否自本月起将汇港经费改寄美金，再折港币发放薪水。即希尊酌示复，至以为感。

五月十六日

〔《北京图书馆馆史资料汇编（1909—1949）》，页 605〕

　　按：此为抄件，无落款。

杭立武覆函先生，告知为王重民在英影照敦煌写经筹措补助实属困难，拟从保存古物项下筹集经费。

守和先生大鉴：

　　本月五日惠示并附王重民君声请书均诵悉。王君影照英国所藏燉煌古本，关系学术，自属重要。敝会此次协助之旨，在救济国内科学工作人员，尚无力顾及海外，惟王君所务弟亦颇欲促成。重承台嘱，现拟于保存古物项下余款设法补助贰千元，俟正式通过后再当奉闻，并将款汇上也。嵩此奉复，祇颂时绥。

弟杭立武

五月十六日

〔中国书店·海淀，四册〕

　　按：此为抄件，落款处先生附笔"杭君来信寄上。外一信请交熊君并与之接洽，如何能使英国方面积极协助。日本地震后，英下院曾补助五万磅恢复'帝大'，专作购书之用，我们亦希望有此事也。"

五月十八日

先生致信张允亮、王访渔、顾子刚，请将平馆存中法工商银行余款查明并送孙洪芬保管，并请转寄函件。

庾楼、子访、子刚先生大鉴：

　　中法工商银行存款原系购书费，应移交孙先生保管，由渠签字支取，除已由法大使馆支去国币叁千伍百肆拾壹元壹角伍分又肆拾五元外，余款若干请查明示复。附上致法大使馆公函，内附致中法工商银行函各一件，即希台察是荷。

五月十八日

〔《北京图书馆馆史资料汇编（1909—1949）》，页 606〕

按：此为抄件，无落款。

先生致信孙洪芬，告知已去函留平人员尽快移交中法工商银行存款，以便支付法文书款。

洪芬先生大鉴：

顷奉五月十一日会中来函并钞件，敬悉一一。本馆所购法文书籍拨付款项一事，业经法大使馆在本馆所存中法工商银行专款内如数照拨，兹将来函录副寄呈，即希鉴核是幸。查此款系中法庚款补助费，指定专购法文书籍之用，因系购书费，故支取时均由尊处签字，弟离平以前曾嘱会计将存折等移交执事，改在上海付款，不悉何以未能照办。兹又函告平馆从速移交矣。专此奉复，顺颂台安。

五月十八日

〔《北京图书馆馆史资料汇编（1909-1949）》，页607〕

按："会中来函"应指中基会公函。此为抄件，无落款。

五月十九日

孙洪芬致函先生，谈郑振铎请平馆购也是园元曲古籍及中基会补助王重民津贴二事。

守和先生大鉴：

关于郑西谛君介绍购买《元曲选》乙事，兹将来往函件照录寄上，至希察览。又附敝执委会对于请给王重民君津贴及购《元曲选》二事之意见，并祈参阅为荷。此颂道祺。

弟洪芬拜上

廿七，五，十九

附件。

加启者，弟定于廿四日来港，叔永兄已代订九龙饭店榻位，届时当走访聆教。

弟洪再白

〔中华教育文化基金董事会信纸。《北京图书馆馆史资料汇编（1909-1949）》，页608〕

按：该函另附郑振铎与孙洪芬往来书信（抄件）各一封，执委会意见书一纸。

五月二十日

先生致信王重民，告知筹集补助进展，其赴美计划可暂缓进行。

　　有三吾弟：

　　　　前寄一信，内附杭立武先生来信。嗣闻住址又变更，未识收到否？兹又寄一复本，中基会补助之壹千元已无问题，孙先生已有信说明也。现专候杭立武来信，即可作为定案，故美洲之行可延至明夏，日内当函告 Hummel 先生也。兹有日本在英宣传机关所印刊物，愿得一份，如能赠最佳，否则请代订一份是荷。顺颂大安。

兄同礼顿首
五月二十

　　发票写北平图书馆，但寄香港。

　　"East Asia News Service", 15 Dartmouth St.

〔中国书店·海淀，四册〕

　　按：该信附杭立武 16 日来函抄件。

五月二十一日

蒲特南覆函先生，告知其已与 *Library Journal*、*Bulletin of the American Library Association* 等刊物编辑沟通并达成一致，建议美国各机构捐赠中国的书刊由史密斯森协会统一收转，恒慕义及东方部馆员也将尽力搜集国会图书馆的复本。

May 21, 1938

Dear Dr. Yuan:

　　A brief note to let you know that your letter of April 2, as well as the general project, have been communicated by me to the Library Journal, and the Bulletin of the American Library Association, with the added suggestion that the Smithsonian Institution is prepared to receive and forward, by international exchange, any books contributed for the purpose.

　　This does not mean that the Library of Congress is equally prepared to receive and assemble gifts of material, but that it would save one transit if, in the first instance, it be addressed directly to the Smithsonian.

　　Dr. Hummel has of course interested himself and his staff in ascertaining what there may be among our own duplicates that could be of any service to depleted libraries in China.

Faithfully yours,

Librarian

〔Librarian of Congress, Putnam Archives, Special File, China: Library Association 1925–1938〕

按:此件为录副。

五月二十七日

先生致信米来牟,提交中国图书馆被毁状况的初步报告,希望美国图书馆协会在其即将举行的年会中以两种方式援助中国。

May 27, 1938

Dear Dr. Milam:

I am submitting herewith a preliminary statement regarding the destruction of Chinese libraries in the course of Japanese invasion. I trust that members attending the sixtieth annual conference to be held in Kansas City will be interested to know the real situation here.

We are compiling a more comprehensive survey of the loss of cultural institutions in China which we hope to publish in the near future.

There are two ways in which the American Library Association can be of great assistance to us at the present juncture: first, some organized effort among American libraries be made to dispose of their duplicate material for this cause; and secondly, to solicit donation of books from the reading public for Chinese libraries.

Donations of books from the United States and Canada should be sent to the Smithsonian Institution which will undertake to forward to China through its International Exchange Service. These books will be kept temporarily in Hong Kong and will be forwarded to educational centers in the interior whenever we feel safe to do so.

We shall be most grateful to you if you will urge your Committee on International Relations to take early action and to convey to each member of the Committee our very heartfelt thanks.

With warmest greetings to you and the annual conference, I remain,

Yours sincerely,

T. L. Yuan,

Chairman

Executive Board

P. S. If you can ask Dr. Bostwick or Mr. Clemons to speak on our behalf at one of the general sessions, we shall be most grateful. As Dr. Bishop has been kept informed about our plans, he may also be willing to lend us the necessary support.

T. L. Yuan

〔The American Library Association Archives, China Projects File, Box 2, Books for China, Folder 1〕

按：此为抄件，另附 3 页报告，题为 Destruction of Chinese Libraries During Japanese Invasion。

德尔格覆函先生，建议将缩微胶片拍摄器材在天津组装并培训合适的人员直至熟练掌握，再将其运往香港开始拍摄。

U. S. Marine Detachment,

Tientsin, China.

27 May, 1938

Dear Mr. Yuan:

I have delayed answering your letter dated 15 March 1938 until such time as I have been able to confer with our Asiatic Fleet Surgeon, Dr. Angwin in regard to my being available to supervise the assembly and installation of the microcopying camera and processing apparatus in Hong Kong.

I believe the best plan would be to have the outfit shipped here together with the remainder of the shop equipment which is still in Paris and set up the camera here in Tientsin with the aid of the personnel who are to operate and care for it in its final location. When the camera is set up and operating properly and the personnel have become thoroughly familiar with its operation it can then be shipped to Hong Kong and installed. I will then be ordered to the U. S. S. Mindanao for duty so that

I will be available part of the time in Hong Kong.

The above plan can be carried out in addition to my regular medical duties here in Tientsin and since we have a ship which operates part of the time in Hong Kong, I can be there from time to time to aid in getting the work started.

In my opinion, it is very important that the personnel who are to operate the camera be carefully selected regarding ability and permanence in order that you may be assured of uninterrupted operation.

I am also writing to Dr. Stevens and Mr. Graves and the Navy Medical school where the camera is stored. We have no transport coming to China for some months which complicates the problem of transportation.

Please let me hear from you regarding your opinion of the plan as outlined.

Yours sincerely,

R. H. Draeger

〔Rockefeller Foundation. Series 601: China; Subseries 601.R: China-Humanities and Arts. Box 47. Folder 389〕

按：该件为录副。

五月二十八日

杭立武覆函先生,告知补助王重民在英影照敦煌写本一事,正在等候古物保存委员会各委员意见。

守和吾兄左右：

五月廿一日惠书奉悉。关于王重民君影照英国所藏燉煌古本,嘱为补助一节,拟即用通信方法征求古物保存委员会各人意见,俟得同意后,再行奉闻。敬先布复,祗颂时绥。

弟杭立武

五,廿八

〔中国书店·海淀,四册〕

按：此为抄件,后寄与王重民。

六月二十五日

先生致信史蒂文斯,附上德尔格五月二十七函,同意其在天津组装、培训的计划,建议与返回美国的顾临商谈协助中国图书馆复兴计划。

June 25, 1938

Dear Dr. Stevens:

I wish to acknowledge with thanks the receipt of your letters dated April 4th and May 12th.

Regarding the microfilm equipment, I fully agree with the American Council that operators should first be trained by experts. I have recently received a letter from Dr. Draeger a copy of which is herewith enclosed for your reference. We are ready to send operators to Dr. Draeger for expert training as soon as the camera is installed.

At the request of your Shanghai office the sum of G $ 2,000, being partial payment of Dr. Bishop's travelling allowance, has been refunded to your Foundation. As soon as permanent peace is restored, we hope the Foundation will reconsider our request in connection with Dr. Bishop's visit to China. In view of the destruction of Chinese libraries, his advice in regard to their restoration would be most urgently needed in China.

I trust you have had an opportunity to discuss matters with Mr. Roger S. Greene who has recently returned to the United States from a flying visit to this country. At the meeting of the Trustees of the China Foundation, the sum of $ 1,800,000 was appropriated for scientific and educational work. A similar amount will be granted by the Trustees of the British Indemnity Board at its annual meeting to be held there next week. In spite of the undeclared war, educational work of permanent nature is going forward.

Your sincerely,

T. L. Yuan

Acting Director

〔平馆(冯平山图书馆转)英文信纸。Rockefeller Foundation. Series 601: China; Subseries 601.R: China-Humanities and Arts. Box 47. Folder 389〕

按:此件为打字稿,落款处为先生签名,于 7 月 22 日送达。

六月三十日

顾子刚致函先生,告知司徒雷登与汤尔和交涉此前新民会查抄平馆馆藏"禁书"的结果。

June 30, 1938

Dear Mr. Yuan:

In one of my former letters, I informed you about the problem of prohibited book. About ten days ago, we were asked to give up our Chinese periodicals and newspapers published 1928 – 37. Dr. Stuart immediately took up the matter with Dr. T'ang Er-ho and the request was quashed. In addition, Dr. Stuart asked that the propaganda material, etc., taken over last time should be returned to us to be sealed in our library. This was also promised us, but it was said that a part of the obviously controversial books, political and social, had already been destroyed. Dr. Stuart said he had already reposted the matter to the China Foundation and Mr. Senn may have informed you already. We have not seen Dr. Stuart since the protest, so I am not well posted about the matter, but he is so busy about Yenching and the other universities, coming into the city two or more times a day, that we have decided it best not to call on him just now.

Yours sincerely,

〔台北"中央研究院"近代史研究所档案馆,〈中华教育文化基金董事会〉,馆藏号 502-01-08-068,页 118〕

按:此件为录副,无落款签名。

六月

先生夫人袁慧熙及子女抵达香港。〔《吴宓日记》第 6 册,页 339〕

七月七日　昆明

先生为*Japan's Aggression and Public Opinion* 撰写序言。

The present collection of fifty-seven articles selected from leading British and American periodicals, and also from a few of the most important ones published in China and elsewhere, embody intelligent and unbiased interpretations of the Sino-Japanese conflict by some of the most outstanding authorities on the Far East. Fully to indicate the trend of public opinion abroad, articles by Chinese writers have purposely been excluded. In making our selection, hundreds of magazine articles have been carefully perused, and the present collection will, we believe, give the reader the alpha and omega on all phases of the Sino-Japanese struggle.

Readers of these articles will invariably be impressed by the precarious situation into which Japan has plunged herself through the intrepid undertaking of her own warlords on the one hand, and the consolidated and growing strength of Chinese resistance on the other. The Japanese people are disillusioned and the army is baffled by the stubbornness and courage of the Chinese soldiers in the act of defending their national honour and existence.

The economic resources of Japan are more and more exhausted as the war is prolonged. A year of relentless campaign against a comparatively weak but determined country finds the Island Empire, inspired by an insatiable lust　for more territory and manacled by military terrorism, not only still remote from her goal, but also sinking deeper and deeper into the morass from which it is extremely hard to extricate herself.

In China there is an increasing conviction that right will finally overcome might and, as the war of attrition is protracted, there has been manifested in the whole nation an indomitable will and power of resistance to the bitter end, in spite of China's immense sacrifice which is the greatest she has ever experienced in the course　of her long history. In the midst of unparalleled tribulations, the Chinese people are fighting with courage and persistence to free themselves from Japanese aggression and to stand before the world as defender of democracy and human decency.

To the sympathetic onlookers, between a united China and a desperate and frustrated aggressor, the future course of events is not hard to foretell; but our readers may form their own conclusions regarding the outcome of the Far Eastern situation. Having observed the first anniversary of the commencement of our war of resistance, we cannot but hope that effective measures will eventually be adopted by democratic powers to stop and end this inhuman war of aggression in order that international peace and justice may be restored.

In the formation of this volume, hearty thanks are due to various publishers who have given special permission for the reproduction of these articles. Credit should be given to the staff of the Library of the National Southwest Associated University in the work of selection and compilation.

〔*Japan's Aggression and Public Opinion*, 1938, pp. iii-iv〕

按：该书由西南联合大学图书馆编辑、出版，正文分为九部分，依次为 Background of Japanese Aggression and Imperialism, Japanese Aggression and International Law, China's Will to Resistance and Its Outlook, Japan's Growing Difficulties, Summary of the War, Japanese Outrages and Atrocities, International Action to Check Japanese Aggression, United States and the Far East, Great Britain and the Far East，书前另冠徐谟（外交部副部长）前言。笔者认为先生序言落款时间应属纪念性质，并不准确，但依照年谱长编惯例系于此日。该篇失收于《袁同礼文集》。

七月十八日

先生致信史密斯森协会，告知收到三十二包交换品，并请该协会随件寄送制式文件以便核对后回寄收讫，且以更经济的方式寄送包裹。

July 18, 1938

Dear Sirs:

We have pleasure in acknowledging the receipt of 32 packages of publications, as listed herewith, which your Service has so kindly mailed to us. We wish to thank you very heartily for your courtesy in forwarding them to this Library.

We shall be doubly thankful to you if you would henceforth send us some form of announcement as to the number of packages you forward to us so that we can check them up and return the form to you after the packages have been received.

If you find it more economical to send the packages by post than freight, please do so, as we can receive the material within a comparatively short period.

Thanking you again for your kind cooperation and assistance, I remain

Yours faithfully,

T. L. Yuan

Acting Director

P. S. Will you kindly forward the enclosed letter for us.

〔平馆(冯平山图书馆转)英文信纸。Smithsonian Institution Archives, Records, 1868–1988 (Record Unit 509), Box 1, National Library, Peiping〕

按：此件为打字稿，落款处为先生签名，于 8 月 15 日送达。

七月二十三日

先生致信王重民，告知中英庚款补助即将汇发，并告自己最近行程安排。

有三吾弟如握：

顷奉七月十四日手书，欣悉种切。中英庚款补助之二千元，决无问题，杭立武君日前在港开会，表示返汉口以后即汇来，现正与中基会接洽按照法定汇率请财政部特允购买外汇，想能办到。现因在港主持留英考试，须下月初方能结束，故又改八月十号赴滇矣。伯希和及 Meuvret 处均不日寄一详信，请将应寄书籍一律寄港，运费可由馆担任也。匆匆，顺颂旅安。

同礼

七月廿三日

熊式一处希再催促。征买书籍可帮 Meuvret 之忙，并约留法同学代为选择。

〔中国书店・海淀，四册〕

按：Meuvret 即 Colette Meuvret(1896–1990)，1923 年起担任巴黎东方语言学院图书馆（Bibliothèque interuniversitaire des langues orientales）馆长。

七月下旬

教育部在香港举行留英同学考试，先生为协助人员之一，因而推迟前往云南的计划。〔中国书店·海淀，四册〕

是年夏秋

先生以中华图书馆协会执行部主席身份致信美国图书馆协会，恳请美国图书馆界捐赠西文书籍。该信部分段落刊登于报纸上，内容如下：

According to a recent survey, over 35 national and private universities in China as well as a large number of cultural institutions have been either destroyed or disorganized in the course of Japanese armed invasion.

Deplorable loss of libraries of Nankai University; Hopei Normal College, Institute of Technology, and School of Commerce and Law; the Great China University; the National Tung Chi University and Kwang Hwa University.

While it may be the feeling of some of our friends abroad that any campaign to collect books for Chinese libraries should be postponed until the armed conflict is over, yet the urgent demand for western literature is so overwhelmingly impelling that we are inclined to think otherwise.

Present hostilities are likely to be long drawn out and may drag on for a considerable time. In the meantime Chinese scholars have to be provided with an adequate supply of material so that there shall be no intellectual stagnation.

〔*The Clinton Journal and Public*, Illinois, Oct. 6, 1938, p. 3〕

按：先生应在信中注明，中国高校亟需的书刊以科学、技术、医学、文学、工具书、学术期刊和政府出版物为主。[1] 收到此信后，美国图书馆协会请各图书馆拣选出对中国学者可能有用的书刊复本，并在 12 月 31 日前付费寄送到史密斯森协会。

先生以中华图书馆协会执行部主席身份致信美国图书馆协会国际关系委员会委员 Alice Anderson，恳请美国图书馆界捐赠西文书籍。该信部分段

---

[1] *The Evening Star*, Washington, D. C., Oct. 3, 1938, p. b-2.

落刊登于报纸上,内容如下:

Not only are we concerned with our Chinese heritage, but we have to continue our work collecting literature on western sciences. The present hostilities may drag on for a considerable time to come. Meanwhile Chinese scholars have to be provided with an adequate supply of material so that there will be no intellectual stagnation.

〔*The Chico Record*, Chico, California, Thursday, Nov. 3, 1938, p. 3〕

按:Alice Anderson 时任加州州立大学奇科分校(Chico State College)图书馆馆长,美国图书馆协会国际关系委员会主席时为 Joseph P. Danton。

八月二日

先生致信伯希和,痛诉日本侵华战争对文教机构的肆意破坏,恳请其敦促法国外交部协助法国图书馆协会募集向中国捐赠书刊,并告知所有援华书籍均可通过法国驻港使馆寄送。

> c/o FUNG PING-SHAN LIBRARY
> BONHAM ROAD
> HONG KONG
> August 2, 1938

Prof. Paul Pelliot

College de France

Paris, France

Dear Prof. Pelliot:

It has been sometime since I have had the pleasure of hearing from you. Although I have been silent for so long, you are constantly in my thoughts and I trust that in our present struggle for national existence, we have your support and sympathy.

The armed invasion of Japan followed by the wanton destruction of our cultural institutions must have been a matter of great interest you have taken in the promotion of close cultural relations between China and France.

With such a large scale destruction of our libraries, we are now, in urgent need of western books and journals. In the name of our Library Association, I sent an appeal to the President of the French Library Association, a copy of his reply is herewith enclosed for your reference. I shall greatly appreciate your assistance if you could speak to Mr. Marx of the Foreign Office and solicit his assistance in speeding up the matter.

I learned from you that the French Government presented a number of French books to various national libraries abroad and a catalogue of these books have already been published. If China has not been presented with such a set, it is time to do so when the need of French publication is especially urgent in this country.

As Hong Kong is free from Japanese aggression, French donations can now be sent to us direct or via the French Consulate General at Hong Kong.

Any assistance from you and your colleagues will be gratefully appreciated.

Your faithfully,

T. L. Yuan

Acting Director

P. S. I enclose a statement regarding the destruction of Chinese libraries. I shall greatly appreciate your courtesy if you will have it circulated among your friends.

〔韩琦《袁同礼致伯希和书信》,页 130-131〕

先生致信 Meuvret 女士,感谢抗战期间法方愿与平馆交换出版品,并表示愿意支付由巴黎寄送香港的书刊运费。

August 2, 1938

Madame Meuvret-Renié

Bibliothécaire

École Nationale des Langues Orientales Vivantes

2 Rue de Lille

Paris, France

Dear Madam:

It has been quite a long time since I have had the pleasure of hearing from you. The armed invasion of Japan followed by the wanton destruction of our cultural institutions must been a matter of great concern to you, especially in view of the great interest you have taken in the promotion of close cultural relations between China and France.

From Mr. Wang Chung-min, we are happy to learn that you have taken steps to gather together a number of French publications for our Library which you are offering as exchanges. I wish to express to you our deep sense of gratitude for your kind assistance rendered to us at a time when the need of French books in China is especially urgent.

I have asked Mr. Wang and his colleagues to collaborate with you in the selection of material. Please command them whenever you need their services.

We shall be very glad to pay the transportation charges from Paris to Hong Kong. Please send all cases to our Hong Kong address with their bill of lading.

With best personal regards and renewed thanks for your courtesy and assistance,

Yours sincerely,

T. L. Yuan

Acting Director

〔中国书店·海淀,四册〕

先生致信卡耐基国际和平基金会主席巴特勒,附金陵大学教授贝德士夫人就日军在南京暴行的报告,并请求其在美呼吁各界力量支持中国、恢复远东和平。

August 2, 1938

Dear Sir:

In view of your humanitarian interest in China's war of resistance, I beg to enclose herewith a confidential report from Prof. M. S. Bates of the University of Nanking. Although it deals with events which took place last

December, yet it gives a graphic picture of the atrocities committed by Japanese troops after their occupation of the Capital, the details of which are not generally known abroad. As Japan's war of aggression is protracted, similar crimes are being repeated elsewhere, only on a larger scale, particularly at outlying places where nationals of third powers are not on hand at the scene to bear witness to these atrocities.

With such a large scale destruction of lives and property as a result of the undeclared war, it has been the unanimous belief of the Chinese people that the stopping of the export of war materials to Japan would be the most effective means to halt Japan's war of conquest. Nothing short of concerted and positive action among democratic powers will stop Japan's ruthless infringement of our right of national existence. It is the only means that will remedy the precarious situation in the Far East.

Realizing our great interest in world peace, we sincerely hope that you will exert some influence in bringing about closer cooperation between government and private organizations towards this objective. As President of the Carnegie Endowment for International Peace, you have contributed a great deal in the promotion of better understanding among nations. We are sure that any effective steps which you will help to bring about in the realization of a permanent basis of peace and international justice and in safeguarding the sovereignty and integrity of China will win the everlasting gratitude of our whole nation.

With assurances with our sincere appreciation of your sympathy and support,

Yours faithfully,

T. L. Yuan

Acting Director

〔平馆(冯平山图书馆转)英文信纸。Columbia University Libraries Archival Collections, Carnegie Endowment for International Peace Record, Box 322, Folder Yuan, T. L.〕

按:Prof. M. S. Bates 即贝德士夫人,时在私立金陵大学外国文学

系任教①,所附报告为 1938 年 1 月 10 日撰写,共 8 页。此件为打
字稿,落款处为先生签名,于本月底送达卡耐基国际和平基金会。

八月十四日　蒙自

晚,先生抵云南蒙自,吴宓听说后即至法国领事馆客厅探访,馆员童明道、
于宝榘、胡某某陪坐。〔《朱自清全集》第 9 卷,页 546;《吴宓日记》第 6 册,页 345〕

　　　　按:胡某某,《吴宓日记》原文作胡□□,或指胡绍声,待考。

八月十五日

九时,先生访吴宓,谈高棣华工作及其薪金情况,约半小时后离去。下午二
时,先生路遇吴宓,同至天南精舍,访贺麟,吊唁其母离世。

晚六时半,朱自清、姚从吾、张佛泉、蔡枢衡四人在法领事馆设宴款待周炳
琳、先生,吴宓作陪。〔《吴宓日记》第 6 册,页 345-346〕

　　　　按:张佛泉(1908—1994),原名张葆桓,天津人,燕京大学哲学系
　　　　毕业,后任《大公报》编辑,1932 年赴美留学,时任西南联合大学
　　　　政治系教授。蔡枢衡(1904—1983),江西永修人,法学家,早年留
　　　　学日本,时任西南联合大学法律系教授。

八月十六日

午后,吴宓来访先生,不值。晚七时复来,先生与之谈平馆南迁交涉、办理
经过,今后迁滇及增设分馆计划,此外谈高棣华工作。先生希望吴宓多多
规劝其踏实、用功工作。吴宓交先生港币十元,为自己购物。〔《吴宓日记》
第 6 册,页 346〕

八月十七日

先生离开云南蒙自。〔《吴宓日记》第 6 册,页 346〕

八月二十八日　贵阳

先生与徐森玉自昆明抵贵阳,中午在庄尚严家聚餐,晚餐食于大十字天津
馆。傅振伦全天陪同,先生嘱其搜集贵州文献图书。〔傅振伦著《蒲梢沧桑·
九十忆往》,上海:华东师范大学出版社,1997 年,页 108〕

八月三十日

卡耐基国际和平基金会覆函先生,此前来信及贝德士夫人报告将待巴特勒
会长归来后转交。

──────────

① 《私立金陵大学一览》,1934 年 6 月,页 385。

August 30, 1938

My dear Dr. Yuan:

In the absence of Dr. Butler, I acknowledge your letter of August 2 with the enclosed report dated January 10 from Professor M. S. Bates of the University of Nanking. Dr. Butler does not plan to return to town until late in September and your letter and the report will be brought to his attention at that time.

Sincerely yours,

〔Columbia University Libraries Archival Collections, Carnegie Endowment for International Peace Record, Box 322, Folder Yuan, T. L.〕

按：该函寄送香港，此件为录副。

九月六日　重庆

李济会同管理中英庚款董事会总干事杭立武、故宫博物院理事王世杰、马衡、先生商定调查故宫博物院古物搬运及存放办法。〔台北"国史馆"，〈古物迁运保存案（二）〉，数位典藏号 014-050000-0034〕

按：9 月 5 日，李济由云南飞赴重庆，9 月 9 日开始工作，依次考察重庆、成都、汉中等处，共费时 31 日，后撰写报告。

阿博特覆函先生，告知已按先生前请将寄送平馆、南京工程参考图书馆、中华图书馆协会的书刊运往香港冯平山图书馆。

September 6, 1938

Sir:

In compliance with your request, the Institution has been forwarding to Hong Kong in care of the Fung Ping Shan Chinese Library packages received here from American establishments addressed to the National Library of Peiping, the Engineering Reference Library and the Library Association of China, the consignments being addressed to the National Library of Peiping.

For your information there is given in the list of contents covering each shipment the name of the sender, the record number and the number of packages. There is enclosed in the announcement an acknowledgment card to be signed and returned by you. No detailed information from you as to the number of packages received is needed here, the card referred to being all that is required.

Very truly yours,

C. G. Abbot

Secretary

〔Smithsonian Institution Archives, Records, 1868–1988 (Record Unit 509), Box 1, National Library, Peiping〕

　　按:该函寄送香港冯平山图书馆,此件为录副。

九月十三日

上午十时,中央古物保管委员会假内政部礼俗司开会,先生、马衡、朱希祖以委员身份到场,另有陈念中、李安为部派员与会。陈念中代主席详细报告各省古物迁移避炸情况,并主张各省古物都应筹备迁移保存,十二时散会。〔《朱希祖日记》,页923〕

九月十七日

先生自重庆乘飞机抵达昆明。〔《民国日报》(云南),1938年9月18日,第4版〕

九月二十日

平馆向教育部呈文一件,题为《为王重民补助在英津贴请转咨财政部按法定汇价准予购买英镑》,具先生名并钤印。

　　　　窃职馆于民国廿六年承管理中英庚款董事会补助国币八千元专作影照英法两国所藏燉煌古写本之用。此项写本卷帙浩繁,势须遴派专家从事选择,凡遇罕见之本,尽先影摄。法国部分既然由职馆馆员王重民影照竣事,自当派其前往英伦继续工作,藉收驾轻就熟之效。预计工作需时一年(廿七年九月至廿八廿八月),该员在国外生活费由职馆津贴国币二千元。拟恳大部转咨财政部按照法定汇价准予购买英镑,俾该员旅外生活得资接济,实为德便。谨呈

教育部长陈

国立北平图书馆副馆长袁同礼

民国廿七年九月二十日

〔中国第二历史档案馆,教育部档案·全卷宗5,国立北平图书馆请拨员工学术研究补助费经常费有关文书,案卷号11616(1)〕

按:12 月 13 日,财政部孔祥熙批准平馆向昆明中央银行购汇 60 英镑,余俟需要时再行申请核办。

九月二十一日

先生致信吴宓,寄送《抗战中之国际舆论》序文、目录,请其帮忙润色、改订。〔《吴宓日记》第 6 册,页 354〕

按:9 月 23 日晚,该信送达。

九月二十三日

国民政府行政院令,任命先生为"美国世界博览会筹备委员会艺术专门文员会委员"之一。

按:"美国世界博览会"即 1939 年纽约世界博览会(New York Expo),此次赴美展览因运输问题,于翌年 6 月作罢,后改为赴苏展出。①

九月二十四日

吴宓覆函先生,寄上修改好的《抗战中之国际舆论》序文、目录,并再荐张敬女士到平馆办事处工作。〔《吴宓日记》第 6 册,页 354〕

按:此函虽以航空信方式寄送,但于 10 月 8 日或 9 日送到,应与先生离港赴昆明有关。

中央古物保管委员会致函先生、李济,请二人协助审查、修正《非常时期保管古物办法》。

径启者:查《非常时期保管古物办法》,前经呈部转奉行政院于二十五年五月通行。现在情势变更,该项办法似有修正必要。经本会在渝委员第二次谈话会决定,推台端等会同审查修正,提出下次会议讨论。相应检同原办法二分,函请查照办理见复为荷! 此致

袁委员同礼、李委员济

　　附《非常时期保管古物办法》二分。

中央古物保管委员会启

九月　日

〔台北"国史馆",〈函袁同礼等审查修正非常时期保管古物办法〉,典藏号 026-011000-0468〕

---

① 《贵州文史丛刊》,1983 年第 1 期,页 62。

　　按:此件为底稿,该函应于 24 日缮就,9 月 26 日封发。

九月二十九日

先生抵达香港。〔中国书店·海淀,四册〕

九月底

先生与匹兹堡大学校长 John G. Bowman 会晤,商讨资助中国学生赴该校
攻读博士学位的可能。〔University of Pittsburgh Library, John Gabbert Bowman,
Administrative Files, Box 2 Folder 13, Chinese Material〕

　　　　按:John G. Bowman(1877-1962),美国教育家,本谱中译作"鲍
　　　　曼"。1911 年至 1914 年为爱荷华大学第九任校长,1921 年至
　　　　1945 年为匹兹堡大学第十任校长,曾主持兴建当时世界最高的
　　　　教育建筑——学习大教堂(Cathedral of Learning)。

十月三日

先生致信王重民,告知中基会补助已按官方汇率寄出,中英庚款亦正在积
极进行,并请其前往曼彻斯特查看 John Rylands Library 所藏摩梭语文献。

　　　有三仁弟大鉴:

　　　　上月廿九日返港,闻尊处曾有航信,业已转滇,竟致相左。在云南
　　　开远晤向觉明,欣悉近况安好,甚慰。惟闻于道泉君经济颇窘,甚为系
　　　念。如研究上仍有留欧之必要,当再设法为之救济,或介绍赴美工作
　　　亦可,请询明示复。尊处应得之补助中基会方面之一千元,已设法按
　　　照法定汇率在沪购买英磅,共合 £ 59.7.6,兹特奉上花旗汇票,希察收
　　　并将收据签字后径寄中基会是荷。此票由沪寄滇适有黔川之行,返滇
　　　不久又携至港,故未能早日奉上。至中英庚款之二千元,刻正设法请
　　　教部转咨财政部,请按法定汇率准予购买外汇,尚未奉到复音,容再函
　　　告。闻向君云 Manchester 之 John Rylands Library 有苗文写本(Moso
　　　mss),请便中前往一观附介绍函一件,一律摄制复本,对于西南文献及英
　　　国新出关于中日战事之书籍及小册,并请随时注意代为搜集。本馆现
　　　决定移滇,希望对于西南文化有所贡献也。专此,顺颂旅安。

　　　　　　　　　　　　　　　　　　　　　　袁同礼顿首
　　　　　　　　　　　　　　　　　　　　　　　十月三日

　　　现定于十日离此赴昆明,嗣后信均寄"昆明迤西会馆,北平图书馆"。
　　　又中英庚款董事会将印行丛书多种,关于《燉煌丛残》拟由吾人

编就,以该会名义印行,除上次寄下提要十种《毛诗音》、《尔雅注》等(照片均存商务)可作一部分外,其余应印者,请先拟一目录寄下,附以提要,再与同人一商。

此外,天主教资料尤其与中英文化有关者,可选数种加入。此事由叶玉虎先生主办也。

〔中国书店·海淀,四册〕

十月七日

先生致信阿博特,感谢其如前信所请将交换品发往香港冯平山图书馆。

October 7, 1938

Dear Sir:

We wish to thank you for your letter of September 6 with regard to the forwarding to Hong Kong packages addressed to the National Library of Peiping, the Engineering Reference Library and the Library Association of China, the consignments being addressed to the National Library of Peiping. We also highly appreciate the information you gave us in the second paragraph of your letter.

In order to help develop the cultural life of the southwestern provinces of China, the National Library has recently established an office at Kunming at the above address.

Pending the erection of a permanent fire-proof building at Kunming, all consignments to the above three institutions should continue to be sent to Hong Kong, even when the parcels are addressed to us at Kunming. We shall greatly appreciate your assistance if the attention of your International Exchange Service could be called to this fact.

With sincere appreciation for your cooperation and assistance,

Yours faithfully,

T. L. Yuan

Acting Director

〔平馆(昆明)英文信纸。Smithsonian Institution Archives, Records, 1868–1988 (Record Unit 509), Box 1, National Library, Peiping〕

按:此件为打字稿,落款处为先生签名,于11月7日送达。

十月上旬

先生离港前往昆明。〔《吴宓日记》第 6 册,页 363〕

十月十六日

先生乘火车抵达昆明,住东寺街花椒巷九号。〔《民国日报》(云南),1938 年 10 月 17 日,第 4 版;《吴宓日记》第 6 册,页 363〕

十月中旬

先生致信吴宓(蒙自),告留高棣华、贺恩慈两位女士留港办事的原因。〔《吴宓日记》第 6 册,页 363〕

　　　　按:此信 19 日送达。

十月十八日

平馆上海办事处钱存训覆函先生,报告订购《申报》及南京工程参考图书馆近况。大意如下:

　　奉到九、廿及廿四日先后由滇、港赐书,至书单数纸均已敬悉。应办各书已分别订购,一俟到齐,当即陆续寄上。《申报》自十、十复刊,由美商哥伦比亚公司经营,俟有余款当为联大订一份直寄昆明。日人所办《新申报》已自本月起试订三月,每日送到此处,拟俟半月或一月汇寄一次。《晨报》改名尚无所闻。自然科学研究所出版之《中国文化情报》(现已出十号),曾委托数家设法,均未购到,据称:"该刊系非卖品,只能赠送日本各机关,无法配得"等语。

　　南京工程图书馆曾托一现在伪教育部之某君前往探视,据云该处房屋完好未毁,惟门口改悬一"中文图书文献整理馆"之牌,有日军守卫,未得入内,闻地质调查所内各书均被该馆接收(见《大美报》载日方消息)。至市上书摊已托请金大工程师齐兆昌先生代为留意搜购矣。

　　京中留居美人,金大方面有 Dr. Mrs. M. S. Bates, Prof. Riggs,金女大方面有 Mrs. M. Vautrin 数人。

　　教会全名单现正觅购下列数种:

　　□□□□□□□□□□
　　□□□□□□□□□□
　　□□□□□□□□□□

　　附上剪报数种,其中资料或可供本馆及协会参考之用也。

　　　　　　〔《北京图书馆馆史资料汇编(1909-1949)》,642-643 页〕

按：上海沦陷后，日军企图以新闻审查为由控制《申报》，该社遂于1937年12月14日宣布停刊。齐兆昌（1880—1956），浙江杭州人，之江大学毕业后赴美留学，入密歇根大学土木工程专业，归国后任金陵大学工程处兼校产管理处主任[1]，时出任金陵大学难民收容所所长。"自然科学研究所"即上海自然科学研究所，由日本政府以庚款设立，其馆址位于法租界祁齐路，以自然科学研究为主，抗战后被中央研究院接收。Prof. Riggs 应指 Charles H. Riggs，中文名林查理，时在农艺系任教；Mrs. M. Vautrin，1919 年至 1941 年在该校任教，长期担任教育系主任。[2] 此件为钱存训所拟底稿，尾处有"注：此函托滇缅路局李女士便带"字样，亦为钱存训亲笔。

十月中下旬

先生撰两信与吴宓，一为决定聘用张敬女士任图书馆中文编目事，月薪七十元；二为请吴宓复校《抗战中之国际舆论》一书序文，并告知自己将缓期赴重庆。〔《吴宓日记》第 6 册，页 363、365〕

按：此两信分别于 22 日、23 日送达吴宓处，张敬自本年 11 月 1 日起在平馆昆明办事处供职。

十月二十日

先生致信王重民，谈法方如能捐赠书刊最好选择免费邮寄，另告其平馆（南馆）与西南联合大学合组成立中日战事史料征辑会。

有三吾弟：

九月六日大札由港转滇，复由滇转港，今日始由港转到，拜悉一一。关于英庚款补助之两千元，曾呈教部九月二十日左右转咨财政部，请求外汇，尚未奉到批示，希望能得政府之允许也。Meuvret 方面已开始进行，甚慰，数目虽不多，但不无小补。刻下政府限制购买外汇，无法购任何西文书。关于运费一节，如能使法邮 M.M 免费最佳，否则请予以折扣，或完全由我方担任，亦无不可。选书事由各专家分任最好，旧书店及冷摊上颇多佳本，但必须有发单方能报账。本馆与联大合组战

---

[1] 《私立金陵大学一览》，1933 年 6 月，页 381。

[2] 《私立金陵大学一览》，1934 年，页 385、399；张连红主编：《金陵女子大学校史》，2005 年，页 307。

史史料征辑会,关于中日战争之各项记载日人方面宣传资料尤重要、照片等
等。中日方面由联大担任,西文方面由本馆担任。凡英法所见之新
书,请特别留意,或择购寄下(均寄昆明)。因香港办事处竭力缩小范
围,仅留三人在彼办事。匆匆,顺颂大安。

　　　　　　　　　　　　　　　　　　兄同礼顿首

　　　　　　　　　　　　　　　　　　十月二十日

　　　　　　　　　　　　　　　〔中国书店·海淀,四册〕

十月二十三日

吴宓致先生两函。一为张敬求职事,表示感谢;一为复校后的《抗战中之国
际舆论》序文,并要求先生将此前随函致周炳琳、贺麟二人信焚毁。〔《吴宓
日记》第6册,页365〕

　　　　按:吴宓与周炳琳、贺麟二人信,所谈应为对《善生周刊》的希望。

十月下旬

先生收西南联大校方公函,先生前请联大承担徐家璧等九位图书馆员薪水
一节,因校方经费困难,恕难应命,仍请平馆(南馆)担任。〔《国立西南大学
史料》第2卷,页72〕

　　　　按:10月26日,该校举行第92次常务委员会会议,其中讨论此项
　　　　议案。

十月三十一日

下午四时,吴宓赴迤西会馆联大图书馆访先生,不值。〔《吴宓日记》第6册,
页369〕

十一月一日

晚,先生在崇义街新云南饭馆设便宴,馆内同仁与席,遇吴宓。〔《吴宓日记》
第6册,页371〕

十一月二日

中午,吴宓来迤西会馆联大图书馆访先生,约明日宴。〔《吴宓日记》第6册,
页372〕

十一月三日

晚五时许,吴宓至东寺街花椒巷九号先生宅,等至六时先生归,谈图书馆近
况、高棣华事,并荐王原真,先生允聘入馆,月薪五十元。随后先生宴吴宓
于共和春,子袁澄、女袁静同往,八时散。〔《吴宓日记》第6册,页372-373〕

十一月七日

先生致信欧美各国学者、学术团体、出版机构,请求各方捐赠再版期刊。

November 7, 1938

Dear Sir:

Ever since Japan's military occupation of Peiping, all national institutions of learning in that historical city have been unable to function. In view of this situation, we have established an office at Kunming, Yunnan. We have been collecting books and journals in order to meet the intellectual needs of Chinese scholars in this hour of distress. As many of our universities and scientific institutions have been deliberately destroyed by Japanese militarists, the need of scientific literature felt by Chinese scholars is especially urgent at the present time.

In order to keep scholars informed as to the recent development of various branches of science, we are building up a special Reprint Collection which will be of great value to investigators engaged in scientific research.

Knowing that you have made notable contributions to learning and cognizant of your intellectual sympathy for China, we earnestly hope that you will find it possible to send us a complete set of your reprints if they are still available for distribution.

As we have to start our work entirely afresh, we are in urgent need of books and periodicals of all kinds, old or new, especially standard works in various fields. Donations of books from American and Canadian authors may be sent to us care of the International Exchange Service, Smithsonian Institution, Washington, D. C., which makes monthly shipment to China. Should any of your friends be willing to lend a helping hand in the rehabilitation of our collections, will you kindly make the necessary contact for us?

As a great deal of scientific work is being carried on in China in spite of the war, your contributions will render a great service to the present and future generations of intellectual workers in this country.

Thanking you in anticipation for your kind co-operation and assistance,

Yours faithfully,

T. L. Yuan

Acting Director

〔平馆（昆明）英文信纸。Smithsonian Institution Archives. Field Expedition Records, Box 11 Folder 18, Yuan, T. L., 1929－1940; Princeton University, Mudd Manuscript Library, AC123, Box 415, Folder Peiping, National Library of, 1937－1944; Harvard University, John K. Fairbank personal archive〕

　　按：此信为打字稿，落款处为先生签名。

十一月十日

下午，吴宓赴迤西会馆，先生外出，故留函而去。是日，先生晤陈福田。〔《吴宓日记》第 6 册，页 376〕

　　按：吴宓、陈福田所谈之事应与《抗战中之国际舆论》有关，似拟将该书列入西南联合大学英文读本。

十一月十三日

晚，云南大学校长熊庆来设宴，孙洪芬、周自新、萧蘧、南□□、闻宥、顾颉刚、先生受邀与席。〔《顾颉刚日记》卷 4，页 161〕

　　按：周自新（1911—1971），江苏江阴人，1929 年赴德留学，1935 年归国，工程师。萧蘧（1897—1949），字叔玉，江西泰和人，清华学校毕业后赴美留学，先后在密苏里大学、哈佛大学学习，归国后在南开大学、清华大学任教。

十一月十四日

先生寄送雨靴、美国细毛浴刷、荔枝与吴宓，并函告已命王原真到图书馆办公。〔《吴宓日记》第 6 册，页 377－378〕

　　按：先生本意，王原真上午为家庭教师，月薪二十元，下午供职图书馆，月薪三十元。

先生致信美国 J. O. Frank 教授，请其捐赠专业图书。〔*The Oshkosh Northwestern*, Dec. 19, 1938, p. 4〕

　　按：J. O. Frank 时任 Oshkosh State Teachers College 教授，收到先

生信后,寄赠八本图书。

十一月十五日

先生致信王重民,答复其前询诸事。

> 有三吾弟如晤:
>
> 连接九月三十日、十月七日及廿一日手书,详悉一切。兹分条答覆如左:
>
> (一)东方语言代购之书,其运费由我方担任,请在照相费内暂垫;寄存本馆之关于远东问题之书,其运费亦请代付。
>
> (二)《大公报》现无能力办副刊,《益世报》将在昆明复刊,将来可向其接洽。因学术机关集中昆明或可易办,俟有确信再奉闻。如不要稿费,该报必欢迎也。万斯年、王育伊不日由平南下均在滇,可主编也。
>
> (三)英伦所照,似以用 Leica film 为佳,总以能复制为上。
>
> (四)协会之报两期,曾寄巴黎,以后改寄伦敦。
>
> (五)王景春、熊式一尚无信来,日内再分别函催。
>
> (六)武昌、长沙相继失守,前途似难乐观,国人深恐为捷克之续也。
>
> (七)英庚款二千元,据教部言财部尚未作覆,已一再函催矣。
>
> 兹乘孙洪芬先生飞港之便。匆匆奉复,即颂旅安。
>
> > 同礼顿首
> >
> > 十一月十五日
>
> 照相支出清单均由香港转到。
>
> 巴黎出版关于云南及苗民之书,便中请开一书目,因此间无工具书也。拟编一云南研究资考,资料需要甚殷也。

〔国立北平图书馆用笺。中国书店·海淀,四册〕

十一月十九日

下午二时,先生访吴宓,谈一时许。〔《吴宓日记》第 6 册,页 379〕

> 按:本日所谈之事似为先生请吴宓帮助改稿,11 月 30 日、31 日、12 月 4 日吴宓用三天为先生校对英文稿件。

先生致信国会图书馆编目部,请求寄赠该部有关云南、贵州及中国西南地区的书目信息。

November 19, 1938

Dear Sir:

The National Library is trying to build up a special collection of books relating to southwestern China. We shall be most obliged to you if you will find it possible to send us a Bibliography of books and articles relating to Yunnan and Kweichow provinces as well as various tribes in southwestern China. If you will kindly comply with our request, your courtesy will be gratefully appreciated.

Thanking you in anticipation for your valuable cooperation,

Yours faithfully,

T. L. Yuan

Acting Director

〔平馆(昆明)英文信纸。Library of Congress, Putnam Archives, Special Files, China: National Library 1930-1939〕

按:此件为打字稿,落款处为先生签名,于1939年1月3日送达国会图书馆秘书办公室,4月20日恒慕义似提交了一份相关书单。

十一月二十一日

平馆上海办事处钱存训覆函先生,请示搜集报纸与资料工作。大意如下:

连奉十、廿九及十一、一日赐书,敬悉一一。谨将嘱办各项奉陈于右:

一、《国会图书馆分类法》原存上海十二册,已于十四日交邮寄上应用,计分装十包(内附《新申报》十五份)。

二、号码机已向青年印刷所购置一具,实价十八元,已嘱该所交邮寄出,连同邮、关等税约需二十余元。一俟该所正式发票送到,当由敝处先为代付。

三、寄下禁书书单一份,已分托沪上书店代觅,现市上不见出售此项书籍,恐难望全数觅到。

四、十、廿九日函嘱购 Smythe-*War Damage in the Nanking Area* 一书,查该书已于前购一批西书中同时购到,于上月廿七日付邮寄上。

五、新复刊之《申报》,闻联大已有函嘱该馆每日寄三份。该馆已函寄出,但款尚未付。据该馆称,倘款未到,将于十二月九日内停寄。来示所嘱代联大订寄两份,恐有重复,故未再订,即请查明前订三份款已付讫否?如未付,当由敝处代为付讫。需订两份抑三份,订费每份半年七元五角,邮费在内。《新闻报》拟自明年一月一日起代订二份寄滇,其他外籍报纸多有美商《华美晨晚报》、《中美日报》(本月一日创刊)、《英商译报》、《导报》、《大英晚报》及《晨刊》(小型,最近发刊)、《循环报》等。《译报》、《导报》闻系共产党机关报,编制尚佳。本馆前已订有《文汇报》及《大美晚报》,联大想无须再订。如有需要,当为联大订《译报》二份寄滇。以上各节均请示办。

六、沦陷区域所出报纸甚多,据查得者有十余种,另附一单。此等报纸要否全数搜罗,抑择要觅购。又江浙一带所用之军用手票、北平联银钞票及印花票等有关史料之实物,要搜集否?

七、本馆购书费前由基金会拨到壹佰元,现尚存廿余元,联大订报、又续购画报、什志及新出抗战书籍等,连同前订日文书一批(送到后即须付款),共尚须百元左右。拟请便中见付若干,以应需要。

八、Devéria: Les Lolos Et Les Miao-Tze 一文约十余页,拟得暇即抄打一份寄上。上海 Photostat 设备尚未询得□□□□□□□□□前来本馆阅书,曾有论文数篇,拟用 Photostat 复印,亦未成功也,闻该所亦无此设备。

〔《北京图书馆馆史资料汇编(1909-1949)》,页 644-646〕

按:"奉陈于右","右"当作"左"。*War Damage in the Nanking Area: December, 1937 to March, 1938* 由金陵大学社会学系教授 Lewis S. C. Smythe 编著,1938 年 6 月刊行。Gabriel Devéria (1844-1899),法国外交官、汉学家,对西夏学颇有研究,1888 年获儒莲奖,Les Lolos Et Les Miao-Tze 直译应为"倮倮族与苗族"。此件为钱存训所拟底稿。

十一月二十五日

先生于昆明翠湖公园遇顾颉刚。〔《顾颉刚日记》卷 4,页 166〕

先生致信史蒂文斯,告知平馆将视纸张供应情况恢复编印中文书籍卡片目录,此外因为运输问题中国政府参加纽约世博会的计划被迫中止,自己因之无法访美。

November 25, 1938

Dear Dr. Stevens:

With reference to the Foundation's grant for the printing of Chinese cataloguing cards, you will recall that, at my request, the payment of the grant was withheld by the Foundation since October, 1937.

In order to help develop the cultural life of Southwestern China, we have established our headquarters at Kunming, Yunnan Province, which is beyond the reach of Japan's arms of war. Since November 1, we have resumed the cataloguing of Chinese new publications and we are now preparing the printing of a classified catalogue similar to the A. L. A. Book-List. We shall resume the printing of catalogue cards as soon as there is a sufficient supply of paper.

I have recently returned from a tour of inspection in the southwestern provinces and I have been very much impressed by the good work accomplished along all lines while the undeclared war is going on. For your information I enclose a list of grants made by the Board of Trustees of the British Indemnity Fund which shows that, in spite of the war, a great deal of scientific work is being carried on. Owing to the depreciation of Chinese dollars, all of us hope that some support could come from the United States.

You have no doubt been informed that China was to participate at the New York World's Fair. Arrangements were completed at this end to send our art treasures to New York to be shown at the Metropolitan Museum and I was appointed chief of the delegation. I have been hoping to have the pleasure of showing you around after the treasures are being properly displayed. But at the last moment the whole project had to be given up on account of the unwillingness of the State Department to send a navy transport ship to bring the collection. In view of Japan's blockade, we feel that it would be too risky to send them by ordinary steamers.

With sincere greetings of the Season,

Yours sincerely,

T. L. Yuan

Acting Director

〔平馆（昆明）英文信纸。Rockefeller Foundation. Series 601: China; Subseries 601.R: China-Humanities and Arts. Box 47. Folder 389〕

按：a classified catalogue similar to the A. L. A. Book-List 与 1939 年 1 月 16 日信中的 monthly bulletin of new Chinese publications 应为同一印刷品，具体情况待考。此件为打字稿，落款处为先生签名，似于翌年 1 月 3 日送达。

十一月

先生致电中华图书馆协会，告知因事务繁忙无法赴重庆参加第四次年会。〔《中华图书馆协会会报》第 13 卷第 4 期，1939 年 1 月 30 日，页 10〕

按：本次年会于 11 月 30 日在重庆川东师范学院大礼堂举行。本次年会筹备十分仓促，约在 10 月 20 日始有此议，由在重庆、成都之会员筹划。

十一、十二月间

先生致信西南联合大学，告因平馆迁滇、事务纷杂，对该校图书馆事业不能兼顾，请辞馆长职务。〔《国立西南联合大学史料》第 2 卷，页 77〕

十二月一日

先生撰写 Memorandum Re the Special War Collection at the National Library of Peiping。原文如下：

The National Library has been building up a special collection of source materials relating to the present undeclared war. The major purpose of this undertaking has been to collect and preserve, not only documents of military and war experiences, but also records of social and political significance resulted from the war.

Our chief endeavor is to gather together various materials as they are being produced from day to day, before they should be lost or forgotten. Lack of space precludes the enumeration of all the types of materials which the National Library has actually been collecting, but the following are the chief features:

Newspapers and periodicals

Publications of learned societies and popular organizations

Private documents, Personal diaries and note-books

Intelligence and secret service reports

Books and pamphlets

Maps and charts

Hand-bills, posters and proclamations

Photographs and films

Propaganda material

Reports and records of medical and relief commissions

Records of various public bodies engaged in war work

Thus, with a view to building up a historical collection that would be of great value and use to future scholars, the National Library feels its duty to assemble widely and to preserve permanently whatever materials of the war that could come within its reach. And for this work, we hereby solicit the active co-operation of the public at large to contribute items and to send in materials to enrich our collection. It is also hoped that the Government will eventually see fit to place and deposit the historical archives of various ministries and commissions in the National Library, for the sake of concentration and completion.

Among the materials to be collected, attention should be called to the small pamphlets, private manuscripts, and other ephemeral material which either do not exist in printed form or do not get into the regular book trade. Materials of this kind will certainly perish if they are not collected immediately. And it is such materials which we believe will be most useful to future historians and students, and which of course will be given the greatest care and thought in the work of preservation.

As this work of collecting will be carried on into an indefinite future, we earnestly hope to receive suggestions from anyone interested in this undertaking and from the public at large, as to the methods and especially as to the types and available sources of war materials. Any assistance extended to the National Library will be gratefully appreciated.

T. L. Yuan

December 1, 1938

The Special Committee consists of the following members:

Dr. T. F. Tsiang　　Prof. Yao Shih-Ao

Dr. Yu-lan Feng　　Prof. Liu Chung-Hung

Dr. Fu Sze-Nien　　Prof. Tsien Tuan-Sheng

Prof. Chen Yin-ko　Prof. Ku Chieh-Kang

Prof. T. L. Yuan

按：the Special War Collection at the National Library of Peiping 即中日战事史料征辑会。特别委员会成员依次为为蒋廷黻、姚从吾、冯友兰、刘崇鋐、傅斯年、钱端升、陈寅恪、顾颉刚、先生。该件附在 1939 年 1 月 21 日先生致胡适信中。

十二月二日

先生覆信 J. Periam Danton，感谢美国图书馆协会国际关系委员会积极呼吁全美各图书馆开展对华捐助书刊的努力。

December 2, 1938

Dr. J. Periam Danton

Sullivan Memorial Library

Temple University

Philadelphia, Penn.

U. S. A.

Dear Dr. Danton:

A week ago, I was in receipt of your letter of October 12th with enclosures for which I wish to extend to you my hearty thanks.

As I wrote you on November 18th, Chinese librarians feel most indebted to you and to your Committee on International Relations for your sympathetic appeal for books for China. It is indeed happy news to all of us that the response to your appeal has been most encouraging. We are confident that libraries as well as other learned institutions in the United States will make a great contribution to this cause under your able leadership.

Your communication arrived just in time for the Joint Conference of

Chinese Educational Organizations held in Chungking November 27 – 30. Our Library Association took an active part in this Conference and your message was read before the participating members of these organizations. They wished me to express to you once more our hearty thanks and gratitude.

We are sorry to learn that Mr. Hu made an appeal in the *Wilson Bulletin*, thus causing confusion with the one conducted by your Committee. We have written to him to the effect that the Book Campaign in America is entirely under the direction of the A. L. A. and that books thus collected are to be sent through the Smithsonian Institution.

I should like to know everything about the Sullivan Memorial Library, and if you publish an annual report, will you kindly send a set to us? I trust Mrs. Danton is still engaged in library work.

With many thanks for your valuable assistance and with sincere greetings of the season,

Yours sincerely,

T. L. Yuan

Chairman

Executive Board

〔平馆(冯平山图书馆转)英文信纸。The American Library Association Archives, China Projects File, Box 2, Books for China 1938–1940〕

按:Joseph P. Danton(1908–2002),美国图书馆学家,1916 年曾随家人来华,1924 年回美国入欧柏林学院(Oberlin College),曾赴德国留学,1929 年获得哥伦比亚大学图书馆学学士学位,后在纽约公共图书馆、德国等处短暂工作,1935 年代获芝加哥大学图书馆学博士学位,时任天普大学(Temple University)图书馆馆长。Mr. Hu,待考。此件为打字稿,落款处为先生签名,以航空信方式寄送。

十二月三日

顾颉刚、容肇祖至迤西会馆,与先生晤谈。〔《顾颉刚日记》卷 4,页 169〕

十二月五日

平馆向教育部呈文一件,题为《呈为呈请拨给专款购置中文图籍藉以充实庋藏便利研究事》,具先生名并钤印。

　　　　窃职馆前奉大部指令迁往昆明继续工作,藉以发扬文化提高学术
等因。当即在昆明设立办事处,除与西南联合大学及其他学术机关密切
合作外,并拟定工作大纲逐步推行,庶不负大部之期望,兹将该工作大纲
另纸呈阅,即希鉴核备案。查滇南前以交通关系,文化落后,图书设备诸
多简陋,刻下学术机关集中昆明,日常阅览尚虞不敷,专门著作参稽尤
难,蒐访购置实不容缓。查职馆购书经费向由中华教育文化基金董事会
拨付,旧都沦陷以来,除北平部分仍由该会继续维持外,昆明部分仅有美
金八千元,指定专购西文崀门期刊之用,关于采购中文书报,迄无专款。
窃查国立图书馆对于中文书籍理当广征博采,尽量搜集,以符名实。矧
自暴日侵华以来,各省市所藏图书多被毁于敌人炮火之下,古今典籍荡
然无存,蓄藏精华悉承灰烬,实为文献上之重大损失。我国经此浩劫,亟
应坚强壁垒,力图恢复。拟请大部体念下情,赐予赞助在二十八年度概
算内特拨两万元,专为职馆购置中文书籍之用,匪特重要典籍可得收归
国有,即抗战期内之学术工作亦不致因之停顿。对于西南文化之发扬与
推进,裨益殊多,是否有当,理合呈请鉴核,施行实为德便。谨呈
教育部长

　　　　　　　　　　国立北平图书馆副馆长袁同礼呈(印)

　　　　　　　　　　　　二十七年十二月五日

〔中国第二历史档案馆,教育部档案·全卷宗五,国立北平图书
馆京沪区及昆明办事处工作报告暨庶务方面的文书,案卷号
11609〕

十二月六日

西南联合大学举行第九十六次常委会议,先生以平馆迁滇事忙为由,辞本
校图书馆馆长之职,改馆长制为主任制,馆务由主任严文郁全面负责。西
南联合大学与平馆组织合作委员会,先生为主席,严文郁、陈岱孙、吴有训
代表校方为该委员会委员。〔《北京大学史料》第3卷,页523〕

　　按:12月9日,该校张贴布告,告知先生辞去图书馆馆长职务。[1]
平馆上海办事处钱存训覆函先生,汇报搜集报纸情况及其他杂事。大意

_____

[1] 《国立西南联合大学史料》第4卷,页17。

如下：

奉到十一、廿日手示，敬悉一一。附书单一纸，当即照购。上月份，联大续到日文书及续购各种画报、什志，合 27.28 元，本馆续到西文书，共 21.11 元。联大书款已向李君支付，本馆书账除支尚存 21.26 元，两项账单均交李君转呈。日前中基会转告，谓如需书款，该处尚可续拨，故昨日在孙先生处续支贰百元，以后联大书账即在该款内垫用。

关于抗战史料，本年以前出版书报现市上已无处觅得，本年内新刊者均陆续购寄。兹将上月份新出书单一份奉上，有关抗战各书，拟先购来。昨悉上海通市馆搜有沪战期内各种刊物、传单及宣传品全套至去年底止，惟均装箱藏于某处。倘能阅及，当抄出目录一份，供协会书目之用。

号码机一架亦于日前寄出，连邮税共计 20.10，此款已先代付，兹将发票收据一并奉上。惟据印刷所称，交邮时误与资源委员会圕蒋一前君所购之卡片包裹互掉（惟包裹封皮并未误写）。倘该包寄到时内系卡片，请饬人向万钟街一○五号蒋君互掉。此间已另函蒋君知照矣。

联大所订《申报》，该馆本允寄至本月九日止。昨复前往交涉，请仍续寄，以免中断。报款，俟尊处复信再行付给。又，该报亦可仿《文汇报》办法送赠本馆一份。请馆中备一公函向该馆总管理处接洽。

沦陷区报纸有十余种，上海可以订到，另附报单一纸。拟均自明年起各搜集一份（先订半年），共约二十余元。

前函寄下禁书书单一份，现沪上各处均无法觅到。昨已转托宁波某书社设法代觅，闻可购到一二十种。此项书籍恐寄递不便，拟先存沪，或俟便人带港转寄。

〔《北京图书馆馆史资料汇编（1909-1949）》，页 647-649〕

按："上海通市馆"当作"上海通志馆"。蒋一前，曾任中华图书馆协会检字委员会委员。此件为钱存训所拟底稿。

十二月九日

蒋梦麟、梅贻琦、张伯苓覆函先生，同意西南联合大学与平馆合作征辑中日战事史料。

守和先生惠鉴：

　　顷由寿民先生转来大函，并征辑中日战事史料办法一份，均敬悉。关于征辑中日战事史料事宜，本校愿与贵馆合作。征辑范围之划分，其属于中日文之资料，拟由本校图书馆担任，属于欧美方面之资料，由贵馆担任。将来整理工作，则由本校历史社会学系依照姚从吾先生所拟计划负责办理。至征辑委员会之组织，俟将来有需要时再行设立。所陈各点，如荷同意，即希赐复，俾便早日开始工作为感。专此，顺颂公绥。

弟蒋梦麟、梅贻琦、张伯苓敬启
廿七，十二，九

〔国立西南联合大学公事用笺。《北京图书馆馆史资料汇编（1909-1949）》，页 619-620〕

　　按："寿民先生"即刘崇鋐（1897—1990），字寿民，福建福州人，清华学校毕业，后赴美留学获哈佛大学文学硕士，1923 年归国，先在南开大学历史系教授西洋史，后转清华大学任教。此函为文书代笔，落款三人均钤各自名章，先生在尾处标记"十二月十日复"。

杭立武覆函先生，谈拟派员协助中日战事史料征辑工作、西康考察团人员组成、战时征集图书委员会等事。

守和吾兄大鉴：

　　奉本月五日惠书，敬聆一一。关于贵馆为征集抗战史料，嘱由敝会就协助科学工作人员案内派人协助一节，原不成问题。惟因来函稍迟，全部人员工作已早派完，现仅有刘金宝君，清华历史系毕业，中正中学史地教员，曾译有《简明欧洲历史图解》等。倘荷同意，即当令其前来贵阳山洞，现正在接洽中。济之兄之建议已由行政院交故宫博物院理事会，提会讨论。至西康考察团已聘定邵逸周兄为团长，黄国璋兄为副团长，团员在各校保送中，专家人选则正与团长商洽。承询征求书籍事，弟等曾以"日内瓦世界学生服务社中国分社"名义将兄前为西南联大所拟之书单送日内瓦总会，此外并未向各方募集。惟另有"战时征集图书委员会"系最近由外交、教育等部发起组织，委员七人，有兄在内，该会由教部郭有守兄负责，尚未向外发

信,因闻图书馆协会已由兄向国外图书馆协会征募,当由郭君征询尊见也。附奉敝会协助科学工作人员一览表,以备台察。余不一一,顺颂时绥。

弟杭立武顿首

中华民国廿七年十二月九日

〔管理中英庚款董事会笺纸。《北京图书馆馆史资料汇编(1909-1949)》,页 616-618〕

按:12 月 6 日,"战时征集图书委员会"举行发起人会议、第一次执行委员会会议,各学术机构、团体、教育部、外交部派人参加,张伯苓为委员会主任委员,四川教育厅厅长郭有守为副主任委员。该函为文书代笔,落款处为杭立武签名。

十二月十二日

先生覆信梅贻琦、蒋梦麟、张伯苓,表示平馆同意西南联合大学所拟征辑中日战事史料办法。

月涵、梦麟、伯苓先生尊鉴:

九日大示,奉悉一一。关于征辑中日战事史料所陈各项办法,敝馆完全同意,极盼分工合作,早日观成。专此布复,顺颂台绥。

袁同礼再拜

十二月十二日

〔梁吉生、张兰普编《张伯苓私档全宗》,北京:中国档案出版社,2009 年,页 1057〕①

按:此信与 12 月 9 日蒋梦麟、梅贻琦、张伯苓来函中先生所注回覆时间有别,究为何故,待考。

十二月十三日

平馆上海办事处钱存训覆函先生,汇报资料搜集工作。大意如下:

奉到十一、廿二日手示,敬悉一一。关于 Hoover War Collection 之记载,*Library Journal* 中仅在 Current Literature 栏中查到介绍短文一则,未知原文载于何处。所存工具书中未能查出,兹将该文抄呈一阅。另将刊中有关战争之文字一并录出奉上。

---

① 该信原件藏清华大学档案馆。

关于战事史料及维新政府文献,所见到者均设法搜集。最近购到大道市《府市公报》全份及维新政府《实业月刊》等数册,其中刊有维新官吏合影多帧,但沪上照相店并无出售,容再留意。又,照相店有上海战事照片册出售,未知要购一份否?

前函嘱查 *Mission de Chine* 即原在北平出版之 *Mission en Chine et du Japon*,现移沪出版后已将日本及东北部分除去,改用今名,除去部分闻另出单行本。《文汇报》赠送本馆全份已向该馆取来,均按月装订成册,并无缺少。现按日送到一份,一并保存。十二、十日交邮寄上代联大续购什志两包,想已收到,亦将书单附上备查。

〔《北京图书馆馆史资料汇编(1909-1949)》,页 649-650〕

按:Hoover War Collection 即"胡佛战争特藏",斯坦福大学胡佛研究所之前身,1919 年创立,为胡佛收集的第一次世界大战战时及战后有关各国政治社会变迁的文件,此处应和平馆与西南联合大学合组成立中日战事史料征辑会有关,或想援引 Hoover War Collection 收藏文献的种类和原则。"大道市府市公报"应指"上海大道市政府公报",即 1937 年底上海出现的傀儡政权的政府公报,1938 年 4 月底即改名"督办上海市政府公署公报"。*Mission de Chine* 即 *Les Missions de Chine*《中国传教区》,原由北平北堂(遣使会)印字馆承印,1936 年起改在上海印行。此件为钱存训所拟底稿。

十二月十四日

先生致信王重民,告平馆昆明办事处通讯地址,请其将稿件寄送《益世报·图书副刊》,并谈自己最近行期计划等事。

有三吾弟:

接十一月十八日航信,详悉一一。本馆在"昆明柿花巷二十二号"设立办事处,以后寄信均寄此处可也。近与《益世报》合作,每两周发行《图书副刊》,需稿颇亟,请尊处将愿发表之稿径寄万斯年君。因下月初旬赴港,须俟月杪方能赴滇。二月中,全国教育会议在渝开会,届时又须前往,生活太不安定。伦敦能照 Micro-film 甚好,即照此进行。英庚款补助之生活费,曾向财部请求外汇,尚无覆音,近又函催矣。任叔永近就中央研究院总干事,向君仍在溆浦,有就武大之意。

战事尚难乐观也。匆匆,顺颂旅安。

同礼顿首

十二月十四日

〔中国书店·海淀,四册〕

按:是年 12 月,任鸿隽接替朱家骅出任中央研究院总干事。

十二月十七日

梅贻琦、蒋梦麟、张伯苓覆函先生,告西南联合大学担任中日战事史料征辑
委员会之人员。

> 守和先生惠鉴:
>
> 　　大函奉悉。中日战事史料征辑委员会,本校方面,已请钱端升、冯
> 友兰、姚从吾、刘崇鋐四先生代表参加。特此函达,即希查照为荷。专
> 此,顺颂教绥。

弟蒋梦麟、梅贻琦、张伯苓敬启

〔《张伯苓私档全宗》,页 1057〕

十二月十八日

先生与陶孟和等人赴昆明西山游览。〔《徐旭生文集》第 9 册,北京:中华书局,
2021 年,页 963〕

> 按:徐旭生访先生,不值,在先生客厅初见贵州红崖磨崖①刻石
> 拓片。

十二月二十日

下午,昆明各界人士百余人在圆通公园欢送美国公使,先生亦出席。〔《竺
可桢全集》第 6 卷,页 632〕

先生致信王重民,告《益世报·图书副刊》可随时投稿,并请其调查西南苗
族之记载及关于安南、缅甸之书等事。

> 有三吾弟如晤:
>
> 　　顷由香港转来二日手书,欣悉一切。本馆与《益世报》合作办理
> 《图书副刊》本星期五创刊,每两周发行一次,每次约八千字,请将大稿
> 随时寄万斯年君为荷。英人捐款事此间尚未接到报告,日内当再函
> 催王景春先生。刻下国币低落,如有西人捐款,当不无小补也。本

---

① 今通作“摩崖”。

馆与联大分地办公,本馆之书虽仍寄存联大,但自己有固定工作,仅派三人前往帮助耳。吕叔湘君刻在云大担任英文文学,尚未晤面。觉明或就浙大,或就武大,尚未决定。英庚款补助,近日又函催教部,一俟有复音即可汇英。以后寄信及稿件可寄港,由港再用平信寄滇。顺颂旅安。

同礼顿首
十二月二十日

关于调查西南苗族之记载及关于安南、缅甸之书,可托下列诸人代为调查:

	法国	翁独健	专治中亚西亚
		高名凯	语言学
	英国	许庆光	人类学
		林耀华	

　　法国　翁独健　专治中亚西亚
　　　　　高名凯　语言学
　　英国　许庆光　人类学
　　　　　林耀华

以上系吴文藻面告,便中可一访或通函一询,并告本馆刻正征集西南苗族之文献,托开书目。

同礼

〔中国书店·海淀,四册〕

按:"许庆光"当作"许烺光"(Francis L. K. Hsu,1909—1999),生于辽宁庄河,人类学家,1923 年入南开中学,1933 年由上海沪江大学毕业,1937 年考取中英庚子赔款奖学金赴英国伦敦政治经济学院就读人类学,师从马林诺夫斯基(Bronislaw Kasper Malinowski),1947 年起任教美国西北大学。林耀华(1910—2000),福建古田人,民族学家、人类学家,1935 年获燕京大学硕士学位,1937 年赴美国哈佛大学学习人类学,1940 年获博士学位,此时并非在英国;该信应先寄送香港,29 日再由港转寄王重民。

十二月下旬

先生致信西南联合大学常务委员会,请该校为中日战事史料征辑会提供文具、桌椅等。〔《国立西南联合大学史料》第 2 卷,页 82〕

　　按:12 月 27 日,西南联合大学常务委员会举行第 99 次会议,就该事项议决,因经费问题难以照办。

十二月二十七日

上午,先生访顾颉刚。〔《顾颉刚日记》卷 4,页 177〕

　　按:此次拜访极有可能与筹组中日战事史料征辑会相关。

十二月二十八日

J. Periam Danton 覆函先生,告知美方积极募集捐赠图书,并将寄赠天普大学图书馆馆务报告、指南等印刷品。

December 28, 1938

Dear Dr. Yuan:

　　I was delighted to learn from your good letter of the second that you feel our efforts on behalf of the Chinese institutions have been worthwhile and that some of what we have been trying to do was transmitted to the Joint Conference of Chinese Educational Organizations held in Chungking November 27 to 30.

　　Please concern yourself no further with the matter of Mr. Hu's statement in the *Wilson Bulletin*. I assure you it made not the slightest difference to us personally, and my only reason for mentioning it at all was the fear that American librarians might be confused by two different appeals.

　　I am glad to tell you that the statement which Miss Gregory, a member of our Committee, is reading on my behalf at the Midwinter meeting in Chicago today reports more than 11,000 items already donated. I have personally seen and checked a considerable number of lists from the contributing institutions and insofar at least as this material is concerned, I believe you will find it of a very high order. At any rate, I know that institutions here would welcome it if they did not already have it.

　　I am enclosing a few reprints of my first report as published in the *A. L. A. Bulletin*; I shall send you copies of those which appear in the future. In accordance with your request, I am sending you under separate cover copies of the last two annual reports-the only ones printed-of this library, sample copies of our monthly publication, "On the Shelf," and a copy of the Library handbook. I think these documents will give you the information you are likely to want about us.

With very good wish for the coming year, I am

Cordially yours,

J. Periam Danton

Chairman

〔The American Library Association Archives, China Projects File, Box 2, Books for China 1938-1940〕

按：该函寄送香港，所附各件不存。此件为录副。

十二月底

先生致片王重民，告行踪并告已调王育伊来滇工作。

《图书副刊》已托孙书万由港寄上，大稿请速寄"昆明柿花巷22万斯年君"。王育伊近亦由平调滇工作。下月二日赴港，二月初返滇。

同礼

〔中国书店·海淀四册〕

按：该片无上款、无落款时间，但应附在 12 月 28 日平馆致王重民公函之内，后者告知教育部训令称财政部批准购汇六十英镑。

十二月三十日

下午四时半，中日战事史料征辑会假柿花巷二十二号平馆昆明办事处召开第一次会议，傅斯年、顾颉刚、刘崇鋐、姚从吾、先生出席，颜泽霡记录。先生被推定为该会主席，冯友兰为副主席。本次会议答复王化成、崔书琴二人来函请予研究便利案，讨论经费、资料征集、保存、编纂等问题，并决定自翌年一月四日起展开工作。〔国家图书馆档案，档案编号 1939-※054-综合 2-001007 至 1939-※054-综合 2-001010；《顾颉刚日记》卷4，页 178〕

先生致信王访渔、顾子刚，告知北平经费汇取办法并指示编印卡片业务变动。大意如下：

关于平馆经费，前曾规定每月实支七千四百元，由沪汇平之经费如有升水，其赢余统归尊处，如有损失则由滇馆担负。日前洪芬先生在此，即以此办法商得其同意。又编印卡片因新书较少，在南方亦不易推销。兹拟自下月起改印丛书子目，凡普通性质之大部丛书均可编印。每片所印之数，至多以二百份为限，即希转告编目组同人，查照办理为荷。专此，顺颂时祉。

下年度平方预算请早日决定后,函示为盼。

〔《北京图书馆馆史资料汇编(1909-1949)》,页621〕

按:此虽为抄件,但为先生亲笔。

先生撰写 Memorandum Re the National Library of Peiping。〔Rockefeller Foundation. Series 601: China; Subseries 601.R: China-Humanities and Arts. Box 47. Folder 389〕

按:先生在该备忘录中坦言虽然中基会在1938年度、1939年度均拨付平馆8000美金用以购买外文期刊,但针对学术界和政府部门提供的参考咨询工作十分繁重,且1938年3月起外汇统制让获取西文科学期刊越发困难,平馆亟需得到美方的援助与支持。

平馆上海办事处钱存训覆函先生,请示所购图书、报刊、器材事。大意如下:

日前由滇附下书单两纸,均已陆续购到寄滇,本月份购书费计本馆付出61.81元,代联大付61.67元外、代购邮票十元、代付号码机一□计二十元○一角(此项发票及收条已于本月六日寄滇),总计91.77元。本馆购书费上月存21.26元外,在中基会续支200元,故除本馆购书费及代联大垫款外,尚存67.68元。两单均一并附上即请查收。

沦陷区报纸在沪订到十三份,各半年。又,《新申报》亦续订半年,均自一日起按日送交此处,各报是否需要全部转滇,抑暂存上海,请示知□□。前函嘱代联大订阅《申》、《新》、《译》各报,据称联大均已各订三份,款亦汇来,故未再另订。

本馆致函《密勒氏评论报》改寄昆明,因注明 via Haiphong,该报嘱补邮费贰元。又函购 *Japanese War in China*, v.2 因已于本月八日由此间购寄,故嘱该报勿再另寄。*North-China Herald* 送来明年份报费单卅五元,此款要否由此间拨付,亦请示知。

Dr. Read 于日前由安南返申,前托代索之《文化情报》,允即代索。馆中函托搜集战事史料及照片,表示甚感兴趣。另又将该所之报告及论文集各三册赠送本馆,已于前日付邮转滇。

半年来(六——十二),此间工作除代本馆及联大购办一部书报外,并随时留意搜集沦陷区刊物及维新政府文献。惟以甚少有关熟人,致□无法办到。最近来馆阅书及借出者亦较增加,准予借出者有中法文化协会、北平研究院药物研究所、中法大学药科、雷氏德医学院、科学社生物研究所等,均备有正式公函介绍。科学社方面编目工作:①新编馆中旧藏美政府刊物一套,约四百余种;②改编　册;③书本目录校本已抄制完成,除分类目录外,并附一著者索引,即将付印,约五百余页。

顷接 Blackwell 来函一件,随函转上。

〔《北京图书馆馆史资料汇编(1909-1949)》,页 651-653〕

按:via Haiphong 即通过越南海防之意。Dr. Read 应指伊博恩(Bernard E. Read, 1887-1949),英国药物学家,1920 年至 1935 年在北京协和医学院任教,1935 年担任上海雷士德医学研究院研究员,以下各处皆同。"文化情报"为此前提及的上海自然科学研究所出版物《中国文化情报》。此件为钱存训所拟底稿。

一九三九年　四十五岁

是年初

先生致信美国商务部（Department of Trade and Commerce），告知平馆更换地址，请其将相关出版品改寄云南昆明。大意如下：

> ……Owing to the present situation in China, we have established an office at Kunming, Yunnan.
>
> All publications intended for the National Library of Peiping should henceforth be sent to the above address……
>
> 〔*The Evening Citizen*, Ottawa, Feb. 4, 1939, p. 4〕
>
> 按：平馆从该部获取之期刊应为 *Commercial Intelligence Journal*。

一月二日

先生乘坐火车由滇越铁路离开昆明，前往海防。〔《民国日报》（云南），1939 年 1 月 3 日，第 4 版〕

一月九日

平馆上海办事处钱存训覆函先生，告知今后日文书报寄送办法并谈购买帐薄、卡片及请款购书事。大意如下：

> 由滇赐书三封，均已先后收到，敬悉一是。此间寄滇日文书报，闻遭扣留，但封皮外并未写"日文书"字样，想系沪方检查时所注明，以后日文书报当径寄史料征辑会，以免注意。
>
> 联大所订《申报》，闻款已由滇直接汇来，订阅八个月，至本年六月止，共三份，该馆均按日寄出。《新闻报》及《译报》亦均系同样情形。来示嘱为史料征辑会再订一份，即照办。自复刊起自六月计每月报费十元，本馆一份，由此间备函接洽，已允自复刊赠送全份存沪。
>
> 嘱购登记簿、薄纸片，拟均托便人带港，邮寄恐须纳税，日文书倘能在沪购得一部，亦当带上。最近在大陆新闻广告中录出此类书报约四五十种，共约日金一百余元，拟先订购。最近闻京沪交通已恢复，惟领取通行证等手续甚为麻烦。日下京杭各地刊物应不甚多，京中曾托

人代觅,并无结果。此时前往,恐所获有限,惟当随时注意,倘遇便人当前往一视,顺便可一探工程图书籍。

联大所购卡片尾数 98.73 元,已在本馆帐内垫付,收据已寄交严先生。前在中基会所付贰百元,顷已用罄,账单业于上月底挂号寄港,便中拟再请通知会中续拨贰百元,以便付中文书账等款为盼。

附日文书单。

〔《北京图书馆馆史资料汇编(1909-1949)》,页 653-654〕

按:"严先生"应指严文郁。此件为钱存训所拟底稿。

一月十日　香港

先生致信王重民,谈牛津大学 Henry N. Spalding 捐款及分配可能,并谈陈寅恪赴欧之目的。

有三吾弟如晤:

在滇寄上陆拾镑汇票,想已收到。旋接上月二日及九日手书,详悉一一。Spalding 捐款购书曾否在任何报纸上有所记载? 极愿一阅。此事照例由郭大使通知外交部,将来必为中央各机关分配无余因翁文灏、蒋廷黻等皆愿购书,吾馆恐未能染指,惟愿致函 Spalding 氏表示谢意。请将其名字、爵位查明速覆,至其牛津住址,想可由 Hughes 转到也。郭大使处亦拟寄一信,表示赠本馆之希望,但伊必推到政府,将来似仍须在重庆设法,最好请第三者出面向伊说项,如熊式一、王礼锡诸先生。注重两点:(一)昆明为学术机关集中之地同济、广州中大、中正医学院均移滇,需要较殷;(二)昆明较重庆为安全。关于法方赠书由英转运公司代运一事,如能办到最佳。兹另寄协会信纸,发信时名字下写一 European Representative 即可。英文图章似无需要,因外人认公文信纸及签字为有效也。剑桥所聘德人汉文教授姓名为何? 陈先生愿赴欧闻尚未决定,目的在到维也纳治眼,此中情形不必为外人道也。本月三十日返滇。顺颂旅安。

同礼顿首

一月十日香港

王育伊今日可到港转滇,渠亦协助编辑《图书副刊》。

《益世报》不肯印单行本,仅赠三十份报,实不敷分配也。

〔国立北平图书馆用笺。中国书店 2013 年秋季书刊资料文物拍卖会〕

按:Henry N. Spalding(1877-1953),本谱中译作"石博鼎"①,1909年起开始在英国海军服务,后与妻子在牛津大学设立有关东方宗教、伦理学、东正教、东方艺术等研究奖学金。王礼锡(1901—1939),字庶三,江西安福人,曾与陈铭枢、梅龚彬、胡秋原等人创办神州国光社,1933年赴欧,1938年底归国。

一月十三日

国会图书馆覆函先生,告知前请寄送该馆所藏有关中国西南书籍、期刊文章目录卡片已获批准,随函寄出。

January 13, 1939

Dear Sir:

In response to your letter of November 19 (received by us on January 3), asking for a bibliography of books and articles relating to southwestern China, we send herewith a collection of cards which the Chief Bibliographer has selected from the Library of Congress Catalog under the various subject headings.

Very truly yours,

Secretary of the Library

〔Librarian of Congress, Putnam Archives, Special File, China: National Library 1930-1939〕

按:此为录副。

一月十四日

平馆上海办事处钱存训覆函先生,报告访购书刊事。大意如下:

顷阅致照亭先生手示,敬悉一一。所嘱代购各书及圕用品均已分别照办,薄纸片一万张已托科学公司切好,价廿六元,中文登录簿二本及导片一百张亦均购好。闻最近寄滇包裹不通,拟得便带港。期刊登录卡片印二千张,未知照何格式(中文抑西文),候示再印。

前寄滇日文书,闻遭扣留,未知能否交涉收回。先后所寄各书封皮外均依遵嘱写私人姓名(昆明拓东路迤西会馆袁守和),藉免此间检查□意。所扣一部想系十一月廿五日所寄三包(内装各书十九册,

① 该人译名,参见《中华图书馆协会会报》第13卷第5期,页15。

见发票),此书系托环球代购,发票系写西南联合大学图书馆(此项单据已于十一月份报销时托李君寄滇,函内将副张寄上备查)。倘与当局交涉似可将此项发票作为证明。又以后所寄各书未知有无缺少,另开一单,以便查核。

以前嘱购各日文书报,因不便以本馆及联大名义与内山书店往来,故转托环球书报社代办(现租界内各书店均与日方书店□化),惟以该社价目汇率开价太高,曾数次去函交涉,后允由 1.75 改按 1.25 计算(曾将该社来函随发票附上寄滇)。惟仍较市价为高,故除前已订各书外,新购各书均用个人名义向内山书店购买。惟该店售价均须按定价加一成,汇价按市价计算后环球可少一角上下,但该店不在虹口,倘沪上□□□□□书外□□,托其向东京配订须付定洋等,甚感不便。

平方汇价较为合算,以后日文书籍拟请寄交平方代购,如不便径寄昆明,可嘱由东京径寄此间代为收转。日前寄上书单三纸,其中有十余种已向内山购到,日内拟托人带港再为寄滇,似较由此间寄发为便也。

前嘱订《申报》已代史料征辑会订一份寄滇(寄报地址该馆不允与收据互异,故亦写史料征辑会,未知报销方面有无困难)。本馆一份由此间接洽,自复刊号起赠一全份,并自本月起按日寄滇,前出各份已送存此间。另,本埠各大报经接洽后,允予赠送者有《华美晨报》、《大英夜报》、《大晚报》,均自一月一日起各送一份。《文汇》、《中美》已各承送一份。

寄来《图书半月刊》已收阅,一俟得暇,当将沪出各版新刊择要介绍。

科学社方面编目工作,数月来已将西文书本目录赶编完成,样本已送排印,除分类部分外并附一 author index。日来正忙于校对。俟西文部分印成后,刘先生意似要再为编印中文部分,此事拟俟西文部分完成再说。因此前拟为本馆编制之西文抗战论文索引,迄未得暇着手,中文部分均已抄成卡片,但亦未有暇整理也。

〔《北京图书馆馆史资料汇编(1909-1949)》,页 655-658〕

按:"迤西会馆"即平馆驻昆明办事处、西南联合大学图书馆所在地。环球书报社(International Bookseller, Ltd.),位于博物馆路

（今虎丘路）。《图书半月刊》似为某种油印刊物,内容为分类目录,类似于美国图书馆协会刊行的 Book-List,参见 1938 年 11 月 25 日先生致史蒂文斯信。此件为钱存训所拟底稿。

费正清致函先生,告知其已在哈佛大学组织捐书委员会,希望将募集到的书籍尽可能的赠予清华大学,并就所需书籍的种类、数量上限、运输渠道等向先生征求意见。

Jan. 14, 1939

Dear Mr. Yuan:

We have organized a committee here to make a collection of books to be sent for use in China. We propose to collect from students in the University textbooks of recent date, and from faculty members books which they have recently reviewed favorably or consider as standard works. We propose to limit this collection largely to books on the social sciences. Prof. K. L. Wildes of the Mass. Institute of Technology, Dept. of Electrical Engineering, is making a collection in that field also and would like the same information which I should like.

1. We propose to have a member of each department pass upon the value of the books selected, to insure their quality.

2. We are particularly interested in making this donation available for the use of Tsing Hua University, and we assume that you can dispose of them with that interest in mind.

3. We plan to make the collection in February at the beginning of the second semester with a view to shipping the books in the spring. We assume that they would in any case be too late for use this school year, but that they can be used for 1939-40 if they arrive in the summer time.

There are a number of questions on which we should much appreciate an answer from you as soon as possible, so that we can carry out this plan in the most effective manner.

1. Do you think our plan a sound one? Can you make any suggestion regarding the type of books most needed, the maximum number desirable, or the mode of selecting them?

2.To what destination and by what agency should we ship them? This is the chief question. The Library here has already made a shipment to the International Exchange Service of the Smithsonian, mentioned in your letter.

We have hopes here that American foreign policy is going to come to life and shut off the supplies to Japan. I think efforts of all kinds in the future to rouse the American public will meet a more active response. At any rate, the University community here is more anxious to help. I hope very much that you will tell me any ideas you may have on things that might be done here, whether there are other things more pressing than books that we could supply.

My wife and I hope to see you in Kunming within a couple of years. I need hardly say that Chinese defense and unity in the past year and a half have given us all a great hope in the future.

With sincerest best wishes,

J. K. Fairbank

〔Harvard University, John K. Fairbank personal archive〕

按:此件为录副。

一月十六日

先生致信史蒂文斯,告知平馆中文新书的月刊即将印行并拟寄送中外各学术中心,并再次提交备忘录希望该基金会考虑援助平馆。

January 16, 1939

Dear Dr. Stevens:

I have already reported to you about our work at Kunming. Our monthly bulletin of new Chinese publications is now in the press and copies will be sent to all sinological centres in China and abroad. It takes the place of the *Quarterly Bulletin of Chinese Bibliography*, although it is printed entirely in the Chinese language. Its pages will show in a concrete way how much scientific work is being done in China during the national crisis.

In order to foster every form of intellectual life, we have been making full use of the limited supply of materials which are placed at our disposal. China's need for Western scientific literature is most urgent at the present time, as set forth in the enclosed memorandum which I beg to submit to you. As China's future depends upon her intellectuals, we sincerely hope that our request will receive due consideration from the Trustees of your Foundation. Any personal assistance which you may extend to us will be gratefully appreciated.

With cordial regards,

Yours sincerely,

T. L. Yuan

Acting Director

〔平馆（昆明）英文信纸。Rockefeller Foundation. Series 601: China; Subseries 601.R: China-Humanities and Arts. Box 47. Folder 389〕

按：此件为打字稿，落款处为先生签名，似于2月中旬送达。

一月十九日

战时征集图书委员会（重庆）致函先生，请中华图书馆协会加入该会征集图书序列中，以便更好开展图书募集与分配工作。

守和先生大鉴：

关于中华图书馆协会向美国图书馆协会征集图书事，经先生之努力，已获该会之同情，允向各方捐赠。我国文化前途，实深利赖。兹全国各学术机关团体，因感觉此项工作之重要，已在政府指导下，联合成立战时征集图书委员会，并拟向各国作大规模之宣传与征集，刻正积极进行。为对国际间表示划一，俾收较宏大之效果起见，经本会第二次执行委员会会议决议："凡在本会未成立以前，已向国外征集图书之团体，均拟请其加入本会统一办理，对于已征集之图书，均请集中本会由教育部作最后之分配"纪录在卷。此项决议，一方面可使国际间明了中国政府对于征集图书已有统一之组织，一方面可将已征得之图书，斟酌各方损失及需要情形，作适当之分配，谅荷赞同。尚祈惠示尊见，以利进行，无任企盼之至。再本会成立经告情形，想已由沈祖荣先生转达。兹特检送本会章程，暨历次会议纪录各一份，以供参考。此颂台祺！

战时征集图书委员会启

一月十九日

〔《中华图书馆协会会报》第 13 卷第 5 期,1939 年 3 月 30 日,页 12〕

　　按:"本会成立经告情形"当作"本会成立经过情形"。"想已由沈祖荣先生转达",1939 年 1 月 14 日、2 月 6 日战时征集图书委员会先后举行第二、三次执行委员会,先生皆请沈祖荣作为代表参加。[①]

George J. Beal 覆函先生,请联系驻沪办事处兰安生,证明昆明办事处为平馆合法代表。

January 19, 1939

Dear Dr. Yuan:

　　We received your letter of November 25th in reference to the Foundation's appropriation for printing of Chinese catalogue cards, payment of which has been withheld since October, 1937. We note that you expect to resume the printing of these cards as soon as there is a sufficient supply of paper. This grant, as you know, expires June 30, 1939, and we assume that in connection with the reopening of the grant you have sent to Dr. Grant in Shanghai information in connection with the legal transfer of the Library from Peiping to Kunming and also financial data in connection with the work to be done and possibilities for the future.

Very truly yours,

George J. Beal

〔Rockefeller Foundation. Series 601: China; Subseries 601.R: China-Humanities and Arts. Box 47. Folder 389〕

　　按:George J. Beal 为洛克菲勒基金会(纽约总部)的审计员。此函寄送昆明。

一月二十日

先生致信詹森大使,请其协助平馆向洛克菲勒基金会申请援助,并附去年十二月三十日撰写的备忘录。

January 20, 1939

---

① 《中华图书馆协会会报》第 13 卷第 5 期,1939 年 3 月 30 日,页 19;《中华图书馆协会会报》第 13 卷第 6 期,1939 年 5 月 30 日,页 18。

Ambassador Nelson T. Johnson

c/o Division of Far Eastern Affairs

Department of State

Washington, D. C.

U. S. A.

Dear Ambassador:

All of your friends in China are extremely glad to learn of Your Excellency's safe arrival at Washington. We are looking forward with keen pleasure to your early return.

Your Excellency will probably recall our talks both at Chungking and Kunming concerning China's urgent need of Western books and journals particularly at the present time due to Government's control over foreign exchange.

At the suggestion of my colleagues, I have submitted a memorandum to the Rockefeller Foundation in the hope that due consideration will be given by the Trustees at their next meeting. I beg to enclose herewith a copy of the memorandum for your reference. Should Your Excellency find it possible to write to President Raymond B. Fosdick to support our application, Chinese scholars will be exceedingly indebted to you.

Being far away from the scene of conflict, the Trustees would naturally adopt a more cautious policy. We shall greatly appreciate your assistance if Your Excellency could explain to the Trustees that amidst all the human conflict and turmoil, a great deal of scientific work is being carried on with renewed vigour and enthusiasm.

With kindest regards to you and Mrs. Johnson,

Yours sincerely,

T. L. Yuan

Acting Director

〔平馆(冯平山图书馆转)英文信纸。Library of Congress, Nelson T. Johnson Papers; Rockefeller Foundation. Series 601: China; Subseries 601.R: China-Humanities and Arts. Box 47. Folder 389〕

按:2 月 11 日,詹森致信洛克菲勒基金会主席 Raymond B. Fosdick(1883－1972),表示先生在备忘录中对中国高校、研究机构的描述与自己在重庆、昆明、贵阳等地所见一致,希望该基金会能够妥善考虑先生申请援助的请求。此件为打字稿,落款处为先生签名,另附备忘录一份,共两页。

一月二十一日

先生致信胡适,告其中日战事史料征辑会工作计划、收集范围、委员构成,希望中基会年会对该项目给予特别资助。

January 21, 1939

Dear Dr. Hu:

Knowing that you will be interested in our special war collection, I enclose herewith a statement regarding its present status as well as our future plans.

Among our desiderata, we are particularly anxious to have copies of your addresses delivered before public bodies in Europe and America. In the case of important documents, we shall treat them as confidential and shall not allow anyone to consult them unless we get from you the necessary permission.

As we are building up a historical collection, any duplicate material which you or your Embassy may wish to dispose of will be most gratefully received.

The annual meeting of the Trustees of the China Foundation is scheduled for April 10th. Should Mr. Greene be able to come out, I hope you will discuss with him about our plans. All members of our Committee hope that US $ 10,000 would be granted by the China Foundation for this purpose and any personal assistance which you will be able to extend to us will be gratefully appreciated.

Professor Yao is mailing to you his unpublished manuscript about our work and he hopes that you would kindly give us some advice.

I wish to add that amidst all the human conflict and turmoil, a great deal of scientific work has been carried on. Through our collection of scientific journals, we have been rendering invaluable services to various government departments and scientific institutions, not to mention a large number of refugee scholars now concentrated at Kunming.

With warmest regards,

Yours sincerely,

T. L. Yuan

〔平馆（昆明）英文信纸。台北胡适纪念馆，档案编号 HS-JDSHESE-0393-011〕

平馆上海办事处钱存训覆函先生，报告图书采访事。大意如下：

昨日奉到一月九日及十二日赐书，敬悉——。附来书单及介绍信件亦均收到，中基会事即当遵嘱前往办理。惟现孙先生以足疾未到会，尚未晤面。因此间每日常存信件及须接洽之事，故拟于每日下午前往。据金先生告，谓本馆购书账及福利储金两项账目甚繁，大约均须交由本馆自理。至时间是否足够支配，拟俟晤孙先生后再议。

前托 Dr. Read 代索之《中国文化情报》，昨收到十二日出版之第十三期一份，已随时转港。以前各期恐已无存，已函请代询矣。

本馆购书事当随时留意，附下日文书单已函内山书店派人前来接洽，作为史料会委托个人代办，不以办事处名义往来可也。联大付款贰百元已收到，以后垫款及本馆书账当分列。本馆搜集资料事，前在 Dr. Read 处曾见馆中所发乙份，其他各处，未知已有何处业经去函接洽请求协助者，盼示知数处，俾易于接洽。

代联大所购日文书报，现尚存沪未寄，未知滇方能否交涉不至扣留，并请示知为幸。

〔《北京图书馆馆史资料汇编(1909-1949)》，页 658-659〕

按："金先生"应指金绍基。此件为钱存训所拟底稿。

一月二十二日

先生访蔡元培，告知平馆文津街馆舍照常开放。清华大学图书馆阅览室住日本伤兵，北京大学第二院未被扰乱，图书馆封存未动。惟缪荃孙旧藏拓片存国学研究院，稍有损失。另，中法大学因受扰停办。〔《蔡元培日记》，页 598〕

按："第二院"即京师大学堂旧址，北大数学系等理科院系所在，旧址在今东城区沙滩后街 55 号院。"国学研究院"，似指北京大学研究院文科研究所。

一月二十四日

平馆上海办事处钱存训覆函先生，报告文具购买、平馆购书账目工作。大意如下：

> 兹托赵善之君赴港之便，带上小包一件，内系薄纸卡片一万张，三组导卡二百张，又战事照片册一部；函内附上托人在京觅得军用手票四种，照片二张，又海关及俄文书目数种，均请一并查收。

> 顷奉十九日手示，得悉尚需五组导片 200 件及登记簿一册（二册已寄滇），当另购寄 National Christian Council 之文件，日内当前往一询。倘能取到，当托任先生之便带港。

> 中基会已自本星期起每日下午前往，购书账已接手办理。孙先生足疾未愈，尚未晤面。日文书购到二十余种，因携带不便，已由沪交邮寄滇（现限定每日每处只能寄两件）。前代本馆所购西文书亦已寄出，书单附上备查。

〔《北京图书馆馆史资料汇编（1909-1949）》，页 660〕

> 按：赵善之，与胡适有旧①，其子赵树林似曾在平馆任职。National Christian Council 即中华全国基督教协进会，其会址位于上海圆明园路 169 号。此件为钱存训所拟底稿。

一月二十六日

先生致信 William A. Simmons，请其在美协助募集再版、新旧书刊以利中国学者在困境中继续研究工作。

January 26, 1939

Dear Sir:

Ever since Japan's military occupation of Peiping, all national institutions of learning in that historical city have been unable to function. In view of this situation, we have established an office at Kunming, Yunnan. We have been collecting books and journals in order to meet the intellectual needs of Chinese scholars in this hour of distress. As many of our universities and scientific institutions have been deliberately destroyed by Japanese militarists, the need of scientific literature felt by the Chinese

---

① 台北胡适纪念馆，档案编号 HS-JDSHSC-1505-001。

scholars is especially urgent at the present time.

In order to keep Chinese scholars informed as to the recent development of various branches of science, we are building up a special Reprint Collection which will be of great value to investigators engaged in scientific research.

Knowing that your institution has made notable contributions to learning and cognizant of your intellectual sympathy for China, we earnestly hope that you will find it possible to ask each member of your scientific staff to send us a complete set of his reprints if they are still available for distribution.

As we have to start our work entirely afresh, we are in urgent need of books and periodicals of all kinds, old and new, especially standard works in various fields. Donations of books from American and Canadian authors may be sent to us care of the International Exchange Service, Smithsonian Institution, Washington, D. C. which makes monthly shipment to China. Should any of your friends be willing to lend a helping hand in the rehabilitation of our collections, will you kindly make the necessary contact for us?

As a great deal of scientific work is being carried on in China in spite of the war, your contributions will render a great service to the present and future generations of intellectual workers in this country.

Thanking you in anticipation for your kind co-operation and assistance,

Yours faithfully,

T. L. Yuan

Acting Director

Mr. William A. Simmons
Association of Business Officers of Preparatory Schools
Tarrytown, N. Y.

〔Smithsonian Institution Archives, Records, 1868－1988 (Record Unit 509), Box 1, National Library, Peiping〕

按：William A. Simmons，该人生平待考。此件为录副。

平馆上海办事处钱存训覆函先生，告知向中华全国基督教协进会等机构索取文献的进展。大意如下：

昨托赵善之君赴港之便，带上卡片包一件及目录函件，日内当可送到。所有书籍因携带不便，均由此间寄滇，其余各书俟有價到，当再寄去。又嘱购德文报及俄文报，自 1937 七月起至 1938 底，嘱查出一份，惟均不全，每月约缺少四五份，是否需要购存，即请示知（每份全年约廿元）。

《期刊日报索引》及《人文月刊》均已托人设法检一全份，《人文月刊》（已出八年）或可允赠送全份，尚在接洽，其余书籍□书店均不□允，容当留意。昨赴 National Christian Council 晤 C. L. Boynton 先生，得悉允予送存本馆之文件尚未整理就绪，其内容大概包括南京、杭州等地之通信及报告，闻此项文件仅有五份，N. Y. State Council, London Embassy, □□□□□及其本人各存一份，其余一份则拟送存本馆。现因一部为各报馆借用，故拟俟整理完备并装订成册，再为送来。其他尚有关于难民救济及捐款文件、广播文稿及 *Bulletin*，谓亦可送存一份。伊谓事甚忙，大约再有数星期当来函通知，届时前往领取。

《译报》已为联大另订一份寄史料会，前预约百期合订本已出版，日内即寄滇。《文汇报年刊》亦为联大预约一册，又前代联大购各画报、什志，因中国图书公司允有办法寄滇不致检查，故均各订半年（共九种），将来即由该公司负责直接寄出，其余新书当随时购寄，勿念。

〔《北京图书馆馆史资料汇编(1909-1949)》，页 661-662〕

按：《期刊日报索引》应指《期刊索引》和《日报索引》，由中山文化教育馆编印，均为月刊；前者涵盖国内期刊二百余种，后者以《申报》、《新闻报》、《时事新报》、《中央日报》、《武汉日报》、《大公报》、《晨报》（北平）、《工商日报》（香港）、《国民日报》（广州）、《星洲日报》（新加坡）等十种报纸为对象。《人文月刊》，1930 年 2 月由钱新之、穆藕初、徐静仁、王儒堂等人创刊，该刊以现代史料为核心，尤其侧重社会经济方面，并以民国大事类表与杂志索引为特色。C. L. Boynton 即 Charles Luther Boynton（1881－1967），美国浸礼宗来华传教士，毕业于纽约协和神学院（Union

Theological Seminary），时任中华全国基督教协进会（National Christian Council）干事。此件为钱存训所拟底稿。

二月二日

平馆上海办事处钱存训覆函先生，报告平馆、联大中西文购书账目信息及采购图书馆文化用品情况。大意如下：

兹寄上一月份本馆及联大购书单据卅一张，清单各二份，计本馆购书账付出 94.32 元，代联大垫付 135.00 元正。兹遵嘱将前中基会拨付三百元作为联大垫款，本月廿一日续付贰百元作为本馆西文书费。兹分别报告如下：

代联大垫付购书费，计十月份 53.40 元及十一月 27.28 元，合计 80.68 元，系由李照亭君在办事处经费内垫付，账已由李君报销。十二月 91.77 元及本月 135.00 元，合计二二六.七七元，则在三百元内扣除，计尚余七十三元二△三分正。

本馆西文书费自上年十月至本年一月止，共付 231.27 元（见清单），除收中基会最近拨付贰百元外，尚不敷卅一元二△七分。兹拟请在联大账内再付贰百元，以便付定购之日文书及什志、报纸等账，则连前合共五百元，可由联大当局正式备函请中基会发款时扣还。另本馆西文书账亦盼再付若干，以便随时应用。至于本馆所购中文书等，以后均将账单交请李君照付，以便与西文书账分列。

上月由港寄下应购日文书单及 1937 至最近之日文什志、报纸等，本嘱内山书店派人前来接洽，迄无回音。故现托圕服务社设法向东京直接往来，价格或可较廉。

前次来示，提及内地需用圕用品甚多，嘱此间商店到滇开设分店，此事曾与圕服务社（现由文华校友陈鸿飞君主持）商洽，大约目前派人到滇甚多困难，倘协会或其他机关能设法代理为最好，可需先付□□若干成。由此间制成大批运滇，售出后由该社给予代理人经售佣金，则西南、西北各内地图书馆需要用品者可径向协会定购，必多便利。此事倘协会认为可办，当再嘱该社将详细办法说明，径向协会接洽可也。

〔《北京图书馆馆史资料汇编（1909-1949）》，页 663-665〕

按：陈鸿飞（1904—?），山东益都人，山东齐鲁大学毕业后留该校图书馆服务。1931 年考取武昌文华图书馆专科学校,与童世纲等人为同学;1936 年至 1938 年任上海市图书馆特藏部主任;1939 年成立"中华图书馆服务社",任理事长;1940 年 2 月赴沙县出任福建省立图书馆馆长。此件为钱存训所拟底稿。

二月七日

先生致信费正清,感谢哈佛大学成立向中国捐赠书籍的委员会,告知平馆亟需国际法、国际关系等领域的图书,对寄赠出版品的可行渠道给出建议,并谈中日战事史料征辑会的工作,请其在美留意相关书刊、报纸。

February 7, 1939

Dear Dr. Fairbank:

Words fail me to express to you my keen pleasure and deep gratitude for your air-mail of January 14th. The news contained in your letter is particularly welcome at a time when Chinese intellectuals are in such urgent need of assistance.

I am delighted to learn that a committee has been organized at Cambridge to make a collection of books for China. The fact that you have already given so much thought on their selection is especially appreciated. I am confident that through the good offices of your Committee, a collection of books representative of American scholarship and learning will be sent to China.

Concerning the type of books needed here, I wish to advise that all standard works in various fields are needed in China especially in view of the loss and destruction of so many scientific libraries. But since you are limiting your selection largely to books on the social sciences, may I request that you make a special effort in gathering material for the National Library in the field of international law and relations? China would need such material as soon as we have the peace conference. For your information, I enclose herewith a memorandum regarding the present status of National Library.

For teaching purposes, books on sociology, economics, statistics, public finance and commerce would be most welcome. Donation of books for Tsing Hua University should be marked in order to avoid any possible confusion. If the number of volumes is not very large, you may like to send them by book-post directly to Tsing Hua at its Kunming address.

The other alternative is to forward the boxes to Hong Kong through the International Exchange Service, Smithsonian Institution, Washington, D. C. which makes monthly shipment to the Library Association of China. Our Association would send by book-post those items especially needed by Tsing Hua. A list of books (in duplicate copies) thus donated should be sent to us for reference.

The freight traffic between Haiphong and Kunming is already too much congested, and with the French way of conducting business, it usually takes three or four months for such boxes to go through Indochina alone! Under these circumstances, it does not seem advisable to send the boxes by freight to Kunming via Haiphong.

The National Library will be very glad to pay transportation charges from Cambridge to Washington, if the books are destined for this Library. I am writing to Prof. K. L. Wildes giving him the same information contained in this letter.

I am also enclosing a statement regarding the special war collection which we have been building up at Kunming. Being a historical scholar, I trust you will be interested in this undertaking. May I, therefore, look forward to your help? Any material published since September, 1931, which your University community may wish to dispose of will be most gratefully received.

I wish to add that in spite of the undeclared war, a great deal of scientific work is being carried on in China. Even amidst all human conflict and turmoil, there is always good news.

All of us feel keenly that if supplies to Japan can be shut off, it would be a most desirable thing and we are sure that public opinion in America is already moving towards the right direction.

With renewed thanks for your assistance in the re-establishment of our intellectual edifice,

Yours faithfully,

T. L. Yuan

Acting Director

〔平馆（昆明）英文信纸。Harvard University, John K. Fairbank personal archive〕

按：此件为打字稿，落款处为先生签名。

二月八日

平馆向教育部陈立夫呈文一件，题为《请转咨财政部准予按照法定汇率再购英镑贴补王重民在英生活费用》，具先生名。

　　案查职馆馆员王重民奉派在英法两国影照燉煌古写本，于学术前途至关重要。其工作费曾于九月间呈请大部转咨财政部购买外汇，当承该部渝钱汇字第九九三号准购外汇通知书节开准，凭该通知书向昆明中央银行购汇英金六十镑在案。查该款仅敷四个月之用，用特再行呈请转咨财政部念此事之重要，准予按照法定汇率再购英金陆拾镑，以便该员继续工作，不致中途辍业，实为德便。崇此上呈，伏希鉴核。

谨呈

教育部长

国立北平图书馆副馆长袁同礼谨呈

廿八年二月八日

〔中国第二历史档案馆，教育部档案·全卷宗5，国立北平图书馆请拨员工学术研究补助费经常费有关文书，案卷号11616（1）〕

先生致信史蒂文斯，报告此前洛克菲勒基金会资助平馆刊印中文书籍卡片目录项目之余额，并表示平馆近期有可能恢复印行，询问未拨付的资助款可否移作购买美国出版的书籍和期刊。

February 8, 1939

Dear Dr. Stevens:

　　With reference to the Foundation's grant of US $ 18,000.00 for the printing and distribution of Chinese catalogue cards, I beg to enclose herewith a statement regarding the receipts and expenditures up to February, 1939.

From the enclosed statement, you will note that out of the grant of US $ 18,000.00, we have received from the Foundation only US $ 7,500.00 which was equivalent to Sh $ 24,930.00. Out of this sum, there is held in the Bank a balance of Sh $ 6,959.28.

As the work of printing and distribution of catalogue cards was suspended under circumstances entirely beyond our control, may I make the following suggestions?

1. Taking advantage of the facilities available at Peiping, we propose to resume the printing of these cards on a smaller scale by our Peiping office. This service and our new bibliographical bulletin would supplement each other and would serve as an essential link between Chinese and Western scholars. I therefore propose that the unexpended balance of Sh $ 6, 959. 28 be used for these two projects.

2. Concerning the balance of US $ 10, 500. 00 not yet paid to the National Library, we venture to request that sympathetic consideration be given to the present difficulty of obtaining American books and periodicals by Chinese educational institutions as a result of Government control over foreign exchange. The reasons for suggesting a diversion of the grant from printed cards to printed books are set forth in the enclosed memorandum.

As you might have received similar requests from other institutions in China, we earnestly hope that conditions would be more favorable this year for a recommendation for changes in these projects necessitated by unforeseen conditions resulted from the war.

But if you do not see your way of acceding to this request, we shall expect that the unpaid balance be held in trust temporarily by the Foundation until permanent peace is restored in China when we shall be able to carry on the work on a larger scale.

With kindest regards, I am

Yours sincerely,

T. L. Yuan

Acting Director

〔平馆(昆明)英文信纸。Rockefeller Foundation. Series 601: China; Subseries 601.R: China-Humanities and Arts. Box 47. Folder 389〕

按:此件为打字稿,落款处为先生签名,随信附 Statement Re the Expenditure of the Rockefeller Foundation Grant for the Printing and Distribution of Chinese Catalogue Cards 两页,Memorandum Re the Establishment of a Bureau of American Bibliography in the National Library of Peiping, Kunming, Yunnan, China 一页。

二月九日

中国驻英大使郭泰祺覆函先生,告先生前此寄送备忘录已获英方人士、机构积极响应,石博鼎等人已捐资购书,并将于最近寄送书刊。大意如下:

> 径启者,阁下前致敝人之备忘录,已在英国获有良好之结果。牛津大学石博鼎先生,已开始发起为中国各大学募集图书。想阁下闻此消息,必感无穷之欣慰。石先生本人愿先捐二千英磅,在英购置图书,以为之倡;并愿继续捐赠三千英磅,如牛津其他人士,亦能凑成同样或更较大之数额。现为此事已成立一委员会,专司选择图书事宜,其第一批捐募之书,并于本月内即可寄出矣。敬颂台祺!

弟郭泰祺谨启

一九三九,二,九。

〔《中华图书馆协会会报》第 13 卷第 6 期,页 12〕

按:郭泰祺(1888—1952),字保元,号复初,湖北广济人,时任中华民国驻英大使,后又改任外交部长、最高国防会议外交委员会主席等职。原函为英文,后被译成中文刊登。

二月十一日

平馆上海办事处钱存训覆函先生,报告接洽《密勒氏评论报》等西方社团组织以获取文献资料的进展。大意如下:

> 在港先后寄下各函及介绍信、书单等件均已收到。兹将各处接洽情形奉告于后:
>
> 《密勒氏评论报》、J. B. Powell 对于本馆征集史料甚表兴趣。该报所载各项照片,均允由本馆翻印一份,惟以并无底片,故复印每张需

费一元至一元五角,如要一全份,约二□张。此项印费似嫌太巨(亦有多数系内地寄来),故与该处商定,俟尊处随时视需选定该片前□要,再为开明接洽专印。上次本拟先择一部文化机关被毁照片添印,然以为数不多亦甚普通(约七八张),故未决定,仅先购日方宣传画照片四种(付价贰元)。至于各项资料,Mr. Powell 允予随时留意,伊复介绍往晤 American Chamber of Commerce 秘书 Mr. Howes,在该处觅得该会所印小册子数种,关于外人在华投资损失情形,曾请其将各方报告录一副份,据称此项情形均保存于美领署,现时尚系秘密文件,恐难索得。关于日方新闻检查制度,American Book Shop 经理 Mr. F. D. Mortimer 或有相当材料供给,日内当前往一询。

又《新申报》等单据,往订时系具名钱公垂,该处误写公□,因系收据不允另补,倘馆中不便报销,请将该条寄下,可嘱圖服务社设法另开一代订发票也。

民 23《中国外交年鉴》、Young-*The International Relations of Manchuria* 等均已觅得旧书,价甚廉。《海关条约》二册可购到,每部 35 元,未知需要否? 又 China Information Committee (原在汉,现迁港) 及 Shanghai Federation of Culture Assn.出有小册多种,未知馆中已有否?

〔《北京图书馆馆史资料汇编(1909-1949)》,页 665-667〕

按:J. B. Powell、Mr. Powell 即 John B. Powell(1919-2008),美国新闻记者,《密勒氏评论报》编辑。American Chamber of Commerce 即驻华美国商务会,位于福州路 209 号,Mr. Howes 即 James Howes,确为该会秘书。American Book Shop 即中美图书公司,其地址位于上海南京路 160 号。[1] *The International Relations of Manchuria* 全称为*The International Relations of Manchuria:a digest and analysis of treaties, agreements, and negotiations concerning the three eastern provinces of China* ,Walter Young 著,1929 年芝加哥大学出版该书,后由蒋景德翻译,书名译作《满洲国际关系》,1931 年 11 月由神州国光社出版,本文第十六封信中亦提及购到此书。"海关条约"应指*Treaties Conventions etc. between China*

---

[1] *The North-China Desk Hong List*, 1939, pp. 51、68.

and Foreign States, 1908 年初版, 由海关总税务司署(Inspectorate
General of Customs)发行, 该书收录了 1689 年至 1908 年间清朝与
各国订立的条约, 按国别分类编次, 各条约均以中西原文对照排
印。China Information Committee 应指中国情报委员会, 国民政府
于 1937 年筹设, 负责对外宣传抗日战争, 其最初办公地点位于上
海, 后经南京、汉口、长沙, 最终于 1938 年迁至陪都重庆, 并在香港
设有分支。钱存训极有可能不清楚内陆情况, 故有"原在汉, 现迁
港"之说。此件为钱存训所拟底稿。

詹森大使覆函先生, 告知已应先生前请致信洛克菲勒基金会主席 Raymond
B. Fosdick, 请后者妥善考虑援助平馆, 并谈个人休假计划。

February 11, 1939

Dear Dr. Yuan:

Your letter of January 20 has just reached me and I shall be glad to
write to Dr. Fosdick in the matter. I took occasion, while in New York the
other day and when talking to people interested in colleges and other
enterprises in China, to say that one of the ways of helping with the work
of education in China would be to send out books and I found people
interested in that. I hope that you will receive a sympathetic response.

I have been very busy here in Washington during the last two weeks
and am now looking forward to the real holiday that is coming when I can
go to Cody and spend a couple of months with the children before
returning to China.

With kindest regards, I am

〔Library of Congress, Nelson T. Johnson Papers〕

按:Cody 似指怀俄明州帕克县(Park County)的度假地。该件为
录副, 无落款。

二月十三日

先生致信鲍曼, 推荐严文兴前往匹兹堡大学学习。

February 13, 1939

Dear Dr. Bowman:

You will probably recall that when you were in Hong Kong last

September, we talked about the desirability of assisting young Chinese scientists to pursue graduate studies at the University of Pittsburgh. It was very kind of you to promise to look into the matter after your return and to see whether something might be done for its realization.

For the past few months, I have been thinking over the matter and I now have the pleasure in enclosing herewith a statement regarding Mr. Yen's academic career.

Under separate cover, I am sending you several professional papers published by Mr. Yen. He seems to be a highly qualified candidate worthy of your consideration and support.

As China needs trained men more than anything else to assist the great task of reconstruction after the war, I sincerely hope that your University may find it possible to offer Mr. Yen a fellowship which would enable him to pursue advanced studies at your great institution. I need hardly say that any courtesy and assistance which your University would extend to him will be gratefully appreciated.

With sincerest thanks and cordial regards,

Yours faithfully,

T. L. Yuan

Acting Director

〔University of Pittsburgh Library, John Gabbert Bowman, Adminis-trative Files, Box 2 Folder 13, Chinese Material〕

按：Mr. Yen 即严文兴（Yen Wen-Hsing, 1909—2012），湖北汉川人，严文郁之弟，1930 年上海圣约翰大学毕业，后入燕京大学研究生院学习化学。该件为录副。

先生致信阿博特，感谢史密斯森协会及其国际交换服务的成员馆给予中国学术界的援助。

February 13, 1939

Dear Dr. Abbot:

We have so far received one hundred and four boxes of books donated by American libraries and institutions which your Institution has so kindly forwarded to this Association. We understand that more boxes will be forwarded to China, as soon as sufficient materials have been accumulated at Washington.

As Chinese universities and scientific institutions have been forced to migrate to the remote West to carry on their work without books and journals, the contributions made by American libraries and institutions will aid materially the cause of education and culture in China particularly at a time of our national crisis.

While we are unpacking the boxes forwarded by your Institution, I hasten to write to express to you our deep sense of gratitude for this scholarly cooperation and assistance. May I convey to you and through you to all members of the International Exchange Service our heart-felt thanks and great admiration for the valuable help you have given to Chinese libraries. Your courtesy and assistance has won our everlasting gratitude.

Yours very sincerely,

T. L. Yuan

Chairman

Executive Board

〔中华图书馆协会（冯平山图书馆转）英文信纸。Smithsonian Institution Archives, Records, 1868-1988 (Record Unit 509), Box 1, Library Association of China, Hong Kong〕

按：此件为打字稿，落款处为先生签名，于 3 月 28 日送达。

二月十五日　昆明

下午四时半，中日战事史料征辑会假平馆昆明办事处召开第二次会议，冯友兰、姚从吾、刘崇鋐、先生出席，颜泽霈记录。讨论请款案、本会工作人员职务分配案。通过决议，推定蒋廷黻为本会名誉委员；姚从吾为总编纂，刘崇鋐为副编纂；函聘郑天挺、钱穆为中文编辑；函聘蔡维藩、雷海宗、皮名举、叶公超、王信忠、傅恩龄、吴达元、邵循正、刘泽荣为外文编辑；颜泽霈为干事。〔国家图书馆档案，档案编号 1939-※054-综合 2-001011 和 1939-※054-综合 2-001012〕

按：蔡维藩（1898—1971），字文侯，南京人，历史学家，1924 年毕业于金陵大学，后赴美留学，1930 年归国在南开大学任教，时任西南联合大学历史系教授，其与雷海宗、叶公超为英文编辑；皮名举（1907—1959），湖南善化人，时任西南联合大学历史系教授，为德文编辑，后又增聘冯文潜①；傅恩龄，字锡永，北平顺义人，1918年留学日本，在庆应大学经济地理专业学习，归国在南开大学任教，时任西南联合大学外文系教授，其与王信忠皆为日文编辑；王信忠（1909—?），江苏南通人，日本史专家，1927 年入清华大学历史系，师从蒋廷黻，后被公派留学日本，抗日战争爆发遂归国在西南联大历史系执教，1943 年 8 月初离开昆明赴美；吴达元（1905—1976），祖籍广东中山，生于上海，清华大学外文系毕业，后赴法国深造，时任西南联合大学外文系教授；邵循正（1909—1972），字心恒，福建侯官人，历史学家，清华大学毕业后赴法留学，师从伯希和，时任西南联合大学历史系教授，与吴达元同为法文编辑；刘泽荣（1892—1970），字绍周，广东肇庆人，早年随父前往俄国，毕业于圣彼得堡大学，时任西南联合大学外文系教授，为俄文编辑。

二月十六日

先生致信王重民，告知刘修业《云南书目》完备后可在上海印刷，并谈离欧前注意事项。

有三吾弟：

顷由港转到二月三日来书，敬悉一一。《云南书目》自以补充完备再付印为是。昆明印刷不易，香港又贵，将来或改在沪付印。Vial已去世，Savina 亦病，其苗族历史在安南亦未觅得，请在各书店书目中随时注意，代为购置一部为盼。燉煌资料在离欧以前应尽量搜集，以后能否赴欧颇是问题。小孩应携至华京寄存教会中或其他教养机关，当托吴光清代为一询，想携美与留巴黎所费相等，而可免将来再赴欧也。况欧局不安，难保一、二年内不发生战事，故稿件及照片亦应送美保存，似较巴黎为安全也。寄去之六十磅系挂号信，想此时已收到。

①《国立北平图书馆、国立西南联合大学合组中日战事史料征辑会工作报告》，1939 年，页 12。

《益世报》需要之文以关于时事者为最欢迎,普通考据之文章只能慢慢付印。三月一号,全国教育会议在渝开会,现定廿五号赴渝。Spalding 捐款事当与张伯苓、杭立武诸先生一谈,看此情形吾人不易染指,现正在美国进行。尊处之余款正与教部交涉,仍请转洽财政部批准售与外汇,但不识又需若干时日耳。顺颂旅安。

同礼顿首
二,十六

外一信阅毕加封寄出。寄 Hummel 之信日内即写。

〔袁同礼家人提供〕

按:Vial 即 Paul Vial(1855-1918),中文名邓明德,法国传教士,长期在云南传教,专门研究彝学。Savina 即 François Marie Savina(1876-1941),法国传教士、人类学家,长期在越南、老挝等地传教。《云南书目》即 A Selected Bibliography of Yunnan and of the Tribes of Southwestern China,后刊于《图书季刊》英文本 New Series Vol. I, No. 1, 3, 4; Vol II, Nos. 3-4,该目本拟分为 8 类,但实际只刊登了前 6 类,分别是概述和游记、自然科学、交通、商贸、回教、历史语言文学,共计 1231 个条目,第 7 西南少数民族和第 8 地图和影集并未刊登。

史蒂文斯覆函先生,重申 RF36072 项目的资助范围,言明该项目款不能挪作《图书季刊》英文本复刊之用,此外先生前此申请基金会资助平馆购买外文书刊的请求不予考虑。

February 16, 1939

Dear Mr. Yuan:

Your letter of January 16 gives welcome news of activities in your new location. I believe that Mr. Beal wrote you on January 19 regarding our grant that expires on June 30, 1939. This was for a three-year period to provide for the development of the card catalogue of current publications 1931 ff., for the visit of the representatives of the American Library Association, and for reproduction of Chinese materials for American scholars. The plan to resume publication of your *Chinese Bulletin of Bibliography* falls outside this grant and would therefore need to be carried on your own funds. You may be thinking of the earlier appropriation for the Bulletin. This was kept open until December 31, 1938, in order that you might give an accounting on the last items of printing. On Mr. Koo's request the account then was closed at the Shanghai office of the Foundation.

On the other matter in your letter, namely the extended purchase of scientific literature beyond what is provided from the China Foundation, I can now only repeat the report of last spring, I greatly regret that it is not feasible for us to recommend extensive purchases of library materials. A considerable service to the National Rural Administration continues through the China program of Mr. Gunn. Beyond that and the aids to various institutions I fear we are now not in a position to go.

Sincerely yours

David H. Stevens

P. S. At our March meeting I will bring up the recommendation to extend the grant for one year and to change the terms for use as indicated in your letter.

〔Rockefeller Foundation. Series 601: China; Subseries 601.R: China-Humanities and Arts. Box 47. Folder 389〕

按:该函寄送昆明,此件为录副。

二月十八日

先生访徐森玉,稍后徐旭生亦来。〔《徐旭生文集》第 9 册,页 985〕

二月二十日

先生致信石博鼎,对其捐款帮助中国各大学购买图书之举动,表示感谢。〔《中华图书馆协会会报》第 13 卷第 6 期,页 11〕

二月二十二日

刘文典邀先生和徐旭生约期晤谈。〔《徐旭生文集》第 9 册,页 987〕

按:24 日,徐旭生忽记起此事。

二月二十四日

先生访徐旭生,提出平馆与国立北平研究院合作办法数条,请其与李书华相商。〔《徐旭生文集》第 9 册,页 987〕

按:晚餐时,徐旭生曾与李书华商谈,后者表示原则上赞成,但其中数项提议须问清。

国际图书馆协会联合会覆函先生，先生前函经联合会主席在大会上代为陈述并引起反响。大意如下：

主席先生：

前接尊处上年六月八日来函，内述关于此次因战事被毁之图书馆恢复藏书一节，业经本联合会主席歌德特先生（Mr. Godet 瑞士国立图书馆馆长）在大会中代为陈述，其讲演词曾印于国际委员会纪录第十卷第三三至三四页，兹随函附上，即希台阅。此项讲演词，曾发生极大之注意，及深刻之印象，用特专函奉达，即希台察。

二月二十四日

〔《中华图书馆协会会报》第 13 卷第 6 期，页 12〕

按：Godet 即 Marcel Godet，1909 年至 1945 年担任瑞士国立图书馆馆长。原函为英文，后被译成中文刊登。

二月二十五日

徐旭生访先生，不值。〔《徐旭生文集》第 9 册，页 987〕

按：徐旭生先后至先生寓所、办公场所，皆未能遇见先生。此时，先生或已动身前往重庆。

先生致信国会图书馆馆长秘书，感谢国会图书馆寄赠中国西南地区书籍卡片，并请寄赠少数民族主题卡片。

February 25, 1939

Dear Madam:

We have pleasure in acknowledging the receipt of your letter dated January 13th as well as a set of cards relating to southwestern China which you have so kindly sent to this Library. On behalf of the National Library, I wish to convey to you and to your Chief Bibliographer my sincerest thanks for the courtesy which you have so kindly extended to this Library.

If it is not too much trouble to you, will you kindly ask your Chief Bibliographer to select for us once more other cards under the following subjects:

Lo-lo, Moso, Miao and other tribes in Southwestern China.,

Languages such as Lai, Khyang, Kaki-Chin and Tibet-Burman languages.

and supply some to us for our use. I need hardly say that any courtesy and assistance from your Library will be gratefully appreciated.

Yours faithfully,

T. L. Yuan

Acting Director

〔平馆(昆明)英文信纸。Library of Congress, Putnam Archives, Special Files, China: National Library 1930–1939〕

按:此件为打字稿,落款处为先生签名,于 4 月 3 日送达国会图书馆秘书办公室。

二月二十六日　昆明—重庆

先生乘坐中航飞机由滇赴渝,同行者有李书华等人。〔《民国日报》(云南),1939 年 2 月 27 日,第 4 版〕

先生抵重庆,致信王重民,告知战时征辑图书委员会内情,并请其转交备忘录。

有三吾弟:

离昆明之前接一月二十八日来函,知近被窃,不知已有线索否? 观来信情形似系熟人又明了情形者所为,如能物归原主,可谓幸极。今日来渝,知重庆组织战时征集图书委员会仍系蒋复聪所为,而对于 Spalding 之捐款显然欲独自染指,而以张伯苓为傀儡,大约张仲述在英活动又不啻暗中帮助蒋慰堂也。闻此委员会曾函熊式一代为帮忙,请速访熊并托其为昆明帮忙。因昆明是学术的,而重庆则完全政治意味也。兹寄上备忘录两份,可以一份交熊,一份交张(对张说话要小心)。昨已寄一份于牛津副校长,并用协会名义函谢 Spalding。关于此类消息请王维诚随时供给是荷。

同礼顿首

二月廿六,重庆

〔袁同礼家人提供〕

按:"并用协会名义函谢 Spalding",参见 1939 年 3 月 30 日《中华图书馆协会会报》第 13 卷第 5 期第 15 页。王维诚(1904—

1964），福建长汀人，1926 年入北京大学理科学习，1928 年转哲学系，1934 年任清华大学哲学系助教，1937 年赴英国牛津大学讲学，1940 年归国任西南联大哲学系教授。

二月二十七日

管理中英庚款董事会函云南省政府，决定补助昆明图书馆建筑费五万元，由该会与省政府合组国立昆明图书馆筹备委员会，函聘李书华为主任，龚自知为副主任，蒋梦麟、梅贻琦、任鸿隽、熊庆来、先生为委员。〔《民国日报》（云南），1939 年 2 月 28 日，第 4 版〕

> 按：龚自知（1896—1967），字仲钧，云南大关人，1917 年北京大学文预科英文乙班毕业[1]，时任云南省教育厅厅长。收到中英庚款董事会来函后，云南省政府以事关文化教育，函覆赞同。该馆本拟于是年秋动工。[2]

二月二十八日

先生致信王重民，告知美方捐赠图书数目，并请其便中赴牛津大学访问修中诚。

> 有三吾弟：
>
> 二月十七日来函顷由香港转到，致 Hughes 信随函奉上。美国方面已寄到 143 箱，有一万三千余册，均暂存香港，将来交教部支配。
>
> Spalding 十一月廿八日致牛津副校长之信今日始见到，此种资料王维诚何以早不供给，便中似须赴牛津一访 Hughes，并托王维诚可也。
>
> 陈寅恪须八九月间方能赴英，主要目的在治眼，不可为外人道也。
>
> 英美期刊关于抗战论文之索引已作完，*Times* 索引已购全份，以后出版者务请随时注意。
>
> Clegg 君已通讯数次，日内再函谢。
>
> 同礼
>
> 二，廿八 重庆
>
> 王礼锡昨日来访，未晤，日内可见面也。
>
> 〔袁同礼家人提供〕

---

[1]《国立北京大学廿周年纪念册》，"学生一览"页 38。
[2]《中华图书馆协会会报》第 14 卷第 2-3 期，页 21。

先生致信萧特会,请卡耐基国际和平基金会对中国教育界予以援助。

Chungking

February 28, 1939

Prof. James T. Shotwell

Carnegie Endowment for International Peace

407 West 117th Street

New York City

U. S. A.

Dear Prof. Shotwell:

With reference to my recent letter, I beg to enclose herewith copy of a communication from Mr. H. N. Spalding. While the amount of the gift is not very large, it has made a most profound impression in China where educational and scientific work is going on steadily in spite of the war.

Since you and I are most anxious to bring China and America closer together, it seems desirable that one or two Foundations in America could see fit to give some practical help to China now and not after the war. I shall be glad to take a trip to New York and talk matters over with you whenever it is necessary.

I came to Chungking yesterday to attend the National Educational Conference which begins its session tomorrow. Presidents of universities and academies, directors of libraries, museums and all scientific institutions have come from all parts of the country. In one of the sessions, a full report of Spalding's gift will be given by the Minister of Education and will no doubt be peculiarly appreciated. It is really painful to see that in this hour of its need, no national institution of learning in China has received any material help from the United States!

Being a graduate of Columbia, I earnestly hope that President Butler and the Endowment could give some practical help to China. The memorandum I sent you could be used as an application. The amount of grant needs not be very large, but an expression of moral support to a victim of Japan's aggression seems most desirable.

With warmest regards, I am,

> Yours sincerely,
>
> T. L. Yuan
>
> Acting Director

〔Rockefeller Foundation. Series 601: China; Subseries 601.R: China-Humanities and Arts. Box 47. Folder 389〕

按:该信应于 3 月中下旬送到,随后萧特会于 3 月 21 日致信史蒂文斯,并表示先生曾是他的学生,请洛克菲勒基金会考虑给予帮助。该件为抄件。

先生致信费正清,寄上石博鼎捐款书信副本并希望哈佛大学及哈佛燕京学社能继续援助中国学术界。

> Chungking
>
> February 28, 1939

Dear Dr. Fairbank:

With reference to my recent letter, I beg to enclose herewith copy of a communication from Mr. H. N. Spalding. While the amount of the gift is not very large, it has made a most profound impression in China where educational and scientific work is going on steadily in spite of the war.

Since you and I are most anxious to bring China and America closer together, it seems desirable that one or two Foundations in America could see fit to give some practical help to China now and not after the war. I am writing to Dr. Graves to-day to the same effect.

I came to Chungking yesterday to attend the National Educational Conference which begins its sessions tomorrow. Presidents of universities and academies, directors of libraries and museums as well as all scientific institutions have come from all parts of the country. In one of the sessions a full report of Spalding's gift will be given by the Minister of Education and will no doubt be peculiarly appreciated. It is really painful to see that in this hour of need, no national institution of learning in China has received any material help from the United States.

Knowing that you are interested in the promotion of Sino-American cultural relations, I earnestly hope that you will urge Harvard University or the Harvard-Yenching Institute to give some practical help to China just as an expression of moral support to a victim of Japan's aggression.

I didn't have time to write to Prof. Wildes before I left Kunming. Since I am going to Chengtu after this conference, will you kindly send a copy of my last letter to him, so that he may be kept informed. Our experience has shown that book-post is much quicker and in the long run is cheaper. The Harvard University Press could be entrusted with such practical matters.

With warmest regards, I am,

Yours sincerely,

T. L. Yuan

Acting Director

〔平馆(昆明)英文信纸。Harvard University, John K. Fairbank personal archive, folder Books for China〕

按：此件为打字稿,落款处为先生签名。

二三月间

先生致信周恩来,征集延安出版的抗战文献。〔《北京图书馆馆史资料汇编(1909-1949)》,页 679-680〕

按：三月初,似由周怡代为回访,但先生出席全国教育会议,不值。

三月一日

上午九时,第三次全国教育会议在川东师范学校开幕,孔祥熙院长、张群副院长、居正院长、张继委员、何应钦部长、王宠惠部长莅临,会议主席为陈立夫,出席代表张伯苓、宋美龄、吴敬恒、颜福庆、先生等二百余人。〔《申报》,1939 年 3 月 2 日,第 15 版〕

按：该次大会会期至 9 日结束,共举行全体会议十次。先生为社会教育组代表之一,该组其他代表有李蒸、李济、吴敬恒、吴景超、吴泽霖、俞庆棠、唐学咏、庄泽宣、陈果夫(王凤喈代)、陈天鸥、陈访先、陈泮藻、陈礼江、晏阳初、宋美龄、蒋复璁、赵太侔、滕固、骆美奂、萧友梅。①

———————

① 《申报》(上海),1939 年 3 月 18 日,第 13 版。

三月四日

上午、下午刘节两次前往英青会访先生,皆不值。〔《刘节日记》,郑州:大象出版社,2019年,页43〕

　　　　按:此次开会,先生与李济同宿重庆英青会。

平馆上海办事处钱存训覆函先生,报告搜集书籍、抗战报纸的进展。大意如下:

　　　　昨接九日手示并附《大陆报》等处函件,均已照收。该报照片三张计洋陆元已付,报纸一份按日送到,1937七月起旧报允俟觅全即送来。*Rules of Procedure for the U. S. Court for China* 预约一部,该书三月初出版后即直接寄滇。兹将收据一并附上,计洋拾捌元正,连上月合计垫付四十九元二△七分。联大书账本月付廿六元○九分,尚余四十七元一角四分。按嘱觅《大公报》,尚未获得,但购到上海战事期间之《救亡日报》(郭沫若等在沪主办)自创刊至停刊止全份,及《战时日报》(上海十种小报联合发刊)。又,《译报》自创刊起239份,共合五元,以后遇此类报纸及全份什志当随时留意收购。代印什志登记卡3000已分寄港(一千张)滇(二千张),指引卡二百张亦寄去,发票单据已交李君报销。

　　　　　　　〔《北京图书馆馆史资料汇编(1909-1949)》,页667-668〕

　　　　按:《大陆报》即 *The China Press*;*Rules of Procedure for the United States Court for China* 该书名称直译"美国在华法庭程序规则",1939年在上海出版,出版方为 A. R. Hager。《救亡日报》1937年8月24日在上海创刊,社长郭沫若、总编辑夏衍,后迁广州,再迁桂林出版,1941年初停刊。《战时日报》1937年10月5日创刊,姚吉光为经理、龚之方任编辑、冯梦云任编辑顾问,该报实为《上海报》《小日报》《大晶报》《金刚钻报》《东方日报》《正气报》《世界晨报》《铁报》《明星日报》《福尔摩斯》十家小报联合出版,1937年12月11日停刊。此件为钱存训所拟底稿。

三月七日

晚六时半,战时征集图书委员会假松柏厅举行第四次执行委员会会议,张伯苓、郭有守、顾毓琇、李迪俊、先生、杭立武、吴俊升、蒋复璁等人出席。议决各案如下:

一、郭有守辞职,由吴俊升继任,并推章益为执行委员;

二、在美征集图书,全权委托中华图书馆协会继续办理,但所得书籍运到香

港后由平馆办事处负责运往内地,再统由本会交教育部分配;

三、在英征集图书,由战时征集图书委员会办理,书籍运到海防后委托国际
出版品交换处负责国内运输费用。

四、各学校、团体送来所需图书目录,推举先生、蒋复璁、沈祖荣三人担任审
查书目委员。〔《中华图书馆协会会报》第 13 卷第 5 期,页 12-13;《中华图书馆
协会会报》第 13 卷第 6 期,页 18-19〕

> 按:章益(1901—1986),字友三,安徽滁州人,早年就读于上海圣
> 约翰大学附属中学,后入复旦大学,1924 年赴美留学,时任教育
> 部总务司司长。李迪俊(1901—?),字涤镜,湖北黄梅人,清华学
> 校毕后留学美国,获威斯康星大学博士学位,时在外交部任职,后
> 曾任"中华民国驻巴西大使"。吴俊升(1901—2000),字士选,江
> 苏如皋人,1928 年赴法留学,1931 年获巴黎大学文科博士学位,
> 1938 年初应陈立夫之邀,担任教育部高等教育司司长。《中华图
> 书馆协会会报》前后两期对本次会议举行时间记载不一,暂依晚
> 六时半,地点松柏厅应在川东师范学校内。

三月八日

刘节来访,谈北平诸旧友近况。先生对谢国桢多有烦言,并言英国庚子退
款似可继续,每月薪俸如有二百元,不妨安于现状。〔《刘节日记》,页 45〕

> 按:此时,刘节与先生已有三年未见,刘节认为先生"情形甚佳",
> 惟因谢国桢擅自由湘返平,遂有不满。此后,刘节确在管理中英
> 庚款委员会从事研究工作。

晚六时,竺可桢与先生、孙洪芬至陕西街留春幄赴孙学悟宴,其他与席者有
黄涵瑞、梅光迪、陈长蘅、李烛尘等,谈至十点半。〔《竺可桢全集》第 7 卷,2005
年,页 45〕

> 按:孙学悟(1888—1952),字颖川,山东文登人,化学家,主持创办
> 了中国第一个化工科研机构——黄海化学工业研究社。

三月十日

先生致信王重民,告其国内各方就向国外征集图书达成妥协,并请其在英
法留意购买中外国际关系史料,以利将来战后与日谈判。

> 有三吾弟:
>
> 在重庆共住十二日。关于向国外征集图书事已与各方商定,美国

方面仍由协会继续办理,英德法方面则由战时征集图书委员会办理(实即蒋慰堂所策动)。该会之事业完全注重 Spalding 及牛津捐款之应付,对于英国圕协会等等机关尚未顾到,盖彼等对于国外情形隔膜殊甚,但既已成立,于协会在英德法之进行殊感困难。英法两国方面除仍由本馆继续进行外,协会之工作似须停止,尊意如何? 希示复。英国方面何处接到该会之申请,亦盼便中一询,想为数甚少也。英国之*Blue Books on China* 已函购,此外有无*Yellow Books*、*White Books*请到 Stationery Office 一询,并在法国政府官书局 Imprimerie Nationale 一询,各买一全份与中国有关者寄滇。本馆刻正搜集近百年来中国国际关系之书,如东北问题、领事裁判权问题、关税问题、租借地问题、中国资源开发及门户开放问题、内外蒙问题、铁路问题等等,请到旧书店及 P. S. King、Stationery Office 诸处查照上列项目一一选购,速同前函所述关于各种书目 bibliographies 一并采购,所需之款当于四月间汇出。刻下英贷款一千万磅,今后如能采其他报复手段,则中日战争结束之期当不在远,吾人亟应准备和平会议时之各种资料,以供政府参考。因外交部书籍、档案遗失不少,故王部长、徐次长均盼本馆协助此事。务祈于离英以前从速办理,而各种有关之书目及索引尤为重要也。顺颂旅安。

袁同礼顿首
三,十日,重庆

第二次应汇之补助费正与财部交涉,盼能早得结果。

〔袁同礼家人提供〕

按:P. S. King 应指英国出版社 P. S. King & Son,1855 年创立,位于伦敦议会街,代售议会出版物;Stationery Office 应指英国财政部文书局,1786 年成立,最初作为政府采购办公用品的机构。Blue Books on China 似指英国政府报告中有关中国之部分,Yellow Books 应指法国官方出版物报告,White Books 待考。"王部长"即王宠惠,"徐次长"应指徐谟。

三月十六日

第十八集团军重庆办事处周怡致函先生,告知将寄送延安出版的抗日文献与平馆。

同礼先生:

　　恩来同志因公赴前方,于月前即已离渝。接奉先生致恩来同志函后,当即趋贵寓拜谒,因先生教育会议忙碌,数次均无缘晤谈。现除将先生大函留交恩来同志外,已函延安方面搜集有关抗战文献,直寄昆明。肃此,即颂公绥。

　　　　　　　　　　　　　　　　　　　　　周怡上
　　　　　　　　　　　　　　　　　　　　　三月十六日

〔《北京图书馆馆史资料汇编(1909-1949)》,页679-680〕

　　按:周怡,湖南新化人,时任第十八集团军驻渝办事处通讯处处长。

三月十八日

平馆上海办事处钱存训覆函先生,报告其在上海征集抗战史料情况。大意如下:

　　接奉由港转到三月三日及十日由渝赐书,敬悉一一。林伯遵先生一函及请款单亦已交去,日内领馆垫付越币卅元已寄还。第四期中文书费四月中发出,届时当请将预支款归帐后(李君三百元,职支五百元,内二百元为西文书费已报销,故应归还六百元),余数转作联大付日文书款。钧处俟收到后再行奉告。

　　前印期刊登录卡已分寄港(一千)滇(二千),孙君来信谓又由港分寄五百张去滇,想均收到。又印日报登录片五百张,沪上拟留用百张,余数当即寄滇。

　　《大公报》顷悉在沪设有办事处,已拟就公函托人接洽,或可觅到。开示购书范围,当随时留意,其中太平洋国际学会出版各种似均需要,兹将该处目录两种附上一阅。中国出版者或可索到,外国出版者该会可以购得。另,又索到《海关图书馆目录》一册,一并另寄并附书单两纸,并请查收。

　　关于史料征集事,连日在各救济团体觅得文件若干。又,日人近日所倡之建设东亚新秩序运动,亦获得一部标贴传单。关于外人投资损失调查,前曾得人介绍,向英大使馆商务参赞公署接洽。关于本馆请求,甚表赞助。惟各项秘密文件,该处未敢擅自做主。前日该署特派副领事 Mr. G. C. Crowe 君来此说明其意,谓已将本馆此项请求送达伦敦 Foreign Office 请示,倘获允许即可照办云云。经连日接洽,结果觉各方对于本馆近况多不甚明了,故拟将日前寄下之启事交由各报发表,俾使各界对此工作有一认识。稿中注明勿与昆明直接接洽,而仍以办事处名义个别接洽,避免公开。

兹有小册等数种,因不易见到,故已先行购下,日内即寄滇,余俟续陈。

顷代本馆购《四川经济参考资料》一部,并代联大订《中外经济拔萃》三卷一年(半价,并送《中外经济年报》一部),一卷二卷有存书,要否请示。

〔《北京图书馆馆史资料汇编(1909-1949)》,页 668-670〕

按:G. C. Crowe 实际应为 C. T. Crowe,该人确为英国商务参赞公署(British Commercial Counsellor)[1]副领事,钱存训在此拼写有误。《四川经济参考资料》,张肖梅编著,1939 年 1 月初版。《中外经济拔萃》,英文名为 *The Economic Digest*,1937 年 1 月于上海创刊,由中国国民经济研究所编辑出版并负责发行工作。此件为钱存训所拟底稿。

石博鼎覆函先生,对中国抵抗日本侵略表示莫大的钦佩,并愿竭尽所能推动英国学术界积极、持续地援助中国各大学。大意如下:

奉到二月二十日函惠,使敝人非常感动! 贵国文化机关能在异常困难环境之中,努力前进,继续工作,钦佩莫名! 此次敝夫妇得稍尽棉薄,深为荣幸!

牛津大学捐赠贵国书籍事,已由评议会正式通过,正在积极办理中,本大学出版部已制一书签,除包括牛津之古塔及校徽外,并有下列文字"一九三八年牛津大学以学术友谊赠与中国各大学",想贵国教育界同仁,必能予以赞同也。

敝馆对于贵国抵抗侵略之伟举,莫不予以极大深切之同情,盖吾人深觉贵国不仅为自由而战,实为拥护全世界人类之自由与人道而战也。倘吾人未能以实力表现吾人之同情,实因今日欧洲局面之紧张,颇阻碍吾人之进行故也。

---

[1] *The North-China Desk Hong List*, 1939, p. 107.

　　因此之故，吾人今日能在文化方面实际援助贵国，藉此表示吾人深切之同情，实深引为欣慰。敝人希望并相信英国其他大学及学术机关必将追随牛津之后，继续援助，刻下已有数处在进行中。

　　英人与贵国人士向有友谊之同情，谅彼此均有同感。牛津中国学生莫不为同人所爱戴，此间一般知名之士，俱深切感觉吾人对于了解中国固有文化，实有迫切之需求，而对贵国今日在抗战期中种种建设之进步，尤为欣佩。又同人等对于中国大哲学家，深致景仰，深信东方哲学，对今日世界政治道德各方面种种问题，均有无限贡献！舍弟在（Brasenose）担任哲学教席，近著有《荀子墨子庄子评论》一书，本年出版后，当举以奉赠。

　　闻贵国教育当局，对于各种科学及其研究方法，正加以新考虑，尤使吾人深感幸趣，如吾人经验能供参考时，则尤为荣幸。吾人对于先生个人工作之成绩——对于学者，对于读书人，对于世界图书馆之贡献——愿表示景仰之意，并盼不久可以晤面也。

　　　　　　　　　　　　　　　　　　　　　　　石博鼎谨启

　　　　　　　　　　　　　　　　　　　　　　　三月十八日

〔《中华图书馆协会会报》第 13 卷第 6 期，页 11-12〕

　　按："舍弟"即 Kenneth J. Spalding（1879-1962），与钱锺书颇多往来，Brasenose 即 Brasenose College，通译作"布雷齐诺斯学院"，创建于 1509 年，为牛津大学下属院校之一，《荀子墨子庄子评论》应指 *Three Chinese Thinkers*，似因欧战爆发并未按信中所言如期出版，后钱锺书主编 International Series of Chinese Studies（《寰宇汉学丛书》）被列为第 1 种[①]，1947 年由国立中央图书馆在南京印行。原函为英文，后被译成中文刊登。

三月中旬

先生赴成都考察文化事业，曾至四川省中山图书馆等处参观。〔《中华图书馆协会会报》第 13 卷第 6 期，1939 年 5 月 30 日，页 11；国家图书馆档案，档案编号 1939-※051-协会 5-001006〕

———————

① 范旭仑《钱锺书不就牛津大学哲学讲师》，《文汇报》，2021 年 6 月 17 日，第 12 版。

三月二十日

先生回抵昆明。〔《民国日报》(云南)，1939 年 3 月 21 日，第 4 版〕

Norma S. Thompson 致函先生，通知洛克菲勒基金会就此前资助平馆 RF36072 的项目期限予以延长。

March 20, 1939

My dear Mr. Yuan:

I have the honor to inform you that at a meeting of the Executive Committee of the Rockefeller Foundation held March 17, 1939, the Foundation's appropriation RF 36072 to the National Library of Peiping was amended to make the unexpended balance available during the period ending June 30, 1942, for development of library services, for purchase of materials, and for production of materials for the Bulletin of Chinese Bibliography, not more than $ 8,000 to be available in any year of the period.

Very truly yours,

Secretary

Norma S. Thompson

〔Rockefeller Foundation. Series 601: China; Subseries 601.R: China-Humanities and Arts. Box 47. Folder 389〕

按：该函中并未注明可支配的余额总数，先生收到后误以为是 10500 美金，即该资助案（RF36072）内针对中文图书目录卡片 18000 美金扣除已支取的 7500 美金，因其他两部分分别为美国图书馆专家访问费用和为美国学术界复制文献资料（拍摄缩微胶片）并未开展，极有可能是出于自律先生直接忽略这两部分的费用——7000 美金。事实上，洛克菲勒基金会修正案可用余额总计 17500 美金，唯一的限制是每年不多于 8000 美金。该函寄送昆明，并抄送上海洛克菲勒基金会办事处。3 月 21 日，洛克菲勒基金会致电其驻沪办事处，告知这一决定。

三月二十一日

先生致信郭有守，请其拟具筹设四川省立图书馆计划书，以便正式向中英庚款董事会提请补助。

有守先生左右：

　　在蓉小留，诸承款待，厚意隆情，无任铭感。去岁管理中英庚款董事会举行年会时，曾经弟建议，在西南诸省，各设图书馆一所，以宏文化。旋经该会决议在滇设立图书馆，在黔设立科学馆各一所，对于川省，独付阙如，不无遗憾。此次弟来蓉视察，深觉图书设备，诸多简陋，极有补充之必要，矧成都为后方重镇，此项设置，似不宜缓，刻下中英庚款董事会本届年会已决定于五月杪在香港举行，除仍由中华图书馆协会继续建议，促其对于川省文化事业积极援助外，拟请贵厅拟具设置省立图书馆详细计划，正式申请，弟能力所及，自当从旁赞助。如何之处，并盼考虑赐覆是荷。专此，顺颂道祺！

〔《中华图书馆协会会报》第 13 卷第 6 期，1939 年 5 月，页 11〕

　　按：同日，中华图书馆协会致函管理中英庚款董事会请在成都筹设一所大规模图书馆。

三月下旬

先生致信王重民，告外汇申请已得圆满结果，开列购书清单，并请其继续在英申请援助。大意如下：

　　顷接三月十四日来函，兹将应复各点列后：

　　（一）向财政部请求外汇六十磅，在重庆时曾托钱币司戴司长帮忙。顷接来信，谓已复教部，一俟教部函到，即购买英磅汇上由 Giles 转，此事经数月之奔走，始能如愿。

　　（二）联大书单系严文郁根据 Mudge: *Guide to Reference Books* 所开，匆促之间错误当不少。此次本馆所开者共三单①近代史及国际关系②国际公法③经济建设，皆寄交 Hughes 转交英伦之委员会。张似旅君研究何种科学，请查明示复处不日当寄一信，拜托一切。

　　（三）张仲述已抵美，此后在英接洽是否即是张似旅君，请询明示复。除牛津外，剑桥、伦敦、爱丁堡诸处有无动静，在离英以前最好到牛津去一次，见见 Spalding 亦好。观渠来信注重大学，而对国立图书馆则未提及，已寄二谢函—用协会名义，一用本馆名义。又牛津副校长及 New College 院长 Fisher 均有谢函寄去也。

　　剑桥史学教授 Temperley 处曾寄一信，请帮忙。

　　关于英国书目，此间甚少，尽可购置，如有重复，可让给联大也。

〔袁同礼家人提供〕

按:此信残,但在右端注有"此信三月廿七日发"字样,据此可以
推断约在三月下旬所写。"戴司长"即戴铭礼(1901—1991),字
立庵,浙江衢县人,1921 年进上海公学商科,曾主编《商学周刊》,
1936 年 3 月起任钱币司司长。张似旅,广东人,毕业于岭南大
学,后赴美国哈佛大学留学,曾任国民政府驻日内瓦国际联盟代
表团秘书、驻美公使随员,后调任驻英国大使馆秘书。Fisher 即
Herbert Albert L. Fisher(1865-1940),英国历史学家,1926 年起担
任 New College 院长。

三月二十五日

下午三时,昆明图书馆筹备委员会假云南教育厅会议室召开成立会议,主
任委员李书华,副主任委员龚自知,委员蒋梦麟、梅贻琦、熊庆来、先生、任
鸿隽出席,白潜叔、张鸿书列席。首由龚自知报告云南省政府筹建图书馆
新馆经过暨拨定专款之收支现况。后讨论议案如下:

(一)本会款项如何保管出纳案。议决,由龚副主任委员负责保管。

(二)建筑地址如何选定案。议决,建筑地址改于昆明大西门外,与学校区
　　接近。

(三)建筑图样如何设计审定案。议决,旧图案已不适用,请余工程师另行
　　设计提会审定。

(四)建筑费如何决定案。议决,以国币十万元为土木工程建筑及水电设
　　备费,国币五万元为购书费。

(五)建筑工程如何实施案。议决,建筑工料招包承办,由会监督建造。

(六)本会办公地点及利用会章印制信封纸案。议决,本会办公地点仍在
　　教育厅内,其余各项由厅派员制备。

此外,临时动议三项,分别为(1)本会筹备之使命及限度,为建筑图书馆及
购买书籍;(2)请先生调查省会各方面现有书籍及以后之需要,作为将来
购书标准;(3)图书馆之性质,本馆收藏书籍以社会科学及普通书籍为主,
供给中、大学生及中学教员参考使用。〔《中华图书馆协会会报》第 13 卷第 6 期,
页 24〕

吴宓致函先生,荐王文漪到平馆昆明办事处任职。〔《吴宓日记》第 7 册,页 9〕

三月二十六日

费正清覆函先生,告知已收到先生此前两信,仍须就所需书籍的内容给予

明确指明,不建议在校内成立正式的组织,并就以上问题致信陈岱孙、刘崇
鋐、钱端升等人。大意如下:

Mar. 26, 1939

Dear Mr. Yuan:

Thank you for your letters of Feb. 7 and 28.

In making a collection here, we find that it is not difficult to get books if we know what books to get. In other words, we must try to ascertain what you need; whereupon we can try to supply it. The community here is tired of campaigns, like those for Spanish Loyalist ambulances or scholarships for German refugees, and we shall not try to have a formal University campaign; we can get just as good results with our informal committee. However, we have decided to expand our efforts, to get books on all subjects, not merely on social sciences.

Could you therefore send me as soon as possible an indication of the present state of your collection and of the Tsing Hua or United University collection? We need to know 1) on what subjects books are needed, 2) what books you already have on those subjects, 3) what kinds of textbooks you want. I am writing to Prof. Deison Chen of Tsing Hua, in Economics, and Prof. Liu Ch'ung-hung, in History, and Prof. Ch'ien Tuan-sheng, Political Science, to ask them the same question. You have already mentioned international law and relations; could we have similar suggestions, if possible more specific?

Until we receive a reply from you, we shall go ahead with the List of Books for College Libraries, Supplement published by the American Library Association, as our chief bibliographical guides⋯⋯

〔Harvard University, John K. Fairbank personal archive〕

按:此件为底稿,只存首页。

三月二十七日

先生致信 George J. Beal,声明平馆昆明、上海、香港办事处的地位和作用,
并表示中文书籍的编目、卡片印刷即将恢复。

March 27, 1939

Dear Mr. Beal:

Thank you for your letter of January 19 which was received while I was attending the National Educational Conference at Chungking. Please pardon this unavoidable delay in answering.

Besides our Library at Peiping which has been holding on ever since Japan's military occupation of the city, we are having three offices at Shanghai, Hongkong and Kunming. In addition to the duty of looking after our book-collections deposited in Shanghai and Hongkong, our offices at these two places have been assisting our Kunming office in the acquisition of material along certain fields in which we are especially interested.

The Kunming office was established in May, 1938, by the order of the National Government and was subsequently approved by the China Foundation. The creation of a new library centre in an interior province has three immediate objectives: first, to give facilities for research to Chinese intellectual workers who have come in large numbers from war-affected areas; secondly, to develop cultural life in Southwestern China which lies beyond the reach of Japan's arm of war; and thirdly, to continue to build up a systematic collection of books of Western learning so that scientific research shall not be interrupted during the national crisis.

It is, therefore, not a "transfer" of the Library from Peiping to Kunming, but an addition to the library resources of the Southwest which is in urgent need of cultural development.

The cataloguing of Chinese new publications started at Kunming in November, 1938, and the printing of cataloguing cards will be resumed at Peiping next month. While it involves some correspondence, our mails have been unusually regular.

The statement concerning the receipts and expenditure in connection with the grant of your Foundation was enclosed in my letter of February 8 to Dr. Stevens and I trust it has received your attention.

Hoping the above information answers the points raised in your letter,

Yours sincerely,

T. L. Yuan

Acting Director

〔平馆(昆明)英文信纸。Rockefeller Foundation. Series 601: China; Subseries 601.R: China-Humanities and Arts. Box 47. Folder 389〕

按:此件为打字稿,落款处为先生签名,该信附于翌日致史蒂文斯信中,于 4 月 19 日送达。

三月二十八日

下午三时,吴宓至柿花巷平馆办事处,先生表示不能聘用王文漪。〔《吴宓日记》第 7 册,页 12-13〕

先生致信史蒂文斯,告知云南省政府和管理中英庚款董事会将共同出资在昆明东北部建立新图书馆,并谈石博鼎捐款及平馆开始筹建四类特藏文献,请洛克菲勒基金会再次考虑资助平馆购买外文文献。

March 28, 1939

Dear Dr. Stevens:

I beg to acknowledge with many thanks the receipt of your letter of February 16.

I trust you have received my letter of February 8 enclosing a statement of the receipts and expenditures of your grant as well as a memorandum re the proposed Bureau of American Bibliography. In the light of information given in that letter, we hope that the whole question of extending assistance to the National Library might be reconsidered by your Foundation.

I enclose herewith a letter addressed to Mr. Beal and shall be obliged to you if you will kindly forward it for us. In this letter, I have tried to explain the legal status of our Kunming office and I hope it answers the points raised in Mr. Beal's letter.

Since writing to you last, several developments have taken place. Knowing that you are interested in the promotion of library services in

China, I wish to submit to you a very brief report.

Firstly, a new library building costing Sh $ 150,000.00 will be built this fall at Kunming. The Provincial Government of Yunnan provides two-thirds of the cost, while the British Boxer Indemnity Trustees contribute the rest at the request of the Library Association of China. The library will be located in the northeastern section of the city which is within easy reach of the two universities and two academies. The National Library is collaborating with this project and all of its books and journals will be deposited in the new library as soon as it is completed.

Secondly, Mr. H. N. Spalding and the University community at Oxford have contributed £ 8,000.0.0. to be used for the purchase of scientific literature for various universities in China. Every book sent to China contains a book-plate with a picture of Oxford and the words:

        "From the University of Oxford to the Universities of China in Fellowship of Learning"

The first consignment of books intended for the National Southwest Associated University at Kunming has already been dispatched. Although the amount of the gift is not very large, this "gesture" from Oxford has a psychological effect on Chinese intellectuals, perhaps even greater than the American credit of $ 25,000,000.00 and the British stabilization loan of £ 10,000,000.0.0. combined.

Since the Oxford gift is limited to Chinese universities, the National Library will not be privileged to have a share which, we feel, is rather unfortunate. However, in spite of intense difficulties, we have been building up four collections at Kunming, viz. (1) Special Collection on the Southwest, (2) Special Collection on the undeclared war, (3) Special Collection on international relations and (4) Special Collection on post-war rehabilitation and reconstruction. Materials of this kind are urgently needed in China and we have been rendering valuable services to the National Government as well as to all research institutions. We are carrying on this work under the unfortunate difficulties of the present hour, especially due to the Government's control over foreign exchange.

Arm in arm with resistance, the Chinese people are carrying out an extensive program of reconstruction particularly in the remote West which lies beyond the reach of Japan's arm of war. If we win the war, we will emerge stronger than we entered it. All of us are confident of our ultimate victory and we are more concerned with the European situation than that of the Far East.

While we do not expect your Foundation to assist us in the extensive purchase of research materials, we earnestly hope that sympathetic consideration might be given by your Trustees to our need of American literature as set forth in my memorandum of February 8. The Foundation will be rendering an invaluable service to the cause of higher education in this country if we were enabled to continue to carry on our work of coordination in the field of library services.

With warmest personal regards,

Yours sincerely,

T. L. Yuan

Acting Director

〔平馆(昆明)英文信纸。Rockefeller Foundation. Series 601: China; Subseries 601.R: China-Humanities and Arts. Box 47. Folder 389〕

按：此件为打字稿，落款处为先生签名，于 4 月 19 日送达。

三月二十九日

徐森玉致函先生，谈故宫南迁文物在安顺等地情形及浦江清借钞《也是园藏古今杂剧目录》事。

守和先生赐鉴：

养病昆垣，诸承照拂，隆情挚谊，感思至今。侧闻台从返滇，博论精研，切实振作，收获良多，欣服无似。宝来安已将一月，建造洞中木质库房，尚未就绪，盖此间工匠玩愒之疾已入膏肓，呼唤无灵，驱策勘效，殊令人烦闷耳。苗夷名称虽繁，大别不过四种，曰苗、曰仲家、曰㑊

伢、曰仡佬,暇时拟加调查^{项已雇一青苗服役,藉可询问一切}。红崖山径崎岖,
须库工完毕后,再往探考也。理会决议渝蓉文物悉数疏散,渝物限一
个月办竣,蓉物限一个半月办竣。叔平先生已在嘉定西乡安谷镇觅得
私人祠宇十余所,又在峨眉县东门外觅得大佛寺一所,容纳二处文物。
日来正在交涉船只,准备于最短期间迁往。刘官谔、李光第二君均调
往渝中帮助^{项接欧阳邦华来函,劝傅维本兄前往}。惜宝股胫之作用尚未恢复,
不能胼胝躬与此役,甚自媿恧耳。邓竹筠兄生计异常困难,倘能特予
提挈,俾竟所学,感同身受。《也是园杂剧目》宝曾手写一份,在途中
遗失,清华浦江清兄书来借钞,无以应之,求将馆中一份暂假渠一阅。
浦君住农校,望通知渠来馆领取为祷。专此,敬请钧安。

弟徐鸿宝再拜
三月廿九日

馆中同仁均此致候。

〔国家图书馆档案,档案编号 1945-※057-综合 5-015003〕

按:"养病昆垣"指 1938 年 10 月中下旬,徐森玉在昆明因从人力
车坠落,髀骨受伤颇重。^①"台从返滇"非指从香港回抵昆明,实
为自渝返滇。傅振伦在《蒲梢沧桑·九十忆往》中亦提到因贵阳
山洞多潮湿、不便保存古物,1939 年 1 月 3 日他与同事前往安顺
华严洞考察,21 日装运古物,翌日运抵安顺。徐森玉于本年 3 月
间抵达安顺,负责督建华严洞库房。刘官谔,抗战前任故宫文献
馆第二科科员;李光第,字绍时,抗战前任故宫总务处第二科书
记。临时大学图书馆从长沙到昆明的撤迁工作结束后,邓竹筠自
香港奉调入滇。

三月三十日

教育部社会教育司致函平馆,令平馆在滇办事处改组为馆本部。

奉部长发下贵馆二月二十五日呈,以在滇仅设办事处尚无组织法
规等情,奉批"该馆现已迁滇,如在滇仅设办事处,殊不足以正观听,亟
应加以调整,将办事处改组为馆本部,并呈送组织法规候核"等因;相
应函达,即希查照遵办为荷。此致

---

① 《徐旭生文集》第 9 册,页 927。

国立北平图书馆

教育部社会教育司启

三十

〔《北京图书馆馆史资料汇编(1909-1949)》,页 683-684〕

按:《北京图书馆馆史资料汇编》《中国国家图书馆百年纪事》均

将此函归在 4 月 10 日,有误。

阿博特覆函先生,告知美国各学术机构曾向史密斯森协会询问拟捐赠援华的文献期刊是否有价值,并谈寄送重庆教育部出版品交换局的箱件数量。

March 30, 1939

Dear Dr. Yuan:

　　The Institution is glad to learn from your letter of February 13 that the consignments of American publications being forwarded to you through the International Exchange Service are reaching you safely. Many organizations in this country, before sending material here for you, ask whether the publications they have to offer are of a character that would be needed. In all such cases the Institution has replied that in its opinion the books or journals in question doubtless would be of value in the work you are undertaking even though some of the material is duplicated.

　　I might add that in July 1938 the Institution forwarded 46 boxes to the Chinese Bureau of International Exchange in Chungking. Those boxes recently were acknowledged and yesterday another shipment consisting of 30 boxes was forwarded to Chungking. Those consignments contained packages from various American establishments for distribution to correspondents throughout China.

Very truly yours,

C. G. Abbot

Secretary

〔Smithsonian Institution Archives, Records, 1868 - 1988 (Record Unit 509), Box 1, Library Association of China, Hong Kong〕

按:此件为录副。

三月三十一日

先生致信章益、陈礼江,请从旁协助将平馆(南馆)经费列入国家预算。

友三、逸民司长惠鉴:

在渝畅聆教言,至为欢慰。关于敝馆购书经费,恳请列入本年度追加预算一案,荷承惠允,无任欣感。敝馆自南迁以来,购书经费业已大减,本年庚款停付,而大部分经费仍用于北平,困难情形想在洞鉴之中。尚希于该案呈送行政院时多加按语、从旁赞助,至为感荷。耑此拜托,顺颂道祺。

弟袁同礼再拜

三月卅一日

又馆员王重民在伦敦摄照燉煌写经工作费请求外汇六十磅,闻已得财政部之允准,尚祈将通知书早日寄下为感。

〔中国第二历史档案馆,教育部档案·全卷宗5,国立北平图书馆请拨员工学术研究补助费经常费有关文书,案卷号11616(1)〕

按:陈礼江,字逸民,时任社会教育司司长。3月30日,蒋梦麟以平馆委员会主席身份亦致信教育部,恳请从旁协助将平馆经费列入国家预算。该信为文书代笔,尾页左侧标注"查该项准购外汇通知书以本部图叁8第6677号训令转发在案。谷馨敬注,四,七。"

四月三日　昆明

中午,先生在厚德福设宴,冯至、吴达元等受邀与席。〔冯至《昆明日记》,《新文学史料》2001年第4期,页27〕

四月五日

平馆驻沪办事处钱存训覆函先生,汇报购书事宜。大意如下:

接奉三月十日由成都及廿五日由滇赐书,并购书单等,均已先后收到。十八日曾有一函寄滇,想达尊览。兹将购书各事奉陈于后:

一、太平洋国际学会赠送本馆全部出版物一套,并有代售各种书籍,均检送一份,计138种,一四〇册(书单附上)。上海现由杨兆延女士主持,刘驭万先生现在港□会,九龙北京道十号四楼设有驻港办事处,谓尚有最近出版刊物均在港,得便向刘先生一洽,或可觅得若干。

二、开示本月购书范围。中文者购得刘彦所著外交史数种《国民政府外交史》□□航□□,《外交年鉴》三年亦均觅得。上海通志馆刊物十种,购一套(尚有《上海市年鉴》及《上海研究资料》(均中华出版),《申报年鉴》需要否?)外交部白皮书、黄皮书及日本研究会各种小册均无法觅到。西文因恐购置重复,附上书单乙纸,请示知再购。Walter Young 之著作,仅购 *Int. Rel. of Manchuria* 一种(二元五△)。除者商务存有此两种,均售原价,要否购下,请示知。又 China United Press 现似迁渝或在港,出有刊物多种,上海尚可购得,请阅附单,示知要否? *Directory of China, Japan* 请在港购。

三、海关出版各种贸易统计,本馆似均应备一份。惟该处各种出版物得托中美、别发及商务代售,未知能否索到。拟请缮一公函,以便持往接洽。《海关条约》如不能索到,商务可允九折。

近来因寄滇包裹拥挤,邮局暂停收寄昆明邮件,故购好各书均无法寄出。是否候通递后再寄,抑托中基会公便带港?请示知照办。又,海关圕及太平洋学会目录未及寄香滇,已改寄香港。《图书季刊》已阅两次,大约十五日以前可以出版。

〔《北京图书馆馆史资料汇编(1909-1949)》,页 671-672〕

按:杨兆延,生平待考,抗战后期曾在交通部任职。[1] 刘驭万(1896—1966),湖北宜春人,清华学校毕业,后赴美留学,获欧柏林学院文学士、威斯康星大学政治学硕士,回国在交通部、经济部任职,时兼任太平洋国际学会中国分会执行干事。"刘彦所著外交史数种"似指《中国近时外交史》《最近三十年中国外交史》等书。China United Press 即联华书报社,原址在上海四川路 299号。"中美"应指中美图书公司(American Book Shop)。该信寄送香港,此件为钱存训所拟底稿。

四月七日

徐森玉致函先生,谈安顺近况并重申不受薪酬等事。

守和先生赐鉴:

前闻台驾返滇,曾寄一书,谅邀青照。侧闻馆中新猷旧绩同时并举,声誉四驰,论者推为西南第一,欢忭之情不可言状。贱体如恒,股胫之间仍未恢复原状,不识何故。安顺四乡土匪出没无常,前数日距

① 《交通公报》第 8 卷第 4 期,1945 年,页 10。

华严洞二里之版桥邮竟遭匪劫,殊令人担忧昨日此间有警报以敲锣为号。因戒备起见,宝所雇之苗人遂不敢用。当此乱世,虽调查工作亦不易进行也仍在蒐访材料,并未息工。木质库房建筑费不过二千元,屡受叔平先生驳诘,故至今不能开工,慕陵、维本两兄已赴贵阳接洽此事矣。平馆金壬父兄前寄赠宝百元,业已设法汇还。兹又由邮局汇来承邓竹筠兄转来,每次汇费十八元,甚不合算,似不能再行汇还,拟暂收下,将来另设他法还渠。前将汇票及信封寄上汇票在金信封内,求饬人代为取回。宝之图章在房东杨文斋处,兹写一片请饬工友取回或托万稼轩、邓竹筠两兄亦可,或请代刻徐森玉三字章亦可。此款不必汇下,寄存尊处为祷。外间寄宝之款,除邢勉之外,尚有张寓锋一百元、葛仲勋四百元、周仲洁一百元、周叔廉一百元、陈茨青二百元,均已一一璧回,费去汇费甚多。成都寄宝拓片二包承邓竹筠兄由邮局取得,亦拟暂寄馆中,种种劳神不安之至,铭感万分。晋陵县各碑摹拓已毕工否? 甚为念念。贵阳朱汉云住竹桐井、陈志书住三版桥两家藏书甚富,均毁于二·四炸灾。宝已托人觅其目录,尚未到手。昆市物价日高,竹筠兄境况极为困难,务恳加以救济,不胜企盼之至。匆此,敬请撰安。

弟徐鸿宝再拜

四月七日

同仁均此致候。

〔国家图书馆档案,档案编号 1945-※057-综合 5-015006 至
1945-※057-综合 5-015008〕

按:"慕陵"即庄尚严,抗战前任故宫古物馆第一科科长,时为故宫驻黔办事处主任;"万稼轩"即万斯年,抗战前任平馆参考组组员;"邢勉之"即邢冕之(邢端),曾就学于保定莲池书院、日本东京帝国大学法律系,解放后出任北京市文史研究馆首任馆长;张寓锋,20 世纪 30 年代初曾任黄郛随从,时亦在西南,1939 年底在云南为徐森玉寻觅适宜疗伤的温泉;葛仲勋,1924 年曾在北京交易所任候补监事,1941 年与徐森玉同为陶剑萍、陈平凡订婚的介绍人;周仲洁,曾任津浦铁路南段浦口特别货捐局局长,后在上海从事房地产业,1943 年 7 月 24 日"上海特别市房地产业同业公会"合组成立,任首届理事;周叔廉,曾任交通银行副经理;陈茨青,待考。"晋陵县"应指昆明西南的晋宁县,因该地方言发音中

N 和 L 不分,且此处颇多碑铭,1939 年起平馆派范腾端等人传拓云南各地石刻,详情可参见《图书季刊》新第 2 卷第 1 期《国立北平图书馆传拓滇南石刻》一文。朱汉云、陈志书二人应为贵阳士绅,具体生平待考,"二·四炸灾"是抗战中贵阳遭受的一次重大浩劫,全市约七分之一被毁。

四月十一日

先生致信费正清,告知国立昆明图书馆筹建的进展、重庆教育部出版品交换局在昆明设办事处、平馆筹设四类特藏等事。

April 11, 1939

Dear Dr. Fairbank:

I am much obliged to you for your letter of March 26 and for various valuable suggestions which you have sent to me.

Since writing to you last, several developments have taken place.

Firstly, a new library building costing Sh $ 150,000.00 will be built this fall at Kunming. The Provincial Government of Yunnan provides two-thirds of the cost, while the British Boxer Indemnity Trustees contribute the rest at the request of the Library Association of China. The library will be located in the northeastern section of the city which is within easy reach of the two universities and two academies. The National Library is collaborating with this project and all of its books and journals will be deposited in the new library as soon as it is completed.

Secondly, Mr. H. N. Spalding and the University community at Oxford have contributed £ 8,000.0.0. to be used for the purchase of scientific literature for various universities in China. Every book sent to China contains a book-plate with a picture of Oxford and the words:

"From the University of Oxford to the Universities of China in Fellowship of Learning"

The first consignment of books intended for the National Southwest Associated University at Kunming has already been dispatched.

Thirdly, the Chinese Bureau of International Exchanges of Publications has recently set up a branch office at Kunming which receives consignments from abroad and distributes them to the interior. Arrangements have been made with the Smithsonian Institution to send shipments to Haiphong from where they are forwarded to the Bureau at Kunming. While the process is slow, yet it is quite convenient to both the sender and the receiver. I would therefore suggest that you send your books through this channel.

I am asking the Librarian and Professors of the Southwest Associated University to send you lists of their books as well as their desiderata. The University would need text-books, while the National Library is interested in sets of journals and other source materials.

Since the Oxford gift is limited to Chinese universities, the National Library will not be privileged to have a share which, we feel, is rather unfortunate. However, in spite of intense difficulties, we have been building up four collections at Kunming, viz. (1) Special Collection on the Southwest, (2) Special Collection on the undeclared war, (3) Special Collection on international relations and (4) Special Collection on post-war rehabilitation and reconstruction.

Under separate cover I am sending you our monthly list of additions to our special war collection. As we collaborate very closely with all the universities and research institutions here in Kunming, we have worked out a scheme for the differentiation of fields. Moreover, we deposit our books and journals in different universities and their reading rooms.

I enclose herewith a list of our desiderata. It could be revised and some additions made. As second-hand copies would serve the purpose equally well, I hope it would not involve too much expense.

At any rate we are grateful to you for your interest and help.

Yours sincerely,

T. L. Yuan

Acting Director

〔平馆(昆明)英文信纸。Harvard University, John K. Fairbank personal archive, folder Books for China〕

按:此件为打字稿,落款处为先生签名,随信附平馆迫切需要书目单(List of Desiderata)3页,以美国各主要大学出版社为单元分别列出。

四月十三日

先生、陶孟和等人乘火车离开昆明,前往香港。〔《民国日报》(云南),1939年4月14日,第4版〕

四月十五日

平馆驻沪办事处钱存训致函先生,汇报在沪收集日伪、英文文献及运滇情况。大意如下:

兹托中基会之便带上在沪蒐集所得各种资料一包,计小册子十七种(附单)、传单标贴等二十五件、又橡皮章一件,关于蒐集情形,附有说明,即祈察核。

又在沪所购各书俟设法运滇,其中有孙述万君嘱购 *Treaties of 1928* 一书恐须用,先行带上。另有请款单三百张,已印好一并带奉,均请查收。

又昨日往晤 Mr. Boynton,本拟将允赠送本馆之一部资料带港,但此君甚忙,尚未整理,现已请其早日办好送来。

《中国文化情报》十三期以后未收到,函询 Dr. Read 亦未得覆,大约亦未收到。

尚有托工部局华人教育处长陈鹤琴君代集各救济团体之文献,尚未完全收到,容当另行带奉。

〔《北京图书馆馆史资料汇编(1909-1949)》,页673-674〕

按: *Treaties of 1928* 似指 Kellogg-Briand Pact(《凯洛格—白里安公约》或《巴黎非战公约》),日本是最初签约国之一,后中华民国也是该条约的签署国之一,但信中所指之书待考。陈鹤琴(1892—1982),浙江上虞人,儿童教育家,清华学校毕业,后赴美国哥伦比亚大学学习并获硕士学位,回国任南京高等师范学校、东南大学等教授。此件为钱存训所拟底稿。

四月十八日　香港

先生访蔡元培,以姚从吾所拟《中日战事史料蒐集及整理之方法》见示,告知平馆现已照此进行,并搜集西南文献,蔡元培认为甚善。〔《蔡元培日记》,

页 612〕

先生致信王重民，汇补助款及购书费，并谈洽购英国私人所藏《永乐大典》
等事。

有三吾弟：

今日到港，接四月三日来书，知日内即返巴黎，尊夫人何日分娩？
极念。美国方面想已有信致尊处，大约九月一日可开始工作。兹寄上
六十磅汇票，系英庚款补助尊处之壹千元，经财政部特许按法定汇率
购买者；壹百磅汇票，系本馆购书费，系以国币二千九百余元购得者。
此信系航空，银行信或稍迟。

《永乐大典》可全数购下，如内容不佳，则请 Moule 再减五磅何
如？上次寄来之书目书单均已查过，除 Subject Jade 已函请大英博物
院捐赠外，其余均已入藏，故不必再买。又 1937 年新出之中国问题书亦
均入藏，但如已购买则寄到昆明后可让给联大也。奉上书目两纸，关于
云南者可请 Madame Meuvret 购买，或由尊处买好向伊请款。关于法国
黄皮书及中法中越关系之书，以及此次奉上之"九一八以后出版之法文
书"，均在此次寄上之壹百磅内购买可也。下月十日返滇，余再函。

同礼顿首

四月十八

已寄张似旅及 Hughes 书单共三种，一、近代史及国际关系，二、国
际公法，三、经济建设，共六百余磅，希望能在 Spalding 捐款内设法。

关于书目之书，请多买专门目录 Special bibliographies，尤注意以
上三种。

〔The Chase Bank(Hong Kong)信纸。袁同礼家人提供〕

按：是年 6 月初，王重民之子王黎敦出生。

先生致信 David H. Linder，告知中国植物学、生物学研究机构和学者的通
信地址。

April 18, 1939

Dr. David H. Linder

Curator, Farlow Reference Library

20 Divinity Avenue

Cambridge, Mass.

U. S. A.

Dear Sir:

　　Your letter of February 24th addressed to the Smithsonian Institute has been referred to us for reply.

　　Owing to the present situation in China, a number of scientific institutions have been forced to move to Southwestern China where they can carry on their work without Japanese interference.

　　Referring to the addresses of several institutions noted in your letter, we beg to give their present addresses as follows:

　　　　Lingnan University, c/o Fung Ping Shan Library, Hongkong.

　　　　Mr. S. C. Teng, Academia Sinica, Institute of Botany and Zoology, Pei Pai, Chungking, China.

　　　　Science Society of China, 533 Avenue du Roi Albert, Shanghai.

　　　　University of Nanking, College of Agriculture and Forestry, Chengtu, China.

　　　　Mr. F. L. Tai, National Tsing Hua University, Kunming, Yunnan.

　　　　Fan Memorial Institute of Biology, Peiping, China.

　　If you will address them in this way, they will be duly received as our mails have been extremely regular in spite of the war.

　　　　　　　　　　　　　　　　　　　　Yours sincerely,

　　　　　　　　　　　　　　　　　　　　T. L. Yuan

　　　　　　　　　　　　　　　　　　　　Acting Director

　　　〔Smithsonian Institution Archives, Records, 1868 - 1988 (Record Unit 509), Box 1, Library Association of China, Hong Kong〕

按:S. C. Teng 即邓叔群(1902—1970),字子牧,福建闽县人,微生物学家;F. L. Tai 即戴芳澜(1893—1973),字观亭,湖北江陵人,植物病理学家、真菌学家。该信于 5 月 19 日送达,此为抄件,收件人用铅笔做标记。

四月十九日

先生访蔡元培,借得《德意志文学》四册及《五十年来之德国学术》二册。

〔《蔡元培日记》,页 612〕

四月二十日

上午十时,中基会图书馆委员会在蔡元培居所开会,蒋梦麟、先生、周诒春、孙洪芬、司徒雷登等人与会,十一时半会毕。〔《蔡元培日记》,页613〕

四月二十一日

先生致信史密斯森协会,附上致哈佛 Farlow Reference Library 信件的副本,并告知最近收到美方赠书的箱件数量。

April 21, 1939

Dear Sirs:

I beg to enclose herewith for your files copy of a letter addressed to the Curator of the Farlow Reference Library at Cambridge.

We have recently received another twenty boxes of books which your Service has recently forwarded to Hongkong. Eighteen more boxes are on their way to China and we hope to receive them very shortly.

May I take this opportunity of expressing to you once more our sincere appreciation and grateful thanks for the most efficient manner in which you have assisted China in the great task of rebuilding our intellectual edifice.

Arm in arm with resistance, the Chinese people are carrying out an extensive program of reconstruction, particularly in the Southwest, which lies beyond the reach of the Japanese arms of war. We have taken special note that the publications are placed in centers where they will be used to the best advantage.

You may be sure of the special care and thought which Chinese libraries will give in preserving them and in making them available to the largest number of interested readers.

With assurances of our sincere appreciation of your cooperation and assistance,

Yours sincerely,

T. L. Yuan

Acting Director

〔中华图书馆协会(冯平山图书馆转)英文信纸。Smithsonian Institution Archives, Records, 1868–1988 (Record Unit 509), Box 1, Library Association of China, Hong Kong〕

按：此件为打字稿，先生略有修改，落款处为先生签名，于5月16日送达。

四月二十二日

国会图书馆覆函先生，告知先生前请寄送西南部族、民族语言卡片已由相关编目员检出并将另邮寄送平馆。

April 22, 1939

Dear Sir:

Your letter of February 25, requesting Library of Congress printed catalogue cards on certain tribes and languages in southwestern China, has had the attention of the Chief Bibliographer, Miss Hellman.

We enclose here memorandum in response, the cards she selected have been sent to you under separate cover and we trust will reach you safely.

Very truly yours,

Secretary of Library

Dr. Hummel, the Chief of our Division of Orientalia, thinks the title on the accompanying card may be of interest to you.

〔Librarian of Congress, Putnam Archives, Special File, China: National Library 1930−1939〕

按：此件为录副。

四月二十五日

章益、陈礼江覆函先生，告知行政院已将本年预算中平馆（昆明图书馆）删除，教部致函中英庚款董事会请协助维持平馆（滇馆）。

守和先生大鉴：

三月三十一日函，承悉。补助贵馆经费，本部原以成立昆明图书馆名义列入二十八年度预算，已承行政院令删除。顷由部另函管理中英庚款董事会商请特予设法拨款维持。如无办法，拟再专案呈请行政院核办。弟等职责所至，自当力助贵馆之发展也。为王重民先生购买外汇事，业由部将准购通知书转发矣。专此承复，顺颂公绥。

弟章○

陈礼○

按:此信应于 4 月 25 日发出,同日教部致中英庚款董事会公函,大意如下,

　　查国立北平图书馆自经迁设昆明后,竭力经营,现已粗具规模,更为保存文献并便联络起见,除北平原馆照常维持外,并于香港、上海各设办事处,积极工作。惟该馆经费,向由中华教育文化基金董事会担任,近以经费锐减,顿感维持为难。而指定购书用费,更限于西文图书,未便够购中文典籍,尤为遗憾。就该馆目前情形而论,在本年度内至少当须增筹中文图书及研究编纂用费两万元,俾利进行,无奈国库支绌,无款可拨,素念贵会对于文化事业,□极扶植,拟请特予设法补助,以资维持,即希查酌见复为荷。
此致
管理中英庚款董事会

　　　　　　　　　　　　　　　　　　　　　部长陈○○

〔中国第二历史档案馆,教育部档案·全卷宗五,国立北平图书请拨员工学术研究补助费经常费有关文书,案卷号 11616〕

四月二十六日

平馆驻沪办事处钱存训覆函先生,报告采购图书资料情况。大意如下:

　　昨日奉到十九日手示,并书单、附件均已照收。

　　(一)徐淑希著作三种,已退还别发。

　　(二)先后开来书单均已购到一部,其中绝版无法觅得者。

　　(三)前后所购各书及太平洋学会刊物约有三十余包,寄港须每包八角,再为转滇,似所费太多。拟再稍待以候邮局通递直接寄滇(大约数日后可通)。

　　(四)沦陷区报纸共订十三种,但有数种仅来数份,其他亦间有缺少。因自虹口送来,屡次函补均无办法,另抄一单附上。其余如《武汉报》等上海无代订。

　　(五)刘纯甫处已遵嘱汇去卅元,并另函说明搜集范围,俟有复信再为函告。

　　(六)存沪各种什志内载关于苗族论文均注明原单,其余均不在沪,科学社亦未藏。

　　(七)《密勒氏评论报》所刊九国公约签字插图,据称亦系从另一

什志上所印出制版（什志名称已查不出）。现因本馆搜藏，特请代为本馆用铜版纸另印数份，以供保存。

〔《北京图书馆馆史资料汇编(1909-1949)》，页 674-675〕

按：徐淑希（Shuhsi, Hsü）"著作三种"似指 *The North China Problem*（《华北问题》，1937）、*Three Weeks of Canton Bombing*（《广州念日记》，1939）、*Documents of the Nanking Safety Zone*（《南京安全区档案》，1939），均由别发洋行（Kelly & Walsh, Ltd.）出版、太平洋国际学会赞助，因前信中提及"太平洋国际学会赠送本馆全部出版物一套"，故此三书可以避免重复购买。"刘纯甫"即刘纯（1894—？），字纯甫，南京人，中华图书馆协会会员，曾任国立中央大学图书馆编纂课课员[1]，时似在南京私立金陵大学任职。"九国公约"——全称为《九国关于中国事件应适用各原则及政策之条约》，1921 年 11 月 12 日至 1922 年 2 月 6 日，美国、英国、日本、法国、意大利、荷兰、比利时、葡萄牙、中国九国在美国首都华盛顿举行国际会议时签订，该条约确认中国的主权和领土完整，迫使日本将山东省的领土控制权归还给中国。此件为钱存训所拟底稿。

四月二十九日

平馆驻沪办事处钱存训致函先生，报告采购图书资料情况。大意如下：

兹将四月份在沪代购书账随函奉上，计代本馆垫付一六五元六角三分，其中有别发账单四笔，因该处催收已先代付，尚有四月五日发票一份，计洋 23.50，前已寄港，即请检出附入。又徐淑希著作三种已退还，改换新发票一纸，亦已付讫矣。

联大三、四两月共付二十五元三角四分，另邮汇刘纯甫君三十元，俟单据收到再为报销。圕服务社代办之日文书报现收到一部书籍及年鉴，什志及报纸尚未寄到，该项单据均另分开，拟俟中基会之款取到，再为一并报销。

Mr. Boynton 送来油印 Bulletin 一套（不全），财政部国定税则委员会送来《上海物价月刊》一套（自 1937 起），俟得便再为带上。日前托

---

[1]《国立中央大学一览第十一种：教职员录》，1930 年，页 11。

林君带港之传单、小册等件，想均收到，其中有日本新友社小册三种，本系别发 share 交来，故前单写明赠送。日前接该店开来票又将该价计入，因为数甚微，故已照付。

〔《北京图书馆馆史资料汇编（1909-1949）》，页 675-676〕

按："林君"应指林伯遵。此件为钱存训所拟底稿。

四五月间

先生在港期间，与顾临晤谈。〔台北胡适纪念馆，档案编号 HS-JDSHSE-0214-011〕

按：顾临应在 4 月中旬赴沪，随后南下香港，两地均停留各十天，其中在香港参加中基会年会，但先生与之见面的次数和具体时间均无法确定。此后，顾临经日本长崎、东京返回美国。

五月一日

晚，许乃波夫妇在大华饭店设宴，纪念二人木婚。陈君葆夫妇、芬尼克、马先生、冯秉芬、劭太太、先生、高小姐等与席。〔《陈君葆日记全集》第 1 卷，页 451〕

按："马先生"应指马鉴，"高小姐"似为高棣华。

先生致信王重民，谈与石博鼎联络捐书情况并请其在英查明其他院校有无捐赠意愿，此外由英寄赠图书至平馆请以付邮方式寄送，无须装箱。

有三吾弟：

前接三月十四日、廿一日、四月三日及十一日来书，曾于十八日复一书，内附汇票二纸，想已收到（寄巴黎）。Spalding 亦有信来，非常客气。开来书目，内中四、六两种，昆明已入藏，其余者北平已入藏。前此未向 Spalding 开此项书目者，因恐伊觉得吾人近在昆明所成立之 Bureau of British Bibliography，系因伊之捐款而藉此谋取书籍，故所开书单仅有三种（一）近代史及国际关系（二）国际公法（三）经济建设，如寄来之书单能照单购买则尤所欢迎，惟 No. 4 及 6 可删去，径告张似旅可也。Spalding 赴美有何职务，能探得一些消息否？英国图书馆协会六月间开年会，届时拟寄一信作进一步之进行，希望能有结果也。Spalding 来信谓英国其他大学亦正步牛津之后尘，援助中国学术界云，未系究为何大学，请询明示知。又前曾函告张似旅谓寄北平馆之书应直接付邮 by book-post，不用装箱运，即恐交换局将寄平馆之书扣下也。如必须大批寄海防，即在箱上注明"出版品国际交换局转北平图

书馆"为要，

National Library of Peiping, Kunming, Yunnan, c/o Bureau of International Exchange of Publications, Kunming, Yunnan (Via Haiphong)

请转告张君 Pirkis 女士担任功课事，最好请伊开一履历，托大使馆写一信介绍较有力量，需要报酬若干，最好亦注明。联大方面已有人满之患，云大或可设法。此间寄英航邮较廉，故此信仍由英伦转。

同礼顿首

五月一日

〔袁同礼家人提供〕

按：Pirkis 应指 Susan Mary Lyne Pirkis(1915—2013)，似为希腊裔，牛津大学毕业，未能如愿来中国工作，1946 年在香港结婚。

五月二日

钱存训覆函先生，谈寄书、购书及薄卡片等事。

守和馆长先生赐鉴：

孙先生带回各件及四月廿七日手示均已照收，敬悉一一。关于本馆消息，嗣后自当审慎。前购各书均遵嘱于昨日付邮寄港，以便携滇，共计卅四件(内十二件系联大中日文书报，邮费另列)，附上书单乙纸，以备查核。至最近寄下应购书单，因不及购寄，拟俟寄滇邮包通后再寄。日前，尊处由滇电嘱购薄卡片三万张带港，此电直至昨日始由孙先生阅及交下，未知何处延误，深以为歉。联大预支之款，昨在本馆中文书账内领到五百元，连前合共八百元(前预支之三百元原在西文书账内支取，顷已由中文书账内拨还，作为共在中文书账内预支八百元)。另还中基会垫付李君一月廿五日预支一百元，又四月廿三日李君另支一百元。联大预支之八百元，倘由该校还到，请尊处赐一收据作为该款转滇，以便察账。顷收到刘纯甫君覆函，随函转奉。专此，敬请道安。

职钱存训谨上

五，二

〔国家图书馆档案，档案编号 1945-※057-综合 5-010002〕

按："孙先生带回各件"应指 4 月 20 日中基金会在港开会后，孙洪芬由港带回沪上的文件。

五月三日

先生致信史蒂文斯,感谢其寄赠有关林肯的剧本,告知《图书季刊》英文本复刊并已寄送欧美各汉学中心,平馆已在北平恢复印制中文书籍卡片目录并请其将此前资助的时间延长一年,美国学术界通过史密斯森协会寄赠了书刊。

Hongkong,

May 3, 1939

Dear Dr. Stevens:

The book "*Abe Lincoln in Illinois*" which you so kindly sent to me has been duly received which I shall read with great interest and pleasure. May I express to you my sincere appreciation of your gift?

Under separate cover, I am sending to your Division a copy of the *Quarterly Bulletin of Chinese Bibliography* which is printed in Shanghai. A glance of these pages will show that in spite of the war, a great number of scientific publications have been produced in China. The Commercial Press has been able to publish one book each day since last winter.

Copies of our *Bulletin* have been sent to all sinological centres in Europe and the United States. I trust that they will be found useful by scholars interested in Far Eastern studies.

The printing of Chinese catalogue cards was resumed last month by our office in Peiping. These cards will be distributed very shortly. We are hoping that the Foundation will extend the term of the grant for another year in accordance with my request of February 8th.

At a recent meeting of the China Foundation held in Hongkong, a total sum of $ 1,800,000.00 was appropriated to educational and scientific institutions for the year 1939 – 1940. The National Library received the same grant as last year. Both Dr. Monroe and Mr. Roger S. Greene attended the meeting and have just returned to the United States.

Over 200 cases of books have been received by the Library Association of China from the Smithsonian Institution. We have been distributing them to various centres in the interior. A report will be sent to the American Library Association for its annual conference at San Francisco.

With many thanks and kindest regards,

Yours sincerely,

T. L. Yuan

〔平馆（昆明）英文信纸。Rockefeller Foundation. Series 601: China; Subseries 601.R: China-Humanities and Arts. Box 47. Folder 389〕

按：*Abe Lincoln in Illinois* 作者为 Robert E. Sherwood（1896－1955），本书为 3 幕的剧本，描述林肯少年时代至其前往华盛顿前的生平事迹，1938 年 10 月 15 日在百老汇剧院首演。此件为打字稿，落款处为先生签名，于 5 月 22 日送达。

五月十日

先生致信王重民，告刘修业所编《云南书目》可印入《图书季刊》英文本，并谈汇款购买《永乐大典》、石博鼎赠书邮寄问题、敦煌写经照片合编目录等事。

有三吾弟：

四月廿一日及廿四日自巴黎来函均收到，张似旅亦有信来。发单亦收到，但内中颇有重复者，已告滇馆于收到后详加检查、转售联大。兹将应复各点列后：

（一）《云南书目》似可印入《图书季刊》，因此刊在上海印，法文部分可令徐家汇天主堂排印，印好后再合钉一本。

（二）《永乐大典》之款共一百磅，于四月十八日航寄巴黎，已收到否？

（三）Spalding 第一次所捐之书，已有四箱到海防，由交换局接收，深恐蒋慰堂中饱，因寄来书目仅有一份，径寄委员会，该会无人负责，即交蒋君也。本馆在海防设办事处一节，限于经费不易办到。今为补救计，已函张似旅，请其①将寄北平馆之书在可能范围内装在一箱之内，上面注明北平图书馆收启字样；②以后寄华之书单均寄两份，一份寄委员会，一份寄平馆，想渠能照办；③寄本馆之书可寄海防中国领事收转，刘领事即委托中国旅行社运滇。

（四）前寄北平所藏燉煌照片目，请将巴黎所藏者汇为一目，以便在《季刊》第三期发表,《云南书目》则入三期或四期。

(五)Pirkis 女士法文程度如何?如月薪在二百元左右,本馆可请他担任征求法文书报事,请暂勿与之商谈,俟返滇后先与云大接洽可也。蒋慰堂托谢寿康在巴黎及比京进行捐书,不知结果如何?希便中一探听示知。

(六)Kegan Paul 寄来一信,内中所开之书多在前寄巴黎之书单内,请查明后已有者不再购径寄该店,告其将书径寄昆明可也。

同礼顿首

五月十日

〔袁同礼家人提供〕

按:"刘领事"应指刘锴。Kegan Paul 为英国出版商,1912 年被 Routledge & Sons 并购,但仍保持原名至 1947 年,本谱中罗家伦将其称为"伦敦克干保罗公司"。

五月十一日

先生致信张元济,请其赐寄也是园旧藏元曲影印选目,并为《图书季刊》约稿。

菊生先生尊鉴:

违教以来,时深渴想。近维起居清豫,著作日宏,为颂为慰。前接郑振铎君来函,欣悉也是园旧藏元曲已委托贵馆影印,甚感甚感。既系选印,想选目业亦酌定,拟请赐寄一份为感。敝馆编印《图书季刊》,业已由沪方办事处奉上一份,尚希教正。倘承惠赐序跋一类之稿件,俾光篇幅,尤为感幸。专此,顺候著祺。

后学袁同礼顿首

五月十一日

香港冯平山图书馆收转。

〔普通红栏信纸。张元济等撰、胡坚整理《校订元明杂剧事往来信札》,北京:商务印书馆,2018 年,页 48〕

按:张元济在该信上作了三处批注,依次为"仅由郑君振铎交到半部""托王君九校订,目亦归伊选定,恐须数日后方能编成""寄去《宝礼堂宋本书录序》一篇",并于 5 月 17 日覆信。《宝礼堂宋本书录序》后刊于《图书季刊》新第 1 卷第 2 期(1939 年 6 月)。

五月十八日

先生致信王重民,请留意英国学术界对华捐款情况并告知将在下年度馆经费中设法为其谋得旅费补助。

有三吾弟:

接 Hughes 来函,知 All Souls College, Oxford 又捐一千磅,分五年拨付。Universities China Committee 则捐一百磅买仪器。凡此消息如有所闻,希随时函示,以便在会报上发表。图书馆补助旅费一节可以办到四月三十来函已收到,但本年六月以前结亏甚多,实无法可想,当在下年度预算中设法,约在八月间径汇美国可也。另寄中日史料会报告及计划书,均寄英伦转。罗都尔住址望示知,拟寄伊一本《季刊》也。Rock 已移居安南,此人不能帮忙中国,实可憾事。

同礼顿首
五月十八

〔袁同礼家人提供〕

按:"罗都尔"应是法人,其姓氏、生平待考。Rock 应指 Joseph Francis Charles Rock(1884-1962),美国人类学家、植物学家,生于奥地利,通译作"洛克",曾多次赴中国西南地区考察,对纳西文化颇有研究。

先生致信 Norma S. Thompson,就洛克菲勒基金将其资助平馆的款项展期表示感谢,并请代转信函给史蒂文斯。

May 18, 1939

Dear Miss Thompson:

I beg to acknowledge receipt of your letter of March 20 stating that at a meeting of the Executive Committee of your Foundation held March 17, 1939, the Foundation's appropriation RF 36072 was amended to make the unexpended balance available during the period ending June 30, 1942.

This action taken by the Trustees of your Foundation will enable the National Library to develop its program of coordination in Library services in China. On behalf of the National Library, I beg to express to you and through you to all members of the Executive Committee our deep sense of gratitude for your courtesy and assistance.

With kindest regards,

Yours sincerely,

T. L. Yuan

Acting Director

P. S. Will you kindly forward the enclosed letter to Dr. Stevens?

〔平馆(昆明)英文信纸。Rockefeller Foundation. Series 601: China; Subseries 601.R: China-Humanities and Arts. Box 47. Folder 389〕

按:此件为打字稿,落款处为先生签名,于 6 月 2 日送达。先生致信史蒂文斯,收到洛克菲勒基金会资助展期的通知,先生对此表示感谢,并附上草拟年度支取计划。

Hongkong

May 18, 1939

Dear Dr. Stevens:

We have recently received a communication from the Secretary of your Foundation stating that at the meeting of your Executive Committee held March 17, the Foundation's appropriation to the National Library was amended to make the unexpended balance available for a further period of three years.

It is with a deep sense of gratitude that this news has been received and I wish to express to you personally our sincere appreciation and heartfelt thanks for your assistance. Your grant is one which is not to be considered merely in terms of an immediate emergency, but of an opportunity for closer intellectual collaboration over a long period of years.

In view of these considerations, we propose to receive the unexpended balance of G $ 10,500.00 by quarterly installments as follows:

For 1939-40　$ 4,000.00

For 1940-41　$ 4,000.00

For 1941-42　$ 2,500.00

I shall write to your Shanghai office to this effect after having discussed the matter with Dr. Grant who will arrive at the Colony this afternoon.

With renewed thanks and kindest regards,

Yours sincerely,

T. L. Yuan

Acting Director

〔平馆（昆明）英文信纸。Rockefeller Foundation. Series 601: China; Subseries 601.R: China-Humanities and Arts. Box 47. Folder 389〕

按：此件为打字稿，落款处为先生签名。

史蒂文斯致函先生，重申已经解除此前资助款的诸多限制，平馆可以自行购买任何所需要的文献，并建议先生与美国图书馆协会联系。

May 18, 1939

Dear Mr. Yuan:

I believe that my report to you of liberalization of use of the balance of the fund to the National Library has made clear the opportunity of using the balance for purposes of the Library in general education. It occurs to me that you will get some aid in purchasing by writing to the office of the American Library Association, 520 North Michigan Avenue, Chicago, Illinois, addressing the letter to the International Committee. This committee is just now starting to lay plans to help popular libraries secure books expeditiously and at certain discounts that would be possible in larger purchases.

If you have at hand the file of other letters from me, please note that the report on liberalization of this balance overrules the statement in my letter of February 16th, for in that letter I was reporting on the terms of the original grant. There is no restriction on the type of material for the Library that you now may secure to the limit of the funds, as reported on March 20 by the Secretary.

Yours sincerely,

David H. Stevens

〔Rockefeller Foundation. Series 601: China; Subseries 601.R: China-Humanities and Arts. Box 47. Folder 389〕

按：该函寄送昆明，此件为录副。

五月十九日

中午，先生与洛克菲基金会驻沪办事处负责人 Marshall C. Balfour 聚餐，谈论平馆、中华图书馆协会在西南地区重新开展工作及其他事宜。具体事宜涉及：一、与中华民国驻海防的领事馆商妥，将此作为中转站向内陆运送图书；二、与牛津大学教授 Radcliffe-Brown 取得联系并收到捐赠的图书；三、美国图书馆协会已寄出 200 箱赠书；四、洛克菲勒基金会已就资助平馆时限延长至 1942 年。〔Marshall C. Balfour's Diaries, Rockefeller Archive Center, Rockefeller Foundation records, Officers' Diaries, RG 12〕

> 按：Marshall C. Balfour(1896–1976)，1926 年加入洛克菲勒基金会国际卫生部(International Health Division of the Rockefeller Foundation)，1960 年退休。Radcliffe-Brown 即 Alfred Reginald Radciffe-Brown(1881–1955)，英国人类学家，结构功能论的创建者，时任牛津大学人类学系主任。

先生致信洛克菲勒基金会上海办事处，告知支取赞助款的初步计划，并请其将支票寄送孙洪芬处。

May 19, 1939

Shanghai Office,

Rockefeller Foundation,

711 Liza Building,

Szechuen Road, Shanghai.

Dear Sirs:

We have recently received a communication from your New York office stating that at the meeting of your Executive Committee March 17, 1939, the Foundation's appropriation RF 36072 to the National Library of Peiping was amended to make the unexpended balance available during the period ending June 30 1942.

Copy of this communication as well as our reply are enclosed herewith for your information.

If it would meet your approval, we propose to receive the unexpended balance of G $ 10,500.00 by quarterly installments for the following years beginning July 1 1939−

For　1939−40　$ 4,000.00

　　　1940−41　$ 4,000.00

　　　1941−42　$ 2,500.00

The checks should be sent to Mr. Clarence L. Senn, Treasurer of the Board of Management of the National Library at Room 404, National City Bank Building, Shanghai.

With renewed thanks for your cooperation,

Yours sincerely,

T. L. Yuan

Acting Director

$ 1000 each 1939−41

$ 625 each 1941−42

〔Rockefeller Foundation. Series 601: China; Subseries 601.R: China-Humanities and Arts. Box 47. Folder 389〕

按：洛克菲勒基金会上海办事处收到此信后，于 5 月 25 日致信纽约史蒂文斯询问资助案余额的确切数字。该件为抄件。

五月二十二日

陈福洪致信先生，详述四川省中山图书馆创办经历、所遭各种劫难，并请中华图书馆协会协助该馆向有关政府机关申请补助。

守和先生惠鉴：

月前承莅馆指导，别来未久蟾圆一度，感光阴之易逝，念故人之遥隔，引领滇池，不禁神驰左右也。兹将敝馆十年经过略为一陈，幸垂察焉。敝馆自民国十六年由洪约集二十八军第三混成旅旅长周绍芝等十余人在成都卧龙桥川北会馆成立中山政治研究社，是年十月二十日由社成立中山图书馆，十七年春迁移岳府街铁路公司旧铁道银行，由中山图书馆名义呈请国民革命军第二十四、八、九三军联合办事处立案，当蒙批准。是年，洪推设中山政治研究社各县分社并办四川中山政治讲习所，造就宣传及组织各县分社人才，四川党务特派员二十四、八、九三军联合办事处委员兼二十四军新编第二师师长向传义忌刻洪此种组织，派兵占住，书籍不敌刀枪，器具悉被炊爨，于是社务解组、学校停办。幸洪早将善本书籍移开,未尽损失。是年七月,愤而离省赴京沪请求同乡会及老同志援助,黄复生、吕汉群两先生分别专函向传义请予维持。十八年,洪同四川革命后援军总司令吕超、副司令罗觐光率部返川,并代表总司令部赴蓉接洽各将领,始将图书馆恢复。奈铁路公司地址被二十四、八、九三军长划为市府办公。十九年春,租定现住馆址将军街开元宫。是年,二十九军戍区成都县成立成都县官公庙会产业处理委员会处理全县庙产,敝馆所住开元宫庙宇处委会登报拍卖,敝馆呈请二十九军部令饬提留划拨,当蒙批准。洪以馆址既定,呈请四川省教育厅及四川省党务指导委员会立案,教厅派吴天爵科员、四川省党委会派黄莘牧科长来馆查明,始将案批准。至基金一层,请各董事分担承认,用符立案手续,并未实行付款。二十年,洪赴京呈请中央党部立案并请补助,中宣部将案批准并分别函令四川省政府及四川省党务指导委员会宣传部请予协助。是年洪由京返馆,呈请二十九军部令饬成都市政府发给管业证,二十年筹款添制大批书柜、桌凳、书籍,始有收藏设备,稍为就绪。国家主义份子二十四军炮兵司令徐孝匡佔住馆内,四川省党务指导委员会委员魏廷鹤、二十八军陈光藻师长、二十四军党务特派员许行怿力为交涉,均无效。迨至是年冬,二十四、九两军巷战,徐始败去。未及两月卷土重来,洪请敝馆董事周绍芝旅长开兵到馆保护,未能入馆。但当徐败去时,馆内损失及几至一空。二十二年,二十一军部兵站第四分处又来佔住,洪电请四川善后督办刘湘令饬迁移,殊兵站方去,督办署子弹库又来佔住,交涉无效。洪赴京呈请军政部令四川善后督办署军委会令四川剿匪总司令部严饬迁移,洪转省交涉,得罪当局代督办李宏锟,竟以枪毙等词骇洪。二十三年,督办署子弹库始移去。因得罪当局,是年三月,四川剿匪总司令部成立四川官公产清理处,敝馆呈验市府所发之管业证,竟谓二十九军部令饬划拨开元宫是拨予使用,复支使开元宫庙宇会首唐德彝等与敝馆起讼。敝馆处于强权威胁之下,只得让步,法院和解,确定敝馆于开元宫有十年使用权。夫市府所发管业证不下千余张,独敝馆一张不生效,其中黑暗令人敢怒而不敢言。二十四年,军方唆使开元宫会首唐德彝等变卖开元宫,幸洪发觉早,呈请四川省党务特派员办事处及蒋委员长行营,双方函请省府制止未成事实,而教厅即藉故将批准立案撤销,使敝馆根本推翻。至敝馆原名中山图书馆,因别省图书馆亦有以中山命名者,二十年由董事会议决增加省名以资识别,分别呈报中央党部及四川省党务指导委员会、四川省教育厅备案。随奉中央党部秘书处及党务指导委员会均蒙批准,教厅独谓应遵图书馆规程第三条定名为私立成都中山图书馆。查图书馆规程第三条第四项载凡私立图书馆应以所在地教育行政机关为主管机关,并无不能用省名之规定。敝馆设在四川省会、四川教育厅所在地,敝馆应以教育厅为主管机关,是时省会尚无市政府,况经教部、教厅批注立案之杭州私立浙江流通图书馆已有成例,兼之敝馆加增省名沿有既久,未便更改。而又早经中央党部、四川省党务指导委员会批准有案,教厅撤销立案,敝馆将以上各由具呈申明,迄今竟无明白批示。二十五年,敝馆之设立系由私人集资及筹措所办,行文以私立四川中山图书馆名义。是年改修书屋、添制大批书柜,刘督办湘正式由督署拨款补百元补助,又为题四川中山图书馆馆名,邓锡侯军长、唐式遵军长亦为题馆名刊挂街口,薛岳总指挥亦为题“创造革命文化,建设强盛国家”一联刊挂。敝馆是年呈请四川省党务特派员办事处拨款补助,随奉党特派处二月十日宣尚字第二八五七号指令开:“呈悉。该馆长苦心经营、奋斗不懈,成绩斐然,殊堪嘉许,惟本处经费亏累已深,一俟整理就绪再行酌予补助可也。此令。”等因在案。奈书屋添修未久,二十一军唐式遵军长所买住宅与敝馆相连,竟向开元宫会首串买,用修私人住宅。敝馆以法院确定十年使用权未满两载,由董事长陈泽霈率同各董事联名专函唐式遵军长说明馆址情形。唐军长遂坚持,乃涉讼,经一、二审唐均败诉,复以武力摧残。洪不得已请中委黄复生、国府参军长吕超援助,蒙两先生分别函电刘主席维持、制止,刘以督办署名义明令唐军长静候最高法院解决,但唐式遵军长已命人将墙垣拆毁,后又摧残。洪又电请军政部制止,军政部函川康绥靖公署核办,摧残得以中止。二十六年,为敝馆十周年纪念,发印刊物、征求题词,并征书籍,孙院长哲生特为题“东壁图书自宏富,西川文化凤瑰琦”一联刊挂。二十七年,各方题词赠书先后寄到,是年将馆舍略为培修,复添制大批阅书椅凳。八月五日,柬请各机关、法团莅馆举行十周年纪念典礼。未久,中委邓家彦、邹鲁及萨镇冰将军先后来蓉,洪均请到馆指导。书籍达四万余册、日报达五十余种,华侨日报亦有八种。是年十一月,应中国学术团体联合年会之约赴渝,便中接洽孙哲生院长。孙院长特电请川省府王治易主席切实扶助,最高法院亦于是年十一月判决敝馆十年使用权不能变更。王主席函孙,反谓敝馆地址未定、纠纷未了、经费无着,虽欲设法补助,窒碍良多,不知馆址已定、纠纷已了,即云经费无着,政府自应协助,并中央于教育一项,指有专款补助而不肯维扶加以补助,恐有得罪于唐式遵耳。但洪以百折不回之初心求遂,发扬主义之宏硕,故愈挫愈奋、不畏强敌、赤手创造,十余年来所用金钱不过万余元,募集之数不过四千余元,其余之数悉由洪挪垫借贷,呈报四川省党部有案可查。月前,鸠工庀材添修书屋数间,所有全体房屋亦加培修刷新,因此一度布置颇改旧观。现刻正筹款添置大批书柜,及呈请市府在成都南门外划拨新村四五亩,扩充建筑。敬请先生由大会专函杨市长请予切实扶助,并电郭有守厅长请予维持原案以利进行,贤者谅必乐予玉成也。窃维中央纪念总理,特设中山文化教育馆,敝馆在四川为纪念总理之唯一图书馆,现在规模已具、成效日著,只待发皇。况当此抗战时期,三民主义教育更应积极推动。奈洪以环境恶劣、才力棉薄、孤掌难鸣,以致发扬主义迄今未遂。务望先生予以指示,俾洪所创办纪念总理之图书馆十余年来惨淡经营成绩不致功亏一篑,尤所盼祷,所拟电稿请予参酌。又凡此实情均不足为外人道,幸勿公诸报端也。如何之处,统希见复。崇此,即颂勋安。

弟陈福洪再拜
五月二十二日

〔四川省中山图书馆用笺。国家图书馆档案,档案编号 1939-※051-协会 5-001006 至 1939-※051-协会 5-001014〕

按:陈福洪,字范畴。[1]"王治易主席"即王缵绪(1886—1960),字治易,四川西充人,1938 年 4 月担任四川省主席。"杨市长"即杨全宇(? —1940),四川西充人,1938 年至 1940 年担任成都市市长,后因"抢米事件"被枪决。

阿博特覆函先生,询问中央研究院各研究所及金陵大学等机构现在的通讯

---

① 中华图书馆协会执行委员会编《中华图书馆协会会员录》,1935 年,页 66。

地址。

May 22, 1939

Dear Sir:

The Smithsonian Institution acknowledges, with thanks, a copy that you have sent here of your letter of April 18 to Dr. David H. Linder, Curator, Farlow Reference Library, 20 Divinity Avenue, Cambridge, Massachusetts, giving various changes of address for establishments in China.

In going over the list it was found that the address changed in connection with the Academia Sinica, was that of the Institute of Botany and Zoology, which was not listed by the Smithsonian Institution for its publications. There was, however, on the mailing list for the Smithsonian Reports the National Research Institute of Psychology of the Academia Sinica. Will you please tell me how that Institute should be addressed, as I find that the various Institutes of the Academia Sinica have been in different towns. It is noted also in the list that the College of Agriculture and Forestry of the University of Nanking is at Chengtu. The college is not listed by the Institution, but the University of Nanking itself is on the mailing list for all Smithsonian publications. The University Library address has now been changed to Chengtu, but if this is not correct will you please inform me.

Very respectfully yours,

C. G. Abbot

Secretary

〔Smithsonian Institution Archives, Records, 1868 – 1988（Record Unit 509), Box 1, Library Association of China, Hong Kong〕

按：此件为录副。

五月二十五日

洛克菲勒基金会上海办事处致函先生，告知该会将于七月一日起如先生前请每季度向平馆汇出美金一千元。

May 25, 1939

Dear Mr. Yuan:

We note from your letter of May 19 that you request us to make payments under the present extension of the Foundation's appropriation RF 36072 to the National Library of Peiping, at the rate of US $ 1,000.00 quarterly, commencing July 1, 1939. Inasmuch as this makes an annual payment of US $ 4,000.00, which is well within the stipulations of the letter from the Secretary, limiting the amount available in any one year to $ 8,000.00, we see no reason why we should not comply with your request.

We will therefore, as be requested, make the first payment on July 1 to Mr. Clarence L. Senn, Treasurer of the Board of Management of the National Library, at Room 404, National City Bank Building, Shanghai.

> Yours sincerely,
>
> C. G. Copley.

〔Rockefeller Foundation. Series 601: China; Subseries 601.R: China-Humanities and Arts. Box 47. Folder 389〕

按:C. G. Copley,生卒年待考,洛克菲勒基金会驻沪办事处人员,曾任 Lincoln Inn 餐厅经理。[1] 该函寄送昆明,此为抄件,寄送给纽约总部。

顾子刚致函先生,告知北平生活日益艰难,留平馆员收入难以维持。

May 25, 1939

Dear Mr. Yuan:

Dr. Stuart came back on the 20th, but he has not yet been in to the library. I suppose he feels there is nothing particular with the last China Foundation meeting.

The CF has replied to our request to pay our monthly allowance to the Chung Foo Bank in Shanghai. Since it has our May and June allowances here already, the consideration of our request has to be

---

① *The North-China Desk Hong List*, 1934, p. 167.

deferred.

The difference in exchange is now about 25%, against 40% at the highest, but the cost of foodstuffs, except flour, has not come down. Indeed mixed millet flour is now 11 ¢ . When exchange was fluctuating badly, the price of all textiles varied <u>from day to day</u>, or rather from morning to evening. The cheapest 竹布 is now 29 ¢ . This is to give you some idea of conditions here. I think conditions in Kunming are no better, if not worse, but our men have their families here, so feel the burden most keenly.

We have done what we can for those below ＄40. Yenching is giving a subsidy based on exchange, and PUMC, a flat 20%. Our people petitioned for the same, but, of course, we could not do anything of the sort. It was explained to them that YC and PUMC had gold income, and consequently their local currency income was greater, while ours was local currency, so we could not follow them. Some even thought our a/c at the City Bank was in Shanghai currency, that we actually have got a profit on exchange. This we dispelled easily by telling them that we paid ¾% in March to change our a/c to local currency, and that the CF had done the same.

The Municipal Government has ordered a ＄3-subsidy to policemen, so we have to pay ＄12 a month extra for our police.

Yours sincerely

顾

〔国家图书馆档案，档案编号 1939-&249-027-1-5-003002〕

五月二十七日

John A. Pollard 致函先生，告知其兄 Robert T. Pollard 逝世，临终前曾全力为中华图书馆协会征集图书。大意如下：

　　径启者，四月二十一日阁下致兄饶伯（Dr. Robert T. Pollard）之函，现已由西雅图转来敝处，因渠不幸业于四月十二日与世长辞矣。自一九三三年以还，先兄即患剧烈心脏病，但渠对于应尽职务，则从来未放弃。迳为贵国各图书馆征集图书，由渠口中所述遗札中所记，余深悉渠实积极赞助。余抵西埠之时，适先兄弥留之际，即闻人言，本年一月初，当渠旧病复发时，至三月十日入医院期间，渠仍躬亲奔走，进行征书及运华事宜,而并未以此委诸他人,足征其热诚之一般。

吾人追思之余,觉渠今所捐躯以赴者,实乃至上仁义感召之所致,而对其过去四十一载之成就,尤引以为荣焉。

阁下来函,辱承申谢先兄协助贵会复兴大业,至为感激。刻下西雅图先兄诸挚友,正筹募纪念金,以为救济中国学生之用,此则余愿以奉告者也。此致
中华图书馆协会袁理事长

约翰·波拉德(John A. Pollard)谨启

一九三九,五月,廿七日,于美国俄亥俄头立多城

〔《中华图书馆协会会报》第 14 卷第 1 期,1939 年 7 月 20 日,页 13-14〕

按:Robert T. Pollard(? - 1939),曾著 *China's Foreign Relations: 1917-1931*,1933 年纽约初版。该函原为英文,后被译为中文刊登。

五月

美国图书馆协会刊登先生来信,感谢美国同仁给予中国图书馆界的无私援助并将编印美国赠书目录。

To the Secretary:

We have been informed by the Smithsonian Institution that over one hundred boxes of books donated by American libraries and institutions have been shipped to China. We understand that more boxes will be sent as soon as sufficient materials have been accumulated at Washington.

As Chinese universities and scientific institutions have been forced to migrate to the southwest to carry on their work without books and journals, this notable contribution will aid materially the cause of education and culture in China.

It is with keen pleasure and sincere appreciation that we are now unpacking the first installment of thirty-six boxes just received. We plan to have a catalog of the American gift of books printed and trust that it will serve as a token of American sympathy as well as a memento of Sino-American cooperation in intellectual work.

It might be a source of gratification to all of our American friends to know that scientific and educational work of permanent nature is going on steadily in China in spite of the war. As the need of books and journals is a pressing one, further gifts from the United States are earnestly solicited.

May I take this opportunity to convey to you and all members of your Committee on International Relations our heartfelt thanks and great admiration for the generous efforts you have made in conducting the book campaign in the interest of Chinese libraries. Your work has won our everlasting gratitude.

T. L. Yuan, Chairman

Executive Board

Library Association

〔A. L. A. *Bulletin* Vol. 33, No. 5 (May, 1939), p. 352〕

按:1939 年收到美国捐赠的书刊后,中华图书馆协会委托九龙海关将存港图书设法运滇,运费由教育部出版品交换局承担,但该处海关以海防仓库无余地、无力转运为由拒绝落实该办法,导致运送效率极低。[①] 原信登载时并未标明撰写时间,暂系于此。

六月五日

先生致信李俨,转寄王重民在法所摄算学古籍照片,并附中日战事史料征辑会计划书及报告等件。

　　乐知先生大鉴:

　　　兹寄上王重民君在巴黎所摄《阿尔热巴拉新法》照片三十八帧,即希查收,并盼见覆。敝馆征辑抗战史料,屡荷赞助,感谢不尽。兹奉上报告及计划书各一册,统祈教正为荷!

　　　尚此,即颂公绥。

弟袁同礼顿首

六月五日

〔韩琦《王重民、向达致李俨信》,《国际汉学研究通讯》第 22 期,2021 年 10 月,页 189〕

按:《阿尔热巴拉新法》由来华耶稣会士傅圣泽(Jean-François

---

① 《中华图书馆协会会报》第 14 卷第 4 期,页 11。

Foucquet, 1665-1741）译出，该书名即"代数"（algebra）一词的音译。先生致信国会图书馆 Louise G. Caton，请寄赠 1800 年以来中外外交关系书籍的卡片目录并就其中重要者标注星号。

June 5, 1939

Miss Louise G. Caton, Secretary

Library of Congress

Washington, D. C.

U. S. A.

Dear Madam:

I beg to acknowledge with many thanks the receipt of your letters of April 22nd and May 2nd enclosing memoranda from the Chief Bibliographer with the cards she has so kindly collected for us. We appreciate very much your assistance in the matter and we wish to express to you and to the Chief Bibliographer our deep sense of gratitude. Please convey our hearty thanks also to Dr. Clark and Dr. Hummel. We are looking forward to the receipt of the books recommended by you from Messrs. Stechert & Co.

We shall be most indebted to you if you will kindly solicit the assistance of the Chief Bibliographer once more for us. We are in need of a list of references on China's foreign relations from 1800 to date from the collections in the Library of Congress and we shall be obliged to you to have a set of cards on this topic. If you could mark with a red star on all the more important works, it will be a great help to us.

May I assure you once more our grateful appreciation of your valuable cooperation and assistance?

Yours faithfully,

T. L. Yuan

Acting Director

P. S. Please send the enclosed letter to Mr. Robert and □□□□.

〔平馆（昆明）英文信纸。Library of Congress, Putnam Archives, Special Files, China: National Library 1930-1939〕

按：Stechert & Co.应指 G. E. Stechert & Company，1872 年在纽约
成立的一家大型国际图书进出口公司，后在伦敦、巴黎、斯图加特
等地设立分支办事处。此件为打字稿，补语、落款均为先生亲笔，
以航空信方式寄送，6 月 22 日送达国会图书馆秘书办公室。

六月六日

先生致信王重民，寄上书单一纸请其购买，并谈昆明被日寇空袭所扰。

　　有三吾弟：

　　　　接五月十五日来书，详悉一切。兹寄书单一纸，请代访购，寄滇
　　或港。在法所购之书，如装箱运华，则均托王景春寄港，因此间随时
　　有被炸之可能也。刻下疏散者日多，但乡间诸多不便，于办事尤感
　　困难也。

　　　　　　　　　　　　　　　　　　　　同礼
　　　　　　　　　　　　　　　　　　　　六，六

　　　　　　　　　　　　　　　　　〔中国书店·海淀，四册〕

　　按：所附书单不存。

六月七日

顾子刚致函先生，告知本月五日其赴天津拜会德尔格的情况，并就缩微胶
片机组装周期、费用、人员培训、运营成本和耗材等方面予以必要的说明。

　　　　　　　　　　　　　　　　　　　　June 7th, 1939

Dear Mr. Yuan:

　　I saw Dr. Draeger in Tientsin on the 5th in connection with the book
camera. The camera parts were all built in America, but they require a
certain amount of machining before they can be put together. This work
will require about four more months, and it is to this that Dr. Draeger
referred to when he mentioned about setting up the machine. The actual
assembling of the finished parts will not take much time.

　　Dr. Draeger kindly explained to me in a general way the operation of
the camera, the personnel and space requirements, and also showed me all
the parts that were ready. Although I had feared the actual operation
would be rather more complicated than the photostat, I found all the
important processes were more or less automatic, so there would be no

difficulty. According to Dr. Draeger, the most difficult part is to keep the machine in order. An article by Dr. Draeger is enclosed for your information.

The following points are presented as a report of my visit:

(1) Home for the Camera. Dr. Houghton had expressed a great deal of interest and had informed Dr. Draeger that PUMC would furnish the necessary space if we couldn't find a suitable home for it. I think for a Rockefeller camera to stay in a Rockefeller institution is about the best arrangement under the circumstances. Moreover, there are certain other advantages, as heating in winter and cooling in summer (for the dark room), the availability of engineers and mechanics, etc. It will also be more convenient for Dr. Draeger to look over the camera at PUMC than at Yenching. The matter will be taken up by Dr. Draeger directly with Dr. Houghton on his return from America. I am therefore not approaching Dr. Stuart.

(2) Equipment. The camera and the darkroom are almost completely equipped. Additional equipment required, besides pipes and some minor things, are the following: an exposure meter, a voltage meter, and a pair of scales for weighing chemicals (other things may be required, as work progresses, but during my visit, we thought of these). The two meters are required to insure correct exposures, for with these we can easily determine and get the amount of light required for particular books, without having to adjust the lens opening or speed. If we were to depend upon the operator's judgment, the results wouldn't be satisfactory, particularly with old Chinese books, whose condition varies so much. The cost of the meters and the scales will be about US $ 50.00.

The Rockefeller Foundation has paid for the parts already made, but Dr. Draeger does not know what other financial provision has been made for expenses in China, and I do not know either. Transportation has been through U. S. government agencies, so we do not have to pay for that, but we have to refund Dr. Draeger for the expenses he is incurring on our behalf. Roughly speaking, the mechanics he now puts on the camera cost about Ch $ 100 a month (to be four months probably), while no idea can yet be formed of the total cost of minor equipment that has to be bought or made. I presume it will also cost something to fix up a darkroom in Tientsin.

(3)Personnel. If the camera is kept in full operation, we shall need two operators and one darkroom man to process the films, besides a mechanic. Owing to the speed of the camera (easily 800 exposures an hour), for even allowing only 3200 exposures a day, due to lower efficiency of Chinese operators, we should still require about 40 Chinese volumes a day. Perhaps we should start with only two men, both to be trained in all the processes, so when we have urgent work, they may both concentrate on filming; after the rush is over, one can do the developing and the other continues with filming. I must find out from Yenching how much material we can borrow there, and know what you want for your end, before deciding on this problem.

For operation, only intelligent workers are required, no white-collar staff, so I shall try to pick two from among our pages. I have in mind one already; since he is quite mechanically minded, I hope he can pick up enough not only to run the camera but also to keep it in condition. According to Dr. Draeger, probably a minimum of four months' training under his direct supervision will be required. Training will begin late in September or early in October.

As to the mechanic, Dr. Draeger thinks PUMC should be able to let us have a part-time man. He can be sent to Tientsin before the camera is ready to be set up, so he can see and learn everything. Since the mechanic will not have as much constant work as the other operators, a part-time man from PUMC is ideal. The checking of films to see that everything is o.k. may be done in the Library.

(4) <u>Finances</u>. Since neither of us know much about the final Rockefeller Foundation grant for operating expenses, we did not discuss finances much, except the cost mentioned in (2) above. The following are entirely my own ideas. We have to provide for the cost of final installation and running expenses. For wages, I think $ 80 a month will be enough; $ 20 to PUMC for the part-time use of one mechanic, and about $ 60 for two operators and one darkroom man (if we keep our men in PUMC, we may have to pay more since its scale is rather high). In PUMC we don't have to pay for electricity and water, and the cost of oil and grease will not be much, if not free. Films and chemicals will have to be paid for in U. S. currency. Since the films for the Library of Congress are to be re-exported, I think we should arrange the supply through official channels in Washington, for it will be a pure waste of money to pay 25 percent import duty on them. At the same time, U. S. official quarters may not be willing. Allowing for 250 working days a year, we require that number of 200 ft. rolls of films annually. According to the *Library Journal* the 100 ft. films cost US $ 2 something; then 200 ft. films should cost US $ 5, or we require US $ 1,000 for films a year. Chemicals may cost one-eighth as much. These are my guess work, merely to let you have some idea of how much of the RF you have to keep in UScy.

We have to decide how the account books should be kept. Probably all US currency disbursements have to be recorded by you, while PUMC should keep the current Chinese currency accounts, or it can give me a nominal appointment to look after the camera and then I can keep the accounts. The National Library here should not have anything to do with the accounts until your return. For this reason, I have not charged my travelling to the Library.

I am sending a copy of this to Dr. Draeger, as I desire his opinion and advice, particularly as to the cost of films and the feasibility of my proposal to arrange for the supply of films through Washington.

Yours sincerely

T. K. Koo.

〔Rockefeller Foundation. Series 300 Latin America-Series 833 Lebanon; Subseries 601. Box 9. Folder 86〕

按：UScy 应指美元（US currency）。此后，该缩微胶片设备的确安装在协和医学院。此为抄件。

六月上旬 昆明

先生路遇傅斯年，后者请先生推荐一位专业图书馆人士到中研院史语所服务。先生告以一人。后傅斯年致信先生，可否请王育伊到所服务，先生快信回绝，但推荐馆员邓衍林代替。〔《傅斯年遗札》，页 1008〕

按：此事最初为傅斯年与李济商量，觉史语所图书室须人服务，故致信先生，请代为物色，但先生并未及时复信。两人路遇时，傅斯年并未记得推荐之人的姓名，但以其资历、学识不佳，不甚满意，先生则告知如推荐图书馆专业（文华图专）毕业生，恐史语所负担薪酬为重。王育伊为王敬礼（字毅侯）之子，燕京大学史学毕业，与邓衍林在平馆服务多年。此事记于 6 月 22 日傅斯年给李济的信中，但并未提及具体时间，暂系于此。

六月十一日

王重民致函先生，告英国文化界及捐书情况。

守和吾师钧鉴：

兹探得 All Souls College 拟派往中国之教授为 A. R. Radcliffe-Brown，教人类社会学，据云与吴文藻颇相识。又今年正月间，伊在 *Times* 发表一论文，述我大学近况，据云其所据材料，为得自吾师者。牛津副校长及各热心教授，又联名发出一函征书（由该大学注册课办理），俟索得原稿，即寄呈。又牛津大学又捐了五十镑。王维诚叟有回国消息（或仍回西南大学），此君胆太小，不敢透漏一点消息，以后均托尤桐代探。伦敦之总委员会为张似旅素志，盖伊不主张中国人出名，让外国去办，内只有一华人主传达消息并接受图书即可。想此总委员会成立后，伊之地位益重要。生一切情形均好。图书馆已发一月薪，共 1200 法郎，实出意料之外。从此每外可得 2200 法郎，有小孩后每月须三千,八月内无所得,然东补西凑,足可很从容的渡过矣。别有一信,寄呈 Stationery Office 所寄 Parliament papers 清单。即请道安!

受业重民敬上。

六月十一日

〔国家图书馆档案,档案编号 1940-※044-外事 3-002051〕

按:"从此每外"当作"从此每月"。"伊在 *Times* 发表一论文"即1939 年 1 月 3 日, *The Times* 刊登之 Chinese Centres of Learning, a sad survey, the policy behind destruction。[1] 尤桐(1897—?),字琴庵,河北完县人,1927 年北京师范大学英文研究科毕业,后任河北省教育厅督学[2],三十年代赴英在牛津大学留学,1940 年有意回国任教,但因海路不通遂前往美国继续深造,后在普林斯顿大学高等研究院担任孙念礼的助理,协助其翻译《汉书·食货志》。

六月十二日

费正清致函先生,告知哈佛大学各院系教员挑选书籍、期刊,并最终寄赠七箱图书、期刊,徐家麟协助编辑了赠书清单。

June 12, 1939

Dear Mr. Yuan,

We are shipping to your address in Kunming, via the Smithsonian Institution and routed through Haiphong, seven cases containing some 1008 - odd selected volumes and some 4807 - odd copies of learned journals, collected from the faculty here during the last few months. I have informed the Smithsonian of your statement in yours of April 11, to the effect that the Chinese Bureau of International Exchange will take delivery of such shipments at Haiphong, and I assume the Smithsonian will be able to route the cases to you without trouble. If such arrangement is not in working order, I shall probably be informed by you or them.

The Engineering School joined in our project in the person of Prof.

---

① 台北"国史馆",〈中国图书馆协会请补助(教育部)〉,数位典藏号 019-030508-0015,页 44-48。
② 《河北省教育厅职员录》,1929 年,页 16。

Lionel Marks, through whom we collected some 200 volumes and 2000 journals (copies) on engineering sciences; I enclose copy of his circular on the subject to the engineering faculty. If and when you have time, perhaps you could write him; but I imagine we might wait until the books arrived, and at that time I shall relay some kind of greeting to the people here, if you will send me a brief statement; this procedure I think will strengthen local interest, and may be considered part of our project as a whole.

These books are selected for value in a reference or teaching library, and I think have fairly high standard of value. Among them are some volumes that might be of particular use to teachers, and with your permission I shall send later in the summer a brief list of volumes which I should like to see put at the disposal of certain teachers at the University. We have a card for each book sent, and so can send a bibliography of the books to be transferred in this way.

Some of the totals now sent run as follow: Physics 919, Science in general 1478, Medical science 74, History 207, Economics 48, Philosophy 209, Geography 420, Literature 134.

I am glad to get this temporarily wound up and go off for a vacation. Mr. C. L. Hsu (Hsu Chia-ling), a graduate of Boone now at Harvard-Yenching, has helped us in cataloguing.

With best wishes as always,

J. K. Fairbank

〔Harvard University, John K. Fairbank personal archive, folder Books for China〕

按：Lionel Marks（1871－1955），英国工程师、航空工程的先驱，1892 年移民美国，1894 年起担任哈佛大学机械工程系教授，直至 1940 年退休。此件为录副。

六月十四日

先生致信哈佛学院图书馆，感谢寄赠书籍。

June 14, 1939

Harvard College Library,

Cambridge, Mass.,

U. S. A.

Dear Sirs:

We have pleasure in acknowledging the receipt of a set of books listed on the enclosed sheet which the faculty and students of Harvard University have so kindly presented to this Library. On behalf of the National Library, I beg to express to you and through you to the faculty and students of your University our sincerest appreciation and heartfelt thanks for your timely assistance.

The various books you so kindly sent to China are extremely valuable to our students and investigators. We shall place them in prominent places in our Library where they will no doubt be used to the best advantage.

It must be a source of gratification to you and your colleagues to learn that in spite of the war, a great deal of scientific and educational work is going forward in China. In the face of great difficulties, the work of scholarship is being carried on.

As the need of Western books and journals is most urgent in China at the present time, further gifts from interested friends in America are earnestly solicited. We shall be greatly indebted to you if you would kindly bear our needs in mind and make the necessary contact for us.

With renewed thanks for your cooperation and valuable assistance in the rebuilding of our intellectual edifice.

Yours sincerely,

T. L. Yuan

Acting Director

〔平馆（昆明）英文信纸。Harvard University, John K. Fairbank personal archive, folder Books for China〕

按：这批捐赠书籍应于 4 月 6 日以挂号信的方式寄出，附收到书目一页，共 14 种。此件为打字稿，落款处为先生签名，于 7 月 25 日送达。

六月十五日

先生致信费正清，告知因昆明邮局失火此前哈佛大学寄赠的一批图书只接收到十四册且无书单及实际寄出方，只得致信哈佛学院图书馆表示感谢，并告平馆寄赠了《图书季刊》英文本。

June 15, 1939

Dr. J. K. Fairbank,

41 Winthrop Street,

Cambridge, Mass.,

U. S. A.

Dear Dr. Fairbank:

We have recently received 14 volumes of books on the Social Sciences from the Harvard College Library. As they are the gift of faculty and students of Harvard University, I hasten to write to express to you our sincere appreciation of your timely assistance. These books are very well selected and are meeting a real need here.

As the local Post Office had a fire inside their building soon after these volumes were received, we have been wondering whether there was any official communication transmitting these volumes to us. In the absence of such a letter and a complete list of books sent to China, we wrote to the Harvard College Library yesterday acknowledging the receipt of these 14 volumes and asking it to convey our thanks to the faculty and students of your University.

I have recently mailed you a copy of the *Quarterly Bulletin of Chinese Bibliography* and hope you will find it useful to your work.

With kindest regards,

Yours sincerely,

T. L. Yuan

Acting Director

〔平馆（昆明）英文信纸。Harvard University, John K. Fairbank personal archive, folder Books for China〕

按：5 月 21 日，昆明当地邮局失火。此件为打字稿，落款处为先生签名，该信附在本日致裘开明信中，于 7 月 17 日送达。

先生致信裘开明，感谢其赠书并表示平馆愿意承担自马萨诸塞州剑桥到华盛顿的邮寄费用，且平馆已寄赠《图书季刊》英文本。

June 15, 1939

Dear Dr. Chiu:

It is a pleasure to learn that you have succeeded in securing some books for Chinese libraries. Please send them to the International Exchange Service, Smithsonian Institution, Washington, D. C. which makes monthly shipment to China.

This Association will be glad to pay the packing and transportation charges from Cambridge and Washington. Please send us the bill in duplicate copies.

I wish to assure you and through you to all of your colleagues that in the face of great difficulties in China, the work of scholarship is being carried on, as you will see from the *Quarterly Bulletin of Chinese Bibliography* which we mailed to your Library recently.

Yours sincerely,

T. L. Yuan

Chairman,

Executive Board

P. S. Please mail the enclosed letter to Dr. Fairbank.

〔中华图书馆协会（冯平山图书馆转）英文信纸。Harvard University, John K. Fairbank personal archive, folder Books for China〕

按：此件为打字稿，落款处为先生签名，于 7 月 17 日送达。

内政部警政司致函先生，告前呈《图书季刊》中文本在昆明复刊申请登记、挂号等未核法令，并检送《修正出版法及施行细则》，请重新办理。

奉部长交下贵馆来呈一件，为《图书季刊》，迁滇续刊，请查明登记证号数，俾便向邮局挂号等情。查杂志迁移别省出版，依法应另填登记声请书，连同原领登记证（登记证如已遗失，应先登报声明作废，连报附呈）呈由新发行所所在地之主管官署（县或市政府）重行声请登记,层转本部核办,始与法令相符。来呈核有未合。样本二册,亦未收到。相应检送《修正出版法及施行细则》一册,函复查照。此致

国立北平图书馆袁同礼先生

　　附《修正出版法及施行细则》一份。

内政部警政司启

六,十五

〔内政部通用笺。国家图书馆档案,档案编号 1943-※041-编印 2-001078 和 1943-※041-编印 2-001079〕

按:该函于 26 日送达,7 月 1 日,平馆(昆明)填具"新闻纸杂志登记声请书",先生为发行人,王育伊、万斯年为编辑。

六月十八日

下午,先生与凌纯声、董作宾访徐旭生、顾颉刚。〔《徐旭生文集》第 9 册,页 1016;《顾颉刚日记》卷 4,页 240〕

六月二十日

先生致信王重民,谈私人、编纂《云南书目》、法国外交部赠书及赵录绰和谢国桢近况。

有三吾弟:

五月三十一日及六月六日及刘女士五月二日函均先后收到六月四日之信尚未收到。兹将各事分别录左:

一、此时想尊夫人已生产,产后应在医院多住数日,不可过于劳碌,将来由法赴美较为简便,到华京后住房极不易觅,因房东多不愿收有小孩者,且对华人态度甚坏,与欧洲情形大不相同,可暂住车站左近小旅馆,徐徐觅房或托吴光清字子明代觅亦可。登岸时须将证明书及 Hummel 来信携在身上。

二、关于托购之法文书,述及云南及苗民生活者请寄滇,其余寄港,吾人在滇仅系临时性质,将来运费亦待考虑也。

三、关于《云南书目》,兹将哈佛大学寄来书目送上用印刷品与 *Selected Chines Books* 一同寄上,请将未收者补入尊目内。

四、近数年中国出版新书曾由顾子刚编—"*Selected Chinese Books in 1933-37* ",已寄张似旅一份,并寄尊处一份。

五、前来函谓法外交部可赠吾馆一万法郎之书,不知是否与赠云大及

燕大完全相同,抑系现款由吾人自由选择。兹又附上书目一纸,请选购。

六、法外交部书及官书局所刻之书,日内即函 Marx 请求赠与,并谢对于执事之优待。

七、赵孝孟及谢国桢均因为东方作提要,先后免职。谢在大中银行作秘书,赵仍在东方办公,通讯处东厂胡同该会转。

同礼顿首

六月二十日

〔袁同礼家人提供〕

按:"吾人在滇仅系临时性质"当作"吾人在港仅系临时性质"。*Selected Chinese Books in 1933-37* 中文题名为《新书选目》,该书在《图书季刊》英文本前四卷之"中文图书"(Selected Publications: I. Books in Chinese)基础上,补充 1938、1939 年出版物,其中 1939 年出版的部分为前 142 页,1940 年 7 月版则补齐正文 143 页至 190 页内容,并撰写序言和缩写清单及作者索引。Marx 即 Jean Marx(1884 - 1972),时在法国外交部任职,主持 Service des Œuvres françaises à l'étranger。

王重民致函先生,谈其在法获取赠书的情况及赴美日程。

守和吾师:

近来无多消息,实因在家事忙,与外人接触较少也。今日由医院介绍一女仆,看护小孩及刘女士数日,明日生又可工作如恒矣。Mme Meuvret 称,伊与外交部图书馆主任颇相识,法国黄皮书,可请他赠吾馆一份,伊说必成。生又问 Imprimerie Nationale 出版物,是否可全要一份? 她说:"不能很快!"牛津捐书启,不知曾见到否? 三两日内,尤桐必能找到一份,当转上。谢礼士即返明星,大约九月以前能返抵北平,因限于时间,恐不能赴昆明一游。杜乃扬女士有时能帮助我们,Bibliothèque Nationale 有她,将来定能予以方便不少。以后馆中所有刊物或其他出版物,可以另外赠伊个人一份。如此次图书季刊新号出版,他人多有接到者,她尚未接到,未免叫她不好过。谢寿康仍在比,闻不久来,来后有动作,非找 Mme Meuvret 不可。美国之事,已算十二分确定,路费百元已寄来,法外部两船票前已允许,刻已选定法邮船 Normandie 请外部代订舱位,八月二十三日开,二十八日抵纽约,二十九日或三十日即能到华盛顿矣。天津事件,法报所载消息亦不少,除 *Le Temps* 外,每天都买四五份报。看情形,英国不起劲,希望就地解决,则不久可完。所买报即可全数寄交史料会。即请道安!

受业重民顿首

六月二十日

〔国家图书馆档案,档案编号 1940-※044-外事 3-002020〕

按:"明星"即新加坡;*Le Temps* 通译为《时报》,1861 年至 1942 年出版,巴黎最重要的报纸之一。1938 年 9 月,日本与英国就天津英租界反日运动产生矛盾,1939 年 4 月 9 日亲日派天津海关监督兼伪华北联合储备银行天津支行经理程锡庚在大光明戏院被暗杀,6 月 14 日,日本正式封锁天津英租界,迫使英租界内生活停顿,史称"天津英租界危机"。此函后附铅笔标识"函谢寿康 Marx: Documents Diplomatiques Français. 3e série",应为先生亲笔。

六月二十一日

先生致信徐旭生,大意为平馆将其一部分馆藏图书寄存国立北平研究院史学研究所,由研究所负责寻找合适场所妥善保管,此部分馆藏的负责人为平馆馆员范腾端。〔《徐旭生文集》第 9 册,页 1017〕

按:21 日,该信由范腾端交予徐旭生,故暂系于此。范腾端(1891—1948),字九峰,湖南湘阴人,湖南群治法政专门学校毕业,1920 年 12 月入京师图书馆工作,后长期在平馆金石部任职。

六月二十九日

晨,傅斯年与先生晤谈,再请先生荐人至史语所服务。先生依旧推荐邓衍林并表示必不放王育伊,二人相谈未果。〔《傅斯年遗札》第 2 卷,页 1011〕

按:本日,傅斯年致信李济,询问意见。

六月三十日

上午十一时,郑天挺来访,与先生晤谈。〔《郑天挺西南联大日记》,北京:中华书局,2018 年,页 162〕

先生致信王重民,告知石博鼎捐赠书籍积压在海防无法运滇,请其将英国赠书交邮寄出。

有三仁弟：

六月四日回信均由香港转到。Lady Brownrigg 拟售之《永乐大典》请即进行，价或不致太昂，前赠之残叶者已寄港否？Spalding 捐款所购之书，第一批四箱于二月间寄出，四月到海防，迟至今日仍在该处，实因交换局办事不力蒋慰堂派陈仲骞世兄陈厚吉在滇设办事处，而滇越路货物堆积如山，且大半专运军火性质之物，故普通货物只得存于海防也。关于本馆之书，请告张似旅仍交邮按 Book-post 寄滇，一切运费由本馆担任。尊处可先付渠二十磅，不敷用时再设法汇寄。如渠愿利用 Blue Funnel 之免费，则由英轮运至海防中国旅行社 national library of peiping, c/o China Travel Service, Haiphong，该社有刘女士之弟在彼办事，但近日恐又他调转交，由馆派人到海防按运行李办法分批运滇亦可，其他机关之书只得令其在海防存储也。前代垫之 £ 18.19.4 $\frac{1}{2}$ 已托孙洪芬先生由沪汇还。此外，请在存款内取出十五磅作为尊处赴牛津、剑桥及 Manchester 之旅费，望先寄下一收据为荷。离英以后关于征募书籍之消息，请委托友人随时以航信报告寄港转交，并可预付其邮费也。P. S. King 之蓝皮书已收到数册并闻。顺颂旅安。

袁同礼顿首

六月三十日

英伦摄影工作请作一报告寄港，以便列入馆务报告内。

〔国立北平图书馆(昆明柿花巷)用笺。袁同礼家人提供〕

按：Lady Brownrigg 本名似为 Beatrice Brownrigg，其丈夫为英国海军少将布朗里格男爵（Douglas Egremont Robert Brownrigg, Fourth Baronet, 1867－1939），该册《永乐大典》应为 G. E. Marinus 旧藏，此人生平事迹待考。

先生致信徐旭生，告知范腾端最近无法赴国立北平研究院史学研究所协助图书阅览工作。〔《徐旭生文集》第 9 册，页 1019〕

按：30 日，该信送交徐旭生，时该所位于昆明北部黑龙潭。

先生致信史蒂文斯，请求洛克菲勒基金会支付李芳馥回国旅费。

June 30, 1939

Dear Dr. Stevens:

I am much obliged to you for your letter of May 18. We shall get in touch with the American Library Association and shall avail ourselves of the new arrangement which you so kindly informed us.

The last letter I received from you was dated February 16. A fire at the local Post Office on May 21 destroyed a number of foreign mails; and I was most anxious to know whether any letters from your Office has been sent to us during the months of March and April. If so, may I request you to send us duplicate copies?

May I take this opportunity to reiterate our previously expressed appreciation for the Foundation's aid toward our program of library development in Southwestern China. Owing to the dispersal of cultural centres from North China and the coastal regions, something like a renaissance is happening here. As we have intimate relationships with all the institutions of higher learning now located in Kunming, your timely assistance is appreciated by all of my colleagues.

China has been showing the utmost determination in building up her shattered seats of learning and this Library is contributing its share in this task. For this reason, I am asking Mr. F. F. Li, now doing cataloguing work at Columbia, to come back to us early in the fall. I trust the Foundation will arrange to pay his travel expenses in order to enable him to come to Kunming by way of Europe. May I express to you and Mr. Marshall once more my sincere appreciation for the assistance which you have so kindly extended to him?

With kind regards,

Yours sincerely,

T. L. Yuan,

Acting Director

〔平馆（昆明）英文信纸。Rockefeller Foundation. Series 601: China; Subseries 601.R: China-Humanities and Arts. Box 47. Folder 389〕

按：此件为打字稿，落款处为先生签名，以航空信方式寄送，7 月 17 日送达。史蒂文斯在该信就李芳馥返华费用处作标记✕。

六月

先生收牛津大学副校长函,其中并附英国赞助委员会致英国、印度、加拿大、澳大利亚各大学公函,号召各处为中国募集书刊资料。〔《中华图书馆协会会报》第 14 卷第 1 期,页 11〕

七月一日

晚六时,先生访吴宓请其改英文稿,吴宓则荐荣琬,先生答应。时吴宓有恙,故请先生代笔作函辞是晚钱锺书宴。〔《吴宓日记》第 7 册,页 22〕

　　　　按:该函误寄松柏厅,未送到钱锺书手中。

七月二日

王重民覆函先生,谈其在法募集款项及图书交换诸事。

　　守和吾师钧鉴:

　　　　六月二十日直寄巴黎之手谕已奉到,聆悉种切,极为快慰。Mme Meuvret 所称一万法郎者,今又仅能预备五千,以后尚有多少,似如再有,至多亦不过五千。此款虽发自外部,似与赠燕大及云大者不同。此五千法郎,现在完全交生支配,所买尽系西南民族等书。又东方语言学校、中国学院、Bibliothèque Nationale、Guimet 四机关,不能出钱,仅将其自己出版物拿出若干,先集中于 Meuvret 处,然后一同装箱。此事在七月内,要完全办清,则八月初方可由生交王景春运华也。窥其情形,完全系报答我方交换图书性质,但不知除吾馆之外,对其他交换机关,如何报答也。Meuvret 下周内可去外交部,到时或更有新消息。关于对我国交换一节,现在似由她一人完全负责也。购书进行颇佳,巴黎似较伦敦稍便宜,而在 Bd. St. Germain 198 号,又有一家 G. P. Maisonneuve,书价本来较他家稍廉,近又将中国实业银行之图书馆全部买来,内英文书亦不少,定价似较伦敦便宜一半,(其书目前天方印出)是一机会,故拟多买一些。Kegan Paul 之书单,尚未往索,因在此既便宜,除非不能找到之书,再给他去信也。此次所买,十之七八为关于云南,种族,抗战者,或将其最急须者,直寄昆明,余交王景春转运。关于那部永乐大典,又由 Moule 出来调说,或可索价 £ 20 也,然 £ 20 似仍太贵。生一切均好,就是太忙了。可补充天主教史料已够作,然一放弃,似又无再来机会,则数年之功,不得结果。故现拟多花一点钱,务期完成。刘女士日内即满月,拟满月之后,多花一点钱雇一女太太来寓看小孩,则刘女士可到图书馆整天抄此史料。六月四日,共发四信,想已收到矣。余再禀,即请道安!

受业重民敬上。

七月二日

〔国家图书馆档案,档案编号 1940-※044-外事 3-002025〕

按:G. P. Maisonneuve 应指 Gustave Maisonneuve 与 Gaston Maisonneuve 新开的书店,全称为"La Librairie orientale et américaine Gustave-Paul Maisonneuve, Successeur"。"那部《永乐大典》"指馆字册(卷 11312-11313),夏鼐在 5 月 24 日记中详述了此册《永乐大典》的内容及特点,如卷首有乾隆御笔,并特意写下"此册未曾收入袁同礼《〈永乐大典〉现存卷目表》颇希望能归回国人手中,惟索价 100 镑,未免过昂,商榷结果,减为 50 镑,函告王君,令其自行决定。"[①]

七月三日

先生致信法兰西学院汉学研究所,告知平馆已寄出《新书选目》并将赠寄《图书季刊》英文本,此外希望平馆能够与之开展出版品交换。

July 3, 1939

Dear Sir:

We have recently mailed to you a copy of the first instalment of *SELECTED CHINESE BOOKS 1933-37* and hope that it may be of some service to you. The second instalment including the author index will be distributed during the summer.

We have placed your name on our mailing list to receive copies of the *QUARTERLY BULLETIN OF CHINESE BIBLIOGRAPHY*, Chinese edition, beginning from new series, vol. 1, no. 1 (March, 1939). We trust that through the medium of these aids, you will be kept informed of the output of Chinese publications issued during recent years.

As we are greatly interested in the scientific work you are doing, it is our earnest hope that you would send us your publications in exchange. The need of western literature is especially urgent in China to-day when,

---

① 夏鼐著《夏鼐日记》第 2 卷,上海:华东师范大学出版社,2011 年,页 247。

arm in arm with resistance, we are carrying out an extensive programme of reconstruction particularly in the vast hinterland of West China. Both culturally and economically these developments are destined to have tremendous importance for the future of the world.

In the face of great difficulty in China, the work of scholarship is being carried on. For this reason, we hope that you will lend us your assistance to our great task of reconstruction by sending us books and journals representative of western scholarship and learning. Any practical help which you might be able to extend to China will be warmly appreciated.

Yours faithfully,

T. L. Yuan,

Acting Director

Secretary

Institut des Hates Études Chinoises

A la Sorbonne

Paris, 5e

France

〔平馆（昆明）英文信纸。法兰西学院图书馆档案〕

七月五日

下午四时许,吴宓至柿花巷平馆,与先生晤谈,先生请吴宓修改英文稿件。
〔《吴宓日记》第 7 册,页 24〕

七月六日

先生致信王重民,谈英国赠书寄送的两种方法,并请其在离欧前委托他人继续留意英法两国消息。

有三仁弟:

兹致张似旅一函,请在存款中取二十磅送去为荷。如大驾能赴英,则可将较笨重之书另装入木箱中,小本之书一律改为邮寄。请告张君北平馆需用之书,较其他方面尤为需要,盼其赞助,速寄为荷。关于英法二国方面消息,请于离欧前委托专人报告为幸。

同礼

七，六

〔中国书店·海淀，四册〕

先生致信张似旅，告知英国捐赠的第一批书尚未运抵昆明，请用王重民所预支的英镑付邮寄送，并请注明平馆收讫。

July 6, 1939

Dr. Chang Su-Lee,

Warden, China Institute,

16 Gordon Square,

London, W. C. l,

England,

Dear Dr. Chang:

The first shipment of books which left London on February 24 arrived at Haiphong early in April. When I wrote to you in May, I thought they were on their way to Kunming, but up to the time of writing, they have not yet been received.

This long delay is most annoying. The reason for it is partly due to the heavy congestion on the narrow-gauged railway between Haiphong and Kunming, and partly due to French inefficiency in handling large scale shipments now accumulated at the small port of Haiphong. While our Committee has been doing its best to tackle the business side of the question, a lot of difficulties have yet to be overcome.

In view of these practical difficulties, I wonder whether you would do us a great favour if you could arrange to send the books desired by the National Library by book-post as suggested in my letter of March 31. I am, therefore, asking Mr. Wang Chung-min to send you 20.0.0. as our advance payment for the postage thus incurred. Additional payment will be sent to you as soon as this sum is being spent.

If, however, you wish to avail yourself of the kind offer of Blue Funnel to carry the cases to Haiphong free of charge, will you send the heavy volumes by freight and address the cases to us as follows:

National Library of Peiping,

Kunming (Yunnanfu),

c/o China Travel Service,

Haiphong.

In this case, we shall send, as each shipment arrives, one of our assistants to Haiphong and arrange to bring the cases to Kunming as a part of his personal luggage. It seems that the first method would be less costly; and in view of the utmost regularity of second-class mails, it should be recommended as a temporary measure pending the solution of the transportation problem between the Southwestern provinces and the outside world.

Hoping the matter will receive your immediate attention,

Yours sincerely,

T. L. Yuan

Acting Director

〔中国书店·海淀,四册〕

按:该信应以航空信方式寄送,并抄送一副本给王重民。

七月八日

先生致信阿里克(Basil M. Alexéiev),介绍故宫博物院赴苏联展出古物的职员傅振伦。

July 8, 1939

Professor Basil M. Alexéiev,

ul. Blohina, 17/1 log. 5,

Leningrad,

U. S. S. R.

Dear Prof. Alexéiev:

I have pleasure in introducing to you Mr. Fu Ch'en-Lun (傅振伦), assistant curator of the National Palace Museum, who is going to Moscow to attend the Exhibition of Chinese art to be held in U. S. S. R. As he is interested in museum management and methods, any assistance which you could extend to him will be greatly appreciated.

With cordial regards,

Yours sincerely,

T. L. Yuan

Acting Director

〔平馆(昆明)英文信纸。国家图书馆善本组手稿特藏〕

按:此件为打字稿,落款处为先生签名。该信存信封,其上有先生所写"阿里克教授",应是给傅振伦写的介绍函,并由傅振伦携带面交,非邮寄。

七月九日

王重民致函先生,告法国外交部再赠价值五千法郎书籍,其已选目,并谈图书交换等事。

守和吾师钧鉴:

礼拜四 Mme Meuvret 赴外交部,称除前所称之五千元外,外部尚拟再赠五千元书,仍可由吾人选择。生当于礼拜六赴外部,由 Mme Meuvret 之绍介,去见 Joubert 先生,伊即 Marx 司内职员也。法外部印有"Livres français choisis à l'intention des Bibliothèques étrangères et des Bibliothèques françaises à l'Etranger"一目,其所赠书,均由此目内选择,燕大、云大皆然。Joubert 氏称再赠吾馆 5000 frs 书,亦可由此目内选,但多一点亦无妨。生当即索两份目录,即日选就,大部分为文史社会科学,今日拟托人打字约在六七千元之间,因恐有不能买到者,冀下礼拜三交 Joubert,伊盼于生离巴黎前买好也。(Joubert 又给以赠云大书目,该目多科学书,故生多选社会科学,俾免重覆。)生又告以普通书籍,皆留北平,亟盼法外部所出刊物,另外各赠一份,伊当下先赠:

1. *Documents diplomatiques sur la Chine*,

2. *Bulletin périodique de la presse chinoise*,

3. *Bulletin périodique de la presse japonaise*.

第一次之五千元书,下周内可有清单,此次所选书,拟打三份,连同清单一同寄呈一份。又生在 Maisonneuve 所选约可二百种,五千元上下由吾馆付款,Kegan Paul 所开,大致在内,连生随时所购拟寄存吾馆者,此四宗凑合起来,亦很可观矣。凡 Bibliothèque Nationale, Guimet,东方语言学校出版者均未买;东校可赠,当无问题,杜乃扬已得 M. Leroy 承认,该馆所出目录,可共赠四千元上下。此外,尚有何好消息,再继续禀闻。

其他工作及照相片等,均各努力进行。盖生此次返法,较以前忙多,今又加小孩之累,实在更忙也。法国工人不易找虽各方托人,而十天之内,竟未找到,下周内不论如何,或有相当解决,则刘女士又可帮同抄稿矣。

专此,即请道安!

受业重民敬上
七月九日

〔国家图书馆档案,档案编号 1940-※044-外事 3-002028〕

按:Livres français choisis à l'intention des Bibliothèques étrangères et des Bibliothèques françaises à l'Etranger 直译为"为外国图书馆和国外法国图书馆选择的法语书目"; *Documents diplomatiques sur la Chine* 直译为《法国对华外交文件》,*Bulletin périodique de la presse chinoise* 直译为《中国报刊定期公报》,*Bulletin périodique de la presse japonaise* 直译为《日本报刊定期公报》,以上四种皆由法国外交部编辑出版。"东校"即巴黎东方语言学校,下同。

七月十二日

阿博特覆函先生,请留心寄送岭南大学出版物,将其检出并送交该校在香港办事处,另告费正清、明尼苏达大学寄送平馆的出版品,请注意将其从重庆国际交换局检出。

July 12, 1939

Dear Dr. Yuan:

The Institution duly received your letter of April 21 and notes the kind words of appreciation expressed therein by you of the part taken by the Smithsonian in rehabilitating the libraries which have been seized or destroyed by the Japanese.

On June 28 there were forwarded to you 27 boxes numbers 2347-73. One of the boxes, namely, number 2375, is for Lingnan University, which, as you no doubt know, has established an office in Hong Kong. I shall be obliged if you will kindly have the box turned over to Lingnan University.

The Institution has received a number of letters from various American correspondents inquiring regarding the sending of publications to China through one of the establishments with which you are connected. Those letters and the Institution's replies, together with announcements from correspondents in this country of the forwarding of publications for you, have been included in the shipment referred to above as you may desire to make some direct acknowledgment to the various senders.

Mr. J. K. Fairbank of the Department of History of Harvard University, Cambridge, Massachusetts, has forwarded to the Institution 6 boxes of books for the National Library of Peiping with the request that the shipment be sent directly to that library through the Chinese Bureau of International Exchange at the National Library's new branch in Kunming, adding that it is your desire that the shipment be so forwarded. The consignment consists of boxes numbered 66 - 71 and is this day being dispatched from the Institution via Haiphong to the Chinese Bureau of International Exchange, Chungking, in care of the Chinese Maritime Customs, Mengtze, Yunnan. The Institution will call the matter to the especial attention of the Chinese Bureau with the request that arrangements be made to have the consignment delivered to the National Library in Kunming instead of having it forwarded on to Chungking. The Institution understands that the shipment contains an especially selected collection of publications of Harvard University, and I would suggest that you also bring the matter to the attention of the Chinese Bureau of International Exchange in order that the boxes, which are large and weigh more than 700 pounds each, be delivered directly to the National Library by the Chinese Maritime Customs.

On June 28 the Institution forwarded to the Bureau of International Exchange in Chungking 12 boxes numbered 2374-85. Two of the boxes, namely numbers 2374 and 2375, contain publications from the University of Minnesota for the National Library of Peiping and should be delivered directly to the National Library instead of being forwarded to Chungking. The shipment left New York June 30 per SS "Van Buren".

Very truly yours,

C. G. Abbot

Secretary

〔Smithsonian Institution Archives, Records, 1868-1988 (Record Unit 509), Box 1, National Library, Peiping〕

按:该信寄送香港,并抄送昆明,此件为录副。

七月十三日

先生致信哈佛学院图书馆,感谢寄赠图书。

July 13, 1939

Harvard College Library,

Cambridge, Mass.,

U. S. A.

Dear Sirs:

I beg to acknowledge with cordial appreciation the receipt from the Faculty and students of Harvard University of the gifts mentioned below, a welcome addition to the collections of the National Library.

Very truly yours,

T. L. Yuan

Acting Director

Birnie, Arthur: *An Economic History of the British Isles*. 1936.

Faulkner, Harold Underwood: *American Economic History*. 1931.

Fullington, James F. ed.: *The College Omnibus*. 1938.

Heaton, Herbert: *Economic History of Europe*. 1936.

〔平馆(昆明)英文信纸。Harvard University, John K. Fairbank personal archive, folder Books for China〕

按:此件为打字稿,落款处为先生签名,于 8 月 22 日送达。

七月十七日

第十八集团军重庆办事处致函先生,告知寄赠书籍。

馆长先生:

兹有周副部长交下书籍数十本,特函附上并付书单一纸,收到后希即赐覆。今后尚有书继续寄上。特此,并祝敬礼！

国民革命军第十八集团军重庆办事处（印）启

七月十七日

〔《北京图书馆馆史资料汇编(1909-1949)》，页 692〕

　　按："周副部长"应指周怡。该函左侧标注"书已点收无讹并已函覆，曾家岩五十号。八月一日"。

王重民致函先生，告其在法谋取赠书及图书交换诸事。

　　守和吾师道鉴：

　　为法外部捐赠吾馆图书事，九日曾上一信，想已蒙鉴察。生依书目，即速速选出社会、语言、历史、图书目录等共值八千二百余元，即于十二日再赴外部谒 Joubert 氏。伊谓并不算很多，可照办。一月以内可买齐，即直送云南，由法领事转赠吾馆，十月底十一月初准可到达。其黄皮书及两 Bulletin，Joubert 当时又加入目内，到时一并装箱。生所选目，曾打三份，谨别将一份，由伦敦转香港，冀省一点邮费。Joubert 已知我方须要图书之殷，临别又谓："再要何书，可给我写信。"Mme Meuvret 已去休假，八月一日回来，伊所存之 5000frs，俟八月初，即可完全支配清楚。法国法律，国立图书馆不能直接向外国买书，必须托书铺办理；然一经书铺之手，则所费不仅一倍。杜乃扬来后，颇欲拓充中文书，又不能直接买，殊以为憾。生因与伊商议，中法两国，可特别交换一万法郎书，即是他们所缺，如三部"四部丛刊"及新出字典辞书之类，由伊开一清单，请北平图书馆将其旧有或特别新买送来，而吾馆开一单要法国何书，伊当速买送去。际此外汇不能办理，用此法买书，于我似甚方便，于彼亦有利不少，似可实行。况我北平如有重份，送到法使馆即可，不必另外花钱也。杜女士学问不大好，但为人勇敢，尚能作事，吾师如赞同此事，请与杜女士一直来信，那时生如未离法，更好办也。上礼拜五已找到一犹太女子看小孩，刘女士已于今日来馆抄天主教史料。云南书目伊即可整理一部分寄上，登入季刊。唯"敦煌相片目"生不能作，八月一日寄不出，只好再推后一期。即请钧安！

受业重民上。

七月十七日

〔国家图书馆档案，档案编号 1940-※044-外事 3-002029〕

七月十九日

先生致信燕树棠,寄上书评样例一份,请于暑期之内撰就《中华民国亲属法大纲》书评。

> 召亭先生大鉴:
>
> 　　关于荷人所著之《中国家族法》一书,前承惠允写一书评,至感厚意。暑假中盼能寄下,以便付印。兹奉上张煜全之书评一篇,未识可供参考否?专此申谢,顺候著祺。
>
> 　　　　　　　　　　　　　　　　　　弟袁同礼顿首
> 　　　　　　　　　　　　　　　　　　七月十九日
>
> 　　　　〔国立北平图书馆(昆明柿花巷)用笺。孔夫子旧书网〕

　　按:"荷人所著之《中国家族法》"即*An Outline of Modern Chinese Family Law*(《中华民国亲属法大纲》),荷兰学者 Marc van der Valk(范可法),辅仁大学《华裔学志》专刊(*Monumenta Serica Monograph Series*)之二,1939 年 7 月魏智(北京法文图书馆)初版。张煜全之书评,待考。此信暂系于此,后并未在《图书季刊》中文本见及该书书评。

John Marshall 致函先生,就前请支付李芳馥归国旅费一事仍待史蒂文斯决定,并告知李芳馥已经离开美国经欧洲回中国。

　　　　　　　　　　　　　　　　　　　　　　　July 19, 1939

Dear Mr. Yuan:

　　In Mr. Stevens's absence, your letter of June 30th has come to me. I learned from Mr. Stevens's secretary that his last letter to you was dated February 16th, so apparently none was destroyed in the fire you mention on May 21st.

　　I was sorry the other day to miss a call from Mr. Li, who in my absence left a message to say that he was leaving. In fact, he is sailing this morning on the "Queen Mary" to return as you hoped by way of Europe. When you see him, will you convey to him my regrets at not being able to see him when he called and best wishes for the success of his work with you at the National Library. Our hope is, as always, that both you and he will find of value the study he carried on while in this country.

With best wishes,

Yours sincerely,

John Marshall

〔Rockefeller Foundation. Series 601: China; Subseries 601.R: China-Humanities and Arts. Box 47. Folder 389〕

按：John Marshall（1903–1980），先后获得哈佛大学英文系学士、硕士学位，1931 年至 1933 年担任美国学术团体理事会编辑，后出任洛克菲勒基金会助理，并兼任大众教育委员会（General Education Board）主任。内文 his last letter to you was dated February 16th 是不准确的，因为 5 月 18 日史蒂文斯寄出一信，并且确定送到先生手中。李芳馥在欧期间恰逢欧战爆发，归国受阻只得返回美国，参见 1939 年 10 月 8 日、1940 年 1 月 2 日王重民致先生函。此函寄送昆明。

七月二十日

上午十一时，吴宓至柿花巷平馆访先生，交送此前修订的英文稿件。十二时，同赴金碧西餐馆，先生设宴，客为吴宓、刘大钧、章元善等人。下午二时半，先生与吴宓返平馆。稍事休息后，吴宓为平馆校改 1936 年至 1937 年度英文报告，约五时许，吴宓出，先生告将赴上海。〔《吴宓日记》第 7 册，页 35〕

按："1936 年至 1937 年"或应为"1937 年至 1938 年"，参见吴宓本年 7 月 31 日日记。

七月二十一日

先生致信王重民，谈公私杂事。

有三吾弟：

前接六月二十及廿一日来书，详悉一一。关于黄皮书及官书局出版书，请先设法觅一目录，官书局在档案局左近（Archives Nationales），离巴黎前亦可前往参观。杜乃扬处曾寄赠《季刊》，不识何以未收到。兹第二期已出版，另加寄一份，寄尊处之《季刊》则改寄华京。前寄 Kegan Paul 书单内多关于云南书籍，不识已收到否？望速示。拟在 Radcliffe-Brown 来华以前，将民族及西南问题书籍搜集成一系统也。馆中进行甚猛，经费亦未核减，惟自庚款停付后中基会已无美金，应付极感困难。罗氏基金会补助本馆美金四千元，可以专购书籍，但亦甚

有限耳。抵美国后,对于外人搜书方法及组织请特别留意。如愿返国
吃苦,则留美一年后仍请回馆办事。此间工作紧张,惟办事人员尚不
敷分配。《馆务报告》下月在沪付印,届时当寄上。大约八九月在沪
港约留月余,寄信均寄香港。Hummel 夫人处,不日拟写一信托其代觅
保育院,俾抵华京后即可安心作事。刻下美金壹元合国币拾贰元,故
刘女士如能在美工作亦不无小补也,此层亦托恒夫人代为留意。前在
伦敦遗失之手饰,不识已获得否? 在美出售必得善价。张似旅第一次
寄来四箱书,在海防滞留三月仍未运滇,焦灼万状,故前请汇张似旅二
十磅,作为邮寄牛津赠本馆书之运费,不识已送去否? 刻下海防货物
堆积如山,而每日火车仅运三百吨,内中以军用品为大宗,故普通货物
不得不滞留于海防也。张伯苓月初在此,对于征集书籍毫不热心。现
在"战时征集会"已全部移入中央图书馆内办公,该会完全为其利用,
故牛津赠本馆之书必须请其交邮寄滇,如此办法不致为人劫留也。二
十磅如不敷用,则再多寄拾磅。笨重之书可告张似旅寄海防,轻便者
一律付邮是荷。

同礼顿首
七月廿一

又 Pirkis 女士事,已与 Reclus 现在云大任法文谈过。据云如渠来滇,必
能为之设法,最好托 Langevin 等写一介绍信致熊校长,先用航邮寄滇,
俾渠有所准备。云大怕被炸,有迁移大理之意,联大则决定不移也。

P. S. King 寄来蓝皮书已到一部分。外致谢理士信,请代发。

〔袁同礼家人提供〕

　　　　按:"廿一日来书"或指 6 月 11 日王重民来函,待考。该信写在普
　　　　通红栏信纸,补语单用半纸,或有部分被裁去。

七月二十五日

上午,郑天挺来访,先生与其一同前往北京大学办事处。〔《郑天挺西南联大
日记》,页 170〕

　　　　按:所谈之事似与借阅平馆藏日本印《朝鲜李氏实录》相关,其书
　　　　存于沪上,但先生仍答应致信调运。

七月二十七日

先生致信王重民,谈平馆与法国交换图书的方法,并请其将去年春夏的工

作报告寄港,以便刊印。

有三吾弟:

顷接十七日航信,欣悉法外交部可捐赠书籍,至慰。惟九日之函尚未寄到。一月以来,国币惨跌,昆明行市均较沪港为高,每美金壹元可换国币十八元,英磅则换八十元,实开破天荒之纪录。与法国交换书籍如大致能按照七七事变前之汇率,则吾人甚为合算,否则太昂,故不如先从小规模作起。敝意中国需要者,先从 1940 年一月以后出版之法国杂志入手,凡能赠或能与中国交换者,由馆直接函索;商家出版之期刊,则由法国方面代订而以之交换中国书籍;至我方所购之书则以新出版之国学、历史、考古有永久价值者为限。选择之权则我方任之,但法方如需要何书亦可开单,本馆仅有二千元可作此用,如选择精审亦可稍有裨益。至法方能出款若干(或五千法郎左右),则请伊等决定,此中情形不必完全告诉杜女士也。兹致伊一函请转交。又《四部丛刊》初、二、三编均需要否? 请函示。现定八月七日到港并拟赴沪,寄信均寄香港为荷。张似旅处前请寄伊二十磅牛津赠书之邮费,已送去否? 并向伊索一收据,以便报账为要。在巴黎影照燉煌工作报告,已将去年二月寄英庚款会者印入上年度报告,至在伦敦工作报告及巴黎 1938 年二月至六月之报告,刻亟待付印入本年度馆务报告内,务于在离法以前寄港为要。致 Mrs. Hummel 信已发出,请代觅一 nursery。匆匆,顺候旅安。

袁同礼顿首

七月廿七日

到纽约后可到 China Institute in America, 119 W. 57th Street, N. Y. City 访问,主任为孟治,至友也。

〔袁同礼家人提供〕

七月二十九日

Foon Sien(温哥华)致函先生,告知将寄赠加拿大出版的有关抗日战争的书籍、册页。

July 29th, 1939

T. L. Yuan, Esq.,

Dear Sir: -

Your kind favor of June 14th. 1939 came to hand. I am advised that your Library is building up a special collection of source materials relating to the present undeclared Sino-Japanese war, and that books, leaflets, posters as well as other printed matters concerning the work should be sent to you. I, therefore, take the opportunity to mail you under separate cover some booklets and letters sent to Canadians in public office as well as organizations by this League. I shall, also from time to time, send you booklets of that nature hereafter.

Sincerely yours,

Foon Sien

Chairman:

Chinese National Salvation League

Headquarters for Canada,

Vancouver, D. C.

〔加拿大云高华中华会馆（The Chinese Benevolent Association, 108 Pender Street East, Vancouver, B. C. Canada）信纸。国家图书馆档案,档号不明〕

按:落款处为 Foon Sien 签名,并钤"驻云埠加拿大中华民国国民抗日救国总会"印。此函右上端标有收讫时间"九月七日"。

七月三十日

王重民覆函先生,告其在法选书交换事。

守和吾师钧鉴:

奉七月二十一日手谕,获详聆种切,殊以为慰。谢礼士数日前尚在巴黎,今已回明星,已将师函转去。伊大概九月初回中国,因开校在即,不能赴昆明,明夏则极愿赴西南一行也。伊已将我最近图书馆界努力情形,写好一文,不久可发表。生明年甚欲返国,追随吾师努力,蒙允仍回馆任职,甚感! 又蒙特赐访书路费,亦谨将收条附上。吾师于生等情形,如此关怀,又拟给恒夫人写信。前得 Hummel 信,允将相片寄存伊馆,伊更拟设法筹款,就我所有 film,加洗一份。俟抵美后看情形如何,如 Hummel 肯让刘女士担任此事,月给三四十美金,即可。已遵嘱寄张似旅二十镑。近接伊秘书来信,称张君正在休假,不在伦敦。本月十八日,曾由巴黎直飞一信至昆明,报告法外部赠书经过,又将选定书单,由伦敦飞寄香港一份。其 Mme Meuvret 处所存 5000 元,已支配清,伊明日回巴黎,作一报告,即可装箱。昨日生谒见 Leroy, Bibliothèque Nationale 赠书,亦已当面说明,八月一二日即可拿出,容再将目录寄呈。王景春来信,八月十八有一期船,故十五日以前,均打箱送 Le Havre。与法再交换 10000 元书事,想必蒙赞同。一请书价按政府外汇合计,二请四部丛刊第一集应索国币千五百元至二千元,生已与杜乃扬说明,第一集久绝版,普通卖两千元,而新印报纸的,则仅三百余元。外交部编印目录,生已挂号寄一份至昆明,将来交换时,依该目选书较方便。Kegan Paul 书单,共 21 部,仅七部未找到,内两部太贵,已去信买五部,请直寄昆明。在此所买一切书,刻正在整理,其各书单,不日可以航寄香港。Pirkis 女士极欲去中国,伊在牛津毕业,Langevin 不易求,请吾师多设法。找人报告消息很不易,在牛津可托尤桐,在巴黎似以杜乃扬较方便也。生等仍在抄辑天主教,尚甚忙。专此,即请道安!

受业重民上。
七月三十日

〔国家图书馆档案,档案编号 1940-※044-外事 3-002031〕

七月三十一日

先生路遇顾颉刚。〔《顾颉刚日记》卷 4,页 261〕

加拿大公共卫生协会覆函先生,该协会将如先生前请寄赠平馆所需期刊。

July 31, 1939

Dr. T. L. Yuan,

Dear Sir:

I have pleasure in mailing to you copies of the *Canadian Public Health Journal* for February 1938 and February 1939, as requested in your letter of June 3rd.

I am sorry for the delay in writing to you. Our supply of these issues was exhausted and we had to try to obtain them from other sources. I regret that thus far we have not been able to obtain a copy of the January 1939 issue for you. I hope, however, to have one for you shortly.

Yours very truly,

R. L. Bandall

Executive Assistant

〔国家图书馆档案,档号不明〕

按:该函右上端标有收讫时间"九月十四日"。

七月

先生撰写《〈永乐大典〉现存卷目表》。〔《图书季刊》新第 1 卷第 3 期,1939 年 9 月,页 246-286〕

按:该篇辑录 367 册信息。

八月一日

上午九时,吴宓赴平馆办事处访先生,送 1937 至 1938 年度平馆英文报告,并托先生赴港时代为打听毛彦文通讯地址。此外,先生为吴宓办理护照事,特撰一信与外交部王占祺处长,并将其交吴宓亲送。〔《吴宓日记》第 7 册,页 42〕

按:王占祺,字禹枚,浙江绍兴人,时应任外交部驻云南特派员。[1] 1942 年 11 月间,先生在重庆晤高棣华,后者告知毛彦文自离港去沪后就一直住在上海,从未再往他地。[2]

先生致信格雷夫斯,附上顾子刚六月七日函,请美国学术团体理事会考虑在美购买缩微胶片摄影机的耗材,并就捐赠图书、仪器的寄送渠道给予建议。

August 1, 1939

Dear Dr. Graves:

　　I enclose herewith a letter from Mr. T. K. Koo of our Peiping office concerning the setup of the microfilm camera at Peiping. In his letter he raised several questions about the equipment and operating expenses. I shall be very grateful to you indeed if you could give some consideration to this matter.

　　We shall be glad to pay the overhead expenses out of our own regular budget, but we shall have great difficulty in buying films and chemicals from the States owing to our Government's control over foreign

---

[1] 外交部编《外交部留部职员名册》,1938 年,叶 13。

[2] 《吴宓日记》第 8 册,页 421。

exchange.

Beginning from this month, a grant of US $ 4,000 will be made to the Library by the Rockefeller Foundation. We are using this sum for the acquisition of materials; largely for subscriptions to current scientific journals. If a part of this sum should be used for the equipment of the microfilm, we shall have to cut down a great number of the purchases.

Although there is a heavy congestion of the narrowed-gauged railway from Haiphong to Kunming, yet things do come through. I would suggest, therefore, that the cases of books and apparatus be addressed as follows:

For books

National Library of Peiping

c/o Bureau of International Exchange of Publications,

Kunming, Yunnan, China

For Scientific Instruments

National Southwest Associated University

c/o Bureau of International Exchange of Publications,

Kunming, Yunnan, China

I understand that the Smithsonian Institution sends them to the above Bureau care of Subira Freres, 44 Boulevard Bonnal, Haiphong, who is the official agent of the above Bureau.

With kindest regards,

Yours, sincerely,

T. L. Yuan

Acting Director

〔Rockefeller Foundation. Series 300 Latin America-Series 833 Lebanon; Subseries 601. Box 9. Folder 86〕

按：Subira Freres 即徐壁雅洋行，法商筹办，信中提及之处应该是其在海防的分店，代理国际出版品交换业务。该信于 9 月 25 日送达，此为抄件。

先生致信费正清，感谢赠书并将致信 Lionel Marks 表示谢忱，另告法币大幅贬值。

August 1, 1939

Dr. John K. Fairbank
41 Winthrop St.
Cambridge, Mass.
U. S. A.

Dear Dr. Fairbank:

I am much obliged to you for your letter of June 12th informing me that you have shipped seven cases of books and journals through the Smithsonian Institution. At a time when Chinese scholars are working under great handicaps, your timely assistance is very much appreciated.

I am writing to Prof. Lionel Marks to-day to thank him for his valuable assistance. As soon as the books arrive, I shall write again. I hope that these volumes will be here before the University opens in October.

During recent weeks the sudden depreciation of Chinese dollar has hit everbody. Since April, 1938, the exchange rate has been Ch $ 6.60 to US $ 1.00, but recently it has jumped to $ 16.00 to $ 18.00. Under these circumstances, it is extremely difficult to get American books and journals. I wish to assure you that the books you so kindly collected will meet our need and will no doubt be used to the best advantage.

I am enclosing a statement about library progress in China which I hope may be of some possible interest to you.

Thanking you very heartily for your assistance and with kindest regards,

Yours sincerely,

T. L. Yuan

Acting Director

〔平馆（昆明）英文信纸。Harvard University, John K. Fairbank personal archive, folder Books for China〕

按：此件打字稿，但先生略加修改，落款处为签名，于 10 月 9 日前送到。

八月二日

国会图书馆覆函先生,告知先生前请该馆寄送十九世纪以来中外关系目录卡片已获批准,目录卡片将通过国际交换服务送达平馆。

August 2, 1939

My dear Dr. Yuan:

　　Your letter of June 5 was received, and its cordial expressions have been noted by the Chiefs of the several divisions mentioned by you.

　　To meet your specific request of references on China's foreign relations from 1800 to date, the Chief of the Card Division has sent to you, through the International Exchange Service, a set of printed catalogue cards covering works on this subject. We trust these will reach you safely.

　　For the Librarian,

Very sincerely yours,

Chief Assistant Librarian

We have had pleasure in sending these cards with our compliments.

〔Librarian of Congress, Putnam Archives, Special File, China: National Library 1930-1939〕

　　按:此件为录副。

八月初

先生离开昆明前往香港。〔《吴宓日记》第 7 册,页 35〕

八月七日

Lyman Hoover 致函先生,请平馆协助提供抗战爆发后有关中国回教协助抗击日寇的文献、信息,以利编辑对外宣传册页。

c/o European Y. M. C. A.

Kowloon, Hongkong

August 7, 1939

Dear Dr. Yuan:

　　Professor Frank Price has asked me to prepare a 35 or 40 page pamphlet on "Chinese Muslims and the War" as one of the series which his committee in Chengtu and Chungking is preparing for publication, in cooperation with various other bodies such as the China Council of the Institute of Pacific Relations. These pamphlets will be used widely abroad, it is hoped, and some will be translated into other languages for widest possible circulation.

If you happened to notice my articles in the November and December 1938 issues of *Asia Magazine* (New York), these will have given you some notion of my interest in this subject. I have been much encouraged in undertaking this present task by Prof. Price's promise that you and your staff would be glad to assist me in the collection of relevant data, and it is because of this promise that I am writing you now.

I shall be most grateful if you will assist me by giving me a bibliography of recent materials on this subject, in English, Chinese, French, or German which you think might be available in Shanghai, where I shall have to do this piece of writing. I shall especially appreciate it if you can secure for me copies of extracts from materials which might not be available in Shanghai (giving sources in each case) covering the following points:

1. Names and positions of Muslim civil and military officials in national and provincial service since 1937 or the outbreak of the war.
2. Detailed evidence regarding assistance being given China's cause by Muslims, including their pronouncements giving their attitude.
3. Detailed evidence and supporting data regarding special consideration and assistance given Chinese Muslims by national and provincial governments during recent years, especially since the war began.
4. Statements made (a) by government leaders regarding Muslims and their part in China's struggle, and (b) by Muslim groups or leaders indicating their hopes, plans, and actual activities in this regard.

I want to try to write a pamphlet which will be thoroughly grounded in facts. Naturally, I shall be interested in any evidence you can give me of Japanese propaganda among Muslims here and abroad and any estimates of the effects which it is having.

If you do not feel it wise to send this material to my Shanghai office, 131 Museum Road, the European YMCA, Kowloon, Hongkong, has kindly agreed to forward materials to me. It will mean a great deal to me if at least part of this material can reach me by September 1st as Dr. Price tells me that the I. P. R. is anxious to use this pamphlet in connection with its coming meetings and that the manuscript should be in his hands by early October. I shall be glad to have you send me these materials in installments, as soon as any part of them is ready, but I hope that a note may be enclosed giving me the list sent to date so I may be sure that everything arrives safely, or perhaps it might be sufficient if the materials were numbered so that any commissions would be self-evident.

I need scarcely say that I shall be deeply grateful for any and all assistance you can give me in this work, which I hope will be of value to China in the period ahead.

With sincere personal regards, I am

Cordially yours,

Lyman Hoover

〔Yale University records, Lyman Hoover Papers, RG 9 Series I, Box: 13, Folder: 280〕

按: Y. M. C. A. 即基督教青年会（Young Men's Christian Association）; I. P. R. 即太平洋国际学会（Institute of Pacific Relations）。Lyman Hoover, 20 世纪 30 年代长期担任基督教青年会驻华机构的行政人员。该函由香港转寄昆明, 但先生彼时已前往上海。在沪时, 先生曾尝试联系 Lyman Hoover, 未果。

八月八日

Marshall C. Balfour 覆函先生, 明确洛克菲勒基金会可支付资助款余额为一万七千五百美金及年度支取上限, 并询问先生是否更改此前的拨付申请。

Shanghai, August 8, 1939

Dear Dr. Yuan,

In further reference to your letter of May 19, and the notification to you by the Secretary of the Rockefeller Foundation under date of March

20, I may call your attention to the fact, after confirmation by Mr. Stevens, that the unexpended balance of the appropriation RF-36072 was US $ 17, 500 as of July 1. The action of the Foundation of March 17, 1939 removed all restrictions except that the unexpended balance available during the period ending June 30, 1942 was for the development of library services for purchase of materials and for production of materials for the bulletin of Chinese bibliography, not more than US $ 8,000 to be available any year of the period. You were advised of the initial advance of US $ 1,000 of the available balance on July 4. Since your letter of May 19 assumed that the balance was US $ 10,500, you may wish to modify your request for instalment payments.

Very truly yours,

M. C. Balfour

〔Rockefeller Foundation. Series 601: China; Subseries 601.R: China-Humanities and Arts. Vol. Box 47. Folder 394〕

按:此函寄送昆明,并抄送给史蒂文斯、胡恒德、耿士楷。

八月十日　香港

先生致信王重民,告其西南运输不便,请设法让法国外交部再赠书,并速将"伦敦影照燉煌写本报告"寄来,另告自己的行踪。

有三吾弟:

到港后接七月二日、九日及三十日手书并法外部书目、牛津征书启事等,均悉一一。关于西南及抗战书邮寄昆明,其余交王景春寄港,因张似旅寄海防之书迄今未到,由海防至昆明之运输尤困难也,存港则较安全。法外部 Marx 之名字 initial 为何,已不记忆函谢外部是否即函 Marx,故尚未写信。应设法请该部再捐一部法国关于《欧战是文件汇编》Documents Francaise, 3rd Series 内中关于重要文件甚多,北平已赠一部,兹昆明仍愿再索一部。刻下需要《伦敦影照燉煌写本报告》颇亟,请从速寄下印入馆务报告内。《永乐大典》二十磅仍嫌太昂,近以国币大跌为理由每磅合国币八十元! 请其再让价何如? 又前寄上之壹百磅系勉强凑成,本年由罗氏基金补助费内陆续归还,请另立一账,随时函告为要。明日赴沪留两星期,九月初返滇。《四部丛刊》第一集当在沪购买,送交法国领事馆。Pirkis 女士事已托 Reclus，请渠再函彼一托。

同礼
八月十日，香港
〔袁同礼家人提供〕

　　按："欧战是文件汇编" 当作 "欧战事文件汇编"，Documents Francaise, 3rd Series 应指*Documents diplomatiques français. 1871-1914. 3e série*，国家图书馆确藏有该书。

八月十五日　上海

先生致信王重民。〔国家图书馆档案，档案编号 1940-※044-外事 3-002038〕

　　按：此时先生的通信地址为上海市江西路九江路花旗银行大楼 404 室中基会。此次赴沪，傅增湘托张元济转交先生一篇题跋，盖先生曾为馆刊向傅增湘索取文稿。后傅增湘又致函先生，请其派平馆留守职员助其录入 "《文苑英华》校记"。[①]

八月十七日

上午，先生与赵万里至开明书店访王伯祥，商议《丛书子目类编》书稿排印事宜。〔王伯祥著《王伯祥日记》第 16 册，北京：国家图书馆出版社，2011 年，页 126〕

　　按：平馆自 1932 年左右开始编纂《丛书子目类编》，最终并未付梓。[②] 此前，似由谢国桢负责与王伯祥接洽此事，但他此时已经脱离平馆。另，《王伯祥日记》中记作《丛书子目汇编》，特此说明。

先生电话联系 Marshall C. Balfour，询问洛克菲勒基金会延长资助的细节，包括资助总额、款项可否用来补助中华图书馆协会。Balfour 将修正案的要点再次予以重申。〔Marshall C. Balfour's Diaries, Rockefeller Archive Center, Rockefeller Foundation records, Officers' Diaries, RG 12〕

　　按：该基金会对平馆资助款项剩余总额为 17,500 美金，比先生此前认为的要多出 7,000 美金，先生想用该款对中华图书馆协会进行紧急援助，为期 10 个月，每月大约 150 港币，总计约 500 美金，但不知是否合乎洛克菲勒基金会的资助条款。Balfour 在日记中并未反对，只是记录自己再次宣读了洛克菲勒基金会的资助原则。

[①]《张元济傅增湘论书尺牍》，1983 年，页 372、373。
[②]《国立北平图书馆馆务报告（民国二十一年七月至二十二年六月）》，1933 年，"编纂" 页 25。

八月十八日

晚,李宣龚在海格路设宴,先生、赵万里、孙楷第、朱师辙、钱锺书、夏承焘等受邀与席,酒馔极丰。〔夏承焘著《天风阁学词日记》(二),杭州:浙江古籍出版社,1992年,页124〕

　　　　按:夏承焘似第一次见先生,故称"始晤"。

八月中下旬

先生访合众图书馆,与顾廷龙晤谈,知"合众"意指及该馆创办目的,先生对此大加赞赏。〔《顾廷龙年谱》,页92〕①

　　　　按:《图书季刊》曾在"学术及出版消息"栏介绍上海合众图书馆,
　　　　颇多褒扬。②

八月二十二日

H. E. M. Chisholm 覆函先生,告知将寄赠平馆所缺的 *Canadian News Letter* 及其他加拿大出版的科学文献。

August 22, 1939

Dear Mr. Yuan:

　　I have your letter of July 8 and take much pleasure in forwarding to you not only the number of the "*Canadian News Letter*" which are missing from your Library, but also some other literature which I think will be of interest from a scientific and educational standpoint so far as your Library is concerned.

　　I was much interested to know that you had been steadily carrying on this work in spite of internal troubles. After all a philosophy of that kind is something which is not very common in the world today.

　　I should be glad if you would let me know of any special literature which you might find useful in your Library. In return for whatever services, we can give you here, I should personally be glad if you would send me some postage stamps, used or unused, as I happen to be a bit of a philatelist.

————————————

① 《顾廷龙年谱》将此事系在本年夏,但考虑到先生此次在沪的时间,特将其可能时间进一步圈定。另,《顾廷龙日记》未存本年8月6日之后的日记,特此说明。
② 《图书季刊》新2卷第2期,1940年6月,页269。

Kindest personal regards.

Yours sincerely,

H. E. M. Chisholm,

Director of Publicity

〔The Department of Trade and Commerce, Canada 信纸。国家图书馆档案，档号不明〕

按：该函寄送昆明，落款处为 H. E. M. Chisholm 签名，右上标注收讫日期为"十月五日"。

八月二十三日

先生致信刘咸，推荐陈贯吾前往中国科学社图书馆协助编纂中文书目。

重熙先生大鉴：

日前晤教为快。昨日本拟来社面谭，适为友人所阻，因之未果。关于贵馆馆务需人协助事，弟能力所及，自当赞助。兹拟派陈贯吾先生来社工作，陈君前在敝馆服务多年，后又主持镇江江苏省立第二图书馆馆务，颇著成绩，对于编目事务定能胜任愉快。尊处中文书目既待完成，即可先从此项工作入手。仍希尊酌，予以指导，至为企盼。专此，顺颂著祺。

弟袁同礼顿首

八月廿三日

允中先生同此致意。

〔上海市档案馆，档案编号 Q546-1-192-53〕

按：先生在此信左下标注"后知陈贯吾君已到社，表谢意"。

王重民致函先生，谈其离法前与各方交接、从法寄送图书情况，并介绍外籍人士来平馆工作诸事。

守和吾师道鉴：

生等刻已离 Le Havre，二十八日便可到纽约了。行前因赶工，实在太忙，未及详为呈报。刻精神仍稍倦，谨先略禀一二，其各种账单书单，明后自当可详为清理，再寄。（前已由伦敦寄上书单一包。）交换书事，是由法外部出钱，而凡得来之书，则为各与中国有关之机关分得，故杜乃扬、Meuvret 等等，莫不欲与我交换而白得书也。生十五日谒 M. Cain 辞行，伊表示赞同，并让生转告 Meuvret，因此事统由

Meuvret 太太主持，Cain 既赞同，她便可执行也。伯希和方面，伊允一定再设法，另外赠我一批书，至于通报、亚洲学报等，伊表示即直寄昆明。生已将吾馆及昆明最近情形奉告一二。据伯希和言，Marx 名 Jean。十六日由巴黎寄书五箱，转利物浦运香港。第一箱：吾馆及法外部五千元所买书。第二箱：王重民寄存书。第三箱：王重民寄存书及杂件。第二箱可打开，第三箱甚乱，可后清理。第四箱：吾馆及法外部五千元购书，又 B. N.赠书。又向达前代购书目一包，赠抗日战报一包，伊本人□画两册。（俟与向君去信，请其自取或索寄。）第五箱：B. N.赠书，东方语言学校赠书。因箱不满，生又实以破衣物及开明二十五史，请托人代为保存。相片及其他杂书，尚有五箱，生携美。Pirkis 女士是无条件愿去中国，薪水多少，在所不计。Reclus 方面，生今日可致 Pirkis 一信，劝其一直去信。她颇愿为吾馆编法文书目，现在所得法文书，亦已值得有一人主其事，吾师前既拟聘伊来馆任事，此地位如未给他人，聘她正好。依生意，如云大不迁而可兼钟点，则给伊 150 元，如不能兼，则给 200 元，伊当甚为满足。她家中不大充足，路费问题，多少有点困难，不知吾师可否致王景春一信，请给她设法办一免票。张似旅闻已返伦敦，然杳无消息。依生之意，此次凡为吾馆所买书，请张似旅统交 Pirkis 女士，托她按行李或按其个人用书，一齐带往昆明，则蒋慰堂更无法矣。不知吾师以为如何？不论云大或吾馆事，Pirkis 愿早有决定，以便整顿行装，凡可实现之点，请吾师径致她一信，Miss Susan L. Pirkis, 57, Kidbrooke Park Road, London, S. E. 3。余再及，即请钧安！

受业重民敬上。

八月二十三日

〔国家图书馆档案，档案编号 1940-※044-外事 3-002035〕

按：此函似未及时寄出，故很有可能晚于王重民 8 月 30 日函送达。

八月二十五日　香港

先生致信王重民。〔国家图书馆档案，档案编号 1940-※044-外事 3-002038〕

八月二十八日

先生致信史蒂文斯，感谢洛克菲勒基金会对平馆的资助并更新每季度支取拨款的数额。

August 28, 1939

Dear Dr. Stevens:

From Dr. Balfour of your Shanghai office, we are glad to learn that the balance of the grant made by your Foundation to the National Library amounts to ＄17,500, not ＄10,500 as we had anticipated. The liberation of this balance contributes greatly to the cause of library development in China and I wish once more to convey to you and through you to your Trustees our heartfelt thanks for your timely assistance. The aid from your Foundation in this hour of need is gratefully appreciated.

As to the payment of the grant, I have arranged with Dr. Balfour that quarterly payment be made to our Treasurer at Shanghai as follows:

For 1939－40　＄7,500 (＄1,875 each quarter)

1940－41　6,000 (＄1,500 each quarter)

1941－42　4,000 (＄1,000 each quarter)

which, I trust, will meet your approval.

With renewed thanks for your interest and assistance,

Yours sincerely,

T. L. Yuan

Acting Director

〔平馆(昆明)英文信纸。Rockefeller Foundation. Series 601: China; Subseries 601.R: China-Humanities and Arts. Box 47. Folder 389〕

按：此件为打字稿，落款处为先生签名，与 29 日信一并寄出，并于 9 月 22 日送达。

八月二十九日

先生致信史蒂文斯，谈个人赴欧美访问计划，请求洛克菲勒基金会给予资助考虑。

August 29, 1939

Dear Dr. Stevens:

In addition to the enclosed letter, may I add a personal one regarding my own plans?

When Mr. F. F. Li returns to China next month, he will be given a position of some responsibility. I am confident that the training which he has received in America through the Foundation's aid will enable him to carry on the work of the National Library to the satisfaction of all concerned.

As soon as I am relieved from routine duties, I hope to be able to visit America and Europe for nine or ten months. One of the projects which I have in mind is to make a survey of the various sinological collections abroad and work out a scheme for closer collaboration in the interchange of source materials. While on the spot I hope also to gather together a systematic collection of materials needed in China for post-war reconstruction and rehabilitation.

I have been writing notes for a Handbook of Chinese Studies and I am anxious to consult some literature which is not available in the Orient. If I could have this handbook published with your aid, it might serve as a useful tool to young American scholars. For this reason, I wonder whether the Foundation would be interested to sponsor this undertaking through a grant in aid.

If I could arrange it, I shall attend the I. P. R. Conference to be held in November at Victoria. Should you feel that such projects as I have in mind might receive some consideration, I shall appreciate a cable from you.

We have been very much concerned over the European crisis. If war should break out, all these plans have to be postponed. Not infrequently the international and domestic setting has upset research and educational work.

With kindest regards,

Yours sincerely,

T. L. Yuan

P. S. My telegraphic address: 7049 Hongkong

〔平馆(昆明)英文信纸。Rockefeller Foundation. Series 601: China; Subseries 601.R: China-Humanities and Arts. Box 47. Folder 389〕

按：Handbook of Chinese Studies 应为 *China in Western Literature*（1958）的最早雏形。I. P. R. Conference 即太平洋国际学会第七届会议，本次会议于 1939 年 11 月 22 日至 12 月 2 日在美国弗吉尼亚海滩（Virginia Beach）举行，其原地会议地点为加拿大的维多利亚市（Victoria）。此件为打字稿，落款处为先生签名。

八月三十日

王重民致函先生，谈其离法前诸事之进展及到美后的情况。

守和吾师道鉴：

生等于八月二十三日早晨离巴黎，午登舟，至二十八日早十时抵纽约。过海关后，即直赴车站。下午六时余到美京。吴光清、房兆颖二君来站迎接，并已找租好房子，故下车后毫无困难。昨日已见 Hummel，并将办公桌子预备好；后天早九时，即正式到馆办事。在巴黎时太忙，临行前数日更忙，故未及写信。离 Le Havre 后，曾作短信，但未及发，已过 Southampton。抵纽约前，又寄回伦敦，或要较此信后数日方收到，请再重述一次。所有相片及 film，共装四大箱，携来美国，在船上及在纽约，均详细查看一次，毫无损失，想明后日即可抵华盛顿，昨已告恒先生，到后即一直运国会图书馆。欧战若不幸而再开，Bibliothèque Nationale 并无地窖来收藏这些卷子，设遭不幸，则此四箱为无价宝矣。（去年危急时，只将十余卷藏地窖。生行前告杜女士，此次再入地窖，应去掉盒子，冀能多藏一些卷子也。）所捐书及所购书，共装五箱，已于八月十六日离巴黎，二十日可抵利物浦，极盼现在已过地中海，则可无危险矣。里面所藏，另附一单，请照点查。生离法时，M. Joubert 正休假，他说九月间可寄出，想现在快要买齐，极望欧战不开，此一批书准能于十月十一月之间收到也。Mme Meuvret 称明年再送一批，十九日见 Pelliot，特向他说明法外交部已送一些，将来能再特别设法？他说将一定要再特别设法，另外更赠一批，他又问明吾馆最近情形，并说通报及亚洲学报以后即直寄昆明矣。Marx 氏之名，伯希和说是 Jean。再交换一批书事，生已能明白个中情形，盖交换事由外部出钱，而将所得分送于各与中国有关之图书馆，故在各图书馆方面，莫不愿交换而白得书也。然主持人则以 Meuvret 太太为总主。杜女士

接到吾师信后,非常高兴,曾找 M. Cain 商谈一次,当然赞成,只待再
向 Meuvret 太太一言。生行前又找 Cain 辞行,他除详问我图书馆界情
形外,又表示十分愿继续交换,并嘱生特将此意转达 M. Meuvret;生当
日见她,她当然很愿帮忙。但 M. Meuvret 太忙,非到最后五分钟不作
事,将来多给杜女士写信,叫她借近催 Meuvret 太太即可。生行后未
清之事,一切托之 Meuvret,给她留下一千一百法郎。除五箱书外,其
与云南、西南民族及抗战有关者,曾由书铺寄去昆明十六包,(也许是
二十六包,记不大清了。包皮上有生手记号码。)后来又打六包,生离
巴黎之前一日,始知有三包过重,不能寄,嘱东校听差再分为五包或六
包寄去。想不至有误。一切单据,在船上未弄清,须稍待再从此一直
寄。前寄来敦煌目录,嘱将后照者补入,依昨日所观察办公情形,及此
工作之不易,恐非短时间所能完成,请先发表这一部分,以后另作如
何? 刘女士"云南目"已收辑很完全,哈佛及其他目,未有在刘女士所
编以外者,现应赶快编号码,以便将来作索引,号码编好后,即可寄上
付印。巴黎抗战材料,当应收辑一点,生手中所得,尚有零星几件,将
来寄上。行前与王海镜详谈,当然他所主持或参与之数机关可送一全
份,惟窥其意似欲借此要一点钱。生表示北平图书馆无外汇,现在非
常困难,兹可留下一百元作寄费,如抗日救国会等需要中国日报,可由
北平图书馆出钱代订;伊均拒绝,盖觉 100 法郎太少也。生即说请袁
先生一直来信奉托。他住,8 rue Toullier, Paris 5ᵉ,王君五六年来,均未
读书,只作政治生活;今年很窘,但八月间似又从容,今年不回国,据云
明年再说。Pirkis 女士事,云大方面,伊当即与 Reclus 一直去一信。此
女士无条件的爱中国,薪水多少,在所不计,尤望今年能成行。云大如
不能成功,或钟点太少,不能维持生活,她极愿为吾馆服务,则吾师早
先计画,如尚未找人,即可聘她编法文书书目,并采访法文各种图书
也。况法文书已得不少,从此亦可继续交换,则必专有一人,来主持此
事,聘她正好。吾师如同意,请一直去信为祷。(Miss Susan L. Pirkis,
57, Kidbrooke Park Road, London, S. E. 3.) Pirkis 女士家中不大从容,
未审可否与王景春先生写一信,给她办一免票,从伦敦到香港。因张
似旅至今无消息,不知他意见如何? 若聘定 Pirkis 女士,即可让她在
伦敦先作好此事,将吾馆所要之书,买齐后叫她随身带去,一则可催张

似旅,一则路上平安也。免票不必须,闻伊已预备好六十镑作路费,但如得到免票,于她帮助实不小也。请一切与 Pirkis 女士一直去信为祷!生等来后,即能租到一房子,总算不错。房一间,厨房一大间,每月＄40,寄存小孩,据恒夫人说不易,因小孩非过十八个月不收,现在恐非自看不可。曾宪三已去哈佛,曾宪文已与裴开明结婚。余再及,即请钧安。

受业重民敬上。

八月三十日

〔国家图书馆档案,档案编号 1940-※044-外事 3-002036 和 1940-※044-外事 3-002037〕

按:是年 7 月 1 日,徐家麟离开哈佛燕京学社汉和图书馆,同日曾宪三入职该馆。[1] 该函应于 9 月 29 日送达。

九月三日

先生和岳父袁道冲访蔡元培。〔《蔡元培日记》,页 634〕

按:时袁道冲在《大公报》服务,住坚道 95 号 3 楼。

九月五日

先生致信王重民,询问其离法前寄出图书情况,并告知购书款均应按照美金当日行市拨还。

有三吾弟如晤:

抵华京后,住处及寄存小孩处所已觅妥否?离法不久即发生战事,幸而避免,可谓万幸。燉煌照片及一切稿件想已携美,惟寄 Havre 转英国之书箱是否于八月中旬已寄交王景春先生,迄未接报告,颇以为念。请速函告王先生或寄华,或改存乡间,恐战事延长,大家更无暇及此也 刻下赴远东之船为数甚少,且有危险。前在巴黎 Maisonneuve 代购各书之单据及书目均已收到,法郎 4855.20 合计英磅二十七磅又八十九法郎,应按当日美汇行市折成美金近日英磅大跌,必须按付款之日之行市计算,以便在罗氏补助费内归还,请查照。另纸所开者,分别查明付款日之行市,一律改用美金拨还。此项拨还之款即另为存储,暂存华京之 Riggs Bank 可也。已定十号返滇,谢理士乘德轮 Potsdam 十六日抵港,恐不能上岸,

---

① 《裴开明年谱》,页 222。

因此间德人均已拘留于收容所内也。顺颂旅安。

同礼顿首

九月五日

〔袁同礼家人提供〕

按：Havre 应指法国海滨城市勒阿弗尔（Le Havre）；Riggs Bank 现通译为里格斯银行，19 世纪成立。

九月六日

先生致信 Lyman Hoover，告知其所询出版物信息将会发送到此前给予的九龙地址，但信息为数甚少。

September 6, 1939

Mr. Lyman Hoover

National Committee, Y. M. C. A.

131 Museum Road,

Shanghai.

Dear Mr. Hoover:

　　Your letter asking for information about Muslim's part in the present war was received while I was in Shanghai. In fact, I called on you at your office, but I was sorry to have missed you.

　　The publications you requested will be sent to your Kowloon address, but I am afraid that the information given in these publications is rather meager.

　　With kindest regards,

Yours very Sincerely

T. L. Yuan

Acting Director

〔平馆（冯平山图书馆转）英文信纸。Yale University records, Lyman Hoover Papers, RG 9 Series I, Box: 13, Folder: 280〕

按：此件为打字稿，落款处为先生签名。

九月十二日

加拿大皇家学会 Theresa Pereira 覆函先生，告知交换品清单上的所有出版物均已寄送北平，如补寄则需额外收费。

Post Office Box, 114

House of Commons,

September 12th, 1939

Dear Sir,

Although your Library is listed on our exchange list as receiving "all parts" of our Transactions, which includes all five sections, I have delayed answering your letter of last June 21st until I had had a chance of checking up the actual plates of our Addressograph machine to see whether your Library was among them. This was done a few days ago, and I can now state that all parts, as published, have been forwarded to your Library.

I do not know whether you understand that our Transactions are only published once a year, because where you quote missing parts, you mention January, March and May, I cannot make it out at all.

The Society's Transactions are published following our annual meeting each year, in Sections I and II (together), Section III, IV, and V. Volume XXXIII is in the hands of the printers at the present time, and, as each part is ready for distribution, it will be mailed to you.

The Society cannot afford to replace any missing parts, but these may be supplied at a cost of ninety cents each, which is a special price quoted to those on our exchange list. The postage is extra.

Yours very truly,

Theresa Pereira

Assistant Secretary-Treasurer

P. S. I have just noted that we have been forwarding your Transactions addressed as "National Library of Peiping, Peiping, China."

〔The Royal Society of Canada 英文信纸。国家图书馆档案，档号不明〕

按：Theresa Pereira 生平待考。此函寄送昆明，右上端标注收讫时间为"十一月一日"。

九月十三日

钱存训覆函先生，谈购买郑振铎藏书等事。

守和馆长先生：

由港赐寄各函，均已拜悉。郑振铎藏书书款计由罗氏基金款内拨兑美金 US＄506.11 元，合成国币柒仟元正，业分两次交付清讫。香港办事处八九两月经费共美金贰佰元，均已寄发，另由孙先生具名正式通知矣。八月份经费，据中基会称已于前日寄滇，惟中文购书费尚未发出，闻将按月在沪拨付。余、金两君拨款当即止付，俟收到后再候示支配。印件香港停转。联大寄来日文书单，是否照购，乞示。温君托带《国际舆论》廿本，尚未收到，已请孙述万君在港查询。专肃，敬请钧安。

职钱存训谨上

九，十三

〔中华教育文化基金董事会信纸。国家图书馆档案，档案编号 1945-※057-综合 5-010001〕

按："郑振铎藏书"即郑振铎所藏戏曲之善本，平馆先后分两批购入，共计 84 种、262 册。[1] "温君"应指温源宁；"国际舆论"应指 *Japan's Aggression and Public Opinion*。

九月十五日

上午，徐旭生来访，请平馆将馆藏中西文文献中有关中国学之书籍借与国立北平研究院史学研究所，先生告查明具体情况后再做决定。〔《徐旭生文集》第 9 册，页 1040〕

按：1940 年 4 月，北京研究院与平馆订立合作办法，后者将昆明办事处所藏关于西南文献之中文书籍全部借予该院史学研究所。[2]

九月十七日

午后，先生访徐旭生，晤谈。〔《徐旭生文集》第 9 册，页 1040〕

晚六时，陈永龄、高棣华在昆明曲园设宴，先生、吴宓、邓衍林夫妇等受邀与席，九时散。〔《吴宓日记》第 7 册，页 72〕

九月二十二日

史蒂文斯致函先生，表示洛克菲勒基金会不会考虑资助先生赴欧美考察。

September 22, 1939

---

[1] 陈福康著《郑振铎年谱（修订本）》，上海：上海外语教育出版社，2017 年，页 737；《文学集林》第 2 辑，1939 年 12 月，页 41。

[2] 李书华《北平研究院第十一年》，《大公报》（香港），1940 年 9 月 12 日，第 3 版。

Dear Mr. Yuan:

Thank you for your letter on the accounts of the National Library. This has been given to the Comptroller of the Foundation. He will write you if there is any added fact to be supplied to him or to the office in Shanghai.

Your question on possible help toward attending the conference in Victoria in November has been answered in the terms of your request for my response. As I did not find it possible to make provision for the trip that you wish and for work on the handbook of Chinese studies, I did not send a cable.

My best wishes to you, and my hope for the continued success of your program of work.

Yours sincerely,

David H. Stevens

〔Rockefeller Foundation. Series 601: China; Subseries 601.R: China-Humanities and Arts. Box 47. Folder 389〕

按：此信寄送昆明，并抄送给洛克菲勒基金会驻上海办事处。

九月二十八日

晚，先生在曲园设宴，吴宓、陈永龄、高棣华、高棣华之母受邀与席，约九时散。〔《吴宓日记》第7册，页79〕

钱存训致函先生，告知最近所寄邮包情况并谈平馆西文《馆务报告》印刷费用。

守和馆长先生：

前昨两日先后寄港转上邮包廿二件，内三件系本馆西文书报（108-110包），余十九包系为联大所购之日文书七十四种及新到什志多种（63-81包），内有十余种系前寄下书单中指购，余系选购。此间新到之书，另单开列详细名称，即请到时查核为幸。西文《报告》各五百册均已印就，兹寄港转上样本二册，即祈察收。一俟名单寄下，即行发出。纸张本拟用白道林，但印价现涨至五百本每页八元（旧估价乙千本每页四元六角），次道林每页六元，因恐印刷费超出预算，故与李君酌定均用次道林印，可省四分之一。惟纸色较黄，未知是否嫌劣，并请示知，以便下册印时照办。中文本排印甚迟，现仅校阅一次，下月中或可印成。中基会九月份经费昨已发出，据闻以后每月可发当月之

款。陈贯吾君薪俸,孙先生嘱尊处再去一正式函件通知,以便在汇滇
经费内扣除。专肃,敬请钧安。

职钱存训谨上
九,廿八

〔国家图书馆档案,档案编号 1945-※057-综合 5-010003 和
1945-※057-综合 5-010004〕

按:"西文报告"似指 1935-1937 年馆务报告。1939 年 11 月 10 日,
昆明办事处曾致信北平留守人员王访渔、顾子刚,告知上海办事处
会寄上十册馆务报告,因纸价高涨只印五百份,须谨慎分配。①

九月三十日

先生致信王重民,请其查明美国国会图书馆所藏《永乐大典》中尚未以
photostat 方式为平馆复制者,并寄上平馆已有影本之清单。

有三吾弟:

　　昨奉八月三十日手书,欣悉抵美后一切情形,甚以为慰。由巴黎
运至利物浦之五箱迄今尚无消息,已函王景春询问,预料不致有何意
外也。由书店径寄昆明之书包,仅收到一包,既系挂号,想陆续必能寄
到,惟英伦拟购之《永乐大典》,未识接洽如何? 刻下欧战方殷,想可
减价,望再与 Moule 一商,以免为他人购去。国会图书馆所藏《大典》
不少,内中尚有四、五本未照相,望查明请 Hummel 为馆制一复本。兹
由上海办事处将本馆所藏国会图书馆入藏之《大典》复本开一清单,
随函寄上,即希备查是荷。顺颂旅安。

同礼顿首
九月三十日

　　向觉明来滇,谓 Robertson 有关于菲律宾著作一种,约五十本,内
中述及中西交通颇详,请为馆中购一部(美国出版),请将书名查出
示复。

〔袁同礼家人提供〕

王重民致函先生,谈其由欧洲寄送图书和书稿诸细节及到美后的工作、生
活等情况。

---

① 《北京图书馆馆史资料汇编(1909-1949)》,页 696。

守和吾师钧鉴：

　　生等于八月二十八日抵华京，三十一日曾作一信，报告托王景春先生所转运之五箱书籍，并 Pirkis 女士愿赴中国，张似旅代买之书，可托她随身带去等节。嗣奉到吾师八月十五日在上海，二十五日在香港所发两手谕。即将经手所购各书，略结账目，到今恰为 £ 100 矣。所有帐单，已于二十五日挂号寄上，兹另附上一清单，以便与寄上之账单相对。生之路费，今亦另开一英文收据，惟张似旅之£ 20，尚未寄来收据，Meuvret 太太处，亦尚欠一清单耳。俟收到后再寄上。伦敦某太太之永乐大典，Prof. Moule 谓£ 20 或有希望者，至今无消息，恐不能成功。因物主由百镑降五十镑，即不肯再让步故也。如再有消息，拟劝 Hummel 买恐须三四十镑，吾人能得一照片足矣。此间所藏大典，生尚未及检查，未照者将来当可继续摄影。戴密微、Meuvret 太太，均有信来，他们自然有相当恐慌，生有一部分稿子，尚存戴先生处，闻已代藏地窖中。截至今日，已炸沉船五十七艘，故欧美交通颇不便，他们都是八月底九月初写的信，一月后方到此，可见大西洋中商船之少矣。前致 Meuvret 太太信，请代索 *Documents diplomatiques français. 1871-1914*，又另外给杜乃扬一信，告以四部丛刊有找齐希望，并请其从旁催促 Meuvret 太太也。欧战再开，法国杂志，想必有一部分停刊，吾人应多开一些，请其代订，至于如何合计，每国币应合多少法郎，吾人心中先按七八法郎计算，届时再向 Meuvret 一说，想很易达到目的。生一月之内，已将此间善本书撰成提要三十余篇，其比较重要者，当即遵嘱，另抄一份寄上，请登馆刊。二十五日还寄上一挂号包裹，内有①刘女士之云南书目第一章，请吾师稍加改正，送上海印入季刊排字应用几号字，或何处用大字，何处用小字，何处用斜体字，请批注一下。②在法所买西南种族书三小册，③伦敦寄来抗战史料。夏间寄来之敦煌影片目录，嘱生补充，预备付印，至今尚未动手。固然携来之照片箱，直至今日，尚未收到。（Hummel 说图书馆秘书处已接到海关消息，不久可到。）即收到后，似亦很难即时编入。依生之意，此目或可先发表，生当另开一极简略之目，预备向中英庚款会作报告如何？将来 Library of Congress 拟加洗一份，势必为其整理，到那时再编详目，方可一举两得。不知吾师以为何如也。得吾师今冬或明春来美消息，殊为喜跃；但欧战既开，图书馆协会理事会，恐不能如期开会，而国际变化如此大，俾日寇得乘机专对付我国，长沙已危，前途不无悲观，殊恐信到之日，昆明亦较危险于今日也。然祖国如能不亡，战事能告一相当段落，则吾师来欧美捐书，正是大好机会。所难者美金狂涨，筹旅费不易耳。协会如能准期开会，生当便中向 Hummel 一言，请其代向罗氏基金会设法。

生来此后，倏倏已一月，考订虽亦费一些气力，作来虽亦有相当趣味，但多是明版书，十之八九为明末无聊文人所辑刻，此对象无多大价值，故总觉不如在英法时花得来。从别一方面想，生年将四十，娶妻生子，实应及早积蓄一点，正如吾师所言，美金狂涨，是一好机会也。图书馆只能聘华人四，现冯家昇已辞职回国，另请朱士嘉继任，闻已首途，不久可到。此外房兆颖、吴先生及生共四人，决不能另聘人。房太太杜联喆曾在馆服务，然最近二年赋闲。自冯家昇走，她暂代，朱士嘉到后，又必赋闲。故刘女士决无插入可能。恒夫人曾代询，寄托小孩虽有机关，然非到十八个月以上不肯收养。刘女士不得不决计自己看顾。但她因不习惯于此，且每贪看书，故终日如此极苦。现在恐无他法，将来再找机会，则她可借 Library of Congress 之便，另编一种专科目录也。据这一月经验，每月有 $100 或多至 $110 美金，足够全家之用。则每月至少可省出四十美金，若月月如此，一二年后，亦可称小康矣。

生在欧洲五年，把全部精力，都用在敦煌材料之整理上。一二年前，已计有三十余种，曾开一目，请张菊生、王云五代为印行，想吾师或尚记得该信，但因抗战，不能施行。生此次来美，颇拟设法得一点印刷费，但未敢语人。在巴黎时，戴密微忽一日欲有言而未言，乃劝生到街上散步，遂谈到伊颇愿写一封信致 Elisséeff，请在哈佛出一笔款为生印费，正与生所蕴蓄于心者相合。伊劝若托伯希和帮忙，必更有效。生因于伯希和为生饯行时，向他一说此意，伊亦非常同情，愿写介绍信。然除戴、伯二先生外，生尚未语他人，因尚未与吾师商议，生亦殊不明了哈佛组织与 Elisséeff 先生之为人也。今冬或明春，吾师能来美，此事当极易办，但事前应稍作准备，可否进行，应如何进行，极愿吾师详为指教也。专此，即请道安！

受业重民敬上。

九月三十日

照相费尚有七八十镑,一俟奉到寄款,即将春间寄来之£100寄回香港。又将来与清华不知如何算账,趁早拿回一点钱(能合国币一千五六百元即可)预备还清华如何?

生在船上给胡适之先生发一信,来后未即往拜见,伊却来电话,请到其公馆吃饭九月初。伊身体已很好,大少爷亦已到此。其手稿及重要书籍已运来几箱,余尚在天津。生之稿件到后,拟每两周写定一种,即请他看,并作序。

〔国家图书馆档案,档案编号 1940-※044-外事 3-002038 至 1940-※044-外事 3-002040〕

按:"伦敦某太太"即 Beatrice Brownrigg。冯家昇(1904—1970),字伯平,山西省孝义人,历史学家、语言学家。杜联喆(1902—1994),天津杨柳青人,1924年燕京大学历史系毕业,随即留校攻读硕士学位,1929年起任职于该校图书馆,协助购买、整理古籍并参与哈佛燕京学社引得工作,后赴美,协助恒慕义编撰《清代名人传略》(*Eminent Chinese of the Ch'ing Period*)。该函及本日刘修业函应于10月2日寄出,首页右上角标注"Nov. 10 到"。

刘修业致函先生,寄上《云南书目》之一部,并谈到美后的生活、工作情况。

守和馆长钧鉴:

读寄重民谕,得知关怀修业,至感。现《云南书目》先寄上第一节,如可继续刊布,当再将其余校正编号寄上,惟现因忙,不能多练习打字,请人又太贵耳。前在英伦读圕行政,季末有实习时,曾作一《巴黎东方语言学校圕参观记》,经 Mr. Cowley 校阅一次,文章间已无大误,将来亦拟寄呈审阅,如可介绍如《天下》月刊等刊布,则请馆中一人代打字后,再将底稿寄下。最近来美,因有小孩杂事多,不能再专心学业,精神上极觉不快,每日清晨忙于各种事务,至午后则体力不支,若再多读写则夜间或至失眠。现惟希望在此有机会找数小时工作,得些津贴则可用以雇黑奴代洗小孩脏布及擦地板等笨重工作,则心力较有余裕,冀再能兼顾课业也。余容再陈,即请钧安。

修业谨上
九月卅日

〔国家图书馆档案,档案编号 1940-※044-外事 3-002043〕

九月

云南民族研究会假云南大学至公堂成立,到者六十余人,云南大学校长熊庆来为会议主席,吴文藻报告筹备经过,继讨论会章并选举职员,龙云被推为名誉会长,周锺岳、熊庆来、李书华、陶孟和为名誉副会长,李济、吴定良、梁思永、罗莘田、顾颉刚、潘光旦、陈达、周云苍、先生、姚寻源、闻宥、凌纯声、吴文藻等十三人被推为理事。〔《申报》,1939 年 10 月 18 日,第 7 版;《总汇报》(上海),1939 年 10 月 16 日,第 6 版〕

> 按:该会推定吴定良为理事长、吴文藻为书记、周云苍为会计,拟通过以下方式推进会务:(一)每月举行演讲会一次、延请中外专家担任;(二)组织编纂西南民族学文献目录及提要委员会;(三)组织云南民物标本委员会;(四)组织西南民族学研究工作调查委员会。

九十月间

先生致信张元济,请其在沪代《图书季刊》等刊物征求稿件。〔《张元济年谱长编》下卷,页 1122〕

> 按:此信于 10 月 15 日送达,翌日张元济致信顾廷龙,请其在合众图书馆藏善本中择要撰写题记。1940 年 2 月 5 日,顾廷龙致信张元济,并附未刊布之序跋十篇①,托其转寄先生,并希望获赠平馆出版物。②

十月二日

先生致信 Foon Sien,感谢其寄赠出版物。

> Dear Sir:
>
> On behalf of the National Library, we have pleasure in extending to you our sincerest thanks for your letter dated July 29 as well as 2 copies of "War in China; what it means to Canada" and 3 copies of "Save China and Save World Peace!" and other leaflets which you have so kindly sent to us.
>
> We are happy to learn that you have been so kind as to put this Library on your mailing list to receive future issues of your valuable publications. We are looking forward with great pleasure to their arrival.

---

① 序跋似指《卷盦藏书记略》,刊《图书季刊》新 2 卷第 3 期,1940 年 9 月,页 338-346。
②《顾廷龙日记》,页 49。

With renewed thanks for your kind assistance,

Yours faithfully,

T. L. Yuan,

Acting Director

Mr. Foon Sien, Chairman,

Chinese National Salvation League,

108 Pender Street East,

Vancouver, B. C.,

Canada.

〔国家图书馆档案，档号不明〕

按：此件为录副。

Lyman Hoover 覆函先生，以未能与先生在上海面谈而深以为歉，并告知此前收到莫余敏卿寄来的参考书目和英法文材料，极具价值。

October 2, 1939

Dear Dr. Yuan:

I greatly appreciated your recent letter and am sorry indeed that I was away at the time when you came to call on me here in Shanghai. I hope we shall have another opportunity for a good visit together. I am planning to leave for the interior within the next two weeks, if possible, I am traveling by way of Ningpo or by some other overland route, but on the way back I hope to visit Kunming and the National Library there.

I am glad to inform you that some days ago, I received a very helpful letter from Mr. M. Y. Mok of your staff, enclosing a very valuable bibliography and several other materials in French and English. He also said that he was sending additional materials in Chinese under separate cover. I hope to receive these soon and am most grateful for this assistance.

With cordial regards, I am

Sincerely yours,

Lyman Hoover

〔Yale University records, Lyman Hoover Papers, RG 9 Series I, Box: 13, Folder: 280〕

按：Mr. M. Y. Mok 应指莫余敏卿，此处应为 Mrs.非 Mr.，10 月 17 日致先生信中亦如此，特说明。① 其寄送的期刊和材料有 China's Mohammedans mobilize support for Central Government, March, 1938;《月华》第 10 卷、《回民论》第 1 卷；Chinese Mohammedans appeal to Moslem World。该函寄送香港。

十月四日

平馆向教育部呈文一件，寄上已购及拟购英文书籍书单并请转咨财政部准予按照法定汇价购买外汇，具先生名并钤印。

> 呈为呈请事。窃职馆为适应目前国家之需要起见，所购之西文书专以有关抗战及战后复兴者为限。兹寄上书单甲乙二份。（甲）单为购到之书，亟待付款者（附 Stechert 公司发单九张），共美金一百二十七元六角七分。（乙）单为拟购之书四十种，共合英磅二十二磅六仙令三辨士。呈请鉴核并乞转咨财政部准予按照法定汇价购买外汇。即希赐予批准，无任感祷。谨呈
>
> 教育部长
>
> 　　　　　　　　　职国立北平图书馆副馆长袁同礼谨呈
> 　　　　　　　　　　中华民国二十八年十月四日
>
> 附书单两份。
>
> 　　　　〔中国第二历史档案馆，教育部档案·全卷宗 5，国立北平图书馆
> 　　　　请拨员工学术研究补助费经常费有关文书，案卷号 11616（1）〕

十月七日

先生派人将馆藏《朝鲜李氏实录》借与郑天挺。〔《郑天挺西南联大日记》，页 196〕

十月八日

王重民致函先生，谈其与法国诸友人的联系，并请先生为王新民在平馆谋一职务。

> 守和吾师道鉴：
>
> 生等在此，生活非常平静。惟因天气太热与相片箱尚未接到，工作方面，尚不能紧张起来。前拟请吾师指教，可否向哈佛请一点款，为

---

① 余敏卿的丈夫即莫泮芹（P. K. Mok），时在西南联合大学文学院任教授。

印行生手辑敦煌丛抄之用。今又拟先将所作题跋,再汇为"巴黎敦煌残卷叙录第二辑",寄北平付印。现在美金价高,印费仍可由生自付,但拟借用吾馆代印名义,不知吾师以为如何?

欧洲前途如何,数日后当可分明,接杜乃扬信,知巴黎文化工作,大致停顿。Bibliothèque Nationale 已关门,善本书或迁城外,或入地窖,敦煌卷子则仅藏了一半。杜女士已迁往乡间,惟不时进城耳。李芳馥开战前赴欧洲游历,刻仍困巴黎。

张似旅来信,称吾人所请邮寄之书,不能照办,须交委员会分配,不知是否蒋慰堂曾和他通消息,抑是张彭春之主张。张君又称自开战以来,捐书事已停顿,惟牛津方面尚有余款,仍可继续买书耳。想此种种情形,伊已有信奉告吾师。又伊用中文开来一£ 20 收条,既不肯为吾馆寄书,此二十镑将来惟有更用以购书耳。

生屡接家信,知乡间土匪横行,殊为焦虑,家严虽已避居白洋淀边,竟非安全之地。刻此间收入较丰,且汇价又高,故拟今年冬间,仍希望全家搬到北平居住。舍弟新民所受教育虽不高,但七八年来,随家父读书,写字与看书程度已不错,为将来永久计,恳请吾师在平馆给伊一"练习书记"名义,写字或在阅览室管出纳书,或看守书库,均能胜任。每月只希望有十五元,以慰高堂,即足!吾馆如尚能有此种机会,而吾师又特别惠助,则明年一月一日,新民即可到馆任职!

倭寇攻长沙已失败,海外闻之,殊为安慰!此月内欧洲不大打,必有大变化,则东方局势,必能随之而变。以往国际情形,对我愈变而愈坏;但生总相信:将来必有一日,愈变而对我愈好也。在巴黎、伦敦所购诸书,想已收到不少;生寄去账单与书单,可令人点查,如有错误,再速速追究也。

专此,即请钧安!

受业重民敬上。

十月八日

上月三十日,曾上一长信,并附寄 Bibliothèque Nationale 赠书单等。

因吾师前有信致恒夫人,她今日下午来寓看视。但称托儿所对中国小孩,非过十八个月不收,仍无办法。

〔国家图书馆档案,档案编号 1940-※044-外事 3-002044 和

1940-※044-外事 3-002045〕

按:"家严"即王步霄,字近宸。①

十月九日

顾颉刚致函先生。〔《顾颉刚日记》卷 4,页 293〕

费正清覆函先生,告知哈佛寄赠图书、期刊七箱,将通过华盛顿史密斯森协会运往中国,并简述书籍、期刊的分类和数量,其中一些书刊请留意转交陈岱孙、刘崇鋐、钱端升三人。

Oct. 9, 1939

Dear Mr. Yuan:

Thank you for your letter of Aug. 1 in answer to my last letter, of June 12, six cases of books were sent in July by the Smithsonian Institution, and a seventh will be sent from here to Washington for similar dispatch in the near future.

The six cases sent contain the following types of

Material	books	Periodicals
Medicine	24	74
Government	71	
Chemistry	15	2
History	176	32
Science in general	12	1466
Education	8	
Physics	95	824
Sociology	23	
Engineering	205	1840
Economics	41	7
Mathematics	9	71
Literature and Dictionaries	134	

---

① 台北胡适纪念馆,档案编号 HS-JDSHSC-0939-009。

Material	books	Periodicals
Biology and related	10	
Geography	2	418
Psychology	15	
Philosophy	134	75
Geology	3	32
Art	21	

Total books 1008, total periodicals 4807, total both 5815.

(We had a card made for all books received and chosen, and my wife tabulated the above results). The card file from which I draw these figures I am sending to you by post in a separate package, in case it may be of some use to your staff. The items in the seventh case are not listed above.

I am sorry this collection is not larger. All the dormitories were canvassed, by the Phillips Brooks House, a student society, and we reached a large part of the faculty informally, without having an official drive. But as you may have noticed before, the American public is like most publics, rather concerned with itself and with things at hand. The European situation has been monopolizing attention and continues to do so, and so the American conduct toward China generally is disgraceful. Another reason for it lies in the continuation of the depression. In the 1920s we would have had no trouble in raising funds. Public spirit is a luxury to many people, who fail to see that intellectual cooperation is a necessity in any case. When I hear from you that the first cases have arrived, I shall circularize interested persons here and see what we can do further.

I would appreciate it if you could, without too much trouble, have a few of the books given to certain teachers in Kunming. The books I have in mind are nearly all textbooks, which would probably be of most use in the possession of teachers, and the individuals concerned are friends to whom I should like to make a special donation. I have therefore taken the liberty of picking out a few cards from the general file and marking them as follows: for Prof. Deison Ch'en, 9 items on economics; for Prof. Liu Ch'ung-hung, if he is in Kunming, 29 items on history; and for Prof. Ch'ien Tuan-sheng 11 items on political science (I have mentioned this arrangement to Prof. Ch'ien). Theses donations are little enough, compared to what we should like to send, but they may be of a little help.

It is unnecessary to say that in all this project it has been a great satisfaction to know that you were in Kunming to take delivery of anything that we could send. Those of us in touch with the situation admire very warmly the work that you have been doing. Every crisis brings forth its leaders, but it is very fortunate when the leaders are of special competence.

With cordial regards,

J. K. Fairbank

〔Harvard University, John K. Fairbank personal archive〕

十月十三日

先生致信 H. E. M. Chisholm（多伦多），感谢其赠书并回赠邮票以表谢忱。

October 13, 1939

H. E. M. Chisholm, Esq.,

Director of Publicity,

The Department of Trade and Commerce,

West Block,

Canada.

Dear Sir:

We have pleasure in acknowledging the receipt of your letter dated August 22nd as well as the following publications which you have so kindly sent to this Library:

2 *Canadian Geographical Journal* Vol. XIX, no. 1, July 1939

2 *Canada's Water Power Wealth*

2 *Canada 1939*

2 *5000 Facts about Canada*

Canadian News Letter

　　Vol.7, nos. 25–28, 32–33, Oct. 7, Dec. 8, 1938

On behalf of the National Library, I beg to convey to you our sincerest thanks for your courtesy.

　　We are happy to learn that you could arrange to send to this Library other Canadian publications. We are sending you herewith our desiderata and shall be most indebted to you if you would kindly procure them for us.

　　As a humble return for your courtesy, we are sending you herewith a set of used Chinese postal stamps. We hope that they will be of some possible use to you.

　　Thanking you for your kind co-operation and assistance, I remain,

　　　　　　　　　　　　　　　　　　Yours sincerely,

　　　　　　　　　　　　　　　　　　T. L. Yuan

　　　　　　　　　　　　　　　　　　Acting Director

　　　　　　　　　〔国家图书馆档案,档号不明〕

　　按:该件为录副。

先生致信 Ontario Research Foundation(多伦多),请该基金会寄赠研究报告及出版物。

　　　　　　　　　　　　　　　　　October 13, 1939

Secretary,

Ontario Research Foundation

Toronto,

Canada.

Dear Sir:

　　As we are very much interested in the valuable work your Foundation has been doing, we take the liberty of writing to you to inquire whether it would be possible for you to send us a copy of your report as well as other publications through the International Exchange Service of the Smithsonian Institution, Washington, D. C. If you would kindly comply with our request, your courtesy will be gratefully appreciated.

Thanking you in anticipation for your valuable assistance,

Yours faithfully,

T. L. Yuan,

Acting Director

〔国家图书馆档案,档号不明〕

按:Ontario Research Foundation 即安大略研究基金会,1928 年成立,主要是该省和制造业协会拨款支持,研究对象多为工科项目。该件为录副。

十月十六日

顾颉刚致电、函与先生。〔《顾颉刚日记》卷 4,页 296〕

按:此日函电应为王育伊调任史语所任职事。

十月十七日

Lyman Hoover 致函先生,告知其收到寄来的中文文献,用毕即奉还。

Oct. 17, 1939

Dear Dr. Yuan,

I am glad to report to you that the package of Chinese materials forwarded me through your help and that of Mr. M. Y. Mok has now been received. These are extremely valuable and there is so much material that it may take me some time to finish my use of these publications. As soon as this is accomplished, however, I will undertake to get them back safely to your Library in Kunming. I am leaving very soon on a trip to the interior, in the course of which I hope to visit Kunming, if necessary, I shall try to deliver these materials there in person.

With cordial regards,

Very sincerely yours,

Lyman Hoover

〔Yale University records, Lyman Hoover Papers, RG 9 Series I, Box: 13, Folder: 280〕

按:此函寄送香港,另有一副本抄送给莫余敏卿。

十月十八日

先生致信胡恒德,同意将缩微胶片拍摄机永久安装在协和医学院,并感谢该院提供空间和机械师，此外就该设备的运行、服务对象以及委员会构成提出意见。

October 18, 1939

Dear Dr. Houghton:

I have just received a report from Mr. T. K. Koo about the meeting held at your residence September 26 concerning the micro-film camera. I am glad to learn of the new arrangement, particularly the fact that PUMC has agreed to provide the necessary space and a mechanic for the camera.

Because of mechanical and other facilities, it is my hope that the camera can be permanently installed in PUMC. It is most desirable that it should be kept in order under the expert supervision of a mechanic.

As to the actual operation of the camera, permit me to offer to you a few of my observations:

Firstly, the National Library will furnish the necessary personnel out of the regular members of its staff. It was our understanding with the Rockefeller Foundation that these operators be trained by Dr. Draeger after the assembling of the camera. Dr. Draeger will be in China long enough to train them and watch its full operation. After they are trained for the work, they are expected to stay on in order to secure a maximum of efficiency.

Secondly, the National Library will supply the funds for the purchase of films and other equipment to be imported from the United States. As we cannot afford to operate the camera at full speed, I suggested that we set aside temporarily US $ 4,000 for three years for this purpose. In these days of financial stringency, strict economy should be observed. But should additional sum to be required, we shall make additional appropriations out of our regular book fund.

In order to conform with our usual procedure, all requisitions should be signed by Mr. T. K. Koo who will send them to our Treasurer at Shanghai for payment.

Thirdly, in addition to film rare books for the Library of Congress, we shall make film copies of books and scientific literature for the migrated libraries now located in Western and Southwestern China, not a few of which have been destroyed by the war. The film copies will be supplied at actual cost. The National Library is anxious to render service of this kind.

In view of the considerations enumerated above, may I venture to suggest that Dr. Draeger and Mr. T. K. Koo be invited to serve on the sub-committee. Mr. Koo will be responsible for the actual operation of the camera under the supervision of the local committee.

I am confident that these suggestions will meet your approval as well as that of the local committee. I sincerely hope that we shall co-operate heartily in this joint undertaking which is destined to play an important part in the diffusion of scientific literature in this country.

With renewed thanks and kindest regards,

Yours sincerely,

T. L. Yuan

Director

〔Rockefeller Foundation. Series 300 Latin America-Series 833 Lebanon; Subseries 601. Box 9. Folder 87〕

按:由该信可知此套缩微胶片拍摄机除为国会图书馆拍摄平馆古籍善本外,本拟为西南地区学术机构拍摄科学文献。该信于11月3日送达,此为抄件。

十月二十二日

王重民致函先生,谈到美后的境况。

守和吾师道鉴:

九月五日自港发来手谕已奉到;想吾师久已安抵昆明。此次长沙胜利,海外闻之,殊为欢抃,昆明在最近的将来,想可少空袭,亟望在此期间,国际上有有利于我之变化。英镑折美金,日内当函询,或到新闻纸部去查美国旧报纸,一两周内再奉陈。接尤桐自牛津来信,知伊曾寄上关于抗战刊物三数册,伊又称自欧战发生,征书委员会,有将总机关迁牛津之说,该会有人邀他加入帮同买书。迁牛津后或将举行一委员会,开会结果如何,伊当有信报告也。接 Kegan Paul 信,知又找到 *Peking to Mandalay* 一书,已直寄昆明。生抵美后,未曾逛书铺,将来如有好书,未审可否代吾馆购买? 但如遇有关云南及西南民族,确知吾馆尚未买者,定当买了寄上。月前曾去信询王景春先生,所托寄之书,刻已离英与否,但未得覆,其信殆已沉大海耶? 不然王先生覆信最快,何以至今无消息? 又不知吾师最近接到关此之消息没有? (该书曾保险两万法郎。)生等日来稍习惯,刘女士有时亦能出来看点书,小孩下午六时即睡觉,故她晚上尤能有整个时间。云南书目已寄上第一篇,其余即可依次清理,拟不久寄昆明,请找一人打字,打好再寄回编号码,期望明春能印成书,最好! 此间中文书总算不少,刘女士已开始簿录中文书中关于西南各民族之著述,冀可与她所编英法文者并行。相片箱已抵华盛顿,还因关税问题,Library of Congress 代交涉,尚未十分清,然已大致无问题矣。余再及,即请钧安!

受业重民上。

十月二十二日

〔国家图书馆档案,档案编号 1940-※044-外事 3-002030〕

按:*Peking to Mandalay* 全称*From Peking to Mandalay: a journey from north China to Burma through Tibetan Ssuch'uan and Yunnan*,庄士敦(Reginald F. Johnston,1874-1938)著,1908 年初版,今译作《从北京到曼德勒:末代帝师中国西南纪行》。

十月二十六日

下午二时,中日战事史料征集会假昆明光华街海棠春召开第三次委员会,冯友兰、陈寅恪、傅斯年、姚从吾、陶孟和、先生出席,张荫麟、王信忠、傅恩龄列席。会议审核本年度工作大纲,决定集中力量先编印(1)《敌情丛刊》、(2)《抗战大事表》、(3)《双月刊》;审议英庚款补助费用途案,其中中日文购书费三千元,西文购书费三千元,编辑出版费四千元;审核并通过借阅书规约、借钞史料规约;聘请张荫麟为英文编辑;决议本会办事人员,非本会特许不得在外发表文章;另聘胡绍声为干事。约三时散。〔国家图书馆档案,档案编号 1939-※054-综合 2-001013〕

按:胡绍声,1928 年毕业于金陵中学,后考入金陵大学,1938 年任西南联合大学图书馆馆员。①

---

① 《国立西南联合大学史料》第 4 卷,页 67。

十一月三日

先生致信王访渔、顾子刚,谈寄来的目录卡片及其定价、销售事。

> 子访、子刚先生大鉴:

> 关于寄来之卡片,编印精良,至为欣慰。惟刻下纸价日涨,每组卡片拟定为六十元或七十元,外加邮费　元,零售则定为每张一分五厘。如何之处,即希查明示复,以便发出通启。又,寄国内国外之卡片发至若干号时,即希函请寄款(第三组)并盼示及。据目下情形观之,亟须力谋大量增加订户,方能挹注。又,寄来之十八份,每有缺少张数情事,请转告高凌汉君特别注意。兹查一八四八号缺三张,请附在来函内寄滇为荷。

> 〔《北京图书馆馆史资料汇编(1909-1949)》,页694〕

> 按:"邮费"与"元"之间的空格,原属有意,请经办人根据实际情况自行决定。高凌汉,北平市人,抗战爆发前任平馆中文编目组书记之一。此件录副,无落款。

十一月四日

先生、梅贻琦、蒋梦麟、张伯苓致信管理中英庚款董事会,寄上征辑中日战事史料会预算书,请予赞助。

> 敬启者,准贵会渝教字第3040号公函,为本馆、校合组之征辑中日战事史料会请求补助一案,业经议决补助壹万元,嘱即编制详细预算送会查核等由;贵会赞助学术,钦感莫名。除将本工作报告陆续寄奉外;兹将该项预算书随函附上,即希察收示复为荷。此致
> 管理中英庚款董事会
> 附预算书壹份。

国立北平图书馆馆长袁○○
国立西南联合大学常务委员梅○○
蒋○○
张○○
中华民国廿八年十一月四日

> 〔国家图书馆档案,档案编号1939-※054-综合2-001167和1939-※054-综合2-001168〕

> 按:该件应为文书拟稿。

先生致信王重民，谈购书、运书以及敦煌照片目录发表等事。

有三吾弟：

前接到美后第一函，多日未接来信，想工作繁忙之故。巴黎 Maisonneuve 寄来廿八包已先后收到，尚有书多种（见另单）而无发票，是否在 Madame Meuvret 处，请查询。至八月十六日转利物浦运港书籍五箱，毫无消息，已函王景春询问；至 Meuvret 及 Joubert 面允九月间可寄赠之一批，想欧战发生后已无希望。Pirkis 女士处恐亦受欧战影响中止来华，故亦未致伊一函。此间经费亦甚困难，实不易设法也。前在寄上之一百磅内，在 Luzac, Kegan Paul 所买各书共 £ 18.19.5，兹折成美金 $ 88.95。又在 Maisonneuve 代购书共 4855.20 法郎，合英磅二十七又四十九法郎£ 27+49frcs，均告中基会在罗氏基金会款内陆续拨还，请收到后仍将原数寄还香港孙述万君冯平山图书馆。此外，尚有《永乐大典》残卷迄无收条寄来，请查明示复。又 Moule 介绍之《大典》，前以索价过昂未成交，近日能否因欧战而落价，亦请进行。《敦煌照片目录》如无暇将两部份合并，则先将孙子书所编部分发表亦可。关于《燉煌卷子叙录》之文章仍可陆续寄来，以便在《季刊》发表。此外，美京所藏中文善本书亦应作一提要登之《季刊》，并交 Hummel 一份，似需要其同意也。关于刘女士之《云南书目》应将华京所藏者一并加入，俾能完备。此外，请其留意新出版关于汉学之书籍及期刊，将来返国后，可约其协助编辑《季刊》也。三期已出版，由沪寄上。朱士嘉已到华京否？为念，顺颂大安。

袁同礼顿首

十一月四日

〔袁同礼家人提供〕

按：Luzac 即 Luzac & Co，伦敦书店、出版商，尤其以东方、佛教书籍为特色。《敦煌照片目录》似指由先生所编《国立北平图书馆现藏海外敦煌遗籍照片总目》，载于《图书季刊》新 2 卷第 4 期，仅截止到卢沟桥事变爆发前平馆所藏者。《燉煌卷子叙录》后只刊登了其中的一篇——《敦煌本董永变文跋》（《图书季刊》新第 2 卷第 3 期）。

十一月十七日

王重民覆函先生，谈此前巴黎寄出五箱书籍的下落及购买《永乐大典》

等事。

守和吾师道鉴：

九月三十日手谕奉到。在巴黎所寄之五箱书，曾得王景春先生信，谓接运该书之船 Lycaon 被英政府征去，未审五箱书曾否上船？刻正在追踪。在巴黎系交 Currie 公司代运，生因离法在即，故发寄人写的 Mme Meuvret，伊已再向该公司探询。此事不一定有大危险，只因正在开战之前夕，办事人手续彼此不接头。吾人甚盼该五箱仍在 Le Havre，未及上船，反更安全也。后有消息，再呈报。

觉明所说之书，如下：

Robertson, (James Alexander) *The Philippine Islands, 1493 - 1803 explorations by early navigators, descriptions of the islands and their peoples, their history and records of the Catholic missions, as related in contemporaneous books and manuscripts, showing the political, economic, commercial and religious conditions of those islands from their earliest relations with European nations to the beginning of the nineteenth century.* 1903 年在 Ohio 出版，共 55 vols.，即当探询价目，再去买。

Library of Congress 所藏大典，拟稍后，俟生编目时，即详为校阅，凡吾馆未有影片之本，当一一代为摄影。照费想系由吾馆付，不是由 Hummel 送礼罢？伦敦之一册，已售出，吾人因外汇关系，不能出高价，为可惜耳！（Dr. Hummel 说，他得此消息后，即拍电报电至英国，信到之前一日，已以 £ 50 出售矣。）

在巴黎所寄书包，甚望能平安收到。Maisonneuve 共寄十六包，生寄三包，Mme Meuvret 代寄五包，（也许是六包，来信未说明包数，仅说共用邮费 93.10 法郎，想不是五包，就是六包。）共二十五包或二十六包全数收到后，请示知。

兹别寄上一邮包，内计：

1. 生所撰此间所藏善本书提要稿，请为季刊补白。

2. 前寄北平之敦煌影片目录。生仅稍稍改其差误，并弁一短序，请先发表。带来此间者，俟编好目录后，再继续发表。（短序附此信封内。）

3. 刘女士所辑云南书目稿，请派人打字，共打两份，一份同原稿再寄下,以便编号码。此事因小孩耽误,□出版者恐须一年,为可憾。第一章曾打好,已将打稿于九月二十五日寄上,想此时已平安收到。

前信嘱查美金与英镑旧汇对律,因已于九月二十五日将账单寄上,手中无账单,不知日期,故请就便在香港一查,如何? 吾馆若有 *London* 或 *New York Times*,亦极易查也。

Kegan Paul 来信,又寄上 Johnston *Peking to Mandalay* 一书,价£ 1-4-0,已由生付。

转瞬又将年终,而来美所作自己工作太少了。明年八九月恐作不完,期望能于十二月或 1941 年春结束,早日归国,与其为人卖气力,不如回去为自己国家作点事,苦乐在所不计也。即请道安!

受业重民上。
十一月十七日

携来五箱影片,已平安运到 Library of Congress。(内一最好之箱,反碰坏,幸相片无大损坏。) Dr. Hummel 贪图得乘机洗一份,从 New York 至华盛顿运费,及在税关储存两个多月之储存费,大概由 Library of Congress 代付了。

〔国家图书馆档案,档案编号 1940-※044-外事 3-002046 和 1940-※044-外事 3-002047〕

十一月十八日

先生致信王重民,谈《云南书目》、《敦煌照片目录》的整理及刘修业女士文稿可代为向《天下》(*Tien Hsia Monthly*)投稿、馆中亟需美金诸事。

有三吾弟:

连接十月二日及八日来书,又刘女士九月三十日来函,欣悉种种。《云南书目》亦同时收到,编辑此目想费时间不少,请将以后部分从速整理寄下以便付印,并拟酬赠壹百元。此款应交国内何人,请示知,并寄下一收据是盼。《燉煌照片目》既无暇整理,拟即先发表子书所整理之一部分。关于向哈佛燕京社请求印刷费一节,最好托伯希和或戴先生写一信二人均有力量,不必再托他人,想因印刷关系,该社必交燕京引得处代印。刘女士《观书记》可交《天下》付印,或可得些稿费,请即寄下。如渠有暇,可留意汉学书籍及杂志,写一介绍登《季刊》仿照第三期格式,但须早日示知,以免重复寄上杂志单,均系本馆入藏者。刻下馆中需用美金甚亟。照相款即汇香港可也。顺颂大安。

同礼顿首

十一,十八

关于 L. C.所藏中文书搜集经过,可读历年《馆务报告》,并访 Dr. Swingle 一谈。

借印《燉煌叙录》可照办。令弟事可在大同书店内为之设法,已函顾子刚。因馆中不能添人,亦不能裁人也。

外一纸交吴光清。

〔国立北平图书馆(昆明柿花巷)用笺。中国书店 2017 年春季书刊资料文物拍卖会〕

按:大同书店实为平馆所开设,由顾子刚负责经营。该信附纸一张,为各外国书店寄书费用清单。

十一月二十日

先生致信 J. Periam Danton,请其在美国图书馆协会执行委员会上代为表达谢意,并询问有无可能捐赠医学类书籍,因为此前获捐的此类书籍相对较少。

November 20, 1939

Dear Dr. Danton:

　　May I write to express to you once more our sincere appreciation and heartfelt thanks for the generous effort you have made in conducting the Book Campaign in the interest of Chinese libraries. If you attend the Mid-winter Conference, will you kindly convey our sense of gratitude to all the members of the Executive Board of the A. L. A. as well as your colleagues on the Committee on International Relations?

　　I understand that several people from China have written to your Association requesting for books on medicine and public health. As we find very few medical books included in your shipment, I have been wondering whether it would be possible for your Association to solicit books in this field for Chinese libraries. Perhaps you may like to get in touch with the Medical Library Association and solicit their help. If this can be arranged, it would undoubtedly prove to be a great service to

Chinese and foreign doctors who are working under handicaps due to the lack of medical literature.

We understand that your Committee has been laying plans to help popular libraries secure books expeditiously and at certain discounts that would be possible in larger purchases. As our libraries are experiencing great difficulties in obtaining scientific literature from America on account of our Government's strict control over foreign exchange as a result of Japan's invasion, we are greatly interested in your undertaking. Will you kindly give me detailed information regarding your plans?

With renewed thanks for your valuable assistance and with Season's Greetings,

Yours sincerely,

T. L. Yuan

Chairman,

Executive Board

〔中华图书馆协会(冯平山图书馆转)英文信纸。The American Library Association Archives, China Projects File, Box 2, Books for China 1938-1940〕

按:此件为打字稿,落款处为先生签名,于翌年1月6日送达。

十一月二十九日

先生致信闻宥,请其撰写书评。

在宥先生大鉴:

Savina 所著《法属印度支那语言指南》一书,顷已寄到,兹随函送上,敬祈尊阅,并盼撰一书评,俾能在下期《季刊》内予以发表是荷。顺候台祺。

弟袁同礼顿首

十一月廿九

〔国立北平图书馆(昆明柿花巷)用笺。闻广、蒋秋华主编《落照堂集存国人信札手迹》,台北:"中央研究院"中国文哲研究所,2013年,页399〕

按:后闻宥确为此书撰写书评,刊登于《图书季刊》新第2卷第1

期。此信为文书代笔,但落款处签名和日期均为先生亲笔。

十二月三日

王重民致函先生,谈《永乐大典》、购书及刘修业所编《云南书目》等事。

守和吾师道鉴:

"馆"字韵之永乐大典,今不知落谁手,为恨。近 Dr. Hummel 又接 Kegan Paul 一信,谓又有一册出售,在"老"韵,亦索价 £ 50,Hummel 说可买,如此价钱,吾馆无法问津,只盼美国买了,我们摄影片耳。Robertson 之 *The Philippine Islands* 一书,只印 100 部,每部有著者签字,想不甚多。曾函询纽约之 Orientalia Inc.,已八九日,尚无覆音,想系书不在手。同时曾与 Kegan Paul 去一信,亦询该书定价如何?馆中照相费等,如张似旅之 £ 20 无用,将来势必退回,则存伦敦者尚约有七八十镑,离欧洲前,未汇成美金;及到华京后,恐金镑太低,将来吃亏,去信往提,已不能提,且有限制,手续亦麻烦。那时每镑已降至四元,想不至再降,故未再设法。不知将来该款应如何处理,寄一点回国,抑仍存伦敦,以待他用。美国新出版书,有关我国者亦不少,不知已否托他公司代购?或以后由生随时购买?寄交王景春先生之书,现在尚无好消息;但那条船无炸沉消息,想尚不至无希望,Mme Meuvret 或能探得好消息也。所得之书,均颇有实用,虽说保险 20000 法郎,与书价相差不远,然再买,一则费时间,再则此机会亦难得也。

刘女士云南书目稿,第一章想已收到,或已送上海付印矣。后又寄上四章,请派人打字。此间尚存三章,有两章已打好,一章未打。望将第一章最末一号码示知,即可再继续编号,继续付印也。季刊西文之部,想已出版,生亦可将所编敦煌目,从 3511 以后,伯希和未编者,再抄一份,为西文本充篇幅。

Pirkis 女士,已在伦敦我驻英大使馆作事,则赴中国之愿,明年再说。生前去一信,称家乡不平安,拟请家严等去北平居住,并请吾师为舍弟新民,在平馆给一练习书记职,看阅览室或书库都可。月薪只有十五元以慰高堂,则感恩无暨矣。该书想已接到。专此,即请钧安!

生重民敬上。

十二月三日

〔国家图书馆档案，档案编号 1940-※044-外事 3-002048 和
1940-※044-外事 3-002049〕

按："望将第一章最末一号码示知"，见翌年 1 月 24 日先生覆信。

十二月十日

王重民覆函先生，报告从美所寄送书信、包裹及其到美后之近况。

守和吾师钧鉴：

敬奉十一月四日手谕，领悉一是为慰。生初抵此，环境稍变，精神
因而不振，致劳惦念。来此所寄上函件，计有：

九月二十五日　寄账单一包，又云南书目第一章及抗战史料等一
包。（共两包）

三十日　信一封，内附书单数纸。

十月八日　信一封

廿二日　信一封

十一月十八日　信一封

二十二日　包裹一件，内有云南书目及敦煌目子书编等。

十二月三日　信一封

以上各件，想已一一收到。购书款孙洪芬先生已寄来两次，第一次之
£ 18-19-5，并未折成美金 $88.95，乃如数寄来英镑。第二次之£ 27
与 frs49 都折成美金 $105.57，显系按十一月间兑价每镑三元多合算，均
未照吾师计画，——按买书时日之汇价合算，不知此事将来如何处理？
第一次之£ 18-19-5 为九月间接到，当时美金已高至每镑换四元一二
角，以英镑不致再多跌，遂将汇票寄存伦敦。（孙先生票寄来美国，而
须在伦敦支取，故寄往英国。）今日曾致伦敦 Westminster Bank，请提出
此数，寄交孙述万先生。这笔款既花汇水，而无形之中，汇价内亦吃亏
不少也。这一两周内，美金又提高（上周 n. s. $8.02 汇国币 $100，今
日 n. s. $,7.50 即可汇国币 $100），拟再稍候，再将此 $105.57 汇
香港。

收到之廿八包书，其有书无单者，想都在生九月二十五日及三十
日所寄两信件内，想收到后已再检查，如再有有书无目者，请再示知。

此间提要稿，前已寄上一些，寄前曾得 Hummel 同意。生在此工

作,每书都有提要,脱稿之后,约可如善本书室藏书志或适园藏书志。惟该两家多抄提要,生有几句话说几句话,只著明其家著录,而不钞袭也。刘女士闻将来可协助编季刊,闻之颇兴奋,以后自当多看西洋人关于国学之著述,冀将来每期以后,均能附一欧美新刊书目,则于国内治汉学者,当大有帮助也。生来此后,曾将在巴黎所发见刘宋时众经别录(此当为佛经录第一部佛经目矣)寄胡适之先生,请其作跋;闻其不日或可写几句话;如写好,即当速速寄昆明,在季刊发表。

朱士嘉先生抵此已一月余,他专司购书事。现因国币贬价,Hummel 几于有书便买,故采访够忙。盖自江浙失陷,故家族谱地志之类,散出不少,现运来华京者,已三四百种矣。

余再禀,即请道安。

生重民敬上。
十二月十日

〔国家图书馆档案,档案编号 1940-※044-外事 3-002050 和 1940-※044-外事 3-002052〕

按:后《图书季刊》中文本自新第 2 卷第 2 期起连载王重民所撰《美国国会图书馆所藏善本书叙录》。有关《众经别录》之文章并未在《图书季刊》中文本及时发表,该卷编号为"伯 3747",1948 年 12 月北京大学建校五十周年纪念时曾展出该卷照片。[①]

十二月十三日

徐旭生赴中日战事史料征集会,遇姚从吾、先生。〔《徐旭生文集》第 9 册,页 1056〕

胡恒德致函先生,告知德尔格将在华北地区停留更多时日足以培训缩微胶片摄影人员,对平馆提交的三年经费预算表示赞同,但希望拍摄时能严格遵守经济原则,并强调该套设备仅限于为美国图书馆和学者拍摄稀见的汉学文献,最后告知顾问会员会及执委会成员。

December 13, 1939

---

① 白化文在《敦煌写本〈众经别录〉残卷校释》中推测"王先生在巴黎写卡片时,尚未明确认出哪个卷子是《众经别录》。1948 年底展览说明中的正确表达,想系归国后与向先生共同研究的结果。"由该信可以知这个说法是值得商榷。

Dear Dr. Yuan:

Reply to your letter of October 18th has been delayed for some weeks because I felt it important to circularize it to the various members of the Advisory Committee for their information before undertaking to answer.

It will be best I think to take up in order the suggestions you have made in your letter and to give you the assurance that they either have already been fulfilled or are in process of being met:

1. Dr. Draeger, fortunately, has had an extension of his assignment to North China and will therefore be here long enough to organize the operating personnel for the camera and to train the people for the work. It is proposed now to assemble a permanent operating team for the camera. It is my understanding that you desire to have people selected as far as possible from the regular members of the staff, and that will be done; the only necessary reservation is that it might be necessary to have an additional person with technical background which library work would not provide.

2. It is understood that the Library will furnish the funds for purchase of film and other equipment to be imported from the United States and that requisitions for these expenses are to be signed by D. T. K. Koo and sent through your Treasurer, Mr. Senn in Shanghai, for payment.

The sum of U. S. $4,000, I note, has been set aside to cover operating expenses for a three-year period, and you ask that strict economy be observed. The designation of these funds and the program of the Library, as suggested, will largely be dealt with by Mr. Koo, who will assume, I understand, the financial responsibility for the Library's program in relation to this photographic work.

3. It is my understanding that the work to be carried out under the Committee's auspices will comprise the micro-film reproduction of rare and valuable sinological material for the use of libraries and scholars in the United States, and that no other activities are to be undertaken at this

time.

It is probable that Mr. Graves has informed you of the composition of the Advisor Committee, but if he has not, I give it below for your information:

Dr. H. S. Houghton, Chairman

Mr. Trevor Bowen, Secretary-Treasurer

Dr. R. H. Draeger

Mr. T. K. Koo

Mr. A. R. Ringwalt

Dr. J. Leighton Stuart

Mr. Koo, together with the officers, constitute an Executive Committee.

I hope you will be reassured as to the spirit with which this informal committee takes up its temporary task of aiding the program of the National Library. During the three years in which the micro-film camera is to be installed in the College I hope we will carry out everything as you wish and help you to make an effective contribution to the various services you have in mind. I should be grateful at any time to have through Mr. Koo your advice and instructions.

Cordially yours,

Henry S. Houghton

〔Rockefeller Foundation. Series 300 Latin America-Series 833 Lebanon; Subseries 601. Box 9. Folder 87〕

按：Trevor Bowen(1886-1960)，英国人，时任协和医学院总务长，中文名博文或鲍文①；A. R. Ringwalt 即 Arthur R. Ringwalt(1899-1981)，美国外交官，中文名林华德，时应任驻华副领事。此件为打字稿，落款处为其签名。

十二月十四日

先生致信震旦大学博物馆，告《图书季刊》英文本即将复刊，请该馆惠赠近

---

① 《私立北平协和医学院教职员一览表》，1939 年，页 14。

两年来的出版物或清单，以挂号寄送平馆香港办事处。

December 14, 1939

Dear Sirs:

The need of a bibliographical publication covering current books and periodicals published in China has long been felt by foreign scholars and scientific institutions. To meet this demand, the *Quarterly Bulletin of Chinese Bibliography* was published from 1934 until 1937 when its publication was interrupted by the outbreak of hostilities between China and Japan.

Since March 1939, we have resumed the publication of Chinese edition. The English edition will appear in March 1940. In resuming the publication of the Bulletin, it is our earnest desire to record every important title of books or serial publications published in China since January 1938. We are addressing this letter to you in the hope that you would extend to us your co-operation and assistance.

In order to make our bibliographical record as complete as possible and in order to review your publications in our Bulletin, we shall greatly appreciate your courtesy if you would send us a set of your publications issued in 1938 and 1939 and place the name of this Library on your mailing list to receive the future issues. After they are reviewed in the *Quarterly Bulletin*, they will be made available to Chinese scholars now concentrated here. If you do not see your way of presenting complimentary copies to the National Library, will you kindly send us a list of our publications?

As the Post Office at your end does not receive book-parcels for Kunming, you are requested to send them by registered post to Hongkong. They will be reforwarded to their destination by our Hongkong office.

Thanking you in anticipation for your co-operation and hoping to hear from you soon,

Yours very truly,

T. L. Yuan

Acting Director

P. S.: Correspondence and printed matter should be addressed as follow: Mr.
T. L. Yuan, c/o Fung Ping Shan Library, 94, Bonham Road, Hongkong.

〔上海市档案馆,档案编号 Q244-1-499〕

按:此件为打字稿,落款处为先生签名。

十二月十六日

晚七时,李书华招宴,陈寅恪、罗文幹、叶公超、先生、李晓生、杨振声、朱君
等与席,钱临照、徐旭生作陪。〔《徐旭生文集》第 9 册,页 1058〕

按:朱君为某医学院院长或主任,新自上海来。钱临照(1906—
1997),江苏无锡人,物理学家,时应在北平研究院物理研究所
工作。

十二月十八日

先生致信董显光,向其介绍荷兰记者 Dirk Kluiver,并表示该人希望获得中
国抗战的最新消息及中国情报委员会印刷品。

December 18, 1939

Dr. Hollington K. Tong,

The Central Publicity Board,

Chungking.

Dear Dr. Tong:

I have pleasure in introducing to you Dr. Dirk Kluiver, journalist and
correspondent of the *"Utrechtsch Nieuwsblad"* Utrecht, Netherlands. Dr.
Kluiver is anxious to obtain first-hand information about conditions in
war-time China as well as some of the publications issued by the China
Information Committee. As he is a stranger here, will you also put him in
touch with foreign correspondents in Chungking. Any courtesy and
assistance which you could extend to him will be gratefully appreciated.

With cordial regards,

Yours sincerely,

T. L. Yuan,

Acting Director

〔国家图书馆档案,档案编号 1939-※044-外事 3-008001〕

按：Dirk Kluiver 生平待考。The Central Publicity Board 即国民党中央宣传部，董显光时任该部副部长，负责抗日战争的国际宣传；*Utrechtsch Nieuwsblad* 直译即《乌得勒支新闻报》。此件为录副。

十二月十九日

先生致信于道泉，谈为其在国内谋求职务事及其归国事宜。

道泉吾兄：

前奉手书，深慰饥渴。欧战发生，未识东方语言学校之经费因之紧缩否？如无意蝉联，似可早日返国。兹将兄之学历及研究旨趣转达于北平研究院，该院亦极愿罗致在史学研究所内由徐旭生主持聘为专任研究员月薪三百五十元，除五十元不折扣外，其余七折，共得二百六十元。惟该院无力担负旅费，兹特致王景春先生一函，请其援向觉明前例，径与轮船公司接洽，谋一免费优待办法。如决定返国，请将该函加封代为付邮，并请王先生将接洽结果径告足下。如无希望，则所藏西藏资料及照片可让给图书馆，因政府统制外汇，实无法汇款至国外也。专此奉达，即希卓裁示复为荷。此颂旅安。

袁同礼顿首

十二月十九

昆明柿花巷二十二号

〔程道德主编《二十世纪北京大学著名学者手迹》，北京：北京图书馆出版社，2003 年，页 102〕

按：后于道泉并未归国，而是前往英国伦敦大学亚非学院执教。

十二月二十六日

先生致信 Lyman Hoover，告寄上一批刊登回教文章的期刊，并嘱其用毕请挂号寄还。

December 26, 1939

Dear Mr. Hoover;

As requested, we are sending you, under separate cover, a set of Chinese journals which contain articles on Chinese Muslims and the war. A list of these journals is herewith enclosed. We hope that they will be of use to you.

As soon as you finish using these materials, will you kindly return them to us from Hongkong by registered book post? If there is anything else we can do for you, please do not hesitate to write to us.

With kindest regards.

Yours sincerely

T. L. Yuan

Acting Director

P. S.: Enclosed herewith please find a list of articles published in western journals.

〔平馆(昆明)英文信纸。Yale University records, Lyman Hoover Papers, RG 9 Series I, Box: 13, Folder: 280〕

按:寄送中文杂志有《边事研究》第 8 卷第 3 期(1938 年 11 月)、《群众》(合订本第 2 册)、《成师校刊》第 5 卷第 7 期(1939 年 8 月)、《回民言论》第 1 卷第 12 期(1939 年 6 月)、《回教大众》第 1 至 7 期(1938 年)、《回教论坛》第 2 卷第 1 至 4 期(1939 年)、《中国回教救国协会会刊》第 1 卷第 1 至 2 期(1939 年)。此件为打字稿,落款处为先生签名,该信寄送香港九龙。

十二月二十七日

先生致闻宥两信。其一,请其掷下书评稿并送还 *Reader's Digest*。

在宥先生:

前承惠允撰一介绍文字,至感厚意。兹派人前来走取,即希连同原书交其携下为感。又 *Reader's Digest* 四册,前托赵诏熊先生送上,如已阅毕,并盼一并掷交去人为荷。专此申谢,顺候教祺。

弟袁同礼顿首

十二月廿七

按:赵诏熊(1905—?),江苏武进人,1921 年常州高级中学肄业,转入北京清华学校就读,1928 年赴美留学,1930 年获麻省理工学院机械工程系学士学位,后转入哈佛大学英文系,1932 年获大学硕士学位,时在云南大学任教。

其二,感谢告知《云南戎事志》出让消息,请将此书送往平馆(昆明)。

在宥先生道席:

顷承送下书评及原书两册,敬谢敬谢。蒙示《云南戎事志》出让事,尤为感荷。此书敝处颇愿入藏,拟请便中送下一阅,书价若干,并乞代为接洽。余容面谢,顺颂大安。

弟同礼顿首

廿七

〔《落照堂集存国人信札手迹》,页397-398〕

按:《云南戎事志》,清佚名所撰地方史。

十二月二十九日

先生致信闻宥,询问《云南戎事志》出售细节。

在宥先生:

手示敬悉。承寄下《戎事志》一册,至感厚意。暂存敝处,日内即行奉上,如前途能将全书送下一阅或示地址,当前往一阅,最所盼望。索价若干,并恳询明见示为荷。琐琐奉渎,顺颂著祺。

弟同礼顿首

廿九

〔《落照堂集存国人信札手迹》,页396〕

十二月三十日

先生签署本年度十月至十二月洛克菲勒基金会36072资助案的财务报告,并寄送该基金会驻沪办事处。〔Rockefeller Foundation. Series 601: China; Subseries 601.R: China-Humanities and Arts. Vol. Box 47. Folder 390〕

十二月

平馆向教育部呈文一件,题为《呈为呈请转咨财政部准予给与内汇事》,具先生名并钤印。

窃职馆每年所购外国之文法理工各科之专门杂志为数九百余种,每年均须继续订购以供研究。刻下请求给与外汇既多困难,势须将此项购置费国币四万三千元,汇至上海以便在黑市购买外汇。事关学术研究,拟请转咨财政部,按照优待国立学术机关内汇办法准予自二十九年一月起由滇汇寄上海,每月四千三百元,以资便利。是否有当,敬

候钧部俯予察核指令祗遵。谨呈

教育部部长陈

国立北平图书馆副馆长袁同礼

中华民国二十八年十二月

附专门杂志清单十九纸。

〔中国第二历史档案馆,教育部档案·全卷宗5,国立北平图书馆
请拨员工学术研究补助费经常费有关文书,案卷号 11616(1)〕

是年冬

白寿彝开始校写《咸同滇变传抄史料》书稿,先生、万斯年给予鼓励至多。
〔《咸同滇变见闻录》(上)自序,重庆商务印书馆,1945 年〕

是年

先生以中华图书馆协会执行部主席身份向美国图书馆协会赠送礼物,以表
示感谢美国图书馆界对中国图书馆的援助。〔"A. L. A. News." *Bulletin of the
American Library Association*, vol. 33, no. 7, 1939, p. 513〕

按:该件礼物于本年 12 月 27 日至 30 日美国图书馆协会芝加哥
会议上展示。

一九四〇年　四十六岁

一月二日

王重民覆函先生，谈汇款及其在美近况。

守和吾师钧鉴：

敬奉去年十一月十八日手谕，领悉一是。寄上刘女士云南书目，拟酬赠一百元，伊闻之非常感谢，非常鼓励！生犹忆在师大肄业时，曾以史记版本和参考书一文呈阅，蒙赐二十元，以作鼓励，从此以后，生始专力于学问，得有今日，十余年来，此恩未忘；今刘女士若亦能从此开始作去，将来或不致有负吾师之盛意。附上收条一纸，该款请径寄伊六姊处，备为伊买零物用。通信处如下：

张君劢太太，上海法租界麦阳路一五六156号。

寄来吾馆所有汉学杂志单，可备刘女士涉阅之参考；至于介绍一事，金毓黻先生所作甚佳，最好仍请伊作；不过近水楼台，让刘女士专作美国出版之杂志及专书如何？不久当寄上几篇以示例。

舍弟新民事，蒙向顾子刚先生绍介，甚感。如能有成，请通知刘树楷君即可。又蒙允许印敦煌叙录用吾馆名义，约本月杪，即可将稿件发付北平去印。

伦敦存款，又曾提 4500 法郎到巴黎，还照相费。前已通知 Westminster Bank 给孙述万寄£ 18-19-5；当时因手中无有英政府外汇证，或须待其寄来，添好，方能照办。昨又去一信，请其再多寄£ 15，按现在法律，或又须寄来外汇证，添好再寄去，则往返须再费一月余，在此时期，办事颇不便也。

王维诚前从英国来，将返国。据云 Spalding 所捐之款，所拿出者并不多，而 Spalding 本人，刻仍在美国，将来再肯拿与否，实未敢必。若 Spalding 不再拿钱，则其他收入实在无几，此事或将从此作罢矣。张似旅处之£ 20，似可要回，不知生可否给他去信，请其直寄香港？俟得覆后，生再遵办！

　　孙洪芬先生寄来之 $105.57，生拟暂不寄回，因伊未按当时美金汇价合算，或可存此作他用，而另向其索美金也。盖在此不时买书要用钱，而将来照永乐大典及其他希见书相片，亦要用钱也。Robertson 之 *Philippine Islands* 一书，现纽约无存者，须另待机会，而有二三种云南及 Lolo 书，日内拟买了寄上。又林语堂之 *Moment in Peking* $2.75 及杜威之 *Freedom and Culture* $2.00，此书为其八十生日时发表两书已买到，明后日即可寄出。今日方见申报亦载林书售四元，如系四元国币，想必是中国版，但若售四美金，又太贵矣。

　　离法前寄上之五箱书，想已收到。昨接 Madame Meuvret 信，称据公司调查，该五箱书已在 Glasgow 由 S. S. Lycaon 转入 S. S. Antilochus 运往中国。盖 Lycaon 既被政府征去，未在利物浦停留，直到 Glasgow 方卸下此五箱，可见开战前之恐慌。

　　Meuvret 太太谓法外部已迁出巴黎一部分，再索新书，恐无人管；而旧赠送之一批，恐最近亦不易送出也。Meuvret 先生已在前线，小姐方三两岁，送去乡间，她的精神很苦恼。

　　又箱子费，运费，保险费以及后来在伦敦续买之书，或尚有 £ 20 上下，俟礼拜日（一月七日）再结清将账单寄上，仍请孙先生寄香港，或较伦敦之三十余镑更快也。

　　前赐生之 £ 15，寄香港甚佳；因此 £ 15，生在巴黎时已花去矣。忆数年以来，吾师所特别助生者很多，而均一一花尽，所余者惟几包稿子耳。哈佛如交引得处印，则不如交商务，因商务另外尚有稿费也。拟给伯、戴二先生信，（一）索美金一千元，（二）此一千元交北平图书馆，专印此项书，以此为条件，成则可办，否则再向商务进行矣。（胡适之先生向商务较可说话。）

　　吴光清先生为人很好，办事颇认真，颇努力，惟学问稍差一点；然在此再练习三二年，必更熟能生巧。他生活有秩序，守法奉公，在图书馆作主任很适宜，将来吾馆平定后，尚须依赖他。李芳馥十月间方从欧洲回来，恐最近尚不返国。朱士嘉在此，与 Hummel 很合得来，二三年内不至离此。冯家昇即因办事不负责，Hummel 不痛快他，因而辞职。裘开明与曾宪三不知若何；惟闻裘聘了于震寰，曾很不痛快。哈佛近有作联合汉文书目片之拟议，可是 Hummel 不赞成，然亦不反对。

生所编善本目,集部大致作完;其经史二部不大多,子部或可与集部相等,但不论如何,今年一年,或能作完也。

余再及,即请道安!

受业重民上。

二十九年一月二日

年前胡适之作生日,伊因乘机叫生去玩,遇到钱端升等。钱先生对伦敦捐书,谓无丝毫成绩。但他正拟和国会图书馆新馆长商议交换事。Hummel 这边已都买,似无可交换。然此事与 Hummel 商议,其力量或更大于馆长也。

〔国家图书馆档案,档案编号 1940-※044-外事 3-002001 至 1940-※044-外事 3-002003〕

按:《史记版本和参考书》,刊于《图书馆学季刊》第 1 卷第 4 期页 555-577。《敦煌叙录》应指《巴黎敦煌残卷叙录》第 2 辑,1941 年 2 月平馆印行,实价国币伍圆。*Moment in Peking* 即《京华烟云》,1939 年纽约 The John Day Company 初版。于震寰抵达波士顿的时间约在 1939 年 12 月 5 日。[1]"国会图书馆新馆长"即 Archibald Macleish,任期为 1939 年至 1944 年。

一月三日

先生、万斯年应方树梅邀请,前往昆明附近的盘龙、万松等名胜游览。〔《北游搜访文献日记》,页 225〕

一月四日　昆明

贺麟、郑昕、冯文潜、姚从吾、陈铨、林同济、杨业治、傅斯年、毛准、先生、严文郁、滕固、徐琥等人迁居才盛巷。〔冯至《昆明日记》,页 31〕

按:此前,先生及家人应宿昆明柿花巷二十二号,才盛巷之新址为西南联合大学教员宿舍。郑昕(1905—1974),字秉璧,安徽庐江人,南开大学毕业,后赴德国柏林大学哲学系学习,时在西南联合大学哲学系任教;冯文潜(1896—1963),字柳漪,河北涿县人,冯至的叔叔,早年赴美、德两国留学,时任西南联合大学哲学系教授;陈铨(1903—1969),字涛西,四川富顺人,清华学校毕业后赴

---

① 《裴开明年谱》,页 236。

美、德两国留学,时应任西南联合大学外文系教授,与林同济等人为"战国策派"代表人物;杨业治(1908—2003),字禹功,上海人,1929年清华大学外文系毕业,后赴美、德留学,时在西南联合大学外文系任教。"徐琥"或书写有误。

中华图书馆协会撰《呈为推进战时文化因经费困难恳请增加补助以利进行事》,具先生名并钤印。〔台北"国史馆",〈中国图书馆协会请补助(教育部)〉,数位典藏号019-030508-0015〕

　　　　按:自1939年5月①至1939年12月,教育部每月补助协会一百元,该文拟请自本年起每月补助二百元,另附《中华图书馆协会二十八年度工作概况》一件,四叶。

先生致信Marshall C. Balfour,请求就RF36071资助案的拨款方式予以调整。〔Rockefeller Foundation. Series 601: China; Subseries 601.R: China-Humanities and Arts. Vol. Box 47. Folder 390〕

一月六日

下午,先生与毛准访郑天挺,恰其正将不用之书装箱,二人片刻即离去。〔《郑天挺西南联大日记》,页230〕

　　　　按:此时昆明防空形势日趋紧张,故郑天挺整理书籍以防不测。

一月七日

先生致信王重民,告收到英法寄来书刊,并请刘修业速将《云南书目》余稿寄来。

　　有三仁弟:

　　　　十一月十七日来书,详悉一一。由利勿浦寄来之书五箱,已于日前到港。巴黎寄来廿四包亦于月前收到。L. C.所藏《大典》,凡未录副者可用Photostat照相,如费用太多则用Microfilm。日机连日轰炸,滇越路今日已不通,不日修理告竣仍能通车,邮件均挂号为妥。《云南书目》已登英文《图书季刊》,二、四、五、六章一俟收到再行奉闻,其第三章自然科学并请速寄,以便打字是荷如不多则寄香港由孙述万打字后再寄回,较简捷。匆匆,顺颂大安。

　　　　　　　　　　　　　　　　　　　　同礼顿首

――――――――――

① 《中华图书馆协会会报》,第14卷第1期,页11。

一月七日

〔中国书店·海淀,四册〕

一月八日

先生致信蔡元培,赠方树梅所著《钱氏族谱》、《盘龙游诗录》,并代其请蔡元培赐墨宝一份,屏条或对联均可,并告可托章元美寄送。〔《蔡元培日记》,页 657〕

> 按:章元美,字彦威,江苏吴县人,南开学校毕业①,时应在中基会工作。

一月十日

先生致信普林斯顿葛斯德中文图书馆馆长,推销《宋会要辑稿》。

January 10, 1940

Dear Sir:

Early in 1936 the National Library published a work of considerable importance. It is entitled: Sung Hui-Yao, which is a compendium on the institutions of the Sung Dynasty. A description of this work is found in the report of the Division of Orientalia, Library of Congress, for 1937, pp. 179–182.

As a very limited number of copies are now in stock, we wonder whether you would like to take advantage of the favorable exchange by securing a copy for your Library.

This work is reprinted by photo-lithographic process from the original manuscript and consists of two hundred volumes. It is being sold at US $ 20.00 plus US $ 5.00 for foreign postage.

Should you desire to avail yourself of this opportunity to purchase a copy, will you place the order immediately. Cheques should be made payable to the Hon. Treasurer, National Library of Peiping, Room 404, National City Bank Building, 45 Kiukiang Road, Shanghai.

Yours faithfully,

T. L. Yuan

---

① 《南开同学录》,1924 年,页 43。

Acting Director

〔平馆(昆明)英文信纸。Princeton University, Mudd Manuscript Library, AC123, Box 415, Folder Peiping, National Library of, 1937–1944〕

按:信文末尾处的地址即孙洪芬在上海的办公场所。此件为打字稿,落款处为先生签名。

一月十一日

先生访冯至,携其稿《评福兰阁教授的李贽研究》而去。〔冯至《昆明日记》,页31〕

按:此文后刊于 1940 年 3 月《图书季刊》新 2 卷第 1 期。

一月十二日

先生致信傅斯年,告知其所托找寻敦煌卷子中有关古谶纬之部分一事,已分函各处代为录副或影照。

孟真先生大鉴:

昨奉本月十一日惠函,敬悉贵所拟从事于古谶纬之搜辑整理,亟须利用敦煌卷子中之若干部分,查影照之巴黎卷子,除一小部分在北平保存外,其余者均暂存美京国会图书馆。尊处所需之资料顷已分别函请平、美两方面代为录副或影照,径寄贵所。如王君未摄此项影片,时已嘱其函托杜乃扬女士(前本馆法籍交换馆员)再行影照矣。耑此奉覆,顺颂著祺。

弟同礼顿首

十二日

叶慈所编 Eumorfopoulos 目录关于铜器部分,请派人送下一阅。

〔国立北平图书馆用笺。台北"中央研究院"历史语言研究所傅斯年图书馆,"史语所档案",昆 7–50〕

按:"Eumorfopoulos 目录关于铜器部分"应指 *The George Eumorfopoulos Collection: catalogue of the Chinese & Corean bronzes, sculpture, jades, jewellery and miscellaneous objects*,叶慈编著,1925 年伦敦出版,该书限量 560 部。该信为文书代笔,落款处为先生签名。傅斯年在首页批注"只能影照,不能录副",第二页则注明"请即影照,费用事面谈,惟请速去函照"。

一月十三日

傅斯年致函先生,商讨史语所在平购书及转寄办法。

守和吾兄左右:

接奉贵馆一月十日大函,关于敝所在平所购图书,拟托贵馆香港办事处代转昆明一事,荷承惠允,至深感谢。承示邮寄办法,自当遵照办理。并已函知在平友人余让之先生矣。其收件人之姓名,拟写"那简叔收",即烦转知贵馆香港办事处于收到此项通知后,径行转下是感。兹为求在北平付邮时之方便起见,拟嘱余君将图书包扎停当后,送请大同书店用该店名义代为付寄,似更妥当。

此事以弟写信至北平诸多未便,拟恳吾兄代函顾子刚先生,托其襄助一切。敝所最近拟在北平购买之书甚多,并请子刚先生帮忙代为物色(书单容当开奉),至感至感。又,敝所汇平之书款,承示汇交大同书店代收一节,亦当遵命办理。一俟将款汇出后,即将数目奉闻,并请贵馆转知该店照付也。专此布达,并申谢悃。即颂日祺。

弟傅○○敬启

一月十三日

〔《傅斯年遗札》,页 1062-1063〕

按:"余让之"即余逊(1905—1974),湖南常德人,余嘉锡之子。此函应于 1 月 14 日发出。

一月十四日

王重民致函先生,谈寄送图书、购书和国会图书馆近况。

守和吾师钧鉴:

近又接王景春先生信,他还不知那五箱图书已在 Glasgow 找到。想 Currie 转运公司说如此,一定是已经找到了;惟现在已否平安抵香港,殊为惦念。

Robertson 之 *The Philippine Islands* 一书,Kegan Paul 有一部,共五十五册,索价 £ 50,连邮费,想每册可 £ 1,共须五十余镑,不为少;然那样大书,每册只一镑,亦不算很贵。吾师如以为可买,请直接去信为祷!

林语堂之 *Moment in Peking* 尚未寄去,因刘女士拟阅一过,即随手作一绍介也。生亦有中文书评数种,将一并寄上。昨天下午适之先生无事,又闲谈了两点半钟,他对于生等所抄辑之天主教目尤为称许,他说一俟稍平静,他保险有款印刷。因此书系目录,若由基金会特别出一笔款,作为吾馆出版物最好。

舍弟事,在顾子刚处最好,如能安插,生再写一信,向他致谢也。此间在二月初,Dr. Hummel 或能通过一笔款,冀凡 L. C.所无之书,有便买,如此大规模购书,则顾子刚处更忙矣。近已将方志、法律、文集、乐书、医书、朱墨印版书六类,将此间所有有开一详目致顾子刚,冀凡不见此目者则都买。(法律书为另外私人所捐款。)

联大与此间交换书事,钱端升、周鲠生很奔走,此事新馆长允办,Dr. Hummel 不愿办。盖因新馆长并不详细购买中国书情形,而 Dr. Hummel 计画颇大,新书皆已买到,很不易言交换故也。然他们进行方法亦不妙,应先与 Hummel 商议,然后在向馆长说,则多少能有一点成绩矣。

账单尚未寄出,拟俟与书评稿同寄。

余再详,即请道安!

受业重民上。
一月十四日

〔国家图书馆档案,档案编号 1945-※057-综合 5-016001 和 1945-※057-综合 5-016002〕

按:王重民所辑天主教书目,胡适极为称许,可参见其 1 月 13 日日记。[1]

一月十八日

Marshall C. Balfour 覆函先生,告知已按照先生要求调整拨款方式。

January 18,1940

Dear Mr. Yuan,

Replying to your letter of January 4, proposing a revision of the payments as proposed by you under the Foundation's appropriation RF 36071, so that they may be as follows:

For　1939-40……　$ 8,000.

---

[1]《胡适日记全集》第 8 册,页 9。

1940-41……5,500.

1941-42……4,000.

Inasmuch as this is in agreement with the limit stipulation laid down in Miss Thompson's letter of March 20 1939, we see no reason why this should not be approved. We have therefore as requested by you, today forwarded to your Treasurer at Room 404, National City Bank, Shanghai, a further check for ＄500.00, in addition to the January payment of ＄1,875.00

It is noted that this money will be utilized to pay the initial equipment for the micro-film camera.

Very truly yours,

M. C. Balfour

〔Rockefeller Foundation. Series 601: China; Subseries 601.R: China-Humanities and Arts. Box 47. Folder 390〕

按:该函寄往昆明,并抄送给史蒂文斯和 George J. Beal。

一月十九日

先生致信王访渔、顾子刚,请其派馆员联系周祖谟,取回此前借出的敦煌卷子《刊谬补缺切韵》照片。

二十六年赵斐云先生经手由中央研究院历史语言研究所借去敦煌卷子《刊谬补缺切韵》照片,计七十页。日前致函该所,即予收回,嗣得覆云"此项照片,前敝所系为助理员周祖谟君所借,现仍存周君手,周君住北平前门外茶儿胡同三号,请派人设法向周君收回"云云。查此项照片既仍在平,拟请尊处即派人前往周君处将该片取回,即交写经组点收见复为荷。

〔《北京图书馆馆史资料汇编(1909-1949)》,页708〕

曾昭燏致函先生,寄赠《大理工作简报》中英文各一份。〔南京博物院编《曾昭燏文集·日记书信卷》,北京:文物出版社,2013年,页86〕

按:"大理工作"似指1939年11月中旬曾昭燏在大理考察佛顶遗址。

一月二十二日

J. Periam Danton 致函先生,告知美国图书馆协会无力应中国同仁的呼吁收集并捐赠医学和公共卫生领域的书刊,另外该委员会欧洲计划是受洛克菲勒基金会资助但无法扩展到东亚地区。

January 22, 1940

Dear Dr. Yuan:

It was good to hear from you again and to know that the material we have been instrumental in having sent to China has been of some help. Mr. Milam is passing on to the Executive Board your thanks inasmuch as your letter did not arrive here until after the Midwinter meeting.

I have referred to the officers of the Medical Library Association your request for books in the field of medicine and public health. I very much fear that the A. L. A. through our Committee will not be able to be of assistance to you this time. There are two reasons for this. One is that we have apparently tapped about as completely as possible for the time being the interest of American libraries in sending material to China. (The European war, especially Finland's share in it, and the needs of neutrals and belligerents alike may of course be partially responsible.) In the second place, I have been advised by the International Exchange Service of the Smithsonian Institution that the Service is no longer making shipments to China. This would rule out at the start almost all gifts, even if we could secure additional donations, since the Committee has no money for shipping charges and individual libraries are generally unable to defray them.

I judge that your reference to the work of our Committee in helping "popular libraries secure books expeditiously⋯" refers to the Books for Europe project whereby the Association, through our Committee and with support from the Rockefeller Foundation, is sending American books to certain countries of northwestern Europe. Unfortunately, this activity is limited to the European countries included in the original project.

Cordially yours,

〔The American Library Association Archives, China Projects File, Box 2, Books For China 1938-1940〕

　　　　按:该函寄送香港。此件为录副,未签名。

一月二十三日

中华图书馆协会撰《为呈覆奉钧部第〇〇一六八八号训令移赠华侨图书馆图书困难情形请予鉴核备案由》,具先生名并钤印。〔台北"国史馆",〈中国图书馆协会请补助(教育部)〉,数位典藏号019-030508-0015〕

　　　　按:该年1月18日,教育部曾令中华图书馆协会酌情将美国捐赠且滞留在港书籍转赠该处华侨图书馆①,协会以捐赠者意愿及书籍性质为由婉拒此令。

一月二十四日

先生致信王重民,告知此前自巴黎寄来的五箱书已收讫,并谈在英存款、其弟新民等事。

　　有三仁弟如握:

　　　　连接十二月三日及七日手书,深以为慰。巴黎寄来五箱业已收到,点收无误。"馆"字韵《大典》,如国会图书馆业已购到,请从速摄影,径寄大同书店以利编纂,内中引用书一律用红铅笔标出为荷。存英伦之款可暂存伦敦,总数共若干,希即示复。美国新版书关于中国者已陆续寄来,惟为避免重复计,可将书名或本馆决不会买者开示或代购,而小册子尤重要也。刘女士《云南书目》第一章已付印,第二、四、五、六章亦收到,只缺第三章。《敦煌目》亦可刊于西文《季刊》,请编好寄下。关于令弟事曾托顾先生设法,复函谓据刘树楷之意,令弟无赴平之意。兹又致顾先生一函,嘱其于令弟何时到平后予以位置,其薪水则在存款内拨付,不必在北平馆经费内支付也。汇港之£18.19.5.已收到,第二次汇去之$105.57亦请即汇香港,用Chase Bank支票较方便,或花旗亦可。寄来之提要,文字方面不甚谨严已代改正,想太辛苦之故。总望星期日多多休息,勿操劳过度是荷。L.C.所购家谱,可请刘女士作一综合的研究,亦一有趣之工作也明家谱已请杨殿珣为之,可专作清代家谱。外一信,请代发。匆匆,顺颂大安。

　　　　　　　　　　　　　　　　　　　　同礼顿首
　　　　　　　　　　　　　　　　　　　　一月廿四

---

① 该馆为国民党驻港澳总支部于1939年冬在香港成立,馆址设在德辅道广东银行四层。

第一章号码为一——三九三（原注）

第二章号码为三九四——四九八（代填）

第三章号码应为四九九——

请托编目部刘女士（哈尔滨人）将俄国出版之关于中日战事之书，开单见示，以便购买。

〔中国书店·海淀，四册〕

按："可将书名或本馆决不会买者开示或代购"当作"可将书名或本馆决对会买者开示或代购"。

一月二十五日

晚五时，先生至叶公超宅，遇吴宓，请其常年校阅《图书季刊》英文本。〔《吴宓日记》第 7 册，页 124〕

按：此刊现由高棣华编辑，故先生委吴宓校阅，但后者对此项工作甚愤怒。

Lyman Hoover 覆函先生，表示尚未收到平馆寄来的书件包裹，并告知其在上海住址。

Jan. 25, 1940

Dear Dr. Yuan:

I am very grateful to you for your recent letter enclosing some valuable materials on the subject in which I am interested. I am also expecting to receive the things sent, under separate cover, within a few days. I shall be most grateful for this and will return them by registered book post as you suggest. I suppose things are delayed in Hongkong somewhat these days by the British censorship regulations. If you feel you would prefer to address things to me directly at this office, I shall be glad to have you do that, or you might use my residence address, 10 - A Route Winling. However, the Hongkong address still holds good if that seems preferable.

Thanking you again and with sincere personal regards, I am

Cordially yours,

Lyman Hoover

〔Yale University records, Lyman Hoover Papers, RG 9 Series I, Box 13, Folder 280〕

　　　　按:10-A Route Winling 即法租界汶林路,1943 年 10 月改为宛平路。

一月二十八日

先生访徐旭生,并在其处午餐。〔《徐旭生文集》第 10 册,页 1068〕

一月

先生收赵万里(北平)函,内附《清代文史笔记篇目索引》契约拟稿。后先生将修订稿径寄上海王伯祥,并感谢开明书店慨允印行此书。〔《王伯祥日记》第 16 册,页 324、352〕

　　　　按:先生信于 2 月 5 日送达。

二月四日

中午,先生访徐旭生。〔《徐旭生文集》第 10 册,页 1070〕

二月五日

先生致信王访渔、顾子刚,告知难以就留平馆员维持每月额外贴补壹仟元,对于冗员可以酌情淘汰。

　　　　顷接十五日航函,拜悉一一。北平物价与日俱增,同人生活闻咸困苦。关于此节,时在系念关怀之中,自当尽最大之努力予以改进。惟本馆经费原有固定之数,目前在年度之中既无法筹措,而中基会自庚款停付后,每月借款度日,亦决无增加之可能。查平馆事务较前减少十分之七,原无聘用如许人员必要,在委员会会议席上屡次有人提议请予缩减,弟为维持同人生活起见,独任其难。故前增加四百元,并由此间担负汇款贴水,今又自本月起再增六百元,以作临时津贴之用。在此经费拮据之秋,每月增加壹千元,至感困难,究能维持若干时日,弟亦无把握也。至阴历年前,加发一个月薪水一节,本馆向无前例,况经费中亦无此预算,碍难照办,即希转告同人为荷。

　　　　近查各部组寄来报告,工作松懈,殊难令人满意(如编目部虽述明编书若干,但在庋藏组入库报告内并无记载),嗣后务请行政委员会随时督促,严密稽核。凡工作不努力者,可随时予以淘汰也。

　　　　　　　　　〔《北京图书馆馆史资料汇编(1909-1949)》,页 708-709〕

　　　　按:此为抄件,似为先生亲笔。

先生致信震旦大学博物馆,感谢寄赠出版品并请将平馆(昆明)列入其邮寄样刊名单。

　　　　　　　　　　　　　　　　　　February 5, 1940

Dear Sirs:

We have pleasure in acknowledging the receipt of the following publications which you have so kindly sent to this Library to be recorded in our *Quarterly Bulletin of Chinese Bibliography* :

Deux nouveaux coléoptères de Chine , par M. Pic.

Deux Nouvelles espèces de longicornes , par Dr. Stephan Breuning.

Musée heude . 70 anniversaire. 1868–1938.

Musée heude. Notes de malacology Chinoise . v. 5, no. 5.

Musée heude. Notes d'entomologie Chinoise . v. 5, no. 7; v. 6, nos. 1–4, 6, 9.

Sur deux sapygides nouveaux pour la faune de Chine et de Mongolie , par Keizo Yasumatsu.

On behalf of the National Library, I beg to convey to you our sincerest thanks for your courtesy.

As we are greatly interested in these publications, we shall be most thankful to you if you would kindly place the name of this Library on your mailing list to receive future issues.

As we wrote you on December 13, the parcels should be sent to us by registered mail to our Hongkong address.

With renewed thanks for your co-operation and assistance,

Yours sincerely,

T. L. Yuan

Acting Director

〔平馆(昆明)英文信纸。上海市档案馆,档案编号 Q244-1-499〕

按:此件为打字稿,落款处为先生签名。

二月六日

下午一时,先生访吴宓,托校阅稿件。〔《吴宓日记》第 7 册,页 128〕

二月七日

王重民致函先生,谈在美近况及账目等事。

守和吾师钧鉴:

伦敦第二次所出卖之永乐大典,Hummel 已以 £ 50 买来。在"老"

韵,为卷11618与11619。刻正送去登记,生拟先作一消息,将来一同照相。每册售至£50,尚须争买,而今,又外汇如此之高,流出国外者,最近不易再购回矣。

接 Westminster Bank 来信,知那£19-1-5已汇交孙述万,可惜事前未接吾师详细指教,该款已汇为港币$303.50,若须用美金,恐须尚转换,如此转换三数次,赔钱实在不少矣。后又让该行汇上£15,想不久亦可收到。张似旅处尚存£20,俟奉指示后,再给伊去信。英款所照相片,尚在等候两收条,俟接到后,即可作总结束矣。

购书账目,刻尚待 Mme Meuvret 处所存之收条;兹先别件寄上一些,以便先向基金会取款。

林语堂、杜威两书,前已寄出,想能先此收到。

账单挂号信内,附上稿件数种,冀为图书季刊补白。西文书介绍,刘女士已试作三篇。现因初次试作,未免生疏,不能很快。且 Library of Congress 此类书,分藏数处,不易找,且有时被人借去,或先存 Smithsonian Institution,一时不能转到图书馆,而刘女士又只有晚上方能分身;然以后一切熟习了,于找书作文,自能均作到快处。未审金毓黻先生与吾馆有无直接关系,如伊不能按期作,将来都让刘女士作,亦可。

此间近无特别消息,生为其编善本书目,亦进行如故。集部即可完,约下周即可开始子部矣。生等在此生活,亦非常平静。

日来倭寇大炸滇越铁路,昆明自受相当惊恐,吾师至人,必能处之泰然;生等在外,反时时惦念也。

谨更将帐单列一项目如下:

G. P. Maisonneuve 邮费打箱费等	625.00frs.
G. Jobert 木箱	600.00frs.
三包书寄费	49.80frs.
F. Charis 打字费	67.30frs.
杂费	375.25frs.
	1717.35frs.

Kegan Paul 购书	第一包	£2-0-6
	第二包	£1-5-3
		£3-5-9

Moment in Peking　　　　　　　　　　　　　$ 2.85

　　巴黎所送之五箱书籍,近来未得 Mme Meuvret 或王景春先生之任
何报告,想刻已平安抵港矣。数月以来,生为此事,殊觉焦心,一俟接
到,速速赐一消息为恳!

　　余再及,即请道安!

　　　　　　　　　　　　　　　　　　　　　受业重民上。

　　　　　　　　　　　　　　　　　　　　　　二月七日

　　　〔国家图书馆档案,档案编号 1945-※057-综合 5-016003 和
　　　1945-※057-综合 5-016004〕

二月九日

冯至将《华裔学志》(*Monumenta Serica*)送还先生。〔冯至《昆明日记》,页31〕

二月十四日

先生致信顾毓琇,请其从旁协助平馆(昆明)申请教育部补助。

　　一樵次长尊鉴:

　　　前奉此书,藉悉李瑞年君已由部派在国立艺专服务,俾能用其所
长,高谊隆情,至为感谢。兹复有恳者,敝馆经常费大部分用于北平,
最近半载以来,北平物价狂涨,职员几无以为生,故最近复请中华教育
文化基金董事会在应汇昆明经费内每月扣除一千元改汇北平,以资接
济。昆明部分之经常费每月仅有二千二百元,实属无法维持。上月立
夫部长来滇曾请大部赐以补助,蒙允返渝后予以考虑。馆中曾于上月
十日将实际需要及本年度计划呈请鉴核谅荷垂察,因念我公对于平馆
事业素所关怀,敬请从旁再进一言,俾获俯允。用特不揣,冒昧专函奉
渎,尚希赐以援助,无任铭感。尚此,敬候道祺。

　　　　　　　　　　　　　　　　　　　　　弟袁同礼拜启

　　　　　　　　　　　　　　　　　　　　　　二月十四日

　　　附平馆行政委员会王访渔来函一件。

　　　　〔中国第二历史档案馆,教育部档案·全卷宗5,国立北平图书馆
　　　　请拨员工学术研究补助费经常费有关文书,案卷号 11616(1)〕

　　按:此前,李瑞年似在西南联合大学事务组担任试用事务员。①

――――――――――

① 《国立西南联合大学史料》第4卷,页81。

该信为文书代笔,落款为先生签名。

二月十五日

先生访冯至,送《图书季刊》稿费二十元。〔冯至《昆明日记》,页31〕

先生致信王访渔、顾子刚,告北平经费汇寄细节并请将《图书季刊》留平费用汇寄上海。抄件如下:

> 顷奉一月十九日及二十七日大函,拜悉一一。中基会汇平一月份经费之汇水,已由该会在汇滇经费内予以扣除,自二月份北平部份经费由中孚银行实拨八千元(详二月五日航函),九月至十二月所扣储金当由该会补汇不误。又,关于《西藏文经》保留费一千九百四十五元五角二分,日前曾请送交大同书店,谅荷台察。顷因《图书季刊》在沪付印需款颇殷,拟请将北平所存之《图书季刊》费三百十五元六角一分汇交李照亭君,以资应用为盼。

〔《北京图书馆馆史资料汇编(1909-1949)》,页709-710〕

二月中上旬

先生致信徐旭生,请其代为联系郭伯恭,聘后者来平馆(昆明)服务。〔《徐旭生文集》第10册,页1073〕

> 按:郭伯恭(1905—1951),原名习敬,以字行,河南南阳人,著有《四库全书纂修考》《永乐大典考》《宋四大书考》等书。2月11日,徐旭生曾致信郭伯恭。先生信于16日送达,后徐旭生再次致信郭伯恭。

二月十六日

王伯祥覆函先生。〔《王伯祥日记》第16册,页366〕

> 按:先生收到后又覆信,并于3月9日前送达。[1]

二月十九日

先生撰写 Memorandum Re the publication fund for the National Library of Peiping,包括两部分,一是 Reprint of rare historical works(善本丛书);一是 Lost works from *Yung-Lo Ta-tien*(《永乐大典》辑佚书),各需要 1500 美金。
〔The Houghton Library, Roger S. Greene Papers, Box 19, Harvard Yenching Institute〕

> 按:该备忘录援引 1932 年哈佛燕京学社批准的 2500 美金资助出

---

[1]《王伯祥日记》第16册,页391。

版《宋会要辑稿》的成功案例,此件应附于 22 日致顾临信中。

二月中下旬

先生致信曾昭燏,并寄《图书季刊》。〔《曾昭燏文集·日记书信卷》,页 88〕

> 按:曾昭燏日记所记为"《北平图书馆季刊》新第三期",应指《图书季刊》新 1 卷第 3 期。

二月二十一日

先生派人送信与吴宓,索要《图书季刊》英文本稿件,并约明日去取。〔《吴宓日记》第 7 册,页 133〕

> 按:翌日,吴宓等先生久不至,故前往送稿,路遇高棣华为先生取稿,二人遂同至平馆办事处。《图书季刊》英文本于 1940 年 3 月在上海复刊。

先生致信史密斯森协会,告知平馆已将错寄至中国的包裹发送给正确的目的地——西班牙。

February 21, 1940

Dear Sirs:

Among the books which you so kindly forwarded to China, we find that there are several packages intended for Spain, therefore, reforwarded them for you to their destination as noted on the enclosed list.

As the amount of postage is very small, please do not bother to refund it to us. We are glad that we can do this little service for you in humble return to your many courtesies.

Yours sincerely,

T. L. Yuan

Acting Director

> 〔平馆(冯平山图书馆转)英文信纸。Smithsonian Institution Archives, Records, 1868–1988 (Record Unit 509), Box 1, National Library, Peiping〕

> 按:此件为打字稿,落款处为先生签名,附两页共计 17 种出版物名称,于 4 月 2 日送达。

二月二十二日

先生撰写 Report of the use of the Rockefeller Foundation's grant for development of library services in China, July-December 1939。〔Rockefeller Foundation. Series 601: China; Subseries 601.R: China-Humanities and Arts. Vol. Box 47. Folder 390〕

先生致信王重民,请刘修业完善《云南书目》,并请她编纂西人关于中国铜器的书刊目录,此外留意西人有关麼些手稿的文章。

> 有三吾弟:
>
> 顷由联大送下关于云南地质论文目录二纸,请转交刘女士加入其《云南书目》内,以期完善。又美国地理学会亦藏有 Mo-So Mss,何日到纽约亦可一商借印为幸。刘女士《云南书目》编制完毕,请对于西人所著之关于中国铜器之书籍及论文编一书目,不日将此间所得者寄上一份,以供参考。又寄来之£ 18.19.5 及£ 29 又 49 法郎尚未收到,如英伦无法寄港,即暂存英伦作购书用可也。匆匆,顺颂大安。
>
> 同礼顿首
>
> 二月廿二日

American Geographical Society, Broadway at 156th St. N. Y.

Francis H. Nicholas mo-so mss 在

1. *Geographical Review* apr. 1937, V. 27, No. 2

2. *Geographical Review* apr. 1916, V. 1 p. 274-285

〔国立北平图书馆(昆明柿花巷)用笺。中国书店·海淀,四册〕

按:Francis H. Nicholas 实为 Francis H. Nichols, 著有 *Through Hidden Shensi* ,1902 年纽约初版,今译为《穿越神秘的陕西》。Mo-So Mss 即麼些手稿,纳西族古旧文献。美国地理学会的两篇文章实为 The Nichols Mo-So Manuscript of the American Geographical Society[1]、The Nichols Mo-So Manuscript[2]。

先生致信顾临,请其寄赠新著并请就平馆向哈佛燕京学社申请资助给予必要的支持。

February 22, 1940

---

[1] Rock, Joseph F. " The Nichols Mo-So Manuscript of the American Geographical Society. " *Geographical Review*, vol. 27, no. 2, 1937, pp. 229-239.

[2] Laufer, Berthold. "The Nichols Mo-So Manuscript. " *Geographical Review*, vol. 1, no. 4, 1916, pp. 274-285.

Mr. Roger S. Greene,

548 Lincoln St.,

Worcester, Mass.,

U. S. A.

Dear Mr. Greene:

In spite of my silence, I have often been thinking of you and your interest in world federation and government. It is, therefore, with great pleasure that I learn of your recent contribution entitled: "*The Price of Peace*" published by the World Citizens Association. As we are interested in everything you write, will you kindly send us an autographed copy for our collection here.

Ambassador Johnson arrived here yesterday after having paid a visit to Peiping and Hankow. While in Peiping he took occasion to visit the Library and was very pleased with the status quo being maintained there. The sudden rise in the cost of living both in Peiping and Kunming has hit hard on our staff. In view of the financial difficulties of the Foundation, I doubt whether we can expect any increase for our budget next year.

In connection with the publication fund for this Library, I have submitted an application for a grant from the Harvard-Yenching Institute. I enclose herewith copy of a memorandum, and I hope you will find it possible to support the application.

Owing to the favorable exchange, the finances of all missionary institutions are much better than before the war. And when we heard that the recent campaign of Associated Boards for Christian Colleges in China has already reached the US $ 100,000 mark in addition to US $ 580,000 raised in 1937-39, it really made us regret that we are not a missionary institution!

Such being the case, I wonder if some of the grants which the Institute makes to various missionary institutions might not be freed for use in favour of the National Library. However, our request is such a humble one that it probably does not call for any readjustment.

Assuring you our sincere appreciation of your interest and with kindest regards to you and Mrs. Greene.

Yours sincerely,

T. L. Yuan

Acting Director

〔The Houghton Library, Roger S. Greene Papers, Box 19, Harvard Yenching Institute〕

按: The Price of Peace 仅为一个册页, 非正式出版物, 约 11 页。

二月二十三日

先生致信史蒂文斯, 附上平馆《工作简报》, 并告知平馆上海办事处将寄赠其福开森的新著。

February 23, 1940

Dear Dr. Stevens:

You have no doubt received our quarterly statements of the expenditure in connection with the appropriation RF36072 through your Shanghai office. For your further information, I now enclose a summary report.

I should like to express to you once more how very grateful we are for your assistance without which the Library would be unable to carry on its program upon the scale of its present operations.

I have sent to you from Shanghai a set of Dr. Ferguson's *Survey of Chinese Art*. When both Europe and the Far East are being occupied with the war, it is a relief to turn to the things of peace for which China is always noted. In spite of the difficulties of war, scholarly works are being produced in this country.

With cordial regards,

Yours sincerely

T. L. Yuan

Acting Director

〔平馆(昆明)英文信纸。Rockefeller Foundation. Series 601: China; Subseries 601. R: China-Humanities and Arts. Vol. Box 47. Folder 390〕

按:该信中附有 22 日所撰馆务报告。*Survey of Chinese Art* 中文书名为《中国艺术综览》,1940 年上海商务印书馆初版。此件为打字稿,落款处为先生签名,以航空信方式寄送。

二月二十四日

先生致信平馆驻香港办事处,指示寄送《暴日侵华与国际舆论》。

一、请寄《暴日侵华》于下列各处:

1.重庆国民政府军事委员会政治部十部_{发票已由滇寄渝,请寄书}。

1.重庆国民政府军事委员会政治部十部 <small>发票已由滇寄渝,请寄书</small>。

2.桂林广西地方建设干部学校资料室两部 <small>收据已由滇寄去</small>。

3.四川江津中白沙国立编译馆一部 <small>附收据一纸</small>。

4.重庆南岸米市街武昌中华大学校一部 <small>款尚未付,发票已由滇寄去</small>。

5.成都华西坝私立齐鲁大学一部 <small>附收据一纸</small>。

右共十五部,附收据二纸请随书寄去。

二、李小缘先生不日寄来港币百元,作为金陵大学文化研究所寄书邮费之用,请另立一账,每月报销一次。

〔《北京图书馆馆史资料汇编(1909-1949)》,页 712〕

按:《暴日侵华》即《暴日侵华与国际舆论》(*Japan's Aggression and Public Opinion*),1938 年底由西南联大出版第一辑。[①] 此为抄件。

二月二十五日

王重民致函先生,请补寄前此寄法书单,并告巴黎局面已恢复正常。

守和吾师钧鉴:

顷接<u>杜乃扬</u>来信,称八月间吾师寄往巴黎之杂志单——即作为交换品,请法方从今年一月份起代为订阅者,Madame Meuvret 弄丢,请速速另寄去一清单,以便代为订阅。现外交部专司交换事之 Joubert 氏已赴前线,其地位暂由一位太太代理。杜女士称吾师去信所索之 *Bulletin périodique de la presse chinoise, Catalogue des Cartes du Service Géographique de l'Armée* 等,以及生所索之 *Document diplomatique* 等均不难凑齐赠送我方。两三月来,<u>巴黎</u>情形颇为平静,其他如罗都尔

———————————

[①]《中日战事史料征辑会工作报告》(1938 年 1 月至 4 月),页 7。《暴日侵华与国际舆论》出版日期,可参考《吴宓日记》(第 6 册,页 365)的相关记述。

等来信罗都尔又生一位少爷，所述情形，可想见一切已复旧观，已不若开战前后之恐慌矣。Bibliothèque Nationale 闻亦仍旧，只是有一部分人去打仗，而剩下的人只能支撑局面，不能有什么工作矣。

Meuvret 太太事情太多，而遇事不是太着急，便堆积起来不办，所以杂志单仍请寄杜乃扬，让她去催 Meuvret 太太，较妥较易生效。生前索之账单，尚未寄下，惟恐亦丢了。

敦煌所出西藏文残卷目录，由一位 Lalou 女士编辑，已有五六年，刻第一册已出版，已去买，可是生拟一阅，还是先寄来美国。

尤桐已有信寄吾师，报告英国捐书情形。似张似旅不肯发邮包，为出于中国人方面之意见，那二十镑，如何处置，请速示知。

余再及，即请道安！

受业重民敬上
二月二十五日

杜乃扬的母亲卧病已三月，近方能起床。家中杂事，都须她照顾，而还要学看护，预备有用时便到医院侍奉伤兵。她写信时，尚未接到云南丛书，不过她还期望能找到一部全四部丛刊。

〔国家图书馆档案，档案编号 1940-※044-外事 3-002007〕

按：*Catalogue des Cartes du Service Géographique de l'Armée* 似指 *Catalogue des Cartes, publiés par le service géographique de l'Armée*（《法国陆军地理署地图目录》）。Lalou 即 Marcelle Lalou（1890-1967），法国西藏学家。“敦煌所出西藏文残卷目录”即 *Inventaire des manuscrits tibétains de Touen-houang: conservés à la bibliothèque nationale*，1939 年刊行第 1 卷，其他两卷分别于 1950、1961 年出版。

二月下旬

先生寄赠《图书季刊》新一卷第四期与曾昭燏。〔《曾昭燏文集·日记书信卷》，页 89〕

按：2 月 28 日，曾昭燏收到该刊，在日记中记为“《北平图书馆季刊》新第四期”。

三月一日

先生致信张元济，感谢其和顾廷龙赐稿，并告合众图书馆前请平馆赠出版物事之结果，另谈也是园旧藏元曲选印之意见。

菊生先生尊右：

　　奉读二月廿一日赐教并《稼轩词跋》两通，又附起潜先生大函及善本题跋十种，拜领之余，无任感谢。起潜先生拟为合众图书馆征求敝馆出版书籍，无任荣幸。除各项藏书目录全部寄赠外（由平交邮寄沪），余者特别予以优待，照码按七折计算，惟《宋会要》所存仅有数部，且系借款所印，未能奉赠，至为怅然。此书现存沪上，即希就近与李照亭君接洽，诸希费神代为转致为幸。又，也是园曲承尊处选印，丰功伟业，至为佩仰。西南学术界同人咸主张仿《元曲选》办法付诸影印，以存其真。如贵馆以成本较重，似可先售预约，敝馆可预定三百部，先行交款，未识尊意以为如何？并希卓裁，见复为感。特此申谢，并祈垂察。临颖依依，无任神驰。专覆，敬请著安。

后学袁同礼拜启
三月一日

《稼轩词》何时出版？如荷检赠，请交李照亭君为荷。

　　　　　　〔国立北平图书馆用笺。《校订元明杂剧事往来信札》，页
　　　　　　464-465〕

　　按：《稼轩词跋》即《毛钞稼轩词甲乙丙丁集跋（一）（二）》，刊《图书季刊》新第 2 卷第 2 期（1940 年 6 月）。此信为文书代笔，落款处为先生亲笔，于 3 月上旬送达，12 日张元济向顾廷龙出示先生信。15 日，顾廷龙访平馆在沪馆员李耀南，接洽购买《宋会要辑稿》。[1]

三月二日

Lyman Hoover 致函先生，告知收到先生由九龙转来的参考文献，并将寄上有关学生救济工作的油印材料。

March 2, 1940

Dear Dr. Yuan:

　　I am glad to inform you that your last package of registered printed matter reached me from Hongkong on Feb. 29th, having been mailed from Kowloon on Feb. 24th. I am very grateful for this material and will

---

[1]《张元济年谱长编》下卷，页 1135；《顾廷龙日记》，页 59。

return it to you as soon as I have had opportunity to go through it carefully.

Under separate cover, I am sending you a few recent mimeographed materials in connection with the Student Relief Work and related matters.

With sincere personal regards,

Cordially yours,

Lyman Hoover.

〔Yale University records, Lyman Hoover Papers, RG 9 Series I, Box 13, Folder 280〕

按：此件为录副。

三月四日

先生致信阿博特，鉴于太平洋时局稳定，建议史密斯森协会恢复由美国发往香港的出版品交换。

March 4, 1940

Dear Dr. Abbot:

For several months we have not received consignments from the Smithsonian Institution. Although we have not been officially informed by your Institution, yet a number of our correspondents in the United States have written to us to the effect that the International Exchange Service is no longer making shipments to China.

Your decision in suspending temporarily the shipment to the Orient is no doubt due to the European war. But while the German submarines have done immense damages to the allied and neutral steamers, yet the travel across the Pacific has been extremely calm and peaceful. The present status quo will be maintained so long as Japan does not fight against Great Britain and the United States.

At a time when Chinese universities and libraries are in urgent need of American books and periodicals, the suspension of the Service will rule out almost all gifts and donations from our correspondents in the United States. Since the shipping facilities between New York and Hongkong are extremely normal, we earnestly hope that you would kindly reconsider your decision. If favorable consideration could be given to this request, we trust you will notify various institutions to this effect.

May I take this opportunity of expressing to you once more our sincere appreciation of your assistance rendered to Chinese libraries in the past and of expressing the fervent hope that shipments to Hongkong will be resumed at an early date? In spite of the war, a great deal of scientific and scholarly work is being carried on in this country, and we hope you will co-operate with us in the efforts which China is making to maintain her intellectual life under the most formidable difficulties.

With renewed thanks and cordial personal regards,

Your sincerely,

T. L. Yuan

Chairman,

Executive Board

P. S.: We recommend that shipments to Haiphong be temporarily suspended, as there is too much congestion of traffic along the Yunnan railway.

〔中华图书馆协会（冯平山图书馆转）英文信纸。Smithsonian Institution Archives, Records, 1868-1988 (Record Unit 509), Box 1, Library Association of China, Hong Kong〕

按：此件为打字稿，先生对内文略有修改，落款处为先生签名，以航空信方式寄送，于 5 月 23 日送达。

三月六日

先生致信震旦大学博物馆，请寄送该馆一九三九年至一九四零年中英文版的学术活动概述。

March 6, 1940

Dear Sirs:

In the *Quarterly Bulletin of Chinese Bibliography*, there is one separate section devoted to the scholarly and scientific work carried on by various institutions in China. The purpose of printing this record in the Bulletin is to keep the scholarly world well informed of the research work carried on in this country in order to have closer co-ordination as well as to avoid possible duplication.

We shall, therefore, be much obliged to you if you would kindly send us a statement concerning the activities of Musée Heude during 1939–40. In order to have the statement recorded in both the Chinese and English editions, will you kindly supply us the required information in both languages?

If you publish anything of scientific interest in the future, kindly send us a sample copy for review in the Bulletin.

Assuring you of our sincere appreciation of your collaboration and thanking you in anticipation for your assistance,

Yours sincerely,

T. L. Yuan

Acting Director

P. S.: Correspondence and printed matter should be addressed as follows: Mr. T. L. Yuan, c/o Fung Ping Shan Library, 94, Bonham Road, Hongkong.

〔上海市档案馆，档案编号 Q244-1-499〕

按：4 月 1 日，该院寄送一份法文版 1939 年至 1940 年学术活动概述。

三月七日

教育部社会教育司致函先生，告知拟补助平馆（昆明）两万元，但须等行政院核定。

奉顾次长发下二月十四日台函，并附王访渔先生原函，藉悉壹是。贵馆请在二十九年度内补助购书款及出版费三万元，已承部长批列两万元，仍候汇案呈请行政院核示。一俟完案，即当令复知照。特先函闻，即希察照！此致
袁守和先生
附检还王访渔先生原函一件。

教育部社会教育司启

〔中国第二历史档案馆，教育部档案·全卷宗 5，国立北平图书馆请拨员工学术研究补助费经常费有关文书，案卷号 11616(1)〕

按:该函拟于 2 月 26 日,3 月 7 日实发。

三月八日

下午五时,吴宓至平馆访先生,表示愿意继续校阅《图书季刊》英文本。
〔《吴宓日记》第 7 册,页 139〕

王重民致函先生,告尚未影照《永乐大典》册数及在国会图书馆编纂善本书目及题跋,并谈《天主教士书目》之进展。

守和吾师钧鉴:

此间所藏永乐大典仅有两册吾馆无影片,更有一册,为馆外人所寄存,须得物主许诺,方能摄影。闻 Dr. Hummel 言,以前赠送吾馆照片,均与原书一般大。此次亦说明要一般大,因用生个人名义,每叶仅收美金一角。俟照好后,即一直寄北平赵斐云。

罗氏基金赠国会图书馆编目用之款,近闻 Hummel 言,明年夏季以后,恐难再继续;(闻系哈佛方面想另设一机关,印中国书卡片,供全美国之用,则可独吞此款。)至于善本书,伊拟仅印目录,不印题跋。生问其原因,系由政府不能印中国字,而送往中国付印,则馆方不易拿钱。经生题醒他,将来此题跋记可由北平图书馆代印代卖算吾馆出版物之一,只要在美筹出印费即可。伊谓一俟编讫后,转请吾师致信罗氏基金会,国会图书馆方面亦一同另去函请求此项印刷费,Hummel 称基金会既有钱请人编目,由馆方请求,由吾师证明,(一要证明编的很好,二要证明藏书很好,中国人都想知道。)此款定能得到。一俟生编的有眉目,此事即可由双方进行,想吾师定能同意。

关于向哈佛要印刷敦煌稿费一节,已与伯希和、戴密微二先生去信,俟得其覆信再说,但此事恐无多大希望。

自来美后,无暇清理旧业,但于编书目之便,随手翻检,在明末清初人著作中,得一些与天主教有关文字,日来翻检益勤,所得益多,则"天主教士书目",或能先敦煌而成。在此故字句有不妥处。(现长短已作三百余篇。)一俟作完之后,恐于文辞方面,还要一度修改。至于个人方面,除随手辑录一点材料外,亦无其他成绩。(所编多是明人著作,辑出一些关于明末天主教材料,有可与巴黎、罗马相印证处。又于敦煌掌故,间亦检一点有可与旧说相发明处。)且与 Dr. Hummel 相处,不算很相得生大不喜欢他的样子,故九月以后工作如何,决不先向他谈起。

依生愚意,此目不论编成与否,他如不坚留,暑假后一定归国;但他如坚留,则须:①L. C.允许回国时给充足路费,②何时编完,便何时愿走何时可走,不必以一年为限。不知吾师以为如何? 最近 Hummel 如谈到此事,愿吾师把"充足路费"提在前边!

生已寄一点钱到北平,一为将来家严等安家之用,二为印"敦煌叙录"第二辑。以后再有钱,尚拟寄到香港一点,预备回国后路费及零用。

余再及,即请道安!

受业重民上。

三月八日

上月二十六日,曾上航空信一封,因去年寄巴黎之杂志单,Mme Meuvret 遗失,请再补一单寄上。外交部 Joubert 已赴前线,刻由一太太代其地位。该航信想不至遗失。

〔国家图书馆档案,档案编号 1940-※044-外事 3-002008 至 1940-※044-外事 3-002009〕

按:"闻系哈佛方面想另设一机关,印中国书卡片"即 1939 年秋哈佛燕京学社汉和图书馆向洛克菲勒基金会提出资助卡片目录编印的申请,后全美 8 所大学预订了 14 套卡片。①

三月九日

王伯祥致函先生。〔《王伯祥日记》第 16 册,页 391〕

按:先生收到后即覆信,内容应为请估算方树梅《滇南碑传集》的印刷费用,该信 4 月 20 日前送达。② 1939 年该书稿完成,顾颉刚认为此书"为云南文献攸关之书",本拟由商务印书馆或齐鲁大学付印,先生听说此书稿后遂致函顾颉刚,请让平馆交由开明书店印行。③

三月十日

晚,先生在曲园招宴。〔《吴宓日记》第 7 册,页 140〕

按:吴宓因赴曾琦宴,故未能赴先生之宴。

---

① 《裘开明年谱》,页 228。
② 《王伯祥日记》第 16 册,页 442。
③ 《北游搜访文献日记》,页 224。

三月十一日

先生致信傅斯年,告知其此前委托购书事并附信一封。

孟真吾兄:

手示敬悉。兹致圣经学院饶牧师一函,即希备用为荷。贵所委托余让之君代购之书已由来薰阁陆续寄港,由港转滇者已有十五包,其他尚在途中。明清史料稿件则由大同书店寄港。尊处需用王重民之《燉煌叙录》及纖纬照片,不日亦可寄到,并以奉闻。顺颂著祺。

弟同礼顿首

三月十一日

〔国立北平图书馆(昆明柿花巷)用笺。台北"中央研究院"历史语言研究所傅斯年图书馆,"史语所档案",李45-5〕

按:"纖纬"当作"谶纬"。"饶牧师"即 Charles Roberts(饶培德),湖南圣经学院第二任院长。该信由文书代笔,落款处为先生签名。

先生致信饶培德。

按:该信似由李光宇(K. Y. Li)带去,内容应为商洽史语所暂存圣经学院的甲骨去留问题。

三月十四日

先生致信博睿(荷兰)出版社,告知将从上海汇出购书费,并订购书籍两种。

March 14, 1940

Messrs. E. J. Brill, Ltd.,

Leyden,

Netherland.

Dear Sirs:

We are asking our Treasurer at Shanghai to remit to you the sum of guilders 24.41 being payment for your invoice dated December 16, 1939. As soon as you receive our remittance, please send us your official receipt in duplicate copies.

Please supply a copy each of the following two books and send them to us by book post via Haiphong, French Indo-China:

Stein, Sir A. *On Old Routes of Western Iran*.

Stuyt, A. M.: *Survey of International Arbitrations 1794- 1938*.

Your prompt attention will oblige,

Yours very truly,

T. L. Yuan

Acting Director

〔谢筠(Yun Xie)个人的外国社交软件 X 账户〕

按:E. J. Brill 是 1683 年在荷兰莱顿成立的学术出版社。*On Old Routes of Western Iran* 全称为 *Old Routes of Western Iran: narrative of an archaeological journey carried out and recorded*,1940 年伦敦初版。Stuyt, A. M.即 Alexander M. Stuyt(1911- 2007),生于荷兰阿姆斯特丹,国际法专家,时任常设仲裁法院(Permanent Court of Arbitration)秘书,其著作 *Survey of International Arbitrations*(《国际仲裁概览》)于 1939 年在海牙初版,后多次增订再版。该信为打字稿,落款处为先生亲笔,应于 4 月 27 日送达。

张元济覆函先生,告也是园元明杂剧宜排印的三个原因。

守和先生阁下:

敬复者,前日奉到本月一日手书,展诵谨悉。前函代合众图书馆祈请赐书,辱蒙慨允拨赠藏书目录全部,余并特别减价,至为感荷。当即转知顾君起潜,径与李君照亭接洽。顾君并嘱致谢。《辛稼轩词》现在正在印装,出版后自当敬祈台览。此书虽经陶、赵二君印行,然卒未见汲古原抄,且敝馆经作家集合众本精密校雠,附撰札记,定能仰邀青睐也。再敝公司承印园元明杂剧,初意亦思影印,无如将全书检阅,觉其窒碍难行之处凡有三点:(一)全书有刻本,有抄本,抄本亦不出一手,行款亦各各不同,且有眉目极不清楚者。若用影印,非特毫无美观,且反令阅者多所迷惘。(二)原书经数人校过,校手或详或略,略者随笔将所校改之字蒙盖在本字之上。若用影印,则原字及所改之字并为墨堆,无从辨别;详者用蝇头细楷左右勾勒,若求清析,非用珂罗版不可。(三)抄者程度过低,致形误声误之字,不胜枚举。(记有一字,似是"顯"字,但记不真确。总之右旁为"頁",原文竟将"頁"旁写在左方,而将"㬎"旁写在右方,岂非笑话)且抄手亦甚粗率,若存原式,适是以彰其劣点,而招世人之薄视。以此三点,不能与精刻且有图画之《元曲选》齐观。故鄙见认为只可改用排版,整理之功已费数月,亦甚不易。因专聘曲学名家王君九先生总司校勘,绝不肯草率从事,而弟亦时时加以纠绳。现已发排,将来阁下定能鉴其不谬也。承示贵馆预定三百部,先行交款,具见提倡盛意,至为感幸。一俟排印稍有端绪,可以约定售价,即行奉闻,并请拨款。先此布谢,顺颂台安。

二十九年三月十四日

〔《张元济全集》第 3 卷,页 3〕

按:《稼轩词》,约在 3 月底正式发行。① "王君九"即王季烈(1873—1952),字晋余,号君九,江苏长洲人,清末曲家,时居北平。

三月二十日

王重民覆函先生,谈公私两方面事。

守和吾师钧鉴:

一月七日、十九日、廿四日三手谕,相连奉到,敬悉一是。在巴黎所寄五箱书籍,已平安到港,闻之尤为欣慰。所欲奉禀者,谨一一详下:

1. 语言历史研究所欲从敦煌卷子辑古谶纬事,生已开一详目,并附一信,请转傅孟真。生所带来者,不久要稍稍整理,即顺便将此类相片拣出,为其制复本。

2. 西南文献,海外所藏虽不少,然大致已发表。且其较有价值者,似为回教石刻,多数藏巴黎,生未暇详检。仅在牛津见一王韬手录本苗疆图说,似有收入西南文献丛刊之价值。惟不知拟排印抑影印? 如影印,生当作一跋,并原片寄上。

3. L. C.所藏永乐大典,生正开始编目,即依前日寄下吾馆已制复本之单,凡未有照片者,赶速摄影,遵命寄平。Photostat 每叶价钱,馆外人两毛五分,馆内职员仅收一毛,用生名义排照,不为贵,不必制 Microfilm 也。

4. 第二次寄来之 $105.57,尚存此地。因存款都在英,在此有时

---

① 《顾廷龙日记》,页 66。

要用钱,如不久即拍照大典与将来回国时运费等,故拟暂存于此,而用伦敦所存,以还前此£ 27 之数。伦敦存款,连张似旅处之£ 20,想尚有三十镑上下。如此办法,不知吾师以为如何?

5. 前寄上林语堂、杜威两书,太普通,想必重复。以后不拟代买;但如买,则间购一二较生僻之书,或如吾师所谓小册子之类。

6. 云南书目第三章,分量不少,盖除第一章外,以此章为最多。现已钞清,再稍校阅,拟还是寄昆明。随时发见有失收或续出之书,不能补入各章,将来或再作一补遗。

7. 编目部刘女士,生只见过一次,不大熟。关于抗战书目,吴先生已催三四次,最末,伊表示不愿作。生与吴先生推测,伊或因吾师未给她一直通信之故。生再往恐亦无益,望吾师向她一直去信为祷!

8. 近已找到一寄托小孩地方,已接洽一次,可收容,惟现在尚无空位,故正在等候中。将来拟每星期寄出三天(每天五角),则刘女士可到图书馆工作三天,作汉学书及期刊介绍,与综合研究清代族谱等,方能有成绩。二月八日曾发出介绍稿数篇,今日接到季刊第四期,见与二月八日以后所作有相重者,故从此以后,请凡美国所出专书及期刊,都不必作,刘女士有时间后,当能更快也。

9. 舍弟新民事,蒙吾师特别位置,实为感激。生便中当再致顾子刚一信。家严因有老母在堂,不忍远游,而祖母今年已九十有四,不堪远道跋涉(曾在保定住一时),此家严所以近来屡游疑而不能决定。生当再商酌,如万不得已,或生让新民赴平供职。

10. 生来美后,工作总是不起劲,所作提要,亦一味求快,最耽误时间者,即为清抄。在未有小孩以前,都是刘女士代钞,现在已不能,每回想存在箱内各种相片,不能清钞校对,辄为恓恓,此所以欲早日归国之重要原因。只因生在此每月仅拿一百五十美金,而归国路费,Hummel 未有明言,此所以耿耿于心,每欲向他说个明白,给路费则好好编完此目,否则八月底便拟东归。伊于商议印刷题跋记时,已非正式的表明期望生留至明年夏季,想将来尚须有正式谈判,到那时,关于路费一节,生非要和他说一下不可。

傅孟真是否也在昆明,关于伦敦所藏敦煌谶纬书史料,现尚未开清目录,但不久当查明,再奉上。

小孩尚未寄出,因无空位。刘女士已开始看族谱。新书介绍,近又作两种,约下礼拜,即可与<u>云南书目——科学</u>一章,一同挂号寄上。

专此,即请道安!

受业重民上。
三月二十日

所作两书介绍如下:

White (W. C.) *Tomb Tile pictures of ancient China*

Creel-Chang: *Selection from the Lun-y ü*, Chicago, 1939

〔国家图书馆档案,档案编号 1940-※044-外事 3-002004 至 1940-※044-外事 3-002006〕

按:*Tomb Tile Pictures of Ancient China* 即《中国古墓砖图考》,作者 William Charles White(1873-1960),中文名怀履光,加拿大圣公会传教士,1897 年来华在福建传教,后赴河南传教,1934 年归国,时任多伦多大学教授并兼安大略皇家博物馆远东收藏部主任,该书于 1939 年多伦多大学初版。*Selection from the Lun-y ü* 即 Literary Chinese by the Inductive Method 第 2 种,由顾立雅、张宗骞(Chang Tsung-ch'ien)和 Richard C. Rudolph 三人编译,1937 年 1 月芝加哥大学发起"中国语文研究计划",旋得洛克菲勒基金会资助,出版《中国文学丛刊》,刘修业将此书译为《归纳法之中国文学丛刊第二集:论语》,该篇刊于《图书季刊》中文本新第 2 卷第 4 期页(685-686)。

三月二十一日

先生致信顾临,告知史密斯森协会寄往中国的书籍多滞于海防、无法送抵重庆或昆明。

March 21, 1940

Dear Mr. Greene:

I trust you have received my air-mail letter of February 22nd sent to you at your Worcester address.

Your letter of February 8 to Mr. Senn concerning the consignment held up at Haiphong has been referred to me for reply.

The consignments in question are those forwarded by the

Smithsonian Institution to the Bureau of the International Exchange of Publications, Ministry of Education, Chungking. All of them have duly arrived at Haiphong, but the Bureau would not acknowledge their receipt until the cases are received and opened at Chungking! Owing to the congestion of traffic on the Yunnan railway, the Bureau has not been able to transport all the cases even to Kunming.

From the very beginning, I have urged the Bureau to set up an office at Haiphong to look after the receipt and transshipment of cases, but owing to the difficulty of obtaining foreign exchange, the Bureau has not been able to take this advice. Since receiving your letter, I have called the attention of the Bureau as to the serious consequences arising out of their inefficiency; and I hope it may produce some effect.

On March 4th I wrote to the Smithsonian suggesting that books for China may be sent to Hongkong. Our office there will be glad to reforward them to their destinations by book-post. Although it is a little more expensive, yet the books are received much quicker than by freight. Thousands of parcels for our library have been received in this way.

If the Bureau could not set up an office at Haiphong, we might consider designating one of our men to service at that port. I shall, however, keep you posted as to future developments.

I have just read your article published in Asia. The views you expressed therein represent exactly those of your Chinese colleagues.

With kindest regards,

Yours sincerely

T. L. Yuan

Acting Director

〔Smithsonian Institution Archives, Records, 1868－1988（Record Unit 509), Box 1, Library Association of China, Hong Kong〕

按：此为抄件。顾临收到该信后，4 月 11 日、16 日致信阿博特。

三月二十二日

毕安祺覆函先生，告知前信已转交佛利尔艺术馆馆长，并询问袁复礼近况。

22 March, 1940

Dear Dr. Yuan: -

Your letter of Feb. 2nd reached me the day before yesterday, and I have already given it to our Director, Mr. John E. Lodge, who has entire charge of all such matters. He will, I am sure, give it prompt attention.

It was pleasant to hear from you, for Mrs. Bishop and I have often wondered where you were, and how you were getting on. We both retain delightful recollections of our former association with you, and with your brother, in Peiping.

Where, and how, is your brother, by the way? I should appreciate it if, when you write or see him, you would kindly offer him our most cordial remembrances. I should be most happy to hear from him.

I am glad to tell you that interest in China is higher in this country than it has ever been, and Mrs. Bishop and I are doing all we can to keep it so. We unite in extending to you our very warm regards, and all good wishes. We shall be delighted to hear from you again when you have time and opportunity to write. As ever,

　　　　　　　　　　　　　　　Yours very sincerely,

　　　　　　　　　　　　　　　C. W. Bishop

〔Smithsonian Institution Archives. Field Expedition Records, Box 11 Folder 18, Yuan, T. L., 1929-1940〕

按：John E. Lodge（1876-1942），1920 年起担任佛利尔艺术馆馆长，此前任波士顿博物馆（Boston Museum of Fine Arts）东亚部主任。该函寄送昆明。此件为录副。

三月二十三日

先生致信王访渔、顾子刚，就临时米贴分配办法做出指示。

刻下北平米价日昂，各物随之涨价。此种现象，举国皆升。本馆增拨之津贴，系属“米贴”性质，自应平均分配，以示大公，而不能以薪金多寡按照比例分配也。近查由沪汇平之款，每月升水甚多，但以后是否如此，则殊难□揣。兹拟定一临时办法，即希自四月份起采纳实行：

一、如汇款升入每月在百分之十以上，则职员每人给予米贴十五元,工友每人十元。

二、如汇款无升水,则职员每人给予米贴十元,工友每人六元。

如下年度预算可望增加,届时再定办法。刻下发电厂既停,每月可省三百元,加以汇款升水,似足敷用。但今后如升水过高,则留待下月分配,或补行政费之不足。盖此种意外之收入,随时可以停止,甚难预言也。总之,弟对于平馆之维持,已尽最大之努力。如同人中以家室所累,仍有不能维持生活者,自可另谋出路也。总之在此困难时期,薪水较高者自应略予牺牲,将此款额外之款分配于低级职员。区区微意,谅荷赞同。用特再行函达,即希台察为荷。

袁署

〔《北京图书馆馆史资料汇编(1909-1949)》,页710-711〕

按:此为抄件。

三月二十四日

上午九时,昆明各界人士在云南省党部礼堂举行追悼蔡元培大会,先生率平馆在滇同人参加。〔《北京图书馆馆史资料汇编(1909-1949)》,页713〕

按:3月5日,蔡元培在香港逝世。

三月二十五日

先生访冯至,送书三册,请其作书评。〔冯至《昆明日记》,页32〕

先生致信上海办事处,通知中英庚款董事会拨付款项购买资料。

一、顷接重庆管理中英庚款董事会来函,内称史料会在沪购书拨付之三千元(联大部分)已函该会副董事长马锡尔爵士就近办理。兹寄上该会介绍李耀南君在沪领款一函,并附英文临时收据一纸,即希到北京路二号马锡尔爵士处将该款如数领回,在银行内另立史料会一户,以后代该会购书,即在此款内拨付。前于二月廿一日寄上之中文临时收据一纸,应即作废,并乞寄滇为荷。为接洽便利起见,可请钱先生前往接洽。

二、另邮上《图书季刊》第二卷第二期稿件一部分(见另单),收到后示复。

〔《北京图书馆馆史资料汇编(1909-1949)》,页713〕

按:马锡尔爵士即 Robert Calder-Marshall(1877-1955),英国商人,上海祥兴洋行创立者,并任上海英国商会会长,兼任管理中英庚款董事会英方董事。此为抄件。

先生致信张元济，告因《稼轩词》改为排印，请其忽略此前预约三百部之说，并请打听瞿启甲藏书有无出让的可能。

　　菊生先生著席：

　　　　昨奉三月十四日赐函，敬悉一切。尊处所印《辛稼轩词》，校雠精审，嘉惠艺林，远道闻之，莫名钦佩。出版后倘承惠寄，甚愿先睹为快也。也是园曲闻已发排，尤为神往，便中并希将选印目录赐寄一份，尤所感盼。承示不能影印之点，尤感厚意。此籍得公加以整理，并有君九先生从事校勘，将来出版之后，必能风行海内，承学之士当视如拱璧矣。前函所述平、沪、川、滇友人拟预约三百部一节，系指影印本而言。今既决定排印，自当候贵馆发售预约时，由愿购者分别办理，即希亮察为荷。近闻良士先生遽归道山，老成凋谢，深为痛惜。其全部藏书，前闻让诸潘丈明训者，颇不在少数。现存之书，如能继续保存，尤所翘企。倘有出让公家之意，散处颇愿为之设法，俾其精华不致散失。区区微意，谅荷赞助。尚希便中询明，赐覆为幸。尚此，敬候著祺。

　　　　　　　　　　　　　　　　　后学袁同礼拜启

　　　　　　　　　　　　　　　　　　三月廿五日

赐覆请寄香港般含道冯平山图书馆。

　　　　　〔国立北平图书馆用笺。《校订元明杂剧事往来信札》，页533-534〕

　　按：该信为文书代笔，落款处为先生亲笔，于4月3日送达，翌日张元济覆函。瞿启甲（1873—1940），字良士，江苏常熟人，铁琴铜剑藏书楼第四代传人。是年1月15日瞿启甲在沪去世，此后铁琴铜剑楼藏书由其第三子瞿熙邦继为主持。[①]

先生致信巴黎大学汉学研究所，请该所发来研究近况概述，《图书季刊》英文本将刊登以利中外学术界交流。

　　　　　　　　　　　　　　　　　　March 25, 1940

Institute des Hautes Études Chinoises,

Université de Paris,

---

① 《申报》，1940年1月30日，第10版。

Paris,

France.

Dear Sirs:

In the Chinese edition of the *Quarterly Bulletin of Chinese Bibliography*, there is a special section devoted to the activities of scientific and learned institutions in China.

In the next issue of the *Bulletin*, we propose to publish a statement concerning the sinological research work carried on in various centres abroad. Such a record would be of great interest to Chinese scholars who are engaged in similar studies.

We shall therefore be greatly indebted to you if you would kindly send us a statement concerning the recent researches in the sinological field carried on by your Institute. If convenient, kindly include names of personnel with their research projects in progress.

Any printed or mimeographed material illustrating the scope of your work which you may be able to send to us will be gratefully appreciated.

Thanking you for your co-operation,

Yours faithfully,

T. L. Yuan

Acting Director

〔平馆(昆明)英文信纸。法兰西学院图书馆档案〕

按:此件为打字稿,落款处为先生签名。

三月二十七日

下午四时,吴宓赴平馆办事处访先生,不值。〔《吴宓日记》第 7 册,页 147〕

按:吴宓留函,推荐学生来馆任职,似为周珏良,时刚从西南联合大学外文系毕业。

三月二十八日

徐旭生致函先生,告知郭伯恭不久来昆明任职。〔《徐旭生文集》第 10 册,页 1083-1084〕

按:3 月 23 日,徐旭生收郭伯恭函,告知决定赴昆明平馆任事,预计下月动身。先生收到是日函后即覆信徐旭生,告自己将赴香港,届时或可与于道泉相见。

三月二十九日

阿博特覆函先生,告知寄送东方的交换品并未因为欧战爆发而受到影响,在美华人响应战事征集图书委员会号召捐赠的出版品将寄送重庆,收件方为平馆者是否应继续寄往香港,或者按照捐赠人的意愿投递昆明,请先生明示。

March 29, 1940

Dear Dr. Yuan:

In reply to your letter of March 4 I would say that until to-day the Institution has received only a few publications for the Library Association of China, which accounts for the infrequent shipments. Consignments to the Orient have not been suspended on account of the European War, but shipments to the Chinese Exchange Bureau in Chungking have been withheld owing to conditions along the Yunnan Railway. On February 23 a shipment consisting of 14 cases was transmitted to Hongkong, and another transmission will be made within a few days.

The Institution has not notified any of your correspondents that it cannot accept packages for transmission to Hongkong. Any statement on this subject that has been made merely referred to China, as you will note by the enclosed form letter which was sent out February 10, 1940. If you think it necessary that your correspondents, be given further information on this subject, I would suggest that you write directly to them regarding the matter.

I might add that, in response to an appeal from China's Culture Emergency Committee for the Solicitation of Books and Periodicals in Chungking, quite a number of publications are being received here from American organizations for Chinese establishments. The forwarding of those publications, as well as others for distribution throughout China, is awaiting a safe channel of transmission to Chungking. If you learn of the opening of such a channel in future, I shall be obliged if you will notify the Institution.

In this connection I beg to ask whether all material received here for the National Library of Peiping-whether consisting of only a few packages or several boxes-shall be forwarded to that Library at its temporary address in Hongkong. In several instances in the past, specific requests have been made that certain boxes for the National Library be forwarded through to Kunming, which request was complied with.

Dr. Harold S. Quigley of the Department of Political Science, University of Minnesota, Minneapolis, has sent the Institution two large packages of books for inclusion with one of its shipments to the Chinese Library Association with the request that you forward the packages in question, which bear Smithsonian Record No. 9515, at your first opportunity to the Institute of Administration, National Peking University, Kunming, Dr. Quigley adds in his letter that the person with whom he has had correspondence regarding the books is Professor Tuan-Sheng Chien, a member of the Faculty of the School of Law at the University. Dr. Quigley further adds that he is notifying the Chinese Embassy in Washington of his action in regard to these materials.

Very truly yours,

C. G. Abbot

Secretary

〔Smithsonian Institution Archives, Records, 1868 – 1988 (Record Unit 509), Box 1, Library Association of China, Hong Kong〕

按:Harold S. Quigley(1889-1968),中文名魁格雷,美国政治学家,1921 年至 1923 年担任清华学校社会科学部教授;[1]Tuan-Sheng Chien 即钱端升,与魁格雷同在清华学校任教。该函寄送香港,此件为录副。

三月三十一日

上午,先生于华山西路遇吴宓,遂同访刘崇鋐、汤用彤、陈寅恪。〔《吴宓日

---

① 《清华年报》,1921 年,页 31。

记》第 7 册, 页 148〕

按: 本日晨, 吴宓为先生改蔡元培先生纪念文之英文稿 (In Memoriam: Dr. Tsai Yuan-pei), 在送稿途中遇先生。

三月

平馆拟印《景泰图经》, 先生嘱方树梅撰写跋文。〔《北游搜访文献日记》, 页 225〕

按:《景泰图经》应指《景泰云南图经志书》, 明代郑颙、陈文纂修, 全书共十卷, 较全面地反映了云南当时的政治、经济、军事、文化 等方面的状况, 其中前六卷介绍云南的地理情况, 后四卷由诗文 组成。

《图书季刊》英文本刊登先生两篇文章, 一是 In Memoriam: Dr. Tsai Yuan-Pei, 一是 Editorial Comment。〔*Quarterly Bulletin of Chinese Bibliography* (New Series), Vol. I, No. 1, pp. i-ii, 1-4〕

按: 后者共六部分, 依次为 To Our Reader, Publishing in War-Time, Preservation of Art Treasures, Scientific and Technical Literature, Friends of the National Libraries, Publication Fund for the National Library。

顾临覆函先生, 告知此前寄来的备忘录已转交叶理绥, 但被哈佛燕京学社 批准的可能性极低, 并请先生就史密斯森协会已寄出的交换品收发情况报 告该协会, 否则该会将暂停寄送交换品。

Mar 1940

Room 710

1420 New York, Ave

Washington, D. C.

Dear Mr. Yuan:

I was glad to receive the other day your letter of February 22. Under separate cover I am sending you reprints of three recent efforts of mine, none of them of a very substantial nature.

With regard to the publication funds of your library, I noted your proposal to the Harvard-Yenching Institute and am referring it to Professor Elisséeff. The Institute Trustees will have a meeting early in April at which this matter may be discussed, but I have a good deal of doubt whether the members will find it possible to make such a grant as you propose. In general, we are very much restricted by the terms of our endowment, which seems to make it impossible for us to contribute to the support of government institutions.

You probably know that some shipments of books to institutes in the interior of China have been held up by the Smithsonian Institute because no report have been received of the safe delivery of earlier shipments made in 1938. If you have not already sent to the Smithsonian Institute a report showing which shipments have been received and which have not come through, I suggest you send such a report at an early date with any new directions that you may have to give as to the route which will be safest for future shipments.

I regret that I am not to be in Hongkong during the meeting of The China Foundation when perhaps you will also be in the city. However, my responsibilities here seem to make it impossible for me to leave the country at present.

Yours sincerely,

Roger S. Greene

〔The Houghton Library, Roger S. Greene Papers, Box 19, Harvard Yenching Institute〕

按：Memorandum Re the publication fund for the National Library of Peiping 似获得哈佛燕京学社的资助，参见本年 6 月 19 日赵万里覆先生函、7 月 29 日先生致王重民信。该件为录副，未注明撰写日。

四月四日

张元济覆函先生，告知将遵嘱托留意瞿氏铁琴铜剑楼藏书之近况。

前月三十日肃上寸函，并附呈新印《稼轩词》一部，托李照亭转递，计登签掌。昨日奉到三月廿五日手教，展诵祇悉。元明杂剧不得已改用排印，仰邀鉴允，甚幸甚幸。迩来纸价太昂，国产尤不易得，不得不缩省工料，冀易流通。现正筹议版式，俟决定后发售预约，当再呈鉴,并乞广为传播,无任感祷。瞿君良士遽尔下世,故交日少,殊有邻笛之感。闻其在日,曾以善本若干种质于潘氏,后货诸王寿山。寿山殁,又售与陈澄中。然瞿氏桥梓与弟为道义之交,从未言及,弟亦未便探问。其季子凤起亦甚知书且爱惜,谅不至藉以疗贫。万一有是,获闻消息,定当密报,冀副盛意。《稼轩词》为海内孤本,倚声家素所推重,遇有同好者,务乞赐以齿芬,至恳至恳。

廿九年四月四日

〔《张元济全集》第 3 卷,页 3-4〕

按:王寿山即王体仁(1873—1938),字绥珊,浙江绍兴人,清末秀才、盐商、近代藏书家。

四月八日

王重民覆函先生,告知收到前信及联大所开目录,照好《永乐大典》影本两册将直寄北平,并谈国会图书馆拟以东巴文写本之相片与平馆交换其所需文献。

守和吾师钧鉴:

奉二月二十二日手谕,并联大所开云南地质论文目录两纸,适云南书目自然科学一章正校讫,即再校对,可补此目者约可三四篇,殊有帮助。所多概在一印度杂志内,在欧洲时未见到,不日到 L. C. 一查,再为补入,即可与刘女士所作书评,一同寄昆明。

永乐大典两册,今日已照讫,共用十三美金,明后日即可直寄北平。为傅孟真所选敦煌纬书片,今日亦送照相部复制,俟照出后再详报告,并直寄昆明。

纽约美国地学会所藏 Mo-So 文,今年暑假如去纽约,当去一看,近 Quentin Roosevelt 年很幼,当是 Theodore 之孙从丽江来,新获 Mo-So 写本不少,上礼拜曾提一箱到 L. C.,让大家看,颇为得意,其经过已在 *National History* 发表。询之 Hummel,此项写本,盖欲售之 L. C.,刻正在议价,想不久可成交。又 Rock 之五千册 Mo-So 文,久已售之 L. C.,现存东方部,现 Rock 氏在 Leiden 付印之件,反为从 L. C. 所摄影矣。则全世界藏 Mo-So 文之富,刻当以 L. C. 为最矣。

生曾向 Hummel 说,拟择要为北平图书馆摄影,观其意,似欲乘此机会,与我方交换。吾师可来信一商,趁生在此,赶快办理。依生所见,我方可作为交换品者:①吾馆善本书或清代人手迹稿本之类,为其所愿要,但此类书刻在上海,不知是否易制 Photostat? ②生从巴黎及 Manchester 所摄 Mo-So 相片,易制复本。俾他方成一较完备之收藏。(Manchester 似共有百余张,巴黎 B. N. 及 Bacot 所藏,共三百余张,生处有 film,在此即可加洗。图书馆有一黑人,近作副业洗相片,不至太贵。)③生离巴黎前,为清华加洗一千余片敦煌写本;若不给清华,作为交换品亦好。请吾师斟酌示覆!

Mo-So 文写本内,重本不少,若择其善,去其复,想五千册,选一千册足矣。每片可照 Mo-So 原书六叶至八叶,一千册至多不过三千片,一片一毛计,合数不过三百美金,请吾师依此数商议。

嘱刘女士作铜器书及论文目录,伊闻之非常快乐,已开始试作。L. C. 取书很快,较在欧洲时方便多多,所恨者,小孩儿尚未寄出,时间仍有所限制耳。

丽江所存 Mo-So 书似尚不少;生返国后,极欲有机会到丽江一行,如能得一些原本,则更善矣!

余再及,即请道安!

受业重民敬上。

四月八日

今年一月以后,所上启如下,不知有无遗失也。

1940 年一月二	日	平信
十 四 日		平信
二月一	日	寄书一包(林语堂及杜威书各一册)
七	日	平信
八	日	寄账单及文稿一包
二十六日		航空信一件
三月八	日	平信
二十二日		平信

接伦敦信,£ 18-19-5 及 £ 15 已寄出。

以前购书费一百镑,俟张似旅所存 £ 20 解决后,生拟将不足之数,再一次寄上。

伦敦寄港	£ 18–19–5	又上海寄港 344.85 法郎。
又	15–0–0	留 Meuvret 付运费保险费
上海寄港	21–5–5	等 1100frs.
王重民访书费	15–0–0	又二月八日寄上之账单,一时
张似旅寄港	20–0–0	未找到存根,总数想已在一百
	£ 90–4–10	十五镑上下。

又上海寄来之二十七镑多,仍存此地,是前后买书运费,已共用去一百四十余镑矣。一切旧账,拟不日作一总结束。

通信处:Mrs. Moore, 4, East 54th street, N. Y.

Spalding, Butler Hall, 400 W. 119th street, N. Y. C.

〔国家图书馆档案,档案编号 1940–※044–外事 3–002008 和 1940–※044–外事 3–002009〕

按:20 世纪 10、20 年代,英国植物学家和探险家福瑞斯特(George Forrest,1873–1932)多次前往中国西南地区收集植物标本,其间经过云南丽江,在那里获得大量东巴经典文献,他先后将其中的 135 册售与 John Rylands Library。

四月十日

先生致信格雷夫斯,感谢寄赠 *Notes on Far Eastern Studies in America* ,并希望美国学术团体理事会考虑捐赠二百二十伏电压的缩微胶片阅读机,如蒙同意,请将该仪器寄送至美国驻昆明领事馆。

April 10, 1940

Dear Dr. Graves:

You very kindly sent us the "*Notes on Far Eastern Studies in America*" Nos. 1–3. Will you arrange to send us the subsequent issues, if already published?

In the Chinese edition of the *Quarterly Bulletin of Chinese Bibliography* copies of which we have been sending to you regularly, we would like to record the progress of Chinese studies made in the United States. I hope you will be good enough to keep us informed from time to time concerning the developments along this line.

Chinese educational institutions removed from the war zones have all settled down. We have done our utmost in providing western scientific literature to various institutions as far as our resources permitted. With the installation of the micro-film camera in PUMC, films of scientific articles will be pouring into Free China. We are now in urgent need of a reading machine to be specially built for our use (220 voltage), which will enable us to render a great service here. Since you are keenly interested in the dissemination of scientific literature, I wonder whether you would find it possible to help us obtain a reading machine which is destined to play an important part in the cultural life in Southwestern China.

Although the traffic along the narrow-gauged Yunnan Railway is congested, yet preference is always given to consignments required by foreign consulates. If you possibly can, please send the machine directly to the American Consulate at Kunming; otherwise send it to the Chinese Consulate at Haiphong and we shall send for it as soon as it arrives.

In a few days, I shall send you and also Dr. Leland the English edition of our *Quarterly Bulletin*. I hope that through the medium of this Bulletin, you will be kept posted concerning cultural developments in China.

With cordial regards,

Yours sincerely,

T. L. Yuan

Acting Director

〔平馆(昆明)英文信纸。Rockefeller Foundation. Series 300 Latin America-Series 833 Lebanon; Subseries 601. Box 9 Folder 87〕

按:此件为打字稿,落款处为先生签名,于 5 月 9 日送达。

四月十一日

姚光致函先生,告知其滞留沪上而金石字画尽遭劫掠,书籍尚存却多污残,并询《图书季刊》发行及平馆善本保存情况。

窃自敝邑金山卫失守之际,弟适有事在沪。变起仓卒,欲归不得,遂栖迟至今,忽忽已二年矣。跼地蹐天,沉闷欲绝。迩者猥承手书下逮,远劳存问,真如空谷之音,欣喜无量。舍间室庐幸存,物件荡然。金石字画,尽遭劫略。书籍则劫余尚多,惟存者多污损残缺也。敝馆亦同此情形。贵馆编印之《图书季刊》,复刊后,在沪已见到四期。国难前见至三卷四期而止,二十六年份有印行否?续有所出其他刊物尚祈随时赐阅,以解寂寥,贵馆善本书目初编所载之书,未知刻置何地?敝处颇多相同之本,亦有原向贵馆录副者,今劫余残缺诸种,异日拟托补钞配全耳。

四月十一日

〔《姚光全集》,页 372〕

王重民覆函先生,谈国会图书馆拟购麽些写本并可能以其相片与平馆交换珍本图书胶片、善本书目编纂进度等事。

11 April 1940

守和吾师道鉴:

前日早晨上一禀,直寄昆明,下午又奉到二月二十七日手谕,知吾师将有香港之行,想已平安在港矣。谨将最近所欲言者,敬述如下:①上礼拜 Theodore 罗斯福之子,携一箱 Mo-So 文写本到 L. C.,盖最近从丽江得来者,拿给大家看,颇呈洋洋自得之色。生即向 Hummel 表示,L. C.应各留一照片,冀北平图书馆亦能得一份也。嗣后又向他重提,始知 L. C.拟全数收买,正在议价,不久可成交。又知 Rock 氏所得之五千册,久已售之 L. C.矣。Rock 在 Leiden 影印之书,反从 L. C.得去照片。生即表示愿为北平图书馆择要摄影。Hummel 表示可以,但愿交换,他意颇佳。生窥知他所欲要者与我们容易拿者,(a)善本书和清人手稿或稿本之类,此类书现在沪,不知易否制 Photostat?(b)生在 Manchester 所得 Mo-So 相片百余张,在 Paris 之 B. N.与 Bacot 私人所藏又三百余片,可送伊复制片,以增益其收藏。Manchester 所得,可在国内复制;巴黎所得,生处有 film,在此找黑人加洗,尚便宜。(c)敦煌相片,生曾为清华复制一千余片,若不给清华,亦可用以交换。惟此五千余本 Mo-So 书,择要去重,值得摄影者不过一千册,每片能照该书六叶至八叶,则一千册 Mo-So 文,有三千相片足办,则一共不过用三百美金(U. S. $300)。我们预备交换品,有三百美金即可。②今日计算生所编善本书,已有四百十余篇提要,共书六千余册,此成绩总算对得住他。将来付印，拟由 L. C.与吾师，双方向罗氏基金会请求印费，作为吾馆出版物之一，前已去信将此事经过禀明，想吾师离昆明前，或已接到该信。此间工作，只善本书，今年九月以前，一定不能完，由今日观之，至早须到今日冬季。编完之后，尚须重新将提要稿覆审一次，恐亦非二三月不为功。Hummel 个人方面，亦曾向生表示，罗氏基金会此项薪水，明年恐不易再行继续，伊期望明年六七月以前，应该作完。生自量脱稿之期，总比他所期望者较早一些。生再留此一年，固然不错；但看 Hummel 情形，因编清代传记关系，早先每年许他请五六人，自去年罗氏基金便毅然不给他钱，生未来之先，他一再声明不给回国路费，生疑他欲用此款，移作聘人临时帮忙修正清代传记稿之用，故乘此声明再延长之际，一定要和他把归国路费说明；他若声明不给，无宁早和他决裂也。此间所编普通书目，汪长炳编第一次，李芳馥又全改了，再编第二次，吴光清来，又废旧重编，现为第三次矣，一书而编三次，故一个目录都无成功。照此下去，不再要十年，至少亦须五年。罗氏基金会有时来人查看情形，Hummel 则着急无钱，哈佛为敌，明年以后无着落，基金会又责其以往工作不佳。生来此以后，置一切稿件而不顾，实实在在的为他作一点工作，而他于生之薪水和归国路费上，若再从中克扣，实为无眼，故乘此机会，非和他说明不可。吾师有何方法，请便中先向其示意。季刊第四期已收到。王育伊既走，以后关于西文书，刘女士可完全担任。惟此间期刊极不易借，国内若有人担任英、法出版之杂志，较佳。天主教史料，生尚拟将欧洲文字书参考一点，期望今秋能写定，再交商务。接戴密微信，他已与 Elisséeff 写信，即说须一千美金，如见允，即与吾师去信，此款由北平图书馆保存支配。舍弟事殊感激，家用一切，由生担任，不在钱多少，在找一地方，练习作事也。生初意给他十五元，吾师付二十元，已出望外矣。大典已照好，共用十三美金，即寄北平。为傅孟真选敦煌相片，正在复制，制好寄昆明。即请钧安！

受业重民敬上。
四月十一日

……不上第一流学者，所以所得传记，在履历和……方面，……到掌故，便不能辨真假，盖所采多系二三流史料也。差误之多，拈手便可指出！然现已开始付印矣。

〔国家图书馆档案，档案编号 1940-※044-外事 3-002012 和
1940-※044-外事 3-002013〕

按："今日冬季"当作"今年冬季"。"Theodore 罗斯福之子"即昆
廷·罗斯福（Quentin Roosevelt II, 1919-1948），实为前泰德·罗
斯福总统（Theodore Roosevelt Jr., 1858-1919）之孙，非是其子，此
处王重民表述有误，但 4 月 8 日函中则为正确表述。1939 年昆
廷·罗斯福中断哈佛艺术历史系学习，出发前往云南丽江探索西
南少数民族文化。"王育伊既走"，指其赴史语所工作。该函似
直寄香港，故较之前数封理应早些收悉。末段系函件第二页抬头
处文字，但因纸张装订，部分文字无法看到，以省略号替代。

四月十六日　香港

下午四时半，平馆委员会会议在香港九龙饭店召开。蒋梦麟、周诒春、任鸿
隽、先生出席，司徒雷登列席，蒋梦麟为主席，先生为书记。因蔡馆长病故，
全体起立致哀。后由司徒雷登先生及先生分别报告平滇两处馆务，并作下
列之决议案：

（一）在本馆为蔡元培馆长立碑以志永久纪念，函请吴敬恒先生撰书碑文，
　　　并在馆中成立蔡氏纪念书藏，收集范围侧重美学。

（二）建议教育部及中华教育文化基金董事会以袁副馆长升任馆长，并取
　　　消副馆长一职。

（三）周诒春、傅斯年两委员本届任满，决议各连任三年。

（四）本委员会职员本届任满者决议各连任一年。

（五）本馆举办之职员福利储金在战事未终了以前暂时停止施行。如职员
　　　中有因事实上之需要，愿提取个人部分之储金者，可以照办，但馆方
　　　担任之储金仍继续存储，暂不退还。

六时散会。〔《北京图书馆馆史资料汇编（1909-1949）》，页 714-715〕

按：1943 年教育部正式任命先生为国立北平图书馆馆长。

四月十八日

先生致信张元济，商谈影印平馆馆藏孤本戏曲并寄上拟目，且请其留意沪
上有无珍本书籍出让情况。

前奉上月三十日及四日赐书，拜悉种种。承赠《稼轩词》壹部，厚

意隆情,至为感谢。《元明杂剧》闻不日可发售预约,尤为翘首,自当广为传播也。敝馆藏有孤本戏曲多种,颇愿委托贵公司影印发行。兹奉上拟目,即希鉴核。书均在沪,随时可以提取。窃念影印之工人经先生多年之培植,已有专长,如继续工作,亦维持其生活之一法。迩来纸价大昂,敝馆为赞助起见,可预约数百部也。又沪上如有珍本书籍出让,敝馆颇愿搜求,尚希随时电告李照亭君为感。敝处经费虽感困难,相遇有善本亦不愿为异族人捷足先登。区区微意,谅荷赞助也。

二十九年四月十八日

〔《张元济全集》第3卷,页4〕

按:《元明杂剧》最终定名为《孤本元明杂剧》,1941年8月由商务印书馆排印出版,共32册,收杂剧144种。另,此次寄上拟目应为20种,未存。

四月中下旬

先生致信刘承幹,介绍馆员前往抄录《遗民传》目录。〔《求恕斋日记》(稿本)〕

按:4月23日,平馆馆员陈贯吾持该信前往拜谒时在上海的刘承幹。

四月二十日

王伯祥致函先生。〔《王伯祥日记》第16册,页442〕

按:该函由卢芷芬转交,先生收到后即覆信,并附《滇南碑传集》印行契约草稿,5月20日送达。

四月下旬

先生致信李耀南。〔《王伯祥日记》第16册,页455〕

按:信中一事为询问王伯祥《滇南碑传集》印行办法,李耀南收到先生信后,写信与王伯祥,4月30日送到,后者表示已于本月20日径覆先生。

先生致信顾廷龙。〔《顾廷龙日记》,页76〕

按:此信于是月29日送达。

四月二十七日　越南海防

先生致信王重民,告此前欲购的 *The Philippine Islands* 已售出、请刘修业以美国出版的汉学书籍及期刊论文为对象撰写书评介绍,并请其回国后在沪负责采访、编辑、出版等事。

有三吾弟：

离港前接四月十一日航函，详悉一切。兹将各事分列于后：

一、Kegan Paul 前曾来函，谓 Robertson：*The Philippine Islands* 售价七十五磅，旋不久即售出，此书如能以五十磅购得原不算贵，但刻下中基会所发之购书费均系国币，实无余力购此书，不如仍拟影照 Micro-film 为是。国会圕现拟照馆藏方志多种，吾人正苦无书可照藉以交换，似可同 Hummel 一商影照此书，暂行记在交换账上，不必付现款也《永乐大典》亦同样办理。（L. C.所需之方志将在北平影照。）

二、刘女士介绍文已在二卷二期刊载，内中如通报关于 Stein 一文，已由翁独健撰就，故仍用翁稿，以后为避免重复起见，拟请专作美国出版之汉学杂志英法德在滇作，如 *Journal of Am. Oriental Society* 自一九四〇年出版者做起（一九三九年出版者已作），*Harvard Journal of Oriental Studies* 四卷三、四期及五卷一期已作介绍（自五卷二起），及其他汉学书籍及各博物馆关于中国美术之著述。又《云南书目》仅收到第一章，已在本期英文本刊载，第二章务希从速寄下为盼。

三、前数年传说 L. C.有章实斋手稿，务希一查究竟有否？L. C.近年购中国法律之书甚多，系由某人捐款购藏，该人姓名为何，可查阅馆务报告或询 Hummel 后示知。该馆如有明刊本方志，亦先寄下一书目。

四、林玉堂书及杜威书均已收到，杜乃扬所需之期刊单早已寄去，所需要之《四部丛刊》亦在配补中，将来由沪寄去。

五、英文《季刊》共印一千五百份，注重美国销路，以期换得外汇。本期收到后可便中一询 Hummel 之意见，此外应赠之人亦可开一单。又胡适之处中西文本均照赠，不知均收到否？便中亦请一询。牛津尤桐之号为何，亦望示知，是否为河北人。

六、令弟事据顾子刚来信，该店现有八人，已无办公余地，且每月二十元实不敷生活。又据刘树楷云，如人离开本乡，家产有被没收之虞。究竟如何，可托刘君详为一询。大约以刻下北方情形论之，在沧陷区内尚可苟安也。

七、本馆近在丽江购到 Mo-So 写本多种，将来均可为 L. C.复制一份。惟照相材料因欧战之故飞涨不已，而国币日跌，三百美金即合五千余元，不如候战事停止后再为 L. C. 复制。刻下不妨先有一交换此项资料之了解，则罗斯福此次所得者亦可为本馆留一复本，而昆明所藏者当亦代 L. C.摄一复本。本馆所购者约二元一张，在丽江买并不贵，但已日见稀少。刻下闻在宥、李芳桂均研究此文，方国瑜为丽江人，现协助本馆托人在丽江搜求此项资料。

八、为清华复制之敦煌照片仍应留交清华，一俟北平之 Micro-film 装置完毕，则吾人为 L. C.影照之书甚多，该馆决不致吃亏。至存沪之善本书，将来再陆续复制。刻下限于地址堆积如山，欲找某书颇不易也。

九、尊处为路费问题不必与 Hummel 决裂，伊之后台为 Dr. Graves，将来有成绩后可与 Graves 多多联络，渠必能帮忙。惟 Hummel 对吴光清等均不给旅费，或不愿开一新例。如明夏 1941 返国，则时间较长自可从容进行也。

十、本馆善本书集中上海，而刻下一切印刷出版亦在该处，亟须有人负责主持，何时大驾返国，拟请即在沪办事，勿须来滇也。刻下上海三人、香港三人，而新散出之珍本书之采购尚无能胜任者，故敢以此事（采访、编辑、出版）奉托也。孙述万处已收到 £ 19.1.5 及 £ 15.,惟均按港币收进。

十一、本馆近与商务订立契约续印《善本丛书》第二集，多系西南史地之书。刻下纸张奇涨，商务要求预定四百部并先付款，只得照办也。

十二、巴黎新出之《敦煌西藏文残卷目录》（Lalou 女士编），如已代购，请刘女士作一介绍登《季刊》，《季刊》请吾弟任特约编辑想荷惠允。二卷一期已收到否？

匆匆，顺颂旅安。

同礼顿首

四月廿七日，海防

〔中国书店·海淀，四册〕

按:"刘女士介绍文"应指刘修业对 *Buddhist Wall-Paintings: a study of a ninth-century Grotto at Wan Fo Hsia*(《万佛峡之佛教壁画》)所作之书评介绍,刊《图书季刊》中文本新 2 卷第 2 期页280-281。方国瑜(1903—1983),字瑞丞,纳西族,云南丽江人,民族学家、历史学家;1923 年赴北京求学,翌年入北京师范大学预科但因病休学返乡,1928 年重回北平入师范大学,1930 年考入北京大学国学门,同时在两校上课,1935 年 9 月回抵云南,翌年起在云南大学历史系执教。

五月三日

张元济覆函先生,表示商务印书馆颇愿承印平馆藏《也是园元明杂剧》及馆藏其他孤本戏曲,请告知预约部数以便核算成本、购纸开工。

> 守和仁兄阁下:
>
> 敬复者,前日奉到四月十八日手教,展诵敬承。影印《也是园元明杂剧》因王君翁近日染恙,尚未将目次编定,故一时未能发售预约。然现时已着手排版矣。蒙示拟将贵馆珍藏孤本戏曲选定二十种,委敝馆印行,藉以维持手民生活,又以现时纸价大昂,俯赐赞助,并定预约数百部,具征盛意,极愿遵行。当即函达李君照亭,即日派人前往检查全书叶数,并察看原本印刷情形。昨据复称,书箱度存他处,开检手续颇繁,约须半月方能检齐云云。故工料价值尚未能估定奉复。既承挚爱,敝馆自当奉行。惟未知贵馆可预定若干部? 可否先祈见示,俾得确计售价。一俟领到全书,核定价格,即行陈报,并乞拨发预约全价,以便购纸开工。此实时势所迫,故敢为此不情之请,既荷玉成,想不责其冒渎也。专此奉恳,顺颂台祺。
>
> 二十九年五月三日
>
> 〔《张元济全集》第 3 卷,页 4〕

按:"王君翁"即王季烈,该目次大约在 6 月中下旬初步编定。①

五月四日

顾廷龙致函先生。〔《顾廷龙日记》,页 77、87〕

按:先生收到后即覆,于 6 月 13 日送达。

---

① 肖伊绯《新发现张元济、王季烈校印〈孤本元明杂剧〉信函辑录》,《文津学志》,2017 年,页 46。

五月六日

下午,先生路遇吴宓,交在港为其购物明细,并还余款越币四元。〔《吴宓日记》第 7 册,页 165〕

五月八日

先生致信阿博特,感谢其仍将寄送平馆、中华图书馆协会的书刊发往香港,因该渠道转运要比海防便利许多,并请史密斯森协会就此情况刊登启事以便美国各机构和个人了解现状。

May 8, 1940

Dear Dr. Abbot:

I am much indebted to you for your letter of March 29th.

We are happy to learn that consignments to Hongkong have not been suspended. On behalf of Chinese Libraries, I beg to express to you once more our sincerest appreciation and heartfelt thanks for the most valuable assistance which the Smithsonian Institution has rendered to us.

Hongkong serves as a convenient center for the reception and transshipment of books. Cases of books reforwarded from Hongkong to Southwestern China reach Kunming much quicker than those delivered at Haiphong. For these reasons, all packages and boxes addressed to the National Library of Peiping as well as to this Association should continue to be sent to Hongkong. This association sends the urgently needed books by book-post to the interior, so that they reach Kunming ten (days) or two weeks later from the date of posting. If your Institution has occasion to issue any statement on this subject, you will perhaps be good enough to make this point known to those individuals and institutions who are interested in sending material to institutions situated in Free China.

This Association will be very glad to reforward the two packages of books sent by Prof. Harold S. Quigley of the University of Minnesota as soon as received.

With renewed thanks for your kind co-operation and assistance,

Yours sincerely,

T. L. Yuan

Chairman,

Executive Board

〔中华图书馆协会（冯平山图书馆转）英文信纸。Smithsonian Institution Archives, Records, 1868-1988 (Record Unit 509), Box 1, Library Association of China, Hong Kong〕

按：此件为打字稿，落款处为先生签名，于6月5日送达。

五月九日

阿博特覆函先生，感谢平馆香港办事处将错寄的交换品发往西班牙，并表示愿意支付相关邮费。

May 9, 1940

Dear Dr. Yuan:

I have your letter of February 21 and beg to thank you for your courtesy in mailing to Spain the packages for that country which were inadvertently included in a consignment of publications sent to the National Library of Peiping.

The institution desires to refund to you the amount of postage incurred in the matter and therefore is enclosing herewith an international money order for ＄1.73, the equivalent in American currency of the amount expended by you.

The enclosed voucher should be signed in the place indicated and returned to the Smithsonian Institution in the enclosed envelope.

Very truly yours,

C. G. Abbot

Secretary

〔Smithsonian Institution Archives, Records, 1868-1988 (Record Unit 509), Box 1, National Library, Peiping〕

按：该函寄送香港，此为录副。

五月十日

午后，徐旭生、袁复礼同赴平馆，与傅斯年、先生晤谈。先生表示郭伯恭既然无法速来此任事，故已找他人替代，请即通知其本人，并告于道泉归国日

期推至七月;此外,先生谓如欲购买飞机票,可请中央银行代为设法。〔《徐
旭生文集》第 10 册,页 1090〕

　　　　按:本日晚些时候,徐旭生与李书华谈,后者表示在中央银行无熟
　　　　人,但可询北平研究院秘书长徐廷瑚①。

五月十一日

先生致信 J. Periam Danton,告知由香港转运书刊至西南各省较由越南海防
中转的方式要迅捷许多,希望其将这一情况转达给美国愿意援助中国图书
馆的机构。

　　　　　　　　　　　　　　　　　　　　　May 11, 1940

Dr. J. Periam Danton, Chairman

Committee on International Relations,

American Library Association,

c/o University of Cincinnati Libraries,

Cincinnati, Oh.,

U. S. A.

Dear Dr. Danton:

　　With regard to the forwarding of books to China through the
Smithsonian Institution, I have just received a letter from Dr. Abbot
stating that consignments to Hongkong have not been suspended, but
shipments to the Chinese Exchange Bureau in Chungking have been
withheld owing to the congestion of traffic along the Yunnan Railway.

　　Hongkong serves as a convenient centre for the reception and
transshipment of books. Cases of books reforwarded from Hongkong to
Southwestern China reach there much quicker than those delivered at
Haiphong. For this reason, we have requested the Smithsonian Institution
to continue to send all packages and cases to Hongkong. This Association
sends the urgent needed books by book post to the interior, so that they
reach Kunming ten days later from the date of posting. If your Committee
has occasion to issue any statement on this subject, will you be good

―――――――――――

① 徐廷瑚,字海帆,时应任北平研究院秘书长。

enough to make this point known to those individuals and institutions who are interested in sending materials to China?

I enclose a list of institutions (41 colleges and universities □□□□) to which we have been distributing material sent over by American libraries. In view of the vastness of the need, further donations of books and periodicals will be gratefully appreciated.

Materials intended for public libraries that have been destroyed by the war, such as those of Shanghai, Hangchow, Tsinan, Nanking, Hankow, etc., are being kept temporarily in Hongkong and will be distributed to them as soon as China is freed from the invaders.

You will no doubt realize the stimulating effect which the American donation of books has produced to the cause of education in China during her present emergency, and you may rest assured that in contributing books to various Chinese libraries, your Committee is doing something of permanent value which no time would destroy. I shall be grateful to you indeed if you could convey our heartfelt thanks to your colleagues attending your annual conference at Cincinnati.

With renewed thanks for your valuable assistance and with best wishes for the success of your Conference,

Yours sincerely,

T. L. Yuan

Chairman,

Executive Board

〔中华图书馆协会(冯平山图书馆转)英文信纸。The American Library Association Archives, China Projects File, Box 2, Books for China 1938–1940〕

按:此件为打字稿,先生对信文有细微修改,落款处为其签名,另附各高校院系名单 5 页。

五月十四日

王重民致函先生,告国会图书馆拟购东巴文写本数量及为傅斯年影照文献等事。

守和吾师道鉴：

　　久未奉手谕，预计吾师在港已公毕，刻或已返昆明矣。阅报知日寇前日又炸昆明，幸损伤不重。深望吾师在昆明或在旅途，诸多保重为祷！此次基金会开会结果，于吾馆经费，能增加一点否？生等在此均好，暑假期内，或将赴波士顿小住，为看彼处藏书及博物馆书画。王韬手稿，闻纽约市立图书馆有人赠藏一些，过时或择其要者摄影。Hummel 将于六月初离华盛顿，任暑期讲演，大约八月中旬方能回来。生之归国旅费一节，不知将来应如何向伊表示？想吾师于六月以前，必有信致伊，并指示生如何办法也。国会图书馆经费今年拟增加，Hummel 为东方部所提很多，其在计画中之买善本书，照敦煌相片以及与吾馆交换 Mo-So 文等用费，均在此新加经费中，如不能通过或不能全数通过，则 Hummel 不能一一如愿以偿。其 Mo-So 文写本，生已调查清楚。经 Hummel 手所买 Rock 的共五百本，采访部买多少，伊不知，尚有一箱未买定今存馆内。小罗斯福送来者，约千余册，拟每册出价一元半至两元，尚未十分说定。又有影片约近千册，不知从何处照来。上回所谓五千本者，是讹传，实则不足彼数。为傅孟真所照相片，已制讫，即别件挂号寄吾师，再转傅先生。照费四元三角，连寄费不过五元，此款请吾师向傅先生索。上礼拜又到胡适之先生家吃饭，他很健康，惟那天偶牙痛。周鲠生仍寓他家，未回国。伊称近接教育部信，称已饬令各大学校将出版物各赠国会图书馆与其他各著名大学一份，冀和他们交换。盖此仍是钱端升和周氏所主张；钱为联大，周为武汉大学也。但直至今日，在此尚无结果。其原因即由找新馆长交涉，伊个人虽表示赞同，而未与各主任接洽，故不能实现也。去年所说之 Pirkis 女士，不知今年能否有机会，为她找一位置？她教书作其他事都可，钱多少与名义如何，不计也。她刻仍在伦敦我大使馆当书记。此间陈参事闻有小误，胡先生已调他去做领事，新调来驻英使馆一等秘书刘凯作参事。生对于敦煌之整理，日来无进展，仅将题跋写定为第二辑，已寄北平付印。此辑即遵吾师意，用吾馆名义出版，印费由生自付。对于天主教史料，到有一点小成绩。缘生所注意者，为明末清初，而在馆所编书籍，十之九为明末刊本，乘编目机会，辑出材料不少，多可与欧洲所得者相印证。（此步工作，陈援庵先生已作一点。）此全部工作，将来可成①欧洲所藏联合书目;②明末奉教九华人集;③明清之间天主教史料(上谕、奏疏及其他文件等);④即在欧洲所复抄及在此从各明清人记载中所得者,编为笔记体,冀巨细并收,以与前三编相印证。兹不管将来能否印刷?此四书能辑成,总约略可为三四百年来此公案作一结账。联合目写定者已有四分之三,若能在暑假期内写成所余四分之一,则今年之底,或可寄呈吾师矣。专此,即请钧安!

受业重民敬上。

五月十四日

刘女士不久寄上之介绍稿,计有:

Harvard Jl. of Asiatic Studies, vol. 5, no. 1, 1940

Jl. of the American Oriental Society, vol. 60, no. 1, 1940

Chinese Bronzes of the Shang through the T'ang Dynasty, N. Y. 1938

按:"刘凯"似应作刘锴,待考。本日王重民亦写信与傅斯年,应附在与先生信之后,由先生转交。该信内容如下,

孟真先生:

　　携来在伦敦所摄敦煌相片,已择其有关古纬书者六种,为覆制相片一份,别件寄上。摄影费＄4.30,寄费＄.43,共＄4.73。用重民个人名义,照费减半,故无收条;为一收条而花＄4.30,谅先生亦不爱也。其已寄北平者,请依向觉明先生所编目,选出后仍可在北平设法。至 Pelliot 3636 一卷,重民虽为作跋,然并不重要,因直接引用书不多也。此卷已为北平图书馆与清华大学各制相片一份,携来此地暂存,因费钱多而无多可取,故未为复制。谨列所复制卷如下:

S. 5614	《日暝占第卅六》等	六叶(原书册叶装)
S. 6015	《易三备》	八叶
S. 3326	《解梦及电经》一卷	十叶
S. 1339		三叶
S. 6261	《白泽精话图》	一叶(与 P. 2682 为同书)
S. 612		十一大张

专此,即请著安!

后学王重民上。

五月十四日

〔国家图书馆档案,档案编号 1940-※044-外事 3-002014 至
1940-※044-外事 3-002016〕

五月十七日

先生致信教育部出版品国际交换处昆明办事处,告知率馆中同仁前往编目
英国捐赠图书的时间安排。

　　径启者:敝处近接战时征集图书委员会四月十六日公函,内开关
于英国捐赠图书编制总目录一案,经四月十三日第十三届执委会决
议,委托敝人负责办理等因。兹定于本月二十日(星期一)上午八时
半,率同馆员前来贵处从事编目,约一星期即可完毕。用特函达,即希
赐以便利为荷。此致
教育部出版品国际交换处昆明办事处

　　　　　　　　　　　　　　　　　　　袁同礼谨启
　　　　　　　　　　　　　　　　　　　五月十七

　　　　〔国立北平图书馆(昆明柿花巷)用笺。台北"中央图书馆"档案,
　　　　档案编号 051-185〕

　　按:此信应为文书代笔,落款处为先生签名。

五月十八日

先生致信王重民,谈《苗疆图说》影印、刘修业所撰书评应以美国出版品为
限等事。

　　有三吾弟:

　　三月八日及二十日两函均收到。兹将各事列后:

　　(一)《苗疆图说》王钧撰仅十九叶,可收入《西南文献丛刊》之内,
请撰一跋文,连同照片一并寄下,以便付印。

　　(二)张似旅已到滇,该款已告其送交王景春处,以便拨付各款。

　　(三)《云南书目》第二章尚未到,恐须候至九月出版之第三期方
能付印。

　　(四)刘女士今后请专作美国出版之新书及期刊之介绍,以免重
复。清代族谱已请杨殿珣作一论文。兹请将国会图书馆所藏之族谱
开一详细书目寄大同书店,托其转交贾芳,因贾芳现作一最完备之族
谱书目也。

（五）Hummel 旅费事可相机进行，不可从之过急。为两馆合作计，应彼此和睦相处，万勿发生恶感，至要至要。

（六）孟真不日到滇，致彼之信当即转交。

余再函，顺颂旅安。

同礼顿首

五，十八

〔中国书店·海淀，四册〕

按：贾芳，字志洁，1929 年 7 月入馆，20 世纪 40 年代后期担任平馆会计。信尾有"寄王重民先生"一语，为先生亲笔。

五月中下旬

先生致信竺可桢。〔《竺可桢全集》第 7 卷，页 362〕

按：此信于 22 日送达。

五月二十二日

王伯祥致函先生，内为《滇南碑传集》印行契约。〔《王伯祥日记》第 16 册，页 482〕

按：先生代表平馆在该份契约上签字，寄回开明书店，于 6 月 15 日前送达。后，平馆将《滇南碑传集》稿本 34 册寄出，7 月 13 日送达开明书店。

五月二十四日

下午三时，吴宓赴平馆送稿并访先生，不值。〔《吴宓日记》第 7 册，页 172〕

先生致信毕安祺，感谢佛利尔艺术馆寄来所藏铜器照片，并告知兄长袁复礼近在西南联合大学任教。

May 24, 1940

Dear Dr. Bishop:

I am most grateful to you for your letter of March 22nd and for your courtesy in referring to Mr. Lodge our request for photographs of Chinese bronzes.

The photographs which Mr. Lodge has so kindly sent to us have been duly received. Will you forward our acknowledgment for us? I am sure that you will convey to him our grateful appreciation much better than we can express in our letter.

I thank you for inquiring about my brother. He is now joining the staff of the National Southwest Associated University located at Kunming after having spent a year of exploration at Sikong. He wishes me to send you and Mrs. Bishop his best regards.

I have often had the occasion to recall our associations both at Peiping and Washington. I am glad to hear that interest in China is much higher, but I am afraid that the war in Europe will force people to forget the needs of China.

With kindest regards to you and Mrs. Bishop,

Yours sincerely,

T. L. Yuan

Director

P. S. I am sending you a copy of our Bulletin.

〔平馆（昆明）英文信纸。Smithsonian Institution Archives. Field Expedition Records, Box 11 Folder 18, Yuan, T. L., 1929-1940〕

按：Sikong 即西康。此件为打字稿，落款处签名及补语均为先生亲笔。

五月二十五日

饶培德覆函先生，询问长沙代存甲骨的去留问题。

Hunan Bible Institute

Changsha, Hunan, China

May 25, 1940

Dear Mr. Yuan:

Thank you very kindly for your letter dated March 11, and handed to me by Mr. K. Y. Li. Thank you, we are able to continue with our work in Changsha, and general conditions in and around the city are very good for which we are grateful.

We enjoyed the visit from Mr. Li and I believe he has now returned to you. While he was here, we urged him to get in touch with the authorities regarding the skeletons moved from Peiping to here by the Academia Sinica. We should like very much to dispose of these "bones", as they may be a source of difficulty at some future date. Have you anyway to bring this matter to the attention of the authorities? We should be most grateful if you would inform us to whom we should send word to.

Thanking you and with kindest regards,

Sincerely yours,
HUNAN BIBLE INSTITUTE
Charles A. Roberts

〔台北"中央研究院"历史语言研究所傅斯年图书馆,"史语所档案",李 45-28〕

五月二十七日

竺可桢覆函先生。〔《竺可桢全集》第 7 卷,页 365〕

先生致信傅斯年、罗常培,请校阅清末江标《笘誃日记》稿本二十七册。〔《郑天挺西南联大日记》,页 277〕

> 按:江标(1860—1899),字建霞,江苏苏州人,光绪朝翰林院编修。罗常培将此事转托郑天挺,参见其 6 月 2 日日记。

五月二十八日

中华职教社昆明指导所与中振会昆明难民总站,为救济昆明各大学贫困学生,在平馆成立昆明市大学生抄书管理委员会,推查良钊、熊庆来、龚自知、喻兆明为名誉委员,并推何崇杰、苏健文、先生为委员,通过该会组织大纲及抄书进行简则,决定会址暂设于职业指导所内,第一期自即日起至六月一日止。抄书时间为每日上午九时到十一时,下午二时到五时,在云南大学内抄写。〔《民国日报》(云南),1940 年 5 月 29 日,第 4 版〕

> 按:喻兆明(1901—1988),字鉴清,江苏南京人,职业教育学家,金陵大学毕业,后留学美国,获加州大学教育学硕士学位,时应任中华职业教育社驻昆明办事处主任,《民国日报》(云南)错排为"喻北明"。何崇杰,时应在振济委员会工作。① 苏健文,时应主持职业指导所工作。

王重民致函先生,谈在美近况并表示愿回国搜集民语文献。

> 守和吾师道鉴:
>
> 久未奉手谕,殊以为念。想吾师已由港返昆明,基金会开会结果

———————————

① 《振济委员会工作概况》,1940 年 3 月,页 1。

如何,在报纸上未公布,再来信时或能示知一二。

生等情形如故,他亦无消息可陈,谨于 *New York Times* 上剪下消息两节,附呈。

图书季刊新二卷一号已收到,睹近来刊物之盛,成绩之佳,颇动归思,尤望到云南后赴丽江一行,若能得到一批 Mo-So 写本书,实为平生一大幸事。又吴子明兄未接到季刊,想系未寄赠;然生与伊同在一处,寄生而不寄吴先生,未免有点令人难为情,亦寄伊一份,似较好!

专此,即请钧安!

受业重民上。

五月二十八日

〔国家图书馆档案,档案编号 1940-※044-外事 3-002017〕

按:信中所提《纽约时报》(*New York Times*)剪报,未存。

五月三十一日

先生致信 Marshall C. Balfour,请求洛克菲勒基金会调整拨付赞助款的方式。〔Rockefeller Foundation. Series 601: China; Subseries 601.R: China-Humanities and Arts. Vol. Box 47. Folder 390〕

六月二日

刘修业致函先生,感激提携并告知在美近况。

守和馆长钧鉴:

近接西文《图书季刊》,《云南书目》蒙先为刊载,至为欣感。此目修业在巴黎时即全部清抄,但以重民懒为早日校阅,竟至第二章未能如期寄到,殊觉歉憾。修业初来美时,因一切不惯,颇以为苦,近来稍觉熟悉,家事之余,尚有时间自修。且屡蒙来书鼓励,使修业研究之兴趣,更觉浓厚。现已将国会圕关于铜器书均已录出,所余惟如期刊单篇论文,方正着手。大概此暑期中,铜器一目,总可先成。此后拟再收集关于中国其他古艺术书目,及中日满洲事件目录,想亦邀蒙赞许。近在家,除作美国出版之汉学研究书籍及期刊之论文介绍外,则专编国会圕所藏族谱提要,并拟为分析研究。如能完成,当再寄呈。至于族谱书目,日内当赴圕抄录一份,直寄贾芳。其余一切情形,已详重民信。专此,敬请钧安。

刘修业敬上

六月二日

〔国家图书馆档案,档案编号 1940-※044-外事 3-002024〕

六月四日

史蒂文斯致函先生,告知洛克菲勒基金会及学术团体理事会已请纽约公共图书馆制作一系列有关戏剧书籍的缩微胶片并购置较为经济的阅览机组件,将由姚莘农携带回国,建议先生与之见面并了解如何使用这一设备。

June 4, 1940

Dear Dr. Yuan:

I am writing to acknowledge for Mr. Graves your letter of April 10 regarding the need of a reading machine in the National Library at Kunming. A few weeks ago, we arranged with the New York Public Library to produce a set of film books on the subject of drama and also to purchase economical reading machine materials for construction in finished form as models for other uses in your country. The particular use of the material now ready is to assist Mr. Yao Hsin-nung, who is returning to China this coming month for work in the normal college for teaching of drama. I anticipate that the next step for you is to see him on arrival and to arrange for common use of the equipment if that is possible, and at least for use of the patterns to construct reading machines. I shall expect to be informed of the outcome of your talk with him, which should come sometime in midsummer.

I am reporting this reply to Mr. Graves. With best wishes,

Cordially yours,

David H. Stevens

〔Rockefeller Foundation. Series 300 Latin America-Series 833 Lebanon; Subseries 601. Box 9. Folder 87〕

按:Yao Hsin-nung 即姚莘农(1905—1991),笔名姚克,安徽歙县人,生于福建厦门,毕业于东吴大学,后致力于外国文学作品的介绍和翻译。此函寄送云南,并抄送给格雷夫斯。函中所谈缩微胶片及设备之后续情况,可参见《图书季刊》(英文本)新7卷(页59)。

六月六日

先生致信傅斯年,告知《图书季刊》寄赠如常,史语所所须敦煌卷业已由北平录副寄来。

孟真吾兄：

手示敬悉。《图书季刊》每期均按期寄赠，内中一卷三期业已绝版，但贵所同人多有不愿保存者（如济之、思永），或愿奉让也。兹接Roberts来信，录副奉上，如何之处，希酌夺办理。顺颂大安。

弟同礼顿首

六、六

又北平自卷子内抄来《类林》，据云系代贵所录副者，兹一并奉上。

〔台北"中央研究院"历史语言研究所傅斯年图书馆，"史语所档案"，昆7-105〕

按：Roberts即饶培德。《类林》为唐初私撰小型类书，作者是唐初宰相于志宁之子于立政，该书原本已佚，近代考古发现的西夏文本和敦煌手抄本等成为后世研究该书的珍贵资料。

是年夏

先生致信孙楷第，请其查明在平敦煌卷子中关于古谶纬者究有几种，并查非敦煌经卷中有无可印之书。

子书吾兄：

孟真借抄敦煌卷子，关于古谶纬之部分，因上次寄来目录已送沪，手下无书可查。拟请查明在平者究有几种，如有请录副寄下为荷。孟真所开五种，二六八三号、二六三五号、二六八二号、二九六四号、三六三六号皆据伯希和写本目，仅一部分，当不只此五种也。前托在非燉煌经卷中详查有无可印之书，结果如何？希示复。贵体想已复原，尚希随时留意是荷。专此，顺颂著祺。

同礼顿首

十一日

〔《中国国家图书馆藏敦煌遗书》，南京：江苏古籍出版社，1999年，第1册卷首〕

按："上次寄来目录已送沪"或指《国立北平图书馆现藏海外敦煌遗籍照片总目》之一部分，该文送上海排印，后刊登于《图书季刊》中文本。

六月十日

张元济覆函先生，已按先生与王云五之约将平馆珍藏孤本戏曲暂缓印行。

守和先生大鉴:

敬复者,奉五月二十日惠书,展诵敬悉。委印贵馆珍藏孤本戏曲,已由敝馆派员与李君照亭接洽,并将各书页数详细检查,其中有若干种纸渝墨黯,制版须特别加工者,另具清单附呈。异日分集尚拟将叶数多寡分别均配,敬祈察核。惟据敝馆驻港办事处来信,谓此书已由王云翁与执事商妥,俟《善本丛书》第二集出书之后再行影印,并承同意等语。现拟将此书暂行阁置,待至可以付印之时,再将工料价值估计奉达,想邀鉴允。专此布复,顺颂公绥。

二十九年六月十日

〔《张元济全集》第3卷,页4〕

按:"《善本丛书》第二集"即《国立北平图书馆善本丛书》第二集,该集并未面世。

Marshall C. Balfour 致函先生,告知已收到纽约转来的 1939 年财务报告,并请先生寄去平馆迄今为止的季度报告及财政年度报表。

June 10, 1940

Dear Mr. Yuan:

Referring to my letter to you of November 14, I regret that due to certain mails going astray, we have only just now received from New York a reply to our enquiry regarding the procedure to be followed in respect of your accounts. It is now confirmed that your financial reports should be rendered to this office. In this connection, it will be sufficient for you to continue to render us quarterly reports as heretofore, with an annual financial statement at the end of the year, together with a narrative report on the work accomplished.

We are attaching in duplicate our regular financial report form, your accounts with us up to the end of March 1940, in accordance with statements provided by you. One is for the period July 1936 to July 1937, and the other, for convenience at the moment, combines your three quarterly statements to date. As your next statement would complete your financial year, this will be an assistance in compiling the annual statement. If these statements are found to be in order, please sign and return one copy to this office. Additional blank forms are sent herewith.

You will note that we have carried forward the balance of LC $ 6,959.28 from your July 1937 report. As we have not yet received any statement from you showing its expenditure, it naturally remains a charge against you on our books. If such accounting was sent to New York, will you kindly provide us with a copy?

We have noted in previous statements such items as "Peking Union Book Store- $ 500"; "Shanghai Office- $ 100"; "Hong Kong Office- $ 300". After consultation with your Hon. Treasurer in Shanghai, I understand that in the case of the Hong Kong office, this represents a fixed allowance or payment, whereas the others are deposits or advances. There is no question that such advances are fully expended, but from an auditing point of view, I believe that in the future, only actual expenditures should be reported and that in the case of advances, they may be reported in the summary as "Outstanding Debits to be accounted for".

Very truly yours,

M. C. Balfour

〔Rockefeller Foundation. Series 601: China; Subseries 601.R: China-Humanities and Arts. Vol. Box 47. Folder 390〕

六月十二日

J. Periam Danton 覆函先生, 表示其将在*A. L. A. Bulletin* 撰写文章, 呼吁美国各图书馆将捐赠中国高校图书馆之图书寄往史密斯森协会。

June 12, 1940

Dear Mr. Yuan:

I am sorry that your good letter of May 11, which I was delighted to receive, arrived too late for presentation at the Cincinnati conference. It is good news to learn that you are carrying on and especially that you have been enabled to send books on to the interior. I am, today, preparing a statement for publication in the *A. L. A. Bulletin* urging our libraries to continue to send materials for the Chinese college and university libraries to the Smithsonian Institution.

With best wishes, I am

> Sincerely yours,
>
> J. Periam Danton, Librarian
>
> Chairman, Committee on International Relations

〔The American Library Association Archives, China Projects File, Box 2, Books for China 1938-1940〕

按:该函寄送香港,此件为录副。

六月十二、十四日

王重民覆函先生,谈先生前信嘱托之事和其在美近况。

守和师鉴:

奉四月二十七日在海防所发手谕,所指示种切,生将次第遵办,谨将已办讫者,一一奉闻。与 L. C.交换相片事,又已向 Hummel 谈过,Robertson: *Philippine Islands* 欲照 Micro-film 亦已说明。伊称 Robertson 亦曾在 L. C.服过务。又说明我方所要,偏重 Mo-So 文相片。惜 L. C.此笔款,至今日还未通过,恐七月以前不能通过了,则最近伊亦无款为我方照相片。方国瑜代买 Mo-So 写本,甚好。方君为生在师大同学,研究小学声韵,颇有成绩。毕业后因在北平不能作事,致不得在学术上多发展,此人诚实坚苦,有机会可重用。云南书目第二章早已寄上,想吾师返抵昆明后,即可见到。英文本季刊第一期已奉到,刘女士见之,又感谢,又快乐。所作绍介,又重了不少,兹将未重者寄上。好在此种工作,俾伊多读书,重了不用,亦无多大关系。新出斯文赫丁所著书,正在作介绍。此后划分疆域,只作美国所出新书及杂志,想不至再重了。现因有小孩不便,暑假拟不他去,且可省一些旅费。假期中,生可隔日看一次小孩,则刘女士可有多时间去搜罗美术书目,其"吉金"一类,拟八九月间,将目录编成。章实斋史籍考稿,L. C.没有,系讹传,生前寄上一短文,批评姚名达目录学史,曾言及章稿由毕沅归谢启昆,由谢归潘世恩,潘聘许瀚、刘毓崧等重修,未刻而毁于火,想已不在人间矣。L. C.藏明本方志目,容编讫再寄呈。捐款购法律书之人,即在本馆,为:Mr. John T. Vance, Law Librarian, L. C. Washington, D. C.,英文季刊已请 Hummel 看,可赠之人,伊开一单,谨另录一份转上。Hummel 已去 Colorado 担任暑期讲演,今年八月中旬方能返华盛顿。尤桐字琴庵,河北完县人。近接来信,拟于今年回国,现地中海已不通,不知能否回去。李云亭有意要他仍回师大,他不愿教英文,愿作点较深的研究,或教一些有趣味的古英文,或比较语言学,因此科目,非师大所有也。伊曾来信,嘱生致信吾师,为伊在联大或中央研究院看看有无机会。生上礼拜为此事,曾给胡适之先生一信。生近接家信,知家乡麦秋颇有丰收希望,家父拟于麦秋后,全家移平居住。乡间实可苟安,或较在北平少麻烦;但有时打游击,不幸遇到,即时丧命,一二年来,只高阳一县,已大小打过四五次,死于非命者,已二千余人矣。生所以催促赴平居住者以此。老人家总是贪田园之利,因请吾师为新民位置一事,以转移其心,故只要有事可学习,不在得钱多少也。到平后用费,生在此稍节一点,即够全家之用矣。命生返国后在上海作事,闻之极为快乐,感荷,所嘱采访编辑等事,均生所乐为,至于吾馆书目,生亦殊有总编之志,上海如有书架,可将书箱打开,暇中便可先从善本作起也。至于归国路费,即遵嘱待机会,同时努力作成绩,待今年年终或明春,即可开始交涉也。(近欧美拟联合将古本书制Micro-film,Hummel 想从中取利,拿此中款来洗敦煌相片。吾人在巴黎照时,每片拿 60 生丁税,此亦借口要路费一机会。)前寄上一王韬手写苗氏图说说明,善本丛书第二集中,未审曾决定收入该书否?该书一因在外国,一因讲苗民,一因王韬手写,正好乘机印入也(全书只十余叶)。嘱生作馆刊特约编辑,非常感谢。余再及,即请道安!

生重民上

六月十二日

……出城外,则危险性较未迁者反大。生尚有 50 卷 Microfilm 留 B. N.,手钞稿件一大批留戴密微家,亦可告安全矣。

十四日又及

〔国家图书馆档案,档案编号 1940-※044-外事 3-002018 和 1940-※044-外事 3-002019〕

按:末段系函件第二页抬头处十四日补语,但因纸张装订之故,部分内容无法看到。

六月十四日

顾廷龙覆函先生。〔《顾廷龙日记》,页 87〕

六月十五日

Marshall C. Balfour 覆函先生,告知已按照先生申请调整了洛克菲勒基金资助拨付方式。

June 15,1940

Dear Mr. Yuan:

Replying to your letter of May 31, requesting that you may be allowed to revise the method of payment for the next two years under the Foundation's appropriation RF 36072 to the National Library of Peiping, so that they may be as follows: －

For 1940－41……. $ 8,000.00 ($ 2,000 each quarter)

1941－42…….   1,500.00 ($ 375 each quarter)

Inasmuch as this is in agreement with the limit stipulation laid down by our New York office, this revision of payments to you is approved.

Very truly yours,

M. C. Balfour

〔Rockefeller Foundation. Series 601: China; Subseries 601.R: China-Humanities and Arts. Vol. Box 47. Folder 390〕

六月十八日

吴宓至平馆访先生,先生劝其勿往西北,谓"抗战期中,一动不如一静。他年再大举可也。"〔《吴宓日记》第 7 册,页 179〕

　　按:本年吴宓屡接西北大学函件,欲聘其为文学院院长兼外文系主任,先生与众人皆劝其勿往,只有贺麟和李赋宁表示赞同。

六月十九日

赵万里覆函先生,谈《善本丛书》选目、南下沪苏购书及雇人抄书等事。

守和先生:

　　正驰念间,忽奉一日、四日赐书,敬悉一一。《善本丛书》所收两《图经》、《桂林郡志》、《滇略》及四库本《桂故》、《滇略》(《滇略》馆藏明刻、存六卷,故据库本补配)共十八册,均于旬日前由司徒先生亲来取去,由渠转寄商务,乞勿念。四库本因此间材料太贵,无法景照,故临时由子刚作主,与其他善本一同托司徒寄沪,较为省事。《桂胜》、《桂故》同是张鸣凤撰,此二者缺一不可,可视为一书《四库提要》地理类即以此二书连贯书之，视为一书也，如此则加入沅公之《百粤风土记》，仍与原数十二种相符。沅公之宣德本《桂林郡志》亦内阁大库书，可补馆本之缺，连同《百粤风土记》共四册，均已借到，即交大同寄商务（由照亭先生收转）。尊函已面交沅公，沅公于丛书拟目颇为称许，盖均为绝无仅有之孤本也。《大典》辑佚书蒙哈佛燕京社补助印费，闻之无任感奋。公之厚爱于里，可谓至矣，自当努力将事早日完成，以符雅望。兹定下星期启程赴沪，即在子刚处支取旅费二百元，到沪后拟住青年会，并拟于下月初赴苏州一行沪苏间往返甚便，因此半年该地出书最多且最佳，平估之在该地者约七八家，且有二三家拟在沪开分店以便收货。今年书市之盛与书体之贵，可称造峰造极，请即函告钱存训兄筹付书款五六千元暂以此数为度，最好能于里到沪时筹付，以免错过机会，以便在苏沪各肆选购，如遇私家大批之书，自当随时函告，再定进行办法。今年方志、政书价格大涨，大半系受燕大景响。燕大曾三次出单征志书，洋洋洒洒近二千种，几乎将《千顷目》及吾馆《善本目》全数抄入，损人而不利己莫此为甚，其愚诚不可及。估人乘机要价，康熙志须四五百元或二三百元，道咸以下亦可值百余元，至明志则无论矣。闻此次燕大过节购书费支出约五六万元。里拟九月初返馆，在沪拟从事抄写《大典》辑佚资料，仍拟录用书记一人，月薪四十或五十元，该款请嘱李先生代付，请即函告李先生准予提用明志总集、别集等书即在科学社楼上检阅，并请予以玉成为幸。慰堂收书单太简，就大体论似远胜以前所收许博明一单也，单中所列瞿氏书以黄校《渑水燕谭录》来单误作《渑山漫谈》最佳。去秋凤起曾来函索六百元，里去函还价三百余，未得覆，今乃知已归慰堂矣。刘世珩玉海堂之《玉海》，元刊元印素有盛名，然吾馆藏本乃元装，视刘本尤佳，故不足艳羡也。叶公之款子刚已收到，新购第五批各书颇多佳本有明嘉靖年蓝笔抄《赵氏宗谱》十大册最佳，附图亦明人所绘也，详目另函寄上，乞鉴核为祷。《糖霜谱跋附校记》须借某君藏原书一勘，故迟迟未寄，现已校竣，与书目同寄，亦请察及。匆匆，敬请道安。

里再拜

六月十九日

〔国家图书馆档案，档案编号 1946-※039-采藏 11-005022 至 1946-※039-采藏 11-005025〕

按:"书体"当作"书价"。

六月二十一日

先生致信王重民,谈《苗疆图说》影印及为李俨查阅美国所藏中国算学书目事。

有三吾弟:

《苗疆图说》可用影印,请作一跋,连照片寄沪"上海亚尔培路五三三号李照亭先生"。日内由平寄上《北平各圕中文算学书联合目录》,凡 L. C. 及美国其他各圕所藏中算书为此目所不载者均请记出,李乐知先生托调查也。寄来稿件已收到,惟 White: *Tomb Tile Picture* 已在一卷三期发表矣。美国会图书馆寄存之《大典》是否 Gilbert Reid 寄存? 此人在国务院服务,便中可一访也_{其父即李佳白}。天主教史料馆中可有款付印,即希整理后寄沪,可分集出版也。顺颂大安。

同礼顿首
六月廿一日

日本或谋取安南,故滇越路有停驶之说,以后寄信可寄沪或寄港,当可用航函转滇也。

〔国立北平图书馆(昆明柿花巷)用笺。中国书店·海淀,四册〕

按:Gilbert Reid 即李佳白本人,其子李约翰(John Gilbert Reid)曾为《图书季刊》英文本撰写过一篇书评,他认为对于那些渴望获取更多有关中国历史参考书目的学生,该刊是一份极为重要的参考资料。①

先生致信纳尔逊·洛克菲勒,请其赐予所藏铜器照片及收藏目录,并寄赠《图书季刊》英文本。

June 21, 1940

Dear Mr. Rockefeller:

In spite of my long silence, I have often been thinking of you and Mrs. Rockefeller. Without a stenographer, letter-writing seems to be a lost art.

---

① Reid, John Gilbert. "Review." *Pacific Historical Review*, vol. 4, no. 1, 1935, pp. 93-94.

I trust your baby has grown up considerably since I saw him last. I shall be delighted indeed if you would send me a snap-shot of the whole family which I shall treasure very much.

Scholarly work has been carried on steadily in China despite of the war. One of the things in which we are now engaged is the study of Chinese bronzes preserved abroad. In order to facilitate our work, we have been collecting photographs of Chinese bronzes. Since you and your distinguished parents have a unique collection of Chinese art, I hope you will be able to arrange to send us the photographs of the bronzes which are preserved in your distinguished collection.

When I was in New York last time, you told me that a catalogue of your collection was in preparation and I have been wondering whether this catalogue has ever been published. If so, we should like so much to receive the copy for review in our *Quarterly Bulletin of Chinese Bibliography*.

Sometime ago, I sent you two copies of our *Quarterly Bulletin*. I hope you will present one copy to your parents. Through the medium of this Bulletin, you will be kept informed of our cultural activities carried on in the midst of war.

With kindest regards to you and Mrs. Rockefeller,

Yours sincerely,

T. L. Yuan

Director

〔平馆（昆明）英文信纸。Rockefeller Foundation, Nelson A. Rockefeller Personal Papers, Box 22 Folder 173〕

按：此时，纳尔逊·洛克菲勒的通讯地址为 810 Fifth Avenue, New York City, U. S. A。此件为打字稿，落款处为先生签名。

王重民覆函先生，表达想回国效力之心并述近况。

守和吾师：

奉六月六日手谕，并拟购书单一纸，知已安返昆明。吾师此次留香港较久，想或因基金会开会之故，此次开会情形，对吾馆如何？经费有无增减,至以为念! 昆明交通虽较沿海大城为不便,然观馆务进行颇积极,工作情形,似较在平时为紧张。生去国已久,很期望于明年回国,追随吾师之后,在国内去努力! 不知吾师意见如何? 再来信示知一二,甚感! 吾馆与联大颇能合作,惟蒋慰堂居于京师之下,时获借中央名义来捣乱;最近若多方联络二张(伯苓、仲述),使知其作用,然后在京师方面,多有一二主要机关作朋友,则蒋君之鬼计或稍敛。刘衡如先生近在何处? 于振寰似已转入中央图书馆,此仅据协会会报猜想,不知然否? Pirkis 女士事,已向云大谈及否? 结果如何,望示知! P. S. King 已将能找到之 Parliament papers 寄昆明。别有生等所开草目,另由巴黎寄出,冀便检查。其 P. S. King 不能找到者,再令馆中一人,将草目打清,或更作详细一点,然后寄 Stationery Office 再查一次,或更再能找出一点。

　　吾师最近身体如何? 以及环境如何? 再来信时,略述一些,至感! 专此,即请道安!

　　　　　　　　　　　　　　　　　受业重民上。

　　　　　　　　　　　　　　　　　六月二十一日

　　　　〔国家图书馆档案,档案编号 1940-※044-外事 3-002021〕

六月下旬

先生致信竺可桢。〔《竺可桢全集》第 7 卷,页 386〕

六月

先生为陈梦家所编《铜器图录》撰写序言。〔《海外中国铜器图录》,上海:商务印书馆,1946 年 5 月〕

　　按:该书后于 1946 年出版,题为《海外中国铜器图录》第一集。

《图书季刊》英文本刊登先生撰写的编者按(Editorial Comment)。〔*Quarterly Bulletin of Chinese Bibliography* (New Series), Vol. 1, No. 2, pp. 117-122〕

　　按:该文分七部分,依次为 Looking Ahead、Scientific Reaserch and National Defence、American Help for Chinese Libraries、Oil for the Lamps of China、500th Anniversary of Printing、*Yung-Lo Ta-Tien*、Friends of the National Library。

七月二日

王重民致函先生,谈《巴黎敦煌残卷叙录》第二辑出版后赠售问题及在法征集铜器拓片诸事。

　　守和吾师道鉴：

　　　巴黎敦煌叙录第二辑正在印刷，想七八月间可出版。共印三百五十本，拟存一百本，暂不卖，一百本交北平图书馆，一百本交莱薰阁代卖。二十五本由生赠人，二十五本由北平图书馆赠人。每册印费约合两元多，将来每册或要定价五元。一俟印讫后，即命刘树楷送 125 册交大同书店，吾师拟如何支配，请与顾先生去信。将来卖完后，一百册之款归生，二十五册不要钱。未审吾师以为如何？

　　　接杜乃扬信，知拟在巴黎征求铜器拓片；此事公家所藏好办，私人所藏恐不易。公家如 Louvre、Guimet、Cernuschi 三博物馆所藏最富，照片均易得。有 Vandier 女士初为 Cernuschi 职员，现在 Louvre 给东方部主任 Georges Salles 作秘书，在国立博物馆联合出版处（相片包括在内）亦非常熟，托她不论真假，凡该三博物馆所藏，均洗一份，颇为容易，或更可打一八折，所费并不多。（生将其底版均看过一次，仅买关于敦煌者，其他未及。）吾师有意买，生可给她写信。此女士颇聪明，明后年可去中国研究，她家很有钱。尚未接到巴黎失陷以后的消息。所存 Micro-films，已由一位小姐捎来；前天已接到，完全无缺损。其敦煌卷均移往巴黎城外，恐反到易出危险。生正待消息。巴黎失陷前，识人都平安，惟据罗都尔说，谢礼士在明星逝世，其致死原因不明。想在中国或已有较详消息。向达拟购之书，W. Campbell: *Formosa made the Dutch*，久绝版，最难找。闻北大有一部，打几部或叫人翻印都可；但如已遗失，或请 L. C. 照一份。B. Laufer:*Sino-Iranica* 吾馆似有之，在美亦不难买也。日来香港非常严重，若仅封闭而不打仗，则吾馆所存书籍可无虞，但情形如此，亦无法再退矣。抗战三年，至今日似已达最紧急时期，英国若不软化，或能于抗战前途大有益也。专此，即请钧安！

　　　　　　　　　　　　　　　　受业重民敬上。

　　　　　　　　　　　　　　　　　七月二日

英文本图书季刊，请赠

Prof. J. Cowley, School of librarianship, University of London, London, W. C. 1, England

Miss Susan L. Pirkis, 57, Kidbrooke Park Road, London, S. E. 3, England

〔国家图书馆档案，档案编号 1940-※044-外事 3-002022 和 1940-※044-外事 3-002023〕

按：Louvre、Guimet、Cernuschi 即卢浮宫、吉美、赛努奇三家博物馆。Vandier 女士应指 Nicole Vandier-Nicolas(1906-1987)，法国汉学家，主要研究中国书法、绘画；Georges Salles(1889-1966)，法国东方学家，曾赴伊朗、阿富汗等地考察，时确任卢浮宫亚洲艺术部主任，后任吉美博物馆馆长。W. Campbell 即 William Campbell (1841-1921)，英国长老会传教士，中文名甘为霖，19 世纪后期在台湾地区南部传教，曾创立全台第一所盲人学校，其书全称为 *Formosa Under the Dutch: described from contemporary records, with explanatory notes and a bibliography of the island* ，1903 年伦敦 Kegan Paul 初版。该信西文部分，王重民拼写错误较多，笔者均已订正。

吴光清、王重民致函先生，建议留平馆员开始编撰普通古籍书目。

守和先生道鉴：

敬启者，光清、重民窃以吾馆普通书籍，搜罗之富，为全国第一。奈至今尚无书目印行，国人有欲作参考者，不得取作标准，遂不得不依八千卷楼、国学图书馆等书目。况国家前途，正未卜将来何若？北平等处，若不能恢复我完全自主权，则此普通书目之编印，似尤为目前急务。二三年前，似已着手预备，未审近来成绩如何？

想自先生南下，平馆工作情形，未免懈怠。为今之计，若能将工作分为若干小组，就各小组，分派在平能通此类书籍之一职员任编目，其较大之组，则一人主之，一人副之，而更以张庚楼或竟以委员会中张、顾、王三君总其成，则事分而责专，其进行必速方志、书目两类已有单本，再稍稍补充即可。至于印刷一节，不必求美观，只求整齐与便于应用。若能用六开版，半页两竖栏横印如邓编参考书目，用四、五、六三号字体，每类附以书名及人名索引，以利检查，所费必不多。值兹平馆人员，无他事可作，集全力以竟此业，正大好机会。任事职员，不必以编目组为限，其善本、写经、采访等组，当均能任此，即其他各组，有能胜此任者，亦未始不可指派。光清、重民会谈之次，有见于此事为目前急务之一，辄陈下意，敬请察鉴！专此,即候近安!

吴光清、王重民仝拜

七月二日

〔国家图书馆档案,档案编号 1940-※044-外事 3-002026 和 1940-※044-外事 3-002027〕

七月六日

先生致信教育部陈礼江,寄呈平馆《组织大纲》等文件,请其代转行政院,以利平馆申请补助。

逸民司长尊鉴:

奉读六月廿九日赐函,祗悉一一。本年一月敝馆请求大部补助经费三万元,蒙鼎力赞助,业经呈请行政院核示,院方对于敝馆情形不甚明了,嘱将概况及本馆《组织大纲》即日奉上,以便分送参考足征。援助盛意,公私均感,兹将该件奉上即希台察,经费核定后并盼早日汇寄,以济燃眉,无任企祷。耑此,敬候道祺。

弟袁同礼顿首

七月六日

附:本馆《概况》二份

《国民政府教育部、中华教育文化基金董事会合组国立北平图书馆办法》二份

《国立北平图书馆委员会组织大纲》二份

《国立北平图书馆组织大纲》二份

〔中国第二历史档案馆,教育部档案·全卷宗 5,国立北平图书请拨员工学术研究补助费经常费有关文书,案卷号 11616〕

按:该信为文书代笔,落款处为先生签名。

七月上旬

先生致信王伯祥,商洽开明书店出版平馆馆藏碑目。〔《王伯祥日记》第 16 册,页 552〕

按:此信寄送平馆驻沪办事处,7 月 19 日陈贯吾将其转交王伯祥。

七月十日

傅斯年致函先生,询问徐森玉今后打算并谈史语所托平馆购书等事。

守和吾兄左右:

兹奉陈数事于后：

一、目下港越交通阻断,森玉先生不能返,应作何计划为宜? 希有以见示。

二、敝所存香港之邮包,现在既无法转滇,拟请函知贵馆香港办事处暂为代存。其后有续到者,并请代存。

三、利玛窦地图,书价三十磅余,敝所实无力购入,方命之处,尚希见谅。此书敝所暂借一阅,如贵馆需用时,祈示知,即行送上。此书原发单兹奉还,即请察收是荷。

专此,敬颂时祺。

弟傅○○谨启

〔台北“中央研究院”历史语言研究所傅斯年图书馆,“史语所档案”,昆7-96〕

七月十一日

先生访冯至,送《亚洲导报》五册,请作介绍文。〔冯至《昆明日记》,页35〕

按:《亚洲导报》即 *Asienberichte*,原名应为 *Berichte des Asienarbeitskreises*,《图书季刊》中文本新2卷第3期确有该刊《亚洲报告》的一篇简短介绍,文章署名“培”,应为冯至所作。

七月十二日

先生致信傅斯年,告知平馆意欲请徐森玉往上海协助购买古籍及史语所在港存放书籍事。

孟真先生大鉴:

奉读七月十日赐书,敬悉一一。港越交通梗阻,森玉先生既一时不能返滇,而久留岛上所费亦颇不赀,敝处拟请其赴上海物色旧籍,斐云业已抵沪,自可商同办理也。但未审森玉先生肯速驾否? 渠拟将木简以航邮寄滇,似觉不妥,未识尊意如何? 贵所寄港之邮包,此时无法转滇,已函嘱代为保存,请释廑念。至利玛窦地图既无需要,拟请便中掷还,因其他学术机关尚拟购置也。尚覆,敬候著祺。

弟袁同礼顿首
七月十二日

〔国立北平图书馆(昆明柿花巷)用笺。台北“中央研究院”历史语言研究所傅斯年图书馆,“史语所档案”,昆7-97〕

按:该信为文书代笔,落款处为先生签名。

七月十四日

朱希祖致函先生,谈国史馆事,并附该馆筹备委员会消息三则。〔《朱希祖日记》,页1203〕

七月十七日

冯至访先生,送书报介绍三篇。〔冯至《昆明日记》,页35〕

七月十八日

教育部陈礼江致函先生,告知已将先生所呈各件转递行政院。

> 守和吾兄大鉴:
>
> 　接奉七月六日手书,诵悉壹是,寄来贵馆概况章则等件,顷已由部转呈行政院核示,并请将补助贵馆经费,迅赐拨发,俟奉令准,当再函奉闻。尚覆,敬候公绥。
>
> 　　　　　　　　　　　　　　　　　　　弟陈礼〇启
>
> 〔中国第二历史档案馆,教育部档案·全卷宗5,国立北平图书请拨员工学术研究补助费经常费有关文书,案卷号11616(1)〕

按:后行政院训令,照准国立北平图书馆廿九年度补助费由。

七月二十六日

冯至致片先生。〔冯至《昆明日记》,页35〕

七月二十九日

先生致信王重民,谈刘修业稿件、平馆经费困难、孙楷第欲离平赴美诸事。

> 友三仁弟:
>
> 　接五月十四、廿八、六月十二来书,并刘女士所作介绍二篇均收到,谢谢。刘女士所作较前大有进步,惟内中关于铜器目录已在二卷二期发表。兹将已进行者另钞清单寄上,以免重复。另外列有三种因书尚未寄到,均请刘女士写介绍可也。中基会因庚款停付,刻下向政府借款度日,再过数年庚款又期满,更感困难。因之兄颇愿在一、二年内赴美筹款,惟旅费无着,颇难如愿耳。Hummel所开的应寄赠《季刊》之人均已赠送过,此外如有新进之学者,并盼随时留意。吾人拟换取美金补助出版费,故销路侧重美国(共印一千五百分但交换的较多)。王韬《苗氏图说》决定付印,请将照片及跋文径寄上海李照亭君是荷。天主教史料馆中亦可付印,近哈佛燕京社补助本馆美金三千元,可用

之专印尊辑各书。《云南书目》自第三期起继续排印（第二期因印《北堂天主教藏书考》一文，故未印），惟该书目尚缺末二章，请速补寄，大约须分三次印完。铜器目录请注重抗战以后国外出版之杂志论文，可查 Art Index 等，此间已有者俟打好寄去，以免重复。尊处旅费事俟返国有期再代为接洽，想今冬或明春接洽不致太迟。大约请彼付旅费颇难如愿，如托其在罗氏基金设法，或多付一、二月之薪水则较容易。Mo-So 写本已购到数百本，每本仅合国币一元，较影照美国所藏须用美金者便宜几二十倍矣。Pirkis 女士可请其专编辑西文《图书季刊》，但此间随时有被炸之虞日人或在安南登陆，而生活日昂，每月非有三百元不能维持生活，不如俟大驾返国后再请其到沪一同办事，因编辑工作均须集中于上海也。晤胡大使时可询邮寄伊之中西文《季刊》均收到否？寄吴子明之中文本《季刊》亦照寄，但恐时有日人扣邮件之事，故寄国外者往往收不到也。寄傅孟真之古纬书迄今尚未收到，邮件之慢令人焦灼。国会图书馆关于敦煌写本之收条误寄北平，兹特挂号寄上，请由尊处妥为保存，将来即凭此据取回原物也。子书来信谓北平生活太昂，所得报酬不易维持，并愿赴美留学，拟托胡大使为之设法，晤面时请一询能否设法。兄曾劝其来滇，联合大学可请其为国文系教授，但渠不愿长途跋涉，奈何刻下中基会各董事均不愿在沦陷区内多用钱，故北平方面仅能维持现状，不易发展。向觉明下年亦在联大任课，前托代购 Laufer: *Sino-Iranica* 一书，已由英伦购到，不必代买矣，嘱为转达。匆匆，顺颂旅安。

　　　　　　　　　　　　　　　　　　同礼顿首

　　　　　　　　　　　　　　　　　　七，廿九日

　　尤桐之事，顷已函询有无著作出版，大约联大、浙大均可设法。近日谣传胡大使有调回专任中央研究院院长之职一说，遗缺由顾少川或宋子文补充，未识确否？

　　　　　　　　　　　　　　　　〔中国书店·海淀，四册〕

　　按："Laufer: *Sino-Iranica* 一书"全称为 *Sino-Iranica: Chinese contributions to the history of civilization in ancient Iran with special reference to the history of cultivated plants and products* ，1919 年芝加哥初版。

七月三十一日

斯文·赫定致函先生,告知将寄赠两种书,如能够顺利送达昆明则会寄送全部科学著作。

Stockholm 31, 7. 1940

Dear Doctor Yuan,

Looking through heaps of letters on my table I find yours of March 22, and don't feel sure whether I have replied it or not. Montell and I have many times spoken of our wish to send you all our publications, but always we have found the political situation so complicated and hopeless that we have postponed all sorts of sending. However, as you say the communication between Stockholm and Kunming is open, we will make an attempt beginning with the American edition of "*The Wandering Lake*" and the Swedish edition of "*Chiang Kai-shek Marshal of China*". The American edition of the latter is not yet published but will appear in the Fall and be immediately sent to you. Copies of our scientific works will be sent to Kunming – you may be quite sure of that.

I hope that the situation in the world will soon be cleared up so far that scientific work may go on undisturbed as before. Every day we are thinking and speaking of China and I am always dreaming of the day when I may come back and pay you a visit again.

Wishing you and all that is dear to you every possible prosperity and with best greetings from Dr. Montell and from me to you and your dear Brother and your Families.

I remain ever yours very sincerely,

Sven Hedin

〔韩琦教授提供〕

按: The Wandering Lake 通常译作《游移的湖》,1940 年 E. P. Dutton & Co.初版;Chiang Kai-shek Marshal of China 即《蒋介石传》,其美国版由 The John Day Company 出版。此件为打字稿,落款处为赫定签名。

七月

《国立北平图书馆现藏海外敦煌遗籍照片总目》编就。〔《图书季刊》新第2卷
第4期,1940年12月,页609-624〕

> 按:该目刊登时,虽注明为先生所编,但据本谱中往来书信,似应
> 为孙楷第负责编写。该目所辑者只限于卢沟桥事变前收到的王
> 重民、向达等人所摄伯希和、斯坦因携走的敦煌遗籍的照片,依经
> 史子集为序,每种分列所藏地、编号、书名、所存章节、照片数量等
> 信息,后该文别出单行本。

八月二日

王重民覆函先生,谈欲编近代来华西人辞典等诸事。

> 守和吾师道鉴:
>
> 　　恭奉六月二十一日手谕,领悉一是。S.133卷,不是世说新语,乃
> 瑚玉集,正与古逸丛书本所残存部分相合。生日内当别致觉明一信。
> 生手录易三备,当可借与傅孟真,拟稍整理,再寄出,并致覆信也。苗
> 疆图说照片,即遵命寄上海。吾馆有款印天主教史料,生闻之极为快
> 乐,当即赶快整理,大约今年年终,即可寄上海付印,冀生回国时能印
> 完,则正好在那时作一索引,附印于书后。缘二三年前,生以曾来吾国
> 之各国使节、教士、商人以及游历考察等人,往往自起一中国名并字
> 号,为使含有华文意义之故,往往与译音不合;近来编译诸书,多不能
> 还其本来名字,甚有一书或一章之内,或遵用其华名,或另为译音,殊
> 为参差,使读者不易捉摸为一人或二人,故有编一此类小辞典之意。
> 将其原名、华名并字,以及生卒、履历、国别、著述等,略作记述,而举其
> 传记于后作参考。(传记有单本者举单本,无单本者举杂志,又如通报
> 卷末往往于一有学问人死后,略志哀悼,并述其履历,则记明在何年何
> 页。)斯事虽体大,然能因前人已成之业,则初步工作,亦可能作到相当
> 好处。如天主教、耶稣教各教士,各有专书,已稍可不大费力。生所作
> 天主教目录,拟于各教士之下,虽不详举其事迹,欲将 Pfister、Cordier
> 诸家所作,记明卷及页数,俾便参考,盖亦含索引之意在内也。年来只
> 管搜罗鸦片战争以后之使节商人等;今正好赶作此一部分,则并可乘
> 机一详校天主教目录,此步工作校完后,此目录即可寄沪付印矣。生
> 编此小辞书一节,尚未禀明吾师,请赐教正;想吾师于最近三二十年中

外人,知之最悉,所曾来往之人,随手记出,便可于生帮助不少也。依生经验,公使领事之类,在民国以前,与中政府来往文件,多用华文,故亦署华名,然无专书记其事,故较难。(公使因清史稿有邦交志,Couling书内有原名表,尚不难对出。)至于海关邮政人员,想有专书,惜生尚不知耳。能期之数年,此书可成为一有用之书也。White之墓砖图录,不刊出那篇介绍文很好,因说起来便可引起一些争论。秦代文化,国人素不注重,而近来外人大为研究,遂不顾时代,不管地域,而统名之为"秦",附和者固多,持异议者亦有人在,如伯希和、高本汉等,对此尚无发表,不知此两大家以为如何也。汉简不知何故未印,适之先生称不久即可运来华盛顿,寄存L. C.,命生点查。此事想系香港有危险之故;如能在美付印,工价虽贵,艺术方面可较美观,未审罗氏基金会能否帮助一点钱否? 存巴黎之film,前由一法国小姐带来,伊所乘之船(Champlain),归途中已沉于英国附近。此次一切东西,完全无损,实足庆幸。刘女士在医院割Tonsil,今日下午或明日上午即可出医院。此一两月来,伊专力收古器物书,如铜器、石刻、玉、瓷、古钱以及漆器等,其图画、法书等,则暂时未及也。铜器一部分,十月中可完成。其流出海外者,以瑞典与美国为多,盖以瑞典为皇太子所好,又逢新出土者多,而美国则有钱也。(英国亦不少。)生休暑假约四礼拜,下礼拜一(八月五日)将仍到L. C.办公。此二十余日中,将所抄敦煌词写定。全唐文附辑唐末五代人所作词,仅得八百余首;生共钞出二百余首,去重覆,共得151首,几可比旧有者多五分之一,亦可算一收获。去年曾以抄稿示适之先生,伊很感兴趣,并说写定后伊愿作一序,拟不日送伊一阅。中央研究院院长已举出否? 是否即胡先生当选? 再有暇,拟写定"全唐诗拾补"。此两书不很大,或可交商务印行也。很希望今年在L. C.能多做一点自己想作的事。去年一年可说为他做事太多了。专此,即请钧安!

受业重民上。

八月二日

Hummel请求之特别购买中国书费,闻原请求十万美金,今已通过三万,并有派伊亲赴中国购买之说。伊现有钱,吾馆拟要之Mo-So等照片,即可向伊要;否则此款用完,伊又无以应我矣。北平方面现已开始为彼方照相片,则吾人亦可开始向伊索交换品矣。

〔国家图书馆档案,档案编号 1940－※044－外事 3－002032 至
1940－※044－外事 3－002034〕

按:Pfister 即 Louis Pfister(1833－1891),法国耶稣会士,中文名费
赖之,清同治六年(1867)来华,曾长期负责上海徐家汇藏书楼,
编著有《明清间在华耶稣会士列传》。Couling 即 Samuel Couling
(1859－1922),英国传教士,中文名库寿龄,"书内"应指 *The
Encyclopedia Sinica*,1917 年初版。

纳尔逊・洛克菲勒覆函先生,告知其母已将所藏中国铜器捐赠给大都会博
物馆,其父收藏的瓷器业已撰成目录限量发行,是否寄赠平馆须等其父归
后才能确定。

August 2, 1940

Dear Mr. Yuan:

I was glad to receive your interesting letter of June 21st and to know
that you are well and still carrying on your important work despite the
tragic circumstances under which the world is struggling today.

I appreciated your thoughtful inquiry concerning our child and am
delighted to tell you that we now have five children and that they are well.

My mother, Mrs. John D. Rockefeller, Jr., had quite an extensive
collection of Chinese bronzes, however, she has recently given her entire
collection to the Metropolitan Museum. I will get in touch with the curator
and see whether he has photographs which he might send to you.

The catalog which was being prepared at the time of your last visit
was a catalog of my Father's collection of Chinese porcelains. This catalog
has been completed and was printed in a limited edition. Unfortunately, at
the moment my father is out of town, however, I will get in touch with
him and ask his permission to send you a copy.

In the meantime, may I take this opportunity to express appreciation
for your thoughtfulness in sending the two copies of your *Quarterly
Bulletin* .

Everyone in this country admires the courage and determination with which your nation has resisted invasion. The world is indeed in a tragic state.

With very best personal regards.

Sincerely yours,

Nelson A. Rockefeller

〔Rockefeller Foundation, Nelson A. Rockefeller Personal Papers. Box 22 Folder 173〕

按：该函寄送昆明，此件为录副。

八月上旬

先生致信王伯祥，请其酌情减印平馆馆藏碑目，并重新估算定价。〔《王伯祥日记》第 16 册，页 597〕

按：此信由陈贯吾转交给王伯祥，于 8 月 22 日送达。当日，王伯祥与章锡琛、徐调孚等人商议，即告陈贯吾调整后的最低价格。

八月十三日

平馆向教育部陈立夫呈文一件，题为《为呈覆本馆移出图书及现有职员人数请予核转由》，具先生名并钤印。

案奉八月三日大部社字第二五四四四号训令，内开"案查关于追加补助该馆经费两万元一案经由部呈请行政院核示并具报该馆概况去后，兹奉指令内开：'呈悉该馆昆明部份究竟移出图书多少职员若干人未据明申述仰即查明具报此令'等因，合行令仰迅速具报以凭核转此令"等因。奉此。窃职馆于民国二十四年一月奉令将所藏中西文善本书籍分批陆续南迁，计已运出者：1.善本甲库全部（即清以前善本书）2.善本乙库全部（即清以后善本书）3.唐人敦煌写经全部 4.内阁大库舆图及参谋本部之地图 5.金石墨本及楚器全部 6.西文善本及专门杂志全部，当时南运经过情形及各项书目曾经呈部备案。惟内阁大库舆图因寄存南京故宫博物院保存库内，首都沦陷以前该院文物西迁未及代为运出，以致因之损失。职馆自迁滇办公以来，职员三十余人，每月经费仅四千元，目前昆明物价高涨，困难情形早在大部洞鉴之中，兹奉前因理合具文呈请大部俯予核转指令祗遵。谨呈

教育部部长陈

国立北平图书馆副馆长袁同礼

民国二十九年八月十三日

〔中国第二历史档案馆,教育部档案·全卷宗5,国立北平图书馆
请拨员工学术研究补助费经常费有关文书,案卷号11616(1)〕

按:后行政院发布训令"核定国立北平图书馆廿九年度补助费由"。
先生撰写Report of the use of the Rockefeller Foundation's grant for
development of Library Services in China, July 1939~June 1940。〔Rockefeller
Foundation. Series 601: China; Subseries 601.R: China-Humanities and Arts. Vol. Box 47.
Folder 390〕

八月十九日

先生致信王访渔、顾子刚,谈缩减平馆经费及馆员辞职补贴办法,并谈《图
书季刊》供稿寄送办法。

查中基会自庚款停付后,维持原有之事业已感困难,因之本馆经
费屡次请求增加,迄今未能如愿。弟虽竭力设法维持全体人员之生
活,但物价日昂,心余力绌,为今之计似须将组织缩小,始能应付目前
难关。近闻尊处提议凡于八月间离馆者,可得五个月之薪金,实于公
私两有裨益,如在此信寄到十日内以后离馆者,亦可特予通融付至本
年年底,以资救济。明年一月势须另筹办法也。

此间同人均将入川,故对于《图书季刊》之编辑势难兼顾,应请以
示诸人,随时供给稿件,由杨殿珣君负责汇集于每星期六,径寄上海陈
贯吾君,俾该刊按期出版,无任企盼。

〔《北京图书馆馆史资料汇编(1909-1949)》,页725〕

按:此为抄件。

八月中旬

教育部函聘先生担任平馆代理馆长。〔《大公报》(香港),1940年8月17日,第4版〕

按:蔡元培馆长去世后,馆务仍赖先生主持,后经平馆委员会推
荐,并由教育部发布正式聘函。

八月二十五日

徐旭生、徐森玉同访先生、乔无忝。〔《徐旭生文集》第10册,页1107〕

按:乔无忝,其父乔曾劬、其母高公浶,其弟乔无遏时在空军服务。①

———————

① 中国近代口述史学会编辑委员会编《唐德刚与口述历史:唐德刚教授逝世周年纪念文集》,页
190-194。

八月二十六日

上午,曾昭燏与胡小石来访,晤先生。〔《曾昭燏文集·日记书信卷》,页102〕

　　　　按:是日,曾昭燏先往云南大学拜见胡小石,后二人同往见先生。
　　　　虽首次见面,但曾昭燏对先生印象甚佳。

八月二十八日

上午,吴宓至平馆访先生,并为改英文稿件。先生劝其用邮包寄书至浙江
大学(贵州),并言竺可桢将于九月十四日至十七日在昆明,或可乘其汽车
前往浙江大学。〔《吴宓日记》第7册,页218〕

九月二日

先生致函平馆驻沪办事处,指示处理诸多馆务。大意如下:

　　　　一、本馆近呈准政府由财政部拨发生活补助费,凡留沪办事同人,
每人每月可领生活费国币二十元,现一月份至七月份者业已领到,计
每人可得壹百肆拾元,应在存款内拨付,如存款不敷即暂在《图书季
刊》账上借用,一俟八月份收到后再行通知。

　　　　二、科学社租房事,近由蒋、任、傅三委员致电科学社,由馆补助二
千元,本馆则有三人借地办公,如仍无效,则只有另租办事处所,存该
社之西文书应点交该社代为保管,惟中文书应一律移入震旦。

　　　　三、中基会不日送来徐家壁、高棣华福利储金,共洋九十三元四角
六分,请收入存款账。

　　　　四、香港办事处日前汇上国币六十七元,应收入《图书季刊》账内。

　　　　五、如移出科学社,则本届中秋节赏勿须付给该社听差,付给震旦
及中基会听差者应在存款内拨付。

　　　　六、《直斋书录解题校记》为《图书季刊》专刊第二种(第一种为孙
楷第之《也是园杂剧》),印刷费可在《季刊》专款内拨付。

　　　　七、六月十五日交此间邮局寄开明书店《滇南碑传集》稿本,该店
迄无复音,请电询是否业已收到,已否付排从速函告。

　　　　八、前由宁波寄滇之《图书季刊》二卷二期迄今未到,如未挂号恐
难寄到,快邮代电纸如有存者,请每次航信内附寄二三张。

　　　　九、二卷三期《季刊》英文目录随函附上,在本期内可将二卷一、
二期目录及二卷四期目录登一广告,中国文化服务社广告已登过二
次,广告费迄今未付,自三期起暂行停止该社之广告。

十、前购之颜色请寄香港办事处,候便携滇,如分量不多可托孙洪芬先生携渝,即存中基会渝办事处,候购者前往走取。

〔《北京图书馆馆史资料汇编(1909-1949)》,页727-728〕

按:此次同科学社之争执似以先生之法暂时解决,参见本谱是年11月5日之记录和翌年2月17日信函。《直斋书录解题校记》由傅增湘撰,先后登载于《图书季刊》新第3卷第1-2期合刊、第3-4期合刊,并未以专刊形式印行。此为抄件。

九月四日

先生致信王重民,请其将拟印行之天主教史料稿件范围略作说明,并告知居延汉简已从香港寄美。

友三吾弟如晤:

关于天主教史料,馆中可以印行,拟请先将此书之范围及内容写一节略,便中寄下。又汉简一箱近由香港寄交胡大使,将来或须寄存于国会图书馆。森玉先生有一详函致胡大使,可取阅也。《云南书目》尚有二部分未承寄下,请径寄钱存训先生可写上海九江路花旗大楼四〇四号 Room 404 中基会转,刻下滇越路阻有日内登陆之说,要信请改用航邮或寄钱君,由渠用航邮寄滇亦可。顺候旅安。

同礼顿首

九月四日

关于汉学书籍之介绍,嗣后均寄钱存训君。

〔国立北平图书馆(昆明柿花巷)用笺。中国书店·海淀,四册〕

九月七日

傅斯年覆函先生,告知宝蕴楼照片及赵万里代钞王国维校本《水经注》已交陈梦家。

守和吾兄:

上月三十日大示敬悉。宝蕴楼照片已遵嘱送交陈梦家君,祈勿念。又弟前借赵斐云君过录王静安校本《水经注》一部十六册,拟请吾兄暂代收存,原书亦已交陈君处。

弟斯

按:原件无落款时间,暂系于此。该件同页附致北平图书馆函之抄件,应为傅斯年亲笔,函文如下,

　　敬启者,前贵馆袁馆长提议,以贵馆所藏利马窦地图及其他最近出版之东方学书籍若干种交换敝所书籍十三种。兹已于昨日(六日)将上项书籍送桃源村贵馆办公处,托由陈梦家先生转交,谅荷收到。则贵馆之利马窦舆图等亦希早日掷下,以便装箱运川,无任感盼。此致
北平图书馆

　　　　〔台北"中央研究院"历史语言研究所傅斯年图书馆,"史语所档案",李 10-11-15〕

九月十一日

先生访冯至并送书,请其作介绍文字。〔冯至《昆明日记》,页 35〕

　　按:时,冯至患流行性感冒。

九月十三日

平馆向教育部呈文一件,请酌情补发迁馆入川费用,具先生名并钤印。

　　前奉钧电,嘱职馆迁入川境地当于本月二日将迁移计划由快邮代电呈请鉴核候示遵行。嗣由中国银行交来大部汇下之迁移费九千九百四十九元二角三分,业经照收,除将收据另寄外敬祈察核。此次迁移承蒙大部发给迁移费用,至为感荷。惟职馆现存昆明书籍以及抗战史料将及四百箱,国内外陆续寄来刊物尚不在内,现在交通困难,人工物价无一不昂贵异常。最近迁川之国立机关所发职员川资均包括眷属在内。职馆在昆职员三十余人,假定三分之二随馆迁川,所需川资即在万元以上,书籍运费以及留设工作站等项费用,依然无着,可否仰恳大部俯念迁移困难之事实,酌加迁移费一万元以利进行,不胜感祷之至。谨呈
教育部部长陈

　　　　　　　　　　　国立北平图书馆代理馆长袁同礼
　　　　　　　　　　　民国二十九年九月十三日

　　　　〔中国第二历史档案馆,教育部档案·全卷宗 5,国立北平图书馆请拨员工学术研究补助费经常费有关文书,案卷号 11616(1)〕

　　按:"钧电"应指 8 月 22 日电。此请后被批准。

晚,先生在曲园招宴,冯至等受邀前往。〔冯至《昆明日记》,页 35〕

　　按:吴宓因事未往。①

---

① 《吴宓日记》第 7 册,页 229。

九月二十四日

先生致信平馆上海办事处,指示馆务各节注意事项。大意如下:

一、财政部拨付八月份之生活补助费,留沪同人每人国币二十元,请在存款内拨付。

二、本馆委托董作宾先生编《甲骨丛编》共十集,须自购纸,照附上之样子约需二百万叶(每集二百叶,十集二千叶,每集拟印壹千部,需纸如上数)。请详细估计约需纸若干,并请各种不同之纸样各检一份寄下,以便定夺。估价单可寄下,便向财政部申请免费汇沪。

三、王重民不日寄来《苗疆图说》照片及跋文,收到后请函告。跋文应抄一份寄滇。又王重民近印《燉煌叙录》由大同书店寄上十五部,除十部暂留沪外,其余五部分配如左:《季刊》编辑部作介绍一部,叶玉虎、张菊生、叶揆初、陈寅恪香港大学中国学院各一部。

四、司徒校长所寄之书,如商务尚未收到,请电大同书店速寄。本馆所印之丛书不可再缓。

五、办事处地址不必在中区,距震旦较近者为宜,可用大同书店分店名义。听差如有得力者,其待遇可增至三十五元。

〔《北京图书馆馆史资料汇编(1909-1949)》,页 728-729〕

按:《甲骨丛编》为《国立北平图书馆考古学丛刊》第五种,该书稿后并未刊行,现仍存于国家图书馆。另,石璋如《古墓发现与发掘》、郭宝钧《中国古器物学大纲——铜器篇本论》分别为《国立北平图书馆考古学丛刊》第六、七种,书稿亦存于国家图书馆。[1]此为抄件。

九月二十八日

先生自大理赴下关,本拟宿滇缅公路招待所,但因无空房不能入住且不允进膳。先生见其内有中国银行住客,探知为卞白眉,遂前往拜谒,后者留先生同膳,并介绍先生往该地中国银行借住。〔《卞白眉日记》第 3 卷,页 29〕

九月

《图书季刊》英文本刊登先生撰写的编者按(Editorial Comment)。〔*Quarterly Bulletin of Chinese Bibliography* (New Series), Vol. I, No. 3, pp. 245-250〕

---

[1] 赵爱学《抗战期间北平图书馆组编〈国立北平图书馆考古学丛刊〉考》,《文津学志》第 14 辑,2020 年,页 185-198。

按：该文分六部分，依次为 Organization of Peace、The Case of Bertrand Russell、Reconstruction in China、Chinese Culture Moves West、Art in War-time、Development of Microphotography。

十月六日　昆明

先生访陈梦家，谈《甲骨丛编》印行计划。〔冯远主编《尺素情怀：清华学人手札展》，北京：清华大学出版社，2016 年，页 289〕

　　按：后，由平馆草拟方案，寄送陈梦家，并由其转交董作宾。

十月七日

先生致信王访渔、顾子刚，告知平兑北平馆失窃损失办法。大意如下：

　　　　奉读九月十三日及二十六日台函，藉悉馆中编目组于职员午餐之际，被贼人割破铁丝纱，窃去第十二号打字机一架以及职员衣物等件，远道闻之，□□□□。查该盗白昼行窃，实属胆大已极，难免不无宵小之徒互相勾结。今后尚希严加防范，随时注意，并请通知全馆同人，嗣后对于保管之馆产尤应格外小心、谨慎负责维护是所至盼。关于兑换损失、设法弥补一节，筹思至再，□此解决办法，嗣后拟请大同书店尽量设法平兑不足之数。自十月份起，则由沪暂汇《图书季刊》编辑费每月六百元（每半年汇平一次），以资弥补，下列诸人薪水可在此次特款内予以拨给，赵万里、孙楷第、杨殿珣、贾芳以上中文，顾华以上西文。

　　　　　　　　　　　〔《北京图书馆馆史资料汇编(1909-1949)》，页 726〕

　　按：此为抄件。

十月十日

先生与陈梦家同访曾昭燏，谈编《考古学丛刊》事。〔《曾昭燏文集·日记书信卷》，页 104〕

　　按：时曾昭燏住靛花巷研究所。12 日，陈梦家独自访曾昭燏，再谈《考古学丛刊》。

十月十四日

钱存训覆函先生，告知已电汇美金至滇并请先生将其垫付书款寄下。

　　守和馆长先生赐鉴：

　　　　昨阅致孙先生函，得悉滇馆需款孔亟，嘱在罗氏基金款内拨汇美金贰佰元，业于昨午电汇，想可早到应用。该款系按 $7\frac{15}{16}$ 折合国币

2519.70 元,上海银行升水,按八五折算每千元贴一百七十六元四△七分,减去电费 $ 10.50,实得 2952 元正。近日美金行市较低,惟上海银行汇兑升水较他处为高。港处美金叁百元明日可以寄出,并请释念。九月份经费,闻于上月廿三日汇出,以后每月底大约可发当月之款也。又职处垫付本馆七、八、九三月购书费三百余元,乞早日赐下,以便周转为幸。专此,即请钧安。

职钱存训谨上
十月十四日

　　近闻史料会在滇展览,如有是项说明,乞寄一阅。日内有书报十余包,暨所集传单标语等,当一并寄上。

〔国家图书馆档案,档案编号 1945-※057-综合 5-010005〕

　　按:1940 年 1 月 2 日至 3 日,中日战事史料征辑会在昆明举行展览。① 此函暂系于 1940 年。

十月中上旬

先生联系美国驻华大使詹森,为安全起见,平馆存沪善本古籍可否交美方舰船运往美国交国会图书馆暂存。〔National Archives, General Records of the Department of State, RG 59, Decimal File, 1940-44, Box 5865〕

　　　　按:此时,先生表示运美古籍箱数大约在 300 箱左右,国会图书馆可以借此机会拍摄该批图书的缩微胶片。10 月 16 日,詹森自重庆致电美国国务卿②,请其尽快联系各方询问此举的可能性。接到此电后,国务院分别联系了国会图书馆和海军部,虽然 10 月 16 日恰好有一艘美军运输船 USS Chaumont 离开旧金山前往远东,但海军部表示该船虽有可能经过上海,但因为空间局促无法承运,希望国民政府利用商船将平馆古籍运往马尼拉,再由美国政府派船送美。

十月中旬

先生致电钱存训,拟派其赴美,具体事宜尚待接洽。〔钱存训致李小缘函(1940 年 11 月 7 日)〕

　　　　按:此时拟派,似为押运存沪善本书赴美。

---

① 《中华图书馆协会会报》第 14 卷第 4 期,页 29。
② 美国国务卿应即 Cordell Hull(1871-1955),任期为 1933 年至 1944 年。

十月二十日

上午,先生访曾昭燏。〔《曾昭燏文集·日记书信卷》,页 105〕

　　按:二人似一起在傅斯年家吃午饭,交谈颇久。

十月二十二日

先生致信斯文·赫定,感谢其寄赠新书两种,并告知昆明已经被轰炸过四次,云南大学和西南联大师范学院损失惨重。

October 22, 1940

Dear Dr. Hedin:

　　I thank you very much for your letter of July 31 which has just been received. Owing to Japan's invasion of Indo-China, the Haiphong route to Free China is temporarily closed, so we have not been able to get foreign mails regularly since July.

　　Please accept my warmest thanks for sending us two of your recent books. I hope we shall be able to get them safely. In the future I suggest that you send us your publications to Hong Kong at the following address:

　　National Library of Peiping,

　　c/o Fung Ping Shan Library,

　　94, Bonham Road,

　　Hongkong.

Our office there can reforward them either by air or through some other channel. You may also send them to Shanghai as advised in my previous letter.

　　With the invasion of Indo-China, Kunming is no longer a safe place for study and research. In the course of the last three weeks, the city has been bombed four times. We had a narrow escape, but the National Yunnan University and the Teachers College of the Southwest Associated University were entirely demolished. So, you see how we have been affected by the French collapse which I think is a most tragic episode of world history.

　　I have sent you copies of our *Quarterly Bulletin* and I hope they have been duly received.

With sincere greetings,

Yours sincerely,

T. L. Yuan

〔韩琦教授提供〕

　　　　按:此件为录副。

十月二十七日

下午,先生访徐旭生,晤谈。〔《徐旭生文集》第 10 册,页 1124〕

十、十一月间

先生致信王伯祥,谈《国立北平图书馆藏碑目》印刷事宜,先生拟用六开毛边纸本。〔《王伯祥日记》第 16 册,页 714 〕

　　　　按:此信由陈贯吾转交,11 月 14 日送达。

十一月四日　　重庆

晚六时许,竺可桢与丁西林至聚兴村访王敬礼、傅斯年、先生,晤谈。〔《竺可桢全集》第 7 卷,页 473〕

十一月五日

下午四时,竺可桢在聚兴村与凌伯遵、先生晤谈,先生告平馆在沪上中国科学社藏书,因保管经费与杨孝述颇有争执,请其代为调解。〔《竺可桢全集》第7 卷,页 474—475〕

　　　　按:杨孝述坚持每本每月五分钱,先生则只欲出两千元,竺可桢拟同意先生之见,表示等孙洪芬来渝后再行说项。“凌伯遵”,此处《竺可桢全集》排印本或有误,似应为林伯遵。

十一月十一日

晚,先生与蒋复璁在行政院偶遇金毓黻,小谈即别。〔《静晤室日记》第 6 册,页4605〕

　　　　按:是日,金毓黻抵重庆,晚至行政院访滕固。

十一月十五日

晚九时,先生给胡适发电报,请其联系美国务院协助沟通平馆存沪善本书运美事宜。

Dr. Hu Shih

　　Education Ministry Agreed Moving Peiping Library Chinese Books in Shanghai to States on Loan. Ambassador Johnson Cabled

State Department Arranging Local Marine Escort and Naval Transport No Reply. Request You Approach State Department If You Think Advisable.

Yuan

〔台北胡适纪念馆，档案编号 HS-JDSHSE-0401-089〕

十一月十六日

先生致信王重民，请其将稿件寄平馆驻沪办事处由开明书店印行，并谈善本书运美计划的进展和问题。

有三吾弟：

　　前接到之《善本书叙录》，决定印入三卷一期，因二卷四期业已付印。近又接九月廿二日来书，详悉种种。尊稿均请寄李照亭，可委托开明印行，本馆略予资助即可。该店排版能力甚佳，且王伯祥亦系学术界人物。商务慢的不堪，但影印及制珂瓀版仍非该店不可。北平局面能维持若干时日，殊无把握，印完寄出亦甚感不便，在沪价廉且交通便利多多也。美国所藏算学书，如有稀见者请钞一目寄李乐知（李照亭转）。现拟派钱存训赴美，如普仁斯敦有机会，请为留意。沪上存货本拟运美，美大使已发三电，而至今仍未覆音，甚以为怪。我方提议者系由 L. C. 借用并用 Naval Transport 运美用商船亦可，以策安全，惟货物在法界，吾人不能搬动，必须美人自搬。美大使怕事，故不敢作主，特请示国务院。前日托翁先生电胡大使，亦尚无覆电。兄在此候美方消息，一俟彼方有确实办法，即赴港。如存货能运美照一份 Microfilm，则亦拟来美一行。闻 Hummel 已不来华，如伊在沪则较易办。国会图书馆有日人某女士系一侦探，如与 Hummel 谈及此事，应托其保持决对秘密，盖消息一漏，则存货均将被人没收。一动尚不如一静也，特此奉托，请便中一询其有无办法。两星期后可到港，来函可寄香港。昆明所存书籍已移乡间，决无虞也。

同礼顿首
十一，十六，重庆

〔中国书店·海淀，四册〕

按："尊稿"内容应为王重民所编《华天主教教士著述目录》。

十一月十九日

云南节约建国储蓄团成立,蒋介石函聘龙云为团长,省内分四百九十一个分团,先生任分团长之一。〔《民国日报》(云南),1940 年 11 月 19 日,第 4 版〕

十一月中旬

先生前往美国驻华使馆,表示平馆存沪善本书现存于法租界,意欲运美者约为三百箱,除十箱属于中央图书馆外,其他皆为平馆所有。此外,恒慕义愿意来华协助运送。〔National Archives, General Records of the Department of State, RG 59, Decimal File, 1940-44, Box 5865〕

　　　　按:11 月 20 日,美国大使詹森致电国务卿,汇报以上信息。

十一月二十日

J. Periam Danton 覆函先生,请先生撰写此前美国向中国捐赠书刊分发、利用的书面声明,以及中国各院校所需书刊类型、数量的情况。

November 20, 1940

My dear Dr. Yuan:

　　It is a long time since we had any word from you and I am wondering how you are getting along. In particular, I wonder how much of the material sent by us to you through the Smithsonian Institution reached you and whether you have been able to distribute any or all of it to the various college and university libraries.

　　When you write I think it would be helpful to our Committee if you would let me also have a statement as to the present possibilities of getting books to the various institutions either via the Burma Road or through Hong Kong, the number of separate institutions needing books and journals and some information as to the amount and type of material needed.

　　With every good wish to you, I am

Sincerely yours,

J. P. D

〔The American Library Association Archives, International Relations Office, Vinton Collection-China〕

按:该函寄送香港冯平山图书馆,此件为录副。

十一月二十二日

翁文灏设晚宴款待詹森及 MacDonald, Weid, Lafoor,杭立武、尹国墉、罗家伦、傅斯年、蒋廷黻、顾毓琇、先生、王化成、任鸿隽、孙洪芬、林伯遵受邀作陪。〔《翁文灏日记》,北京:中华书局,2014 年,页 583-584〕

> 按:尹国墉(1903—1963),字仲容,湖南邵阳人,1925 年毕业于南洋大学电机工程系,后供职于交通部电政司,时应任国家资源委员会纽约国际事务所主任,参与国防物资的采购。王化成(1902—1965),江苏丹阳人,清华大学毕业后赴美留学,获芝加哥大学博士学位,归国后历任北京大学讲师、清华大学教授,时应在外交部服务。

十二月初

先生因疟疾数日,心境发狂,后医治得愈。〔中国社会科学院近代史研究所中华民国史研究室编《胡适来往书信选》中,北京:社会科学文献出版社,2013 年,页 758、760、763〕

十二月十日①

先生访翁文灏,表示病情已痊愈,欲以中国政府代表名义赴美募集款项。〔《翁文灏日记》,页 594〕

> 按:先生去美之意在相当范围内传播。王世杰有意增派先生往中央社在美分社服务,因此前所派卢启新在其看来对中国政治缺乏深刻认识。②

十二月十五日

先生致信纳尔逊·洛克菲勒,告自己即将访美。

Chungking, China
December 15, 1940

Dear Mr. Rockefeller:

I was very much delighted to have your letter of August 2 which has just been received here owing to the interruption of postal service as a result of Japan's invasion at Haiphong. I am particularly happy to learn that you are now having a family of five children. I am so eager to see

---

① 此次拜访,《翁文灏日记》与《胡适来往书信选》记录时间不一,后者为 12 月 11 日,本谱暂依前者。
② 王世杰著、林美莉编辑校订《王世杰日记》,台北:"中央研究院"近代史研究所,2012 年,页 315。

them as soon as I arrive at New York.

As I regard New York as my second home, I have been hoping to visit you and your family all these years. But since I have been tied up with my work in China, I could hardly find it possible to take even a short trip. It is with peculiar satisfaction that I am glad to inform you that I have just obtained the permission from our Government to enable me to visit America on a cultural mission next month. I shall certainly look forward with keen pleasure to seeing you and all members of your family. I shall be accompanied by a Chinese archeological expert, Professor Hsu, who will help me in making a survey of Chinese objects of art in the private and public collections in the United States.

All of your friends in China are greatly touched by the expression of good-will on the part of the American government in granting a credit loan of $100,000,000. The news reached the war capital on December 2nd and I can bear witness to the enthusiasm with which the news was received. All of us here are overwhelmed with great joy. I sincerely hope that similar support will be forthcoming in promoting Sino-American cultural relations as soon as the war situation is more clarified.

With very best personal regards,

Sincerely yours,

T. L. Yuan

Wishing you and Mrs. Rockefeller a Merry Christmas and Happy New Year.

〔Rockefeller Foundation, Nelson A. Rockefeller Personal Papers. Box 22 Folder 173〕

按：Professor Hsu 应指徐森玉。此件为打字稿，补语、落款均为先生亲笔。

十二月二十日

先生致信鲍曼，告知将于明年春访美，询问匹兹堡大学中国纪念堂是否需要中式家具、文房陈设。

Chungking, China

December 20, 1940

Dear Chancellor:

During my last trip to the United States, the Cathedral of Learning, then under construction, was perhaps the most impressive structure in the academic world which has lingered in my mind all these years. When you visited Hongkong in the summer of 1938, I assured you of my earnest desire to visit your University at the earliest possible moment. Since then, I have been tied up with my work in China and I have been obliged to postpone my trip until early next year.

I am glad to inform you that my Government has asked me to head a cultural mission to the United States, so I am looking forward with keen pleasure to seeing you as well as all members of your faculty. I shall arrive sometime in February or March and shall remain in the States for half a year.

As I am greatly interested in the China Memorial Room in the Cathedral of Learning, I shall consider it a great honor if you will allow me to present on behalf of the Chinese Government an appropriate gift to your University. I have in mind a set of red-wood tables, chairs, paintings, books, carpets as well as other stationery representative of a Chinese scholar's study room. But since I am not quite sure what you have had already, I hope sincerely that you will tell me frankly what special things you desire to have, so that the things we send over will be exactly the ones that you need. As the time is getting short, I shall appreciate a cable reply from you to be sent to my Hong Kong address. I shall probably come by clipper after having heard from you.

With sincere greetings of the season and with my very best personal regards,

Sincerely yours,

T. L. Yuan

〔 University of Pittsburgh Library, John Gabbert Bowman, Administrative Files, Box 2 Folder 13, Chinese Material〕

　　　　按:此件为打字稿,落款处为先生签名。

十二月二十二日

先生访翁文灏,谈赴美计划,拟偕徐森玉、李瑞年等四人同行。〔《翁文灏日记》,页 598〕

十二月

《图书季刊》英文本刊登先生撰写的编者按(Editorial Comment)。〔*Quarterly Bulletin of Chinese Bibliography* (New Series), Vol. 1, No. 4, pp. 349–350〕

　　　　按:该文为两部分,一为 A Word of Appreciation,一为 A Means Serves Both Ends。